THE HENRY DAVIS GIFT

THE HENRY DAVIS GIFT

A Collection of Bookbindings

VOLUME III

A Catalogue of
South-European Bindings

Mirjam M Foot

THE BRITISH LIBRARY
and
OAK KNOLL PRESS
2010

First published in 2010 by
The British Library
96 Euston Road
London NW1 2DB
and
Oak Knoll Press
310 Delaware Street
New Castle, DE 19720

Text © Mirjam Foot 2010
Images © the British Library 2010

Cataloguing-in-Publication Data
A catalogue record for this book is available from
The British Library and Library of Congress

ISBN 978 0 7123 5054 9 British Library
ISBN 978 1 58456 272 6 Oak Knoll Press

Typeset by Norman Tilley Graphics Ltd
Black-and-white reproductions by Dot Gradations Ltd
Printed and bound in Great Britain by Henry Ling Ltd
at the Dorset Press, Dorchester DT1 1HD

Contents

Introduction 7

Books and articles referred to, with abbreviated titles 13

FRENCH BINDINGS
(nos. 1–222)
page 27

SWISS BINDINGS
(nos. 223–236)
page 277

ITALIAN BINDINGS
(nos. 237–393)
page 295

SPANISH AND PORTUGUESE BINDINGS
(nos. 394–408)
page 469

MISCELLANEOUS BINDINGS
(nos. 409–421)
page 491

ADDITIONS
(nos. I–II)
page 508

Index of Binders 515
Index of Owners 518

Introduction

Thirty years have gone by since volume I of *The Henry Davis Gift: Studies in the History of Bookbinding* appeared. During this time much work has been done and several books and articles have been published, especially dealing with French and Italian bindings, the main subjects of this volume. New attributions to binders or binders' shops have been proposed and earlier attributions have been corrected. Although the most frequently used method for attributing decorated leather or parchment bindings to binders' shops remains the identification of tools and groups of tools used for their decoration, more archival work has been done and the results have changed our concept of how the fine binding trade was organized and – especially in France – how production was divided between forwarders and finishers. Consequently, some of the attributions suggested in that volume have been revised here.

More recent study of the bindings made for the French kings, from Louis XII onwards, has helped to shed light on some of the royal binders and their role. Some nicknames in use in the older literature have been supplanted by real names of identifiable people, or have been changed altogether.

As the literature on French named and nicknamed binders of the first half of the sixteenth century remains confusing, it may be useful to set out here (in condensed form) the current state of knowledge (as at January 2007).

The names in **bold** are those adopted in the present volume of the Catalogue.

The **Atelier Louis XII/François I** =[equals] Simon Vostre.

Pierre Roffet (active 1511–33): bookseller and royal binder; his widow: Jeanne Cassot (1533–37) took over with the help of their son André. Meanwhile their son:

Etienne Roffet (probably 1533, but at least 1537–49) set up separately. He became royal binder (1539–47) (= 'binder of the Estienne Bible'); he ceased to be royal binder in 1547 (see below: Gommar Estienne), and died at the end of 1548 or at the beginning of 1549.

The **'Fleur-de-lis binder'** (who worked among others for Jean Grolier, c. 1538–40), was at work probably by 1536 (= 'Bayfius binder').

The 'Fontainebleau binder' is now called the **'Salel binder'**.

The 'Entrelac binder' (= 'Claude Picques with solid tools') now equals **Jean Picard** (c. 1540–7), bookseller and binder. He was the Aldine representative in Paris, responsible to Grolier; he left in 1547. Bindings formerly attributed to Claude Picques with open tools and some of those attributed to Claude Picques with hatched tools have now also been attributed to Picard.

Laffitte & Le Bars attribute bindings made for the French kings (François I and Henri II) after 1545 to the **Atelier de Fontainebleau**, using solid, hatched and open tools (all formerly attributed by Nixon to Claude Picques). Picard used the solid tools that were also used in this atelier. **Gommar Estienne** was in charge of the atelier from 1547 and Claude Picques (see below) probably from 1556. The Atelier de Fontainebleau was at work at Fontainebleau from 1545 till 1552; then the 'relieur du roi' moved to Paris, where Gommar Estienne was still in charge until c. 1556 (or 1559).

Bindings with (mainly) hatched tools formerly attributed to Claude Piques are now attributed to Gommar Estienne, who became the representative of the Aldine shop from 1548. Already in November 1547 he was called 'binder to the king'; in 1548 he was called 'bookseller to the king'. Other documents of 1550 and 1554 called him 'binder to the king'; he is last mentioned in a document of June 1556. According to Laffitte, 'Le grand doreur de Henri II' (= 'Claude Picques with hatched tools') now equals two ateliers: the 'Atelier de Fontainebleau' (1547–52) and the 'Atelier du relieur du roi' (from 1552). But both used the same tools.

Claude Picques, bookseller and binder, 1539; in 1548 he was called 'doreur' (finisher); in 1553 he became bookbinder to the queen (in 1557 he was still called 'bookseller to the queen'). In a document of 1556 he was called 'binder to the king', and he was certainly binder to the king in 1559. In 1567 he was called 'binder and finisher to the king'. He remained royal binder (under Henri II, François II and Charles IX), and was still mentioned as binder to the king in 1574 (Henri III). He was succeeded by **Nicolas Ève** (called bookseller and binder in 1560), who became royal binder sometime between August 1574 and November 1578 (when Ève was called 'binder to the king').

Attribution to named French binders is made more difficult by the fact that in France forwarding and finishing were two separate professions, so that structural features cannot be used to attribute bindings with certain finishing tools to specific ateliers. Moreover, it is likely that the 'relieur du roi' organized the binding of the royal books, and probably specified the designs to be used in their decoration, but that he did not himself stand at the bench, using instead the best forwarders and finishers at work in Paris at the time. Alternatively, Laffitte & Le Bars suggest that the royal librarian specified the binding designs, but that the finishing tools belonged to the Atelier de Fontainebleau and the Atelier du relieur du roi, and were used by a succession of royal binders. The same tools are also found on bindings for other collectors, and either the royal binder worked also for other collectors (in slack periods) or the latter also patronized the same finishing atelier in Paris. (See also below under Jean Picard: French bindings no. 23, Gommar Estienne: French bindings no. 64, and Claude Picques: French bindings no. 69).

The work of Italian binders who produced fine bindings during the late fifteenth, the sixteenth and the seventeenth centuries has also been studied much more widely and here, too, archival study and a more general historical approach have made a noticeable contribution to our knowledge both of binders' shops and of their patrons. New literature has helped me to confirm or to change attributions made in volume I of *The Henry Davis Gift*, and especially to bring some order to the vast majority of the Italian bindings in this Gift that had remained uncatalogued in detail.

The title of this volume of the Catalogue is somewhat misleading. 'Southern Europe', consisting of France, Italy, Spain, Portugal and Switzerland, forms indeed the main part of this volume, with 222 entries for France, 157 for Italy, 15 for the Iberian Peninsula and 14 for Switzerland. But there are also three bindings from Eastern Europe, eight from the Near and Middle East, and two from the New World, one from Mexico, the other from New York. Moreover, two bindings overlooked when volume II was compiled have been added here. This last section, headed 'Miscellaneous bindings', has gained from some comparatively recent publications dealing with Oriental bindings.

How useful much of the research published during the past thirty years has been to me in the compilation of this volume is clear from the references, literature and comparative material given in each entry. The list of 'Books and articles referred to with abbreviated titles' (pp. 13–25) is not a complete bibliography. It lists only those works that are of direct relevance to the bindings described, and that have been given abbreviated titles in the entries. Books and articles that have been mentioned only once or are relevant only to one particular binding have been given their full title, etc. in the entry itself.

A few uncertainties remain: within the French section there is a binding (no. 53) with strong Italianate characteristics, as well as one (no. 88) that may well have been made in Switzerland; within the Swiss section there is a binding (no. 234) that might have been made in northern Italy, while a binding in the Italian section (no. 331) may have been produced in Switzerland; the tooling of no. 372 (also in the Italian section) is somewhat suggestive of Spain: all literally borderline cases.

Like volume II, *The Henry Davis Gift: A Catalogue of North-European bindings*, volume III of the Catalogue has been arranged according to country and within each country chronologically.

However, the work of a particular binder or binder's shop, and, to a lesser degree, that done for a particular owner, has been kept together; related binders or binderies have also, where possible, been listed sequentially, thereby overriding a strict date order.

As 25 years have passed since volume II was published, it is hardly surprising that my views about binding description and what it ought to contain have changed. I now regret that in volume II structural features were omitted and descriptions were kept to a bare minimum. Having meanwhile taught several generations of students, I have come to realize that better verbal descriptions, side by side with illustrations, are indeed helpful, and my own research over the past 25 years has brought it home to me how inseparable structure and decoration are when trying to date and locate bookbindings. Consequently, the descriptions of the decorative aspects given in this volume are more extensive than those in volume II (including those of board edges and turn-ins), but, more importantly, several structural elements, such as sewing techniques, endbands and endleaves, have been described –albeit, for practical reasons, still too briefly. Edge treatments and fastenings, mentioned in volume II, are of course included.

When volumes I and II were written, the Henry Davis books had not yet been given a British Library press mark. Since then each volume has been given a number (as opposed to Henry Davis's habit of numbering by title). These numbers are quoted in the entries of this volume, but the old Davis accession numbers are given in parentheses, so that bindings referred to in volume I can still be found. Future researchers are encouraged to use the 'Davis' numbers and not the P or M numbers.

Having given some indication of binding structures in this volume, it may be worth while drawing attention to some comparable and different binders' practices as evident from the fine bindings made in Italy and France during the sixteenth and seventeenth centuries, but not without emphasizing that such practices have been observed in a collection of fine and decorated bindings, splendid objects, made at and for the top end of the market, and that they can not therefore be taken as characteristic of the total binding production in those countries. Structural changes and especially those aimed at simplification are more readily observed in trade bindings and in the run-of-the mill products meant for a wider clientele.

From the tenth century onwards, most western bindings were sewn on alum-tawed leather supports, split over the width of the spine and sewn round in a variety of patterns. By the fifteenth century we also find bindings sewn on split tanned leather supports, while cords, made of flax or hemp (as already used in Carolingian bindings) were reintroduced during the fifteenth century. Thinner, single tawed and tanned leather supports came into use during the sixteenth century. Sometimes tanned and tawed supports can be found in combination, and parchment sewing supports were also used.

From the fine French and Italian bindings in the Henry Davis Gift it is clear that split alum-tawed supports were still commonly used in France in the 1550s. Split tanned leather supports are also found, but far less often, while cords were used more and more, becoming the norm in the early seventeenth century. Nevertheless, alum-tawed supports are still occasionally evident during the 1560s and were exceptionally employed as late as the 1580s. In Italy, too, alum-tawed leather was the most commonly used material for sewing supports, persisting longer than in France. Such supports were still much in evidence in the 1560s, gradually dying out during the 1570s, although turning up occasionally as late as the early 1590s. Tanned leather supports were used as well, especially in the 1570s, 1580s and 1590s, and cords are found from the early 1550s, but only becoming more common towards the end of the sixteenth and during the early seventeenth century. A characteristic of Italian bindings is the use, from c. 1518 onwards, of decorative false bands, thin pieces of cord, stuck onto the backs of the sections between the sewing supports and showing on the spine as smaller and lower bands alternating with the higher and larger bands formed by the structural supports. The French equivalent was the habit, from the 1530s onwards, of emphasizing the kettle stitches as bands.

Sewing supports, usually cords, could be recessed, that is lying in grooves sawn into the backs of the sections, thus creating a smooth spine and giving greater opportunity for achieving a variety of decorative effects, an opportunity by no means always grasped. Recessed supports were introduced into Europe in the sixteenth century and were commonly used in France from the mid-1540s, becoming more and more frequent and lasting well into the 1640s, although raised cords start to take over before 1630. They were much less popular in Italy, where raised bands remained the norm, although recessed cords are on occasion found there from the second decade of the seventeenth century.

Alum-tawed strips were also frequently used for the sewn endbands that are found almost invariably on fine bindings. Endbands can be double or single and were often finished with a bead. Primary sewing in white thread, followed by secondary decorative sewing in coloured silks was common in France until c. 1535, after which sewing with coloured silks only became the norm, with a few exceptions as late as 1540. In Lyon we continue to find primary-sewn endbands in the 1540s and 1550s. *Per contra*, primary and secondary sewing of endbands remained normal practice in Italy all through the sixteenth century and is still found in the first half of the seventeenth century, when it started to diminish, all but disappearing during the second half of the century. Other materials were also used for endband cores. We find tanned leather and cord cores and, from c. 1640, but more frequently during the eighteenth century in France, cores made of rolled paper. In Italy cord remained the favourite material, although rolled paper cores were used during the nineteenth century. We also find in Italy during the later part of the eighteenth century endbands that were not worked on the book, but were stuck onto the spine. Such endbands were of course used far earlier and were far more common on simpler trade bindings. During the first decades of the sixteenth century, the cores were usually laced into the boards, although by now most have broken at the joints. Even in fine bindings there are signs of simplification; by the 1540s the ends of the cores were no longer as a rule laced in, although the sewing thread and silk was almost always tied down either in or between the sections, but even that habit wore off and in France in the 1640s we find more and more that the endband sewing was only tied down in the first and last sections.

The treatment of the edges of the boards gradually became a decorative feature. In France the board edges were tooled, first in blind from c. 1535; this rapidly became standard practice and from the 1540s onwards the edges of the boards were almost invariably tooled in blind or gold. Although we find gold tooling on board edges in Italy from c. 1540, and although blind-tooled board edges are in evidence earlier, the habit of decorating the edges of the boards was much less prevalent here than in France. In Spain, too, we find tooling on board edges and turn-ins from c. 1540 onwards. However, the number of Spanish bindings in the Henry Davis Gift is too small to enable us to come to useful conclusions. Doublures too are rarely found in Italy, while in France they adorned the finest collectors' pieces from the 1550s onwards.

ACKNOWLEDGEMENTS

From the references, literature lists and comparative material mentioned in the individual entries, it will be clear how much I owe to those who have made more detailed studies of specific segments of the history of bookbinding, and I have used their work, often with admiration, always with gratitude. I owe a great deal too to the unfailing helpfulness of friends and colleagues in all major libraries in the UK and in a host of libraries abroad. The list of individuals is too long to enumerate, but my gratitude to them all is profound.

My main obligation, however, is to the staff of the British Library. In particular to those in Early Printed Collections who have allowed me a locker and a few shelves on which to store my card indices and boxes of rubbings; to Philippa Marks for making the collection of rubbings available and for her help with finding the photographs used in this volume; and to Karen Limper, without whose help in getting the Henry Davis books out on a regular basis, I would not have been able to recatalogue this part of the collection in under two years. My gratitude also goes out to David Way of British Library Publications, who has been a model of patience.

I am very grateful to Dr Anthony Hobson for discussing some of the Italian bindings with me, to my many friends who have put up with neglect and occasional irritability, and, most of all, to my husband whose understanding and support have, as always, been limitless

MIRJAM M FOOT
September 2009

Books and Articles Referred to,
with Abbreviated Titles

Andrews, *Bibliopegy*:
  W L Andrews, *Bibliopegy in the United States and Kindred Subjects*, New York, 1902.
Aussen-Ansichten:
  B Wagner (ed.), *Aussen Ansichten. Bucheinbände aus 1000 Jahren aus den Beständen der Bayerischen Staatsbibliothek München*, Wiesbaden, 2006.
Austin:
  G Austin, *The Library of Jean Grolier: A Preliminary Catalogue*, New York, 1971.
Barber 1994:
  G Barber, 'From Baroque to Neoclassicism: French eighteenth-century bindings at Oxford', in: D Rhodes (ed.), *Bookbindings and other Bibliophily*, Verona, 1994, pp. 33–64.
Barber, 'Around the Padeloup and Derome workshops':
  G Barber, 'Around the Padeloup and Derome workshops', in: Foot, *Eloquent Witnesses*, pp. 171–205.
Barber, 'La reliure':
  G Barber, 'La reliure', in: H-J Martin and R Chartier, *Histoire de l'édition française*, vol. II: *1660–1830*, Paris, 1984, pp. 162–71.
Barber, 'Parisian fine binding trade':
  G Barber, 'The Parisian fine binding trade in the last century of the *ancient régime*', in: R Fox and A Turner (eds), *Luxury Trades and Consumerism in Ancien Régime Paris*, Aldershot, 1998, pp. 43–62.
Barber & Rogers:
  G Barber and D Rogers, 'Some seventeenth-century straw bindings', *Bodleian Library Record*, vol. 8, no. 5 (1971), pp. 262–5.
Benvenuti, *Dizionario*:
  F Sforza Benvenuti, *Dizionario biografico cremasco*, Crema, 1888.
Beraldi, *XIXe siècle*:
  H Beraldi, *La Reliure du XIXe siècle*, 4 vols, Paris, 1895–7.
BFAC, 1891:
  Burlington Fine Arts Club Exhibition of Bookbindings, London, 1891.
Bignami Odier:
  J Bignami Odier, *La Bibliothèque Vaticane de Sixte IV à Pie XI* (Studi e Testi, 272), Vatican City, 1973.
Bodley, *Exhibition*:
  Fine Bindings 1500–1700 from Oxford Libraries, Bodleian Library, Oxford, 1968.
Bookbinding in America:
  H Lehmann-Haupt (ed.), *Bookbinding in America; Three Essays*: Hannah D French, 'Early American bookbinding by hand'; J W Rogers, 'The rise of American edition binding'; H Lehmann-Haupt, 'On the rebinding of old books', New York, 1967.
Bosch, *et al.*, *Islamic Bindings*:
  G Bosch, J Carswell and G Petherbridge, *Islamic Bindings and Bookmaking*, Chicago, 1981.
Brera:
  F Macchi, *et al.*, *Arte della legatura a Brera*, Biblioteca Nazionale Braidense, Cremona, 2002.
Bridwell:
  E Marshall White [and others], *Six Centuries of Master Bookbinding at Bridwell Library*, Dallas, 2006.

Briquet:
: C-M Briquet, *Les Filigranes* (ed. A. Stevenson), 4 vols, Hilversum, 1968.
Brooker, *Book Collector*, 1997:
: T K Brooker, 'Paolo Manutio's use of fore-edge titles for presentation copies (1540–1541)', *The Book Collector*, 46 (1997), pp. 27–68, 193–209.
Brooker, *Bulletin du bibliophile*, 1997:
: T K Brooker, 'Bindings commissioned for Francis I's "Italian library" with horizontal spine titles', *Bulletin du bibliophile*, 1997, 1, pp. 33–91.
Brugalla:
: E Brugalla, 'El arte en el libro y en la encuadernación', *Memorias de la Real Academia de Ciencias y Artes de Barcelona*, xlii.5 (1973), pp. 189–266.
Brugalla, *Tres ensayos*:
: E Brugalla, *Tres ensayos sobre el arte de la encuadernación*, Barcelona, 1945.
Brunet:
: G Brunet, *La Reliure ancienne et moderne*, Paris, 1884.
Caro & Crespo:
: C Caro and C Crespo, 'La sección de manuscritos, incunables y raros de la Biblioteca Nacional de España', *Encuadernación de arte*, 1 (May 1993), pp. 4–6.
Carrión Gútiez, 'Incunables':
: Manuel Carrión Gútiez, 'La encuadernación española en los siglos XVI, XVII y XVIII', in: H. Escolar (ed.), *Historia ilustrada del libro español. De los incunables al siglo XVIII*, Madrid, 1994, pp. 385–445.
Carrión Gútiez, 'Manoscritos':
: Manuel Carrión Gútiez, 'La encuadernación española en la edad media', in: H Escolar (ed.), *Historia ilustrada del libro español; los manoscritos*, Madrid, 1994, pp. 365–400.
Castañeda, *Ensayo*:
: V Castañeda, *Ensayo de un diccionario biografico de encuadernadores españoles*, Madrid, 1951.
Cavalli & Terlizzi:
: M Cavalli and F Terlizzi, *Legature di pregio in Angelica, secoli XV–XVIII*, Rome, 1991.
Chacon:
: A Chacon, *Vitae et res gestae pontificum Romanorum et S.R.E. cardinalium*, 4 vols, Rome, 1677.
Chain, Dufour & Moeckli:
: P Chain, A Dufour and G Moeckli, *Les Livres imprimés à Genève de 1550 à 1600* [extracted from: *Genava*, new ser. 7, 1959, pp. 235–94].
Cockx-Indestege & Storm van Leeuwen, *Quaerendo*, 1987:
: E Cockx-Indestege and J Storm van Leeuwen, 'Spaanse boekbanden te Brussel', *Quaerendo*, 17, 3 & 4 (1987), pp. 232–82.
Conihout, *Bulletin du bibliophile*:
: I de Conihout and P Ract-Madoux, 'Ni Grolier, ni Mahieu: Laubespine', *Bulletin du bibliophile*, 2004, 1, pp. 63–88.
Conihout, *Henri III mécène*:
: I de Conihout, J-F Maillard and G Poirier, *Henri III mécène des arts, des sciences et des lettres*, Paris, 2006, pp. 317–29.
Conihout & Ract-Madoux:
: I de Conihout & P Ract-Madoux, *Reliures françaises du XVIIe siècle, chefs d'oeuvre du Musée Condé*, Paris, 2002.
Coppens, 'The prize is the proof':
: C Coppens, 'The prize is the proof: four centuries of prize books', in Foot, *Eloquent Witnesses*, pp. 53–105.

Critien:
> Fra' J E Critien, M Camilleri, J Schirò, *Fine Bookbindings from the National Library of Malta and the Magistral Palace Library and Archives, Sovereign Military Order of Malta, Rome*, [Valletta], 1999.

Crollalanza, *Dizionario*:
> G B di Crollalanza, *Dizionario storico-blasonico delle famiglie nobili e notabili italiane*, 3 vols, Pisa, 1886–90.

Culot, *La Reliure en France*:
> A R A Hobson and P Culot, *Italian and French Sixteenth-Century Bookbindings. La Reliure en Italie et en France au XVIe siècle*, Brussels: Bibliotheca Wittockiana, 1990.

Culot, 'Quelques reliures de l'atelier Lemonnier':
> P Culot, 'Quelques reliures de l'atelier Lemonnier', in: A de Coster and C Sorgeloos (eds), *Bibliophiles et reliures. Mélanges offerts à Michel Wittock*, Brussels, 2006, pp. 192–201.

Culot, *Relieurs et reliures romantiques*:
> P Culot, *Relieurs et reliures décorées en France à l'époque romantique*, Brussels, 1995.

Culot, *Wittockiana*:
> P Culot, et al., *Bibliotheca Wittockiana*, Ghent, 1996.

Dacier:
> E Dacier, *Les plus belles reliures*, Paris, 1929.

Dacier, 'Les premières reliures françaises':
> E Dacier, 'Les premières reliures françaises à décor doré, l'atelier des "Reliures Louis XII"', in: E Dacier (ed.), *Trésors des bibliothèques de France*, V (1933–5), pp. 7–40.

Dacier, 'Une treizième reliure de Louis XII':
> E Dacier, 'Une treizième reliure de Louis XII', in: E Dacier (ed.), *Trésors des bibliothèques de France*, V (1933–5), pp. 186–92.

Dalla bottega:
> [M R Grizzuti, ed.], *Dalla bottega allo scaffale*, Rome, 1990.

Davies, *Fairfax Murray*:
> H W Davies, *Catalogue of … Early French Books in the Library of C. Fairfax Murray*, London, 1910.

De Marinis:
> Tammaro de Marinis, *La legatura artistica in Italia nei secoli XV e XVI*, 3 vols, Florence, 1960.

De Marinis, *Alcune legature*:
> Tammaro de Marinis, *Di alcune legature fatte per Paolo III, Alessandro e Ranuccio Farnese*, Milan, 1938.

De Marinis, *Appunti*:
> Tammaro de Marinis, *Appunti e ricerche bibliografiche*, Milan, 1940.

De Marinis, *Fürstenberg*:
> Tammaro de Marinis, *Die italienischen Renaissance-Einbände der Bibliothek Fürstenberg*, Hamburg, 1966.

De Marinis, *Rilegature veneziane*:
> Tammaro de Marinis, *Rilegature veneziane del XV e XVI secolo*, Venice, 1955.

De Ricci, *Schiff*:
> Seymour de Ricci, *French Signed Bindings in the Mortimer L. Schiff Collection*, New York, 1935.

De Toldo:
> V de Toldo, *The Italian Art of Bookbinding*, London, 1925.

Devauchelle:
> R Devauchelle, *La Reliure en France*, 3 vols, Paris, 1959–61.

Devaux:
> Y Devaux, *Dix siècles de reliure*, Paris, 1977.

Els vestits del saber:
    Els vestits del saber: enquadernacions mudèjars a la Universitat de València, Valencia, 2003.

Encuadernaciones españolas:
    Encuadernaciones españolas en la Biblioteca Nacional (text: Isabel Riuz de Elvira Serra), [Madrid], 1992.

Ettinghausen, 1954:
    R Ettinghausen, 'The covers of the Morgan *Manâfi* manuscript and other early Persian bookbindings', in: D Miner (ed.), *Studies in Art and Literature for Belle da Costa Greene*, Princeton, 1954, pp. 459–73.

Fine Bookbindings from the National Library of Malta and the Magistral Palace Library and Archives, Sovereign Military Order of Malta, Rome: see Critien.

Fletcher, *Foreign*:
    W Y Fletcher, *Foreign Bookbindings in the British Museum*, London, 1896.

Fléty:
    J Fléty, *Dictionnaire des relieurs français ayant exercé de 1800 à nos jours*, Argenton-sur-Creuse, 1988.

Fogelmark:
    S Fogelmark, *Flemish and Related Panel-Stamped bindings, Evidence and Principles*, New York, 1990.

Folger Catalogue:
    F A Bearman, N H Krivatsy and J F Mowery, *Fine and Historic Bindings from the Folger Shakespeare Library*, Washington, 1992.

Foot, 1977:
    M M Foot, 'Twentieth-century bindings in the Henry Davis Collection' [uncorrected], *Designer Bookbinders Review*, 9 (1977), pp. 2–5.

Foot, *Book Collector*, 1975:
    M M Foot, 'Some bindings for foreign students in sixteenth-century Paris', *The Book Collector*, 24 (1975), pp. 106–10 (reprinted in Foot, *Studies*, pp. 324–8).

Foot, *Book Collector*, 1979:
    M M Foot, 'English and foreign bookbindings 9. A binding by Gabriel de Sancha, c. 1790', *The Book Collector*, 28 (1979), pp. 256–7 (reprinted in Foot, *Studies*, pp. 234–5).

Foot, *Book Collector*, 1987:
    M M Foot, 'English and foreign bookbindings 41. A binding by Pierre-Lucien Martin, 1961', *The Book Collector*, 36 (1987), pp. 244–5 (reprinted in Foot, *Studies*, pp. 94–5).

Foot, *Davis*:
    M M Foot, *The Henry Davis Gift: A Collection of Bookbindings*, vol. I: *Studies in the History of Bookbinding*, London, 1978; vol. II: *A Catalogue of North-European Bindings*, London, 1983.

Foot, *Eloquent Witnesses*:
    M M Foot (ed.), *Eloquent Witnesses: Bookbindings and their History*, London/New Castle, 2004.

Foot, 'Geneva Kings' binder':
    M M Foot, 'The Geneva Kings' binder and other 16th-century bindings decorated with masks', in: Association Internationale de Bibliophilie, *XXIVe Congrès 2005 en Suisse. Actes et communications*, Weinfelden, 2006, pp. 17–29.

Foot, *Marsh*:
    M M Foot, *The Decorated Bindings in Marsh's Library, Dublin*, Aldershot, 2004.

Foot, *Mirror*:
    M M Foot, *The History of Bookbinding as a Mirror of Society*, London, 1998.

Foot, *Revue française*:
    M M Foot, 'Les reliures françaises de la collection Henry Davis', *Revue française d'histoire du livre*, 36 (1982), pp. 371–87.

Foot, 'Some bookbindings in the Herzog August Bibliothek':
: M M Foot, 'Some bookbindings in the Herzog August Bibliothek', in: Association Internationale de Bibliophilie, *12e Congrès international des bibliophiles 1981 à la Herzog August Bibliothek de Wolfenbüttel. Actes et communications*, Göttingen, 1984, pp. 87–130.

Foot, *Studies*:
: M M Foot, *Studies in the History of Bookbinding*, Aldershot, 1993.

Fumagalli:
: G Fumagalli, 'Di Demetrio Canevari medico e bibliofilo genovese e delle preziose ligature che si dicono a lui appartenute', *Bibliofilia*, iv and v, Florence, 1903–4, iv: pp. 300–16, 390–400; v: pp. 33–42, 80–90, 149–61.

Fumagalli, *L'arte della legatura*:
: G Fumagalli, *L'arte della legatura alla corte degli Estensi, a Ferrara e a Modena, dal sec. XV al XIX*, Florence, 1913.

Gid:
: D Gid, *Catalogue des reliures françaises estampées à froid XVe–XVIe siècle de la Bibliothèque Mazarine*, Paris, 1984.

Gid: 'Un atelier lyonnais vers 1500':
: D Gid, 'Un atelier lyonnais vers 1500. L'atelier au compas', in: G Colin (ed.), *De libris compactis miscellanea*, Brussels, 1984, pp. 117–31.

Gid & Laffitte:
: D Gid and M-P Laffitte, *Les Reliures à plaques françaises*, Turnhout, 1997.

Glénisson:
: J Glénisson, 'Le livre pour la jeunesse', in: H-J Martin and R Chartier, *Histoire de l'édition française*, III, Paris, 1985, pp. 417–43.

Goldschmidt:
: E P Goldschmidt, *Gothic and Renaissance Bookbindings*, London, 1928.

Gottlieb:
: T Gottlieb, *K. K. Hofbibliothek, Vienna, Bucheinbände*, Vienna, [1910].

Grolier Club, *Exhibition*, 1937:
: *Exhibition of Renaissance Bookbindings*, Grolier Club, New York, 1937.

Gruel:
: L Gruel, *Manuel historique et bibliographique de l'amateur de reliures*, 2 vols, Paris, 1887–1905.

Guigard:
: J Guigard, *Nouvel armorial du bibliophile*, 2 vols, Paris, 1890.

Guignard, 1966:
: J Guignard, 'L'atelier des reliures Louis XII (Blois ou Paris?) et l'atelier de Simon Vostre', in: *Studia bibliographica in honorem Herman de la Fontaine Verwey*, Amsterdam, 1966, pp. 202–39.

Guignard, 1968:
: J Guignard, 'Premières reliures parisiennes à décor doré', in: *Humanisme actif: mélanges d'art et de literature offerts à Julien Caen*, Paris, 1968, II, pp. 229–49.

Guignard, 'A propos d'un Grolier inédit':
: J Guignard, 'A propos d'un Grolier inédit. La date des reliures à plaquettes: Etienne ou Jean Grolier', in: *Mélanges d'histoire du livre et des bibliothèques offerts à Monsieur Frantz Calot*, Paris, 1960, pp. 191–216.

Gumuchian, 1930:
: *Catalogue de reliures du XVe au XIXe siècle, en vente a la librairie Gumuchian & Cie*, Paris, [1930].

Haebler:
: K Haebler, *Rollen- und Plattenstempel des XVI. Jahrhunderts* (Sammlung Bibliothekswissenschaftlicher Arbeiten, Heft 41–2), Leipzig, 1928, 1929.

Haldane:
: D Haldane, *Islamic Bookbindings in the Victoria and Albert Museum*, London, 1983.

Harthan, *V&A Bookbindings*:
: J P Harthan, *Victoria and Albert Museum. Bookbindings*, London, 1961 (paperback, 1985).

Hobson, *Additions et corrections*:
: A R A Hobson, *Additions et corrections; supplément à l'ouvrage 'Les reliures à la fanfare …' de G D Hobson*, Amsterdam, 1970 [supplement to the second edition of G D Hobson, *Les Reliures à la fanfare*, Amsterdam, 1970].

Hobson, *Apollo and Pegasus*:
: A R A Hobson, *Apollo and Pegasus. An Enquiry into the Formation and Disposal of a Renaissance Library*, Amsterdam, 1975.

Hobson, 'Bookbinding in Bologna':
: A R A Hobson, 'Bookbinding in Bologna', in: Luisa Avellini and Rosaria Campioni, *Notizie dei beni culturali. Schede umanistiche*, 1998, no. 1, pp. 147–75 [the English version, with some different illustrations, of Hobson, *Legature bolognesi*].

Hobson, *Book Collector*, 1975:
: A R A Hobson, 'Two Venetian bindings for Diego Hurtado de Mendoza', *The Book Collector*, 24 (1975), pp. 33–6.

Hobson, *Bulletin du bibliophile*:
: A R A Hobson, 'Les livres reliés pour Thomas Mahieu: I', *Bulletin du bibliophile*, 2004, 2, pp. 239–70.

Hobson, 'Buyers of books':
: A R A Hobson, 'Some sixteenth-century buyers of books in Rome and elsewhere', *Humanistica Lovaniensia*, vol. xxxiva (1985), pp. 65–75.

Hobson, *French and Italian*:
: A R A Hobson, *French and Italian Collectors and their Bindings*, Oxford, 1953.

Hobson, *Humanists*:
: A R A Hobson, *Humanists and Bookbinders*, Cambridge, 1989.

Hobson, 'Italian fifteenth-century bookbindings':
: A R A Hobson, 'Italian fifteenth-century bookbindings', *Renaissance studies*, vol. 9, no. 2 (1995), pp. 129–36.

Hobson, *Italian Sixteenth-Century Bookbindings*:
: A R A Hobson and P Culot, *Italian and French Sixteenth-Century Bookbindings. La Reliure en Italie et en France au XVIe siècle*, Brussels: Bibliotheca Wittockiana, 1990.

Hobson, *Legature bolognesi*:
: A R A Hobson and L Quaquarelli, *Legature bolognesi del Rinascimento*, Bologna, 1998 [for a version in English of the chapter by A R A Hobson, with some different illustrations, see Hobson, 'Bookbinding in Bologna'].

Hobson, 'Plaquette and medallion bindings':
: A R A Hobson, 'Plaquette and medallion bindings: a second supplement', in: D Pearson (ed.), *For the Love of the Binding*, London, 2000, pp. 67–79.

Hobson, *Renaissance*:
: A R A Hobson, *Renaissance Book Collecting: Jean Grolier and Diego Hurtado de Mendoza, their Books and Bindings*, Cambridge, 1999.

Hobson, 'Two early sixteenth-century binder's shops':
: A R A Hobson, 'Two early sixteenth-century binder's shops in Rome', in: G Colin (ed.), *De libris compactis miscellanea*, Brussels: Bibliotheca Wittockiana, 1984, pp. 79–98.

Hobson, 'Was there an Aldine bindery?':
    A R A Hobson, 'Was there an Aldine bindery?', in: D S Zeidberg (ed.), *Aldus Manutius and Renaissance Culture. Essays in Memory of Franklin D Murphy*, Florence, 1998, pp. 237–45.

G D Hobson, *Cambridge*:
    G D Hobson, *Bindings in Cambridge Libraries*, Cambridge, 1929.

G D Hobson, 'Dr Theodor Gottlieb':
    G D Hobson, 'The late Dr Theodor Gottlieb and his Grolierstudien', in: G D Hobson, *Studies in the History of Bookbinding*, London, 1988, pp. 229–69.

G D Hobson, *Fanfare*:
    G D Hobson, *Les Reliures à la fanfare: le problème de l'S fermé*, London, 1940.

G D Hobson, *Maioli*:
    G D Hobson, *Maioli, Canevari and Others*, London, 1926.

G D Hobson, 'Parisian bindings':
    G D Hobson, 'Parisian bindings 1500–1525', *The Library*, 4th series, xi (1931), pp. 393–434.

G D Hobson, *Thirty Bindings*:
    G D Hobson, *Thirty Bindings … Selected from the First Edition Club's Seventh Exhibition*, London, 1926.

G D Hobson, *Trésors*:
    G D Hobson, 'Une reliure aux armes d'Henri III', in R Cantinelli and E Dacier (eds), *Les Trésors des bibliothèques de France*, Paris, 1926–46, III, pp. 147–57.

Hoe, *176 Bindings*:
    R Hoe, *176 Historic and Artistic Book-Bindings*, New York, 1895.

Holmes, *Windsor*:
    R R Holmes, *Specimens of Royal, Fine and Historical Bookbindings, Selected from the Royal Library, Windsor Castle*, London, 1893.

Hueso-Rolland:
    F Hueso-Rolland, *Exposición de encuadernaciones españolas, siglos XII al XIX*, Madrid, 1934.

ISTC:
    Incunabula Short Title Catalogue, database with records of all fifteenth-century printing.

James:
    David James, *Qur'ans and Bindings from the Chester Beatty Library*, London, 1980.

Jolly, *Histoire*:
    C Jolly (ed.), *Histoire des bibliothèques françaises. Les Bibliothèques sous l'Ancien Régime*, Paris, [c. 1988].

Jolly, *Siècle d'or*:
    C Jolly (ed.), *Le Siècle d'or de l'imprimerie lyonnaise*, Paris, 1972.

Klepikov, 1962:
    S A Klepikov, 'Russian bookbinding from the middle of the 17th to the middle of the 19th century', *The Book Collector*, 11 (1962), pp. 437–47.

Klepikov, 1966:
    S A Klepikov, 'Historical notes on Ukrainian bookbinding', *The Book Collector*, 15 (1966), pp. 135–42.

Labarre, *Revue française*:
    A Labarre, 'Les reliures des anciens livres de prix', *Revue française d'histoire du livre*, 37 (1982), pp. 477–88.

Laffitte:
    M-P Laffitte, *Reliures royales du département des manuscrits (1515–1559)*, Paris: BNF, 2001.

Laffitte & Le Bars:
    M-P Laffitte and F Le Bars, *Reliures royales de la Renaissance; la librairie de Fontainebleau 1544–1570*, Paris: BNF, 1999.

La Reliure originale, 1959:
    [Bibliothèque Nationale], *La Reliure originale, exposition de la Société de la Reliure Originale* [with a show of bindings from the library of Jean Grolier], Paris, 1959.
La Reliure originale, 1961:
    La Reliure originale: Modern French Bookbindings, Exhibition at the Arts Council Gallery, London, 15 March – 22 April 1961 [Work by members of the Société de la Reliure Originale. Intro. by Professor J Millot].
La Reliure romantique:
    Société des bibliophiles et iconophiles de Belgique, *La Reliure romantique*, Bibliothèque Albert I, Brussels, 1961.
Laucevičius:
    E Laucevičius, *Lithuanian Library Bookbindings in the 15th–18th centuries*, Vilnius, 1976.
Le Bars, 'Reliures Henri III':
    F Le Bars, 'Les reliures de Henri III', in: Conihout, *Henri III mécène*, pp. 228–47.
Le Biccherne:
    L Borgia, E Carli, *et al.*, *Le Biccherne*, Rome, 1984.
Legature papali:
    Legature papali da Eugenio IV a Paolo VI, Biblioteca Apostolica Vaticana, Vatican City, 1977.
Libri, *Monuments inédits*:
    G Libri, *Monuments inédits ou peu connus faisant partie du cabinet de Guillaume Libri*, London, 1862.
Lings & Safadi:
    M Lings and Y H Safadi, *The Qur'an*, London, 1976.
López Serrano, 1942:
    M López Serrano, *La encuadernación en España*, Madrid, 1942.
López Serrano, 1972:
    M López Serrano, *La encuadernación española. Breve historia*, Madrid, 1972.
López Serrano, *Biblioteca de Palacio*:
    M López Serrano, *Biblioteca de Palacio. Encuadernaciones*, Madrid, [1950].
Macchi, *Dizionario*:
    F and L Macchi, *Dizionario illustrato della legatura*, Milan, 2002.
Malaguzzi, *Aosta*:
    F Malaguzzi, *Legature di pregio in Valle d'Aosta*, Turin, 1993.
Malaguzzi, *Il Canavese*:
    F Malaguzzi, *De libris compactis. Legature di pregio in Piemonte: Il Canavese*, Turin, 1995.
Malaguzzi, *Il Cuneese*:
    F Malaguzzi, *De libris compactis. Legature di pregio in Piemonte: Il Cuneese*, Turin, 2006.
Malaguzzi, *Il Vercellese*:
    F Malaguzzi, *De libris compactis. Legature di pregio in Piemonte: Il Vercellese*, Turin, 1998.
Malaguzzi, *La Valsesia*:
    F Malaguzzi, *De libris compactis. Legature di pregio in Piemonte: La Valsesia*, Turin, 1997.
Malaguzzi, *Legature romantiche*:
    F Malaguzzi, *Legature romantiche piemontesi*, Turin, 1998.
Malaguzzi, *Monferrato*:
    F Malaguzzi, *De libris compactis. Legature di pregio in Piemonte: Il Monferrato e l'Alessandrino*, Turin, 2002.
Malaguzzi, *Preziosi*:
    F Malaguzzi, *Preziosi in biblioteca. Mostra di legature in raccolte private piemontesi*, Turin, 1994.

Malavieille, 'La mechanisation de la reliure':
    Sophie Malavieille, 'La mechanisation de la reliure', in: H-J Martin and R Chartier, *Histoire de l'édition française*, III, Paris, 1985, pp. 64–5.
Malavieille, *Reliures et cartonnages*:
    Sophie Malavieille, *Reliures et cartonnages d'éditeur en France au XIXe siècle*, Paris, 1985.
Mattingley, *Coins*:
    H Mattingley, *Coins of the Roman Empire in the British Museum*, 5 vols, London, 1923–50.
Mazal:
    O Mazal, *Europäische Einbandkunst aus Mittelalter und Neuzeit; 270 Einbände der Österreichischen Nationalbibliothek*, Graz, 1970.
Médard:
    P Culot and D Rouger (eds), *Louis Médard et les relieurs de son temps*, Bibliothèque Municipale, Lunel, 2003.
Méjanes:
    [Jean-Marc Chatelain], *Un cabinet d'amateur à la fin du XVIIIe siècle: le Marquis de Méjanes bibliophile*, Avignon, 2006.
Meunier, *BN*:
    C Meunier, *Cent reliures de la Bibliothèque Nationale*, Paris, 1914.
Michon:
    L-M Michon, *La Reliure française*, Paris, 1951.
Michon, *Reliures mosaïquées*:
    L-M Michon, *Les Reliures mosaïquées du XVIIIe siècle*, Paris, 1956.
Miner, *Baltimore*:
    D Miner, *The History of Bookbinding, 525–1950 A.D. An exhibition … organised by the Walters Art Gallery and presented with the co-operation of the Baltimore Museum of Art*, Baltimore, 1957.
Miquel y Planas:
    R Miquel y Planas, *Restauración del arte hispano-árabe en la decoración exterior de los libros*, Barcelona, 1913.
Molinier:
    E Molinier, *Les Bronzes de la Renaissance. Les Plaquettes. Catalogue raisonné*, 2 vols, Paris, 1886.
Morazzoni:
    G Morazzoni, *La rilegatura piemontese*, Milan, 1929.
Moss:
    W E Moss, *The English Grolier*, Worth: Manor House Press, 1941–2.
Munby, *Book Collector*, 1952:
    A N L Munby, 'Query no. 2. Early trade bindings', *The Book Collector*, 1 (1952), pp. 128–9.
Nardelli:
    F P Nardelli, *La legatura italiana*, Rome, 1989.
Nardelli, 'Legatori Vaticani':
    F P Nardelli, 'Legatori Vaticani', in: F P Nardelli, *Fra stampa e legature*, Viterbo, 2000, pp. 253–61.
Needham, *Twelve Centuries*:
    P Needham, *Twelve Centuries of Bookbindings: 400–1600*, New York, 1979.
Nixon, 1985:
    H M Nixon, 'Quelques reliures d'un intérêt particulier pour les Polonais dans les bibliothèques anglaises', in: K Dymkowska and J Pasztaleniec-Jarzyńska (eds), *VIIIe Congrès international des bibliophiles, Varsovie, 23–29 juillet 1973*, Warsaw, 1985, pp. 64–9.
Nixon, 'Binding forgeries':
    H M Nixon, 'Binding forgeries', in: *VIth International Congress of Bibliophiles, Vienna, September 29–October 5*,

1969: Lectures, Vienna, 1971, pp. 69–83.
Nixon, *Book Collector*, 1962:
    H M Nixon, 'Grolier's Chrysostom', *The Book Collector*, 11 (1962), pp. 64–8.
Nixon, *Broxbourne*:
    H M Nixon, *Broxbourne Library. Styles and Designs of Bookbindings from the Twelfth to the Twentieth Century*, London, 1956.
Nixon, *Grolier*:
    H M Nixon, *Bookbindings from the Library of Jean Grolier*, British Museum, London, 1965.
Nixon, *Pierpont Morgan Library*:
    H M Nixon, *Sixteenth-century gold-tooled Bookbindings in the Pierpont Morgan Library*, New York, 1971.
Nixon, *Twelve Books*:
    H M Nixon, *Twelve Books in Fine Bindings from the Library of J.W. Hely-Hutchinson*, London, 1953.
Nixon, 'Wingfield':
    H M Nixon, 'French bookbindings for Sir Richard Wingfield and Jean Grolier', in: *Gatherings in Honor of Dorothy E. Miner*, Baltimore: Walters Art Gallery, 1974, pp. 301–15.
Nuvoloni, 'Commissioni Dogali':
    L Nuvoloni, '*Commissioni Dogali*: Venetian bookbindings in the British Library', in: D Pearson (ed.), *For the Love of the Binding*, London, 2000, pp. 81–109.
Oddos, *Revue française*:
    J-P Oddos, 'Reliures du XVIIe siècle à la Bibliothèque Municipale de Troyes', *Revue française d'histoire du livre*, 37 (1982), pp. 543–63.
Oldham, *Shrewsbury School*:
    J B Oldham, *Shrewsbury School Library Bindings*, Oxford, 1943.
Olivier:
    E Olivier, G Hermal and R de Roton, *Manuel de l'amateur de reliures armoriées françaises*, Paris, 1924–38.
Papantonio:
    Early American Bookbindings from the Collection of Michael Papantonio, New York, 1972.
Parent:
    A Parent, *Les Métiers du livre à Paris au XVIe siècle*, Geneva, 1974.
Parent-Charon:
    A Parent-Charon, 'Nouveaux documents sur les relieurs parisiens du XVIe siècle', *Revue française d'histoire du livre*, no. 36 (1982), pp. 389–408.
Passola:
    J M Passola, *Artesanía de la piel. Encuadernaciones en Vich*, Vich, 1968.
Penney:
    C L Penney, *An Album of Selected Bookbindings*, New York, 1967.
Pinto, 'Legatura di epoca aragonese':
    A Pinto, 'Legatura di epoca aragonese nella Biblioteca Nazionale di Napoli', *Bulletin du bibliophile*, 2001, 2, pp. 239–69.
Pitti, exhibition:
    F Rossi, *Mostra storica della legatura artistica in Palazzo Pitti*, Florence, 1922.
Plantin-Moretus, 1938:
    Gothieke en Renaissance boekbanden uit private verzamelingen tentoongesteld in het Museum Plantin-Moretus 12–27 November 1938, [Antwerp, 1938].
Portalis, *Longepierre*:
    Baron Roger Portalis, *Bernard de Requeleyne baron de Longepierre (1659–1721)*, Paris, 1905.

Quaritch, *Facsimiles*:
: B Quaritch, *A Collection of Facsimiles from Examples of Historic or Artistic Bookbindings*, London, 1889.

Quilici:
: P Quilici, *Legature antiche e di pregio*, 2 vols, Rome, 1995.

Quilici, 'Legatoria romana':
: P Quilici, 'La legatoria romana dal Rinascimento al Barocco', in: Tolomei, *Legatura romana barocca 1565–1700*, Rome, 1991, pp. 15–26.

Raby & Tanindi:
: J Raby and Z Tanindi, *Turkish Bookbinding in the 15th Century*, London, 1993.

Ract-Madoux, 'Essai de classement':
: P Ract-Madoux, 'Essai de classement chronologique des étiquettes de Derome le jeune', *Bulletin du bibliophile*, 1989, 2, pp. 382–91.

Rahir, *Riches reliures*:
: E Rahir (Damascène Morgand), *Livres dans de riches reliures*, Paris, 1910.

Ramsden, *French*:
: C Ramsden, *French Bookbinders 1789–1848*, London, 1950.

Regemorter, *Chester Beatty*:
: B de Regemorter, *Some Oriental Bindings in the Chester Beatty Library*, Dublin, 1961.

Renouard:
: P Renouard, *Marques typographiques parisiennes*, Paris, 1926.

Rietstap:
: J B Rietstap, *Armorial général*, Gouda, 1884–7; *Planches de l'Armorial de J B Rietstap par H [et] V Rolland*, The Hague, 1938.

Romme, *Book Collector*, 1969:
: M M Romme [Foot], 'Contemporary collectors xliv: The Henry Davis Collection I', *The Book Collector*, 18 (1969), pp. 23–44 (this article was updated and reprinted in Foot, *Studies*, pp. 355–83).

Romme, *Book Collector*, Spring 1971:
: M M Romme [Foot], 'Foreign bookbindings ix: a binding for Jacques Malenfant', *The Book Collector*, 20 (1971), p. 69.

Romme, *Book Collector*, Summer 1971:
: M M Romme [Foot], 'Foreign bookbindings x: a binding by Claude de Picques', *The Book Collector*, 20 (1971), p. 227 (these two articles were updated and reprinted in Foot, *Studies*, pp. 336–9).

Romme, *Book Collector*, 1972:
: M M Romme [Foot], 'Foreign bookbindings xiii: a binding by Devers, c. 1770–83', *The Book Collector*, 21 (1972), p. 107 (this article was reprinted in Foot, *Sudies*, pp. 224–5).

Ruysschaert, 'Le legature romane':
: J Ruysschaert, 'Le legature romane della Regina Christina di Svezia e la bottega degli Andreoli', in: Tolomei, *Legatura romana barocca*, pp. 27–30.

Ruysschaert, *Les Frères Andreoli*:
: J Ruysschaert, *Les Frères Andreoli relieurs de Chigi*, Vatican City, 1992.

Sarre:
: F Sarre, *Islamic Bookbindings* (trans. F D O'Byrne), Berlin, n.d. [1923].

Schäfer:
: M von Arnim, *Europäische Einbandkunst aus sechs Jahrhunderten*, Schweinfurt, 1992.

Schonath:
: W Schonath, 'Polnische Bucheinbände in der Graf von Schönbornschen Schlossbibliothek Pommersfelden', *Gutenberg Jahrbuch*, 1962, pp. 507–11.

Schunke, 1959:
: I Schunke, 'Der Meister der Estiennebibel und die Renaissance-Buchbinder in Paris', *Bibliothèque d'humanisme et renaissance*, xxi (1959), pp. 595–605.

Schunke, *Gutenberg Jahrbuch*:
: I Schunke, 'Begegnungen mit Grolier', *Gutenberg Jahrbuch*, 1950, pp. 381–8.

Schunke, *Palatina*:
: I Schunke, *Die Einbände der Palatina in der Vaticanischen Bibliothek*, 3 vols (Studi e Testi, 216–18), Vatican City, 1962.

Schunke, 'Venezianische Renaissance-Einbände':
: I Schunke, 'Venezianische Renaissance-Einbände. Ihre Entwicklung und ihre Werkstätten', in: *Studi di bibliografia e di storia in onore di Tammaro de Marinis*, Verona, 1964, vol. iv, pp. 123–200.

Shipman:
: A-J V Le Roux de Lincy, *Researches Concerning Jean Grolier, his Life and his Library*, ed. Baron Portalis, trans. and rev. Carolyn Shipman, New York, 1907.

Sonntag:
: C Sonntag, *Kostbare Bucheinbände des XV. bis XIX. Jahrhunderts*, Leipzig, 1912.

Spawn:
: W Spawn, *Bookbinding in America 1680–1910 from the Collection of Frederick E Maser*, Bryn Mawr, 1983.

The Italian Book:
: J Irving Davis, *The Italian Book 1465–1900*, National Book League, London, 1953.

Thoinan:
: E Thoinan, *Les Relieurs français (1500–1800)*, Paris, 1893.

Thomas:
: H Thomas, *Early Spanish Bookbindings XI–XV centuries*, London: Bibliographical Society, 1939.

Thompson, *Libri*, 1960:
: L S Thompson, 'Introductory notes on the history of bookbinding in Spanish America', *Libri*, vol. 10, no. 1 (1960), pp. 10–22.

Tolomei, 'I ferri':
: G V Tolomei, 'I ferri e le botteghe di legatori', in: Tolomei, *Legatura romana barocca*, pp. 31–46.

Tolomei, *Legatura romana barocca*:
: G V Tolomei, *Legatura romana barocca 1565–1700*, Rome, 1991.

Tolomei, 'Reliures romaines':
: G V Tolomei, 'Reliures romaines d'archives des XVe et XVIe siècles', *Bulletin du bibliophile*, 1993, 2, pp. 294–320.

Toulet, 'L'école lyonnaise':
: J Toulet, 'L'école lyonnaise de reliure', in: C Jolly (ed.), *Le Siècle d'or de l'imprimerie lyonnaise*, Paris, 1972, pp. 131–58.

Toulet, 'Les reliures':
: J Toulet, 'Les reliures', in: R Chartier and H-J Martin, *Histoire de l'édition française*, vol. I: *Le Livre conquérant*, Paris, 1982, pp. 530–9.

Treasures, 1965:
: D Flower and H M Nixon, *Treasures from Private Libraries in England ... Shown at the National Book League*, London, 1965.

Weale:
: W H J Weale, *Bookbindings and Rubbings of Bindings in the National Art Library, South Kensington*, 2 vols, London, 1898, 1894.

Whitehead, *BLJ*:
: H Whitehead, 'Antonio de Sancha, 1720–1790: a tentative list of holdings', *The British Library Journal*, IX, 2 (1983), pp. 140–60.

Whitney Hoff:
: A Boinet, *Bibliothèque de Madame G Whitney Hoff*, 2 vols, Paris, 1933.

Wittockiana, *Ocho siglos*:
: *Ocho siglos de encuadernación española; Huit siècles de reliures en Espagne; Spaanse boekbanden uit acht eeuwen*, Brussels: Bibliotheca Wittockiana, 1985.

Wormsley:
: H G Fletcher *et al.*, *The Wormsley Library. A Personal Selection by Sir Paul Getty, K.B.E.*, London, 1999.

FRENCH BINDINGS

1 *An early thirteenth-century (Parisian) Romanesque binding*

[Gospels of St Matthew and St Mark, glossed], MS on parchment; four historiated initials; decorated initials in red and blue; written in Paris, c. 1200. fol.

361 × 240 × 65 mm. (M 72) Davis 386

Brown calf over wooden boards, tooled in blind to a design of three concentric frames, built up of individual stamps, with a vertical strip of tools in the centre. The same design on both covers, but effected with different tools. Those on the upper cover include a kneeling elder, two birds in curved lines, two birds face-to-face, a griffin biting its tail, a mounted horseman, and a dog in front of a tree. Traces of four pairs of clasps, hinging on the upper cover, closing on pins, c. 45 mm. from the fore-edge and c. 50 mm. from head and tail edges, on the lower cover. Boards cut flush with the edges of the leaves. Edges: plain.

Resewn on four supports; spine restored with most of the original leather preserved; new headcaps. New endbands.

Endleaves: parchment pastedowns and one free parchment leaf, at both ends (free endleaf conjugate with pastedown of lower cover).

Repairs: at covers and spine.

PROVENANCE: Manuscript inscription: 'Hec sunt euangelia mathi et marcj. que sunt andree de S[an]c[t]o eugendo' [word erased], i.e. Andrew of St-Oyan; abbey of St-Claude du Jura; Louis Fière of Romans, Drôme; Antoine Pol (book plate); Sotheby's, 31.v.1960, *1* (pl.).

REFERENCES: A R A Hobson, 'A new Parisian Romanesque binding', *Burlington Magazine*, CII (1960), pp. 263–4, pls 41–2; E Kyriss, 'Vorgotische verzierte Einbände der Landesbibliothek Karlsruhe', *Gutenberg Jahrbuch*, 1961, p. 284; Romme, *Book Collector*, 1969, p. 27, note 25, pl. vi (lower cover); H M Nixon, 'The binding of the Winton Domesday', in: M Biddle (ed.), *Winchester Studies I. Winchester in the Early Middle Ages*, Oxford, 1976, p. 536, note 2; Foot, *Revue française*, p. 371; C de Hamel, *Glossed Books of the Bible and the Origins of the Paris Booktrade*, Woodbridge, 1984, pp. 67, 68, 72, 77, 82; Schmidt-Künsemüller, *Die abendländischen romanischen Blindstempeleinbände*, Stuttgart, 1985, no. 84.

LITERATURE: G D Hobson, *English Binding before 1500*, Cambridge, 1929, chapter 1; G D Hobson, 'Further notes on Romanesque bindings', *The Library*, 4th series, xv (1934–5), pp. 161–211; G D Hobson, 'Some early bindings and binders' tools', *The Library*, 4th series, xix (1938–9), pp. 202–49; G D Hobson, 'Trois reliures romanes', in: E Dacier (ed.), *Trésors des bibliothèques de France*, IV (1933), pp. 101–7; Jeanne Dupic, 'Reliures du XIIIe siècle à la bibliothèque de Rouen', *Trésors des bibliothèques de France*, XXI (1936), pp. 81–7; Nixon, *Broxbourne*, no. 1.

Note: The historiated initials have been attributed to the 'Almagest' atelier (also named the 'Master of the Sorbonne Ptolemy'). The book forms a pair with the Gospels of St

Luke, glossed, Lons-le Saunier 4, given to the abbey of St-Claude du Jura by Andrew of St-Oyan, archpriest of Treffort, in the 13th century. The binding has been attributed by G D Hobson and C de Hamel to a group of 'closely related and miscellaneous' bindings, associated with the 'Starry Griffin' bindings.

2 A Paris binding, c. 1502

Dante Alighieri, *Le terze rime. Lo'nferno, e'l purgatorio, e'l paradiso*, Venice: Aldus, August 1502. 8vo.

163 × 100 × 35 mm.   (P 1361) Davis 318

Brown sheepskin over paste boards, tooled in blind with a floral roll around a panel, depicting on the upper cover the Virgin and Child (legend partly illegible: MVLIER.AMICTA SOLE/ET LVNA/ SVB PEDIBVS.EIVS) and on the lower cover St John the Baptist, carrying a lamb, a ?bull's head between his feet (legend partly illegible: EGO VOX CLAMANTIS/IN DESERTO PARATE/VIAS D[OMI]NI). Both panels have heads in medallions at the four corners and in the lower border a shield with the monogram GIR. Traces of two pairs of ties. Small squares. Edges: gilt and gauffered (probably later).

Sewn on three whittawed split leather supports, laced in and stuck down beneath pastedown; supports show as raised bands on the spine, tooled in blind with lines; four compartments, tooled in blind with lines.

Endbands: single with a bead; pink and blue silk (probably later) over tawed leather cores (laced into the boards at an angle).

New endleaves: paper pastedowns and one free leaf conjugate with the pastedown, at both ends.

Repairs: at corners of the covers and head and tail of spine.

PROVENANCE:	On title-page in manuscript: Henry D[?P]rietree(?); Dyson Perrins (book plate and number 160; sold: Sotheby's, 17.vi.1946, *99*); J R Abbey (book plate; 'J.A.3067/ 17:6:1946'; sold: Sotheby's, 21.vi.1965, *243*).
REFERENCES:	Foot, *Revue française*, p. 378.
LITERATURE:	G D Hobson, 'Parisian bindings', p. 400, pl. 1a; R Brun, 'Guide de l'amateur de reliures anciennes', *Bulletin du bibliophile et du bibliothécaire*, new series, 5 (1936), pp. 104–6 (attributing GIR-signed panels to Guillaume Le Rouge); Gid & Laffitte, pp. 127, 343 (nos. 134, 236).
Compare:	Weale, R. 504, 506, 508, 512.
Note:	Guillaume Le Rouge: printer and bookseller in Paris, 1493–1517; Gid & Laffitte attribute these panels to Paris, c. 1501–8.

3 A Paris binding from the 'Atelier Louis XII' – Simon Vostre, c. 1505–15

Jean de Pins, *Divae Catherinae Senensis, simul et clarissimi viri Philippi Beroaldi Bononiensis vita*, Bologna: Benedictus Hectoreus, 22 September 1505; rubricated in red and blue. 4to.

221 × 158 × 26 mm.   (P 1525) Davis 362

Brown calf over paste boards, tooled in blind with traces of gold tooling, to a panel design with a border

of rectangular floral diaper tools, fleurs-de-lis at the corners; an inner border of strap-work tools, fleurs-de-lis tools and half-circular tools; the centre panel is filled with vertical strips of floral diaper tools and strap-work. Traces of two pairs of ties. Small squares. Edges: gilt and gauffered (possibly later) with large stylized flowers.

Rebacked; sewn on four supports, laced in, showing as raised bands on the spine; title tooled in blind in second compartment (modern). New endbands.

Endleaves: paper pastedowns at both ends; at the front: one free leaf plus a parchment stub; at the end: two free paper leaves.

Repairs: at corners; rebacked.

PROVENANCE: On title-page in manuscript: 'Collegij/Congregat[ion]is/Anneciacensis [Annécy]/S.Pauli' and 'Sum ex libris Phaedris(?)'; on verso of last page of text: 'frustra opponuntur Divinae Voluntati in humana consilia'; on pastedown of lower cover: 'Emptus 12 assib 1569'; on endleaf: 'Nee l'an 1347'; Jean Baptiste Marduel, vicarius of St-Nicetius in Lyon (book plate); duc de la Vallière (*Catalogue des livres de la bibliothèque de feu M. le Duc de la Vallière*, pt. iii, 1788, *4761*); Henry Harris (sold: Sotheby's, 22.vi.1936,

	112, pl.); J R Abbey (book plate; 'J.A.1334/16:7:1936'; sold: Sotheby's, 23.vi.1965, *549*, pl.).
REFERENCES:	Nixon, *Broxbourne*, p. 36, note 1; *Treasures*, 1965, 71; Guignard, 1966, pl. II.5, p. 206, no. 2, p. 232, no. 2; Romme, *Book Collector*, 1969, p. 27, note 24; Foot, *Revue française*, p. 378.
LITERATURE:	Dacier, 'Les premières reliures françaises', pp. 7–40; Guignard, 1966, pp. 202–39; Guignard, 1968, pp. 229–49; Nixon, *Pierpont Morgan Library*, no. 3; Nixon, 'Wingfield', pp. 305–7; Needham, *Twelve Centuries*, pp. 135–9; Devaux, pp. 53–4, 57; Hobson, *Humanists*, pp. 172–4; Jean-Marc Châtelain, 'Les reliures parisiennes de l'atelier de Simon Vostre', *Bulletin du bibliophile*, 1993, 1, pp. 99–111.
Note:	Jean de Pins: 1470–1537, bishop of Rieux, French ambassador to Venice and Rome; presented a collection of manuscripts to the royal library at Fontainebleau. Atelier Louis XII: the first French bindery to use gold tooling, active in Paris: c. 1503–21; this atelier also carried out work for François I and has been equated with the workshop of Simon Vostre, after whose death in 1521 the contents of the bindery were sold (1523) to Pierre Roffet, but Nixon, 'Wingfield', doubts whether Roffet ever used Vostre's tools. See also: Introduction, p. 7.

4   *A Paris binding, c. 1510*

Martinus de Lauduno, *Epistola exhortatoria*, [Paris]: J. Badius Ascensis, 15 March 1507; rubricated initials; illuminated border. 4to.

196 × 140 × 15 mm. (P 924) Davis 363

Brown sheep over paste boards, tooled in blind with fillets and a large panel, showing a wide border with the Virgin and Child (top), the three Magi (right-hand side), the Massacre of the Innocents, a shield with a roundel, and a soldier (bottom), King Herod, Emperor Augustus, and the Sibyl (left-hand side). In the centre a full-size crowned and bearded man holding a sword and an orb, having been interpreted as: an emperor, Charlemagne, Charles V, or God the Father. Traces of four pairs of ties. Edges: plain.

Sewn on four split alum-tawed supports, laced in straight, showing as raised bands on the spine; five compartments, tooled in blind with lines. No endbands.

Endleaves: white paper pastedowns and three free leaves, at both ends.

Repairs: at the corners of the covers, at the joints and at head and tail of the spine.

PROVENANCE:	On the pastedown of the upper cover in manuscript: 'S. Tiersonnier 1704'. Notes in a different and later hand to the effect that the binding was made in Venice by Jean (Giovanni) Bernardi [a misattribution]. Book plate with the initials B O; Michael Tomkinson (book plate); E P Goldschmidt (Catalogue 80, *62*); bought: Goldschmidt, 26.vii.1948.
REFERENCES:	Goldschmidt, no. 68, pl. xxx.
LITERATURE:	H Lempertz, *Bilderhefte zur Geschichte des Bücherhandels*, Cologne, 1853–65, pl. c4; Weale, R. 498; A Ledieu, *Les Reliures de la bibliothèque communale d'Abbeville*, Paris, 1891, pl. 12; E G Duff sale: Sotheby's, 16.iii.1925, *29, 79, 95*; G D Hobson, 'Parisian bindings', pp. 417–19, pl. vii; Devaux, p. 42; Gid, no. 620; Fogelmark, p. 130 (b); Gid & Laffitte, pp. 126–7 (no. 82).
Compare:	Weale, R. 499.

5   *A Paris binding, c. 1510 with panels signed by André Boule*

Nicolaus de Gorra, *Fundamentum aureum omnis anni sermonum*, [Paris]: M N de la Barre, n.d. [1509]; ruled in red. 8vo.

167 × 102 × 35 mm. (P 1362) Davis 319

Brown calf over wooden boards, tooled in blind with lines, and panels depicting, on the upper cover within a three-sided border with floral and vine branches, wyverns and a running animal: the martyrdom of St Sebastian; along the bottom: ANDRI:BOVLE; on the lower cover within a border with acorn, vine and floral branches, a wyvern and a (?)dragon: the crucifixion with St Thomas Aquinas and St Catherine of Siena, beneath which: ANDRI BOVLE. Traces of two pairs of clasps, hinging on the upper cover. Edges of boards have been tooled later, probably in the 18th century. Edges: gilt and gauffered with flowers and 'frere/gedeoni/pesant'.

   Sewn on four split alum-tawed supports, laced in, showing as raised bands on the spine, tooled in blind with lines; five compartments showing rope marks; later (possibly 19th century) paper label

in second compartment. Later endbands: single with a bead; sewn in red and white.
  Endleaves: paper pastedowns at both ends; at the front: a stub; at the end: three free leaves.
  Repairs: at corners, edges of boards, joints, and head and tail of spine.

PROVENANCE:	Frère Gideon Pesant; on title-page in manuscript: 'Bachelier 1582'; in a different hand: 'Sr Jacobus (?) Despr(?)id(?) (?)ibat (?)'; J R Abbey (book plate; 'J.A.1240/8:4:1936'; sold: Sotheby's, 22.vi.1965, *351*).
REFERENCES:	Foot, *Revue française*, p. 378.
LITERATURE:	Gruel, I, p. 59 (pl.); *BFAC*, 1891, Case B, no. 23; Thoinan, p. 211; K Westendorp, *Die Kunst der alten Buchbinder*, Halle, 1909, pl. 13; H Martin, *Exposition du livre français*, Paris, 1923, pl. opp. p. 136; Goldschmidt, no. 56, pl. xxiv; G D Hobson, 'Parisian bindings', p. 427, no. 44, p. 426, no. 13, pp. 406–7, 430, no. 6, p. 431, no. 23; Plantin-Moretus, 1938, no. 74; Michon, p. 34, pl. xi; Devaux, p. 43; Gid, nos. 325, 473; Fogelmark, p. 129, note 257; Gid & Laffitte, pp. 97–101, 286 (nos. 67, 195).
Same panels on:	BL, C.67.a.1 (Paris, 1513); Canterbury Cathedral, chapter library, L.4–19 (Paris, Jehan Petit, n.d.).
Compare:	Weale, R. 494, 495; R. 496, 497.
Note:	Gid & Laffitte attribute these 'Andri Boule' panels to Paris, c. 1500–23; André Boule was a bookseller and binder in Paris: c. 1499–1543; he gave his daughter in marriage: 1523.

6 *A Paris binding, c. 1515*

J J Pontanus, *Opera*, Lyon: for Barth. Troth, February 1514. 8vo.

178 × 105 × 43 mm. (P 828) Davis 320

Dark brown calf over paste boards, tooled in blind with a panel showing, within a border with floral branches, wyverns, birds and artichokes: St John the Evangelist at Patmos, writing while an eagle holds his inkpot and pencase; below: a shield with a goat or ram with a star, between two wyverns. Traces of four pairs of ties; remnants of whittawed ties visible beneath pastedowns. Edges: plain and lightly gauffered (three rows of roundels).
  Rebacked; sewn on four supports. New endbands.
  Endleaves: at the front: paper pastedown and one (original) free leaf pasted onto a new leaf plus a second new free leaf; at the end: new paper pastedown and two new free leaves.
  Repairs: at covers; rebacked.

PROVENANCE:	Erased manuscript inscription on pastedown of upper cover; manuscript notes on original endleaf; on title-page in manuscript (17th century): 'Ex libris Joannis Filleau Antecessoris pictavien[sis] et fisci advocati'; E Gordon Duff; E P Goldschmidt (Catalogue 75, *127*); bought: Goldschmidt, 20.ix.1944.
REFERENCES:	Goldschmidt, no. 78.
LITERATURE:	*BFAC*, 1891, pl. x; G D Hobson, 'Parisian bindings', p. 427, no. 35; Needham, *Twelve Centuries*, pp. 128–30.
Note:	Pictaviensis: from Poitiers.

7 A binding made c. 1520–25

Juvenal, *Iuvenalis familiare commentum cum Antonij Mancinelli … explanatione*, Paris: in aedibus Ascensianis, 9 March 1505. 4to.

210 × 142 × 45 mm.　　　　　　　　　　　　　　　　　　　　　　　　　　　　(P 587) Davis 364

Brown calf over wooden boards, tooled in blind to a panel design with blind lines along the border and in the centre of the upper cover: two impressions of a panel [i.e. two casts of the same panel] depicting St John the Baptist, preaching, and on the lower cover two impressions of a panel [ditto] showing St James of Compostela with a hanged man. Remnants of two pairs of clasps, hinging on the upper cover. Edges: plain.

Sewn on three split tanned leather supports, laced in straight, showing as raised bands on the spine, tooled in blind with lines; four compartments showing rope marks. Endbands: primary sewing over leather cores (broken off; no visible tie-downs), covered by headcaps, sewn through.

Later endleaves: paper pastedowns and one free leaf conjugate with the pastedown, at both ends.
Repairs: at spine and corners.

THE HENRY DAVIS GIFT

PROVENANCE: On title-page in manuscript: 'Jo: faictonerus (?) 90'; 'Skotus' [or 'Skofus'; partly erased]; Exeter Cathedral Library, 1749 (book plate); bought: Quaritch, 12.iii.1942.
LITERATURE: E G Duff sale: Sotheby's, 16.iii.1925, *178* (both panels); G D Hobson, 'Parisian bindings', p. 426, no. 30, p. 427, no. 32, p. 401.
Compare: Weale, R. 419 (St John panel: not identical).
Note: G D Hobson, 'Parisian bindings', states that these panels were used in England, a statement contradicted by J B Oldham, *Blind Panels of English Binders*, Cambridge, 1958, p. 4. However, as Fogelmark has shown, these panels were cast and not engraved and casts could therefore have been used anywhere.

8 *A binding probably made in Angers, for or by Clement Alexandre, c. 1522*

Joannes de Selva, *Tractatus de beneficio*, Lyon: J Moylin, 14 February 1521. 4to.

200 × 138 × 43 mm. (P 825) Davis 365

Brown sheep over paste boards, tooled in blind with a border roll with Renaissance ornaments, a two-headed bird and the cipher of Clement Alexandre of Angers; the central panel filled with vertical impressions of a roll with flies and a smaller version of Clement Alexandre's cipher. Remnants of four pairs of tanned leather ties. Edges: plain.

Sewn on three split alum-tawed supports, laced in straight, showing as raised bands on the spine, tooled in blind with lines; four compartments, tooled in blind with lines. No endbands.

New endleaves: paper pastedowns and one free leaf, at both ends.

Repairs: at joints and at top and tail of spine.

French Bindings

PROVENANCE: On title-page in manuscript [erased]: 'Ex libris Martinij Ru [?z or ig?]e'; different hand: 'Ex libr. Joan. Civ[?b]moise'; on pastedown in manuscript: 'P.H. Pauncefort Daucombe'; E P Goldschmidt (sold: 20.ix.1944).
REFERENCES: Goldschmidt, no. 112, pl. cv, pp. 34, 48; Foot, *Revue française*, p. 379.
LITERATURE: Gruel, I, p. 41, II, p. 19; Weale, pp. lxxii–iii; Michon, p. 36; J-M Arnoult, 'Angers', in: *Repertoire bibliographique des livres imprimés en France au 16e siècle*, tom. 1, Baden-Baden, 1989, 6.
Note: Clement Alexandre (1509–1538), bookseller, son of Jean (1485–1505), publisher/bookseller in Angers. Clement was stationer to the University of Angers, master of the mint and receiver general of the town: 1522–38.

9 *A Paris binding by Jehan Norvi(n)s, c. 1525*

Desiderius Erasmus, *Paraphrasis in Evangelium Matthei*, Paris: Pierre Vidou for Conrad Resch, 1523; printed in red and black. (long) 24mo.

114 × 56 × 30 mm. (P 824) Davis 321

Dark brown calf over paste boards, tooled in blind. On the upper cover a panel depicting St Michael slaying Satan, below which a strip with two woodhouses and a shield with the initials IN; on the lower cover a panel depicting Bathsheba in her bath, King David behind her, below the scene is a strip signed: IEHAN : NORVIS. Edges: gilt and gauffered (large branches and flowers).

Sewn on four split alum-tawed supports, laced in at an angle, showing as raised bands on the spine, tooled in blind with a line; five compartments, head and tail compartment tooled in blind with hatching. Endbands: single with a bead; primary sewing over (?)rolled leather cores (broken at the joints), tied down; secondary sewing of blue silk.

Endleaves: paper pastedowns and three free paper leaves, at both ends.

PROVENANCE: On title-page in manuscript: 'Sebastiani Schefferi 1661'; Dr Sebastianus Schefferus (book plate); Ashburnham collection (sold: Sotheby's, 25.vi.1897, *1500*); G Dunn (book plate; sold: Sotheby's, 3.ii.1914, *1054*); E P Goldschmidt (book plate; Catalogue 75, *66*); bought: Goldschmidt, 20.ix.1944.
REFERENCES: Goldschmidt, no. 130, pl. cvi; Foot, *Revue française*, p. 378 (title and date misprinted).
LITERATURE: Gruel, II, p. 122; Weale, R. 517, 518; Gumuchian, 1930, no. 14, pl. xi, xlv; G D Hobson, 'Parisian bindings', pp. 404, 432; Plantin-Moretus, 1938, no. 72; Michon, p. 35; Hobson, *French and Italian*, p. 5; D Shaw, 'Books printed by Pierre Vidoue in 24° format', *Gutenberg Jahrbuch*, 1974, pp. 117–22; Fogelmark, pp. 139–40; Foot, 'Some bookbindings in the Herzog August Bibliothek', p. 100. See also Davis 322 (identical panels on same book) and 323 (nos. 10–11 below).
Compare: Needham, *Twelve centuries*, no. 38.
Note: Jehan Norvis (Norvins?): bookbinder, possibly bookseller in Paris: c. 1523–45; according to Hobson, *French and Italian*, he moved to Louvain in the 1530s. These two panels occur on several copies of Erasmus's *Paraphrasis ... Matthei* (Vidou, 1523).

10 *A Paris binding by Jehan Norvi(n)s, c. 1525*

Desiderius Erasmus, *Paraphrasis in Evangelium Matthei*, Paris: Pierre Vidou for Conrad Resch, 1523. (long) 24mo.

115 × 56 × 30 mm. (P 1089) Davis 322

Possibly rebound with the original covers retained: see below. Dark brown calf over paste boards, tooled in blind with on the upper cover a panel depicting St Michael, slaying Satan, signed IN; on the lower cover a panel showing Bathsheba and David, signed IEHAN : NORVIS (see Davis 321, no. 9 above). Edges of boards tooled with blind lines and dashes, probably later. Edges: gilt and gauffered (see Davis 321, no. 9 above).

Rebacked; part of original sewing retained: sewn on four split alum-tawed supports, laced in at an angle. Endbands: single with a bead; primary sewing over (invisible) cores, tied down; secondary sewing of blue silk.

Endleaves: paper pastedowns at both ends; at the front: one (later) free paper leaf; at the end: two free paper leaves.

Repairs: possibly rebound (boards look new) with original covers onlaid; certainly rebacked, although part of the original sewing has been retained.

PROVENANCE: On title-page in manuscript: 'Ph. Schneider, stud. theol. Erlangen 1847'; in red ink on pastedown of upper cover: '5.C.'; Thomas Brooke (book plate; sold: Sotheby's, 27.v.1921, *496*); A Kay (book plate; sold: Sotheby's, 27.v.1930, *300*); Eduardo J Bullrich (book plate); bought: Sotheby's, 17.iii.1952, *143*.
REFERENCES: Foot, *Revue française*, p. 378 (title and date misprinted).
LITERATURE: Davis 321 (no. 9 above; and literature cited there); Davis 323 (no. 11 below).

French Bindings

10 11

11   *A Paris, or possibly Louvain, binding by Jehan Norvi(n)s, c. 1540*

C V A Juvencus and C Sedulius, *Historiae Evangelicae*, Cologne: Eucharius, July 1537 [and] F Bonadus, *Eximii prophetarum antistitis regia Davidis oracula*, Paris: C Wechel, 1531. 8vo.

163 × 101 × 34 mm.   (P 615) Davis 323

Brown calf over paste boards, tooled in blind with two lines outlining a panel, depicting within a border of flower branches, wyverns and thistles: two rows of crested acorns, signed: JEHAN : NORVIS. Traces of two pairs of ties. Edges plain.

   Rebacked with part of the original spine strip retained; sewn on four alum-tawed supports, laced in straight (traces), showing as raised bands on the spine, tooled in blind with lines; five compartments showing rope marks. Endbands: single; primary sewing over (probably) leather cores (once laced in), tied down.

   Endleaves: parchment manuscript (Latin) pastedowns at both ends; at the front: remnant of free paper leaf, parchment and paper stubs round first and last sections; at the end: one free paper leaf.

   Repairs: at edges of boards; rebacked.

PROVENANCE: On title-page in manuscript: 'Carthusianoru[m] in Lovanio; E P Goldschmidt (book plate, Catalogue 71, *102*); bought: Goldschmidt, 19.v.1943.

37

REFERENCES: Foot, *Revue française*, pp. 378–9.
LITERATURE: Gruel, I, p. 137, *BFAC*, 1891, pl. x; Weale, p. lxxv; Goldschmidt, no. 131, pl. xlix; G D Hobson, 'Parisian bindings', p. 432; Plantin-Moretus, 1938, no. 71; Michon, p. 35; Gid, no. 602; Devaux, p. 44; Gid & Laffitte, pp. 143–4 (no. 95); Foot, *Marsh*, p. 77, fig. 3.3. See also Davis 321 (no. 9 above).
Note: The Louvain provenance and Hobson's assumption that Norvis moved to Louvain in the 1530s (*French and Italian*, p. 5) make it possible that this is a Flemish, Louvain, binding, although panels that were cast and not engraved cannot provide evidence for the place where they were used.

12 *A binding probably made in Paris with the arms and salamander of François I, c. 1531*

Alberto Pio, *Tres et viginti libri in locos lucubrationum variarum D. Erasmi*, Paris: Badius Ascensius, March 1531. fol.

341 × 219 × 38 mm. (P 1526) Davis 388

Brown calf over paste boards, tooled in gold with blind lines, to a panel design with an outer border of repeated, large interlacing-circles tools; a second border with smaller interlacing-circles tools; stylized fleurs-de-lis on the corners of the central panel, which is surrounded by a border with smaller interlacing-circles tools. In the centre panel from top to bottom: the royal arms of France, made up of separate tools, a circle of scallop shells around four fleurs-de-lis, the crowned salamander badge of François I, a circle of flame tools around four fleurs-de-lis, and the royal arms of France. Traces of four pairs of ties. Edges: gilt and gauffered (compare Davis 321, 322, nos. 9 and 10 above).

Rebacked with part of the original spine strip retained. Sewn on seven split supports (material invisible), showing as raised bands on the spine, tooled in blind with lines; kettle stitch bands, tooled in blind with dashes; ten compartments, tooled in blind with lines. Endbands: new.

Endleaves: paper pastedowns and two free paper leaves at both ends (probably later).

Repairs: at corners; rebacked.

PROVENANCE: On title-page in manuscript: 'Bibliothecae Augudusis ff Erdni (?) S.Augustini f. Dominicus Brabant prive(?)'; in a different hand: 'Justus Anthoni Erem: Augusti'; Michel de Bry (on pastedown: his red goatskin label tooled in gold: 'Pro captu lectoris'; sold: E Ader, *Bibliothèque d'un humaniste*, Paris, Hôtel Drouot 1966, *83*, pl. v); bought: Hôtel Drouot, 5/6.xii.1966.
REFERENCES: Romme, *Book Collector*, 1969, pp. 26–7, note 23; Foot, *Revue française*, p. 378.
Compare: Dacier, 'Les premières reliures françaises', pp. 7–40; Dacier, 'Une treizième reliure de Louis XII', pp. 186–92; Guignard, 1966.
Note: The tools on this binding are similar to those used by Simon Vostre and by Pierre Roffet, but they are not identical with those of either of these two shops. François I of France: 1494–1547.

12

13   *A binding possibly made in Paris, c. 1535*

M Valerius Martiali, *Epigrammaton libri xiiii*, Lyon: S Gryphius, 1534. 8vo.

154 × 99 × 27 mm.   (P 1312) Davis 324

Brown calf over paste boards, tooled in gold, with blind lines, to a panel design; fleurons in the corners, fleurs-de-lis and stylized flowers in the border and a central panel (block) depicting (top half) a floral ornament and (bottom half) a squatting naked figure between giant fir cones and leafy ornaments. Traces of two pairs of ties. Edges: gilt and gauffered, with on the fore-edge: MARTIALIS XIIII EPI; on the top edge: IE LE VEULT; and on the tail edge: PLVS OVLTR[E].

Sewn on four alum-tawed supports, laced in straight, showing as raised bands on the spine; five compartments tooled in blind with lines and in gold with alternating stylized flowers and fleurs-de-lis. Endbands: double; red and undyed thread over alum-tawed cores (laced in), tied down.

Endleaves: paper pastedowns at both ends; at the end: one free conjugate paper leaf. Manuscript visible beneath pastedown of lower cover, parchment stub; parchment manuscript stub pasted down onto pastedown of upper cover.

PROVENANCE: Lord Clinton (sold: Sotheby's, 3.vii.1946, *344*, pl.); J R Abbey (book plate; 'J.A.3020/3:7:1946'; sold: Sotheby's, 23.vi.1965, *470*, pl.).
REFERENCES: Hobson, *French and Italian*, no. 12 (pl.).
Note: French Renaissance gilt panels are uncommon. Better known examples are Tory's 'pot cassé' panels in two sizes. Compare also Davis 342–6 (no. 35 below) for a later and more symmetrical floral panel.

14   *A Paris binding by Etienne Roffet, c. 1535–40*

L C Firmianus Lactantius, *Divinarum institutionum libri vii* [and other works], Venice: Aldus & A Socerus, April 1515. 8vo.

170 × 100 × 50 mm.   (P 339) Davis 327

Olive-brown goatskin over paste boards, tooled mainly in silver (oxidized) to an overall geometrical design, with lines in blind and gold, bent curving tools and small hatched fleurons. Edges of boards: tooled with a blind line. Edges: plain gilt.

Sewn on five supports (material not visible), laced in straight (kettle stitches not emphasized), showing as raised bands on the spine, tooled in blind with lines; six compartments, tooled in blind with lines. Endbands: single with a bead; dark and pale green silk over alum-tawed cores (broken or cut off at the joint), tied down.

Endleaves: paper pastedowns and three free paper leaves, at both ends.

Repairs: small repairs at the top corners and at the head of the spine.

PROVENANCE: On title-page in manuscript in various hands: 'Ex libris (?)'; [over the first name:] 'Petri Augustini'; '1746' [crossed out]; 'Alexandri Deschamps Rethoris / Catalogo Inscriptus' '1777' [crossed out] '1779' [crossed out] '1847'; on pastedown (upper cover) in manuscript: (monogram?); 'Ar(?)del' [changed to:] 'Arl[l]el'; on endleaf: 'Ex libris Petri

13

14

Aug. Alex. Deschamps Catalogo Inscriptus 1774'; endleaf (near back): 'Deschamps 1774'; on pastedown (lower cover): 'D.Vig(?)ux(?) [crossed out]; notes in French and Latin in a 19th-century hand; bought: Martin Breslauer, i.xii.1941.

REFERENCES: Foot, *Revue française*, p. 374.

LITERATURE: Michon, p. 53 ff.; Miner, *Baltimore*, no. 249; Schunke, 1959; Guignard, 1968, p. 248; Nixon, *Pierpont Morgan Library*, no. 9; Nixon, 'Wingfield'; Hobson, *Humanists*, pp. 178, 207–9; Laffitte & Le Bars, pp. 39–40, nos. 2–10; Laffitte, p. 86; see also Davis 367 (no. 15 below).

Same tool on: Sotheby's, 23.iii.1936, *118* (Basel, 1538: with the ownership inscription of Giorgio Teodoro Trivulzio).

Note: Etienne Roffet (= the 'binder of the Estienne Bible'): son of Pierre Roffet, worked independently probably from 1533, but at least from 1537; royal binder: 1539–47; died between 1548 and June 1549.

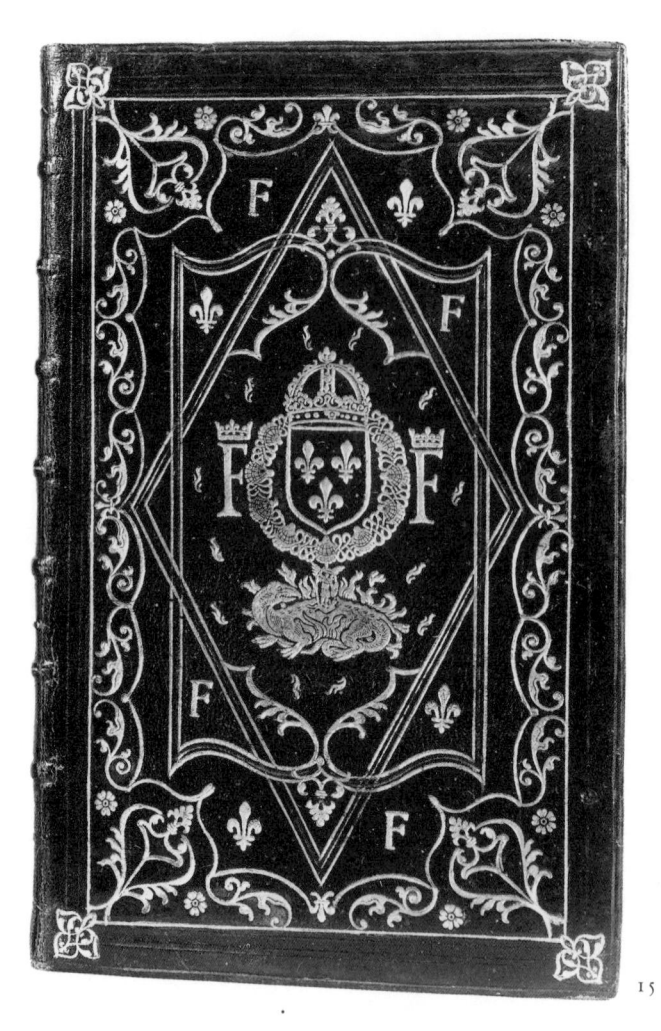

15   *A Paris binding by Etienne Roffet for François I, c. 1542*

Charles de Bouelles, *Livre singulier et utile ... de geometrie* [and] Vitruvius, *Raison d'architecture antique ... traduit d'Espagnol* [by D de Sangredo], Paris: S de Colines, 1542; illustrated, engraved title-page and initials [Sangredo]; ruled in red. 4to.

240 × 155 × 21 mm.   (P 1087) Davis 367

Dark brown goatskin over paste boards, tooled in gold, with blind lines, to a panel design with fleurons at the outer corners, a large composite ornament in the corners, lotus tools and floral tools along the border of the panel, which is formed by straight and curving lines, with in the corners a fleur-de-lis or a capital F; curving branch tools; in the centre the arms, salamander and crowned cipher of François I. Traces of two pairs of ties. Edges of boards: tooled with a blind line. Edges: gilt and gauffered with curving lines and a decorative pattern.

    Sewn on seven (probably split) alum-tawed supports, laced in straight, showing as raised bands on the spine, tooled with alternating gold and blind lines; two kettle stitch bands, tooled with gold and blind dashes, one extra tooled 'band' near the tail to look like the kettle stitch bands; eleven compartments, tooled in gold and blind with (various) solid flower tools, flame tools, fleurs-de-lis and F-tools.

16

Endbands: single with a bead; primary sewing over leather cores (cut off [later?]), tied down; secondary sewing of brown silk. Endleaves: paper pastedowns and two free paper leaves at both ends.

PROVENANCE: On endleaf at the end in manuscript in red: '3' [in a circle] 'H.L/'; comte de Lignerolles; Robert Hoe (book plate); Lardanchet (Catalogue 45, *866*); bought: Lardanchet Bridel/ Howes, 15.i.1952.

REFERENCES: Hoe, *176 bindings*, no. 24; *Treasures*, 1965, no. 73; Romme, *Book Collector*, 1969, p. 26, note 22, plate iiib; Nixon, *Pierpont Morgan Library*, p. 35; Foot, *Revue française*, p. 374; Brooker, *Bulletin du bibliophile*, 1997, p. 38, note 1.

LITERATURE: Davis 327 (no. 14 above, and literature cited there); Guigard, I, p. 6; Toulet, 'Les reliures', pp. 532–5; Brooker, *Bulletin du bibliophile*, 1997, pp. 33–91.

---

16 *A Paris binding by the Pecking Crow binder, c. 1535–40*

Theocritus, *Idyllia ... Epigrammata ... Bipennis & Ala* [Greek] [and] Theocritus, *Idyllia ...Latino carmine reddita, Helio Eobano Hesso interprete*, Basel: A Cratander, September 1531. 8vo.

165 × 112 × 30 mm.   (P 1092) Davis 333

Brown calf over paste boards, tooled in gold, with blind lines, to a panel design with fleurons at the corners and a hand holding a flowering branch with a small bird perched on top, the whole surmounted by a crown, in the centre. Edges: gilt and gauffered to a pattern of curving branches and a flower vase; traces of red paint.

43

Sewn on five split alum-tawed supports, laced in and taken sideways (parallel with the spine), showing as raised bands on the spine, tooled in blind with lines; two kettle stitch bands (of which only one left; see 'repairs'), tooled in blind with dashes; eight compartments, tooled in blind with lines. Endbands: single with a bead; pink and blue silk over cord cores, cut off (see 'repairs'), tied down.

Endleaves: paper pastedowns and one free paper leaf, at both ends; at the front: the free leaf has been tipped onto the title-page; at the end: the free leaf is conjugate with the pastedown.

Repairs: new upper joint; lower joint repaired; top and tail compartments of spine repaired (tail compartment: row of kettle stitches still present).

PROVENANCE: On pastedown of upper cover in manuscript: 'N.191'; Eduardo J Bullrich (book plate; sold: Sotheby's, 19.iii.1952, *373*).

REFERENCES: Foot, *Davis*, I, pp. 132, 137 (no. 5).

LITERATURE: Foot, *Davis*, I, pp. 129–38 (and literature mentioned there); Culot, *La Reliure en France*, no. 32; Laffitte & Le Bars, p. 52; see also Davis 369, 335, 334, 336 (nos. 17–19, 38 below).

17 *A Paris binding by the Pecking Crow binder, c. 1537–40*

François I (King of France), *Exemplaria literarum*, Paris: Robertus Stephanus, September 1537; decorated initials; ruled in red. 4to.

224 × 150 × 24 mm. (P 1221) Davis 369

Brown stained calf over paste boards, tooled in gold, with blind lines, to a panel design with fleurons at the corners, a border composed of interlinking-circles tools and in the centre a circular ornament with an arabesque pattern surrounded by a circle of flames. Edges: gilt and gauffered, rather coarsely, with curving lines.

Sewn on six (?)alum-tawed supports, laced in straight; two rows of kettle stitches; seven compartments. Endbands (not original): single; white silk over (?)alum-tawed or leather cores (cut off), tied down.

Endleaves: paper pastedowns at both ends; on that of the upper cover: a broad strip of paper pasted on to strengthen the joint; at the front: one free paper leaf; at the end: a pair of free conjugate paper leaves and one free leaf conjugate with the pastedown.

Repairs: at the corners of the covers; on the upper cover; at the joints; and at the tail of the spine (new headcap).

PROVENANCE: On title-page in manuscript: 'H
               A. R
                  A' [with slash through tail of A]; list of contents and page numbers in manuscript; bought: Sotheby's, 6.vii.1955, *67*.

REFERENCES: Foot, *Davis*, I, pp. 132, 138 (no. 15).

LITERATURE: Foot, *Davis*, I, pp. 129–38 (and literature mentioned there); Davis 333 (no. 16 above); see also Davis 335, 334 (nos. 18–19 below).

French Bindings

17

18 *A Paris binding by the Pecking Crow binder, c. 1540*

Arsenius, *Scholia in septem Euripidis Tragoedias* [Greek], Venice: L Iunta, 24 December 1534. 8vo.

170 × 113 × 48 mm.   (P 1215) Davis 335

Brown calf over paste boards, tooled in gold, with blind lines, to a panel design with fleurons at the corners, a border composed of interlinking-circles tools, and in the centre within a wreath a coat of arms, possibly those of Beaulieu. Two pairs of silk ties. Edges of boards: tooled in blind with a line. Edges: gilt.

   Sewn on five split alum-tawed supports, laced in straight, showing as raised bands on the spine, tooled in blind with lines; two kettle stitch bands, tooled in blind with dashes; eight compartments. Endbands: single with a bead; pink and blue-green silk over cord cores (laced in at an angle), tied down.

   Endleaves: paper pastedowns at both ends; at the front: one free leaf conjugate with the pastedown; at the end: a pair of free conjugate paper leaves and one free leaf conjugate with the pastedown.

   Repairs: at head and tail of the spine; at the joints; and small repairs at the corners of the covers.

THE HENRY DAVIS GIFT

18

PROVENANCE: On leaf NN7 verso in manuscript: 'Monsieur de bressiens'; 'Madame de bressiens'; two Bs interlaced; 'Monsieur de (?)Lareche [erased]; on NN8 recto: 'Monsieur le bar'; Count Oberndorff (sold: Sotheby's, 6.vii.1955, *18*, pl.).
REFERENCES: Nixon, *Pierpont Morgan Library*, p. 67; Foot, *Davis*, I, pp. 132, 137 (no. 8).
LITERATURE: Foot, *Davis*, I, pp. 129–38 (and literature mentioned there); Davis 333 (no. 16 above); see also Davis 369, 334 (no. 17 above, no. 19 below).
For arms see: Salvaign de Boissieu sale, Grenoble, 1897, *605*; Hobson, *French and Italian*, p. 180, no. 7; Pierpont Morgan Library, 48492 (mentioned in Nixon, *Pierpont Morgan Library*, pp. 66–7); Gennadius Library, Athens (Euripides [Greek], Basel, 1537).

19 *A Paris binding by the Pecking Crow binder, c. 1540*

Primasius, *In omnes D. Pauli epistolas commentarii*, Lyon: S Gryphius, 1537; ruled in red. 8vo.

182 × 122 × 43 mm. (P 1313) Davis 334

Brown calf over paste boards, tooled in gold, with blind lines, to a panel design with a fleuron at the corners, a border composed of interlinking-circles tools and in the centre, in a large diamond, a profile

46

19

portrait of Holofernes, lettered DOLLOFERNES. Traces of two pairs of ties. Edges of boards: tooled in blind with a line. Edges: gilt.

Sewn on five split alum-tawed supports, laced in straight, showing as raised bands on the spine, tooled in blind with lines; two kettle stitch bands; eight compartments, head and tail compartment tooled in blind with cross-hatching; the other six compartments tooled in blind with lines and in gold with alternating stylized flowers and small birds. Endbands: single with a bead; blue silk, possibly over cord cores (cut off), tied down.

Endleaves: paper pastedowns at both ends; at the front: a pair of free conjugate paper leaves and one free paper leaf; at the end: one free leaf conjugate with the pastedown and one free paper leaf.
Repairs: at the corners of the covers.

PROVENANCE: On title-page in manuscript: 'frater Joannis Petrus le gros'/ 'le gros'; On endleaf: notes in Latin in a 16th-century hand; manuscript note in Latin in a 17th-century hand, including the name 'patris Guillelmi' and the date '1620'; manuscript notes in French in a 19th-century hand; bought: Breslauer, 4.vii.1957.

REFERENCES: Foot, *Davis*, I, pp. 129, 131 (pl.), 133, 138 (no. 13); A Jammes, 'Un bibliophile à découvrir, Jean de Gagny', *Bulletin du bibliophile*, 1996, 1, pp. 68–70 (pl.).

LITERATURE: Foot, *Davis*, I, pp. 129–38 (and literature mentioned there); Needham, *Twelve Centuries*, no. 53; Davis 333 (no. 16 above); see also Davis 369, 335 (nos. 17–18 above).

Dollofernes tool on: A binding formerly belonging to Earl Stanhope, at: Chevening, XLIII.D.7 (F. Alunno, Venice, 1543)

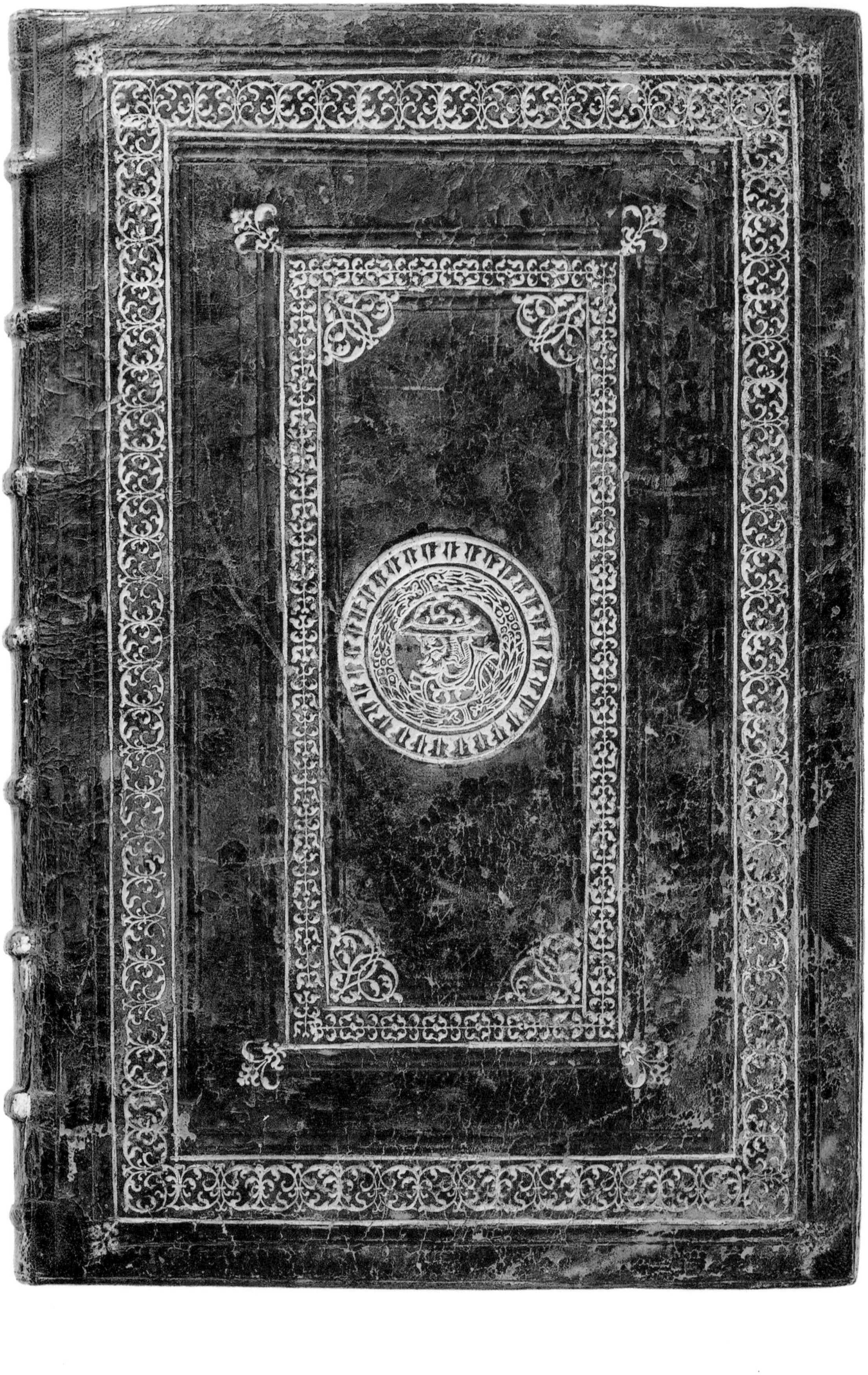

20

20   *A Paris binding by the Fleur-de-lis binder, c. 1536*

Gulielmus Budeus, *De asse et partibus eius*, Paris: in typographia Ascensiana, April 1532; ruled in red. fol. 335 × 228 × 33 mm. (P 1483) Davis 389

Brown calf over paste boards, tooled in gold, with blind lines, to a panel design with small fleurons at the outer corners, a border filled with interlacing-circles tools, larger fleurons at the corners of the panel, a second border composed of small leafy ornaments, a large two-interlacing-circles tool in the corners of the centre panel; in the centre: a medallion portrait within a laurel wreath surrounded by a circle with flames and rays, depicting on the upper cover: Mars and on the lower cover: Dido. Traces of four pairs of ties. Edges of boards: tooled in blind with a line. Edges: gilt and gauffered with curls and leafy ornaments.

Sewn on seven split alum-tawed supports, laced in at an angle, showing as raised bands on the spine, tooled in blind with lines; two kettle stitch bands, tooled in blind with dashes (repaired); ten compartments, tooled in gold with a small fleuron in each (probably later). Endbands: single with a bead; yellow and green silk over (?)alum-tawed cores (cut off), tied down.

Endleaves: paper pastedowns and two free paper leaves, at both ends.

Repairs: small repairs to the covers, repairs at corners; head and tail compartments renewed; new joints; repairs at spine.

PROVENANCE: J R Abbey (book plate; 'J.A.1736/23:5:1938'; sold: Sotheby's, 19.vi.1967, *1721*, pl.).
REFERENCES: Foot, *Revue française*, p. 378.
LITERATURE: Davis 366 (no. 21 below; and literature cited there). For medallion portraits see: G D Hobson, *Cambridge*, xxiii; see also Davis 325 (no. 22 below).
Same tools on: Davis 366 (no. 21 below).

21   *A Paris binding by the Fleur-de-lis binder, c. 1536*

L Bayfius, *Annotationes in libri II de captivis, et postliminio reversis*, Paris: R Stephanus, 1536; illustrated. 4to. 232 × 172 × 30 mm. (P 1320) Davis 366

Brown calf over paste boards, tooled in gold, with blind lines, to a panel design with fleurons at the outer corners, a border composed of interlaced-circles tools, large ornamental fleurons in the corners of the centre panel; the panel filled with a pattern of solid tools (fleurons, leaf tools, branch tools, curls, etc.). Traces of two pairs of ties. Edges: gilt and gauffered to an arabesque pattern of curving lines and leaf shapes.

Rebacked with parts of the original spine strip retained. Sewn on five cords, laced in straight (could be the original sewing), showing as raised bands on the spine, tooled in blind with lines; kettle stitch bands; eight compartments, tooled in blind with lines. Endbands: single with a bead; primary sewing over (?)cord cores (evidence of having been laced in?), tied down; secondary sewing of blue silk.

Endleaves: paper pastedowns and one free paper leaf, at both ends.

Repairs: rebacked.

PROVENANCE: On pastedown in manuscript: 'E6.40'; Sunderland Library, Blenheim Palace (book plate; sold: Sotheby's, 4.xii.1881, *1046*; bought by Quaritch); Paul Hirsch (book plate); J R Abbey (book plate; 'J.A.2032/11.4.1939'; sold: Sotheby's, 21.vi.1965, *115*, pl.).

21

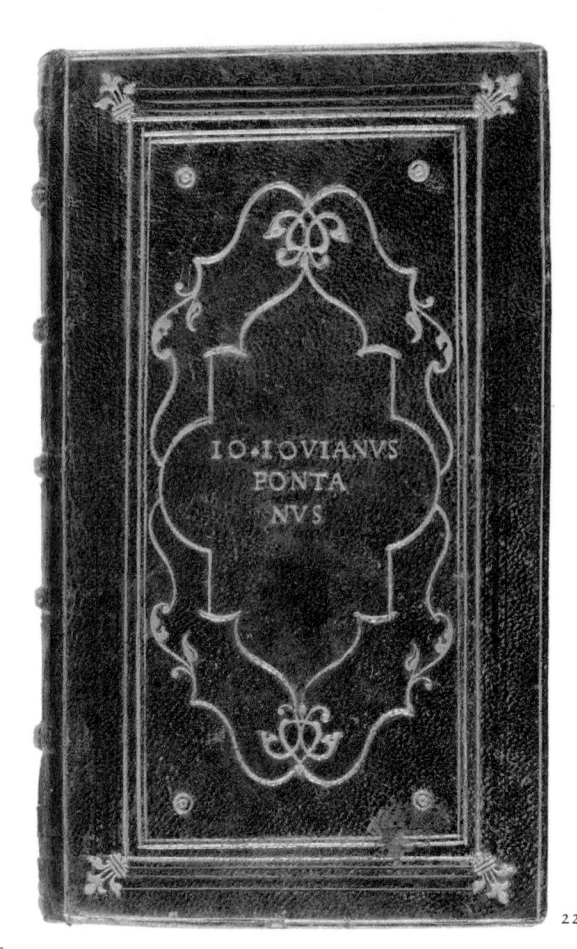

22

REFERENCES: I Schunke, *Das Leben und Werk Jakob Krauses*, Dresden, 1940, pl. 4; Foot, *Revue française*, p. 378.

LITERATURE: Schunke, *Gutenberg Jahrbuch*, 1950, pp. 385–8; Hobson, *French and Italian*, no. 2; Nixon, *Grolier*, pl. 12 (identical tools); pl. B (tools 6, 7, 11a–b, 14, 19); Hobson, *Renaissance*, p. 58; see also Davis 389 (no. 20 above) and 325 (no. 22 below).

22 *A Paris binding by the Fleur-de-lis binder for Jean Grolier, c. 1538*

J J Pontanus, *Opera*, Venice: Aldus, 1513. 8vo.

170 × 100 × 32 mm. (P 1064) Davis 325

Brown goatskin over paste boards, tooled in gold, with blind lines, to a panel design with stylized fleurs-de-lis at the corners; curving lines, lotus tools and fleurons around a frame formed by curving and straight lines, with in the centre of the upper cover: IO.IOVIANVS/PONTA/NVS and on the lower cover: GROLIERII/ET AMICO/RVM. Edges of boards: tooled in blind with a line. Edges: gilt.

50

Sewn on five split alum-tawed supports, laced in straight, showing as raised bands on the spine, tooled in gold with lines; kettle stitch bands, tooled in gold with dashes; eight compartments, tooled in gold with a star and in blind with lines. Endbands: single with a bead; green silk over (?)alum-tawed cores (broken off), tied down.

Endleaves: parchment pastedowns at both ends; at the front: two free paper leaves; at the end: five paper leaves.

Repairs: at joint and head of spine.

PROVENANCE: Jean Grolier; Laurent Rabot (on the title-page in manuscript: IO.GROLERIVS COPIARVM GALLICA/RVM QVAESTOR LAVRENTIO RABOTO/ D.D.); D de Salvaing de Boissieu, Château de Sassenage; marquis de Bérenger (sold: Grenoble, 1897, *534*); M C D Borden (book plate; sold: New York, 17.ii 1913, *289a*, pl.); W D Braeker (sold: New York, 26.xi.1935, *349*); Lucius Wilmerding (sold: New York, Parke Bernet, 29.x.1951, *426*).

REFERENCES: Shipman, 432; Nixon, *Grolier*, no. 17; Romme, *Book Collector*, 1969, p. 26, note 17; Austin, 432; Hobson, *Renaissance*, p. 224, no. 432.

LITERATURE: Zedler, *Universal Lexicon*, vol. 30, Leipzig and Halle, 1741, col. 468; Schunke, *Gutenberg Jahrbuch*, 1950, pp. 385–8; Nixon, *Grolier*, pl. B (tools 15, 18, 20, 21a–b, 25); Devaux, pp. 55–65; Toulet, 'Les reliures', pp. 532–4; Hobson, *Humanists*, Appendix 7; Culot, *La Reliure en France*, nos. 29–30 (but see *Note* below); Hobson, *Renaissance*, chapter 3 (esp. p. 58); see also Davis 389 and 366 (nos. 20 and 21 above).

Note: Jean Grolier (c. 1489/90–1565), notary and secretary to the king, treasurer and receiver general of the duchy of Milan (1509–12 and 1515–21); treasurer of France: 1532. (The literature on Grolier is extensive; for the latest research, see Hobson, *Renaissance*, chapters 1–3.)

Laurent (or Lorentz) Rabot: councillor to the Parlement of Grenoble; for another binding presented by Grolier to Rabot see Sotheby's, 20.xii.1954, *101*; see also Davis 380 (no. 55 below).

M Culot believes the Fleur-de-lis binder to have been Etienne Roffet.

23 *A Paris binding by Jean Picard for Jean Brinon, c. 1538*

[C Estienne], *De re hortensi libellus*, Paris: R Stephanus, 6 April 1536 [and] *Seminarium sive plantarium*, ibid., 12 July 1536 [and] *Vinetum*, ibid.: Franciscus Stephanus, 1537 [and] *Arbustum. Fonticulus. Spinetum*, ibid., 1538 [and] *Sylva. Frutetum. Collis*, ibid., 1538. 8vo.

173 × 112 × 39 mm.   (P 1308) Davis 350

Brown calf over paste boards, tooled in gold, with blind lines, to a panel design with small solid fleurons at the outer corners, a border filled with small tools and ivy-leaf tools in the corners, fleurons in the corners of the centre panel, which has an arabesque pattern built up with curving lines, lotus tools, fleurons and curving and straight lines; in the centre: IO.BRINONII/ET.AMICO/RVM. Edges: gilt and gauffered to an arabesque pattern with a vase and fleurons.

Sewn on five split alum-tawed supports, laced in straight, showing as raised bands on the spine, tooled in gold with lines; two kettle stitch bands tooled in gold with dashes; eight compartments, tooled

23

24

in gold and blind with lines. Paper label with title in manuscript. Endbands: single with a bead; blue silk over cord cores (laced in at an angle and frayed out), tied down.

Endleaves: paper pastedowns at both ends; at the end: a pair of free conjugate paper leaves and one free leaf conjugate with the pastedown.

Repairs: at corners.

PROVENANCE: Jean Brinon; on title-page (and elsewhere in the book) in manuscript: 'Vt Angelus'; on title-page in manuscript (different hand): 'Ex bibliotheca Tibuaul pts'; at the end of the last index in manuscript: 'Rien me change ou m'allege'; J R Abbey (book plate; 'J.A.3656/23:5:1947'; sold: Sotheby's, 22.vi.1965, *318*, pl.).

REFERENCES: L Scheler, 'Jean de Brinon, bibliophile', *Bibliothèque d'humanisme et renaissance*, XI (1949), pp. 215–18, pl.; Hobson, *French and Italian*, no. 10; Foot, *Davis*, I, p. 174.

LITERATURE: Nixon, *Grolier*, pl. C (tools 8a–b,10,12,16), pl. D (tools 42, 43); Hobson, *French and Italian*, nos. 10, 11; Nixon, *Broxbourne*, no. 28; Foot, *Davis*, I, pp. 174, 180, notes 34, 35; Parent, pp. 154–5; Hobson, *Humanists*, pp. 267–71; Culot, *La Reliure en France*, p. 91;

Note: Hobson, *Renaissance*, pp. 59–61, 224–7; Laffitte & Le Bars, pp. 54, 79, 94, 96; Laffitte, pp. 26, 128; *Méjanes*, no. 55; see also Davis 374, 353 (nos. 24–5 below).

In 1540 Gian Francesco Torresani d'Asola, brother-in-law to Aldus Manutius, came to Paris and appointed Jean Picard, bookseller and binder, the Aldine agent in Paris; Torresani imported books in Greek and Latin, which were kept in a shop with the Anchor and Dolphin sign in the Rue St Jacques. Picard had to give account of the sales of Aldine books to Jean Grolier (treasurer of France) to whom the Aldine Press had entrusted their interests in Paris. In 1547 Picard and his wife absconded (owing money) (see Parent). Hobson (*Humanists*) has argued that all bindings on Aldine imprints made for Grolier between 1540 and 1547 were the work of Jean Picard. The tools used on these bindings were formerly attributed (by Nixon) to Claude Picques 'with solid tools'. Laffitte and Le Bars have established a link between Picard and their 'Atelier de Fontainebleau'.

Jean Brinon de Villaines (d. 1554), 'conseiller du roi' in the Parlement of Paris in 1544; was a friend and patron of the Pléiade poets.

24 *A Paris binding by Jean Picard for Jean Grolier, c. 1540*

Z Ferreri, *Hymni novi ecclesiastici*, Rome: L Vicentinus & Lautitius Perusini, February 1525. 4to.

213 × 133 × 22 mm. (P 207) Davis 374

Dark brown goatskin (or possibly hair sheep) over paste boards, tooled in gold to a design of interlacing ribbons decorated with black paint, solid tools, fleurons, lotus tools, arabesque ornament, curved and straight lines, with in the centre of the upper cover: ZACHAR.FERRERII/PONT.GARDIEN./HYMNI.; and on the lower cover Grolier's motto: PORTIO MEA DO/MINE SIT IN/TERRA VI/VENTI/VM. At the foot of the upper cover is Grolier's ownership inscription: IO.GROLIERII. ET.AMICORVM. Edges of boards: tooled in gold with a line, small dashes and small s-shaped leafy tools. Edges: gilt.

Sewn on six (invisible) supports, laced in straight, showing as raised bands on the spine, tooled in gold with lines; two kettle stitch bands, tooled in gold with dashes; nine compartments, tooled in gold with lines. Endbands: single with a bead; (?)primary sewing of brown thread over (?)leather cores (laced in at an angle), tied down; secondary sewing of beige silk.

Endleaves: (later) paper pastedowns and one free leaf conjugate with the pastedown and one free paper leaf, at both ends.

Repairs: at joints and at upper cover.

PROVENANCE: Jean Grolier; Librairie D Morgand (1893); H G Selfridge (sold: Sotheby's, 11.viii.1941, 59, pl.).

REFERENCES: Shipman, no. 196; G D Hobson, *Thirty Bindings*, pl. IX; Nixon, *Grolier*, no. 35; Romme, *Book Collector*, 1969, p. 25, note 13; Austin, no. 196; Foot, *Davis*, I, p. 174; Hobson, *Renaissance*, p. 225, no. 196.

LITERATURE: *La Reliure originale*, 1959, pl. xvi, fig. 9; Nixon, *Grolier*, pl. C (tools 4, 8a–b), pl. D (tool 26), pl. E (tools 49 a–b); Needham, *Twelve Centuries*, no. 42; Laffitte & Le Bars, pp. 60, 79; see also Davis 325, 350 (nos. 22–3 above; and literature cited there), 353 (no. 25 below).

25 *A Paris binding by Jean Picard, c. 1545–7*

Sperone Speroni degli Alvarotti, *Dialogi*, Venice: Aldus, 1543; ruled in red. 8vo.

167 × 98 × 27 mm. (P 581) Davis 353

Black goatskin over paste boards, tooled in gold with a border filled with small leafy s-shaped tools; a geometrical design formed by interlacing ribbons; gouges, small solid and open tools. Edges of boards: tooled in gold with lines, dashes and small leaf-tools. Edges: gilt.

Sewn on five (recessed) supports (?cords), of which at least the centre three have been laced in (possibly all five have been laced in); smooth spine, tooled in gold with strips of leafy s-shaped tools and cross-hatching in the compartments. Endbands: single with a bead; pink and blue silk over cord cores (laced in), tied down.

Endleaves: paper pastedowns at both ends; at the front: one free paper leaf with a conjugate stub, and one free leaf conjugate with the pastedown; at the end: one pair of free conjugate paper leaves, and one leaf conjugate with the pastedown.

PROVENANCE:	On endleaf in manuscript: 'No 1524'; on pastedown of lower cover in manuscript: '9680'; Paul Hirsch (book plate); bought: Sotheby's, 3.ii.1943, *454* (pl.).
REFERENCES:	J Baer, Catalogue 750, no. 268, pl. 39; Foot, *Davis*, I, p. 177 (for reattribution see Davis 350, no. 23 above).
LITERATURE:	Nixon, *Grolier*, pl. D (tools 28, 29); Davis 350 (no 23 above; and literature cited there); see also Davis 374 (no. 24 above).
Compare:	Hobson, *Renaissance*, fig. 27b.

26

26 *A Paris binding by the 'Salel binder', c. 1540*

C Suetonius Tranquillus, *XII Caesares. Sexti Aurelii Victoris a D. Caesare Augusto usq. ad Theodosium exerpta* [etc.], Venice: Aldus & A Socerus, May 1521. 8vo.

171 × 105 × 50 mm. (P1307) Davis 329

Brown calf over paste boards, tooled in gold, with blind lines, to a panel design with ivy-leaf tools at the outer corners, a border of repeated hatched tools with fleurons in the corners, the centre panel filled with arabesque ornaments. Edges of boards: faint traces of a blind-tooled line. Edges: gilt.

Sewn on five split supports (possibly double cords), laced in and taken sideways (parallel to the spine), showing as raised bands on the spine, tooled in blind with lines; two rows of kettle stitches (not emphasized as kettle stitch bands); six compartments, tooled in gold with leaf tools. Endbands: single with a bead; green silk over cord cores (laced in at a slight angle), tied down.

Endleaves: paper pastedowns and one free paper leaf at both ends (conjugate with the pastedown at the end).

PROVENANCE: On title-page in manuscript: '58.'; C S Ascherson (book plate); Vernon-Holford collection (sold: Sotheby's, 9.xii.1927, *770*); J R Abbey (book plate; 'J.A.2707/2.1.1946'; sold: Sotheby's, 23.vi.1965, *638*, pl.).
REFERENCES: Foot, *Revue française*, p. 374.
LITERATURE: Michon, pp. 54–5; Nixon, *Broxbourne*, no. 23; Miner, *Baltimore*, no. 250; Schunke, 1959, pp. 595–605; Nixon, *Pierpont Morgan Library*, nos. 7, 9; Needham, *Twelve Centuries*,

	nos. 46–7; Hobson, *Humanists*, chapter 8; Laffitte & Le Bars, pp. 53, 55–8; Laffitte, pp. 21–2.
Same tools on:	Davis 330, 328 (nos. 27–28 below); for structure compare Davis 328 (no. 28 below).
Note:	Bindings with these tools were formerly attributed to the 'Fontainebleau binder'. His tools are not identical with those used by Etienne Roffet. Laffitte and Le Bars have renamed this atelier the 'Salel binder'; this atelier was active at least c. 1540–45.

27 *A Paris binding by the 'Salel binder', c. 1540*

C Plinius Caecilius Secundus, *Epistolarum libri x* [and other works], Venice: Aldus & A Socerus, June 1518. 8vo.

171 × 102 × 33 mm.   (P 400) Davis 330

Brown goatskin over paste boards, tooled in gold, with blind lines, to a panel design with fleurons at the corners, ivy-leaf tools in the corners, solid lotus tools and fleurons in the corners of the panel, in the centre within a large diamond: an arabesque ornament. Edges of boards: tooled in blind with a line. Edges: gilt.

Sewn on five split alum-tawed supports, laced in straight, showing as raised bands on the spine, tooled in blind with a line; two rows of kettle stitches; six compartments, tooled in blind with lines and in gold with fleurons. Endbands: single with a bead; blue-green silk over cord cores (laced in almost parallel with the edges of the boards), tied down.

Endleaves: paper pastedowns and a pair of free conjugate paper leaves and one free leaf conjugate with the pastedown, at both ends.

Repairs: at spine and covers.

PROVENANCE:	On endleaf in manuscript: 'Elizii Bories' (repeated, once in Greek script); Charles Edward H Chadwyck-Healey (book plate; sold: Hodgson, 16.iv.1942, *184*).
REFERENCES:	*BFAC*, 1891, Case E39, pl. xxxii; Foot, *Revue française*, p. 374.
LITERATURE:	Davis 329 (no. 26 above; and literature cited there); see also Davis 328 (no 28 below).
Same tools on:	Goldschmidt, no. 197, pl lxxi; Bodleian Library Oxford, Broxbourne 24.4 (= Nixon, *Broxbourne*, no. 23); Needham, *Twelve Centuries*, no. 46.

28 *A Paris binding (?)by the 'Salel binder', c. 1540*

M T Cicero, *Epistolae familiares*, Lyon: Sebastian Gryphius, 1539. 8vo.

166 × 110 × 32 mm.   (P 565) Davis 328

Dark olive goatskin over paste boards, tooled in gold, with blind lines, to a panel design with ivy-leaf tools at the corners and in the centre. Edges of boards: tooled in blind with a line. Edges: gilt.

Sewn on five (?)split alum-tawed supports, laced in straight, showing as raised bands on the spine, tooled in blind with lines; two rows of kettle stitches; six compartments, tooled in blind with lines and in gold with a stylized flower; title lettered in gold on second compartment. Endbands: single with a bead; green silk over cord cores (laced in almost parallel with the edges of the boards), tied down.

27   28

    Endleaves: paper pastedowns and a pair of free conjugate paper leaves, and one free leaf conjugate with the pastedown, at both ends.

PROVENANCE: On title-page in manuscript: '43'; on endleaf: long inscription in French (19th-century hand); bought: Sotheby's, 1.xii.1942, *96*.
REFERENCES: Foot, *Revue française*, p. 374.
LITERATURE: Davis 329 (no. 26 above; and literature cited there).
Same tool on: Davis 329, 330 (nos. 26–7 above).

29 *A Paris binding, c. 1540*

Hore secundum ritum ecclesiae Romanae, Paris: Simon Sylvius, n.d. [1527] [and] *Suffragia plurimorum sanctorum & sanctarum,* n.p., n.d. [Paris: Simon Sylvius]; woodcuts, said to be by Hans Weiditz; woodcut initials; ruled in red. 8vo.

146 × 100 × 22 mm.   (P 907) Davis 326

Brown calf over paste boards, tooled in gold, with blind lines, to a panel design with fleurons at the outer corners, a border composed of small solid tools and in the centre of the upper cover: a medallion head of François I, lettered F/REX and on the lower cover: a medallion head of a woman, lettered .DIDO., each surrounded by a circle of flames within an outer circle of fleurs-de-lis. Traces of two pairs of ties. Edges of boards: tooled in blind with a line. Edges: gilt and gauffered with a curling, leafy branch pattern.

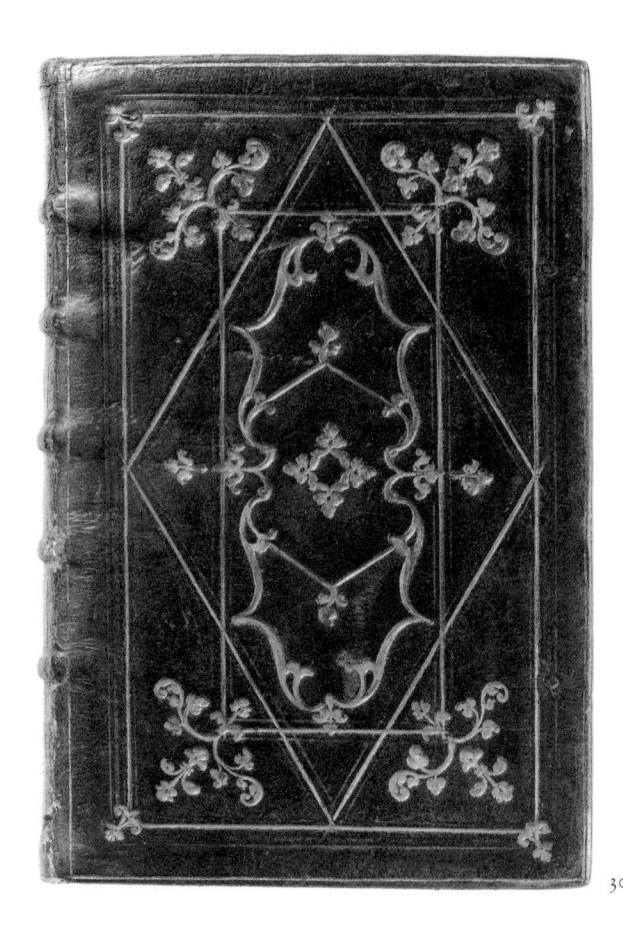

Rebacked with the original sewing and spine strip retained. Sewn on five (probably split) alum-tawed supports, laced in straight, showing as raised bands on the spine, tooled in blind with a line; two kettle stitch bands, tooled in blind with dashes; eight compartments, tooled in blind with lines. Endbands: single with a bead; blue silk, tied down.

Endleaves: paper pastedowns and two free paper leaves, at both ends.

Repairs: at edges of boards and corners; rebacked.

PROVENANCE: On pastedown of upper cover in manuscript in red: '31.'; C W Dyson Perrins (book plate; sold: Sotheby's, 5.xi.1946, *472*, pl.); bought: Quaritch, 7.vi.1948.

LITERATURE: G D Hobson, *Cambridge*, no. xxiii, p. 69, no. 8; Nixon, *Pierpont Morgan Library*, no. 9 (identical medallions); Hobson, *Humanists*, pp. 135–6.

Same tools on: J and J Leighton, *Catalogue of early-printed, and other interesting books, manuscripts and fine bindings*, London, 1905, no. 2598 (*Horae*, Paris: S Sylvius for P Roffet, [1527]).

Note: The book contains a letter, dated 17 August 1909, from Campbell Dodgson of the British Museum Department of Prints and Drawings, to Dyson Perrins, attributing the woodcuts to Weiditz.

30 A Paris binding, c. 1540

C Degrassalius, *Regalium Franciae libri duo*, Lyon: Heredes Simon Vincentius, 1538 [*Liber secundus* has a separate title-page; colophon: Ex officina calcographica Joannis Crispini Typographi]; woodcuts. 8vo.

185 × 125 × 27 mm. (P 1310) Davis 331

Black goatskin over paste boards, tooled in blind and silver (oxidized), to a panel design with small fleurons at the corners, intersecting lines forming a rectangle and a diamond; ornaments built up of solid fleuron and lotus tools in the corners and curving tools, small fleurons and ivy-leaf tools in the centre rectangle. Traces of two pairs of ties. Edges of boards: tooled in blind with a line. Edges: red, painted in gold with a pattern of leaves and fleurons (outlined in black).

Sewn on five split alum-tawed supports, laced in and taken sideways (parallel to the spine) (see Davis 329, no. 26 above), showing as raised bands on the spine, tooled in gold with lines; two kettle stitch bands; eight compartments, tooled in gold with lines. Endbands: single with a bead; blue-green silk over cord cores (laced in), tied down.

Endleaves: paper pastedowns and two free paper leaves, at both ends.

PROVENANCE: Jean Louis Prieur, priest, Paris 1731 (inscriptions in French and Latin throughout the book, one stating that he was born in Paris, his father came from Troyes and his mother from Rheims); bought: Sotheby's, 17.x.1960, *853*.

Note: The taller fleuron and the ivy-leaf tool are similar to but not identical with those used by the 'Salel binder'; the tall fleuron seems very similar to one used on Laffitte & Le Bars, pl. 9, attributed to the 'atelier d'Etienne Roffet?', but none of the other tools match.

31 A binding made in Lyon for Benoît Le Court, c. 1540–50

Henricus Cornelius Agrippa, *De incertitudine et vanitate scientiarum declamatio invectiva*, n.p. [Cologne], 1537. 8vo.

167 × 105 × 30 mm. (P 1117) Davis 332

Brown calf over wooden boards, tooled in blind and silver (oxidized) to a panel design; decorated with black paint in the border and in the border of the panel; fleurons at the corners of the panel; solid curving ornaments, lotus tools and fleurons, with the arms of Benoît Le Court within a double circle tooled in gold in the centre. Remnants of two pairs of clasps, hinging on the upper cover. Edges: plain.

Sewn on four split alum-tawed supports, laced in straight and pegged, showing as raised bands on the spine, tooled in blind with lines; two rows of kettle stitches (showing as a kettle stitch band near the tail); six compartments, five of which are tooled in gold with a stylized flower; top compartment repaired. Endbands: single; primary sewing over (?)leather cores (lacing-in invisible), tied down; secondary sewing of blue and (?)pink silk.

Endleaves: paper pastedowns and one free leaf conjugate with the pastedown, at both ends.
Repairs: at top and tail of spine, at joints and at corners of the covers.

31

PROVENANCE: Benoît Le Court; on title-page in manuscript: 'aegidij tarobiis' (?); (different hand): 'Dordos'; blue stamp with: 'A. Ricordeau'; on A1 recto: stamp: 'DC'; on last leaf of text: a lengthy manuscript note in Latin; bought: Goldschmidt, 3.iii.1952.
REFERENCES: Goldschmidt, Catalogue 97 (1952), no. 4; Foot, *Revue française*, p. 374.
LITERATURE: Olivier, 2091 (two different arms blocks, see also Davis 368, no. 32 below); Rahir, *Riches reliures*, 1910, no. 44 (pl.); Gottlieb, pl. 38a; Goldschmidt, nos. 202, 203, pl. lxxvi; Michon, pp. 75–6; Hobson, *French and Italian*, p. 26, p. xv; Nixon, *Pierpont Morgan Library*, p. 169; Toulet, 'L'école lyonnaise', pp. 147–8; Gid, nos. 544bis (arms) and 601 (arms and identical tools); Gid, 'Un atelier lyonnais vers 1550', pp. 117–31; *Méjanes*, nos. 52, 53; Christie's Paris, Catalogue: *Collection Michel Wittock*, pt. iii, 7.x.2005, 4; see also Davis 368 (no. 32 below).
Note: Benoît Le Court (c. 1500–c. 1565), lawyer, scholar, author and public figure in Lyon in the 1540s and 1550s.

32 *A binding made in Lyon for Benoît Le Court, c. 1540–50*

Claudius Ptolemaeus, *Centum sententiae ad Syrum fratrem. Libri xiiii de rebus coelestibus. Liber etiam de luna imperfectus*, Venice: Aldus & A Socerus, September 1519. 4to.

217 × 132 × 44 mm. (P 810) Davis 368

Brown calf over wooden boards, tooled in blind and gold to a panel design with a twisted-rope roll in blind in the border, gold-tooled corner fleurons and the arms of Benoît Le Court within a wreath tooled in gold in the centre. Edges: plain; on the top edge in manuscript: '1519'.

32

Rebacked in sheepskin; original sewing supports retained. Sewn on five split alum-tawed supports, laced in straight; two kettle stitch bands. Endbands missing (one blue silk thread, tied down).

Endleaves: paper pastedowns and one free paper leaf, at both ends. A strip of parchment manuscript visible at the end.

Repairs: upper cover partly replaced (very damaged), repair at lower cover; rebacked.

PROVENANCE:	Benoît Le Court; on pastedown of upper cover in manuscript: 'V S° AC'; bought: Goldschmidt, 4.viii.1944.
REFERENCES:	Goldschmidt, Catalogue 73, no. 221; Foot, *Revue française*, p. 374.
LITERATURE:	Davis 332 (no. 31 above; and literature cited there).
Same tools:	(arms block, wreath and border roll) Gid, no. 367; Gid, 'Un atelier lyonnais vers 1550', tools 1 and E.
Compare:	Gid, 'Un atelier lyonnais vers 1500', pl. Schéma no. 1, reliure, no. 23 (fleuron).

33 A Paris binding dating from the 1540s

Cuthbert Tunstall, *De arte supputandi libri quattuor*, Paris: R Stephanus, 16 November 1538. 4to.

213 × 150 × 23 mm. (P 785) Davis 384

Rebound with the original covers and spine strip retained. Brown calf over paste boards, tooled in gold, with blind lines, to a panel design with fleurons at the corners and in the centre a medallion head, showing on the upper cover: Mars and on the lower cover: Lucretia (both lettered). Edges: plain.

Sewn on five supports, laced in (unsure whether resewn as well as rebound, i.e. recovered), showing as raised bands on the spine; two kettle stitch bands; eight compartments, head and tail compartments: tooled in blind with cross-hatching; other compartments: tooled in gold with a flower, and in blind with lines. New endbands: single with a bead; red and blue silk over (?alum-tawed) cores (cut off), tied down.

New endleaves: paper pastedowns and one pair of free conjugate paper leaves, at both ends.

Repairs: rebound with original covers and spine strip retained.

PROVENANCE: George Dunn of Wooley Hall, near Maidenhead (book plate; in manuscript: 'δλη / G.D./ May 1905'; sold: Sotheby's, 29.xi.1917, *3836*); John Burns (in manuscript: 'John Burns.m/Feb/5/1918'; sold: Sotheby's, 24.iv.1944, *572*).

REFERENCES:	Romme, *Book Collector*, Spring 1971, p. 69, note 7; Foot, *Davis*, I, pp. 160, 168, 171 (but see *Note* below).
LITERATURE:	G D Hobson, *Cambridge*, p. 69.
Note:	In Foot, *Davis*, I, section 12, I included this binding in the group of bindings by Malenfant's binder (who may have been Claude Picques). However, the only tool linking Davis 384 with this group is a fleuron that also occurs on British Library, G 295 (Paris, 1552, for de Malenfant) and I am now (2008) not absolutely sure that these two tools are identical. Moreover, the style of Davis 384 suggests an earlier dating than the Malenfant – (?)Picques group.

34 *A Paris binding, c. 1545*

Demosthenes, *Orationes prima pars* [Greek], Venice: F Bruciolus, 1543; woodcut initials. 8vo.

161 × 102 × 30 mm. (P 1119) Davis 341

Brown calf over paste boards, tooled in gold, with blind lines, to a panel design with a fleuron at the corners and in the centre an oval plaquette, depicting Amphitrite's triumph. Edges of boards: tooled in blind with a line. Edges: gilt.

Sewn on five split alum-tawed supports, laced in straight; two kettle stitch bands, tooled in blind with dashes; eight compartments, tooled in blind with lines and in gold with a stylized flower. Endbands: single with a bead; green and brown silk over cord cores (still partly laced in, almost straight, parallel with the head and tail edges, partly cut or broken off), tied down.

Endleaves: paper pastedowns and a pair of free conjugate paper leaves, and a third free leaf conjugate with the pastedown, at both ends.

PROVENANCE:	Manuscript notes in Greek on endleaf and in text; manuscript note in Latin on pastedown of lower cover; manuscript note in Latin about the contents on endleaf; on pastedown in manuscript: 'Sept. 9. 1720 Collat. & perfect.'; Lord Sandys (book plate; sold: Sotheby's, 23 ii.1953, *78*, pl.).
REFERENCES:	Hobson, *Humanists*, p. 245, no. 117d) (lot 295 in the Sotheby's sale of 23.vi.1953, quoted by Hobson, is a different book, but with the same plaquette: Hobson, no. 117 e)).
LITERATURE:	Molinier, no. 289 (attributes the plaquette to Valerio Belli of Vicenza); E F Bange, *Die italienischen Bronzen der Renaissance und des Barock*, Berlin-Leipzig, 1922, no. 874; S de Ricci, *The Gustave Dreyfus Collection. Reliefs and Plaquettes*, Oxford, 1931, no. 369; J W Pope-Hennessy, *Renaissance Bronzes from the Samuel H Kress Collection*, London, 1965, no. 39; Hobson, *Humanists*, pp. 133–5, 245.
Note:	The plaquette has been attributed to Giovanni Bernardi da Castelbolognese; it was used from c. 1537/8 until the 1560s.
Same fleuron on:	King's College, Cambridge, M.38.11 (Paris, 1543); Pembroke College, Cambridge, 4.I.13–14 (Eusebius, Paris, 1544).

35   *Five gilt-panel bindings, c. 1545–50*

[Bible in Hebrew] *Exodus, Leviticus, Deuteronomium, Numeri, Quinque libri legis*, 5 vols, [Paris: R Estienne, 1544]; ruled in red. 16mo.

104 × 70 × 18/20 mm.   (P 1301) Davis 342–346

Brown calf over paste boards, blocked in gold with a panel showing a pattern of interlacing ribbons, flowers, leaves and birds; the central rectangular compartment is left empty. Edges of boards: tooled in gold with a small diamond roll. Edges: gilt.

   Sewn on three thin alum-tawed supports, laced in straight; smooth spines, tooled in gold: those of vols I and IV have a curling leaf pattern; vols II and V have a pattern of diapers and fleurons; vol. III has small curls and solid tools. Endbands: single with a bead; blue and pink silk over rolled leather cores (once laced in), tied down.

   Endleaves: paper pastedowns, two free paper leaves at the beginning of the text (near lower cover) (conjugacy invisible); one free paper leaf near end of the text (near upper cover).

   Repairs: small repairs at the joints and at tails of spines.

PROVENANCE: Vol. III : on endleaf in manuscript: 'F. Webber from her affct. Mother' (19th-century hand); bought: Pratley, 15.vi.1965.

36   *A binding, probably made in Paris, c. 1546–50*

Psalterium universum carmine elegiaco redditum et explicatum per H Eobanum Hessum, Paris: P Galterus, 1546 [and] C V A Iuvencus, *Historia evangelica*, Paris: P Galterus, 1545; ruled in red. 16mo.

122 × 80 × 29 mm.   (P 1090) Davis 347

Black calf over paste boards, tooled in gold with interlacing ribbons to a geometrical pattern; small solid tools. In the centre oval on the upper cover: E/IA./AGI/TE.EX./ANIMO/DOMINO/EXVLT/EMVS./QVAN/TES.; on the lower cover: Q/VI./SOL/VS.NO/STRAE/.IVRA./SALVT/IS.HA/BET. Edges of boards: tooled in gold with a line, dashes and s-shaped tools. Edges: gilt and gauffered with fleurons and leaves.

   Sewn on three (recessed) cords; two rows of kettle stitches (lacing-in: invisible); smooth spine, tooled in gold with lines to suggest bands, filled with s-shaped leafy tools; 'compartments' tooled with lines in a cross-hatched pattern. Endbands: single with a bead; pink and green silk over (?)leather core (cut or broken off), tied down.

   Endleaves: paper pastedowns at both ends, at the front: a pair of free conjugate paper leaves; at the end: a free paper leaf.

PROVENANCE: On endleaf in manuscript: 'Michael He [?meni..y?]' [erased]; 'Ex legato D: Equitij Antonij Francisci Marmij'; 'Cajus Vettius Aquileius juvencas V.C. Presbyter'; on title-page: a stamp with: 'M'; and a stamp of the 'Pub. Florentinae Biblioth.'; Madame T Belin (sold: Paris, Giraud Badin, 1936, *57*, pl. xlviii); Eduardo J Bullrich (book plate; sold: Sotheby's, 17–8.iii.1952, *180*).

35　　　　　　　　　　　　　　　36

37　*A Paris binding by Wotton binder A, c. 1543–5*

M T Cicero, *De philosophia, prima pars*, Paris: R Stephanus, 1543. 8vo.

180 × 108 × 30 mm.　　　　　　　　　　　　　　　　　　　　　　(P 976) Davis 337

Olive goatskin over paste boards, tooled in gold to a geometrical design of interlacing ribbons with small ivy-leaf tools, gouges, open tools and hatched tools. In the centre of the upper cover: an inlay with: M.T.C./PH.V.I; in the centre of the lower cover: an inlay of different (?)later leather, with two wings and the initials A.B. Edges of boards: tooled in gold with a line and small s-shaped tools. Edges: gilt.

　Sewn on five split alum-tawed supports, laced in straight, showing as raised bands on the spine, tooled in gold with lines; two kettle stitch bands; eight compartments, tooled in gold with lines and fleurons. Endbands: single with a bead; pink and blue silk over cord cores (laced in at a slight angle), tied down.

　Endleaves: paper pastedowns and one free paper leaf at both ends. The free leaf may be conjugate with a wide stub pasted beneath the pastedown.

37

PROVENANCE: 'A.B.'; on endleaf in an 18th- or 19th-century hand: 'No 840'; bought: Sotheby's, 26.ii.1951, *67* (pl.).
REFERENCES: Foot, *Davis*, I, pp. 143, 148 (note 27).
LITERATURE: Foot, *Davis*, I, pp. 143–4 (and literature mentioned there); see also Davis 336 (no. 38 below).

---

38 *A Paris binding by Wotton binder A (?the Pecking Crow binder) for Thomas Wotton, c. 1547*

M A Lucanus, [*Pharsalia*] *De bello civili libri decem*, Lyon: S Gryphius, 1542; ruled in red. 8vo.

167 × 108 × 22 mm.   (P 804) Davis 336

Brown calf over paste boards, tooled in gold to a geometrical design of interlacing ribbons, painted black; the compartments filled with large dots; open tools at the corners; hatched tools in the border and above and below a centre compartment, with two open tools above and below the tooled ownership inscription: THOMAE WOTT[O]NI/ET AMICORVM. Edges of boards: tooled in gold with lines, dashes and floral sprays. Edges: gilt.

   Rebacked; original sewing supports retained. Sewn on five split alum-tawed supports, laced in

38

straight; traces of two rows of kettle stitches. Endbands: the tail band is probably original: single with a bead; blue (with a few threads of white) silk, possibly over cord cores (cut off [in the rebacking]), tied down.

Endleaves: paper pastedowns and one free paper leaf, at both ends; at the front: the free leaf is conjugate with the pastedown; at the end: it has been tipped onto the last leaf of the last section.

Repairs: at covers; rebacked.

PROVENANCE: Thomas Wotton; manuscript note in a 19th- or early 20th-century hand attributing the binding to Grolier; John Evans (book plate; sold: Sotheby's, 17.iii.1911, *571*); bought: Sotheby's, 17.vii.1944, *149* (pl.).

REFERENCES: Moss, no. 27; *BFAC*, 1981, case L, no. 24; Foot, *Davis*, I, p. 148 (note 22).

LITERATURE: Foot, *Davis*, I, pp. 139–55 (and literature mentioned there); for Wotton binder A (Group I) see also Needham, *Twelve Centuries*, no. 53; for the connection between Wotton binder A (= Nixon, Group I) and the Pecking Crow binder, see Foot, *Davis*, I, pp. 133–4; see also Davis 337 (no. 37 above), 370, 390, 338, 371, 392, 393, 340 (nos. 39–41, 45–8 below).

Note: Thomas Wotton (1521–1586/7), of Boughton Malherbe (Kent); scholar, book collector, staunch Protestant, in and out of favour at Court; sheriff of Kent (under Elizabeth I); twice married. Wotton collected all his best bindings in Paris, which he visited in 1547, 1549 (or soon thereafter), 1551 and possibly also in 1552. For a binding made for him in England, see Foot, *Davis*, II, no. 39.

THOMÆ·WOTTONI
ET·AMICORVM

39 A binding for Thomas Wotton, c. 1547

R Agricola, *De inventione dialectica libri tres*, Paris: S Colinaeus, July 1542; ruled in red. 4to.

235 × 162 × 40 mm.   (P 311) Davis 370

Brown calf over paste boards, tooled in gold to a geometrical design with an interlacing ribbon, painted black; fleurons at the corners; a semis of dots; gouges forming a four-petalled flower (or star) in circles; decorated with black paint. In the centre: THOMAE.WOTTONI/ET.AMICORVM. Edges of boards: tooled in gold with a line, dashes and s-shaped tools. Edges: gilt.

Rebacked. Sewing invisible, but six supports have been laced in straight, lying in triangular slots, showing as raised bands on the spine. Endbands: probably renewed at the time of rebacking: single with a bead; white and blue silk over (?)leather or (?)alum-tawed cores (cut off), tied down.

Endleaves: paper pastedowns and two free paper leaves, at both ends (the pastedowns and the first free leaves are new).

Repairs: at covers; rebacked.

PROVENANCE: Thomas Wotton; Clement J Smythe of Lest[?l]ed Lodge, Chart, Kent; manuscript note: 'this came from my Uncle Clement Smythe'; Godfrey J Bird, Illington Rectory, Thetford, 1861–92; bought: Quaritch, 31.x.1941.
REFERENCES: Nixon, *Twelve Books*, p. 40 (note 5); Foot, *Davis*, I, p. 144.
LITERATURE: Foot, *Davis*, I, pp. 139–55 (and literature mentioned there); see also Davis 337, 336, 390, 338, 371, 392, 393, 340 (nos. 37–8 above, nos. 40–1, 45–8 below).
Note: Although most bindings with Wotton's ownership inscription come from Wotton binder A, this example has no tools in common with any binding from this group.

40 A Paris binding by Wotton binder B, possibly for Thomas Wotton, c. 1550–1

Diodorus Siculus, *Bibliothecae historicae libri*, Basel: H Petrus, March 1548; woodcut initials; ruled in red. fol.

318 × 202 × 34 mm.   (P 1085) Davis 390

Brown calf over paste boards, tooled in gold to a design formed by interlacing ribbons, painted black, forming large knot-like corners, a border and a square centre compartment; dots, gouges and open tools, decorated with black paint. Edges of boards: tooled in gold with lines, dashes and s-shaped tools. Edges: gilt.

Sewn on six (?)split (?)alum-tawed supports, laced in straight, showing as raised bands on the spine, tooled in gold with lines; two kettle stitch bands, tooled with s-shaped tools; nine compartments, the head and tail compartments tooled in gold with cross-hatched lines, the other six tooled in gold with solid acorn tools. Endbands: single with a bead; blue and white silk over (?)alum-tawed cores (cut off), tied down.

Endleaves: paper pastedowns and one free leaf conjugate with the pastedown, at both ends.

Repairs: at spine and joints.

PROVENANCE: (?)Thomas Wotton; the earl of Carnarvon (sold: Sotheby's, 8.iv.1919, *211*); manuscript

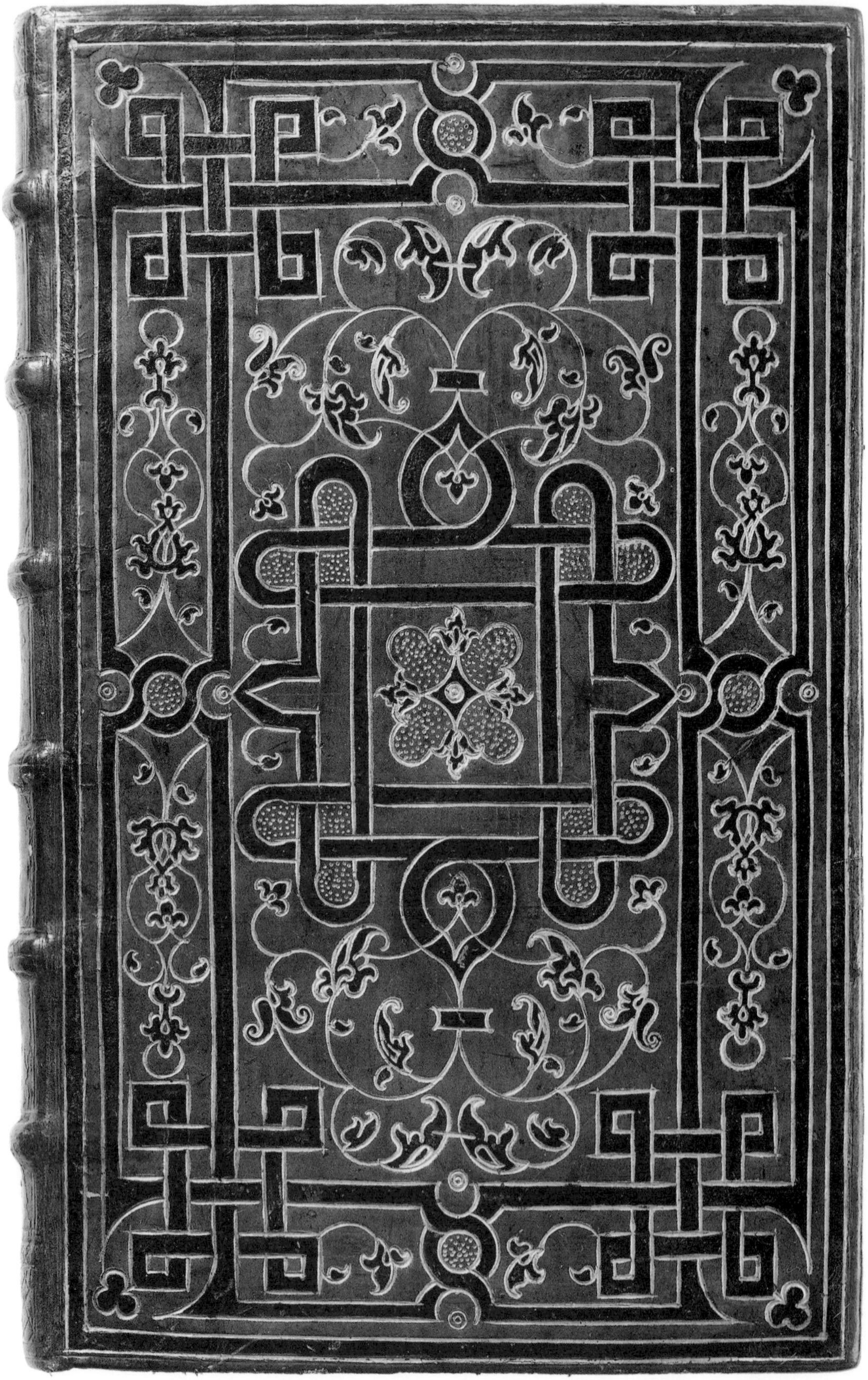

French Bindings

note on flyleaf: 'Superb Wotton binding'; in different hand: a note describing this as a Wotton binding from the Chesterfield library; Lucius Wilmerding (sold: Parke-Bernet, 31.x 51, *940*, pl.).

REFERENCES: Moss, no. 77; Grolier Club, *Exhibition*, 1937, no. 73; Foot, *Davis*, I, p. 149 (note 39).

LITERATURE: Foot, *Davis*, I, pp. 139–55 (and literature mentioned there); see also Davis 336, 370, 338, 391, 371, 392, 393, 340 (nos. 38–9 above, nos. 41–2, 45–8 below).

Note: Wotton binder B = Nixon, *Twelve Books*, pp. 36–48, Group IIA; although this binding does not have any ownership mark, the earl of Carnarvon inherited the Bretby library, from his mother, daughter of the 6th earl of Chesterfield, descendant of Philip Stanhope, 1st earl of Chesterfield, whose son Henry had married Catherine Wotton, great-granddaughter of Thomas Wotton; see also Davis 338, 391, 392 and 393 (nos. 41, 42, 46, 47 below).

---

41 *A Paris binding by Wotton binder B for Thomas Wotton, c. 1550–1*

Gasparo Contarini, *De elementis et eorum mixtionibus libri quinque*, Paris: N Dives, 1548 [and] Georgius Valla, *In Ciceronis Partitiones commentaria*, Paris: F Gryphius, 1534; ruled in red. 8vo.

168 × 102 × 30 mm.   (P 302) Davis 338

Brown calf over paste boards, tooled in gold with interlacing ribbons, painted black, gouges, open and hatched tools and dots; Wotton's coat of arms (with four quarterings), tooled in silver and decorated with black paint, in the centre. Edges of boards: tooled in gold with a line, dashes and s-shaped tools. Edges: gilt.

Sewn on five (possibly split?) alum-tawed supports, laced in straight, showing as raised bands on the spine, tooled in gold with lines; two rows of kettle stitches, tooled in gold with dashes; six compartments, tooled in gold with an acorn tool. Endbands: single; primary sewing over cord cores (cut off), tied down; secondary sewing of blue silk.

Endleaves: paper pastedowns and one free leaf conjugate with the pastedown, plus a second free paper leaf tipped on, at both ends.

Repairs: at joints and corners.

PROVENANCE: Thomas Wotton; Stanhope, earl of Chesterfield (book plate with in manuscript: '£:2:'); the earl of Carnarvon (sold: Sotheby's, 8.iv.1919, *15*, pl.); bought: Quaritch, 31.x.1941.

REFERENCES: Moss, no. 76; Foot, *Davis*, I, p. 149 (note 38).

LITERATURE: Foot, *Davis*, I, pp. 139–55 (and literature mentioned there)
For provenance note: see Davis 390 (no. 40 above); see also Davis 336, 370, 391, 371, 392, 393, 340 (nos. 38–9 above, nos. 42, 45–8 below).

41

42 *A Paris binding by Wotton binder B, possibly for Thomas Wotton, c. 1550–1*

Aristoteles, *Politicorum libri octo* [and other works], Paris: S Colinaeus, 1543 [and] Jacques Le Fèvre, *In Politica Aristotelis introductio* [and] Xenophon, *Oeconomicon, a Raphaele Volaterrano traductum*, Paris: S Colinaeus, July 1535; ruled in red. fol.

301 × 210 × 38 mm. (P 1084) Davis 391

Brown calf over paste boards, tooled in gold to a design of interlacing ribbons, painted black, forming a border, knot shapes in the corners and a centre compartment; acorn tools at the corners, gouges, dots, open and hatched tools, decorated with black and silver paint. Edges of boards: tooled in gold with lines, dashes and s-shaped tools. Edges: gilt.

Sewn on six split alum-tawed supports, laced in straight, showing as raised bands on the spine, tooled in gold with lines; two kettle stitch bands, tooled in gold with dashes; nine compartments, two of which near the head and two of which near the tail are tooled in gold with roundles; the other five are tooled in gold with an open tool, decorated with black paint. Endbands: single with a bead; primary sewing over cord (or ?alum-tawed) cores (cut off), tied down; secondary sewing of blue silk (remnants), tied down.

Endleaves: paper pastedowns and one free leaf conjugate with the pastedown, and a free paper leaf, at both ends.

PROVENANCE: (?)Thomas Wotton; the earl of Carnarvon (sold: Sotheby's, 8.iv.1919, *178*); on endleaves and pastedown in manuscript (?19th-century hand): '289' '319' '269' '278'; Lucius Wilmerding (sold: Parke-Bernet, 31.x.1951, *939*).

REFERENCES: Moss, no. 34; Grolier Club, *Exhibition*, 1937, no. 71; Romme, *Book Collector*, 1969, p. 25, note 10; Foot, *Davis*, I, pp. 139, 141, 149 (note 39).

LITERATURE: Foot, *Davis*, I, pp. 139–55 (and literature mentioned there); for provenance note: see Davis 390 (no. 40 above); see also Davis 336, 370, 390, 338, 371, 392, 393, 340 (nos. 38–41 above, nos. 45–8 below).

42

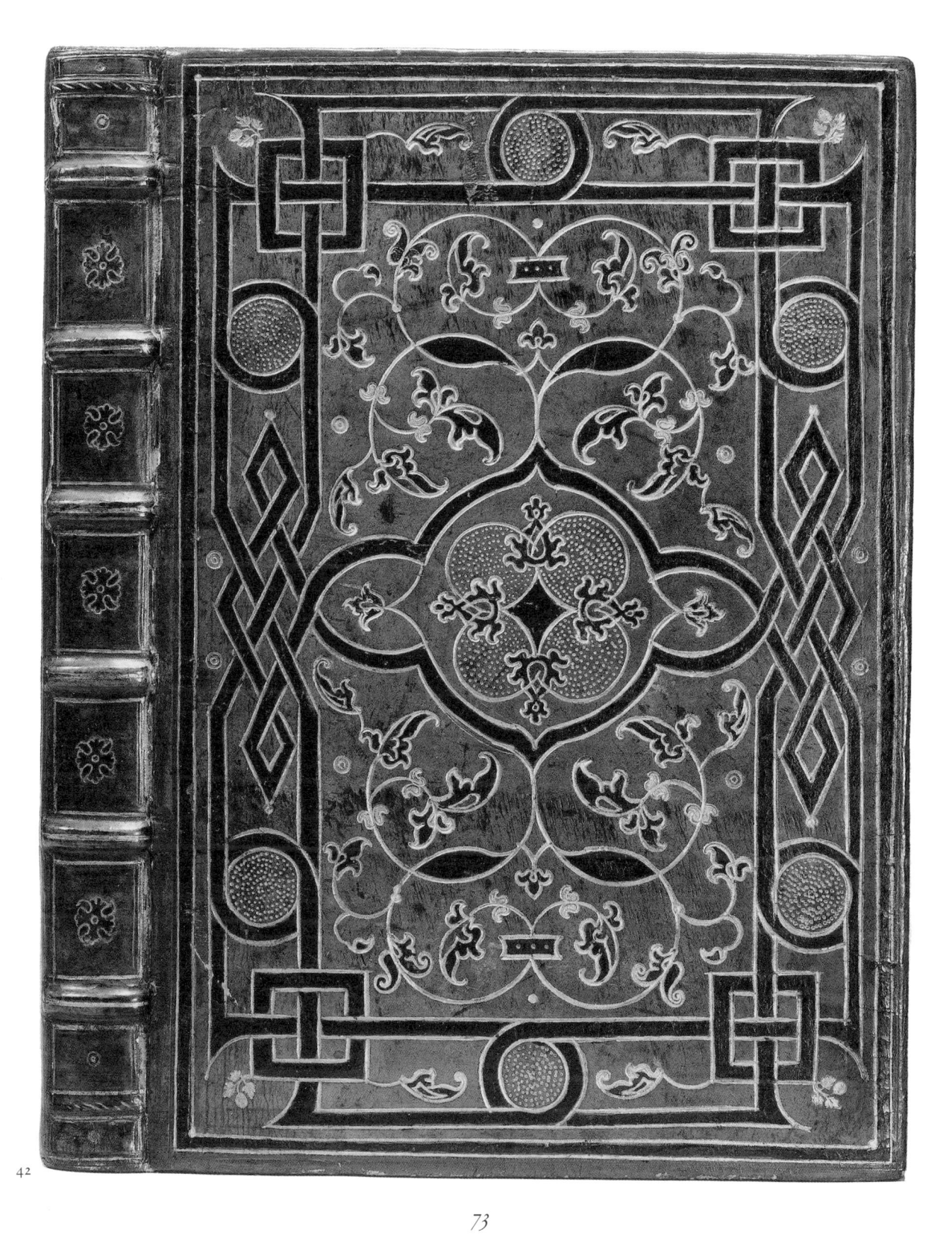

43 *A Paris binding by Wotton binder C, given by Theoderic von Thüngen to Richard von der Kher, c. 1546–50*

Testamenti novi, Lyon: S Gryphius, 1544; woodcut illustrations; ruled in red. 16mo.

126 × 80 × 40 mm. (P 1304) Davis, 348

Brown calf over paste boards, tooled in gold to a geometrical design of interlacing ribbons, painted black; gouges and open tools; in the centre of the upper cover: RICHARDO/A KHER/CANONICO/WVRCZE/BVRGEN; on the lower cover: THEODERICVS/A THVNGEN/NEPOS EX/SORORE/D.D. Two pairs of blue silk ties. Edges of boards: tooled in gold with a line, dashes and s-shaped tools. Edges: gilt and gauffered with leaves and fleurons.

Sewn on four supports (invisible; probably laced in straight), showing as raised bands on the spine, tooled in blind with lines; five compartments, tooled in gold with a small flower. Endbands: single with a bead; primary sewing over cord cores (one side still laced in, rest broken off), tied down; secondary sewing of pink-beige silk, tied down.

Endleaves: at the front: paper pastedown and one free leaf conjugate with the pastedown; at the end: new endleaves.

Repairs: at spine; new joints. With a ticket: 'Repaired for Paul Hirsch by Douglas Cockerell & Son. 1937'.

PROVENANCE: Richard von der Kher (or Kehr), given to him by Theoderic von Thüngen; on the title-page in manuscript: 'Fratrum Marchtallensium' [Marchthal: an abbey near Württenberg]; in a different hand: 'Huius libri possessor est Bartholomeus Hern(?) Were(?)as'; Paul Hirsch (book plate); bought: Breslauer, 1.i.1963.

REFERENCES: P Hirsch, *Eine kleine Bücherschau*, [Frankfurt am Main], 1920, no. 177; Foot, *Davis*, I, p. 151, Appendix III, no. 5.

LITERATURE: G C Knod, *Deutsche Studenten in Bologna*, Berlin, 1899, no. 3861; Foot, *Davis*, I, pp. 144–7 (and literature cited there).

Note: Theoderic von Thüngen (1530–1572); canon of Würzburg: 1541; studied in Paris: 1546; in Bologna: 1550; magistrate in Neustadt an der Saale: 1555–c. 1562; councillor of Würzburg: 1563. His father, Simon, was married to Margaretha von der Kehr and his grandfather, Bernhardt (brother of Conrad, bishop of Würzburg), was married to Freye von der Kehr [a letter from Hubert von Thüngen to Paul Hirsch, dated 25 December 1923].
Wotton binder C = Nixon, *Twelve Books*, pp. 36–48, Groups IIB and III; Davis 348: tools as on Nixon, Group IIB.

44 *A Paris binding by Wotton binder C, possibly for Marcus Fugger, c. 1548–50*

Caius Valerius Flaccus, *Argonautica*, Lyon: S Gryphius, 1548. 16mo.

127 × 75 × 27 mm. (P 1060) Davis 349

Olive-brown goatskin over paste boards, tooled in gold to a panel design; fleurons at the corners; fillets forming a border, painted black; in the centre a laurel wreath with, on the upper cover: VALE/RII/

French Bindings

43 44

FLAC and on the lower cover: four impressions of an open tool; decorated with black paint. Edges of boards: tooled in gold with lines, dashes and s-shaped tools. Edges: gilt.

Sewn on two (?recessed) cords, laced in; two rows of kettle stitches; smooth spine, tooled in gold with interlacing-circles tools. Endbands: single with a bead; green silk over (?)cord cores (cut off), tied down.

Endleaves: paper pastedowns and a pair of free conjugate paper leaves, and one free leaf conjugate with the pastedown, at both ends.

PROVENANCE: Marcus Fugger (on pastedown of upper cover in manuscript: 'Marx Fugg.' [in Fugger's hand]; in a different hand: 'Arc:153/Nro:327' [shelf mark of Fugger's library]); on title-page: library stamp of Oettingen-Wallerstein (sold: Karl & Faber, *Auktion VIII (II Teil)*, 6–7.xi.1933, *361*); Lucius Wilmerding (book plate; sold: Parke-Bernet, 31.x.1951, *385*).

REFERENCES: Foot, *Davis*, I, p. 153, no. 28.

LITERATURE: Foot, *Davis*, I, pp. 145–7, 176–7 (and literature mentioned there); Needham, *Twelve Centuries*, no. 63; Schäfer, p. 42; see also Davis 348, 371, 392, 393, 340, 404, 339, 372, 373 (no. 43 above, nos. 45–52 below); see also Davis, 339 (no. 50 below), 419 (no. 57 below), 379 (no. 66 below), 422, 590 (Swiss, nos. 224, 225).

Note: Marcus Fugger (1529–1597), son of Anton Fugger; educated at Louvain; councillor of Augsburg; banker; book collector. Davis 349: tools as on Nixon, *Twelve Books*, pp. 36–48, Group III.

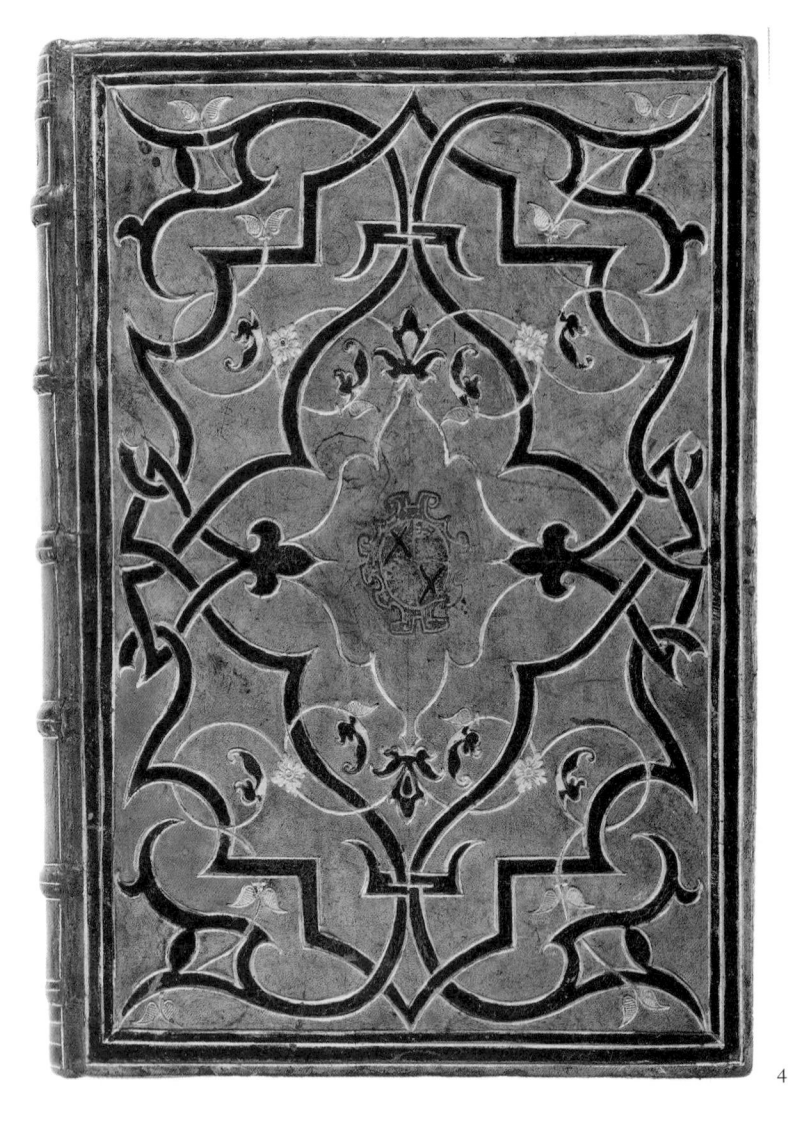

45 *A Paris binding by Wotton binder C for Thomas Wotton, c. 1549–51*

B Ochino, *A Tragoedie or Dialoge of the uniuste usurped Primacie of the Bishop of Rome ... translated out of Latine ... by ... John Ponet*, London: for Gwalter Lynne, 1549; illustrated title-page and initials; ruled in red. 4to.

203 × 143 × 19 mm. (P 389) Davis 371

Light-brown calf over paste boards, tooled in gold to an arabesque pattern of interlacing ribbons, painted black; gouges, solid stylized flowers, open and hatched tools, decorated with black paint; in the centre the arms of Thomas Wotton tooled in silver and decorated with black paint. Edges of boards: tooled in gold with lines, dashes and s-shaped tools. Edges: gilt.

Sewn on five supports, laced in straight, showing as raised bands on the spine, tooled in gold with lines; two kettle stitch bands; eight compartments, the head and tail compartments tooled in gold with lines and decorated with black paint, the other six compartments tooled in gold with lines and flower tools. Endbands: (?)new; single with a bead; black and red silk over (?)leather cores (cut off).

Endleaves: paper pastedowns and two free paper leaves at both ends (possible conjugacy invisible).

PROVENANCE: Thomas Wotton; Lord Amherst of Hackney (book plate; sold: Sotheby's, 25.iii.1909, *646*); Milliner collection (sold: Sotheby's, 15.vii.1924, *406*, pl.); bought: Sotheby's, 25.iii.1942 (there is no Sotheby's book sale catalogue for this date).

REFERENCES: *BFAC*, 1891, Case L, no. 26; Quaritch, Catalogue 1889, p. 129, no. 955, pl. 33; H H Mulliner, *The Decorative Arts in England*, London, 1923, fig. 216; Moss, no. 90; Nixon, *Twelve Books*, p. 41; *Le Livre anglais*, exh. cat., Bibliothèque Nationale, Paris, 1951, no. 393; Nixon, *Broxbourne*, p. 62; Foot, *Davis*, I, p. 149 (note 43).

LITERATURE: Foot, *Davis*, I, pp. 139–55; see also Davis 336, 370, 390, 338, 391, 392, 393, 340 (nos. 38–42 above, 46–8 below).

Note: Davis 371: tools as on Nixon, *Twelve Books*, pp. 36–48, Group IIB.

46 *A Paris binding by Wotton binder C, possibly for Thomas Wotton, c. 1551*

J Omphalius, *De officio et potestate principis in republica* [and] *De usurpatione legum*, Basel: I Oporinus, August/September 1550; woodcut initials; ruled in red. fol.

312 × 202 × 37 mm.   (P 997) Davis 392

Brown calf over paste boards, tooled in gold to an arabesque pattern of interlacing ribbons, painted black; gouges, dots, hatched and open tools, decorated with black and silver paint. Edges of boards: tooled in gold with lines, dashes and s-shaped tools. Edges: gilt.

Sewn on six split alum-tawed supports, laced in straight, showing as raised bands on the spine, tooled in gold with lines; two kettle stitch bands, tooled in gold with dashes; nine compartments, the head and tail compartments tooled with a small solid diamond tool, the other seven tooled in gold with hatched and open tools, decorated with silver paint. Endbands: single with a bead; blue silk over (?)alum-tawed cores (cut off), tied down.

Endleaves: paper pastedowns and one free leaf conjugate with the pastedown, at both ends.

PROVENANCE: (?)Thomas Wotton; the earl of Carnarvon (sold: Sotheby's, 8.iv.1919, *358*); engraving of Thomas Wotton in his 72nd year inserted; lengthy manuscript note (20th-century hand, same hand as in Davis 393, no. 47 below), describing this binding as having belonged to Wotton and coming from the Chesterfield library; Lucius Wilmerding (book plate; sold: Parke-Bernet, 6.iii.1951, *489*).

REFERENCES: Moss, no. 94; Grolier Club, *Exhibition*, 1937, no. 74 (at which time this volume contained a letter by Thomas Wotton, dated 11 September 1574; now lost); Foot, *Davis*, I, p. 149 (note 44).

LITERATURE: Foot, *Davis*, I, pp. 139–55 (and literature mentioned there); see also Davis 336, 370, 390, 338, 391, 371, 393, 340 (nos. 38–42, 45 above, nos. 47–8 below).

Note: Davis 392: tools as on Nixon, *Twelve Books*, pp. 36–48, Group IIB.

46

47

47 *A Paris binding by Wotton binder C, possibly for Thomas Wotton, c. 1551*

Valerius Anselmus Ryd, *Catalogus annorum et principum sive monarchum mundi*, Bern: [M. Apiarius], 1550 [and] Wolfgang Lazius, *Vienna Austriae. Rerum Viennensium commentarii in quatuor libros distincti*, Basel: I Oporinus, September 1546; ruled in red. fol.

315 × 202 × 33 mm.   (P 999) Davis 393

Brown calf over paste boards, tooled in gold to an arabesque design of interlacing ribbons, painted black; gouges, open and hatched tools; decorated with black and silver paint. Edges of boards: tooled in gold with lines, dashes and s-shaped tools. Edges: gilt.

    Sewn on six split alum-tawed supports, laced in straight, showing as raised bands on the spine, tooled in gold with lines; two kettle stitch bands, tooled in gold with dashes; nine compartments, tooled in gold and blind with lines; the head and tail compartments are tooled in gold with a small solid trefoil; the other seven are tooled in gold with hatched and open tools, decorated with black paint. Endbands: single with a bead; primary sewing over alum-tawed cores (cut off), tied down; secondary sewing of blue-green silk, tied down.

    Endleaves: paper pastedowns and one free leaf conjugate with the pastedown, at both ends.
    Repairs: at spine.

PROVENANCE: (?)Thomas Wotton; the earl of Carnarvon (sold: Sotheby's, 8.iv.1919, *377*); engraving of Thomas Wotton in his 72nd year inserted; on pastedown lengthy manuscript note (20th-century hand; same hand as note in Davis 392, no. 46 above), describing this as a binding made for Wotton, from the Chesterfield library; on endleaf manuscript note (20th century): 'Bretby Park library'; Lucius Wilmerding (sold: Parke-Bernet, 6.iii.1951, *581*).

REFERENCES: Grolier Club, *Exhibition*, 1937, no. 72; Moss, no. 93; Foot, *Davis*, I, p. 149 (note 44).

LITERATURE: Foot, *Davis*, I, pp. 139–55 (and literature mentioned there); see also Davis 336, 370, 390, 338, 391, 371, 392, 340 (nos. 38–42, 45–6 above, no. 48 below).

Note: Davis 393: tools as on Nixon, *Twelve Books*, pp. 36–48, Group IIB.

48 *A Paris binding by Wotton binder C for Thomas Wotton, c. 1552*

Polybius, *Historiarum libri quinque*, Lyon: S Gryphius, 1548; ruled in red. 16mo.

129 × 74 × 34 mm.   (P 727) Davis 340

Brown calf over paste boards, tooled in gold with a block showing a pattern of interlacing ribbons around the date 1552 in the centre. Edges of boards: tooled in gold with a line, dashes and s-shaped tools. Edges: gilt.

    Sewn on four split alum-tawed supports, laced in straight, showing as raised bands on the spine, tooled in gold with lines; two kettle stitch bands, tooled in gold with dashes; seven compartments, tooled in gold with lines and a flower tool. Endbands: single with a bead; green silk over cord cores (cut off), tied down.

    Endleaves: at the front: one pair of conjugate paper leaves; at the end: two pairs of conjugate paper

48

leaves, quired inside one another. Spine strengthener of parchment (manuscript) visible: three stubs at the front and one parchment and four paper stubs at the end.

Repairs: at corners of covers, joints, and head and tail of spine.

PROVENANCE: Thomas Wotton; Philip, Baron Wharton (on a2 recto in manuscript: 'Ex Dono Honoratissimi Viri Philippi Baronis Wharton, Amici mei emeritissime colendi'); armorial library label with, in manuscript: '41'; Maggs (Catalogue 407, 1921, *29*); Colonel W E Moss (sold: Sotheby's, 8.iii.1937, *1157*, pl.); bought: Sotheby's, 16.xi.1943, *164* (pl.).

REFERENCES: Moss, no. 83; Nixon, *Twelve Books*, p. 42, note 3; Foot, *Davis*, I, pp. 145, 147, 155, no. (b).

LITERATURE: Foot, *Davis*, I, pp. 145–7 (and literature mentioned there); Nixon, *Pierpont Morgan Library*, no. 27; Bridwell, pp. 42–3 (another Wotton C binding with a block and 1552 on Calvin, Geneva, 1545); see also Davis 336, 370, 390, 338, 391, 371, 392, 393 (nos. 38–42, 45–7 above).

Note: Philip, Baron Wharton's third daughter, Margaret, married Edward, first Baron Wotton (eldest son of Thomas Wotton). Davis 340: tools as on Nixon, *Twelve Books*, pp. 36–48, Group III.

49   *A Paris binding by Wotton binder C, for the duc de Guise, before 1550*

Appian, *Des guerres des Rommains livres xi*, Lyon: for A Constantin, 20 October 1544; woodcut title-page and initials. fol.

332 × 210 × 40 mm.   (P 1042) Davis 404

Brown calf over paste boards, tooled in gold to a design with interlacing ribbons forming large knots in the corners, borders and an oval in the centre, decorated with dark blue and black paint; gouges and open tools, decorated with silver, white, blue and black paint; in the centre: the painted arms of the duc de Guise. Edges of boards: tooled in gold with lines, dashes and s-shaped tools. Edges: stained dark and gauffered with an arabesque pattern of lines, leaves and fleurons.

Sewn on seven split alum-tawed supports, laced in straight, showing as raised bands on the spine, tooled in gold with lines; eight compartments, tooled in gold with lines, roundles and open tools, decorated with black paint; cross-hatching near head and tail. Endbands: single with a bead; pink and white silk over leather cores (cut off), tied down (sporadically).

Endleaves: paper pastedowns and two free paper leaves at both ends.

Repairs: at joints and at the lower corner of the upper cover.

PROVENANCE: François de Lorraine, duc de Guise; J-L Techener (sold: Paris, 1887, *644*); Robert Hoe (book plate; sold: New York, Anderson Galleries, April 1911, *286*); E Rahir (book plate; sold: Paris, 1930, *13*, pl.); Lucius Wilmerding (sold: Parke-Bernet, 5.iii.1951, *40*, pl.); bought: Robinson, 17.x.1951.

REFERENCES: J-L Techener, *Histoire de la bibliophilie*, 1861, pl. 25; Hoe, *176 Bindings*, no. 35; Grolier Club, *Catalogue of Book Bindings*, New York, 1895, no. 35; Shipman, p. 74 (1); Grolier Club, *Exhibition*, 1937, no. 18; Hobson, *French and Italian*, no. 20; Romme, *Book Collector*, 1969, p. 26, note 19; Foot, *Davis*, I, pp. 144–5, 151, Appendix III, no. 6; Culot, *La Reliure en France*, p. 125.

LITERATURE: Foot, *Davis*, I, pp. 144–7 (and literature mentioned there); see also Davis 348, 349, 371, 392, 393, 340, 339, 372, 373 (nos. 43–8 above, nos. 50–2 below).

Note: François de Lorraine, duc de Guise (1519–1563); Davis 404: tools as on Nixon, *Twelve Books*, pp. 36–48, Group IIB.

---

50   *A Paris binding by Wotton binder C, possibly for Marcus Fugger, c. 1550*

Philippe de Comines. *Cronique et histoire … contenent les choses advenues durant le regne du Roy Loys unzieme … en France*, Paris: Estienne Mesviere for Galliot du Pré & I de Roigny, June 1546. 8vo.

175 × 112 × 35mm.   (P 1059) Davis 339

Brown calf over paste boards, tooled in gold with a border formed by fillets, gouges, solid star and flower tools, open and hatched tools. Edges of boards: tooled in gold with lines, dashes and s-shaped tools. Edges: gilt and gauffered with leaves and fleurons, on a red-painted background.

Sewn on four (?recessed) cords, laced in; two rows of kettle stitches; smooth spine, tooled in gold with strips of interlaced-circles tools and 'compartments' filled with cross-hatching and brick-work tooling. Endbands: single with a bead; pink and blue silk over (?)tanned leather cores (cut or broken off), tied down.

49

THE HENRY DAVIS GIFT

50

Endleaves: paper pastedowns and a pair of free conjugate paper leaves, and a third free leaf conjugate with the pastedown, at both ends. Strengtheners, or possibly part of the spine lining, visible beneath the pastedown of the lower cover.

Repairs: at the joints.

PROVENANCE: Marcus Fugger (on pastedown of upper cover in manuscript: 'Marx Fugg' [in Fugger's hand]; in a different hand: 'Arc.293.Nro.303. [shelf mark of Fugger's library]); on title-page: library stamp of Oettingen-Wallerstein (sold: Karl & Faber, *Auktion VIII (II Teil)*, 6–7.xi.1933, *172*); on pastedown in a later hand: 'X943'; Lucius Wilmerding (sold: Parke-Bernet, 30.x.1951, *384*).

REFERENCES: Foot, *Davis*, I, p. 153, no. 22.

LITERATURE: Foot, *Davis*, I, pp. 145–7, 176–7 (and literature mentioned there); see also Davis 348, 349, 371, 392, 393, 340, 404, 372, 373 (nos. 43–9 above, nos. 51–2 below).

Note: Davis 339: tools as on Nixon, *Twelve Books*, pp. 36–48, Group III.

51

51 *A Paris binding by Wotton binder C, c. 1556*

Les Ordonnances royaux, sur le faict et iurisdiction de la prevosté des marchans, et eschevinage de la ville de Paris, Paris: for G Merlin & V Sertenas, 1556; ruled in red. 4to.

235 × 160 × 25 mm.   (P 1135) Davis 372

Brown calf over paste boards, tooled in gold to an arabesque design on a background semé with dots, gouges, hatched and open tools, decorated with red, white and black paint, around a centre oval ornament surrounded by a border, lettered: .DVM.TVA.TE.FORTVNA.SINET. Traces of two pairs of ties. Edges of boards: tooled in gold with lines, dashes and s-shapes tools. Edges: gilt.

    Rebacked with the original spine strip and (possibly) the original sewing supports retained. Sewn on three alum-tawed supports, laced in straight; smooth spine, tooled in gold with interlacing-circles tools. Endbands: single with a bead; blue and pink silk over (?)leather cores (cut off), tied down.

    Endleaves: paper pastedowns and one free leaf conjugate with the pastedown, and a second free paper leaf, at both ends.

    Repairs: rebacked; repair to upper cover.

THE HENRY DAVIS GIFT

PROVENANCE: On endleaf in manuscript: 'Joan. De Bourges medicus Parisiensis'; 'Surreau 1569'; in a 20th-century hand: 'Bibliothèque de la Pere de Faucigny-Lucinge'; bought: Pierre Berès, 29.i.1954.
REFERENCES: Needham, *Twelve Centuries*, p. 223; Foot, *Davis*, I, p. 154, no. 53.
LITERATURE: Foot, *Davis*, I, pp. 145–7 (and literature mentioned there); see also Davis 348, 349, 371, 392, 393, 340, 404, 339, 373 (nos. 43–50 above, no. 52 below).
Note: The De Bourges were a family of doctors; Jean de Bourges was physician to Charles VIII and Louis XII; two more likely candidates are: Jean de Bourges, doyen of the medical faculty in Paris c. 1654 and Jean de Bourges, physician at the Hôtel Dieu in Paris, d. 1684. Davis 372: tools as on Nixon, *Twelve Books*, pp. 36–48, Group III.

52 *A Paris binding by Wotton binder C, c. 1560*

Enea Vico, *Augustarum imagines … vitae quoque earundem … enarratae*, Venice, 1558; illustrated title-page and illustrations throughout. 4to.

250 × 172 × 28 mm.   (P 575) Davis 373

Brown goatskin over paste boards, tooled in gold with large corner pieces and a large oval centre block on a semis of solid stylized flower tools. Edges of boards: tooled in gold with a line and dashes. Edges: gilt and gauffered to an intricate pattern of arabesque lines and curving shapes.

Sewn on five supports, four of which are laced in straight; smooth spine tooled in gold with gouges, hatched fleuron tools, dots and tiny flower tools; hatching at head and tail; paper labels (top label with: '1216/3'). Endbands: missing.

Endleaves: paper pastedowns, a pair of free conjugate paper leaves, and a free leaf (?)conjugate with the pastedown, at both ends; manuscript spine strengthener visible beneath pastedowns.

PROVENANCE: On title-page in manuscript: 'Collegij Paris.Soc.JESV'; on pastedown in manuscript: 'Act 1099R3 / xx:9' on endleaf: '1729'; Renouard (sold: Evans, 23.vi.1834, *1425*); bought: Quaritch, 21.ii.1942.
REFERENCES: Foot, *Davis*, I, p. 154, no. 54.
LITERATURE: Foot, *Davis*, I, pp. 145–7 (and literature mentioned there); see also Davis 348, 349, 371, 392, 393, 340, 404, 339, 372 (nos. 43–51 above).
Note: Davis 373: tools as on Nixon, *Twelve Books*, pp. 36–48, Group III.

53 *A binding made in France or possibly Italy, c. 1550*

Alessandro Piccolomini, *Cento sonetti*, Rome: V Valgrisi, 1549; woodcut initials. 8vo.

172 × 105 × 18 mm.   (P 919) Davis 361

Light brown goatskin over paste boards, tooled in gold, with blind lines, to a panel design with fleurons at the outer corners, a border composed of leafy s-shaped tools; the panel filled with an interlacing diamond and rectangle; small fleurons, small s-shaped tools; in the centre two ornaments with the initials A.S; above and below a crowned dolphin. Traces of two pairs of ties. Edges of boards: tooled in blind with a line. Edges: gilt.

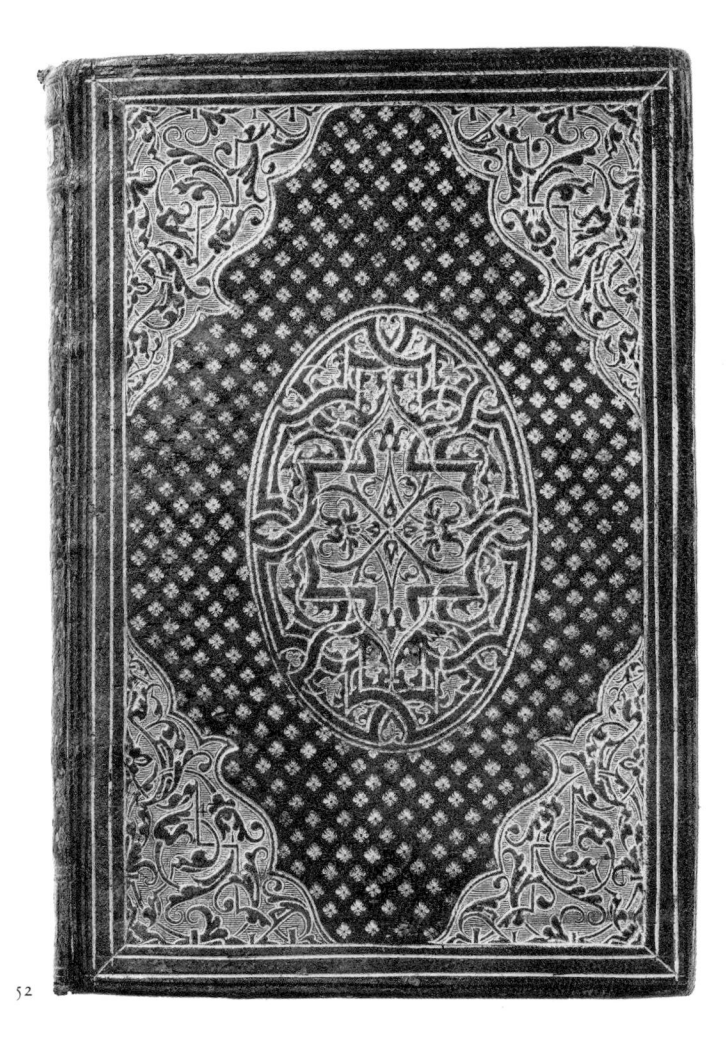

Sewn on four split (?)tanned leather supports, laced in straight (possibly taken sideways parallel with the spine: difficult to see); two rows of kettle stitches. The supports show as raised bands on the spine, tooled in gold with lines; five compartments, tooled in blind with lines and in gold with small fleurons. Endbands: single with a bead; pink and blue silk over tanned leather cores, cut or broken off (traces of lacing-in holes in the edge of the upper board), tied down.

Endleaves: paper pastedowns and one free leaf conjugate with the pastedown, at both ends.

PROVENANCE: A.S.; Landau collection (book plate with '47779'); sold: Sotheby's, 13.vii.1948, *90* (pl.).
REFERENCES: Pitti, exhibition, no. 517; De Marinis, *Appunti*, p. 142, no. 80, pl. cclxxi.
LITERATURE: A R A Hobson, 'Une note sur le fer de reliure d'un dauphin', *Bulletin du bibliophile*, 1990, 1, pp. 139–42.
Same border tools on: De Marinis, I, pl. cxliii (Venice, 1547).
Compare: (centre ornament) John Rylands University Library, Manchester, R16379 (I a Lasco, London, 1552) (?identical tool).
Note: Dr A R A Hobson tells me that this binding was made in France rather than in Italy; I am grateful for his opinion.

54   *A gold-blocked binding made in Paris or Lyon, c. 1550*

Horae in laudem beatissimae virginis Mariae, ad usum Romanum, Paris: R & C Chaudière, 1549; ruled in red; decorated borders. 4to.

232 × 168 × 25 mm.   (P 989) Davis 500

Brown calf over paste boards, blocked in gold (block used upside down on lower cover), showing an intricate design of interlacing ribbons and shells with in the centre of the upper cover the Sacred Monogram and on the lower cover MA (for Maria); on both covers the letters .F. .B. The block is decorated with blue, green, red, black, pink and white paint (repainted). Traces of four pairs of ties. Edges of boards: tooled in gold with a line, dashes and small curling tools. Edges: gilt and gauffered with arabesque lines and leaf shapes.

Sewn on five (recessed) cords, laced in straight; smooth spine, tooled in gold with open tools, decorated with black paint. Endbands: single with a bead; green and yellow silk over (?)rolled leather cores (cut off), tied down.

Endleaves: paper pastedowns and one free leaf conjugate with the pastedown, and one free paper leaf tipped on.

Repairs: at edges of boards; generally restored.

PROVENANCE: F.B.; (?)Bigot (sold: Paris, July 1706?); Lucien Gougy (sold: Paris, Hôtel Drouot, I, 5-8.iii.1934, *144*, pl. xi); Lucius Wilmerding (book plate; sold: Parke-Bernet, 5.iii.1951, *312*).
REFERENCES: Needham, *Twelve Centuries*, p. 200, note 2; Foot, *Revue française*, p. 375, note 14.
LITERATURE: Needham, *Twelve Centuries*, no. 61; Toulet, 'L'école lyonnaise', fig. 144.
Same block: H Joly, *Exposition de reliures*, Lyon, 1925, no. 56, pl. 12; Needham, *Twelve Centuries*, no. 61.
Compare: (similar blocks) Cambridge University Library, SSS.6.16 (*Heures* [1515], illustrated in Quaritch, Catalogue 1889, *131*, pl. 38; G D Hobson, *Cambridge*, pl. xxxii); National Library of Scotland, Bdg.5.43; Libri, *Monuments inédits*, pl. xxxi (Paris, 1549); Gougy sale I, Paris, 5-8.iii.1934, *64*, pl. vi (Florence, 1549), also with the initials F.B. and the ex-libris of Louis-Emeric Bigot; Bibliothèque B* sale: Giraud Badin, 1934, *61*; Madame Th. Belin sale: Paris, Giraud Badin, 1936, *7*; Esmerian sale I, Paris, 6.vi.1972, *29*.

55   *A binding made in Paris (or possibly in Lyon?), c. 1550*

Gulielmus Postellus, *De magistratibus Atheniensium liber*, Venice: I A & P de Nicolinis de Sabio, 1541; on blue paper. 8vo.

205 × 124 × 18 mm.   (P 1331) Davis 380

Black goatskin over paste boards, tooled in gold, with blind lines, to a panel design with two gilt and two blind fillets along the border and outlining the panel; very small leaf tools at the corners, in the centre an interlacing onlay of brown goatskin, tooled in gold with dots and a gold-tooled lozenge shape with small leaf tools. Edges of boards and turn-ins: tooled in blind with lines. Edges: gilt.

Sewn on five, possibly split, alum-tawed supports, laced in straight, showing as raised bands on the spine, tooled in gold with lines; two kettle stitch bands; eight compartments, tooled in gold with lines. Endbands: single with a bead; green silk over cord cores (laced in), tied down.

54 55

Endleaves: blue paper pastedowns and one pair of free conjugate blue paper leaves, plus one free leaf conjugate with the pastedown, at both ends.

PROVENANCE: Guillaume du Choul (on pastedown in manuscript: GVILIERMI. CAVLII /LVGD: ET. AMICORVM); Laurent Rabot (on endleaf in manuscript: 'Guillielmus Caulius Alpium provinciae Praeses Laurentio Raboto D.D'); Jesuit College in Paris (on title-page in manuscript: 'Colleg. Paris. Societ. JESV'); on pastedown in manuscript: '839.[erased]/1563./Hh 53.I.'; Manuscript note by J J de Bure l'aîné, 1833; (in manuscript in a later hand: from the sales of Crevenna and de Bure); Count Henry Chandon de Briailles, 1898–1937 (book plates); Amherst of Hackney (book plate; sold: Sotheby's, 5.xii.1908, *702*); in manuscript: 'A Barbet 249a' (sold: Giraud Badin, 13.vi.1932, *131*); bought: Breslauer, 20.iv.1956.

LITERATURE: Nicolas Bourbon, *Nugae*, Lyon, 1538, p. 148 (for Rabot); Hobson, *Renaissance*, p. 61 (for Grolier and Du Choul).

Compare: (a binding with a similar centre decoration) Sotheby's, 23.vi.1965, *469* (= Hobson, *Humanists*, p. 191, pl.: on a binding with hatched tools as used by Gommar Estienne).

Note: Guillaume du Choul: antiquary, archaeologist and writer in Lyon; c. 1555 he dedicated a manuscript to Henri II (see Sotheby's, 8.vii.1959, *661*); Grolier gave him a Roman silver coin. Laurent (or Lorentz) Rabot, councillor to the Parlement of Grenoble; Grolier presented books to him (see Davis 325, no. 22 above; see also: Sotheby's, 20.xii.1954, *101*).

56 *A binding dating from the 1550s*

Sperone Speroni, *Dialoghi*, Venice: Aldus, March 1546. 8vo.

160 × 98 × 25 mm. (P 361) Davis 418

Brown calf over paste boards, tooled in silver (oxidized) with an interlacing ribbon, gouges, hatched and open tools. Remnants of two pairs of ties. Edges of boards: tooled in blind with a line, dashes and s-shaped tools. Edges: stained black.

Rebacked with the original spine strip retained. [Now] sewn on four recessed cords, laced in, probably straight (lacing-in pattern hidden by a piece of manuscript or printed waste beneath the pastedown); smooth spine, tooled in silver (oxidized) with strips of leafy s-shaped tools; the compartments between these: tooled with cross-hatching. Endbands: single with a bead; traces of primary sewing over cord cores (cut off), tied down; secondary sewing of green and yellow silk, tied down.

Endleaves: paper pastedowns at both ends; at the front: one free leaf conjugate with the pastedown, and one free paper leaf (tipped on); at the end: a pair of free conjugate paper leaves, stub conjugate with the pastedown.

Repairs: rebacked, head and tail renewed; repair at corner of lower cover.

PROVENANCE: On front pastedown in manuscript (19th-/20th-century hand): 'Powis'; (later hand) 'M 500'; lower-cover pastedown price code in 20th-century hand; '13274'; bought: Quaritch, 15.xii.1941.

57

57 *A binding dating from the 1550s*

C Galenus, *Methodus medendi, vel de morbis curandis libri xiii*, Lyon: G Rouillé, 1549. 16mo.

123 × 78 × 45 mm. (P 1061) Davis 419

Olive goatskin over paste boards, onlaid in citron goatskin to an arabesque pattern of interlacing ribbons, outlined in gold; gold-tooled lines along the border. Edges of boards: tooled in gold with a line, dashes and s-shaped tools. Edges: gilt.

Sewn on three (?)cords or flat supports, laced in; smooth spine, tooled in gold with 'bands' of leafy s-shaped tools and a fleuron in each 'compartment'. Endbands: single with a bead; pink and blue silk over cord cores (frayed out beneath the pastedowns; one side possibly laced in), tied down.

Endleaves: paper pastedowns and a pair of free conjugate paper leaves, and one free leaf conjugate with the pastedown, at both ends.

PROVENANCE: Marcus Fugger (on pastedown in manuscript: 'Marcus Fugger' [in Fugger's hand]; in a different hand: 'Arc.134./Nro.249' [shelf mark of Fugger's library]); on title-page: library stamp of Oettingen-Wallerstein (sold: Karl & Faber, *Auktion VIII (II Teil)*, 6–7.xi.1933, *433*); in manuscript (later hand): 'Y.920'; Lucius Wilmerding (sold: Parke-Bernet, 30.x.1951, *386*).

REFERENCES: Grolier Club, *Exhibition*, 1937, no. 69; Foot, *Revue française*, p. 375.

LITERATURE: Foot, *Davis*, I, pp. 176–7 (and literature mentioned there); see also Davis 349, 339 (nos. 44, 50 above), 379 (no. 66 below), 422, 590 (Swiss, nos. 224, 225).

Same spine tools: (and a similar onlaid pattern) Lardanchet, Catalogue 44 (1950), *98* (Lyon, 1550).

58 *A Paris binding of the 1550s*

Herodianus, *Historiae de imperio post Marcum* [and other works by various authors, edited by Angelus Politanus], Venice: Aldus, July 1498 [text starts on L1 verso]. fol.

321 × 214 × 36 mm. (P 962) Davis 395

Brown goatskin (or possibly hair sheep?) over paste boards, tooled in gold to a complex arabesque pattern of interlacing ribbons, painted black, onlays of black goatskin in the corners and at the four sides of a central oval, which is onlaid in dark brown goatskin; gold-tooled gouges and dots; smaller black and brown onlays; black paint. Edges of boards: tooled in gold with lines and dashes. Edges: gilt.

    Sewn on five alum-tawed supports, laced in straight; smooth spine, tooled in gold with interlacing ribbons, painted black, and compartments filled with dots. Endbands: single with a bead; dark green silk over cord cores (taken down beneath pastedowns), tied down.

59

Endleaves: paper pastedowns at both ends; at the front: a pair of free conjugate paper leaves; at the end: two pairs of free conjugate paper leaves, quired inside one another.

Repairs: at corners of covers; at spine; at head and tail of spine.

PROVENANCE: On L1 recto, in manuscript: 'Lafond Laferté'; Quaritch (Catalogue 1921, *100*, pl. xxxii); Lardanchet, Catalogue 44 (1950), *246* (pl. pp. 40–1); bought: Lardanchet, 22.vi.1950.
REFERENCES: Romme, *Book Collector*, 1969, p. 26, note 20, pl. v; Foot, *Revue française*, p. 375, note 12.
Compare: (design) G D Hobson, *Maioli*, pl. 44.

---

59 *A binding dating from the 1550s*

Ovidius, *Metamorphoseon libri xv*, Venice: Haeredes Aldi & A Soceri, September 1533 [title-page: 1534]; ruled in red. 8vo.

165 × 102 × 26 mm.   (P 1008) Davis 420

Brown goatskin over paste boards, tooled in gold to a geometrical design with an interlacing ribbon, painted black, gouges, open tools and dots; in the centre: a six-pointed star, lettered on the upper cover: META/MORPHO/SEON; on the lower cover: OVIDII; decorated with black, green and fawn paint (repainted). Traces of two pairs of ties. Edges of boards: tooled in blind with a line. Edges: gilt and gauffered with a fleuron, leaf and lines pattern.

Sewn on five supports, laced in straight, showing as raised bands on the spine, tooled in gold with lines; six compartments, tooled in blind with lines and in gold with solid fleuron tools. Endbands: single with a bead; primary sewing over alum-tawed cores (?cut off, or possibly taken down to the kettle stitch), tied down; secondary sewing of pink silk.

Endleaves (later): paper pastedowns and one pair of free conjugate paper leaves and a stub conjugate with the pastedown, at both ends.

Repairs: head and tail of spine: renewed; small repairs at corners of covers and at covers.

PROVENANCE: On pastedown in 20th-century hand: 'Library H.1'; Seligman of Newton Hall, Cambridge (book plate with in manuscript: 'JS'); Theodore Seligman (sold: Sotheby's, 2.v.1951, *608*).

60 *A binding dating from the 1550s*

Luigi Alamanni, *Gyrone il Cortese*, Paris: R Chaudière, 1548; illustrated title-page and initials; ruled in red. 4to.

232 × 164 × 32 mm. (P 917) Davis 501

Brown goatskin (or possibly hair sheep) over paste boards, tooled in gold to an intricate pattern of interlacing ribbons, gouges, hatched lines and dots. Traces of four pairs of ties. Edges of boards: tooled in gold with lines and small leaf tools. Edges: gilt.

Sewn on three (recessed) cords, laced in straight; smooth spine, tooled in gold with solid tools. Endbands: single with a bead; blue and pink silk over alum-tawed cores (cut off), tied down (tailband missing, fragment of blue silk tie-down remains).

Endleaves: paper pastedowns, two pairs of free conjugate paper leaves, quired inside one another, plus a fifth free leaf conjugate with the pastedown, at both ends.

PROVENANCE: On endleaf in manuscript: 'Questo libro è di Nicolaio Novini(?) di Pisa'; in manuscript: 'Ex libris Valeriani francisci de Bapsitsinis'(?); G C Galetti of Florence (on endleaves and in text: library stamps: 'Bibl. Gust. C. Galetti Flor.'); Franciscus Riccardus de Vernaccia (book plate); Signora H. Finali of Florence; library label with 'No 62 A.I.3'; Landau (book plate with '47663 47664'; sold: Sotheby's, 12.vii.1948, *3*, pl.).

REFERENCES: Pitti, exhibition, no. 375; De Marinis, *Appunti*, pl. ccxxvii; Foot, *Revue française*, p. 375, note 11.

Note: Notwithstanding the four ties and the early Italian provenance, this binding is more likely to have been made in France. I am grateful to Dr A R A Hobson for his opinion.

61 *A Paris binding, probably made for Diane de Poitiers, c. 1550–5*

Dante Alighieri, *La comedia … con … espositione di Alessandro Vellutello*, Venice: F Marcolini, June 1544; ruled in red. 4to.

242 × 163 × 57 mm. (P 1246) Davis 502

White kid over paste boards, tooled in silver (now oxidized) to a complex arabesque design of interlacing ribbons, gouges, open tools, dots, crescents, the monogram HDD (or HCC: see *Note* below) and in the centre a quiver; traces of brown (once black?) and green paint. Traces of four pairs of ties. Traces of title frame on the inside of the upper board. Edges of boards: tooled in silver with lines and

60 61

dashes. Edges: gauffered and painted (in red and black) with a design of interlacing ribbons, curving lines, crescents, bows and arrows, and the HDD monogram.

Sewn on five alum-tawed supports, laced in; smooth spine, tooled in silver with bows and arrows, crescents, three-interlaced-crescent tools, and the HDD monogram. Endbands: single; a few remnants of silver thread over cord cores (laced in at an angle). Remnants of a blue silk bookmarker.

Endleaves: paper pastedowns at both ends; at the front: one free leaf conjugate with the pastedown and one free paper leaf conjugate with a stub beneath the pastedown; at the end: one free leaf conjugate with the pastedown (remnant stub).

PROVENANCE: (?)Diane de Poitiers; on endleaf in manuscript several inscriptions, mostly unreadable: 'Jo pagata Calama (?) deso per (?) marh di (?)Senem (?) 9 agost 1588'; manuscript inscription in Italian; (?)Quarré d'Aligny (armorial book plate; see Olivier, 1390); E Rahir (book plate; sold: Paris, 7.v.1930, 66, pl.); bought: Pierre Berès, 23.i.1956.

REFERENCES: Nixon, *Pierpont Morgan Library*, pp. 142–3; Foot, *Davis*, I, p. 174.

LITERATURE: J. Porcher, 'Les livres de Diane de Poitiers', in: *Les Trésors des bibliothèques de France*, vol. vii, fasc. xxvi, 1946, pp. 78–89, pls xxi, xxii; De Marinis, *Appunti*, pl. cclxi; Nixon, *Pierpont Morgan Library*, nos. 36–7; Needham, *Twelve Centuries*, no. 68.

Note: The monogram used on this binding and also on bindings for Henri II can be read as HCC (Henri and Cathérine) and as HDD (Henri and Diane). On this binding it is most probably HDD. Diane de Poitiers (1499–1559), favourite of Henri II; married Louis de Brézé (d. 1531); became Henri II's mistress, probably c. 1536; duchesse de Valentinois: 1548.

62 *A strap-work binding, c. 1550–5*

M F Quintilianus, *De institutione oratoria libri xii*, Venice: Aldus & A Socerus, August 1514. 4to.

217 × 135 × 39 mm. (P 935) Davis 503

Brown calf over paste boards, tooled in gold to a strap-work pattern of interlacing ribbons, dots and gouges. Edges of boards: tooled in gold with lines. Edges: gilt.

Sewn on five cords, laced in; smooth spine, tooled in gold with lines forming strips filled with small knot tools; hatched and cross-hatched lines near head and tail; 'compartments' between the strips tooled with a brick-work pattern. Endbands: single with a bead; blue and beige silk over cord cores (laced in), tied down sporadically.

Endleaves: paper pastedowns and one free paper leaf at both ends.

Repairs: at lower joint.

PROVENANCE: On endleaf in manuscript: note signed 'J.Wright', dated 'Ap. 1723'; book plate with: 'Ex libris Di de St Maurice in suprema Rationum curia presidis', motto: 'In soletudine solamen', arms: unidentified; on pastedown of lower cover, in manuscript: 'a3 6tt'; on pastedown of upper cover in manuscript: 'B.3.17'; bought: Davis and Orioli, 27.iv.1949.

REFERENCES: Foot, *Revue française*, p. 373, fig. 2, p. 375.

The group of bindings that follow (nos. 63–73) have all been decorated with the same tools. These were used by the Atelier de Fontainebleau (1545–52) and the Atelier du relieur du roi (Paris, 1552–late 1560s), by Picard (1540–47), Gommar Estienne (1547–1556/9) and Claude Picques (early 1550s–1574/8), all three in Paris. I have attributed the following bindings, when possible, to named binders, but when uncertain to the 'Atelier de Fontainebleau' or to the 'Atelier du relieur du roi'.

63   *A binding by the Atelier de Fontainebleau with the arms of Henri II, c. 1550*
Le Livre des statuts et ordonances de l'ordre Sainct Michel, n.p., n.d. [Paris, c. 1550]; printed on parchment; 4to.
223 × 159 × 18 mm. (P 580) Davis 378

Brown goatskin over paste boards, tooled in gold, with blind lines, to a panel design with fleurs-de-lis at the corners, bow tools in the middle of each side, quiver tools in the corners and in the centre the arms of Henri II. Traces of two pairs of ties. Edges: gilt.
   Sewn on five split alum-tawed supports, laced in, showing as raised bands on the spine, tooled in blind with lines; two kettle stitch bands; eight compartments, tooled in blind with lines; top and tail compartments: blind lines; on third compartment: pale brown label, title lettered in gold; rest of compartments: blind lines and a fleur-de-lis in gold. Endbands: single with a bead; green and yellow silk over cord cores (laced in at an angle and frayed out), tied down.

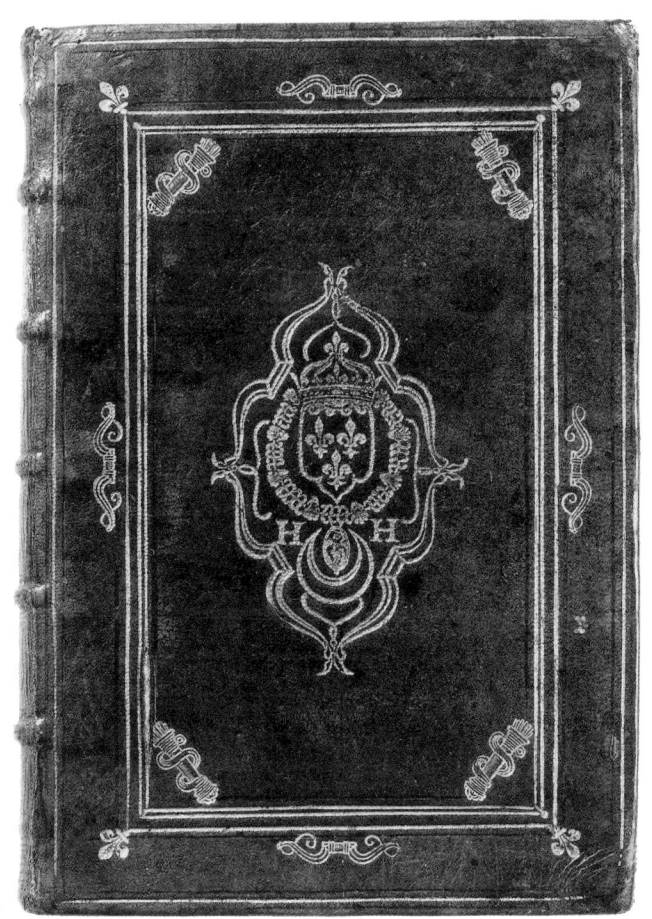

63

Endleaves: parchment pastedowns at both ends; at the front: one free parchment leaf conjugate with the pastedown.
Repairs: small repairs at the corners.

PROVENANCE: Member of the Order of St Michel; Bibliotheca Electoralis Publica (book plate and library stamp); Landesbibliothek of Dresden (library stamp); on the verso of the front endleaf in manuscript: 'No 569'; on pastedown of lower cover in manuscript: 'g.117' Paul Hirsch (book plate; sold: Sotheby's, 3.ii.1943, *453*).
REFERENCES: Foot, *Davis*, I, pp. 172, 182 (no. 22).
LITERATURE: Culot, *La Reliure en France*, p. 99; Laffitte & Le Bars, pp. 72–145 (and literature mentioned there); Laffitte, pp. 85–94; Christie's Paris, *Collection Michel Wittock*, pt. III, 7.x.2005, *36*; see also Davis 351 (no. 64 below; and literature mentioned there).
Note: The royal arms block is the one most frequently used by the Atelier de Fontainebleau, see Laffitte & Le Bars, nos. 41, 42c, 43a, 50–71, 74–6; for the bow tool see Laffitte & Le Bars, nos. 62, 65, 66, 75; for the quiver tools see Laffitte & Le Bars, nos. 59, 62, 66, 75. All these are from the Atelier de Fontainebleau while Gommar Estienne was royal binder. It is more than likely that the copies of the *Livre des statuts* were bound for the members of the Order of St Michel and not for the library of Henri II.

64 *A Paris binding by Gommar Estienne, c. 1550*

P Terentius Afer, *Comoediae*, Venice: P Manutius, Aldi Filio, July 1545. 8vo.

159 (171) × 95 × 32 mm. (P 1379) Davis 351

A Greek-style binding of dark brown goatskin (or possibly hair sheep) over wooden boards, tooled in gold, with blind lines, with a centre onlay of citron calf, with on the upper cover tooled in gold: NEMINEM/LAEDENS,/NEMINEM/TIMEBIS and two ivy-leaf tools; the lower cover tooled in gold with solid and hatched tools and dots. On the upper cover painted in gold: BERR. On both covers the gold-tooled arms of BERRVYER have been added. Two pairs of clasps on plaited leather straps, hinging on the lower cover and fastening on pins protruding from the edge of the upper board. Edges of boards: grooved. Edges: gilt.

Sewn on four supports (probably recessed; lacing-in invisible); smooth spine with raised headcaps, tooled in blind with crescents. Endbands: Greek style: primary sewing, tied down in the centre of the text block and beneath the pastedowns (in bundles), the cores are invisible, but taken over the edges of the boards laced into the grooves; two rows of secondary sewing in pink and white silk, each with a bead; upper row: sewn vertically downwards; second row sewn at an angle.

Endleaves: parchment pastedowns and two pairs of free conjugate paper leaves, at both ends.

PROVENANCE: Berruyer; printed label: 'From the collection of Charles Butler of Warren Wood Hatfield'; bookseller's ticket of Leighton, 40 Brewer Street; Sotheby's, 10.xii.1957, *461*; bought: Breslauer, 14.i. 1958.
REFERENCES: Foot, *Davis*, I, p. 177.
LITERATURE: Nixon, *Grolier*, pl. E (tools 51, 59), pl. F (tools 66a, 68a); Nixon, *Pierpont Morgan Library*, nos. 10, 20, 25; Parent, pp. 155, 193–4; Parent-Charon, pp. 401–8; Hobson, *Humanists*,

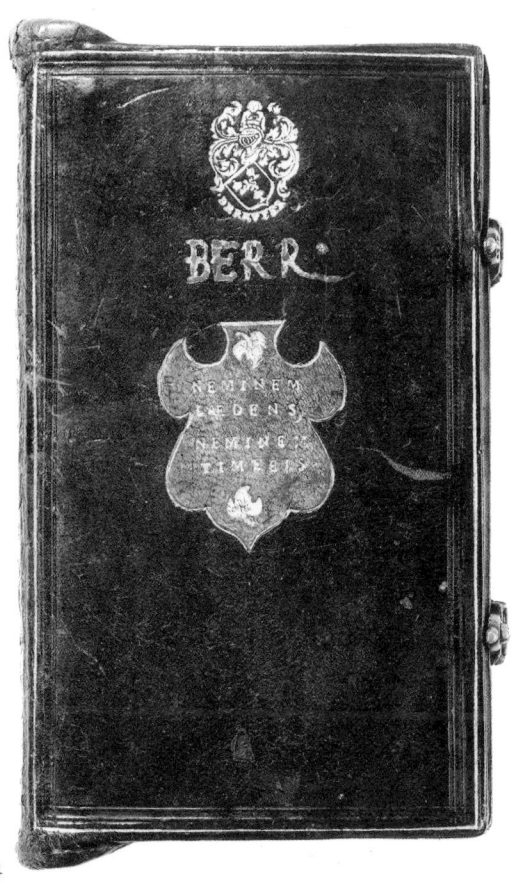

64

pp. 189–211 ('Grand Doreur' and Gommar Estienne); Schäfer, pp 40, 41; Laffitte & Le Bars, pp. 34, 94–7, 128, 148–50, 153–5, 173, 210; see also Davis 378, 352, 379, 354–5, 375–7 (no. 63 above, nos. 65–8 below). For Greek-style bindings with similar structures see Davis 379, 396 (nos. 66, 69 below).

Note: Gommar Estienne is first mentioned as 'relieur du roi' in November 1547; he was in charge of the Atelier de Fontainebleau (1547–1552); a contract of 10 June 1548 mentions him as bookseller to the king and a contract of 9 July 1550 as binder to the king; in 1548 he became the Aldine representative in Paris, an agreement that was renewed for three years in 1550; in the early 1550s he had a house in Paris and from mid-1552 the Atelier de Fontainebleau closed and the 'relieur du roi' had an atelier in Paris (or used a finisher in Paris). Gommar Estienne remained royal binder until at least 1556 (when Claude Picques acting as godfather at the baptism of Gilles Sertenas is first called 'relieur du roi': see Laffitte & Le Bars, p. 149) or until 1559 (when Piques was certainly royal binder). Gommar Estienne also bound for other collectors, such as Jean Grolier, Thomas Mahieu, Marcus Fugger, Marc Laurin, Anne de Montmorency, Diane de Poitiers and others. Between 1547 and 1552 the Atelier de Fontainebleau produced a very large number of bindings for the royal library; it is unlikely that this atelier had spare time to provide for the needs of other collectors. The presence, on bindings for other collectors, of the same tools that were used in the

Atelier de Fontainebleau may suggest that either Gommar Estienne had an atelier in Paris where he had work done for other (non-royal) collectors, or that he used a Paris finisher, both for the royal bindings and for bindings for non-royal collectors. As there is a distinct connection between the tools used by Jean Picard, Gommar Estienne and Claude Picques, it is perhaps most likely that all three used this same Paris finisher.

65 *A Paris binding by Gommar Estienne for Marc Laurin, c. 1550*

M T Cicero, *Orationes*, Paris: S de Colines, 14 December 1543; decorated title-page border; ruled in red. 16mo.

121 × 74 × 40 mm.   (P 994) Davis 352

Brown calf over paste boards, tooled in gold with lines forming a border decorated with black and silver paint; interlacing ribbons decorated with black and white paint; gouges, solid and hatched tools, decorated with red paint. In the centre of the upper cover: .M.T.C./ORATIO/NVM./VOL.I.; in the centre of the lower cover the motto of Marc Laurin: VIRTVS/IN/ARDVO; along the lower edge of the upper cover: M. LAVRINI ET AMICORVM. Edges of boards: tooled in gold with a line. Edges: gilt.

Rebacked with the original spine strip retained. Sewn on three (probably recessed) supports (no visible lacing in); smooth spine, tooled in gold with gouges, solid and hatched tools, an ivy-leaf tool in the centre. Endbands: single with a bead; blue and white silk over cord cores (laced in), tied down.

Endleaves: paper pastedowns, a pair of free conjugate paper leaves, and a stub conjugate with the pastedown, at both ends.

Repairs: rebacked.

PROVENANCE: Marc Laurin; Leon Double (book plate; sold: 1863, *354*); Victorien Sardou, Bibliothèque de Marly (sold: 1909, *67*); Hector de Backer (book plate; sold: 1927, *2865*); Lucius Wilmerding (book plate; sold: Parke-Bernet, 6.iii.1951, *370*).

REFERENCES: *Messager des sciences historiques ou archives des arts et de la bibliographie de Belgique*, Ghent, 1865, p. 481 (pl.); Goldschmidt, no. 206, pl. lxxix (list no. 19); Grolier Club, *Exhibition*, 1937, no. 76 (pl.); Romme, *Book Collector*, 1969, p. 25, note 14; Nixon, *Pierpont Morgan Library*, p. 138; Foot, *Davis*, I, pp. 176, 222.

LITERATURE: Foot, *Davis*, I, pp. 220–9 (and literature mentioned there); Davis 351 (no. 64 above; and literature mentioned there); Nixon, *Grolier*, pl. E (tools 52, 53, 55a–b, 59, 62a–b), pl. F (tools 69, 72); Schäfer, p. 49; Hobson, *Renaissance*, p. 65; see also Davis 497–9 (no. 82 below).

Note: Marc Laurin (Lauryn, Lauweryn), seigneur of Watervliet, Bruges (1530–1581), antiquary and collector of books, manuscripts, coins and medals; visited Paris: 1550.

65

66 *A Paris binding by Gommar Estienne for Marcus Fugger, c. 1550–5*

Epistolae Graecae [variorum auctorum], Venice: Aldus, March 1499. 4to.

220 (228) × 150 × 59 mm. (P 990) Davis 379

A Greek-style binding of brown goatskin over wooden boards, tooled in gold, with blind lines, to an arabesque design of interlacing ribbons, gouges, dots, and solid and hatched tools. In the centre of the upper cover: an oval onlay of light brown goatskin, tooled in gold with hatched fleurons, and with the title in Greek tooled in silver (now oxidized). In the centre of the lower cover: an oval onlay of red goatskin, tooled in gold with fleurons, a flower tool and: O.R.V.E./M.F. [Omnium Rerum Vicissitudo Est. Marcus Fuggerus: the motto and initials of Marcus Fugger]. Two pairs of clasps and traces of two more, with three plaited leather straps hinging on the lower cover and fastening on pins protruding from the edges of the upper board. Edges of boards: grooved. Edges: gilt and gauffered with gouges and an arabesque pattern of leaves and fleurons.

Sewn on four (recessed) supports, laced in and pegged; smooth spine with raised headcaps, tooled in gold with an interlacing ribbon, dots, gouges, hatched and solid tools. Endbands: Greek style: primary sewing (over invisible cores), tied down frequently in the sections and beneath the pastedowns (in bundles); secondary sewing of blue and pink silk in two rows, each with a bead.

Endleaves: paper pastedowns and one pair of free conjugate paper leaves, plus one free leaf (possibly conjugate with the pastedown), at both ends.

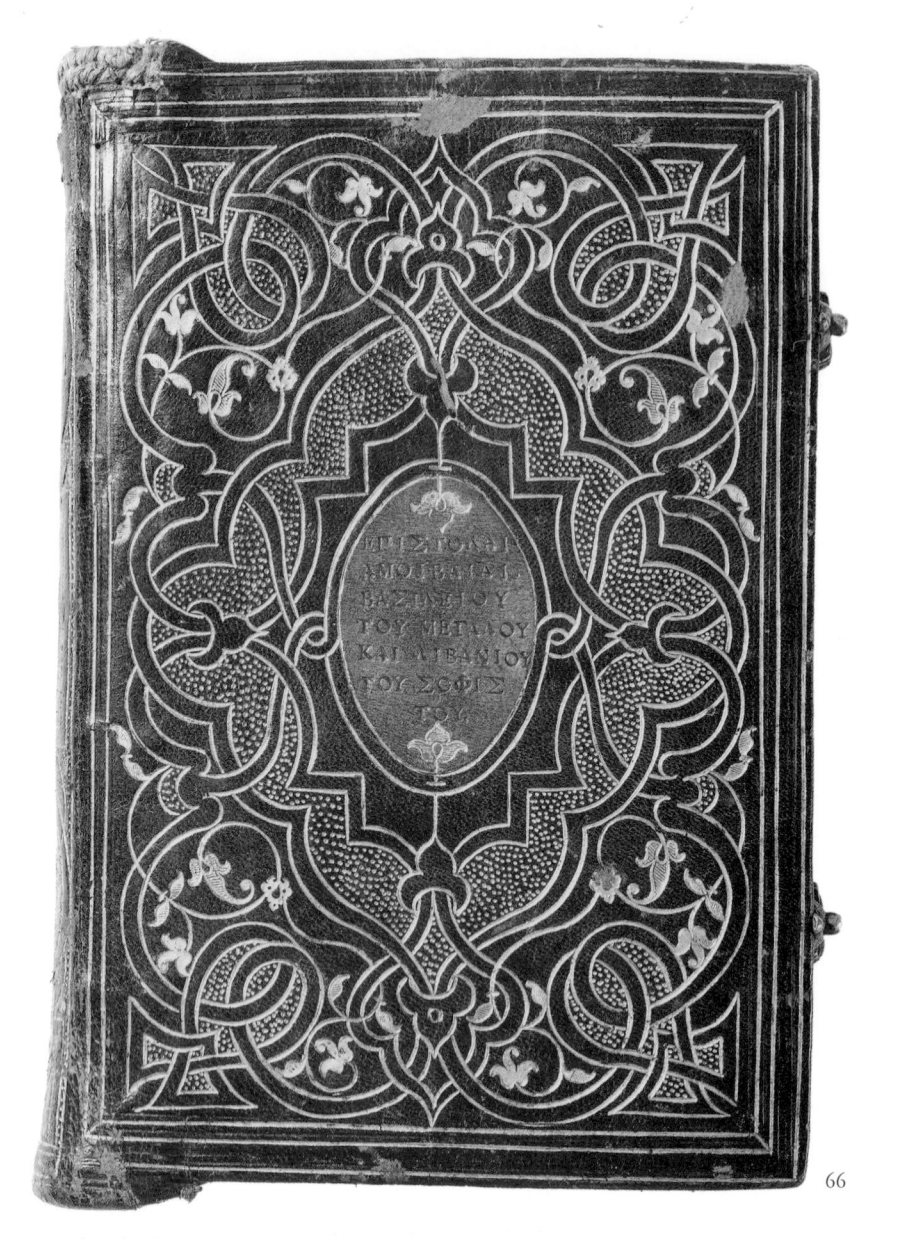

PROVENANCE: Marcus Fugger (on pastedown of upper cover in manuscript: 'Marcus Fuggerus'; sold: Karl & Faber, *Auktion VIII (II Teil)*, 6–7.xi.1933, *29*); library stamp (partly erased); Lucius Wilmerding (book plate; sold: Parke-Bernet, 5.iii.1951, *261*).

REFERENCES: Grolier Club, *Exhibition*, 1937, no. 64; Romme, *Book Collector*, 1969, p. 25, note 11, pl. IIIa; Foot, *Davis*, I, pp. 170, 175 (pl.), 176; Hobson, *Humanists*, p. 210 (note 124).

LITERATURE: Foot, *Davis*, I, pp. 176–7 (and literature mentioned there); Nixon, *Grolier*, pl. E (tools 52, 56a–b), pl. F (tools 66a–b, 69); Needham, *Twelve Centuries*, no. 63; Schäfer, pp. 41, 42; see also Davis 351 (no. 64 above; and literature mentioned there). For Greek-style bindings with similar structures see Davis 351 (no. 64 above), 396 (no. 69 below); see also Davis 349 (no. 44 above; and literature mentioned there).

67   *Paris bindings by Gommar Estienne, c. 1551–5*

Xenophon, *Opera*, 2 vols, Lyon: S Gryphius, 1551; ruled in red. 16mo.

125/126 × 75/76 × 34/40 mm.　　　　　　　　　　　　　　　　　　　(P 1024) Davis 354–355

Brown goatskin over paste boards, tooled in gold to different arabesque designs on both volumes, with interlacing ribbons, gouges and hatched tools (some tools are the same on both volumes, some are different, but all come from the same atelier). Traces of two pairs of ties. Edges of boards: tooled in gold with lines, dashes and s-shaped tools. Edges: gilt.

    Sewn on three (recessed) cords, laced in through two pairs of holes, at an angle (compare Davis 385, no. 73 below); smooth spine, tooled in gold with an interlacing ribbon, gouges and hatched tools. Endbands: single with a bead; green silk over cord cores (laced in at an angle and frayed out), tied down.

    Endleaves: vol. I: paper pastedowns at both ends; at the front: one free paper leaf tipped in; at the end: a stub, conjugate with the pastedown; vol. II: paper pastedowns at both ends; at the front: one free paper leaf; at the end: a pair of free conjugate paper leaves and one leaf (invisible whether or not conjugate with the pastedown); printer's waste visible beneath the pastedowns.

PROVENANCE: On pastedown of lower cover of vol. II in manuscript: 'B'; Ormathwaite (armorial book plate with the motto: 'veritas et virtutis vincunt'); Lardanchet, Catalogue 44 (1950), *314* (pl.); bought: Lardanchet, 29.v.1951.
REFERENCES: Foot, *Davis*, I, pp. 160, 172, 177.
LITERATURE: Nixon, *Grolier*, pl. E (tools 53, 57, 63), pl. F (tool 69); see also Davis 351 (no. 64 above; and literature mentioned there).
Note: It is possible that by the time this binding was made Claude Picques was working in the Atelier du relieur du roi and could use its tools for other clients; see no. 64 (above): *Note* and no. 69 (below): *Note*.

68   *Paris bindings by Gommar Estienne, c. 1552–5*

J Froissart, *Des croniques de france, dangleterre, descosse*, 4 vols bound as 3, vols I and II: Paris: for Antoine Vérard, n.d.; vol. III: Paris: for François Regnault [with the device of Guillaume Eustace], n.d.; vol. IV: Paris: for Guillaume Eustace, 1514 [vols III and IV bound together]; woodcut initials; ruled in red. fol.

266/268/267 × 190 (I, II)/194 × 40 (I, II)/47 mm.   (P 156) Davis 375–377

Vols III and IV: bound together in plain brown calf over paste boards, tooled in gold with a double and a single fillet around the border. Edges of boards: tooled in gold with lines and dashes. Edges: gilt. Rebacked (not illustrated; see below).

    Vols I and II: Brown calf over paste boards, some black staining (having caused surface damage), tooled in gold to a corner and centre design (different designs on these two volumes) with large corner and centre compartments, tooled with gouges and dots; arabesque tooling with gouges, solid and hatched tools. Traces of two pairs of ties. Edges of boards: tooled in gold with lines and dashes. Edges: gilt and gauffered in a strap-work pattern.

Rebacked (with later leather spine strips]). Vols I and II: sewn on five alum-tawed supports, laced in straight; vols III/IV: sewn on five (recessed) thin double cords, laced in through three holes; all three volumes have smooth spines, and have been tooled later to match. Endbands (all three volumes): double with a bead; primary sewing over (?)leather cores (cut off), tied down; secondary sewing of blue and pink silk (in vols III/IV tied down).

Endleaves: paper pastedowns and one free leaf conjugate with the pastedown, plus a second free paper leaf, at both ends, except at front of vol. II: only one free paper leaf (not conjugate with the pastedown).

Repairs: rebacked.

PROVENANCE: Sir William Curtis Bart. (book plate); bought: Quaritch, 31.i.1941.
REFERENCES: Foot, *Davis*, I, p. 177.
LITERATURE: Nixon, *Grolier*, pl. E (tools 47, 53, 56a–b, 57, 58a–b, 63), pl. F (tools 64b, 67a–b, 69, 72, 77a–b); see also Davis 351 (no. 64 above; and literature mentioned there).

69 *A Paris binding by the Atelier du relieur du roi, c. 1553–5 or possibly 1556–9*

L B Alberti, *L'Architecture et art de bien bastir* [translated from the Latin by Ian Martin], Paris: for I Kerver, 2 August 1553; woodcuts. fol.

352 (358) × 225 × 43 mm.   (P 1491) Davis 396

A Greek-style binding of brown calf over wooden boards, tooled in gold to a complex pattern formed by interlacing ribbons, culminating in a large centre cartouche, on a background powdered with dots; a border with twisted-rope tooling; gouges, solid, open and hatched tools. Four pairs of clasps on three plaited leather straps, hinging on the lower cover and fastening on pins protruding from the edges of the upper board. Edges of boards: grooved. Edges: gilt and gauffered to a knot-work pattern.

Sewn on five supports (either thin alum-tawed supports, or recessed cords), laced in; smooth spine with raised headcaps, tooled in gold with interlacing ribbons and gouges on a dotted background. Greek-style endbands: primary sewing over cord cores (taken over the edges of the boards and down into the grooves), tied down in the sections and pegged down into the boards beneath the pastedowns (in bundles); secondary sewing of pink and blue silk in two rows, each with a bead.

Endleaves: paper pastedowns at both ends; at the front: one pair of free conjugate paper leaves and one free leaf conjugate with the pastedown; at the end: there may be three free paper leaves (not conjugate).

Repairs: at corners and at edges of boards.

PROVENANCE: Lardanchet, Catalogue 56 (1963), *1* (pl.); bought: Lardanchet, 13.vi.1963.
REFERENCES: Foot, *Davis*, I, p. 177.
LITERATURE: Nixon, *Grolier*, pl. D (tools 28, 29), pl. E (tools 52, 53), pl. F (tools 64a–b, 72, 77a–b); Laffitte & Le Bars, pp. 194–5 (attribute bindings with cartouches, derived from architectural motifs, to the years 1556–9); see also Davis 351 (no. 64 above; and literature mentioned there), 394 (no. 70 below; and literature mentioned there). For Greek-style bindings with similar structure see Davis 351, 379 (nos. 64, 66 above).

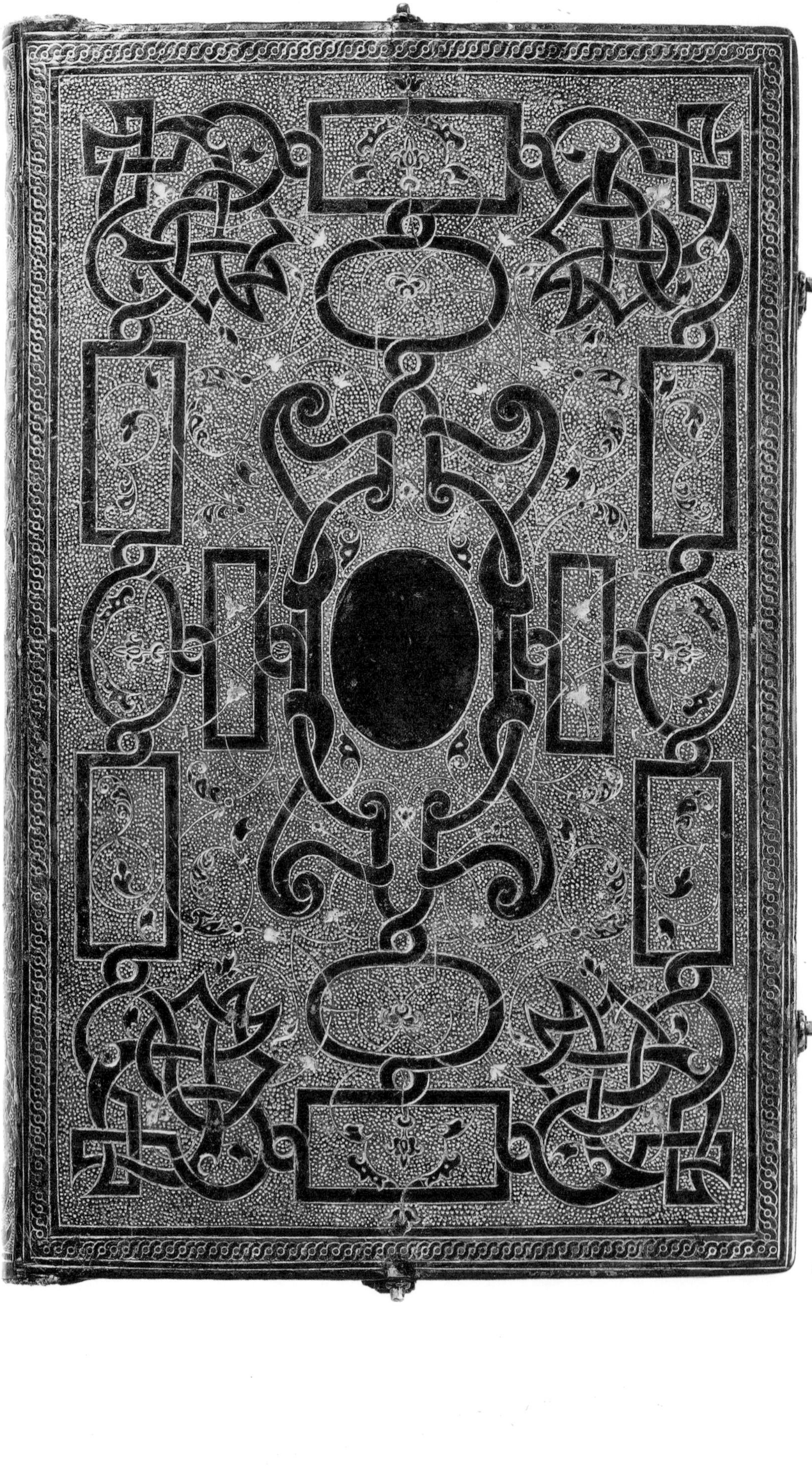

Note: In 1552 the Atelier de Fontainebleau closed and the royal bindery (Atelier du relieur du roi) moved to Paris under the direction of Gommar Estienne. By the time this binding was made Claude Picques was connected with this atelier and it is impossible to say who was responsible for it: Estienne or Picques or the Paris finisher whom both may have used.

Claude Picques: born in Paris c. 1510; in 1539 he is mentioned as bookseller and binder; in 1540 his sister married the bookseller and binder Claude Micart, and in the same year Piques wrote and produced a mystery play; in November 1543 he moved to the rue St Jacques, where he remained for the rest of his active life. He is mentioned as finisher in an act of 1548; in the 1550s he entered the service of the royal court and in 1553 he is called binder to the queen. Picques was Godfather to Gilles Sertenas, at whose baptism in March 1556 he is called 'relieur du roi'. In 1559 Claude Piques is mentioned as 'relieur du roi' on the title-page of a Psalter published for him. The following year, his fortune made, bookseller, and binder to the king, he married the daughter of a draper. He kept his position as royal binder during the reigns of François II and Charles IX and is still mentioned as such in an act of 1574 (under Henri III). Sometime between August 1574 and November 1578 he was succeeded by Nicolas Ève. Royal bindings dating from before 1556–9 cannot be attributed to Claude Picques, but it is possible that, from the early 1550s, he could use the tools of the Atelier du relieur du roi when binding for other collectors. Alternatively, he (like Picard and Estienne) used the same Paris finishing shop (see Davis 351, no. 64 above). **NB: the attributions made to Claude Picques in Foot, *Davis*, I, section 13, have been overtaken by later research, as set out here and above.**

70   *A Paris binding by Claude Picques, c. 1560*

Breviarium Romanum, Lyon: Haeredes I Iunctae, 1556; woodcut initials; ruled in red. 4to.

295 × 216 × 44 mm.   (P 1051) Davis 394

Red goatskin over paste boards, with an onlaid border of black goatskin and an onlaid centre cartouche of olive goatskin; tooled in gold to an arabesque pattern of gouges, solid and hatched tools, decorated with black and silver paint and a large oval block in the centre. Edges of boards: tooled in gold with lines and dashes. Edges: gilt, gauffered and painted (in red), to an arabesque pattern with leaves and fleurons.

Sewn on five (recessed) cords, laced in; smooth spine, onlaid in olive goatskin and tooled in gold with gouges and hatched tools; decorated with black and silver paint. Endbands: single with a bead; green and yellow silk over cord cores (cut off), tied down.

Endleaves (later): paper pastedowns and one free leaf conjugate with the pastedown, at both ends.
Repairs: small repairs at the corners.

PROVENANCE: Samuel Putnam Avery (book plate; sold: New York, Anderson Galleries, 10–12.xi.1919, *156*); Lucius Wilmerding (sold: Parke-Bernet, 29.x.1951, *162*).
REFERENCES: Romme, *Book Collector*, 1969, p. 26, note 15; Foot, *Davis*, I, pp. 170, 173 (pl.), 178, 222.
LITERATURE: Foot, *Davis*, I, pp. 170–81 (and literature mentioned there); Nixon, *Grolier*, pl. E (tools

70

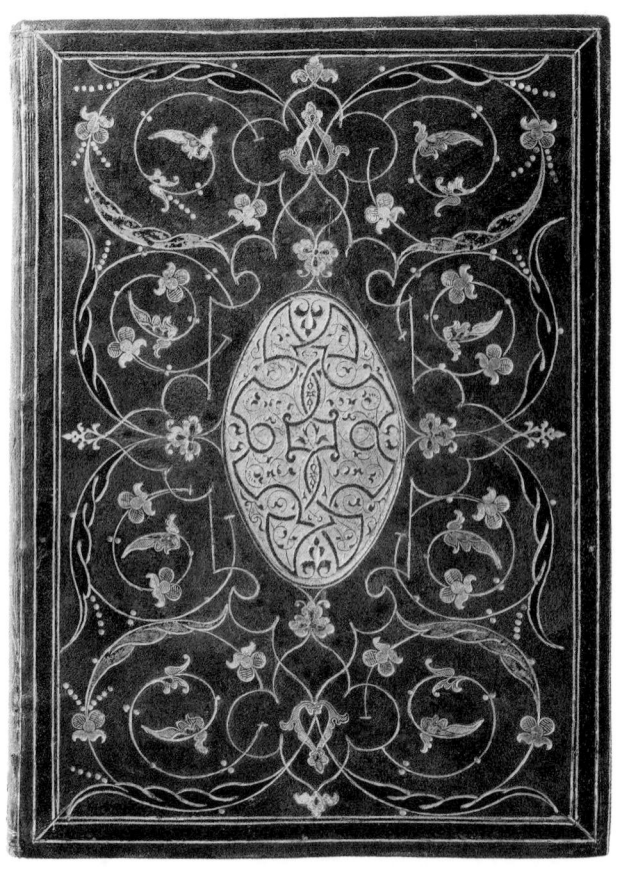

47, 57), pl. F (tools 67a–b, 70a–b, 72); Parent, pp. 173, 189, 190; Parent-Charon, pp. 394–400; Hobson, *Humanists*, pp. 211–13; Laffitte & Le Bars, pp. 34–5, 149–50, 210, 221, 232; see also Davis 351 (no. 64 above; and literature mentioned there); Davis 396 (no. 69 above: *Note*).

---

71 *Paris bindings, probably made by Claude Picques, c. 1560–65*

J J Pontanus, *Opera omnia*, 3 vols, Venice: Aldus and A Socerus, June 1518, April 1519, September 1519; manuscript initials painted in gold and outlined in red. 4to.

219/217 (II, III) × 140 × 44/40 (II, III) mm. (P 1076) Davis 381–383

Red goatskin over paste boards, tooled in blind with lines and in gold, with lines, small corner blocks, a large centre block with a fleuron at both ends, all on a semis of three-dot tools. Edges of boards: tooled in gold with a line. Edges: gilt.

Vols I and III: sewn on five split alum-tawed supports; vol. II sewn on five alum-tawed supports; laced in straight, showing as raised bands on the spine, tooled in gold with dotted lines; two kettle stitch bands (barely emphasized), tooled in gold with dashes; eight compartments. The spine was re-tooled in the 17th century. Originally probably only tooled in blind and gold with lines and dashes; 17th-century tooling partly over the original tooling on the kettle stitch bands and in the compartments: corner curls and centre ornaments built up of small tools; title and volume numbers in the second

71

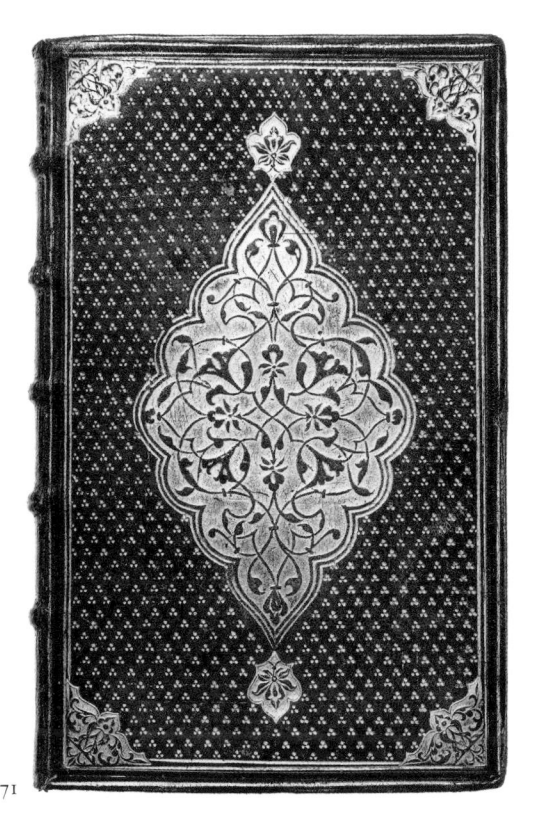

compartment (c. 1630s–40s). Endbands: single with a bead; green silk over cord cores (laced in), tied down.

Endleaves: paper pastedowns and one pair of free conjugate paper leaves, and one free leaf conjugate with the pastedown, at both ends. Manuscript waste visible beneath pastedowns.

PROVENANCE: Jean Ballesdens (on title-page in manuscript: 'Ballesdens' surrounded by three 'S fermés'); Colbert (in manuscript: 'Bibliothecae Colbertinae'); Renouard (*Catalogue de la bibliothèque d'un amateur*, Paris, 1819, p. 282); Lord Vernon collection; Holford collection (sold: Sotheby's, 8.xii.1927, *658*, pl.); Lucius Wilmerding (sold: Parke-Bernet, 31.x.1951, *740*, pl.).

REFERENCES: Foot, *Davis*, I, pp. 177, 178.

LITERATURE: G D Hobson, *Fanfare*, pp. 90–1, 119 (the 'S fermé' is now interpreted as 's-clavo', 'esclavo': see Davis 448, no. 113, below); *Dictionnaire de biographie française*, vol. iv, Paris, 1948, 1425–7; Hobson, *French and Italian*, pp. xix, xxi; see Foot, *Davis*, I, pp. 177–8, 181 (literature mentioned in notes 63–9 for attribution of the tools); see also Davis 396 (no. 69 above: *Note*).

Note: Although centre and corner blocks may have been cast, those used on this binding occur on a number of bindings in combination with tools used by Gommar Estienne and Claude Picques.

Jean Ballesdens (c. 1600–1675): a member of the Académie Française, secretary to Chancellor Pierre Séguier and prior of St-Germain d'Alluyes; he owned a number of Grolier's and Mahieu's bindings. Jean-Baptiste Colbert (1619–1683), minister under Louis XIV, councillor of state, friend of Cardinal Mazarin.

THE HENRY DAVIS GIFT

72 *A Paris binding for Ludwig zur Gilgen, possibly made by Claude Picques, 1566*

A du Pinet, *Historia plantarum ... ex Dioscoride*, [and] P Dioscorides, *Simplicium medicamentorum*, Lyon: G Coterius, 1561. 16mo.

127 × 77 × 44 mm.   (P 885) Davis 429

Brown calf over paste boards, tooled in gold, with a blind line, with lines along the border, fleurs-de-lis in the corners and a central cartouche with the arms of Ludwig zur Gilgen tooled in silver (now oxidized), above and below in a frame with curved sides, on the upper cover: LVDOVICVS/A LILIIS and on the lower cover: LVTETIAE 26.IVNI./ANNO 1566. Edges of boards: tooled in blind with a line. Edges: gilt, gauffered and painted with an arabesque pattern; on the fore-edge a bird's claw; on the top and tail edges: the arms of Ludwig zur Gilgen.

Sewn on four split alum-tawed supports, laced in straight, showing as raised bands on the spine, tooled in blind with lines; two kettle stitch bands, tooled in gold with dashes; seven compartments, tooled in blind with lines and in gold with a hatched fleuron. Endbands: single with a bead; pink and blue silk over (?)alum-tawed cores (cut off), tied down.

Endleaves: paper pastedowns at both ends; at the front: one pair of free conjugate paper leaves; at the back: one free leaf conjugate with the pastedown and one free paper leaf tipped on.

Repairs: small repairs at joints and at corners of edges.

PROVENANCE: Ludwig zur Gilgen; Yemeniz, Lyon (book plate; no. 732); Eugene Waillet (book plate); Henry Yates Thompson (on endleaf in manuscript: 'Insigni Hortorum Harroviensium Cultori d.d. Henricus Yates Thompson a.d. 1916'); Miss Carol Graham; bought: Sotheby's, 29.vii.1946, *158*.
REFERENCES: Foot, *Book Collector*, 1975, pp. 106–7; Foot, *Davis*, I, p. 177.
LITERATURE: Foot, *Book Collector*, 1975, pp. 106–10 (and literature mentioned there).
Note: Ludwig zur Gilgen (1547–1577), from Lucerne, Switzerland; studied in Freiburg: 1560, Dôle: 1563, Paris: 1565–6 and Orléans: 1567. Back home he filled various public functions and formed a library.

73 *A Paris binding, probably made by Claude Picques, c. 1568*

Isocrates, *Enseignements d'Isocrates et Xenophon ... pour bien regner en paix et en guerre* [and] Aristotle, *Les Politiques* [translated by Louis le Roy], Paris: Michel Vascosan, 1568; woodcut initials. 4to.

245 × 172 × 75 mm.   (P 1335) Davis 385

Olive-brown goatskin over paste boards, tooled in gold, with blind lines, with an egg-and-dart border, corner blocks and a large centre block with fleurons at both ends, on a background with a semis of three-dot tools; decorated with silver paint. Remnants of two pairs of ties. Edges of boards: tooled in gold with lines and dashes. Edges: gilt.

Sewn on five (recessed) cords, laced in through two pairs of holes (straight and angled; compare Davis 354–5, no. 67 above); smooth spine, tooled in gold, six strips filled with an egg-and-dart roll, the compartments filled with a semis of three-dot tools; title label of orange goatskin, tooled in gold with

French Bindings

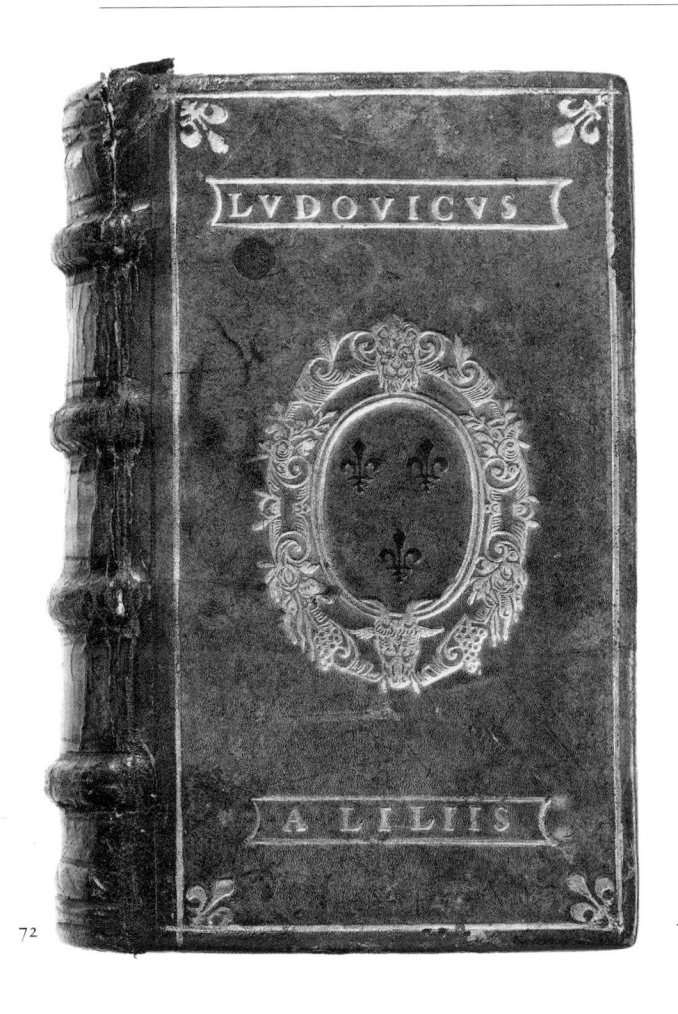

72 73

the title and two sun tools (probably later). Endbands: single with a bead; green silk over (?)alum-tawed cores (laced in), tied down.

Endleaves: two pairs of free conjugate paper leaves at both ends (not pasted down).

PROVENANCE: On the inside of the upper board in manuscript: 'D̄/214'; Charles, Lord Maynard (book plate); J R Abbey (book plate; 'J.A.2217/1:12:42'; sold: Sotheby's, 21.vi.1965, *46*).
REFERENCES: Foot, *Davis*, I, p. 178.
LITERATURE: Foot, *Davis*, I, p. 181, note 64.
Same fleuron on: Sotheby's, 21.vi.1965, *552*; Miner, *Baltimore*, no. 271; Davis 381–3 (no. 71 above).

III

THE HENRY DAVIS GIFT

The six bindings that follow (nos. 74–9) have tools in common with those used by Claude Picques, hence their place in this sequence.

74   *A binding made in Paris for Queen Elizabeth I of England, c. 1562*

N Gilles, *Annales et croniques de France*, vol. I, Paris: G Buon, 1562; ruled in red. fol.

344 × 210 × 45 mm. (P 1063) Davis 397

Brown calf over paste boards, tooled in gold to a fanfare design with interlacing 'fanfare' ribbons and gouges on a semis of dots; in the centre an oval, filled with gouges and open tools around the arms of Queen Elizabeth I of England; decorated with dark paint. Traces of two pairs of ties. Edges of boards: tooled in gold with small s-shaped tools. Edges: gilt and gauffered with fleurons and leaf shapes on a semis of dots; traces of the title in ink on the fore-edge.

Rebacked with parts of the original backstrip retained. Sewn on six supports (material invisible), laced in straight; smooth spine tooled in gold with gouges and a semis of dots; traces of dark paint. Endbands: new (woven and stuck on; not worked); a fragment of a tie-down of an original green silk tailband.

Endleaves: paper pastedowns at both ends; at the front: one free paper leaf, probably tipped on and covered by a paper joint or guard; at the end: two free paper leaves, tipped on, paper joint or guard.

Repairs: rebacked; new endbands; repairs at corners of covers and at edges of boards.

PROVENANCE: Mrs Elizabeth Vesey (manuscript note: 'from the library of Mrs Elizabeth Vesey 1715–91, the first of the blue stockings'; book plate); in manuscript: 'No 231'; on title-page in manuscript: '.e.'; on endleaf near lower cover manuscript notes:
'2. 143 [or: £43]
   22. B.74:at.
   09';
Lucius Wilmerding (sold: Parke-Bernet, 30.x.1951, *405*, pl.).
REFERENCES: Goldschmidt, no. 231, pl. xci; Grolier Club, *Exhibition*, 1937, no. 17; Romme, *Book Collector*, 1969, p. 26, note 21; Foot, *Davis*, I, pp. 160, 164 (note 31), 171.
LITERATURE: Nixon, *Pierpont Morgan Library*, p. 168 (PML 1123: Aristophanes, 1498: with identical tools); Needham, *Twelve Centuries*, pp. 223, 225 (note 2); Foot, *Davis*, I, pp. 160, 162: for the attribution of this binding to Malenfant's binder, whose tools are identical to those used by Claude Picques; see also Davis 356, 357 (nos. 75–6 below; and literature mentioned there).

75   *A Paris binding, possibly made by Claude Picques for Jacques de Malenfant, 1566*

L C Lactantius, *Opera*, Lyon: I Tornaesius & G Gazeius, 1561; decorated title-page; ruled in red. 16mo.

126 × 75 × 33 mm. (P 1065) Davis 356

Brown calf over paste boards, tooled in gold with hatched corner blocks, gouges and open tools, and a large hatched centre block with the arms of Jacques de Malenfant with his name: IACOBVS. MALINFANTIVS.T., and his motto: ANΩ.ΚΑΙ.ΜΗ.ΚΑΤΩ. Traces of two pairs of ties. Edges of

112

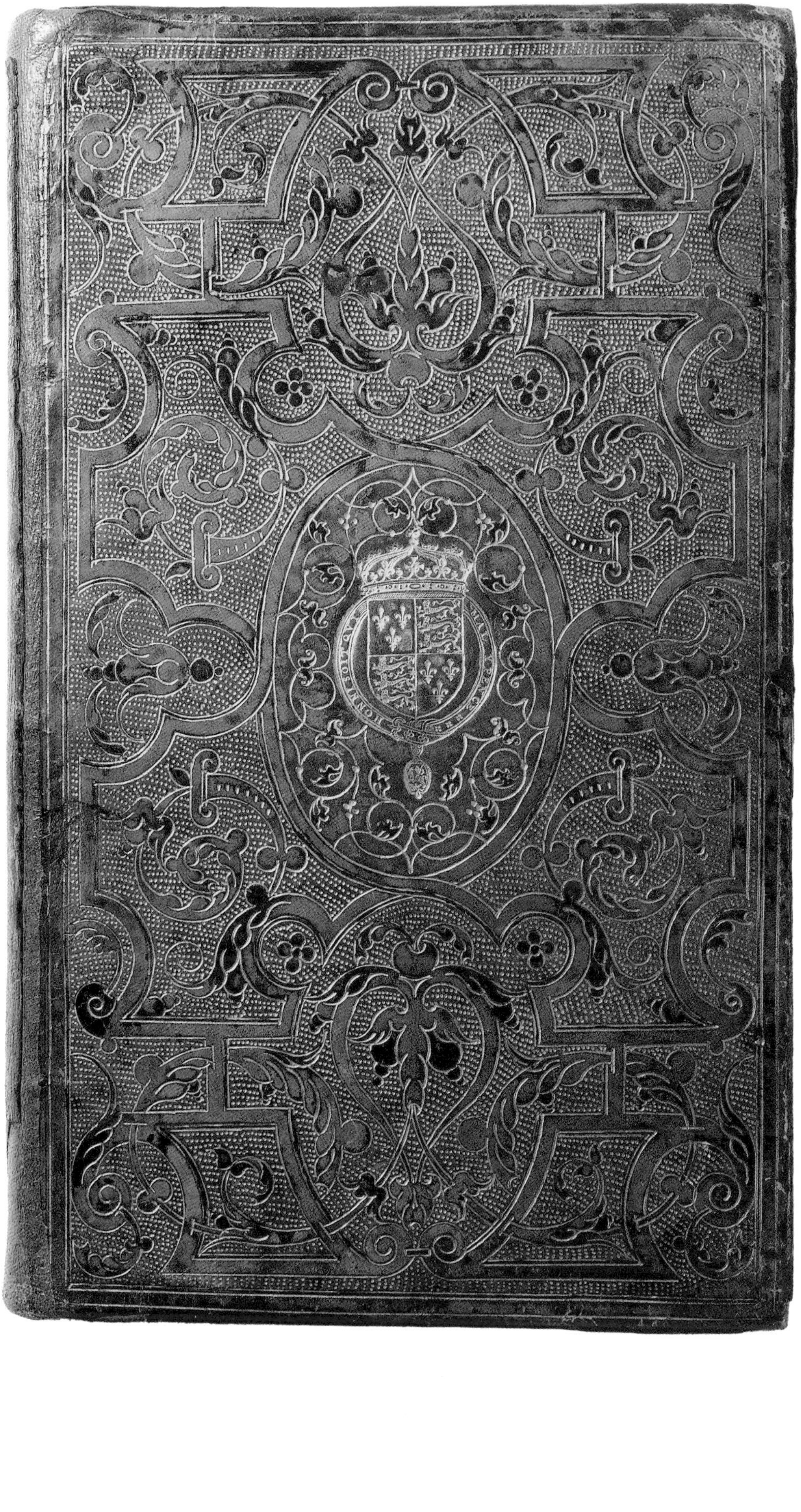

75   76

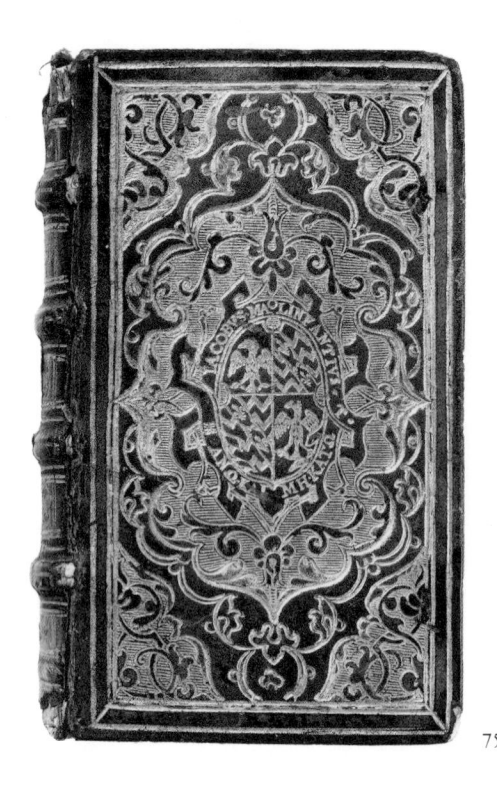

boards: tooled in gold with lines and dashes. Edges: gilt and gauffered to an arabesque pattern of leaves and fleurons with on the top edge: a caryatid; on the fore-edge: two naked figures, one carrying the other; decorated with red paint.

Sewn on four split alum-tawed supports, laced in straight, showing as raised bands on the spine, tooled in gold with lines; two kettle stitch bands; tooled in gold with dashes; seven compartments, tooled in gold with lines and open tools; title lettered in gold in the second compartment. Endbands: single with a bead; blue-green and yellow silk over cord cores (cut off), tied down sporadically.

Endleaves: paper pastedowns and a pair of free conjugate paper leaves, and one free leaf (may have been conjugate with the pastedown), at both ends. Manuscript waste visible beneath pastedowns.

PROVENANCE: Jacques de Malenfant (on upper pastedown in manuscript: 'Ex libris Iacobi Malinfātij Tolosani Lutetiae. 1566. Ανω και μη κάτω'); on flyleaf (in the same hand): 'Horat. Paulũ sepultae distat inertiae celata virtus Pressac.'; Sir Lyonel Tollemache (on endleaf in manuscript: 'Lionellus Tolmachius'), Ham House library (sold: Sotheby's, 31.v.1938, *206*, pl.); Lucius Wilmerding (sold: Parke-Bernet, 30.x.1951, *496*).

REFERENCES: Hobson, *French and Italian*, p. 49, note 1, no. 8; Foot, *Davis*, I, pp. 156, 159 (pl.), 166 (Appendix I, no. 10), 171; Culot, *La Reliure en France*, pp. 134, 135 (note 5).

LITERATURE: Foot, *Davis*, I, section 12 (and literature mentioned there); Culot, *La Reliure en France*, no. 56; Christie's, *The Michel Wittock Collection*, pt. I, 7.vii.2004, *53, 55, 59*; Christie's Paris, *Collection Michel Wittock*, pt. III, 7.x.2005, *12, 49*; see also Davis 357 (no. 76 below).

Note: Jacques de Malenfant, seigneur de Preyssac of Toulouse: almoner to Marguérite d'Angoulême, queen of Navarre; in Paris: 1546–c.1567; back in Toulouse: 1570. Tools used on bindings for de Malenfant link with those used by Claude Picques.

76 A Paris binding, possibly made by Claude Picques for Jacques de Malenfant, c. 1566

M T Cicero, *Rhetorica*, Lyon: I Frellonius, 1560; ruled in red. 16mo.

125 × 70 × 30 mm. (P 1054) Davis 357

Brown calf over paste boards, tooled in gold with hatched corner blocks, a semis of small fleurons and a large hatched centre block with the arms of Jacques de Malenfant, with his name and motto (see Davis 356, no. 75 above). Traces of two pairs of ties. Edges of boards: tooled in gold with lines and dashes. Edges: gilt and gauffered to an arabesque pattern of leaves and fleurons; traces of paint.

Sewn on four split alum-tawed supports, laced in straight, showing as raised bands on the spine, tooled in gold with a line; two kettle stitch bands, tooled in gold with dashes; seven compartments, tooled in gold with lines; the two top and tail compartments: small flowers; the two centre compartments: an egg-and-dart roll; second compartment: title lettered in gold. Endbands: single with a bead; blue and yellow silk over leather cores (cut off), tied down.

Endleaves: paper pastedowns and a pair of free conjugate paper leaves, at both ends; at the front: one free leaf conjugate with the pastedown; at the end: one free leaf (no longer conjugate with the pastedown). Manuscript waste visible beneath pastedowns.

PROVENANCE: Jacques de Malenfant; Sir Lyonel Tollemache, Ham House library (sold: Sotheby's, 31.v.1938, *206*); Lucius Wilmerding (book plate; sold: Parke-Bernet, 30.x.1951, *213*).
REFERENCES: Hobson, *French and Italian*, p. 49, note 1, list no. 7; Romme, *Book Collector*, Spring 1971, p. 69 (pl. opposite p. 69); Foot, *Davis*, I, pp. 163 (note 10), 171; Culot, *La Reliure en France*, pp. 134, 135 (note 6).
LITERATURE: Foot, *Davis*, I, section 12 (and literature mentioned there); see Davis 356 (no. 75 above; and literature mentioned there); see also Davis 359 (no. 79 below: for egg-and-dart roll).

77 A Paris fanfare binding by the binder who worked for Jacques de Malenfant (possibly Claude Picques), c. 1565–70

Q Horatius Flaccus, *Carmina; Epodi liber; Ars poetica; Epistolae; Sermones*, Venice: Aldus, May 1501. 8vo.

166 × 100 × 21 mm. (P 937) Davis 358

Brown goatskin over paste boards, tooled in (oxidized) silver to a fanfare design with gouges and hatched tools. Edges of boards and turn-ins: tooled in blind with lines. Edges: gilt.

Sewn on five split alum-tawed supports, laced in, showing as raised bands on the spine, tooled in blind with a line; two kettle stitch bands, tooled with dashes; eight compartments, tooled with lines and hatched tools; lettered on the second compartment: HORA/TIVS. Endbands: double with a bead; primary sewing over alum-tawed cores (laced in), tied down; secondary sewing of purple and yellow silk; cord crowning cores.

Endleaves: paper pastedowns at both ends; at the front: one free paper leaf conjugate with a stub, and one free leaf conjugate with the pastedown; at the end: a pair of free conjugate paper leaves, and one free leaf conjugate with the pastedown.

77

PROVENANCE: On the pastedown of the upper cover in manuscript: 'D10:52'; Charles Spencer, 3rd earl of Sunderland (sold: Puttick and Simpson, 20.vii.1882, *6371*); de Montgermont collection; E Rahir (sold: sale I, Paris, 1930, *107*); bought: Davis and Orioli, 27.iv.1949.
REFERENCES: Foot, *Davis*, I, pp. 162, 168 (Appendix IV, no. 9), 171.
LITERATURE: Foot, *Davis*, I, section 12 (and literature mentioned there); G D Hobson, *Maioli*, pl. 35, pp. 38–9 (Group II); G D Hobson, *Fanfare*, pl. xxixa, p. 59; Hobson, *French and Italian*, no. 21 (same tools); Nixon, *Pierpont Morgan Library*, no. 44; Needham, *Twelve Centuries*, no. 81 (same tools); Conihout, *Bulletin du bibliophile*, fig. 14, p. 83; see also Davis 409–10 (no. 78 below).
Note: The tools used on this binding (Hobson's Maioli Group II) link with those used on bindings made for Jacques de Malenfant; these, in turn, link with tools that were used by Claude Picques: see Davis 356, 357, 359 (nos. 75–6 above, 79 below).

78 *Paris bindings by the binder who worked for Jacques de Malenfant (possibly Claude Picques) for Claude III de Laubespine, c. 1567–70*

M T Cicero, *Opera*, 4 vols bound as 2, Paris: B Turrisanus, 1565–6. fol.

400 × 272 × 92/95 mm. (P 915) Davis 409–410

Golden-brown goatskin over paste boards, tooled in gold to a fanfare design with gouges and hatched tools. Edges of boards: tooled in gold with a line. Edges: gilt.

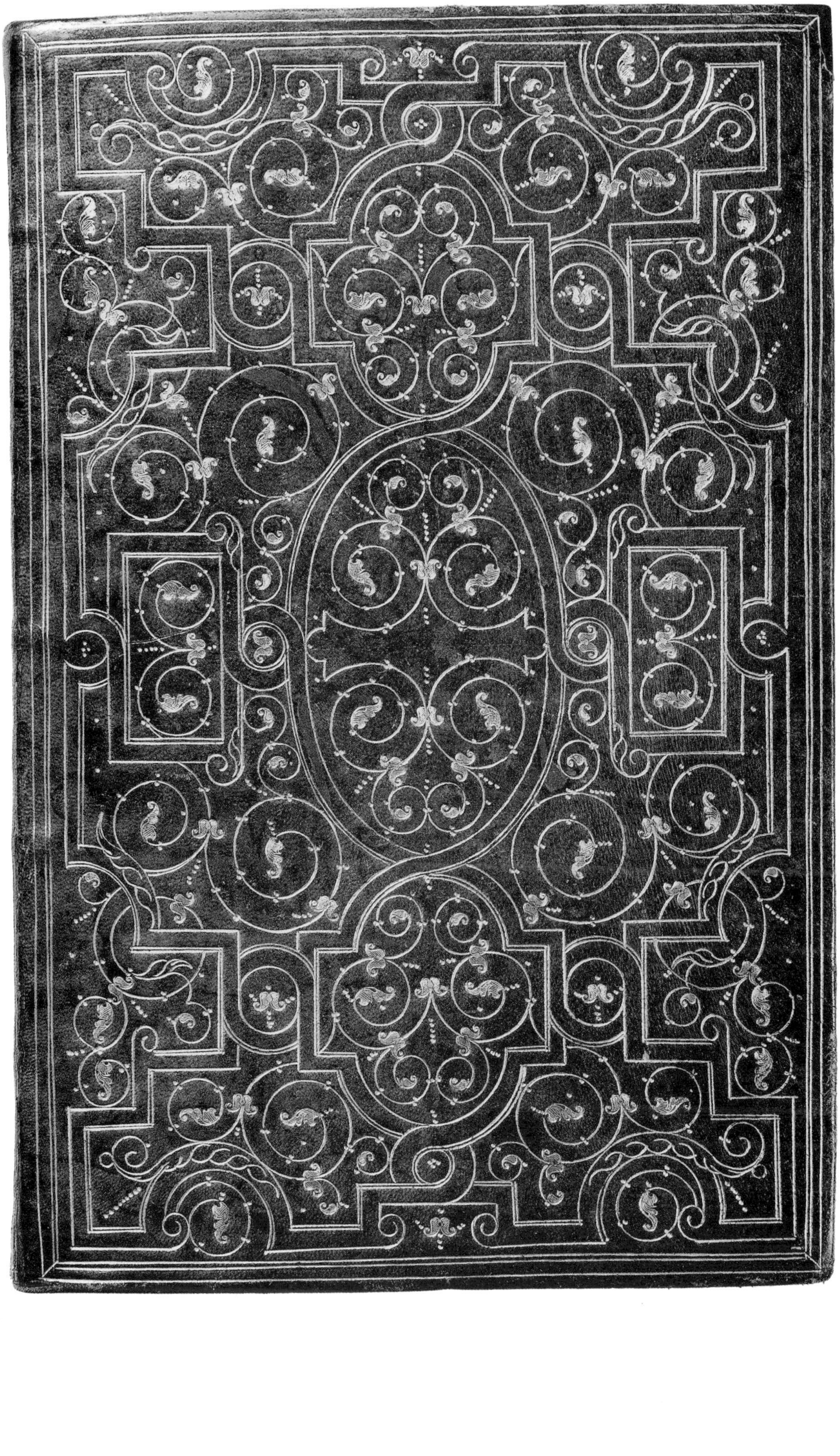

Sewn on five alum-tawed supports, laced in; smooth spine, tooled in gold to an arabesque design with gouges and hatched tools and in the centre of the spine: a cartouche with title, author and volume numbers. Endbands: single with a bead; green silk over cores made up of bundles of thin twine (now cut off), tied down occasionally.

Endleaves: paper pastedowns and a pair of free conjugate paper leaves, and one leaf (?formerly) conjugate with the pastedown, at both ends; fragments of manuscript parchment strengthener.

Repairs: at corners, joints and at head and tail of spine.

PROVENANCE: Claude III de Laubespine; (?)Madeleine de Laubespine-Villeroy; Villeroy ('cote brune': vol. I: '5'; vol. II: '6'); on pastedown of vol. I in manuscript: 'L 1–4'; George Gostling (book plate in vol. I); C M Cracherode (on endleaf in manuscript: 'CMC 1774'); J M Smith; bought: Sotheby's, 28.vi.1948, *174* (pl.).

REFERENCES: *BFAC*, pl. lviii; G D Hobson, *Fanfare*, no. 18; Romme, *Book Collector*, 1969, p. 25, note 8; Nixon, *Pierpont Morgan Library*, p. 175; Foot, *Davis*, I, pp. 156, 161 (pl.), 162, 167 (Appendix III, no. 13), 171; Needham, *Twelve Centuries*, p. 254; Conihout, *Bulletin du bibliophile*, p. 83, fig. 3.

LITERATURE: Davis 358 (no. 77 above; and literature mentioned there); Conihout, *Bulletin du bibliophile*, pp. 63–88; I de Conihout, 'A propos de la bibliothèque aux cotes brunes des Laubespine-Villeroy', in: *Italique; Poésie italienne de la Renaissance*, vii (Droz, 2004), pp. 137–59.

Note: Claude III de Laubespine (1545–1570), secretary to the king, one of four secretaries of state, confidant of Charles IX; his sister Madeleine (1546–1596), admired by Ronsard and Desportes, married Nicolas de Villeroy: 1559; inherited her brother's books which thereby entered the Villeroy library at Conflans. The 'cotes brunes' are inventory numbers of these books that form the nucleus of the Conflans library (see Conihout).

79 *A Paris binding, possibly made by Claude Picques for Claude Berbis, c. 1570*

Heures de Nostre Dame a l'usage de Rome, Paris: J Kerver, 1569; woodcut initials and illustrations [and] *Les Recommandaces des trespassez*, Paris: Jean le Blanc for Jacques Kerver, 1567 [and] *Propositions, dicts et sentences*, Paris: J Kerver, 1567; ruled in red. 8vo.

175 × 110 × 42 mm. (P 1309) Davis 359

Brown calf over paste boards, tooled in gold with hatched corner blocks, a semis of trefoils and a hatched centre block with open tools at its four points and in the centre an oval, lettered on the upper cover: CLAV/DE and on the lower cover: BER/BIS; decorated with dark and silver paint. Edges of boards: tooled in gold with lines and dashes. Edges: gilt.

Sewn on five split alum-tawed supports, laced in straight, showing as raised bands on the spine, tooled in gold with a line; two kettle stitch bands, with gold dashes; eight compartments, seven of which tooled in gold with an egg-and-dart roll; decorated with silver paint. Endbands: single with a bead; yellow and blue-green silk over (?)alum-tawed cores (cut off), tied down.

Endleaves: paper pastedowns and one free leaf conjugate with the pastedown, at both ends.

79　　　　　　　　　　　80

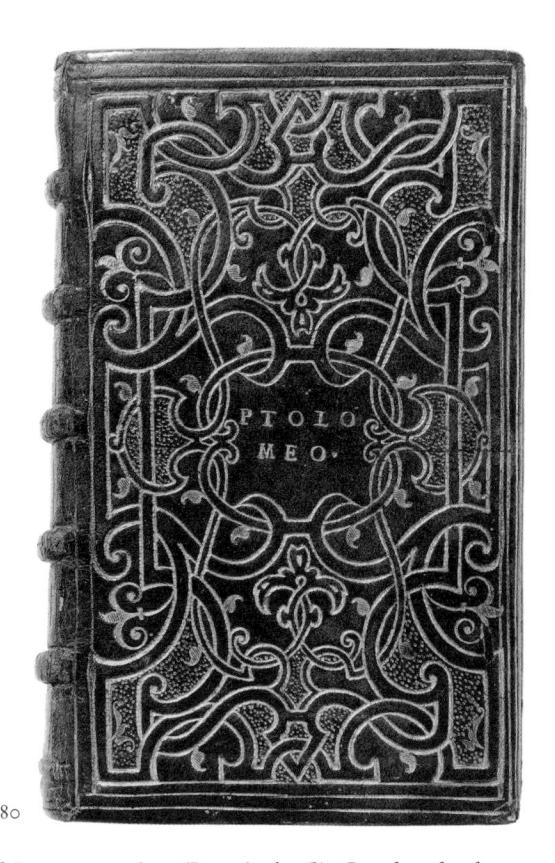

PROVENANCE: Claude Berbis; Datigni (on endleaf in manuscript: 'Je soix le (?) Gendre de dame Claude Berbis ma bisaieulle, femme de françois Guarre ... a dijon le 30 mai 1662 Datigni [?Daligni]'); J R Abbey ('J.A.4677/17:1:1950'; sold: Sotheby's, 22.vi.1965, *397*).
REFERENCES: Hobson, *French and Italian*, no. 22; Romme, *Book Collector*, Spring 1971, p. 69; Romme, *Book Collector*, Summer 1971, p. 227; Foot, *Davis*, I, pp. 157–8, 168 (no. 25), 171; Culot, *La Reliure en France*, p. 134.
LITERATURE: Foot, *Davis*, I, section 12 (and literature mentioned there); see also Davis 356, 357 (nos. 75–6 above).
Note: This binding has tools in common with the binder who bound for Jacques de Malenfant, whose tools in turn link with those used by Claude Picques.

80　*A Paris binding by the Cupid's Bow binder, c. 1550*

C Ptolemaeus, *La Geografia di Claudeo Ptolomeo ... ridotta in ... italiano da M. Pietro Andrea Mattiolo*, Venice: Nicolo Bascarini for Giovanni Baptista Pedrezano, 1548 [colophon October 1547] [and] *Tavole* [Venice, N Bascarini for G B Pedrezano], n.d.; woodcut initials and illustrations; ruled in red. 8vo.

178 × 110 × 54 mm.　　　　　　　　　　　　　　　　　　　　　　　　　　(P 249) Davis 360

Brown calf over paste boards, tooled in gold with a large block of an arabesque pattern, dots and hatched tools; in the centre of the upper cover: PTOLO/MEO.; gouges and hatched tools in the centre of the lower cover. Traces of two pairs of green silk ties. Edges of boards: tooled in blind with lines. Edges: gilt.

Sewn on five split alum-tawed supports, laced in, showing as raised bands on the spine, tooled in blind with a line; two kettle stitch bands, with traces of gold dashes; six compartments, four of which tooled in gold with an ivy leaf; on the second compartment: a red goatskin label with the title lettered in gold; on the sixth compartment: a red goatskin label with gold-tooled lines and the date '1548' tooled in gold (both labels probably added later). Endbands: single with a bead; pink and blue silk over leather cores (cut off), tied down. Green silk bookmarker.

Endleaves (later): paper pastedowns and one free leaf conjugate with the pastedown, at both ends.

PROVENANCE: On the verso of the title-page in manuscript: 'JL'; on title-page in manuscript: 't/ 24—'; Wilmot, earl of Lisburne (book plate; label inscribed: 'North Side/Case 1. Shelf 7. N 26'); in manuscript: 'Quaritch/May 1899'; Henry Yates Thompson (book plate, in manuscript: '193/re.e.e'; sold: Sotheby's, 19.viii.1941, *297*).

REFERENCES: Foot, *Revue française*, pp. 372 (fig. 1), 374.

LITERATURE: Nixon, *Book Collector*, 1962, pp. 64–8; Nixon, *Grolier*, p. 58, pl. G (tools 3, 19) pl. I (tools 55a–b); Nixon, *Pierpont Morgan Library*, no. 34; Needham, *Twelve Centuries*, nos. 66, 67; Schäfer, p. 39; Hobson, *Renaissance*, pp. 61, 65, 227–8; Laffitte & Le Bars, pp. 150, 211, 214; Laffitte, pp. 99–100; see also Davis 402, 497–499 (nos. 81–2 below).

Note: The Cupid's Bow binder was active from c. 1545 to c. 1555/6.

81 *A Paris binding by the Cupid's Bow binder, c. 1550*

Georgius Agricola, *De mensuris et ponderibus Romanorum atque Graecorum libri* [and other works], Basel: H Froben & N Episcopium, March 1550 [and] Henricus Loritus Glareanus, *Liber de asse et partibus eius*, Basel: M Isengrin, 1550. fol.

329 × 206 × 30 mm. (P 300) Davis 402

Brown calf over paste boards, tooled in gold with interlacing ribbons painted yellow, black and white; gouges and open tools decorated with white and green paint; in the centre of the upper cover: GEORGIVS AGRI/COLA/DE MENSVRIS ET PONDE/RIB. ROMANOR. ATQ./GRAECORVM./ETC.; in the centre of the lower cover: gouges and open tools decorated with green and white paint on a black painted ground. Edges of boards: tooled in gold with lines, dashes and small tools; turn-ins: tooled in gold with a line. Edges: gilt.

Rebacked in the 19th century: sewn on six supports, showing as raised bands on the spine, compartments tooled in gold and decorated with paint. Endbands: (new) green silk, single with a bead; green silk bookmarker (new).

Endleaves (later): paper pastedowns and one free leaf conjugate with the pastedown and a second free paper leaf tipped on, at both ends.

Repairs: rebacked; new endbands and bookmarker; repairs at corners of covers.

PROVENANCE: Jacques-Auguste de Thou (on endleaf in manuscript: 'Ex lib. Jac. Augusti Thuani'); John Dent (sold: Evans, 29.iii.1827, *142*); Christie-Miller, Britwell Court (sold: Sotheby's, 4.v.1920, *465*); bought: Quaritch, 31.x.1941.

REFERENCES: Quaritch, Catalogue 1921, *98*, pl. xxxiv; Shipman, no. 9 (but see *Note* below); Austin, no. 8/9; Foot, *Revue française*, p. 374, note 4.

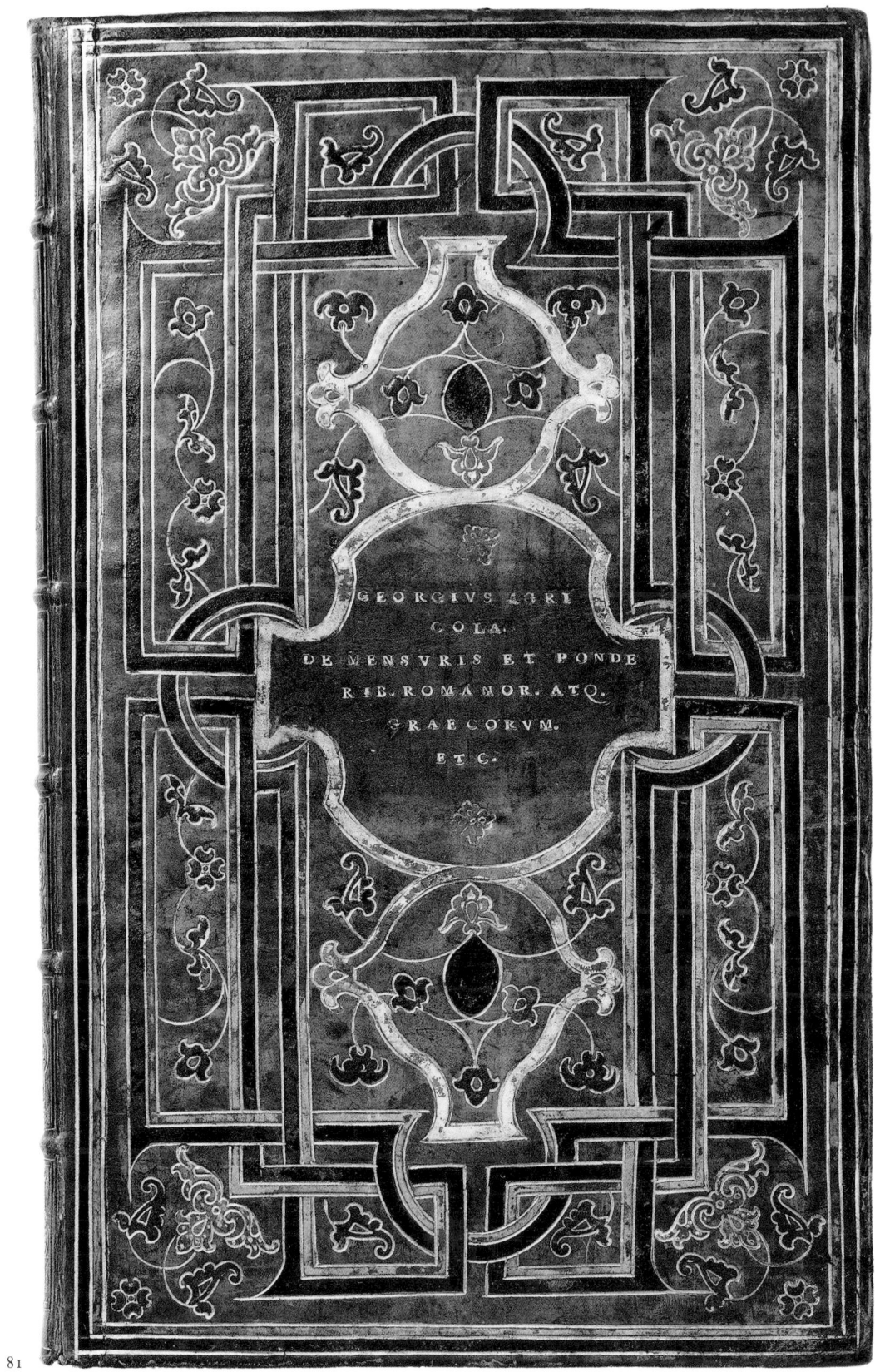

GEORGIVS AGRI
COLA.
DE MENSVRIS ET PONDE
RIB. ROMANOR. ATQ.
GRAECORVM.
ETC.

THE HENRY DAVIS GIFT

LITERATURE: Nixon, *Grolier*, pl. G (tools 7, 8, 9a–b, 11, 13, 14a–b, 16, 17, 25), pl. H (tool 26), pl. I (tool 54); see Davis 360 (no. 80 above; and literature mentioned there); see also Davis 497–499 (no. 82 below).

Note: Jean Grolier owned another copy of this book, also bound by the Cupid's Bow binder (Nixon, *Grolier*, no. 115; Austin, no. 7; Hobson, *Renaissance*, p. 227, list V (a), no. 7). W Clarke, *Repertorium bibliographicum*, London, 1819, p. 242 mentions two copies of this book, both having belonged to Grolier, one of which [i.e. Davis 402] belonged to de Thou; Shipman also mentions two copies (nos. 8–9), however Austin (no. 8/9) states that Davis 402 did not belong to Grolier and only one copy is listed by Hobson. Jacques-Auguste de Thou: statesman, historian and bibliophile (1555–1617): see Davis 449 (no. 115 below).

82 *Paris bindings by the Cupid's Bow binder for Marc Laurin, c. 1550*

J J Pontanus, *Opera omnia*, 3 vols, Venice: Aldus and A Socerus, June 1518, April 1519, September 1519. 4to.

212/210 × 137/135/138 × 42/40 mm.   (P 1152) Davis 497–499

Black goatskin over paste boards, tooled in gold, with blind lines, to a panel design with solid fleurons at the corners, gouges and open tools. Vols II and III are identical; vol. I is somewhat different (but comes from the same shop). On the upper cover (of all three volumes) lettered in gold: IO.IOVIANI PON/TANI OPERVM/ VOLVMEN (respectively vol. I:) PRIMVM. (vol. II:) SECVN/DVM. (vol. III:) TERTI/VM.; beneath this in a frame: M.LAVRINI ET/AMICORVM.; in the centre of the lower cover: VIRTVS/IN AR/DVO [Marc Laurin's motto]. Edges of boards: tooled in gold with a line. Edges: gilt.

Sewn on five split alum-tawed supports, laced in, showing as raised bands on the spine, tooled in gold with a line; two kettle stitch bands; eight compartments, tooled in gold and blind with lines and in gold with an open stylized flower. Endbands: single with a bead; green silk over cord cores (laced in), tied down occasionally.

Endleaves: paper pastedowns and a pair of free conjugate paper leaves, and one free leaf conjugate with the pastedown, at both ends.

Repairs: at head and tail of spines.

PROVENANCE: Marc Laurin; H de Backere (on endleaf of vol. I in manuscript: 'S Emi haec 3 vol. Bruxellae/ in auct. 1 Junij 1618/ H. de Backere t,2„3'; in vol. II: 'S t,2„4'; in vol. III: 'S t,2„5'); John Bridges (on endleaf in manuscript: 'J Bridges'; in vol. III: '1706/7'; in vol. I on endleaf in manuscript: '1706/7 E. Bibliopolio Varenni 3 Vol.' [?a price erased]; sold: *Bibliothecae Bridgesianae Catalogus*, London,1725, *305*); bought: Breslauer, 6.vii.1954.
REFERENCES: Nixon, *Pierpont Morgan Library*, p. 136; Foot, *Davis*, I, p. 229 (Appendix, no. 9).
LITERATURE: Nixon, *Grolier*, pl. G (tools 11, 17), pl. H (tools 26, 29a–b); Nixon, *Pierpont Morgan Library*, no. 35; Hobson, *Renaissance*, p. 65; see Davis 360 (no. 80 above; and literature mentioned there); see also Davis 402 (no. 81 above); for Laurin see Foot, *Davis*, I, pp. 220–9 (and literature mentioned there; a list of bindings for Laurin by the Cupid's Bow binder: p. 229, Appendix); see also Davis 352 (no. 65 above).

82

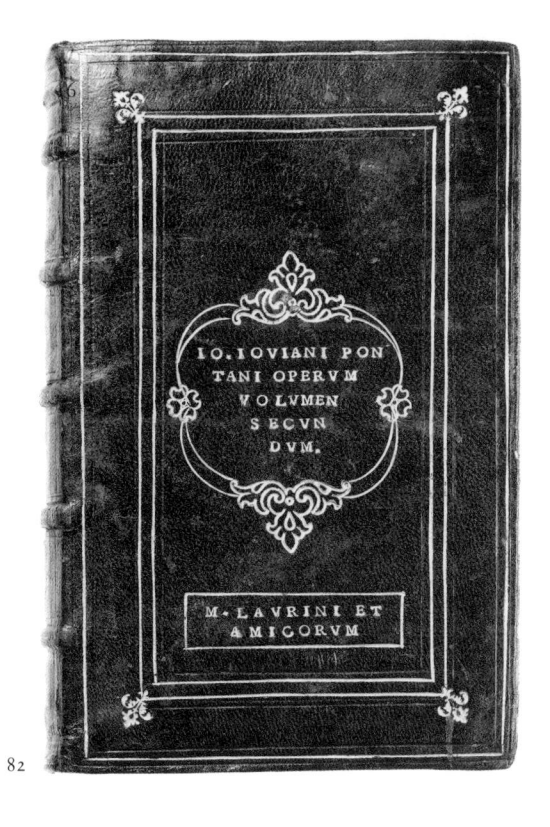

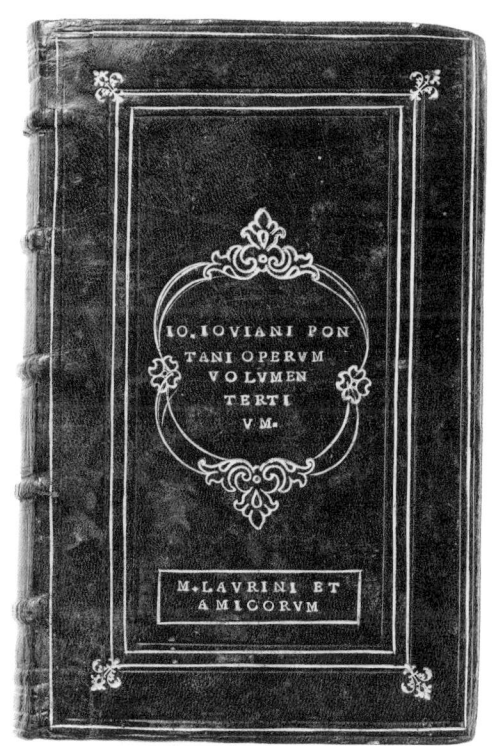

82 82

83

83 *A binding for Sir William Pickering, probably made in Paris, c. 1550–3*

Dante Alighieri, *La comedia ... con la nova espositione di Alessandro Vellutello*, Venice: F Marcolini, 1544; ruled in red. 4to.

240 × 160 × 61 mm. (P 312) Davis 505

Brown calf over paste boards, tooled in gold, with blind lines, to a panel design, with fleurons at the corners and a large cartouche with the arms of Sir William Pickering in the centre. Traces of four pairs of ties. Edges of boards and turn-ins: tooled in blind with lines. Edges: gilt.

Sewn on five split alum-tawed supports, laced in, showing as raised bands on the spine, tooled in gold with a line; two kettle stitch bands, tooled in gold with dashes; eight compartments, tooled in gold and blind with lines; the top and tail compartment with a small solid tool; the other compartments with a fleuron in gold. Endbands: single with a bead; beige and blue silk over cord cores (cut off), tied down occasionally.

Endleaves: paper pastedowns and one free leaf conjugate with the pastedown, at both ends.
Repairs: at the joints.

PROVENANCE: Sir William Pickering; the earl of Carnarvon (sold: Sotheby's, 8.iv.1919, *206*); Quaritch (Catalogue, December 1921, *305*, pl. lxxiii); bought: Quaritch, 31.x.1941.
REFERENCES: Foot, *Revue française*, p. 374, note 3.
LITERATURE: Maggs Bros, Catalogue 489: *Bookbindings* (1927), no. 28 (similar cartouche; Pickering arms in different surround); Goldschmidt, no. 219, pl. lxxxviii (with very similar cartouche; W Pickering's arms and motto); I G Philip, 'Sir William Pickering and his books', *The Book Collector*, 5 (1956), pp. 231–8.
Pickering arms also on: BL, C.47.l.16 (Paris, 1549), C.68.f.5 (Paris, 1552), C108.e.10 (Paris, 1550).

Note: Sir William Pickering (1516–1575); ambassador of Edward VI in France; in Paris: 1551–3; travelled in Italy; while in France was indicted for treason: 1554; back in England: 1555; ambassador of Queen Elizabeth I in the Netherlands and Germany: 1558–9; courtier and bibliophile. His (illegitimate) daughter, Hester, married Edward Wotton, son of Thomas Wotton; their granddaughter, Catherine, married Henry, Lord Stanhope (son of Philip, 1st earl of Chesterfield); through this line of descent the book came into the possession of the earl of Carnarvon (see also Davis 390, no. 40 above).

84 *A Paris binding with the motto of Thomas Mahieu, c. 1550–8*

Claudius Ptolemaeus, *Almagestum seu magnae constructionis mathematicae opus*, Venice: L Iunta, 1528. fol.

318 × 215 × 25 mm.   (P 1337) Davis 406

Semi-limp white parchment (over very thin [?paper] boards), tooled in gold to an arabesque design of interlacing ribbons, with gouges and dots; decorated with black and pink paint. In the centre of the upper cover: CLAVDII/PTOLEMAEI/ALMAGESTVM SEV/CONSTRVSTIONIS/ MATHE-MATICAE/MAGNAE; in the centre of the lower cover, Mahieu's motto: INGRATIS/SERVIRE/NEPHAS. Edges: gilt and lightly gauffered.

Sewn on four cords, laced through the parchment covers and frayed out and stuck down beneath the pastedowns; supports showing as low bands on the spine; five compartments, tooled in gold with fillets forming diamonds painted black and pink, a gold-tooled dot in each. Endbands: single with a bead; pink and beige silk over parchment cores (laced through the covers), tied down.

Endleaves: paper pastedowns at both ends; at the front: one free paper leaf.

PROVENANCE: Manuscript notes (about the text) in the margins; Thomas Mahieu; on pastedown of upper cover in manuscript: 'No. 34'; on free endleaf in manuscript: '32'; bought: Sotheby's, 14.iii.1961, *440* (pl.).
REFERENCES: Foot, *Davis*, I, p. 186; Hobson, *Bulletin du bibliophile*, p. 268, fig. 2.
LITERATURE: Foot, *Davis*, I, pp. 183–91 (and literature mentioned there); Needham, *Twelve Centuries*, nos. 57, 58; F. Adams, 'Maioli's mottoes and monograms', in: M von Arnim (ed.), *Festschrift Otto Schäfer*, Stuttgart, 1987, pp. 451–9; Culot, *La Reliure en France*, nos. 37, 47; Jeanne Veyrin-Forrer, 'Notes sur Thomas Mahieu', in: D Rhodes (ed.), *Bookbindings and other Bibliophily*, Verona, 1994, pp. 321–49; Hobson, *Renaissance*, pp. 65–9; Laffitte & Le Bars, pp. 98, 148, 151, 173; Hobson, *Bulletin du bibliophile*, pp. 239–70; see also Davis 403, 504 (nos. 85–86 below).
Note: Thomas Mahieu, possibly of Italian origin, became secretary to Queen Cathérine de' Medici (1549–1560); signed royal privileges for printed books: 1552–4; became treasurer of France for the Languedoc: after 1560, probably till 1571; book collector, friend and protégé of Grolier, went on collecting at least until 1588. According to Adams, the 'Ingratis' motto was used from 1550 to 1558. Hobson (*Bulletin du bibliophile*) suggests that Mahieu bought this book already bound; however, the statement that this is the only book that Mahieu owned that was bound in parchment is not correct (see Davis 504, no. 86 below and Adams, p. 458).

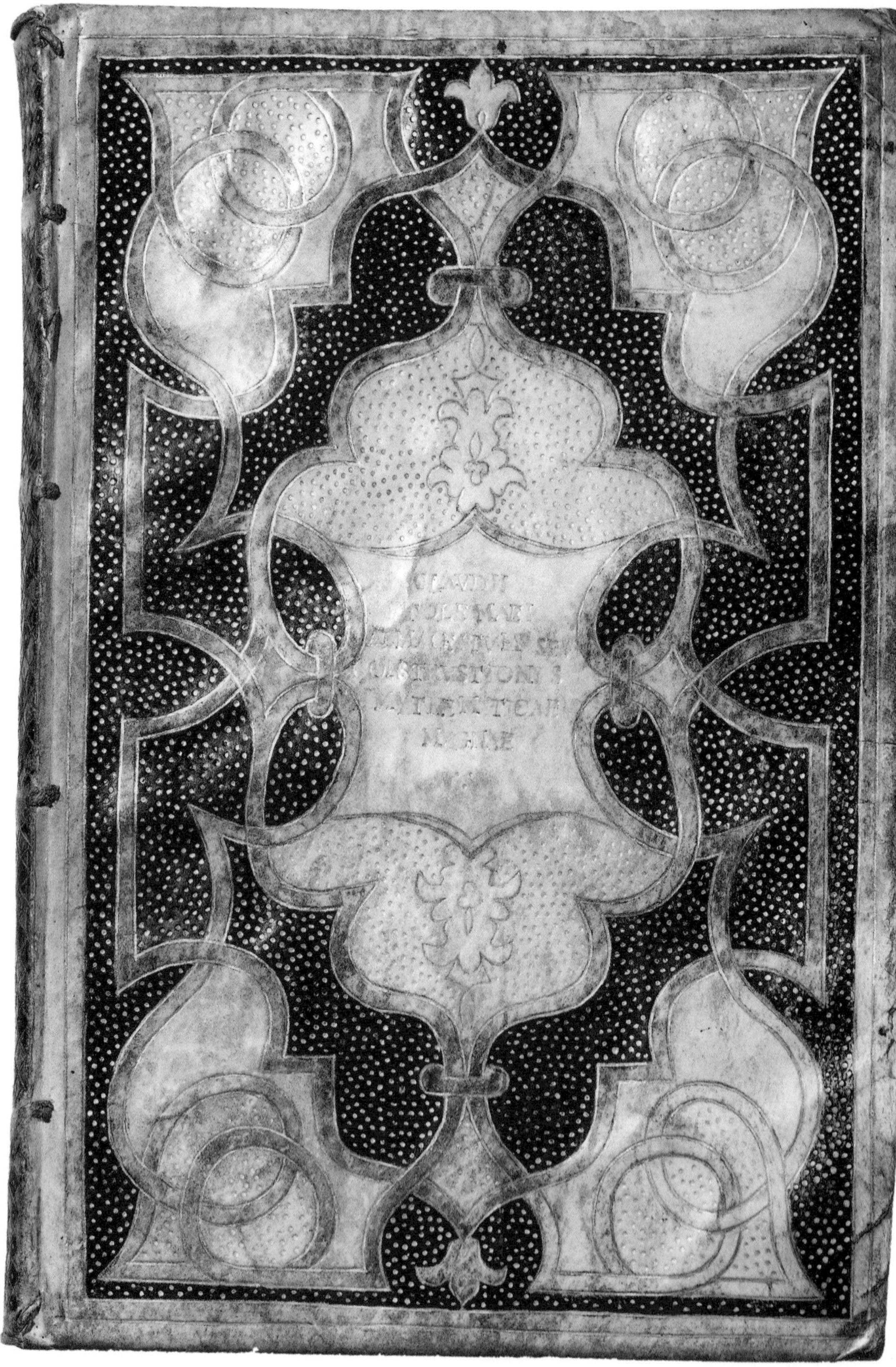

PAVSANIAE·
VETERIS·
GRAECIAE·
DESCRIPTIO·

THO·MAIOLI·ET·AMICOR·

85   *A Paris binding for Thomas Mahieu, c. 1560*

Pausanias, *Veteris Graeciae descriptio* [translated by Romulo Amaseo], Florence: L Torrentinus, 1551. fol.

354 × 229 × 53 mm.   (P 1069) Davis 403

Red-brown goatskin over paste boards, tooled in gold to a fanfare design with gouges. In the centre of the upper cover: PAVSANIAE./VETERIS./GRAECIAE./DESCRIPTIO.; in the centre of the lower cover, Mahieu's (second) motto: INIMICI.MEI./MEA.MIHI./ NON.ME./MIHI. On the upper cover along the lower edge: THO.MAIOLI.ET.AMICOR. Edges of boards: tooled in gold with a line; turn-ins: tooled in blind with a line. Edges: gilt.

    Sewn on six alum-tawed supports, laced in straight; smooth spine, tooled in gold to a fanfare design with gouges; traces of a (?later) title label. Endbands: single with a bead; blue and yellow silk over alum-tawed cores (now cut off; traces of lacing-in), tied down.

    Endleaves: paper pastedowns and a pair of free conjugate paper leaves, and one free leaf conjugate with the pastedown, at both ends.

PROVENANCE: Thomas Mahieu; Lt Col. E R Pratt (Ryston Hall, Norfolk; sold: Sotheby's, 27.vii.1925, *70*, pl.); Maggs; Henry Yates Thompson (sold: Sotheby's, 19.viii.1941, *490*, pl.); Lucius Wilmerding (sold: Parke-Bernet, 31.x.1951, *578*, pl.).

REFERENCES: G D Hobson, *Maioli*, no. lxiv (Group V, class A); Romme, *Book Collector*, 1969, p. 26, note 18, pl. iv; Nixon, *Pierpont Morgan Library*, p. 162; Foot, *Davis*, I, pp. 183, 185 (pl.), 187; Foot, *Mirror*, fig. 67; Hobson, *Bulletin du bibliophile*, pp. 260–1, no. 82.

LITERATURE: Foot, *Davis*, I, pp. 183–91 (and literature mentioned there); see also Davis 406 (no. 84 above, and literature mentioned there), 504 (no. 86 below).

Note: According to Adams the 'Inimici' motto was used from 1558 to 1565.

86   *A Paris binding for Thomas Mahieu, c. 1584*

Caspar Peucer, *Les Devins, ou commentaire des principales sortes de devinations*, Antwerp: H Connix, 1584. 4to.

242 × 162 × 40 mm.   (P 1336) Davis 504

Semi-limp white parchment (over very thin boards), tooled in gold with two lines along the border, in the corners the monogram of Thomas Mahieu: DTM and in the centre within a wreath made by two laurel branches, the monogram of Mahieu. Traces of two pairs of ties. Edges of boards: yap edges. Edges: gilt.

    Sewn on four (possibly alum-tawed) supports, laced in; smooth spine, tooled in gold with lines, oval laurel wreaths and the monogram of Mahieu in the centre oval. Endbands: single with a bead; blue and pink silk over alum-tawed cores (laced in), tied down occasionally.

    Endleaves: paper pastedowns and one free leaf conjugate with the pastedown, at both ends.

PROVENANCE: Thomas Mahieu (on the title-page in manuscript in Mahieu's hand: 'Cest a Mahieu et a ses amys' and 'Portio mea domine sit in terra viventium' [Grolier's motto]); in a different hand: 'Cest a lussau et ses amys'; William Beckford (sold: Sotheby's, 2.vii.1883, *680*); Aldenham House, Herts (book plate; sold: Sotheby's, 24.iii.1937, *278*); J R Abbey (book plate; 'J.A.1494/24:3:1937'; sold: Sotheby's, 23.vi.1965, *544*).

86

REFERENCES: *BFAC*, Case I, no. 39; Hobson, *French and Italian*, no. 17; Foot, *Davis*, I, pp. 184, 186, 187; F Adams, 'Maioli's mottoes and monograms', in: M von Arnim (ed.), *Festschrift Otto Schäfer*, Stuttgart, 1987, pp. 454, 457, 458; Hobson, *Renaissance*, p. 69, note 102; Hobson, *Bulletin du bibliophile*, p. 270 (part II of this study, forthcoming, may provide more information about this binding).
LITERATURE: Foot, *Davis*, I, pp. 183–91 (and literature mentioned there); see also Davis 406, 403 (nos. 84–5 above; and literature mentioned there).
Note: Mahieu's monogram: see Adams, motto III; Mahieu adopted here Grolier's motto, according to Hobson, in homage of his late mentor and friend.

---

87 *A Paris binding by the Mansfeld binder for Peter Ernst, Count von Mansfeld, c. 1552–7*

Vincent de Beauvais, *Le Quart Volume de Vincent miroir hystorial*, [Paris]: Jehan Petit, n.d. [and] *Le Cinquiesme Volume de Vincent miroir hystorial*, Paris: N Couteau for Jehan de la Garde, 16 March 1531. fol.

335 × 215 × 58 mm. (P 1002) Davis 405

Dark brown calf over paste boards, tooled in silver; within a border of fillets, decorated with green-blue paint, an arabesque design of gouges, open tools and flower tools around a large cartouche, with in the

129

centre tooled in gold: the arms of Peter Ernst, Count von Mansfeld, on a gold-dotted ground; decorated with black, red, green and blue paint; above the cartouche Mansfeld's initial and motto: M/.FORCE.MEST.TROP; below it: .MANSFELT., lettered in gold. Edges of boards: tooled in blind with lines and dashes. Edges: gilt and gauffered with gouges.

Sewn on five supports, laced in; smooth spine, tooled in silver with gouges, flower tools and open tools, decorated with green and red paint; lines and hatching near head and tail. Endbands: single with a bead; pale blue and pink silk over leather cores (cut off), tied down occasionally.

Endleaves: paper pastedowns at both ends; at the front: one free leaf conjugate with the pastedown, and two free paper leaves (repaired at the joint; conjugacy invisible); at the end: one free paper leaf (repaired at the joint; conjugacy invisible), and one free paper leaf tipped on; stub before last section (impossible to see whether or not conjugate with either of the free leaves).

Repairs: at joints, and at head and tail of the spine.

PROVENANCE: Peter Ernst, Count von Mansfeld; René de Chalon; Anne de Gros (on endleaf in manuscript: 'Tandem/ Ce livre apertient ['ce livre' erased] a rene de Chalon/ et a mon amie Anne de Gros.1607. 4me de Mars/ De feu mon gran pere. Le prince et Conte/ de Mansfelt. Pier Ernest.'); on title-page in manuscript: 'Collegij Soctis Jesu Nivellis' [Nivelles: south of Brussels] and 'Dono Dñae de Chalon. Ora pro illa/1627' and 'Chalon'; Ambroise Firmin-Didot (book plate; sold: Paris, 6.vi.1878, *715*); Joseph Baer & Co., Frankfurt; Lord Forbes; Sotheby's, 9.xi.1931, *192* (pl.); Gabriel Well; Lucius Wilmerding (book plate; sold: Parke-Bernet, 6.iii.1951, *649*).

REFERENCES: Brunet, pl. 57; J. Pearson, *500 Important Books*, London, [1910–11], no. 493 (pl.); G A E Bogeng, *Die grossen Bibliophilen*, Leipzig, 1922, vol. II, pl. 155; Grolier Club, *Exhibition*, 1937, no. 77; Nixon, *Pierpont Morgan Library*, p. 122, no. 2; E van der Vekene, *Graf Peter Ernst von Mansfeld als Büchersammler und Bibliophile*, Luxembourg, 1976, pp. 85, 87; E van der Vekene, *Les Reliures aux armoiries de Pierre Ernest de Mansfeld*, Luxembourg, 1978, no. vi (ill.); Foot, *Revue française*, p. 374, note 2.

LITERATURE: J. Massarette, *La Vie martiale et fastueuse de Pierre-Ernest de Mansfelt*, Paris, 1930; Nixon, *Pierpont Morgan Library*, no. 32; E van der Vekene, *Bemerkenswerte Einbände in der Nationalbibliothek zu Luxemburg*, Luxembourg, 1972, pp. 42–9; E van der Vekene, *Les Reliures aux armoiries de Pierre Ernest de Mansfeld*, Luxembourg, 1978; Needham, *Twelve Centuries*, no. 64; E van der Vekene, *Reliures des XVIe et XVIIe siècle ... à la bibliothèque nationale de Luxembourg*, Luxembourg, 2000, nos. 84–8.

Note: Peter Ernst, Count von Mansfeld (1517–1604); born in Saxony; page at the court of Ferdinand, king of Naples; made governor-general of the duchy of Luxembourg by Emperor Charles V: 1545. Mansfeld collected antiquities and books; his Parisian bindings were acquired while he was a prisoner in Vincennes: 1552–7.
The Mansfeld binder = Grolier's Arnobius binder.

M
·FORCE·MEST·TROP·

·MANSFELT·

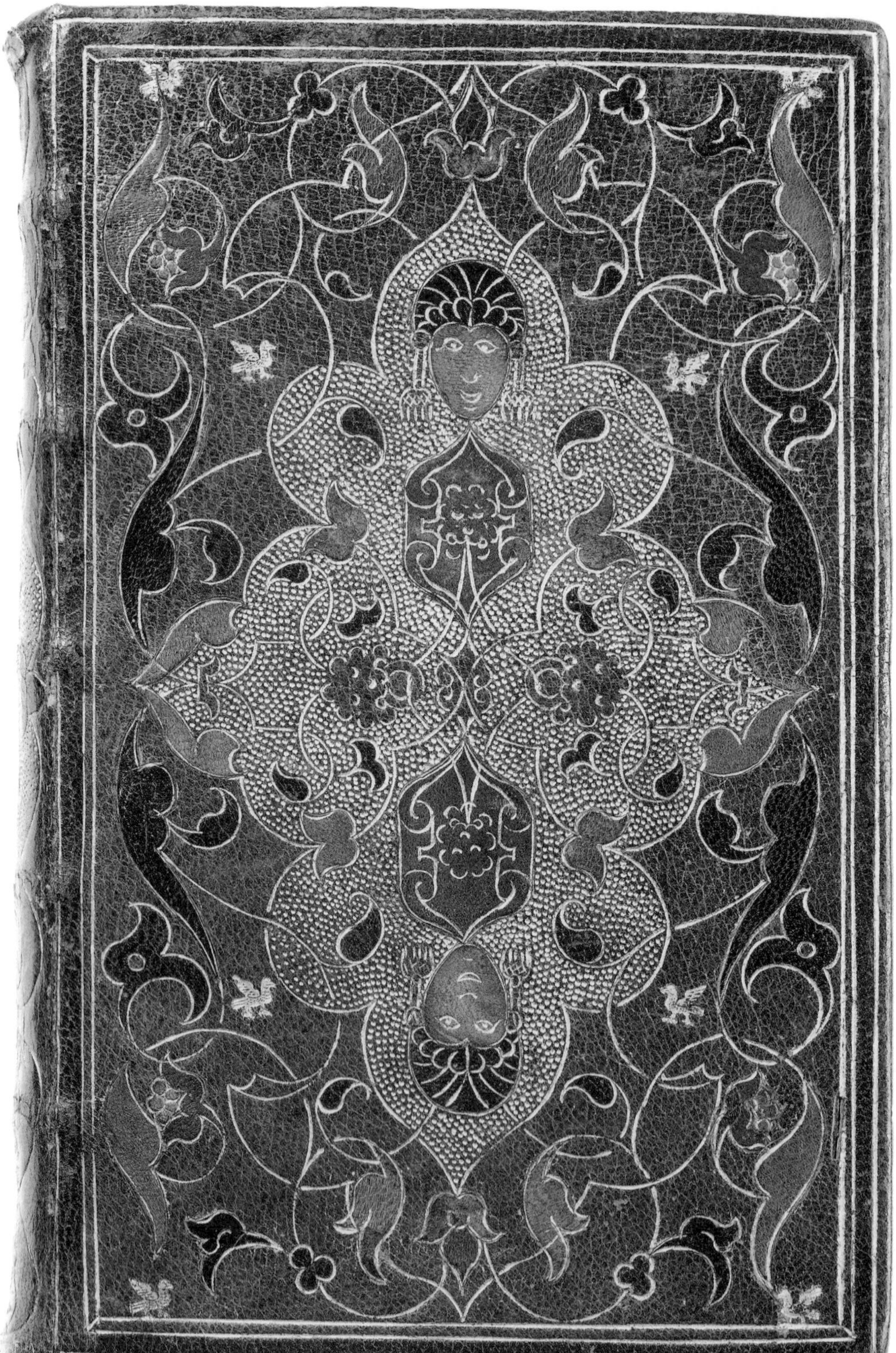

88

89

88 *A binding, possibly made in Paris or Geneva, c. 1555*

G Vasari, *Le vite de piu eccellenti architetti, pittori et scultori italiani*, Florence: [L Torrentino], 1550; decorated initials and title-page. 4to.

217 × 139 × 42 mm. (P 1099) Davis 507

Brown goatskin over paste boards, onlaid in black, red, citron and olive-brown goatskin and tooled in gold to an arabesque pattern of gouges and small bird tools around a large centre cartouche, tooled with gouges, lions' masks and human masks, all on a dotted ground; decorated with dark brown paint. Traces of two pairs of ties. Edges of boards: tooled in gold with lines and dashes; turn-ins: tooled in blind with lines. Edges: gilt.

Sewn on five double cords, laced in; smooth spine (supports showing), tooled in gold with gouges, fleuron shapes and dots, and decorated with dark paint. Endbands: single with a bead; blue and beige (natural) silk over cord cores (cut off), tied down through the spine lining and through the sections, only at the beginning and end of the text block.

Endleaves: paper pastedowns and one free leaf conjugate with the pastedown, at both ends.

In a slipcase, signed: DUPRES LAHEY.

PROVENANCE: Bought: Sotheby's, 31.iii.1952, *156* (pl.).
REFERENCES: Foot, *Revue française*, p. 375, note 16.
Note: Bindings with masks of this kind were made in Paris, Lyon and Geneva. The paucity of tools makes an attribution difficult and uncertain.

---

89 *A binding possibly made in Paris, c. 1555*

Q Curtius Rufus, *De rebus gestis Alexandri Magni regis Macedonum, libri decem*, Lyon: M Sylvius for I Frellonius, 1555; ruled in red. 16mo.

125 × 79 × 23 mm. (P 1055) Davis 423

133

Dark brown goatskin over paste boards, tooled in gold with three lines along the border, a semis of small dolphins and in the centre a cartouche with a crowned dolphin. Traces of two pairs of ties. Edges of boards: tooled in gold with lines and small tools. Edges: gilt.

Sewn on three (?recessed cord) supports, laced in; smooth spine, tooled in gold with lines and small dolphins. Endbands: single with a bead; green silk over cord cores (cut off), tied down sporadically.

Endleaves: paper pastedowns at both ends; at the front: two free paper leaves (pasted together: possible conjugacy invisible); at the end: one free leaf conjugate with the pastedown, plus one free paper leaf tipped on.

Repairs: at spine (new joints and new head) and at corners.

PROVENANCE: On last page of text in manuscript: 'GJ ?S'; Claude des Maisour; Guillaume des Maisour (on last blank leaf in manuscript: 'Ce quint-Curce à été acheté le 28 Novembre 1821 chez M. Thomas libraire ... il a appartenu a Claude des maisour en 1679 à Guillaume en 1821'); Maggs Bros (Catalogue 407, 1921, no. 46, pl. xx); Lucius Wilmerding (sold: Parke-Bernet, 30.x.1951, *258*)
LITERATURE: A R A Hobson, 'Une note sur le fer de reliure d'un dauphin', *Bulletin du bibliophile*, 1990, 1, pp. 139–42 (the Q Curtius of 1555 mentioned there is Davis 423).
Note: François II (1544–1560), when dauphin (1547–59), used a crowned dolphin.

---

90   *A strap-work binding, c. 1555*

Raymundus Rufus [Raymond le Roux], *Duplicatio in patronum Molinaei*, Paris: Benoit Prévost for Poncet le Preux, 1555. 8vo.

177 × 110 × 17 mm.   (P 1025) Davis 421

Brown calf over paste boards, blocked in gold, with a block of a complex strap-work design. Edges of boards: tooled in gold with a line; turn-ins: tooled in blind with a line. Edges: gilt.

Sewn on four (recessed) cords, laced in (at least three of the four cords have been laced in); smooth spine, tooled in gold with gouges. Endbands: single with a bead; yellow and green silk over (?)leather cores (cut off), tied down occasionally.

Endleaves: paper pastedowns and one free leaf conjugate with the pastedown, plus a second free paper leaf tipped on, at both ends.

Repairs: small repairs at corners.

PROVENANCE: On the pastedown a manuscript note in French about the author of this book; Lardanchet (Catalogue 44, 1950, *166*, pl.); bought: Lardanchet, 29.v.1951.
REFERENCES: Foot, *Revue française*, p. 375, note 15.

90

91 *A Paris binding by Mahieu's Aesop binder for Claude II or François de Laubespine, c. 1555*

Thucydides, *L'Histoire de Thucydide Athénien, de la guerre, ... entre les Peloponnesiens et Athéniens* [translated by Claude de Seyssel], Paris: Josse Badius, 10 August 1527. fol.

333 × 215 × 42 mm.   (P 392) Davis 407

Brown goatskin over paste boards, tooled in gold with two parallel intersecting fillets forming a rectangle and a diamond; solid tools at the corners; in the centre the arms of Claude II de Laubespine within a large decorative wreath. Edges of boards: tooled in gold with a line and small s-shaped tools; turn-ins: tooled in blind with a line. Edges: gilt.

Sewn on six split supports (invisible), laced in, showing as raised bands on the spine, tooled in gold with a line; seven compartments, tooled in gold, six of which with lines and open tools; title lettered in the second compartment. Endbands: single with a bead; yellow and blue silk over leather cores (cut off), tied down sporadically.

Endleaves: paper pastedowns and one free paper leaf (conjugate with a stub beneath the pastedown), at both ends.

Repairs: at corners of covers and at head and tail of spine.

PROVENANCE:	Claude II de Laubespine; bought: Sotheby's, 25.iii.1942 (from G D Hobson: no sale catalogue).
REFERENCES:	Foot, *Davis*, I, p. 191, Appendix, no. 1; Culot, *La Reliure en France*, p. 112.
LITERATURE:	Olivier, 1553; G D Hobson, *Maioli*, pls 32, 33 (Group I); Nixon, *Pierpont Morgan Library*, no. 31, and p. 84; Foot, *Davis*, I, pp. 188–9 (and literature mentioned there); Needham, *Twelve Centuries*, p. 203; Culot, *La Reliure en France*, no. 47; Conihout, *Bulletin du bibliophile*, pp. 71–3, 79, 84; see also Davis 408 (no. 92 below).
Same arms on:	Glasgow University Library, Hunt. Di.2.14 (Venice, 1545); Sotheby's, 28.ii.1966, *34* (pl.) (Venice, 1553).
Note:	Mahieu's Aesop binder worked for Mahieu as well as for Grolier and Anne de Montmorency; this shop was active from c. 1555 till c. 1568. The books with this coat of arms belonged either to Claude de Laubespine or to his brother François (see Conihout). Claude II de Laubespine (1510–1567) married Jeanne Bochetel: 1543; became one of the four secretaries of state: after 1547; played an important part in diplomatic and political affairs; became the principal councillor to Cathérine de' Medici: after 1560; owned the castle of Chateauneuf-sur-Cher; father of Claude III, book collector (see Davis 409–10; no. 78 above). François de Laubespine (d. c. 1572), president of the Grand Conseil, owner of the castle of Bois-le-Vicomte.

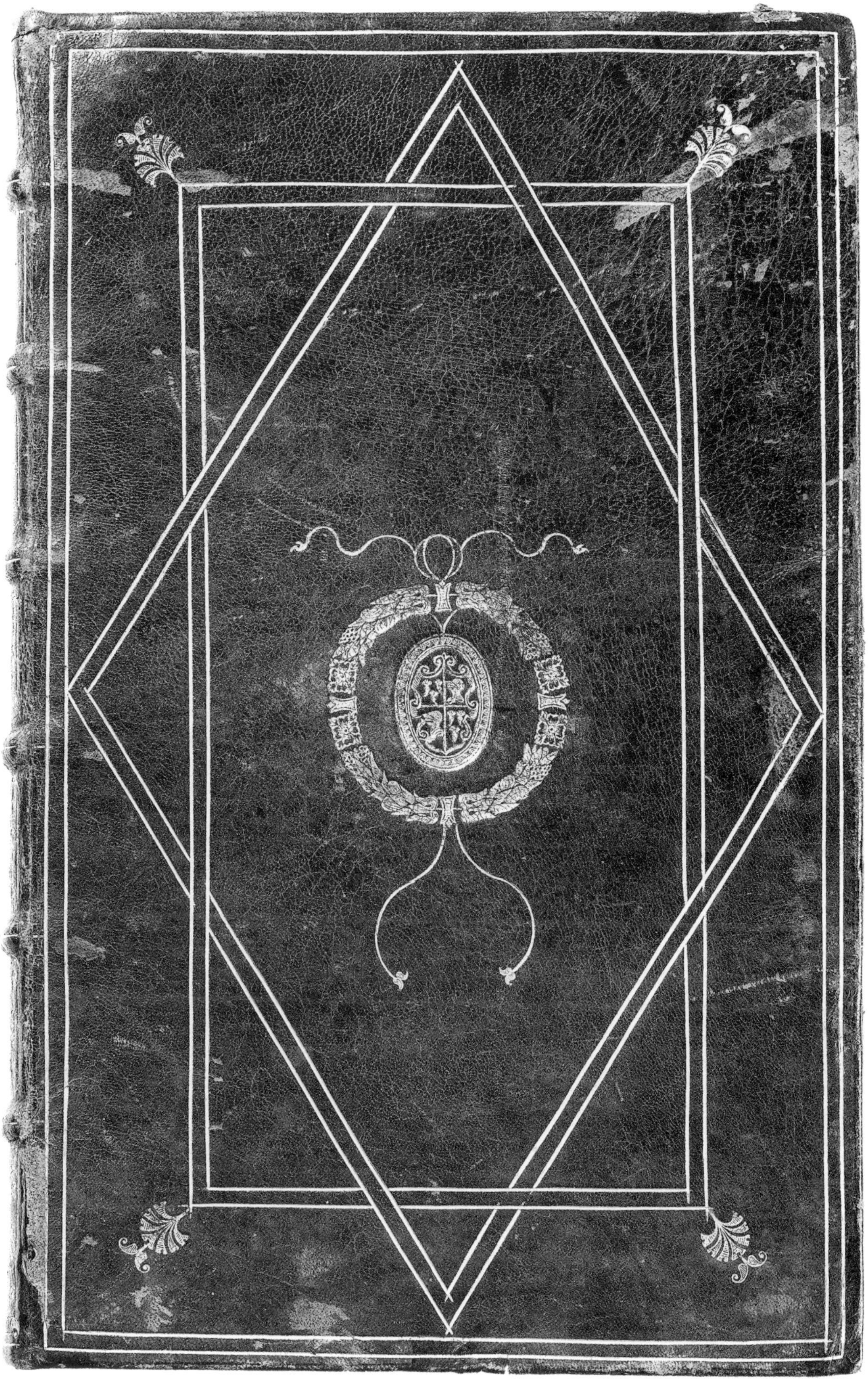

91

92

92   A Paris binding by Mahieu's Aesop binder, c. 1567–8

L Guicciardini, *Descrittione di tutti Paesi Bassi*, Antwerp: G Silvius, 1567; hand-coloured plates, title-page and borders. fol.

340 × 238 × 33 mm. (P 246) Davis 408

Olive goatskin over paste boards, tooled in gold to a forerunner of the fanfare design, with interlacing ribbons, gouges, solid, open and hatched tools. Edges of boards: tooled in gold with a line and small s-shaped tools. Edges: gilt.

Sewn on six (?alum-tawed) supports, laced in; smooth spine (supports visible beneath spine strip), tooled in gold with lines, gouges and solid tools; title lettered onto the spine. Endbands: single with a bead; blue and beige silk over cord cores (laced in), tied down.

Endleaves: paper pastedowns at both ends; at the front: one free leaf conjugate with the pastedown and a second free paper leaf; at the end: a pair of free conjugate paper leaves and a free leaf conjugate with the pastedown.

Repairs: at the joints and at head and tail of spine.

PROVENANCE:	Ballesdens (on the title-page in manuscript: signature of Ballesdens with three S fermés and 'geog.'); Leighton (sold: 14.vii.1897); Henry Yates Thompson (book plate; 'no. 67'; sold: Sotheby's, 18.viii.1941, *268*, pl.).
REFERENCES:	Foot, *Davis*, I, p. 191; Conihout, *Bulletin du bibliophile*, p. 83.
LITERATURE:	G D Hobson, *Maioli*, pl. 31, pp. 37–8 (Group I); see Davis 407 (no. 91 above; and literature mentioned there); for Ballesdens: see G D Hobson, *Fanfare*, pp. 90–1, 119; Hobson, *French and Italian*, p. xxi.
Same tools on:	BL, C.132.h.49 (Paris, 1543); Rahir sale II, Paris, 1931, *514*; Sotheby's, 19.vi.1967, *1701* (pl.); as well as on bindings mentioned in the literature (cited above).

93   A binding possibly made in Paris, c. 1555–60

Polybius, *Historiarum libri priores quinque, Nicolao Perotto Sipontino interprete*, Lyon: S Gryphius, 1554. 16mo.

127 × 75 × 47 mm. (P 1143) Davis 424

Brown calf over paste boards, tooled in gold, with blind lines, with lines along the border and in the centre an oval with a pelican in her piety [the device of Jerome de Marnef]. Edges: gilt.

Sewn on four split alum-tawed supports, laced in, showing as raised bands on the spine, tooled in blind with a line; two kettle stitch bands; seven compartments, tooled in blind with lines and in gold with fleurs-de-lis. Endbands: single with a bead; white and blue silk over cord cores (laced in), tied down occasionally.

Endleaves: paper pastedowns at both ends; at the end: a stub conjugate with the pastedown.

Repairs: small repairs at corners and at head and tail of spine.

PROVENANCE:	On the title-page in manuscript: 'S(?)euret J' [or: '3']; G Brédeault, Presbyteri (book plate); L de Montille (book plate); bought: N Rauch, 29.iii.1954, *198* (pl.).
REFERENCES:	G Colin, 'Marques de libraires et d'éditeurs', in: D E Rhodes (ed.), *Bookbindings and other Bibliophily*, Verona, 1994, p. 103 (A.1).

93   94

LITERATURE:	P Renouard, *Marques typographiques parisiennes*, Paris, 1926, nos. 723–7, 729–30, 733–40; Gruel, II, p. 119, fig. A: device as on Davis 424, fig. B: a different device (same motif) for Jerome de Marnef; Goldschmidt, no. 230, pl. cviii (device with pelican facing left); see also E Kyriss, 'Pariser Einbände', *Börsenblatt für den deutschen Buchhandel*, 51 (June 1969), fig. 5d; also table I, 11 and 12.
Note:	Jerome de Marnef: bookseller and printer/publisher in Paris: 1546–95.

94 *A Paris binding, c. 1555–60*

St Augustine, *Las confessiones … traduzidas … en romance castellano*, Antwerp: Martin Nucio, 1555. 12mo.

130 × 64 × 33 mm.   (P 1521) Davis 425

A Greek-style binding of red-brown goatskin over wooden boards, onlaid in black and tooled in gold; the border is onlaid in brown, the arabesque centre- and corner-design is onlaid in black and outlined in gold. Two pairs of clasps on plaited leather straps, hinging on the lower cover and fastening on two pins protruding from the edge of the upper board. Edges of boards: grooved and tooled in gold with a line. Edges: gilt.

Sewn on three (recessed) cords, laced in; smooth spine with raised headcaps, onlaid in black and tooled in gold to an intricate arabesque pattern. Endbands: Greek-style endbands: primary sewing over cord cores (laced in), sporadically tied down; secondary sewing of blue and yellow silk in two rows each with a bead.

95

Endleaves: paper pastedowns at both ends; at the front: one free paper leaf; at the end: a pair of free conjugate paper leaves, and one free leaf (probably conjugate with the pastedown [difficult to see]).

PROVENANCE: On endleaf in manuscript: '10 Louis'; L. Gruel (sold: April 1896, *516*); J R Abbey (book plate; 'J.A.4691/24:1:1950'; sold: Sotheby's, 21.vi.1965, *104*, pl.).
REFERENCES: Romme, *Book Collector*, 1969, p. 25, note 12; Foot, *Revue française*, p. 375, note 13; Foot, *Mirror*, fig. 26.

---

95 *A binding possibly made in Lyon, c. 1556–60*

Biblia sacra, Lyon: S Gryphius, 1556. 16mo.

127 × 77 × 36 mm. (P 760) Davis 426

Brown calf over paste boards, tooled in gold with three lines along the border, hatched corner blocks, a large centre block (upside down on the lower cover) and two small open tools. Traces of one pair of ties. Edges: gilt and gauffered to a strap-work pattern.

Rebacked with the original spine strip retained. Sewn on three (recessed) cords, laced in; smooth spine, tooled in gold with solid tools (head and tail compartments tooled later). Endbands: missing.

Endleaves: (later) paper pastedowns and one free leaf conjugate with the pastedown, at both ends; at the front: a pair of (original) free conjugate paper leaves; at the end: a pair of free conjugate paper leaves and one free paper leaf (original).

Repairs: rebacked; top of spine: renewed; extensive repairs at edges and corners of covers.

PROVENANCE: Bought: Sotheby's, 26.i.1944, *588*.
Same corner and centre blocks on: Rahir sale I, Paris, 1930, no. 179 (Lyon, 1559) = Kraus (New York), Catalogue 98 [1961]: *Catalogue of French Books*, no. 58 = N Rauch, Catalogue 7 (1961), no. 56 = Esmerian sale I, Paris, 6.vi.1972, *97*.

141

96 *A binding probably made in Paris, c. 1560*

[Vincent de la Loupe], *Premier et second livre des dignitez, magistrats, et offices du royaume de France*, Paris: Guillaume le Noir, 1560 [and] *Cronique abregee des faitz, gestes, et vies illustres des roys de France*, Paris: Guillaume le Noir, n.d. [privilege dated 1560] [and] *La Cronique des roys de France*, Paris: René Avril for Galiot du Pré, 1553. 8vo.

170 × 102 × 32 mm. (P 1066) Davis 427

Brown calf over paste boards, tooled in gold, with blind lines, with two lines along the border and in the centre: a gold-tooled arabesque centre piece with a cut-out profile portrait of Henri II, tooled on leather, onlaid. Edges: gilt.

Sewn on five split alum-tawed supports, laced in, showing as raised bands on the spine, tooled in blind with a line; two kettle stitch bands, with dashes in blind; eight compartments, six of which are tooled in blind with lines and in gold with a flower tool. Endbands: single with a bead; pink and blue silk over leather cores (cut off), tied down sporadically.

Endleaves: paper pastedowns and one free leaf conjugate with the pastedown, at both ends.

PROVENANCE: Yemeniz (Lyon, book plate); Firmin-Didot (book plate); E Rahir (book plate; sold: sale II, Paris, 6.v.1931, *573*); Mensing (sold: Sotheby's, 15–17.xii.1936, *342*, pl.); Lucius Wilmerding (sold: Parke-Bernet, 30.x.1951, *512*).
REFERENCE: E Droz, 'Les reliures à la médaille de Henri II', in: *Trésors des bibliothèques de France*, IV (1931), pp. 16–23, p. 22 (8e série, a); Hobson, *Humanists*, p. 243, no. 104 (c).
LITERATURE: Nixon, *Pierpont Morgan Library*, no. 38; Hobson, *Humanists*, pp. 136–40.

97

97 *An early fanfare binding, probably made in Paris, c. 1560*

Evangelium secundum Matthaeum, Marcum, Lucam [et] Iohannem; Acta Apostolorum [and] *Pauli Apostoli Epistolae; Epistolae Catholicae; Apocalypsis B. Iohannis* [and] *Index Epistolarum et Evangeliorum*, Paris: R Stephanus, October 1541; ruled in red. 8vo.

148 × 94 × 41 mm.   (P 220) Davis 428

Black goatskin over paste boards, tooled in gold to a fanfare design with hatched tools. Edges of boards: tooled in gold with lines and dashes. Edges: gilt.

Sewn on five split alum-tawed supports, laced in, showing as raised bands on the spine, tooled in gold with a line; two kettle stitch bands, with gold dashes; eight compartments, tooled in gold with lines and hatched and open tools. Endbands: double with a bead; primary sewing over cord cores (laced in), tied down; secondary sewing of pink and beige silk.

Endleaves: paper pastedowns and one free leaf conjugate with the pastedown and one free paper leaf tipped on, at both ends.

PROVENANCE: On a blank after ddiii in manuscript: 'Co(?)r Cabazac P. anno dni 1717'; A Firmin-Didot (book plate; sold: Paris, June 1882, no. 63); bought: Sotheby's, 11.viii.1941, *129* (pl.).

LITERATURE: G D Hobson, *Fanfare*, pp. 3–6 ('type primitif'); see also Nixon, *Pierpont Morgan Library*, nos. 41, 44; and Needham, *Twelve Centuries*, nos. 80, 81.

143

98

98   *A binding made c. 1565*

C Sigonius, *De republica Atheniensium libri iiii*, Venice: V Valgrisi, 1565. 8vo.

164 × 110 × 23 mm.   (P 1197) Davis 818

Dark olive-brown goatskin over paste boards, tooled in gold with two lines along the border and in the centre a plaquette showing the profile (to the right) of a bearded man, bare-shouldered. Edges: gilt and gauffered to a pattern of diamonds and dots.

    Sewn on four leather supports, laced in straight, showing as raised bands on the spine, tooled in gold with a line; two kettle stitch bands, tooled in gold with dashes; eight compartments, tooled in gold with lines and stylized flowers.

    Endbands: single with a bead; blue and pink silk over alum-tawed cores (cut off), tied down.

    Endleaves: white paper pastedowns and two free conjugate white paper leaves and one leaf conjugate with the pastedown, at both ends; manuscript parchment lining: visible beneath lower cover pastedown with a stub after the third endleaf (at the back).

PROVENANCE: Unidentified armorial book plate; on upper cover pastedown in manuscript: '2037';
                          bought: Karl & Faber, 12.v.1955, *486*.
REFERENCES: Hobson, *Humanists*, p. 249, no. 138a.

---

99   *A binding possibly made in Lyon, c. 1566–70*

J Chaumeau, *Histoire de Berry*, Lyon: A Gryphius, 1566; engraved initials; ruled in red. fol.

342 × 217 × 30 mm.   (P 244) Davis 398

Brown calf over paste boards, tooled in gold to an arabesque design of interlacing ribbons with gouges forming animal heads at the long sides of the central oval, dots, small circles and small stars; decorated

99

with black paint. Edges of boards: tooled in blind with lines, dashes and small tools; turn-ins: tooled in gold with a line. Edges: gilt and gauffered to a strap-work pattern.

Rebacked with the original backstrip retained; possibly also resewn. Sewn on four cords, laced in; smooth spine, tooled in gold with lines, dots, hatched fleuron tools, small s-shaped tools and large knot shapes decorated with black paint. Endbands: single with a bead; yellow silk over cord or alum-tawed cores (cut off), tied down occasionally.

Endleaves: paper pastedowns and a free leaf (?)conjugate with the pastedown, and a second free paper leaf, at both ends. The watermark is similar to those used in Clermont Ferrant (1584) and Lyon (1518-87).

Repairs: rebacked; small repairs to covers.

PROVENANCE:	Earlier ownership inscriptions erased; in manuscript: symbols (with S fermés) and 'Zu[?n]o fata'; at end of text in manuscript: 'vingt neuf' and (?)monogram; Gruel (sold: 22.x.1899); Henry Yates Thompson (book plate with in manuscript: '66'; sold: Sotheby's, 18.viii.1941, *238*, pl.).
LITERATURE:	Briquet, 13211, 13074 (similar watermarks).
Compare:	(for similar bindings tooled with interlacing ribbons ending in animal heads on dotted backgrounds) Rauch, Catalogue 5 (1956), *50* (another copy of this same book); Lardanchet, Catalogue 50 (1956), *3638* (Lyon, 1558, with the date 1559 on the cover).

100 *A 'primitive fanfare' binding, probably made in Paris, c. 1568.*

Synesius Cyrenaeus, *Hymni vario lyricorum versuum genere* [Greek and Latin], Geneva: Henricus Stephanus, 1568; ruled in red. 32mo.

84 × 53 × 14 mm. (P 1263) Davis 430

Brown goatskin (or possibly hair sheep) over paste boards, tooled in gold to a forerunner of a fanfare design with interlacing ribbons, gouges and hatched tools. Remnants of two pairs of pink silk ties. Edges of boards: tooled in gold with a line. Edges: gilt.

Sewn on three (?recessed cord) supports, laced in through three holes; smooth spine, tooled in gold with gouges and hatched fleuron tools; later red goatskin label with title lettered in gold. Endbands: Greek-style: raised; double with a bead; primary sewing over cord cores (laced in), tied down; secondary sewing of purple and yellow silk.

Endleaves: paper pastedowns and a pair of free conjugate paper leaves, and one free leaf (probably) conjugate with the pastedown, at both ends.

PROVENANCE:	In the centre oval on both covers in manuscript: R.C. with small hearts above and below; on endleaf in manuscript: 'R.C.D.L.T./1677'; Narcissus Luttrell (on the verso of the title-page: his monogram (stamp) with, in manuscript: '1709'); bought: Sotheby's, 19.ii.1957, *390*.
LITERATURE:	G D Hobson, *Fanfare*, no. 34, pl. xxviii (possibly same tool).
Note:	Narcissus Luttrell (1657–1732), analyst and bibliographer, book collector.

101   *An onlaid binding, probably made in Paris, c. 1568*

F Guicciardini, *Histoire des guerres et choses advenues … sous Charles VIII*, Paris: B Turrisan, 1568. 8vo.

173 × 110 × 31 mm. (P 991) Davis 431

Brown goatskin over paste boards, onlaid in black, dark brown and red, outlined in gold tooling, forming a centre- and corner-design, with cornucopias as corner pieces and a floral-arabesque centre piece, all onlaid and tooled with gouges. Traces of two pairs of ties. Edges of boards and turn-ins: tooled in blind with lines. Edges: gilt and gauffered to an arabesque pattern.

 Sewn on five (invisible) supports (possibly double cords), laced in, showing as raised bands on the spine, tooled in gold with a line; six compartments onlaid in black and red and tooled in gold with lines and gouges. Endbands: single with a bead; blue and pink silk over cord cores (laced in), tied down.

 Endleaves: paper pastedowns and a pair of free conjugate paper leaves, and one free leaf conjugate with the pastedown, at both ends.

PROVENANCE: On endleaf in manuscript: 'No, 2445'; A A Renouard (on title-page in manuscript: 'Ant. Aug. Renouard'); Holford collection (sold: Sotheby's, 6.xii.1927, *337*, pl.); Cortlandt F Bishop (book plate; sold: New York, Anderson Galleries, 1938, *944*); Lucius Wilmerding (book plate; sold: Parke-Bernet, 5.iii.1951, *292*).

REFERENCES: A A Renouard, *Catalogue de la bibliothèque d'un amateur*, 4 vols, Paris, 1819, vol. iv, p. 124; G D Hobson, *Thirty Bindings,* no. xiv; G D Hobson, *Maioli*, p. 21 C; *Treasures*, 1965, no. 74.

Compare: G D Hobson, *Maioli*, pl. 28; J Porcher, 'Les livres de Diane de Poitiers', in: *Trésors des bibliothèques de France*, VI, 26 (1946), pl. xxiii.

102 *A binding, probably made in Lyon for François or Antoine Grolier, c. 1568*

Joachim du Bellay, *Divers jeux rustiques* [and] J du Bellay, *Epithalame*, Paris: F Morel, 1568. 8vo.

166 × 107 × 22 mm. (P 1146) Davis 432

White sheepskin over paste boards, tooled in gold with a single line along the border; stylized flowers at the corners; in the centre: the arms and motto, NEC ARBOR NEC HERBA, of Antoine Grolier de Servières. Traces of two pairs of ties. Edges: plain (traces of red paint?)

Sewn on four alum-tawed supports, laced in, showing as raised bands on the spine; two kettle stitch bands, tooled in gold with dashes; small head and tail compartments and five compartments, tooled in gold with lines and a flower tool. Endbands: single with a bead; blue and pink silk over (?)cord cores (cut off), tied down occasionally.

Endleaves: paper pastedowns and one free paper leaf (at the end conjugate with the pastedown?), at both ends.

PROVENANCE:	François (or Antoine) Grolier; N Rauch (Catalogue I, 1948, no. 36; sold: 29.iii.1954, *131*, pl.).
LITERATURE:	Guigard, II, 248; Shipman, pp. 24–7; Olivier, 1135 (attributes these arms and this motto to François Grolier, the father of Antoine, while both Guigard, Rauch and Shipman attribute the arms and motto to Antoine); Hobson, *Renaissance*, pp. 7, 51 (mentions Antoine Grolier, an uncle of Jean and Antoine Grolier, a nephew of Jean. The latter died in 1527, well before this book was printed and bound); Christie's Paris, 7.x.2005, *44*.
Note:	Antoine Grolier de Servières (1545–1610), magistrate in Lyon, ambassador to Switzerland and Turin, treasurer of France. His father, François (d. 1577), was secretary to the king and five times councillor of Lyon: 1545–71; another Antoine was the father of François, consul in Lyon in 1508.

148

103 *A Paris fanfare binding for Nicolas de Villeroy, c. 1570–5*

Isocrates, *Enseignements d'Isocrate et Xenophon … pour bien regner en paix et en guerre* [translated by Loy le Roy, dict Requis de Costentin] [and] Aristotle, *Les Politiques*, Paris: M Vascosan, 1568; ruled in red. 4to.

253 × 170 × 66 mm.   (P 1068) Davis 508

White parchment over thin paste boards, tooled in gold to a fanfare design with leafy sprays, gouges, hatched curl and fleuron tools, and volutes; in the corners the monogram of Nicolas de Neufville de Villeroy (NDN); in the centre a large oval with a painted scene showing a landscape with a tree between rocks and (remnants of) De Villeroy's motto: PER ARDVA SVRGO. Edges: gilt.

Sewn on six alum-tawed supports, laced in straight and sandwiched between two layers of board (or possibly between the board and a stub of paper pasted onto the outside of the board); smooth spine, tooled in gold to a fanfare design with volutes and hatched tools. Endbands: yellow thread over alum-tawed cores (laced in), tied down through a piece of parchment (possibly once a spine panel lining; tie-downs may have pulled loose).

Endleaves: at the front: parchment strengthener; stub of a paper leaf conjugate with the fourth free paper leaf, a pair of free conjugate paper leaves (the third leaf torn off, leaving a sizeable stub); a fourth

THE HENRY DAVIS GIFT

free paper leaf (conjugate with the stub); at the end: parchment manuscript strengthener; two pairs of free conjugate paper leaves, quired inside one another.

PROVENANCE: Nicolas de Villeroy; erased manuscript inscription on DDDiij recto; on endleaf: manuscript note in French about the book; book plate with 'ME' and 'cum consomaverit homo, tunc incipiet'; Lucius Wilmerding (book plate; sold: Parke-Bernet, 31.x.1951, *545*).
REFERENCES: Conihout, *Henri III mécène*, p. 320, fig. 2, pl. xxxviii.
LITERATURE: G D Hobson, *Fanfare*, pp. 61–2, pls xxia (Hobson, no. 66a), xi (no. 94a), vii (no. 58), p. 61, fig. 49k; Conihout, *Henri III mécène*, pp. 318–29.
Same tools on: BL, C.19.b.12, C.19.b.13, C.19.b.16 (three volumes of a set of Aristotle in six volumes, 1552, with the arms of J-A de Thou as bachelor).
Note: Nicolas de Neufville de Villeroy (1543–1617), secretary of state and principal minister to Henri III; friend of Ronsard; married Madeleine de Laubespine: 1559; owned a fine library (see also Davis 409–10, no. 78 above).

104 *A Paris binding, c. 1570–80*

C J Caesar, *Rerum ab se gestarum commentarii*, Paris: M Vascosan, 1543 [and] F Vegetius Renatus, *De re militari*, Paris: C Wechel, 1553; ruled in red. fol.

346 × 222 × 45 mm.   (P 1490) Davis 399

Olive-brown goatskin over paste boards, tooled in gold with lines forming a wide border filled with leafy branches, small stylized flower tools, shields, and in the corners: palmette tools; in the centre a fanfare design with scrolls, palmette tools, leafy branches, fleurons and small stylized flower tools. Edges of boards: tooled in gold with a line and dashes. Edges: gilt.

Sewn on six (?)cords, laced in through three holes; smooth spine (but supports visible), tooled in gold with leafy branches, a fanfare ribbon forming an oval, hatched tools and volutes; title lettered on spine. Endbands: double with a bead; primary sewing over cord cores (laced in), tied down; secondary sewing of blue and (faded) pink silk.

Endleaves: paper pastedowns at both ends; at the front: a pair of free conjugate paper leaves, plus a free leaf conjugate with the pastedown; at the end: trace of a free paper leaf torn off, but conjugate with the second free paper leaf, plus one free leaf conjugate with the pastedown. Printed waste visible beneath the pastedown of the lower cover.

PROVENANCE: On endleaf in manuscript: 'D3:64'; on pastedown in manuscript: '3 10 tt'; bought: Marlborough Fine Arts, 22.xi.1960 (Catalogue 43), *28*.
LITERATURE: G D Hobson, *Fanfare*, p. 28, fig. 26, pls x, xi, p. 40 (fig. 44), pp. 59–60; Culot, *La Reliure en France*, no. 60 (for a very similar binding with identical tools).
Note: For small hatched fleurons see Davis 445 (no. 107 below; and see references to other bindings there).

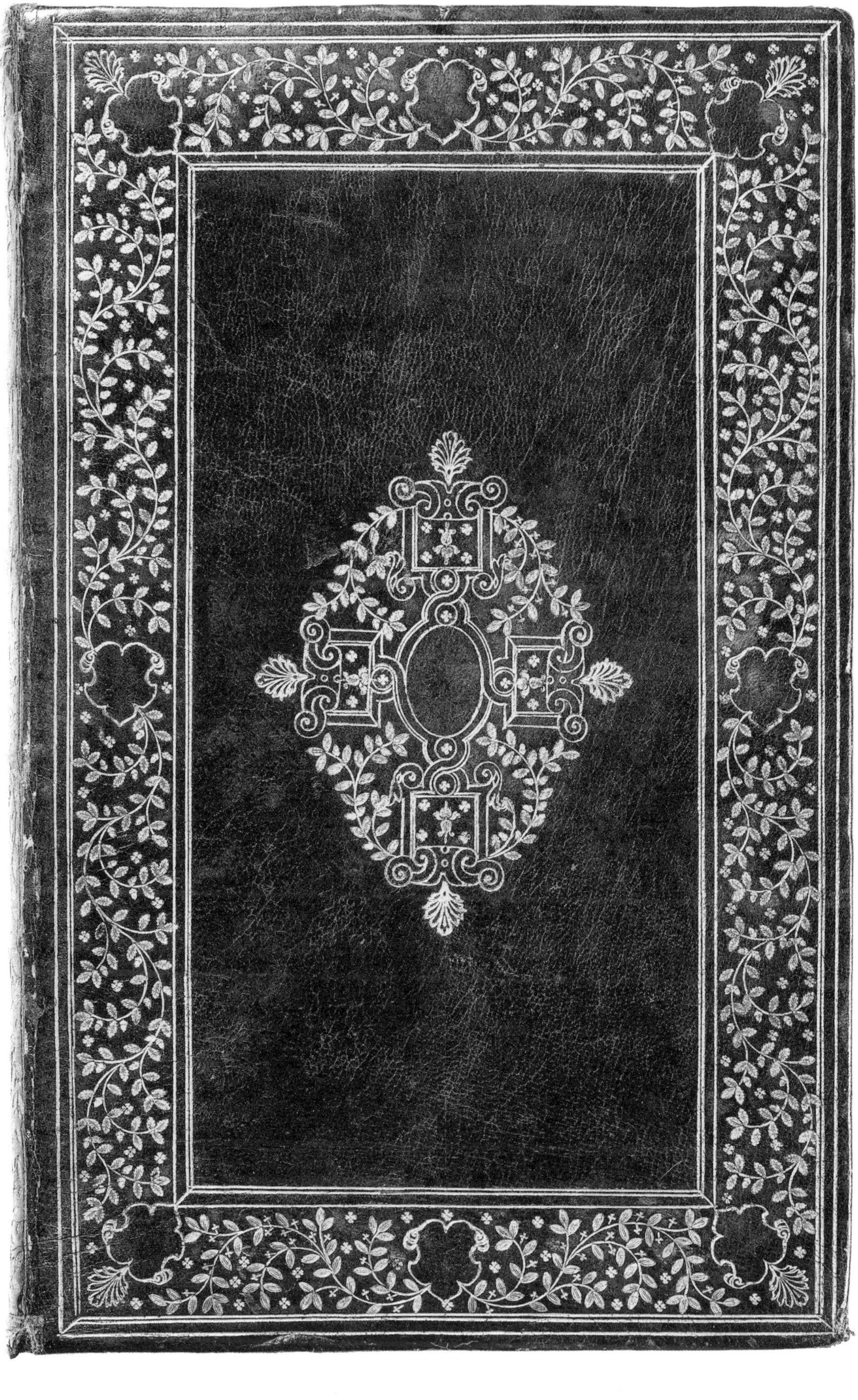

105

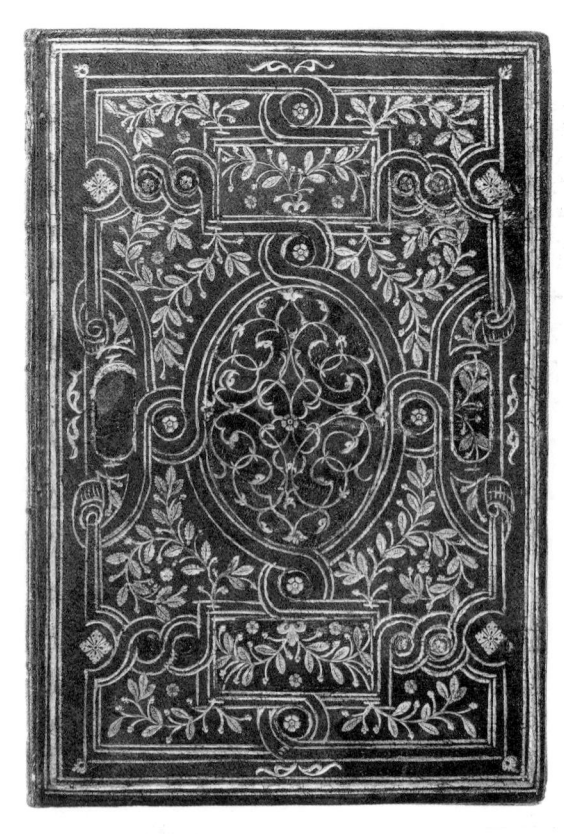

105   *A Paris fanfare binding, c. 1574*

P C Tacitus, *La Vie de Jules Agricola, descripte à la verité par Cornelius Tacitus, son gendre* [translated by Ange Cappel], n.p., n.d. [Paris: D du Pré, 1574]; dedicated to Elizabeth I of England; ruled in red. 4to.

228 × 160 × 9 mm. (P 1086) Davis 509

Brown goatskin over paste boards, onlaid in red and brown and tooled in gold to a fanfare design with leafy sprays, fleurons and flower tools, gouges and small solid tools. Doublures of brown calf, tooled in gold to a fanfare design with leafy sprays, gouges, fleurons and small flower tools; in the centre of the doublure of the upper cover: the royal arms of England, onlaid and tooled in gold; in the centre of the doublure of the lower cover: a Tudor rose tooled in silver. Traces of two pairs of ties. Edges of boards: tooled in gold with lines and dashes; turn-ins: tooled in blind with lines. Edges: gilt.

Sewn on four (invisible) supports, showing as bands on the spine; five compartments, tooled in gold with lines and a semis of small stars. Endbands: lacking.

Endleaves: new: one free marbled leaf (backed) and two free paper leaves, one of which is conjugate with the backing paper, at both ends.

PROVENANCE: (?)Queen Elizabeth I of England [possibly the dedication copy]; marquess of Lothian (in a box with his arms; sold: New York, Anderson Galleries, 27.i.1932, *84*, pl.); Gabriel Wells (sold: Parke-Bernet, 13.xi.1951, *516*, pl.).

REFERENCES: G D Hobson, *Fanfare*, pp. 18 (list no. 88), 30, 33 (list no. 88), 43; Foot, *Revue française*, p. 379, note 26.

106

106 *A binding decorated with a block, c. 1575*

M T Cicero, *Rhetoricorum ad C Herennium* [and] *Rhetoricorum secundus tomus*, Lyon: A Gryphius, 1570 [title-page of vol. I damaged]. 16mo.

124 × 74 × 36 mm. (P 1420) Davis 434

Brown calf over paste boards, blocked in gold with a large block showing an arabesque design on dotted ground; centre oval: tooled in blind with two hatched tools. Traces of two pairs of ties. Turn-ins: tooled in blind with lines.

Sewn on three tanned leather supports, laced in, showing as raised bands on the spine, with traces of gold tooling; two kettle stitch bands; four compartments, tooled in gold with small rolls (or pallets) and curly tools. Endbands: single with a bead; primary sewing over cord cores (now cut off), tied down; secondary sewing of yellow and (faded) pink silk.

Endleaves: paper pastedowns and one free leaf conjugate with the pastedown, at both ends.

Repairs: at corners of covers, at lower joint, at head and tail of spine.

PROVENANCE: On title-page in manuscript: 'J.M. Montis (...?)'; (a signature at the bottom of the title-page has been torn off); bought: Sotheby's, 28.ii.1966, *38*.
Same block on: Belin, Catalogue: *Riches reliures*, Paris, 1910, *645* (Paris, 1555); Gumuchian, 1930, no. 99 (Lyon, 1569); Bodleian Library Oxford, Broxbourne R1813, Bodl. 13.20 (Venice, 1572).

107 *A Paris fanfare binding, c. 1580*

P P Statius, *Sylvarum libri v* [and other works], Venice: Aldus & A Socerus, January 1519. 8vo.

158 × 95 × 36 mm. (P 1080) Davis 445

Dark brown goatskin over paste boards, tooled in gold to a fanfare design, with leafy sprays, gouges, and small hatched and solid tools; in the centre oval of the upper cover: STA/TIUS. Edges of boards: tooled in gold with a line and dashes. Edges: gilt.

Sewn on four (?)alum-tawed supports, laced in; smooth spine, tooled in gold to a fanfare design with hatched fleurons and small cherub's heads. Endbands: double with a bead; primary sewing over cord cores (now cut off), tied down; secondary sewing of pink and white silk.

Endleaves: paper pastedowns and one free leaf conjugate with the pastedown, plus one parchment leaf tipped on, at both ends.

PROVENANCE: William Loring Andrews (book plate; sold: New York, Anderson Galleries, 18–19.iv.1891); Cortlandt F Bishop (book plate; sold: New York, American Art Association, Anderson Galleries, April–November 1938, *2142*); Lucius Wilmerding (sold: Parke-Bernet, 31.x.1951, *867*).
LITERATURE: Culot, *La Reliure en France*, no. 59.

108

Note: Fanfare bindings with very small hatched tools are commonly found on bindings dated to the 1570s and 80s. The same tools as occur on Davis 445 also occur on, or link with tools occurring on, e.g.: Cambridge University Library, SSS.57.18 (n.p., n.d.); Cambridge University Library, SSS.17.30 (Paris, 1501); National Art Library, Victoria & Albert Museum, London, Drawer 43, W138 (Verona, 1531); Fitzwilliam Museum, Cambridge (Lyon, 1551); Davis 399 (no. 104 above; Paris, 1543–53); John Rylands University Library, Manchester, 1789 (Bologna, 1555); Bodleian Library Oxford, Broxbourne R1105, Bodl. 26.7–15 (Paris, 1543–57); V&A, Drawer 42, W132 (Paris, 1557); BL, C.19.b.10 (for de Thou, 1570); V&A, Drawer 42, W135 (Paris, 1572). Compare also G D Hobson, *Fanfare*, p. 7, fig. 3 (not identical with that found on Davis 445 and this group).

---

108 *Ten bindings made in Lyon or possibly Geneva, c. 1580*

M T Cicero, *Opera*, 10 vols, Lyon: A Gryphius, 1571–9. 16mo.

Epistolae ad Atticum, ad Brutum et ad quintum fratrem, 1571		
126 × 77 × 38 mm.	(P 985)	Davis 435
Epistolae familiares, 1578		
124 × 81 × 29 mm.		Davis 436
Orationum volumen i, 1576		
126 × 80 × 32 mm.		Davis 437
Orationum volumen ii, 1576		
126 × 80 × 30 mm.		Davis 438
Orationum volumen iii, 1576		
125 × 80 × 29 mm.		Davis 439

De officiis, 1578
125 × 78 × 29 mm.   Davis 440
De philosophia, vol. i, 1579
125 × 78 × 33 mm.   Davis 441
De philosophia, vol. ii, 1579
124 × 77 × 31 mm.   Davis 442
Rhetoricum ad Herennium [and] *De inventione libri*, 1579
124 × 78 × 23 mm.   Davis 443
Rhetoricorum volumen ii, 1578
123 × 77 × 30 mm.   Davis 444

Brown calf over paste boards, tooled in gold to a panel design with lines and small flowers in the border, hatched tools in the corners and in the centre, and a semis of stylized flower tools. Edges of boards: tooled in gold with lines, dashes and small scroll tools. Edges: gilt.

Sewn on four (recessed) supports, laced in (440, possibly 442, and 444: sewn on four alum-tawed supports, laced in); smooth spines, tooled in gold with lines, cross-hatching, scroll tools, hatched tools and solid floral tools (part of a roll?). Endbands: single with a bead; primary sewing over leather cores (cut off), tied down; secondary sewing of blue silk.

Endleaves: paper pastedowns and a pair of free conjugate paper leaves, and one free leaf conjugate with the pastedown, at both ends (438: at the end: paper pastedown and one free leaf conjugate with the pastedown, plus one free paper leaf).

PROVENANCE: 437: On endleaf in manuscript: 'Gw(?u)i Lambonne (?)'; earl of Carysfort, Elton Hall (book plate in all volumes with library numbers: G/8/17–26); Lucius Wilmerding (book plate in 443; all volumes sold: Parke-Bernet, 5.iii.1951, *174*).

109   *A binding made in Paris, possibly by the Ève bindery, c. 1581–5*

[Book of Hours in Latin (use of Tours) with calendar]. MS on parchment; decorated initials in gold and colours, [France, 16th century]; ruled in red.

157 × 97 × 23 mm.   (M 35) Davis 446

Dark red goatskin over paste boards, tooled in gold to a centre and corner design; corner pieces incorporating a cherub's head and leafy sprays; leafy sprays forming a centre oval with, on the upper cover: N and on the lower cover: A; parachute-shaped tools; a semis of fleurs-de-lis. Traces of two pairs of ties. Edges of boards: tooled in gold with a line and dashes. Edges: gilt.

Sewn on five split alum-tawed supports, laced in, showing as raised bands on the spine, tooled in gold with a line; six compartments, tooled in gold with lines and curling hatched tools. Headband (tailband missing): single with a bead; green and red silk over cord core (cut off), tied down.

Endleaves: parchment pastedowns and a pair of free conjugate parchment leaves, and one free parchment leaf conjugate with the pastedown, at both ends.

PROVENANCE: (?)N A; bought: Sotheby's 17.vii.1944, *78*.
REFERENCES: Foot, *Revue française*, p. 379.

109   110

LITERATURE: W Y Fletcher, *Foreign*, pl. xxxvi (arms of Henri III); G D Hobson, *Fanfare*, p. 38, fig. 43, pp. 51–4; Oldham, *Shrewsbury School*, pl. xviii; N Rauch, Catalogue 8 (1954), 40; Sotheby's, 5.xii.1955, *3a* (pl.) (arms of Henri III); E Kyriss, 'Pariser Einbände', *Börsenblatt für den deutschen Buchhandel*, 51 (June 1969), fig. 6, L2; For the Ève bindery see: Michon, pp. 79–84; Nixon, *Pierpont Morgan Library*, nos. 56, 57; Needham, *Twelve Centuries,* no. 94; Laffitte & Le Bars, p. 149.
Same tools on: BL, C.68.h.11, G.6455 (both for Henri III), C.29.f.16 (dated 1599), Add. MS 35221 (French devotional manuscript); Le Bars, 'Reliures Henri III', p. 239 (fig. 12).
Note: Nicolas Ève: mentioned as bookseller and bookbinder: 1560; succeeded Claude Picques as royal binder between August 1574 and November 1578; royal binder to Henri III; died: 1581. Clovis Ève, probably the son of Nicolas, worked: 1584–1634; royal binder to Henri IV and Louis XIII.

---

110   *A binding made in Paris, possibly for a member of the Congrégation des Pénitents, after 1583*

Liber Psalmorum et Hymni Ecclesiastici, Paris: G Chaudière, 1582. 8vo.

181 × 114 × 31 mm.   (P 1311) Davis, 447

Red goatskin over paste boards, tooled in silver (oxidized) with a line along the border and a central oval plaque depicting the Presentation of Christ in the Temple; lettered on the upper cover: A.MR.LEVESQVE.DE.CLERMONT./POVR.LEGLISE. Edges of boards and turn-ins: tooled in blind with lines. Edges: plain.

Sewn on four (recessed) cords, laced in through three holes; smooth spine, tooled in silver (oxidized) with lines, dividing the spine into compartments, in which a skull, a fleur-de-lis and the royal arms, and the motto: 'spes mea deus' [emblems and motto of the Congrégation des Pénitents or a similar confraternity]. Endbands: double with a bead; red and white silk over cord cores (laced in), tied down occasionally.

Endleaves: paper pastedowns and a pair of free conjugate paper leaves, and one free leaf (?)conjugate with the pastedown, at both ends.; at the end: a further, smaller, paper leaf tipped in.

PROVENANCE: Bishop and church of Clermont; on flyleaves in manuscript: prayers, psalms and litanies in Latin and French; bought: Paris, Pierre Berès, July 1956, *319A*.

LITERATURE: Michon, pp. 81–2; G D Hobson, *Fanfare*, pl. xix (nos. 225a, 226a: same spine tools); Hobson, *French and Italian*, no. 26; Culot, *La Reliure en France*, no. 62; see also Davis 510 (no. 111 below; and literature mentioned there).

Note: Davis 447 and 510 come from the same atelier (possibly Ève?). As well as the Congrégation des Pénitents, Henri III founded several other religious and penitential confraternities. It is possible that the emblems and motto on this (and many other) binding(s) denoted ownership by a member of one of these groups.

111 *A Paris binding, possibly made for Henri III or for a member of the Congrégation des Pénitents, c. 1584*

Heures de Nostre Dame, à l'usage de Rome, Paris: J Mettayer, 1584; ruled in red. 4to.

257 × 190 × 37 mm. (P 1077) Davis 510

Brown goatskin over paste boards, tooled in blind to a fanfare design with leafy sprays, small hatched tools and scroll tools; in the centre of the upper cover: an oval plaque depicting the Presentation of Christ in the Temple; in the centre of the lower cover: the arms of Henri III; crowned H in the corners. Edges of boards: tooled in blind with lines and dashes. Edges: plain.

Sewn on four (recessed) cords, laced in ; smooth spine, tooled in blind to a fanfare design with leafy sprays, small tools and a skull in the centre compartment. Endbands: double with a bead; beige silk over cord cores (cut off).

Endleaves: paper pastedowns and one free leaf conjugate with the pastedown, and a second free paper leaf, at both ends.

Repairs: at edges of boards and at joints.

PROVENANCE: (?)Henri III or a member of the Congrégation des Pénitents; J P F Double, Montpelier (book plate with: 'Doct. Med. Monsp.'); Baron Léopold Double (book plate; sold: *Catalogue des objets d'art, tableaux anciens, livres*, Paris, 30–31.v.1881, *livres*, 4); Monseigneur P M M Double, bishop of Tarbes (book plate, 1883); A Barbet (signature and in manuscript: '294–d'; sold: Paris, Giraud Badin, 1932, *100*); Lucius Wilmerding (sold: Parke-Bernet, 31.x.1951, *748*, pl.).

REFERENCES: M Michel, *La Reliure française*, Paris, 1881, p. 74; Hobson, *Additions et corrections*, p. 10*, no. 144a; Foot, *Revue française*, p. 379, note 27.

LITERATURE: Guigard, I, p. 18; Holmes, *Windsor*, pl. 83 (Paris, 1585); Hoe, *176 bindings*, pl. 72 (Paris,

111

                1576); Olivier, 2491; G D Hobson, *Fanfare*, pls xvi, xix, p. 29, fig. 38a, pp. 51–5, nos. 102, 139, 145a, 175, 192, 225a, 226a (all Paris, 1576–1611); Michon, pp. 79–83; Nixon, *Pierpont Morgan Library*, nos. 55, 56; Needham, *Twelve Centuries*, no. 82; see also Davis 447 (no. 110 above; with the same plaque and the same skull tool).

Compare: Le Bars, 'Reliures Henri III', p. 242 (fig. 15).
Note: Henri III (1551–1589) founded the Congrégation des Pénitents de l'Annonciation Notre-Dame: 1583. It is possible that this binding was made for Henri III by Clovis Ève.

---

112   *A Breton binding, c. 1584*

B d'Argentré, *Coustumes generalles du pays et duché de Bretagne*, Paris: I Dupuys, 1584; ruled in red. 4to.

244 × 168 × 30 mm.   (P 1045) Davis 511

Brown calf over (very thick) paste boards, tooled in gold to a corner and centre design, with large hatched corner blocks, fleurs-de-lis and ermine tools, scroll tools along the sides; a semis of stars; a centre piece composed of scroll tools, flowers, fleurons, lotus tools and dots around the painted arms of the Kergounadech family; decorated with black paint. Traces of two pairs of ties. Edges of boards: tooled in gold with s-shaped tools. Edges: gilt and gauffered to a diaper pattern with fleurons (or stylized flowers).

112

Sewn on five recessed cords, laced in; smooth spine, tooled in gold with at head and tail: s-shaped tools; lines dividing the spine into compartments and strips, filled with egg-and-dart roll; fleurons, hatched tools, curls, lines forming a knot; dots. Endbands: remnant of red and blue silk tie-downs at front and back.

Endleaves: paper pastedowns and a pair of free conjugate paper leaves, at both ends; at the end: a free leaf conjugate with the pastedown. Printed waste beneath the pastedowns.

Repairs: at joints and corners near tail of spine, at tail of spine; head of spine: renewed.

PROVENANCE: Kergounadech family (Brittany); on title-page in manuscript: 'T'APARTIEN S[fermé] A SS[two S fermés]/ ESCVIER FR:DE LANGAN' (in smaller script:) 'SR. DÉSTIVAL'; arms of Brittany (drawn in ink); on pastedown of lower cover in manuscript: 'In Mundo Lumen Accipit Claudine fèr(?)la Sancti-Remigi-/Episcopi, dies lune primi Octob. Undecima quasi Nocte/ Hora. Anno Grat. Milegesi Sexagesim. Septim. [1607] ED [monogram] S[four S fermés]'; Gramont (sold: Paris, 18.xii.1933, *22*); Lucius Wilmerding (book plate; sold: Parke-Bernet, 29.x.1951, *44*).

LITERATURE: Olivier, 2006, 1164; Hobson, *French and Italian*, no. 25.

160

113 *A binding made for Henri, king of Navarre, c. 1585*

P de Mornay, *De la verité de la religion chrestienne*, Paris: C Micard, 1585; dedicated to Henri, Roy de Navarre. 8vo.

174 × 112 × 37 mm. (P 1314) Davis 448

Red goatskin over paste boards, tooled in gold to a panel design with a single and a double fillet and a dotted line along the border and also outlining the panel; a double fillet and two dotted lines connecting the corners of the panel with those of the border. In the centre of the upper cover a monogram: HRR and four S fermés; in the centre of the lower cover two interlaced Ωs and five S fermés. Edges of boards: tooled in gold with a line. Edges: plain.

Sewn on four (recessed) cords, laced in through three holes; smooth spine, tooled in gold with lines and dots; title lettered in gold. Endbands: double with a bead; blue and (faded) pink silk over alum-tawed main core (was laced in), tied down occasionally; cord crowning core (laced in).

Endleaves: paper pastedowns at both ends; at the front: a pair of free conjugate paper leaves; at the end: two free paper leaves (conjugacy uncertain) and a third free paper leaf.

Repairs: small repairs at corners and at head and tail of spine.

PROVENANCE: Henri, king of Navarre (later Henri IV); bought: Breslauer, 23.iv.1957.
LITERATURE: Guigard, p. 22; G D Hobson, *Fanfare*, pp. 85–96, esp. p. 88; A Cioranescu, 'La reliure à l'esclave au XVIIe siècle', *Francia*, 3rd series, 17 (1976), pp. 34–9 (for a new interpretation of the S fermé).
Note: Henri of Navarre (1553–1610), son of Antoine de Bourbon, married Marguerite, daughter of Henri II: 1572; king of Navarre: 1572; became Henri IV, king of France: 1594; married Marie de' Medici: 1600. The S fermé, a common French device, at one time interpreted by G D Hobson as 'fermesse', symbolizing loyalty, but more recently believed to stand for 's-clavo', 'esclavo', indicating the user of the symbol to be a slave to love.

114

114 *A Paris fanfare binding, c. 1586*

Le Pseaultier de David, Paris: I Mettayer, 1586; ruled in red. 4to.

287 × 205 × 40 mm. (P 998) Davis 400

Brown goatskin over paste boards, tooled in gold to a fanfare design with gouges, leafy sprays, solid and hatched tools, fleurons and flower tools; in the corners a St Esprit tool. Edges of boards: tooled in gold with lines and dashes. Edges: gilt.

   Sewn on five (recessed) cords, laced in through three holes; smooth spine, tooled in gold to a fanfare design with leafy sprays, fleurons, flower tools and St Esprit tools. Endbands: double with a bead; primary sewing over (?)cord cores (cut off), tied down; secondary sewing of red and grey silk.

   Endleaves: paper pastedowns and one free leaf conjugate with the pastedown and one free paper leaf tipped on, at both ends.

PROVENANCE: Robert Samuel Turner (book plate); comte de Sauvage; Lebeuf de Montgermont; E Rahir (sold: *La Bibliothèque de feu Edouard Rahir*, 6 vols, Paris, 1930–8, vol. iv, 1936, *1028*, pl.); Lucius Wilmerding (book plate; sold: Parke-Bernet, 6.iii.1951, *524*).

LITERATURE: G D Hobson, *Fanfare*, pp. 28–9 (figs 18b, 28), 61 (figs 49e, 49kk, 49j); pls vii, viii, xi, xva, xxib, xxxiv).

Some same tools on: Quaritch, Catalogue December 1921, *110*.

162

115

115 *A Paris binding for J-A de Thou, after 1587*

B Ochino, *Prediche; Sermones; Epistola; Responsio* [8 works bound together], n.p. and Geneva: J Bourgeois, 1542–4 [and] Hieronymus Lucensis, *Epistola ad Bern. Ochinum Senensem*, Geneva: I Girardus, 1543. 8vo.

142/48 × 85 × 65 mm.   (P 574) Davis 449

A Greek-style binding of red goatskin over wooden boards, tooled in gold to a panel design with lines, small flower tools at the corners of the panel, and in the centre the arms of J-A de Thou within a wreath formed by leafy sprays. Two pairs of clasps with plaited leather straps, hinging on the upper cover, fastening on two pins protruding from the edge of the lower board. Edges of boards: grooved; tooled in gold with a line. Edges: gilt.

Sewn on four (recessed) cords, laced in; smooth spine with raised headcaps, tooled in gold with lines and IAM monograms (the monogram used by de Thou after his marriage to Marie de Barbançon); title lettered on spine (later). Greek-style endbands: two sets: single with a bead and double with a bead, extending well over the edges of the boards; primary sewing (cores invisible, laced in), tied down; secondary sewing of blue and pink silk.

Endleaves: parchment pastedowns and two pairs of free conjugate paper leaves, quired, plus one free parchment leaf, conjugate with the pastedown, at both ends.

PROVENANCE: Jacques-Auguste de Thou; Rohan-Soubise library (on pastedown in manuscript: '3.C.P.T.2.N.38'); on pastedown (in red ink): '3893'; on endleaf in manuscript: 'Belti[?o or ?e] (?)Greyshire 761'; bought: Quaritch, 2.xii.1942.

REFERENCES: Foot, *Revue française*, p. 379, note 28.

LITERATURE: G D Hobson, *Fanfare*, pp. 79–80; Hobson, *French and Italian*, pp. xviii–ix, no. 24; Bodley, *Exhibition*, nos. 84–5; Nixon, *Pierpont Morgan Library*, no. 59; Needham, *Twelve Centuries*, no. 95; Toulet, 'Les reliures', p. 538; A Coron, 'Notes sur les cotes dites de la

	bibliothèque de Thou', *Bulletin du bibliophile*, 1982, pp. 339–57; A Coron, '"Ut prosint aliis": Jacques-Auguste de Thou et sa bibliothèque', in: C Jolly (ed.), *Histoire des bibliothèques françaises: Les bibliothèques sous l'Ancien Régime 1530–1789*, Paris, 1988, pp. 101–26.
Note:	Jacques-Auguste de Thou (1553–1617); married Marie de Barbançon: 1587; Gasparde de la Chastre: 1601. The small arms block as found on Davis 449 was used by de Thou while he was still a bachelor, and it occurs frequently on fanfare bindings for de Thou; also on: e.g. BL, C.19.a.8, C.19.a.33, C.19.b.10–16, C.19.f.23, C.65.a.18–19, C.68.f.9; the combination of the bachelor arms and the married cipher is also found on other small books, e.g. BL, G.9407, probably because no arms block of de Thou impaling that of his first wife exists that is small enough to fit.
	The 'cote' was added after 1789, when de Thou's books ended up in the Rohan-Soubise library. The present 'cote' indicates that this book was in room 3, case 2, shelf N (A started at the bottom), no. 38 on the shelf.

116 *A Paris binding for Pietro Duodo, c. 1594–7*

St Ambrosius, *Officiorum libri iii*, Paris: S Nivellius, 1583, 16mo [and] Epictetus, *Enchiridion*, Antwerp: C Plantin, 1585, 16mo [and] Boethius, *De consolatione philosophiae libri*, Leiden: Plantin, 1590, 12mo [and] I L Vives, *Excitationes animi in Deum*, Lyon: S Gryphius, 1556, 16mo; ruled in red.

127 × 78 × 35 mm. (P 278) Davis 450

Red goatskin over paste boards, tooled in gold to an all-over design, with a border framed with lines and filled with leafy sprays; the centre panel filled with leafy ovals containing naturalistic flowers; in the centre of the upper cover the arms of Pietro Duodo; in the centre of the lower cover: three lilies with Duodo's motto: EXPECTATA.NON ELVDET. Edges of boards: tooled in gold with a line. Edges: gilt.

Sewn on three (recessed) cords, laced in through three holes; smooth spine, tooled in gold with a border with leafy sprays and a centre strip of leafy ovals, two containing a flower and three containing the titles. Endbands: double with a bead; primary sewing over (?)cord cores (cut off), tied down; secondary sewing of white and pink silk.

Endleaves: paper pastedowns and a pair of free conjugate paper leaves and a free leaf, conjugate with the pastedown, at both ends (conjugacy uncertain at the end). Manuscript strengthener visible beneath pastedown of lower cover.

Repairs: small repairs at head and tail joints.

PROVENANCE:	Pietro Duodo; Thomas Brooke, FSA, Armitage Bridge (book plate); Paul Hirsch (book plate); bought: Heffer, 29.ix.1941.
REFERENCES:	Romme, *Book Collector*, 1969, p. 25, note 9; Foot, *Revue française*, p. 379, note 29; Foot, *Mirror*, fig. 71.
LITERATURE:	L Bouland, 'Livres aux armes de Pierre Duodo, Vénitien, et non pas de Marguerite de Valois', *Bulletin du bibliophile*, 1920, pp. 68–80; G D Hobson, *Fanfare*, pp. 70–1; Hobson, *French and Italian*, p. xviii, no. 30; Bodley, *Exhibition*, nos. 92–4; G Barber and D Rogers, 'Bindings from Oxford libraries II: A "Duodo" pastiche binding by C Lewis', *Bodleian*

116 117

Library Record, viii.3 (February 1969), pp. 138–44; Nixon, *Pierpont Morgan Library*, pp. 233–4; R Esmerian, 'Trois reliures aux armes de Duodo 1554–1611', Esmerian sale I, Paris, 6.vi.1972, pp. 94–6; Needham, *Twelve Centuries*, no. 98; Culot, *La Reliure en France*, no. 66; Schäfer, p. 72; Christie's, 18.iii.1998, *215*.

Compare: (for very similar bindings) e.g. BL, C.19.a.15, C.19.a.19, C.69.bb.18.
Note: Pietro Duodo: Venetian ambassador to Henri IV of France: 1594–7. Duodo, who had his books bound in Paris, chose colours for the bindings that denoted their contents. Red was used for theology (as in Davis 450), philosophy, law and history. Davis 450 could have been part of a travelling library. Esmerian attributed bindings for Duodo to Clovis Ève.

---

117 *A Paris binding, c. 1596*

Heures de Nostre Dame a l'usage de Rome, Paris: for A L'Angelier, 1584 [and other prayers; engravings added] [and] *Le Formulaire des prières*, Paris: G Buon, 1596; ruled in red. 8vo.

178 × 115 × 58 mm.   (P 1018) Davis 451

Brown goatskin over paste boards, tooled in gold and silver, with a border framed by lines and filled with leafy sprays, corner pieces built up of small hatched and solid tools; in the centre a fanfare ornament with flower tools, fleurons, hatched tools, gouges and dots around a central oval, cut out and filled with parchment, painted with, on the upper cover: the head of Christ (in profile), on the lower cover: the head of Mary. Edges of boards: tooled in gold with some very small tools. Edges: gilt.

165

Sewn on four (recessed) cords, laced in; smooth spine, tooled in gold and silver with curl and flower tools and a fanfare centre ornament with curl tools, flowers and pears. Endbands: double with a bead; white (beige?) and silver thread over cord cores (cut off), tied down.

Endleaves: paper pastedowns at both ends; at the front: a pair of free conjugate paper leaves and a free leaf conjugate with the pastedown; at the end: a free leaf conjugate with the pastedown.

Repairs: at the upper joint and at corners of covers and spine.

PROVENANCE: Grace Whitney Hoff (with manuscript note by L Gruel pasted onto the pastedown of upper cover); bought: A Rau, 28.v.1951.
REFERENCES: Whitney Hoff, no. 101, pl. xliii (lower cover).

118 *A late sixteenth- or early seventeenth-century binding*

[Blank book with a set of 14 plates by Lucas van Leyden, signed 'L 1521', depicting the Passion, pasted in]. large 4to.

265 × 188 × 15 mm. (P 905) Davis 513

Brown goatskin over paste boards, tooled in gold with a border made with lines, small quatrefoils and dots; the covers filled with various kinds of large leafy sprays; a double fillet running down (part of) the centre of the covers. Remnants of two pairs of brown silk ties. Edges of boards: tooled in gold with dots. Edges: gilt.

Sewn on four (invisible, probably recessed) supports, laced in; smooth spine, tooled in gold with leafy sprays. Endbands: single with a bead; red and grey silk over alum-tawed cores (cut off), tied down occasionally.

Endleaves: coloured (red, blue, green, yellow) feather-marbled pastedowns at both ends.

PROVENANCE: Gancia collection (sold: Paris, 27.iv.1868, *225*); W H Corfield (book plate; sold: Sotheby's, 21.xi.1904, *215*, pl.); C W Dyson Perrins (book plate; sold: Sotheby's, 9.ii.1948, *242*, pl.); bought: Quaritch, 7.vi.1948.
REFERENCES: Quaritch, Catalogue 657 (1948), *171* (pl.).
Compare: (similar spine decoration) Sotheby's, 30.v.1938 (Ham House sale), *55* (Paris, 1547, with the arms of Louis XIII); G D Hobson, *Fanfare*, pl. xxx (Paris, [1584]); Oldham, *Shrewsbury School*, pl. xviii (Venice, 1581).

119 *A binding, possibly made in Paris, c. 1609*

Th.A.I.C. [Morton Eudes], *Tradition catholique ou traicté de la croyance des chrestiens d'Asie, d'Europe, d'Afrique*, [Paris], 1609. Dedicated to Henry, Prince of Wales; dedication signed in manuscript: 'Marsan'; ruled in red. 8vo.

167 × 104 × 23 mm. (P 1056) Davis 452

Red goatskin over paste boards, tooled in gold with a border outlined with lines and filled with alternating rampant lions and leopards. Traces of two pairs of ties. Edges: gilt and gauffered, with traces of paint.

118 119

Sewn on four alum-tawed supports, laced in (parallel to the spine); smooth spine, tooled in gold with alternating rampant lions and leopards. Endbands: double with a bead; pink and blue silk over leather cores (cut off), tied down.

Endleaves: paper pastedowns and two pairs of free conjugate paper leaves (quired inside each other), and one free leaf conjugate with the pastedown, at both ends.

Repairs: at head and tail of spine and at corners of covers.

PROVENANCE: On endleaf in manuscript: 'Jos: Brereton', followed by six pages of notes about this book and its author (said to be Marsan), quoting from a letter from Sir George Carew to Henry Prince of Wales, dated 4 March 1608 (Harl. MS 7007) to show that 'This Copy was probably the very Dedication Book or a Present to Sir George Carew, or the Earl of Salisbury'; (at the end:) five more pages of notes in the same hand repeating the same information; on endleaf in manuscript: 'Moira. London Jan y 26.1789—'; Thomas Brooke, FSA, Armitage Bridge (book plate); library label with: 'HHi'; Lucius Wilmerding (book plate; sold: Parke-Bernet, 30.x.1951, *325*).

LITERATURE: T Birch, *The Life of Prince Henry*, London, 1760, pp. 146–8 (where a letter from Sir George Carew, ambassador in Paris, 1605–9, to the Prince of Wales is quoted, in which he sends a book on Christian religion, dedicated to the Prince, with a recommendation. Carew claimed to have met the author of the book, 'his name is Marsam, which in his printed subscription he dissembleth'. The letter is dated Paris, 4 March, 1608).

Note: The author of Davis 452 is Th.A.I.C [= Morton Eudes]; the dedication to Henry prince of Wales is signed in print: 'TH.A' and in manuscript: 'Marsan', the imprint date is 1609 (new style), while Carew may have followed the old style (Julian Calendar) still in use in England. Carew's arms are three leopards; it is possible that Carew had this copy bound in Paris for Henry, prince of Wales, before sending it.

120 *Possibly a prize binding for the Collège de Lyon, with the arms of Charles de Neufville Halincourt, c. 1615*

St Bernardus (of Clairvaux), *Expositio in cantica canticorum*, Lyon: Iuncta, 1588. 16mo.

122 × 74 × 38 mm. (P 979) Davis 453

Brown goatskin over paste boards, tooled in gold with lines, small corner curls, a semis of 'croix ancrées' and in the centre the arms of Charles de Neufville Halincourt, duc de Villeroy, marquis d'Alaincourt; near the top and bottom edge of both covers the cipher of the Collège de Lyon: λλ and cc interlaced. Traces of two pairs of ties. Edges of boards: tooled in gold with dots. Edges: gilt.

Sewn on four (recessed) cords, laced in; smooth spine, tooled in gold with two small rolls, lines and the cipher of the Collège de Lyon, as well as 'croix ancrées'. Endbands: double with a bead; yellow and blue silk over (?)alum-tawed cores (cut off), tied down. Green silk bookmarker.

Endleaves: paper pastedowns and one free leaf conjugate with the pastedown, at both ends.

PROVENANCE: Charles de Neufville Halincourt; (?)Collège de Lyon [no sign of prize inscription]; Mr J Renard (book plate, in manuscript: 'no 34 du 2e catal. Mai 1884'); Joseph Nouvellet [of] St André de Covey (Ain) (book plate); Lucius Wilmerding (book plate; sold: Parke-Bernet, 5.iii.1951, *91*).
LITERATURE: Guigard, II, 379–80; Olivier, 172; Labarre, *Revue française*, pp. 477–88.
Same arms on: BL, C.47.d.2 (Lyon, 1620); (arms and cipher:) Esmerian sale II, Paris, 8.xii.1972, *74* (where the cipher is said to be that of Charles de Neufville Halincourt).
Note: Charles de Neufville Halincourt, duc de Villeroy, marquis d'Alaincourt (1566–1642), 'prévost des marchands' of Paris: 1592; governor of Lyon: 1608; marquis de Villeroy: 1615. French prize bindings of the 17th century were often elaborately tooled and could bear the arms of the benefactor of the school.

121 *An embroidered binding for Marie de' Medici, c. 1615*

Jean de Loyac, *L'Euphème des François et leur homonie*, Bordeaux: S Millanges, 1615; ruled in red. 4to.

250 × 180 × 37 mm. (P 336) Davis 514

Purple velvet over paste boards, embroidered with gold and silver thread and coloured silks, with a fleur-de-lis or a crowned M in the corners and in the centre the crowned arms of Marie de' Medici, wife of Henri IV of France. Edges: gilt and gauffered to a fanfare design and painted with red and blue flowers.

Sewn on four (?recessed) cords, laced in; smooth spine, embroidered with silver thread and silk with fleurs-de-lis. Endbands: double with a bead; metallic blue and pale blue silk over alum-tawed cores (cut off), tied down.

Endleaves: green silk doublures and one free green silk leaf (backed) conjugate with the doublure, at both ends; at the front: two pairs of free conjugate paper leaves and one free leaf conjugate with the backing paper; at the end: three pairs of free conjugate paper leaves.

Repairs: at spine and corners.

PROVENANCE: Marie de' Medici (with a letter from Marie de' Medici to her cousin Cardinal d'Este, dated Paris, 15 February 1603; and another letter on parchment, dated Blois, 10 January 1618, signed by Marie de' Medici and Phelypeaux); Samuel Putnam Avery (book plate; sold: New York, Anderson Galleries, 10–12.xi.1919, *618*, pl.); Cortlandt F Bishop (two book plates; sold: New York, American Art Association, Anderson Galleries, April–November 1938, *1384*); bought: Sawyer, 27.xi.1941.

REFERENCES: Grolier Club, *Catalogue of books from the libraries or collections of celebrated bibliophiles and illustrious patrons of the past*, New York, 1895, no. 62; *Treasures*, 1965, no. 79; Romme, *Book Collector*, 1969, p. 24, note 5, pl. iia; Foot, *Revue française*, p. 379, note 30; S Coron and M Lefèvre, *Livres en broderie*, Paris, 1996, no. 21; Conihout & Ract-Madoux, p. 18.

LITERATURE: H Bouchot, *Les Reliures d'art à la Bibliothèque Nationale*, Paris, 1888, pl. lviii (a similarly bound copy of the same book for Louis XIII); Guigard, I, p. 94; R Grannis, 'Jewelled and embroidered bookbindings at the Grolier Club', *Bulletin of the Needle and Bobbin Club*, April 1920, pp. 19–23; S Coron and M Lefèvre, *Livres en broderie*, Paris, 1996, pp. 61–3.

Note: Marie de' Medici (1573–1642) married Henri IV of France as his second wife:1600; Louis XIII was her son.

122

122 *A Paris binding, c. 1616–20*

L'Office de la Vierge Marie, Paris: I Laquehay, 1616; ruled in red. 8vo.

186 × 110 × 38 mm. (P 1315) Davis 454

Brown goatskin over paste boards, tooled in gold to an all-over design of small lozenges with parallel horizontal or vertical lines. (?)Traces of two pairs of ties. Edges of boards: tooled in gold with dots. Edges: gilt.

Sewn on three (recessed) cords, laced in; smooth spine, tooled in gold to an all-over design of lozenges. Endbands: double with a bead; pink and blue silk over alum-tawed cores (cut off), tied down; crowning core of (?)tanned leather.

Endleaves: paper pastedowns and a pair of free conjugate paper leaves and one free leaf conjugate with the pastedown, at both ends.

Repairs: at covers and corner of upper cover.

PROVENANCE: Bought: Breslauer, 11.ii.1957.
Note: An all-over pattern of lozenges with parallel lines (vertical or horizontal), alternating with fleurons, is found quite commonly on French bindings of the first quarter of the 17th century, e.g. Lucien Graux sale (Paris, Charpentier, 26.i.1937, *87*: Antwerp, 1622); Breslauer, Catalogue 87 (1957), *118*, pl. vi (Paris, 1621–3); Breslauer, Catalogue 92 (1960), *107A* (Antwerp, 1622); Lardanchet, Catalogue 55 (1962), *125* (15th-century manuscript); Folger Catalogue, p. 199; Davis 516 (no.126 below: spine).

170

123

123 *A binding, possibly made in Paris, c. 1620*

N Caussin, *De symbolica Aegyptiorum sapientia (Polyhistor symbolicus, electorum symbolorum, et parabolarum historicarum stromata)*, [with an additional title-page, (engraved): *Electorum symbolorum et parabolarum historicarum syntagmata*], Paris: R de Beauvais, 1618. 4to.

246 × 175 × 57 mm. (P 1101) Davis 515

Citron goatskin over paste boards, tooled in gold to a panel design with an ornamental border with lines and small tools; fleurons at the corners of the panel, the panel outlined with lines and two small rolls; fleurons and quarter fans in the corners; fleurons, circular fans, various small tools, with in the centre an oval fan built up of segments and small tools. Traces of two pairs of red ties. Edges of boards: tooled in gold with dots. Edges: gilt.

Sewn on five (recessed) cords, laced in; smooth spine, tooled in gold with a small border, triangular and diamond-shaped ornaments, oval fan and various small solid tools. Endbands: double with a bead; pink and blue silk over cord cores (cut off), tied down.

Endleaves: paper pastedowns and a pair of free conjugate paper leaves, at both ends; at the front: one free leaf conjugate with the pastedown; at the end: one free paper leaf conjugate with a stub pasted to the pastedown, plus the remnant of a free leaf (that was) conjugate with the pastedown.

Repairs: at head and tail of spine.

PROVENANCE: On endleaf: manuscript notes in French (about the author) and English (about the edition); label with in manuscript: '1276'; bought: Quaritch, 21.iv.1952.
Compare: (French 17th-century fan designs) G D Hobson, *Thirty bindings*, pl. xix; Lardanchet, Catalogue 45 (1951), *1032* (Paris, 1609); Devaux, p. 130; Davis 516 (no. 126 below).

124

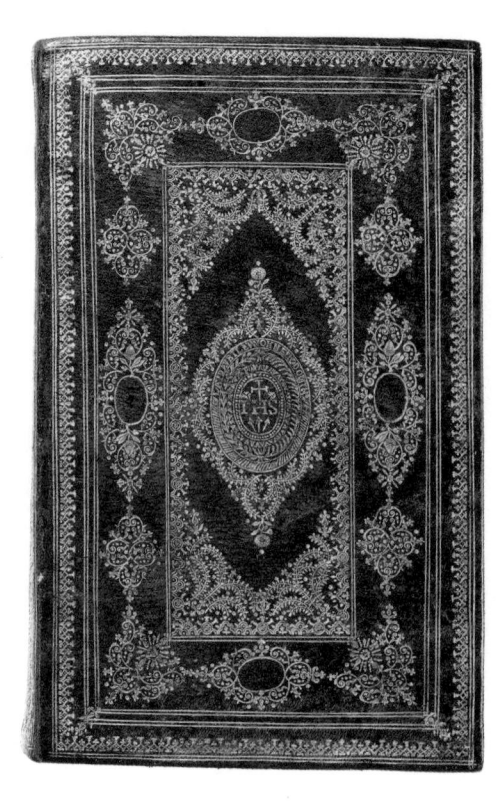

124 *A Paris binding, c. 1621*

Titus Livius, *Romanae historiae*, Lyon: P Marniolles for T Soubron, 1621. 4to.

252 × 160 × 61 mm. (P 1316) Davis 517

Brown goatskin over paste boards, tooled in gold to a panel design with lines, a small roll along the outer border, ornaments composed of solid tools (curls, acorns) in the inner border; a small roll inside the panel; in the corners: leafy sprays, and in the centre, surrounded by leafy sprays and with a flower tool above and below, on the upper cover: the Sacred Monogram surrounded by the legend: LAVDABILE IN OMNE DOMINE[?I], on the lower cover: the arms of Louis XIII of France. Traces of two pairs of ties. Edges: gilt.

Sewn on four (invisible) supports, laced in; smooth spine, tooled in gold to a (long) panel design with lines, a small border roll, corner ornaments built up of solid curl tools and fleurons, and a central ornament built up of solid curl tools and small solid tools. Endbands: single with a bead; blue and white silk over (?)alum-tawed cores (cut off), tied down.

Endleaves: paper pastedowns at both ends; at the front: two free paper leaves (pasted together at the joint); at the end: one free leaf conjugate with the pastedown.

PROVENANCE: Cortlandt F Bishop (book plate; sold: New York, American Art Association, Anderson Galleries, 25.iv.1938, *1336*); M Bridel (Catalogue 11: *Beaux livres XIV–XIX*, 1950, *124*, pl.); bought: Breslauer, 4.vii.1959 (Catalogue 88, *66*, pl. iv).
REFERENCES: *Dix siècles de livres français*, exh. cat., Musée des Beaux-Arts, Lucerne, 1949, *363*.
LITERATURE: Olivier, 2493.
Note: Louis XIII (1601–1643).

172

125

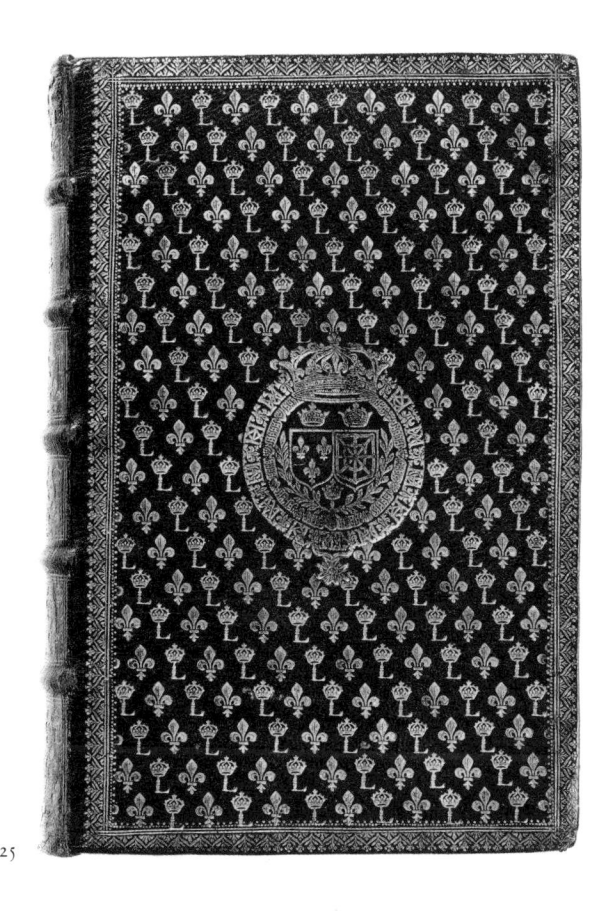

125   *A Paris binding with the arms and cipher of Louis XIII, c. 1621*

Titus Livius, *Romanae historiae*, Lyon: P Marniolles for T Soubron, 1621. 4to.

246 × 165 × 66 mm. (P 225) Davis 518

Red goatskin over paste boards, tooled in gold with lines, dots and a zig-zag roll forming the border, a semis of crowned Ls and fleurs-de-lis, and in the centre the arms of Louis XIII of France. Edges of boards: tooled in gold with a zig-zag roll. Edges: gilt.

Sewn on five cords, laced in, showing as raised bands on the spine, tooled in gold, six compartments, tooled in gold with lines, dots and a semis of fleurs-de-lis and crowned Ls; title lettered in second compartment. Endbands: double with a bead; pink and white silk over cord cores (cut off), tied down.

Endleaves: comb-marbled pastedowns and one free comb-marbled leaf conjugate with a stub pasted beneath the pastedown, at both ends; at the front: one free white paper leaf conjugate with a stub; at the end: a pair of free conjugate white paper leaves.

PROVENANCE: On endleaf in manuscript: '12 tt'; bought: Sotheby's, 11.viii.1941, *193*.
REFERENCES: Foot, *Revue française*, p. 379.
LITERATURE: Guigard, I, pp. 22–4; Olivier, 2493; Michon, pp. 82–3 (Clovis Ève: royal binder to Henri IV and Louis XIII); E Ader, *Bibliothèque d'un humaniste*, Paris, Hôtel Drouot, 1966, no. 93, pl. VII (marriage contract of Louis XIII and Anne of Austria); see also Davis 517 (no. 124 above).

THE HENRY DAVIS GIFT

126 *A prize binding given by Antoine de Leoncourt, c. 1622–3*

Petrus Faber, *Agnosticon*, Lyon: T Soubron & Mosis a Pratis, 1595. 4to.

248 × 156 × 42 mm. (P 1195) Davis 516

Brown goatskin over paste boards, tooled in gold to a panel design with three borders made with lines, two sun rolls and repeated circles-and-square tools. A stylized flower and quarter fans in the corners; in the centre the arms of Antoine de Leoncourt, 'abbé commendataire' of Beaupré, primate of Nancy, surrounded by the sun roll. Traces of two pairs of ties. Edges of boards: tooled in gold with dots. Edges: gilt.

Sewn on five (recessed) cords, laced in; smooth spine, tooled in gold to an over-all pattern of striped lozenges and solid tools. Endbands: single with a bead; white and blue silk over alum-tawed cores (cut off), tied down.

Endleaves: paper pastedowns at both ends; at the front: one pair of free conjugate paper leaves; at the end: one free paper leaf.

Repairs: small repairs at both covers.

PROVENANCE: Joannes Mahuet, prize given by Antoine de Leoncourt at the Jesuit College of Pont-à-Mousson (on endleaf in manuscript: 'Ex liberalitate & munificientia (…?) ac Reverendissime Domini D. Antonii a Lenoncourt S.R.J. Comitis a Lotharingia Primatis Joannis Mahuet quod primas orationis solutae Latinae in Tertia anno 1622 tulisset. Hoc libro in praemium publice donatus est anno 1623.'); below this: a piece of paper with the impression of the seal of the Jesuit College of Pont-à-Mousson, pasted on; in a different hand: 'Ita est Carolus Sanesin (?) Soc[ietat]is Jesu studiorum in collegio Mussipontano praefixtus'; a signature in a different hand: erased; Villers, Off[ici]er D'artillerie (library label); bought: Karl & Faber, 12.v.1955, *466*.

LITERATURE: Guigard, I, 310; Olivier, 875; Labarre, *Revue française*, pp. 477–88.

Compare: Hoe, *176 Bindings*, pl. 85 (Paris, 1620) (?same sun roll); G D Hobson, *Thirty bindings*, pl. xxii; Lardanchet, Catalogue 45 (1951), *1032* (Paris, 1609) (similar fans, not identical); Davis and Orioli, Catalogue 146 (1953), *22* (similar fans, not identical); for spine tools: Davis 454 (no. 122 above).

Note: Antoine de Leoncourt, primate of Nancy: 1607; primate of Lorraine; died: 1636; Mussipontanus: Pont-à-Mousson (on the Moselle).

127 *A binding, probably made in Paris, c. 1630*

P Bertius, *De aggeribus et pontibus hactenus ad mare exstructis digestum novum*, Paris: I Libert, 1629; ruled in red. 8vo.

178 × 110 × 21 mm. (P 203) Davis 456

Red goatskin over paste boards, tooled in gold with lines along the border and a semis of fleurs-de-lis. Edges of boards: tooled in gold with dots. Edges: gilt.

Sewn on three (recessed) cords, laced in; smooth spine, tooled in gold with lines along the edges and a semis of fleurs-de-lis (a size smaller than those used on the covers). Endbands: double with a bead; white and blue silk over rolled alum-tawed cores (cut off), tied down; cord crowning cores.

126   127

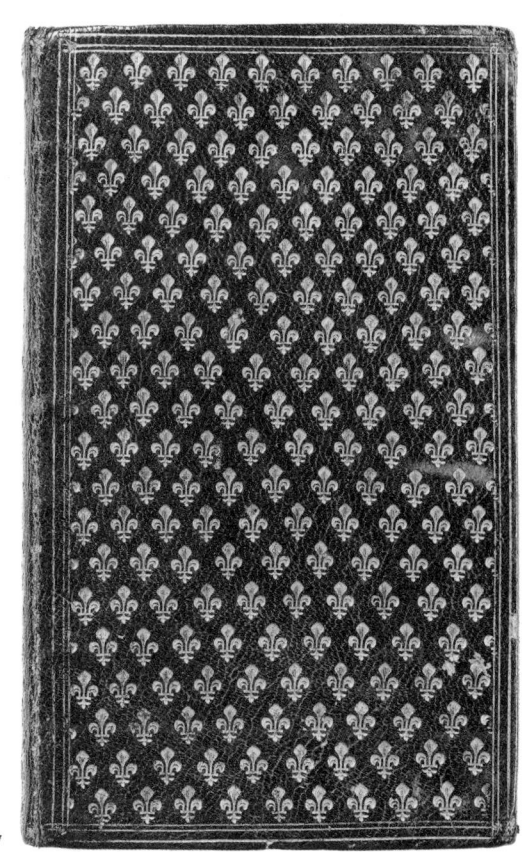

Endleaves: comb-marbled pastedowns at both ends; at the front: one free white paper leaf and a pair of conjugate white paper leaves; at the end: two pairs of free conjugate white paper leaves (quired).

PROVENANCE: H Gordon Selfridge (sold: Sotheby's, 11.viii.1941, *15*).
LITERATURE: Hobson, *French and Italian*, no. 33, p. 65; Esmerian sale II, Paris, 8.xii.1972, nos. 48–50; Oddos, *Revue française*, p. 552, fig. 15; Schäfer, p. 76.

---

128 *A late fanfare binding probably made in Paris, c. 1634*

Speculum poenitentiae, Paris, 1634; MS on parchment, written by Pierre Bierri; decorated title-page; gilt frames to text; initials in red; octagonal book.

145 × 140 × 36 mm.   (M 46) Davis 455

Red goatskin over paste boards, tooled in gold to a fanfare design with gouges and small (mainly) solid tools. Edges of boards: tooled in gold with a small zig-zag roll; turn-ins: tooled in gold with a small half-circles roll. Edges: gilt.

Sewn on two (?)alum-tawed supports, laced in; smooth spine (70 mm. high), tooled in gold to a fanfare design. Endbands: double with a bead; pink and blue silk over (?)alum-tawed cores (cut off), tied down.

Endleaves: multi-coloured fine comb-marbled pastedowns at both ends.

175

128

PROVENANCE: Claude Colurieu [?Colurien]; Pierre Huberdeau (on last blank parchment leaf in manuscript: 'Pierre Huberdeau a eu ces heures du Sr. Claude Colurieu [?Colurien] en l annee 1660 Elles ont este escrites de la main de Pierre Bierri bourgeois de paris en 1634. S' [fermé]); bought: Léon Gruel, 14.v.1954.
LITERATURE: G D Hobson, *Fanfare*, pp. 55–7, compare pls. xiiib, xviii, xix.
Spine tool: See Davis 458, 463 (nos. 132, 134 below).

129 *A late fanfare binding, made in Aix-en-Provence by Simeon Corberan for Nicolas-Claude Fabri de Peiresc, c. 1635*

J A Petramellarius, *Ad librum Onuphrii Panvinii de summis pontiff[icis] et S.R.E. cardinalibus ... continuatio*, Bologna: Haeredes I Rossi, 1599. 4to.

234 × 160 × 50 mm. (P 1332) Davis 519

Red goatskin over paste boards, tooled in gold to a fanfare design with gouges, leafy sprays, wreaths with feurs-de-lis, flowers, birds, small fleurons and dots; in the centre the cipher of N-C Fabri de Peiresc. Edges: painted with chevrons in red.

Sewn on four split alum-tawed supports, laced in, showing as raised bands on the spine, tooled in gold with a line; five compartments, tooled in gold with lines, and a flower with bird tool; title lettered in second compartment. Endbands: single with a bead; pink and blue silk over alum-tawed cores (cut off), tied down.

Endleaves: paper pastedowns and one free paper leaf (at the end: conjugate with the pastedown), at both ends. Parchment manuscript strengthener.

PROVENANCE: Nicolas-Claude Fabri de Peiresc (his cipher stamped on the title-page); in manuscript: '719'; 'H 1672'; label with: '341', 'R29'; J R Abbey (book plate; 'J.A. 4797/5.4:1950'; sold: Sotheby's, 23.vi.1965, *540*).
REFERENCES: N Rauch, Catalogue I (1948), *108*; Hobson, *French and Italian*, no. 36; Hobson, *Additions et corrections*, no. 168b.
LITERATURE: G D Hobson, *Fanfare*, p. 28, fig. 21, pp. 24, 40, no. 191; Michon, pp. 88–9; J-M Arnoult,

129

'Peiresc et ses livres', in: C. Jolly (ed.), *Histoire des bibliothèques françaises. Les Bibliothèques sous l'Ancien Régime*, Paris [c. 1988], pp. 128–9; J-M Arnoult, 'Catalogue du fonds Peiresc de la Bibliothèque municipale de Châlons-sur-Marne', in: *Mémoires de la Société d'agriculture, commerce, sciences et arts du département de la Marne*, 89 (1974), pp. 149–205, 90 (1975), pp. 131–84, 94 (1979), pp. 153–73; J-M Arnoult, 'Les livres de Peiresc dans les bibliothèques parisiennes', *Revue française d'histoire du livre*, 24 (1979), pp. 591–610; Edith Bayle, Agnès Bresson and J-F Maillard, *La Bibliothèque de Peiresc*, Paris, 1990; Pierre Gassendi, *Peiresc 1580–1637*, Paris, 1992; Isabelle Battez [et al.], *L'Universel epistolier: Nicolas-Claude Fabri de Peiresc (1580–1637)*, Carpentras: Bibliothèque Inguimbertine, 1998; Agnès Bresson, 'Les livres et les manuscrits d'un "chercheur". La place de la bibliothèque dans le cabinet de Peiresc', *Bulletin du bibliophile* (2007), pp. 280–310.

Note: N-C Fabri de Peiresc (1580–1637), born in Aix-en-Provence; educated at the Jesuit College in Avignon and at the College of Tournon; studied in Padua: 1599; then in Montpellier; graduated (law) at Aix: 1604; went to Paris: 1605; travelled in England and Flanders; member of the Parlement in Aix: 1607; back to Paris (as secretary to Du Vair); back in Provence: 1623; scholar and book collector; owned mostly simple bindings decorated with his cipher, but also several fanfare bindings; after his return to Provence he employed Simeon Corberan, (probably the son of a Paris binder), who was part of Peiresc's household from 1625 till Peiresc's death; he was still in Aix in 1639.

THE HENRY DAVIS GIFT

130   *A binding made c. 1640*

[Lancelot Andrewes], *Tortura Torti: sive, ad Matthaei Torti librum responsio*, London : R Barker, 1609 [and] [Lancelot Andrewes], *Responsio ad apologiam Cardinalis Bellarmini*, London: R Barker, 1610 [and] I Casaubon, *Ad Frontonem Ducaeum S.J. theologum epistola*, London: I Norton, 1611. 4to.

224 × 160 × 48 mm.   (P 482) Davis 520

Black goatskin over paste boards, tooled in gold to a panel design with lines, solid fleurons at the corners of the outer panel and at the corners of the inner panel, solid curl tools in the corners of the inner panel; a centre ornament built up of pointillé curls and fleurons, dots. Edges of boards: tooled in gold with a leafy zig-zag roll; turn-ins: tooled in gold with a zig-zag roll. Edges: gilt.

  Sewn on five cords, laced in, showing as raised bands on the spine, tooled in gold with a zig-zag pallet (or part roll); six compartments, tooled in gold with lines and pointillé curls and fleurons; titles lettered in second compartment. Endbands: double with a bead; pink, white and blue silk over rolled white paper (or ?parchment) cores (cut off), tied down.

  Endleaves: fine comb-marbled pastedowns and two pairs of free conjugate white paper leaves (quired), at both ends.

PROVENANCE: Manuscript notes in Latin about the text on endleaves; bought: Sotheby's, 19.viii.1942, *434* (pl.).
LITERATURE: Oddos, *Revue française*, p. 549, fig. 6; compare Conihout & Ract-Madoux, no. 12.
Note: Bindings of this kind seem to have been produced in France in the 1640s; the solid and pointillé curls and fleurons occur in many variants and are difficult to identify with absolute certainty. See e.g. Schiff sale: Sotheby's, 8.xii.1938, *2117* (doublure); Lardanchet, Catalogue 59 (1960), *221*; Davis 521 (no. 139 below: corner fleuron).

131   *A binding, possibly made in Paris, c. 1640–56*

B van Haeften, *Schola cordis, sive aversi à Deo cordis*, Antwerp: I Meurs & H Verdussen, 1635. 8vo.

158 × 100 × 37 mm.   (P 217) Davis 457

Red goatskin over paste boards, tooled in gold with a small border roll; corners outlined by gouges and filled with solid curls and fleurons; a large centre ornament outlined by gouges, making four half circles, and filled with solid curls and fleurons around a four-leaf centre; dots, small marguerites and solid fleurons. Edges of boards: tooled in gold with a zig-zag roll. Edges: gilt.

  Sewn on five tanned leather supports, laced in, showing as raised bands on the spine, tooled in gold; six compartments, tooled in gold with lines, corner curls and centre fleurons; title lettered in second compartment. Endbands: double with a bead; pink and white silk over (?)alum-tawed cores (cut off), tied down.

  Endleaves: comb-marbled pastedowns and a pair of free conjugate white paper leaves, at both ends.

PROVENANCE: On endleaf in manuscript: 'Sc. solutae orationis/ Lat. In [?tr] Reth.' [possibly a school prize]; in manuscript: '10100—9#'; bought: Sotheby's, 11.viii.1941, *79* (pl.).
Compare: Conihout & Ract-Madoux, nos. 27, 30; (fleuron tools) BL, C.46.a.6 (Charenton, 1656), C. 68.f.7 (arms of Lionne: 1611–71); Waddesdon Manor (I Grévin, Paris, 1567).

130

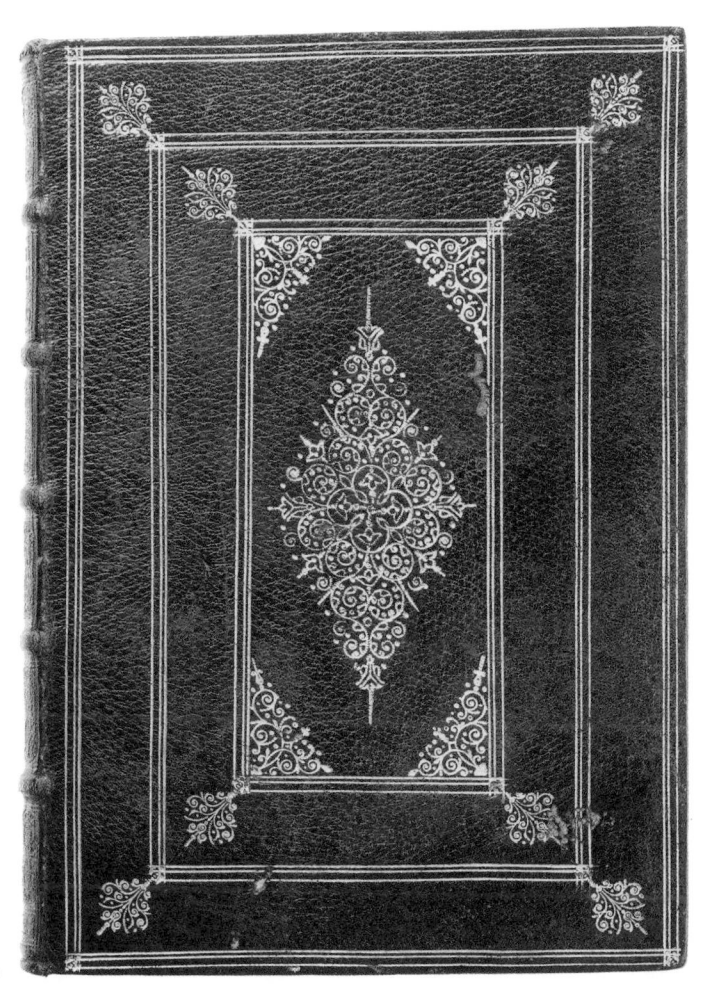

131

THE HENRY DAVIS GIFT

132   *A Paris binding by Antoine Ruette for Louis XIV, c. 1644*

L'Office de la Semaine Sainte, Paris: A Ruette, 1644; ruled in red. 8vo.

185 × 124 × 27 mm.   (P 1020) Davis 458

Brown goatskin over paste boards, tooled in gold to a fanfare design with lines, a small zig-zag border roll, gouges, solid and pointillé curls and fleurons, leafy sprays surrounding crowned Ls and crowned fleurs-de-lis; the arms of Louis XIV in the centre. Traces of two pairs of ties. Edges of boards and turn-ins: tooled in gold with small zig-zag rolls. Edges: gilt.

Rebacked with the original spine strip retained. Sewn on five alum-tawed supports, laced in, showing as raised bands on the spine, tooled in gold; six compartments, tooled in gold with fanfare ribbons, small pointillé curls and fleurons, a crowned L or two small fleurs-de-lis. Endbands: single with a bead; pink and blue silk over alum-tawed cores (cut off), tied down.

Endleaves: comb-marbled pastedowns and a pair of free conjugate white paper leaves and one free white paper leaf, at both ends.

Repairs: rebacked; repairs at corners of covers.

PROVENANCE: Library of Louis XIV; Edouard Kann (sold: Paris, Andrieux, 17–19.xi.1930, *129*, pl. xxi); Grace Whitney Hoff (book plate); bought: A Rau, 28.v.1951.
REFERENCES: Whitney Hoff, *165*, pl. lx; G D Hobson, *Fanfare*, p. 64, no. 244; Foot, *Revue française*, p. 379, fig. 3.
LITERATURE: Gruel, I, pp. 160–1, pl. opp. p. 160; Guigard, I, pp. 22–4; Hoe, *176 Bindings*, no. 77; Olivier, 2494 (2); Michon, pp. 90–1; Sotheby's, 2.v.1951, *598*; Nixon, *Broxbourne*, no. 69; Esmerian sale II, Paris, 8.xii.1972, pp. 55–63; Devaux, p. 142; Conihout & Ract-Madoux, no. 10; see also Davis 455 (no. 128 above: spine); Davis 464, 463, 465 (nos. 133–5 below).
Note: Antoine Ruette: became master binder in 1637; royal binder to Louis XIII and Louis XIV: 1643–69; succeeded his father, Macé Ruette, a little before 1644. Louis XIII (1601–1643); Louis XIV (1638–1715).

133   *A Paris binding, probably made by Antoine Ruette, 1650s*

Le Nouveau Testament [and] C Marot & T de Bèze, *Les Pseaumes de David, mis en rime françoise*, Charenton: A Cellier & P des-Hayes, 1647; ruled in red. 12mo.

144 × 82 × 23 mm.   (P 858) Davis 464

Red goatskin over paste boards with olive and citron onlays and tooled in gold with lines, dots, gouges, tailed volutes, pointillé curls, stylized flowers and fleurons; decorated with silver paint. Two pairs of silver clasps with shell-shaped catches on leather thongs, hinging on the lower cover. Edges of boards and turn-ins: tooled in gold with a small roll. Edges: gilt.

Sewn on five supports (?cords), laced in, showing as raised bands on the spine, tooled in gold; six compartments, tooled in gold with pointillé tools and decorated with silver paint. Endbands: double with a bead; pink, blue and white silk over (?)alum-tawed cores (cut off), tied down.

Endleaves: fine comb-marbled pastedowns and one free comb-marbled leaf conjugate with the pastedown, and a pair of free conjugate white paper leaves, at both ends.

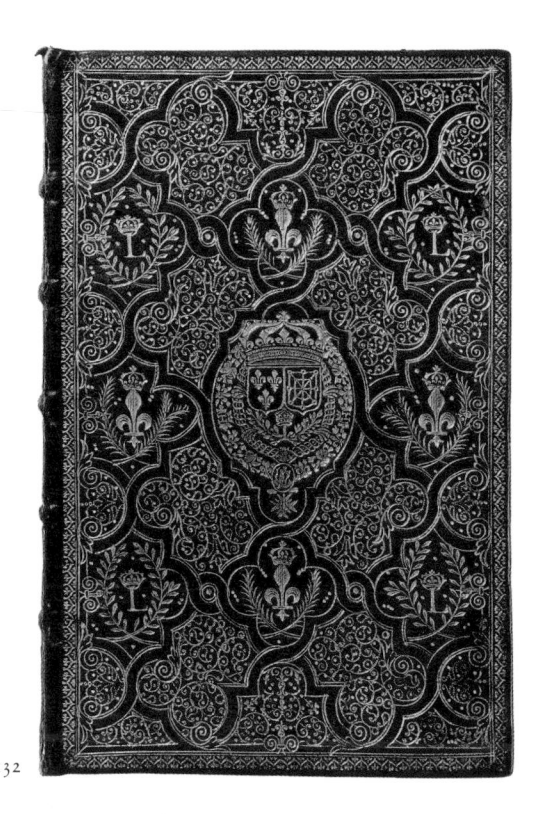

132  133

PROVENANCE: On endleaf in manuscript: 'Ex libris [name erased]'; in manuscript: 'ffor mr Samuell'; Britwell Court library [Christie-Miller]; bought: Sotheby's, 16.x.1945, *2110*.
REFERENCES: Foot, *Revue française*, p. 384, note 31.
LITERATURE: Davis 458 (no. 132 above; and literature cited there); see also Davis 463, 465 (nos. 134–5 below).

---

134 *A Paris binding, probably made by Antoine Ruette, c. 1655*

Le Nouveau Testament, Charenton: A Cellier & P des-Hayes, 1647 [and] C Marot & T de Bèze, *Les Pseaumes de David, mis en rime françoise*, Charenton: A Cellier, 1654; ruled in red. 12mo.

143 × 84 × 25 mm. (P 221) Davis 463

Red goatskin over paste boards, tooled in gold with lines, a small zig-zag border roll, gouges forming corner and centre compartments, filled with pointillé curls, stylized flowers and fleurons, tailed volutes and small fleurons. Edges of boards and turn-ins: tooled in gold with small zig-zag rolls. Edges: gilt.

Sewn on five cords, laced in (at an angle), showing as raised bands on the spine, tooled in gold; six compartments, tooled in gold with lines, dots, pointillé stylized flowers. Endbands: double with a bead; pink, white and blue silk over (?)cord cores (cut off), tied down.

Endleaves: comb-marbled pastedowns and one free comb-marbled leaf conjugate with the pastedown, and a pair of free conjugate white paper leaves, at both ends.

PROVENANCE: A catalogue description with lot no. 141 pasted in (not traced); bought: Sotheby's, 11.viii.1941, *131* (pl.).

134   135

REFERENCES: Foot, *Revue française*, p. 384, note 31.
LITERATURE: Davis 458 (no. 132 above; and literature cited there); see also Davis 464, 465 (nos. 133 above, 135 below).
Compare: Schiff sale: Sotheby's, 25.iii.1938, *482*.

135 *A Paris binding probably made by Antoine Ruette, c. 1655–60*

C Marot and T de Bèze, *Les Pseaumes de David, mis en rime françoise*, Charenton: P des-Hayes & A Cellier, 1655; ruled in red. 12mo.

142 × 84 × 15 mm.   (P 1021) Davis 465

Red goatskin over paste boards, onlaid in citron and tooled in gold with lines, a small zig-zag border roll, profile heads in the corners; gouges forming corner and centre compartments, pointillé fleurons, stylized flowers and curls; large dots. Remnants of two pairs of clasps hinging on the lower cover. Edges of boards and turn-ins: tooled in gold with a small roll. Edges: gilt.

Sewn on five cords, laced in, showing as raised bands on the spine, tooled in gold; six compartments, tooled in gold with lines, dots and pointillé tools. Endbands: single with a bead; pink, blue and white silk over alum-tawed cores (cut off), tied down.

Endleaves: fine comb-marbled pastedowns, at both ends; at the front: a pair of free conjugate white paper leaves; at the end: one free white paper leaf.

PROVENANCE: On endleaves in manuscript: prayer in French; Grace Whitney Hoff (book plate); bought: A Rau, 28.v.1951.
REFERENCES: Whitney Hoff, no. 183, pl. lvii; Foot, *Revue française*, p. 384, note 31.
LITERATURE: E Dacier, 'Autour de Le Gascon et de Florimond Badier', *Trésors des Bibliothèques de France*, X (1929), pp. 77–90 (for the profile head: a different tool from that used on Davis 465); see Davis 458 (no. 132 above; and literature cited there); see also Davis 464, 463 (nos. 133–4 above).

136

136 *A binding made in Paris, in or after 1644, possibly for Nicolas Fouquet*

[Adam Blackwood], *Martyre de la royne d'Escosse, douairiere de France*, Edinburgh [Paris]: J Nafeild, 1588. 12mo.

141 × 81 × 30 mm. (P 1071) Davis 243

Brown calf over paste boards, tooled in gold with lines along the border and a large rampant lion in the centre. Edges: stained red.

Rebacked, original spine panels retained; sewn on five (invisible) supports, laced in, showing as raised bands on the spine (new); six compartments, tooled in gold with lines; compartments 3 and 5 have two interlaced ΦΦs [cipher used by Nicolas Fouquet], compartments 1, 4 and 6 have the Sacred Monogram [used as cipher by the Jesuits], title lettered in second compartment. Endbands: (new) single with a bead; brown and red silk.

Endleaves: (new) paper pastedowns and one free leaf conjugate with the pastedown, at both ends; at the front: two free paper leaves; at the end: one free paper leaf.

Repairs: rebacked; repairs at corners of covers and edges of boards.

PROVENANCE: (?)Nicolas Fouquet; Jesuit College in Paris (on title-page in manuscript: 'Collegii paris. Soc. Jesu'; in a different hand: '1644'); further ownership note(?) cut off; library stamps of: 'Collegium Ludovici (?)Pa…'; on pastedown of upper cover in manuscript: 'Pp. 29' '173.4.17'; manuscript notes about Nicolas Fouquet in two different (modern) hands; Hamilton-Bruce (stamp with motto: 'ride thro, be trew'; monogram: 'RTHB'; crest: horse's head); Lucius Wilmerding (sold: Parke-Bernet, 31.x.1951, *616*).

LITERATURE: Guigard, II, p. 224; Olivier, 1398; Oddos, *Revue française*, p. 563, fig. 16 (books acquired by the College of Clermont with money left by Fouquet); Labarre, *Revue française*, pp. 477–88, esp. p. 478; Coppens, 'The prize is the proof'; for Fouquet, see also: Davis 523 (no. 142 below).

Note: Nicolas Fouquet (1615–1680), viscount of Melun and Vaux, marquis of Belle Isle; 'procureur-général' of the Parlement of Paris: 1650; superintendent of finance and

183

minister of state under Louis XIV: 1653; built the castle of Vaux-le-Vicomte; fell out of favour with the king, was arrested: 1661, and imprisoned for life. The greater part of his library became part of the French royal library. Fouquet gave a large fund for buying books to the Jesuit College in Paris, which out of gratitude (according to Guigard) stamped the bindings with his cipher.

137 A binding, probably made in Paris, c. 1645

Dionysius Petavius [Denis Petau], ... *Rationarium temporum in partes duas*, Paris: S Cramoisy, 1641. 8vo. [title-page of pt. II and *ij misbound between viij and viiij].

179 × 114 × 63 mm. (P 1234) Davis 459

Red goatskin (or possibly hair sheep) over paste boards, tooled in gold to a panel design with lines, two border rolls, an ornament at the corners of the panel, two small rolls around the panel, corner pieces built up of solid curl tools; in the centre a diamond-shaped ornament built up of solid curls and fleurons round a four-leaf-clover shape. Traces of two pairs of ties. Edges of boards: tooled in gold with a zig-zag roll. Edges: gilt.

Sewn on five cords, laced in, showing as raised bands on the spine, tooled in gold; six compartments, tooled in gold with lines, dotted lines, corner curls and a centre oval with fleurons; title lettered in second compartment. Endbands: double with a bead; white, blue and pink silk over (?)cord (or rolled) cores (cut off), tied down at back and front.

Endleaves: comb-marbled pastedowns at both ends; at the front: one free white paper leaf; at the end: two free (non-conjugate) white paper leaves, one of which is conjugate with a stub.
Repairs: at head and tail of spine.

PROVENANCE: On title-page verso in manuscript: 'LDLP. 1726.12.1'; bought: Sotheby's, 6.vii.1955. *134*.

138 A binding made in Paris, c. 1645

L Laspeirères, *L'Academie des philosophes sur l'amour*, Paris: F Targa, 1642; ruled in red. 8vo.

176 × 115 × 25 mm. (P 1007) Davis 460

Red goatskin over paste boards, tooled in gold to a panel design with lines and small rolls along the border, pointillé stylized flowers at the corners of the panel and flowers, fleurons and solid dots in the wide border around the panel, decorated with silver paint (repainted); small roll and lines to outline the panel; corner pieces and centre piece: onlaid in citron goatskin; panel filled with pointillé curls, fleurons, stylized flowers, decorated with silver paint (renewed), and solid dots; in the centre a monogram: RM (in two different colours of gold). Edges of boards and turn-ins: tooled in gold with small rolls. Edges: gilt and marbled beneath the gold.

Sewn on five cords, laced in, showing as raised bands on the spine, tooled in gold with dashes; six compartments, tooled in gold with lines, small curls and pointillé stylized flowers; decorated with silver paint (renewed). Endbands: double with a bead; pink, white and blue silk over cord cores (cut off), tied down.

137 138

Endleaves: comb-marbled pastedowns and one free comb-marbled leaf conjugate with the pastedown and two pairs of free conjugate white paper leaves (quired), at both ends (at the front: white leaves 1 and 4 are conjugate; not certain whether 2 and 3 are conjugate).

PROVENANCE: RM; on flyleaf in manuscript: 'Library N.1'; Newton Hall, Cambridge (book plate); T Seligman, New York (sold: Sotheby's, 2.v.1951, *499*).

---

139 *A binding made c. 1656*

G Viole, *La Vie, les vertus et les miracles du grand Saint Germain Evesque d'Aucerre*, Auxerre: G Bouquet, 1656. 4to.

224 × 174 × 28 mm. (P 1317) Davis 521

Red goatskin over paste boards, tooled in gold to a panel design with lines, and mainly solid tools; a wide border tooled with fleurons, fleurons at the corners of the panel; in the corners small solid tools, gouges forming a scalloped strip, filled with curl tools; a square centre with corner curls and surrounded by corner curls, fleurons and two pointillé stylized flower tools. Edges of boards and turn-ins: tooled in gold with a small roll. Edges: gilt.

Sewn on five cords, laced in, showing as raised bands on the spine, tooled in gold; six compartments, tooled in gold with lines, corner curls and fleurons; abbreviated title lettered in second compartment. Endbands: single with a bead; pink and white silk over rolled (?)leather or possibly paper cores (cut off), tied down.

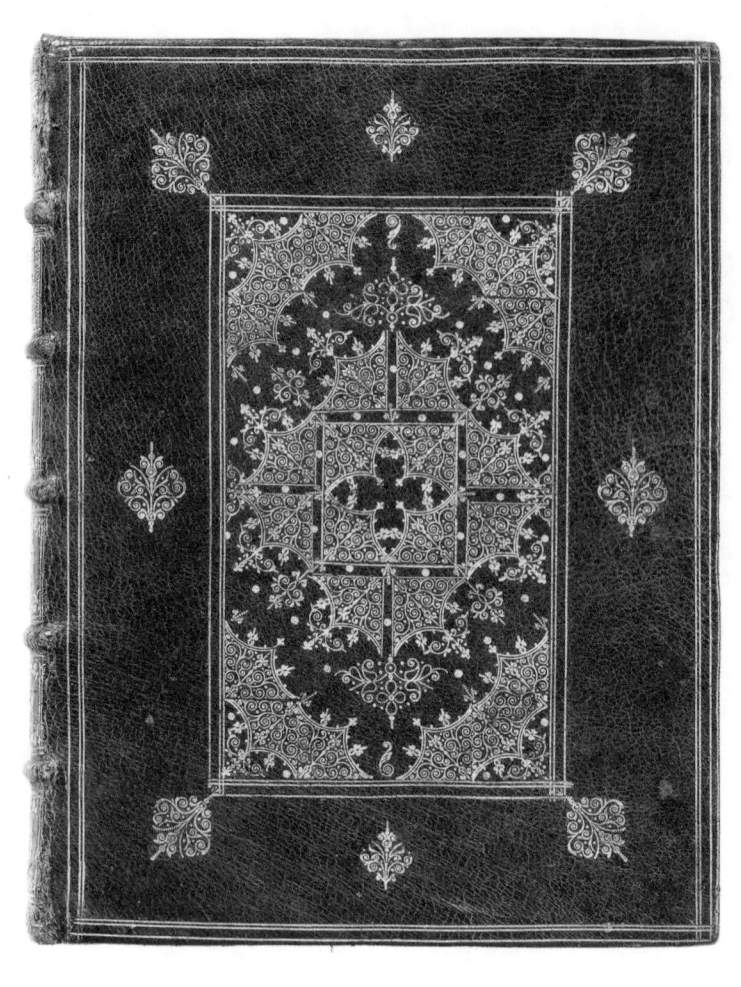

Endleaves: comb-marbled pastedowns and one free comb-marbled leaf conjugate with the pastedown, at both ends; at the front: one free white paper leaf tipped on.

PROVENANCE: Signature on title-page (unreadable); catalogue entry with no. 2372 pasted in; bought: Breslauer, 15.xi.1957.
Compare: Manchester College, Oxford (*Le Nouveau Testament*, Paris, 1647).

---

140 *A binding made in Charenton or Paris, c. 1657*

Le Nouveau Testament, Charenton: A Cellier & P des-Hayes, 1656 [and] C Marot & T de Bèze, *Les Pseaumes de David, mis en rime françoise*, Charenton: P des-Hayes & A Cellier, 1657; ruled in red. 12mo.

148 × 85 × 31 mm.   (P 762) Davis 466

Red goatskin over paste boards, tooled in gold with lines, a small border of half circles and a small border of three dots; fillets and gouges forming a rectangle and half-circle design with pointillé fleurons at the corners, pointillé curls in the corners and curls and fleurons around a central four-leaf-clover shape with small fleurons. Edges of boards and turn-ins: tooled in gold with a small roll. Edges: gilt.

140

Sewn on five cords, laced in, showing as raised bands on the spine; six compartments, tooled in gold with small pointillé curls and fleurons. Endbands: (headband only remains; of tailband a pink silk tie down remains) double with a bead; pink, white and blue silk over (?)alum-tawed core (cut off), tied down; cord crowning core.

Endleaves: comb-marbled pastedowns and one free comb-marbled leaf conjugate with the pastedown, at both ends.

Repairs: at head and corners of spine; at corners of covers and at lower cover.

PROVENANCE: On endleaf in manuscript: 'Wm. Wilsons Book Huntly 1837'; bought: Sotheby's, 26.i.1944, 588.
LITERATURE: Foot, *Marsh*, pp. 95–7 (on Charenton bindings, but tools not identical).

---

141 *A binding given by Antoine Druot to the College of Chalon-sur-Saône, 1658*

M T Cicero, *Opera omnia*, Geneva: P & I Chouët, 1646. 4to.

235 × 163 × 70 mm. (P 1318) Davis, 522

Brown goatskin over paste boards, tooled in gold to a panel design with lines, dots and zig-zag border rolls, a wide border with the arms of France and the arms of Chalon-sur-Saône and pointillé fleurons; fleurons at the corners; small curl tools filling the corners of the panel, and in the centre: curls and fleurons above and beneath a laurel wreath, in which: EX./DONO.D/ANTONII/DRVOT./1658. Edges: gilt.

Sewn on five cords, laced in, showing as raised bands on the spine, tooled in gold; six compartments, tooled in gold with solid curl tools. Endbands: single with a bead; pink and blue silk over alum-tawed cores (cut off), tied down.

Endleaves: comb-marbled pastedowns at both ends; at the front: several stubs (one marbled and ?three white); at the back: two free white paper leaves (conjugacy uncertain).

PROVENANCE: Antoine Druot; College of Chalon-sur-Saône [school prize]; bought: Sotheby's, 6.vii.1955, *116*.

LITERATURE: Olivier, 1578; Labarre, *Revue française*, pp. 477–88; Coppens, 'The prize is the proof', especially pp. 65–73, fig. 2 (prize binding for the College of Chalon-sur-Saône, given by Claude Tapin, 1655).

Other prize bindings for this college: BL, C.47.a.4 (Antoine Druot, 1598), C.46.b.11 (Antoine Druot, 1640); Fitzwilliam Museum, Cambridge (Claude Tisserand, 1627); BL, C.67.a.5 (Claude Tisserand, 1648), C.57.b.37 (no name, 1661).

Note: Prize books for the College of Chalon-sur-Saône were provided by several benefactors, among whom Antoine Druot, Claude Tapin and Claude Tisserand. Antoine Druot was sommelier to the king and captain of Germoles; gifts by him are dated: 1598, 1629, 1640, 1644, 1647, 1658, 1659.

142

142   *A Paris binding for Nicolas Fouquet by the Atelier 'Rocolet', c. 1659–60*

Marin Cureau de la Chambre, *Les Charactères des passions, volume III*, Paris: P Rocolet, 1659. 4to.

257 × 184 × 48 mm.   (P 1058) Davis 523

Brown goatskin over paste boards, tooled in gold to a panel design with lines, zig-zag and small-circles rolls, fleurs-de-lis at the corners of the panel; lines and small rolls outlining the panel; a wide border with crowned Ls, fleurs-de-lis, solid fleurons and small curl tools; an inner panel with half circular extensions, at the corners: pointillé curls and stylized flowers; corner pieces formed by gouges and filled with a semis of fleurs-de-lis; pointillé stylized flowers and fleurons around a central oval with the arms of Nicolas Fouquet. Edges of boards and turn-ins: tooled in gold with small rolls. Edges: gilt.

    Sewn on five cords, laced in, showing as raised bands on the spine, tooled in gold; six compartments, tooled in gold with a semis of fleurs-de-lis; title lettered in second compartment. Endbands: double with a bead; blue, pink and white silk over alum-tawed cores (cut off), tied down; cord crowning cores.

    Endleaves: comb-marbled pastedowns at both ends; at the front: a pair of free conjugate white paper leaves; at the end: one free white paper leaf conjugate with a stub.

    Repairs: small repairs at corners.

PROVENANCE:	Nicolas Fouquet; on pastedown in manuscript: 'Jourdin'; in a different hand: 'J'ai commencé L'Ecole le 29.9bre 1830'; on title-page in manuscript: 'Ex libris L. Dupuis'; in a different hand: 'Mathurin Baudaire 1712 1713'; manuscript notes on endleaf; Lucius Wilmerding (sold: Parke-Bernet, 31.x.1951, *346*).
REFERENCES:	Foot, *Revue française*, p. 384, fig. 4.
LITERATURE:	Olivier, 1398; Michon, pl. xxxv (= Dacier, pl. 31: 1 with the arms of Louis XIV), p. 93; George Chrétien, Catalogue 132 [June 1960], no. 339 (a remboîtage of a[nother?] volume of *Les Charactères des passions* has been replaced by P Bouhours, 1676) with arms of Fouquet; (same design, ?same tools as Davis 523); Esmerian sale II, Paris, 8.xii.1972, pp. 47–8, no. 35; Devaux, pp. 142, 144; Schäfer, pp. 80–1; Conihout & Ract-Madoux, nos. 18, 23 (the latter with same design and same tools as Davis 523); see also Davis 243 (no. 136 above: for Fouquet).
Note:	This atelier worked for Pierre Rocolet (printer and bookseller, 1618–62) from c. 1638 to 1662. Nicolas Fouquet (1615–1680), 'procureur-général' of the Parlement of Paris: 1650; superintendent of finances and minister of state: 1653; fell out of favour with Louis XIV: 1661, arrested and banned. Many bindings with his coat of arms are known, e.g. BL, C.46.h.7 (Paris, 1655).

143 *A Paris binding for Hélie Dufresnoy, by his first binder, c. 1662–8*

Publius Terentius Afer, *Comoediae sex ... cum ... notis ... Corn. Schrevelio*, Leiden: F Hackius, 1651. 8vo.

184 × 117 × 43 mm. (P 1082) Davis 462

Red goatskin over paste boards, tooled in gold with lines, fillets and gouges forming a rectangle and half-circle design with fleurons at the corners, curl tools in the corners, solid curls and fleurons in the half circles, and in the centre the arms of Hélie Dufresnoy, above and below which: his monogram, incorporating his name (HELI FRESNOY). Edges of boards and turn-ins: tooled in gold with a small roll. Edges: gilt and marbled in red and blue beneath the gold.

Sewn on five (invisible) supports, laced in, showing as raised bands on the spine, tooled in gold, six compartments, tooled in gold with lines, corner curls and the Fresnoy monogram; title lettered in second compartment. Endbands: double with a bead; blue, white and pink silk over rolled (?)leather cores (cut off), tied down.

Endleaves: fine comb-marbled pastedowns and one free comb-marbled leaf conjugate with the pastedown and one pair of free (?)conjugate white paper leaves, at both ends.

PROVENANCE:	Hélie Dufresnoy; on endleaf in manuscript: 'c.a. Boisset' 'Harwood. p. 187'; Holford collection (sold: Sotheby's, 9.xii.1927, *796*); Lucius Wilmerding (book plate; sold: Parke-Bernet, 31.x.1951, *883*).
LITERATURE:	Guigard, II, 190–1; Hoe, *176 Bindings*, no. 92; Olivier, 963; Michon, p. 94; Hobson, *French and Italian*, p. xx; Esmerian sale II, Paris, 8.xii.1972, pp. 69–70; Devaux, pp. 138–9.
Other Dufresnoy bindings with same tools:	Lardanchet, Catalogue 45 (1951), *787* (Paris, 1651); Sotheby's, 4.xi.1958, *249* (Amsterdam, 1665), *250* (Amsterdam, 1672), *253* (Leiden, 1653). Design: compare Conihout & Ract-Madoux, nos. 27, 28, 30.

143 144

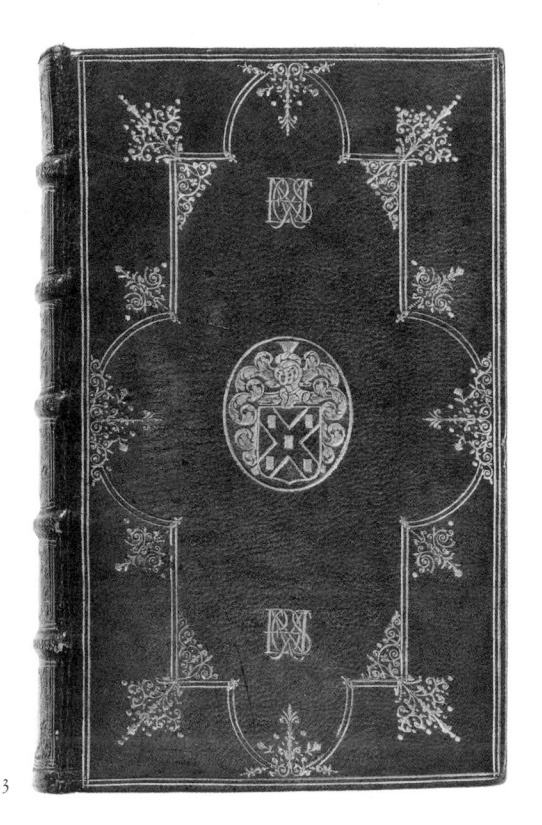

Note: Hélie Dufresnoy (Elie du Fresnoy) (1614–1698), son of an apothecary in Paris; held government posts under Chancellor Le Tellier and the marquis de Louvois; married in 1663/4; probably used two different binders, one: 1662–68/70, the other: c. 1668/70–90.

---

144 *A Paris binding with the arms and cipher of Louis XIV, c. 1666–1700*

L'Office de la Semaine Sainte, Paris: F Grange, n.d. [c. 1666]; engraving signed Landry; ruled in red. 8vo.

194 × 128 × 31 mm. (P 1022) Davis 469

Brown goatskin over paste boards, tooled in silver (oxidized) to a fanfare design, with a small half-circle roll and lines along the border; gouges, pointillé curls and fleurons, tailed volutes, small solid tools, stylized flowers and dots; the monogram of Louis XIV and in the centre his arms.

Sewn on five cords, laced in, showing as raised bands on the spine; six compartments, tooled in silver with lines, dots, a 'fanfare' knot, small solid tools and a fleur-de-lis in the centre. Endbands: double with a bead; silver thread and pink silk over alum-tawed cores (cut off), tied down. Three pale blue silk bookmarkers.

Endleaves: silver paper pastedowns and one free silver paper leaf (backed), conjugate with the pastedown, and two free white paper leaves (probably not conjugate), at both ends.

PROVENANCE: Grace Whitney Hoff (book plate; Whitney Hoff, no. 213); bought: A Rau, 29.v.1951.
REFERENCES: Foot, *Revue française*, p. 384.

LITERATURE: Brunet, no. 69 (arms of Louis XIII); Guigard, 25; Olivier, 2494 (8); 2494 (21); G D Hobson, *Fanfare*, pp. 63–6 ('type tardif'), pl. xxiib (arms of the duchesse d'Orléans); Devaux, p. 128.
Same tools on: BL, C.46.e.19 (arms of Du Cambout de Coislin, bishop of Orleans, 1636–1706), C.46.d.17, C.67.e.7 (arms of James II); Cambridge University Library, SSS 37.2 (Paris, 1774); Bodleian Library Oxford, Broxbourne R941 (Paris, 1686); Phillips, March 1983 (*Office*, Paris n.d.); Davis 526 (no. 154 below).
Compare: (spine) Esmerian sale II, Paris, 8.xii.1972, nos. 42–3 (Atelier des Caumartins).
Note: Louis XIV (1638–1715); king: 1643; consecrated: 1654.

145   *Two bindings made c. 1667*

Le Nouveau Testament ... en françois. Les Epistres de S. Paul, les epistres canoniques, l'Apocalypse, 2 vols, Mons: G Migeot, 1667. 8vo.

166/165 × 101 × 32/29 mm.   (P 222) Davis 467–468

Red goatskin over paste boards, tooled in gold with lines, dotted lines, fanfare ornaments in the corners filled with pointillé fleurons and curls; pointillé curls along the sides. Edges of boards and turn-ins: tooled in gold with small zig-zag rolls. Edges: gilt.

Sewn on five cords, laced in, showing as raised bands on the spine, tooled in gold; six compartments, tooled in gold with lines, dotted lines and fanfare ornaments, small solid and pointillé tools near head and tail; title lettered in second compartments. Endbands: triple with two beads; pink, blue and white silk over leather (possibly alum-tawed) cores (cut off), tied down; cord crowning cores.

Endleaves: fine-comb-marbled pastedowns and a pair of free conjugate white paper leaves and one free paper leaf (conjugate with a stub in Davis 468; tipped on in Davis 467), at both ends.

Repairs: vol. I: at joint with lower cover and at tail of spine.

In goatskin slipcases.

PROVENANCE: Lord Gosford (ex-libris with motto: 'inter folia fructus'); Count L Clément de Ris (on endleaf in manuscript: 'Cte L. Clément de Ris – 5 Mai 1882/ Vente d'un Amateur Anglais No. 13–260"/ Avec l'Ex-Libris de Lord Gosford'; on endleaf of vol. II in manuscript: 'Cte L. Clément de Ris. 1882.'); H Gordon Selfridge (sold: Sotheby's, 11.viii.1941, *132*, pl.).
LITERATURE: G D Hobson, *Fanfare*, pp. 63–6: 'Type tardif'.

146   *A binding for Charles de Castellau, c. 1670*

Plautus, *Comoediae xx. quarum carmina magna ex parte in mensum suum restituta sunt*, Venice: Aldus & A A Socerus, July 1522; ruled in red. 4to.

217 × 133 × 40 mm.   (P 977) Davis 524

Red goatskin (or possibly hair sheep) over paste boards, tooled in gold with lines along the border and in the centre the arms of Abbot Charles de Castellau. Edges of boards: tooled in gold with a line. Edges: gilt.

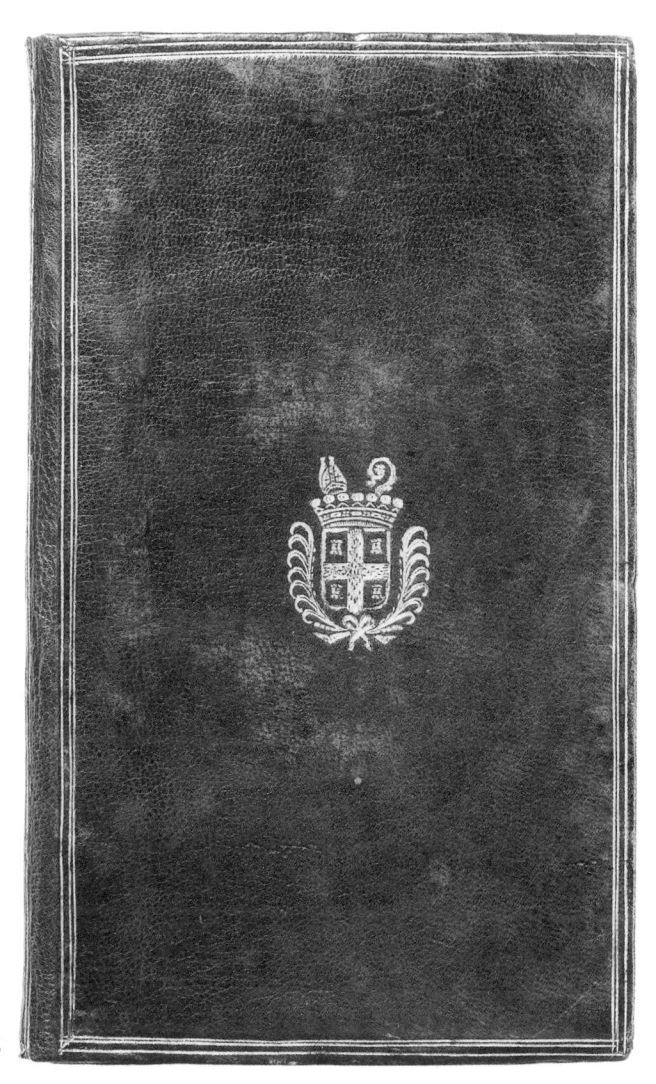

Rebacked with the original spine strip retained; sewn on five recessed cords, laced in through three holes; smooth spine, tooled in gold with a semis of two monograms (2 Bs; 2 Ys) and fleurs-de-lis; near the head : PLAVTVS. Endbands: double with a bead; white and green silk over (?)alum-tawed cores (cut off), tied down.

Endleaves: paper pastedowns and one free leaf conjugate with the pastedown and one free paper leaf tipped on, at both ends.

Repairs: rebacked; upper joint renewed; repairs at lower cover and tail of spine.

PROVENANCE: Abbot Charles de Castellau; on title-page in manuscript: 'MJusani'(?); ownership inscription erased; manuscript notes in the margins of the text; manuscript note in red about the book (19th century); Mr J Renard (book plate); bought: Sotheby's, 27.ii.1951, *209*.
LITERATURE: Olivier, 802 (2).
Note: Charles de Castellau, abbot of St Epure of Toul: 1663; died in Paris: 1676/7.

147 *A Paris binding with the arms and cipher of Louis XIV, c. 1676*

P F Chifflet, *Dissertation touchant Saint Denys l'Areopagite, evesque de Paris*, Paris: Jean de la Caille, 1676. 12mo.

157 × 90 × 14 mm. (P 1053) Davis 470

Red goatskin over paste boards, tooled in gold with lines, the crowned cipher of Louis XIV between two palm branches in the corners, and his arms surrounded by a wreath of leaves, flowers and a small sun, in the centre. Edges of boards and turn-ins: tooled in gold with a small zig-zag roll. Edges: gilt.

Sewn on five cords, laced in, showing as raised bands on the spine, tooled in gold; six compartments, tooled in gold: compartments 1, 4 and 6 with a sun tool, 3 and 5 with Louis's cipher; title lettered in second compartment. Endbands: double with a bead; white and blue silk over alum-tawed cores (cut off), tied down (a pink silk tie-down is also visible).

Endleaves: fine-comb-marbled pastedowns and one free fine-comb-marbled leaf conjugate with the pastedown, at both ends; at the front: two pairs of free conjugate white paper leaves (quired); at the end: three pairs of free conjugate white paper leaves (quired) (whites: same watermark as text block paper).

PROVENANCE: Benedictine monastery in Paris (on title-page in manuscript: 'Aux R.ges benedictines de ladoration perpetuelle du tres Saint Sacrement du premier monastere de paris rue cassette'); Lucius Wilmerding (sold: Parke-Bernet, 30.x.1951, *206*).
REFERENCES: Foot, *Revue française*, p. 384.
LITERATURE: Olivier, 2494.

148 *A Paris binding of the last quarter of the seventeenth century, possibly made for Baron de Longepierre*

L A Florus, *Ex recensione N Blanckardi. Accedit eiusdem ex omnium observationibus editis, ac ineditis Salmasii commentarius*, Leiden: A Wijngaerden, 1648. 8vo.

186 × 113 × 30 mm. (P 1057) Davis 461

Black goatskin over paste boards, tooled in gold with lines along the edges, a rose tool at the corners and the badge of the Golden Fleece in the corners and in the centre. Edges of boards: tooled in gold with a line; turn-ins: tooled in gold with a small floral roll. Edges: gilt and marbled in blue and red beneath the gold.

Sewn on five (invisible) supports, laced in, showing as raised bands on the spine, tooled in gold with a line; six compartments, tooled in gold with lines and the badge of the Golden Fleece; title lettered in second compartment. Endbands: double with a bead; pink silk over (?)cord cores (cut off), tied down. Pink silk bookmarker.

Endleaves: comb-marbled pastedowns and one free comb-marbled leaf (backed) conjugate with the pastedown, plus one free white paper leaf, conjugate with the backing paper, at both ends.

147   148

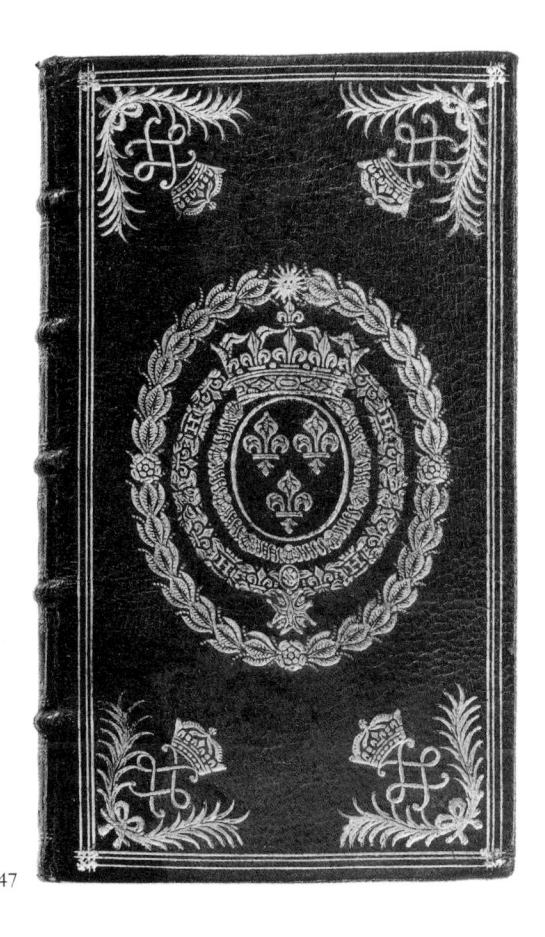

PROVENANCE: (?)Baron de Longepierre; on endleaf in manuscript: '12 0 3 5286'; comte de Lurde (book plate); Edouard Rahir (book plate; sold: pt iv, Paris, 1936, *1051*); Lucius Wilmerding (sold: Parke-Bernet, 31.x.1951, *341*).

LITERATURE: Gruel, p. 132 (illustrates three Golden Fleece badges, the third one of which = that on Davis 461; all are said to have been made for Baron de Longepierre); Portalis, *Longepierre* (gives two badges, the larger of which may be identical with that on Davis 461); *Livres anciens précieuses reliures*, sale: Paris, Hôtel Drouot: C Galantaris, 27.xi.1987, no. 68 (same badge as on Davis 461, said to be for Baron de Longepierre); see also Davis 471, 472 (nos. 149–50 below).

Note: Hilaire-Bernard de Requeleyne, Baron de Longepierre (1659–1721): a mediocre poet, born in Dijon; wrote *Médée*, a tragedy, and it is said that in memory of this work he had his books decorated with the badge of the Golden Fleece; his coat of arms also had a sheep. There are at least three different badges: a long-legged version which appears to come in three sizes; two short-legged versions, a thin and a fatter sheep, both of which come in two sizes. The largest of the long-legged version is that used on Davis 461. The two smaller sizes of the long-legged version occur on e.g. BL, 676.a.22 (Paris, 1649), 676.a.23 (Paris, 1649), 676.a.16 and 17 (Amsterdam, 1675).

149 *A Paris binding of the last quarter of the seventeenth century, made for Baron de Longepierre, possibly by Luc-Antoine Boyet*

Quintus Curtius Rufus, *Historia Alexandri Magni*, Leiden: Elzevier, 1633. 12mo.

130 × 72 × 20 mm. (P 1078) Davis 471

Red goatskin over paste boards, tooled in gold with lines along the edges and the badge of the Golden Fleece in the corners and in the centre; doublures of red goatskin tooled in gold with lines and a small border roll; the badge of the Golden Fleece in the centre. Leather inside joints. Edges of boards: tooled in gold with a line; turn-ins: tooled in gold with a small roll. Edges: gilt and (lightly) marbled beneath the gold.

 Sewn on five (invisible) supports, laced in, showing as raised bands on the spine, tooled in gold with a line; six compartments, tooled in gold with the badge of the Golden Fleece; author's name lettered in second compartment. Endbands: double with a bead; white, pink and blue silk over (?)cord cores (cut off), tied down. Green silk bookmarker.

Endleaves: two free comb-marbled leaves, pasted together, and a pair of free conjugate white paper leaves, at both ends.

PROVENANCE: Baron de Longepierre; Belton House library (book plate; pasted over another book plate: now invisible); Lucius Wilmerding (book plate; sold: Parke-Bernet, 31.x.1951, 753).
REFERENCES: Foot, *Revue française*, p. 384.
LITERATURE: Gruel, pp. 60–1, 132 (does not illustrate the badge as used on Davis 471; refers to Longepierre bindings with doublures as extremely rare); Portalis, *Longepierre*;

	Esmerian sale II, Paris, 8.xii.1972, no. 70 (attributed to L-A Boyet); Davis 461 (no. 148 above; and literature cited there); see also Davis 472 (no. 150 below). For Boyet see Davis 473 (no. 152 below).
Same badge on:	BL, C.19.f.3 (Venice, 1503), 679.b.29 (Paris, 1709). There are two versions of the small badge: a slightly thinner one (as on Davis 471) and a slightly fatter version (as on Davis 472), as well as three sizes (two sizes are used together on Davis 472).

150 *A Paris binding of the last quarter of the seventeenth century, made for Baron de Longepierre*

P P Statius, *Sylvarum libri quinque* [and other works], Venice: Aldus, August 1502. 8vo.

168 × 100 × 34 mm. (P 1125) Davis 472

Brown calf over paste boards, tooled in gold with a line, a smaller version of the badge of the Golden Fleece in the corners and a (slightly) larger version of the same badge in the centre. Edges of boards and turn-ins: tooled in gold with a zig-zag roll. Edges: gilt and marbled beneath the gold.

Sewn on five (invisible) supports, laced in, showing as raised bands on the spine, tooled in gold; six compartments, tooled in gold with lines, corner curls and the (smaller version of) the badge of the Golden Fleece; in the second compartment: a red goatskin label, lettered: STATII/ORTOGRAP. Endbands: double with a bead; pink silk over alum-tawed cores (cut off), tied down. Pink silk bookmarker.

Endleaves: fine-comb-marbled pastedowns and one free fine-comb-marbled leaf (backed), conjugate with the pastedown and one free white paper leaf conjugate with the backing paper, at both ends.

Repairs: at both joints and at head of spine.

PROVENANCE:	Baron de Longepierre; on title-page in manuscript: '34'; on endleaf in manuscript: 'Dg:88'; pencil note in a 20th-century hand about the collation, signed: 'C.C./RD'; also in a 20th-century hand: 'Exemplaire de Longepierre'; bought: N. Rauch, 29.vi.1953.
REFERENCES:	Foot, *Revue française*, p. 384.
LITERATURE:	Gruel, p. 132, second badge; see Davis 461, 471 (nos. 148–9 above; and literature cited there).
Same badge on:	BL, 673.a.14 (Leiden, 1650), 676.b.2 (Paris, 1652).

151 *A binding probably made in Paris, c. 1683*

François le Gras, [Acknowledgement of suzerainty from Chevalier François le Gras to the duc de Vendôme over his lands, etc.]; manuscript on parchment, signed and dated: Le Gras, 10 November 1683, n.p.

248 × 190 × 22 mm. (M 58) Davis 525

Red goatskin over paste boards, tooled in gold with lines and dotted lines; a wide border filled with a semis of fleurs-de-lis. Edges of boards and turn-ins: tooled in gold with a small zig-zag roll. Edges: gilt.

151

Sewn on five (invisible) supports, laced in, showing as raised bands on the spine; six compartments, tooled in gold with lines and a semis of fleurs-de-lis. Endbands: double with a bead; blue and pink silk over (?)cord cores (cut off), tied down.

Endleaves: marbled pastedowns and one free marbled leaf conjugate with the pastedown and a pair of free conjugate white paper leaves, at both ends; at the end: a pair of free conjugate parchment leaves.

PROVENANCE: (?)Duc de Vendôme; in text (on most rectos): stamp with GEN O DE/TOVRS/DIX SULZ; bought: Breslauer, 4.vii.1957 (Catalogue 88, no. 101, pl. v).

Note: Louis Joseph, duc de Vendôme (1654–1712), grandson of Caesar, natural son of Henri IV (duc de Vendôme: 1598), general under Louis XIV; governor of Provence: 1681; lieutenant general: 1688.

---

152 *A Paris binding made for Marie Marguerite de Cossé-Brissac, duchesse de Villeroy, probably by Luc-Antoine Boyet, c. 1690*

Le Pseautier distribué selon l'ordre des heures canoniales, Cologne: P. Laville, 1684; ruled in red. 8vo.

164 × 104 × 20 mm. (P 1423) Davis 473

White vellum over paste boards, tooled in gold to an over-all design with lines and dotted roll along the border; gouges forming compartments filled with pointillé curls, fleurons and stylized flowers; solid bunches of flowers, garlands, leafy sprays and flower heads, dots and stars; in the corners the arms of

198

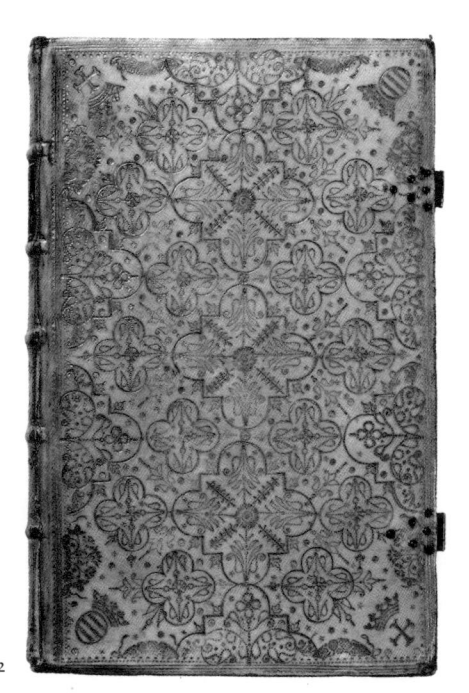

152

Cossé-Brissac and those of Neufville de Villeroy. Two pairs of silver clasps, hinging on upper cover. Edges of boards and turn-ins: tooled in gold with zig-zag roll. Doublures of red goatskin, tooled in gold to an over-all design with lines and dotted roll along the edges; gouges forming compartments filled with pointillé fleurons, curls and stylized flowers; solid bunches of flowers, leafy sprays and flower heads, dots and stars. Edges: gilt and marbled beneath the gold.

Sewn on five (?)cords, laced in, showing as raised bands on the spine, with traces of gold tooling; six compartments, tooled in gold with lines, the same heraldic charges as occur on the covers; title lettered on red goatskin label in second compartment. Endbands: single with a bead; dark blue and silver twist, pink and white silk over alum-tawed cores (cut off), tied down. Pink silk bookmarker.

Endleaves: a pair of free conjugate white paper leaves and a third free paper leaf, at both ends.

PROVENANCE: Marie Marguerite de Cossé-Brissac, duchesse de Villeroy; on endleaves in manuscript: prayers in Latin and French; Michel de Bry (his red goatskin label with: 'Pro captu lectoris'; sold: E Ader, *Bibliothèque d'un humaniste*, Paris, Hôtel Drouot, 1966, no. 168, pl. L).

LITERATURE: Gruel, pp. 60–1; Olivier, 176; Beraldi sale I, Paris, 1934, no. 40 (identical tools, attributed to Boyet); Conihout & Ract-Madoux, nos. 42–3 (attributed to Boyet).

Same tools on: Esmerian sale II, Paris, 8.xii.1972, no. 60 (attributed to L-A Boyet), also possibly same tools on Esmerian sale II, nos. 51, 53, 54 (Ateliers Eloy Levasseur–L-A Boyet); same design with very similar (?not identical) tools on: Whitney Hoff, no. 227 (pl. LXIV) (attributed by Michon, p. 95, to Boyet); Giraud-Badin, *Catalogue Bibliotheque B** (Paris, 1934), no. 65; Sotheby's, 14.vi.1955, *282*; for a binding with doublures tooled with a semis of the arms of Cossé-Brissac and Villeroy, see: Esmerian sale II, no. 64.

Note: Marie Marguerite de Cossé-Brissac married François de Neufville, duc de Villeroy, maréchal de France: 1662
Luc-Antoine Boyet, binder in Paris: 1680–1733.

153

153 *A binding, possibly made for Le Riche, c. 1690–1700*

C Guichard, *Funerailles et diverses manieres d'ensevelir des Rommains, Grecs et autres nations*, Lyon: I de Tournes, 1581. 4to.

247 × 159 × 40 mm.　　　　　　　　　　　　　　　　　　　　　　　　　　　　(P 1194) Davis 512

Black goatskin over paste boards, tooled in gold with lines, dotted lines and a small roll forming the border, fleurs-de-lis at the corners; a design of circular fans, built up of small tools, garlands of fruit and leaves, and small solid tools. Edges of boards and turn-ins: tooled in gold with a roll with fleurons. Edges: gilt and marbled beneath the gold.

Sewn on six (?cord) supports, laced in, showing as raised bands on the spine, tooled in gold with a zig-zag roll; seven compartments, tooled in gold with small corner curls and a centre fleuron; title lettered in second compartment. Endbands: double with a bead; red, pale blue and beige silk over leather cores (cut off), tied down.

Endleaves: whorl-marbled pastedowns and one whorl-marbled free leaf (backed), conjugate with the pastedown, and one free white paper leaf conjugate with the backing paper, at both ends.

PROVENANCE:　On title-page in manuscript: 'Le Riche'; bought: Pierre Berès, 15.iv.1955.
REFERENCES:　Romme, *Book Collector*, 1969, pl. IIb, p. 24, note 6 (wrongly dated); Conihout & Ract-Madoux, p. 83.
LITERATURE:　Conihout & Ract-Madoux, nos. 34–6, pp. 66–7.
Same tools:　and a very similar design, also with the name of Le Riche in manuscript, on: Gougy sale I, Paris, 5-8.iii.1934, *213*, pl. xviii (Paris, [1519]).
Note:　Antoine Le Riche (1643–1715), secretary to the king: 1687.

154

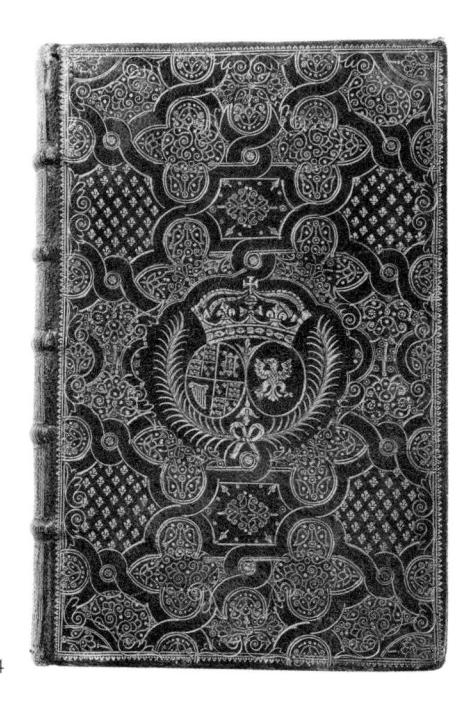

154 *A Paris binding for James II and Mary of Modena, c. 1691*

Office de la Semaine Sainte à l'usage de Rome, Paris: A Dezallier, 1691; ruled in red. 8vo.

198 × 132 × 38 mm. (P 1522) Davis 526

Red goatskin over paste boards, tooled in gold to a fanfare design, with a small roll and lines along the border; gouges, pointillé curls and fleurons; small solid tools, dots and fleurs-de-lis; in the centre the arms of James II, impaling those of Mary of Modena, his second wife. Edges of boards and turn-ins: tooled in gold with a zig-zag roll. Edges: gilt.

Sewn on five (possibly alum-tawed) supports, laced in, showing as raised bands on the spine, tooled in gold; six compartments, tooled in gold with lines, a 'fanfare' knot, small solid tools and a fleur-de-lis in the centre; zig-zag roll along head and tail. Endbands: double with a bead; pink, blue and white silk over alum-tawed cores (cut off), tied down.

Endleaves: marbled pastedowns and one free marbled leaf (backed) conjugate with the pastedown, and one free white paper leaf conjugate with the backing paper, at both ends.

PROVENANCE:	James II and Mary of Modena (on endleaf in manuscript: '1693 JR'); in a later hand: 'PII picc.46'; C Fairfax Murray; Krishaber (sold: Sotheby's, 27.vii.1943, *390*, pl.); J R Abbey (book plate; 'J.A. 2321/27:7:1943'; sold: Sotheby's, 23.vi.1965, *515*).
REFERENCES:	Davies, *Fairfax Murray*, no. 400 (pl.); G D Hobson, *Fanfare*, p. 65; Romme, *Book Collector*, 1969, p. 24, note 7; Foot, *Revue française*, p. 384, note 32.
LITERATURE:	G Barber, '"Il fallut même réveiller les Suisses": Aspects of private religious practice in a public setting in eighteenth-century Versailles', in: N Aston (ed.), *Religious Change in Europe 1650–1914*, Oxford, 1997, p. 84; see also Davis 469 (no. 144 above; and literature cited there).
Note:	James II of England (1633–1701) married Mary of Modena (1658–1718) as his second wife: 1673; king: 1685; abdicated: 1688.

155

155 *Four bindings dating from the end of the seventeenth century*

C Gilbert, *Recueil abregé des principales familles du royaume*, n.p., 1693, illuminated MS on parchment; 4 vols.

244/242 × 174/172/173 × 47/45/50 mm. (M 44) Davis 527–530

Brown stained calf over paste boards. Tooled in gold with three lines along the border and stars at the corners. Edges of boards: tooled in gold with two lines; turn-ins: tooled in gold with slanting lines and dots. Edges: gilt.

Sewn on five recessed cords, laced in; smooth spine, tooled in gold to an over-all pattern of solid curls; title lettered on brown goatskin label. Endbands: single with a bead; blue-green and white silk over rolled paper cores, tied down. Green silk bookmarkers.

Endleaves: whorl-marbled paper pastedowns and one free whorl-marbled paper leaf (backed), conjugate with the pastedown and one free white paper leaf conjugate with the backing paper, at both ends.

PROVENANCE: Mortimer Schiff (book plate in vol. I; sold: Sotheby's, 23.iii.1938, *517*); Lucius Wilmerding (book plate in vol. IV; sold: Parke-Bernet, 31.x.1951, *593*).
LITERATURE: R Portalis, 'Nicolas Jarry et la caligraphie au XVIIe siècle', *Bulletin du bibliophile*, 1896/7.
Note: Charles Gilbert (1642–1728): calligrapher, pupil of Jarry.

156

156 *A Paris binding by Duseuil or possibly by A-M Padeloup, c. 1707–15*

Offices ou pratiques de dévotion, Paris: C de Hansy, 1707; ruled in red. 12mo.

118 × 75 × 23 mm. (P 1305) Davis 474

Brown goatskin over paste boards, tooled in gold with a small outer border, lines, gouges, flower tools in the corners, small solid and pointillé curls, fleurons and flame tools, stars and dots. Edges of boards: tooled in gold with a small roll. Doublures of red goatskin, tooled in gold with a border roll. Edges: gilt and marbled beneath the gold.

Sewn on five cords (lacing in not visible), showing as raised bands on the spine, tooled in gold; six compartments, tooled in gold with small tools; title (PRIERE/ DE LA/ SEMAINE) lettered in second compartment. Endbands: double with a bead; blue, pink and white silk over (barely visible) cores (cut off), tied down occasionally. Two pink and one blue silk bookmarkers.

Endleaves: a free gilt-paper leaf (backed), at both ends; at the end: one free white paper leaf tipped on.

In a (later) brown goatskin case.

PROVENANCE: Mortimer Schiff (book plate; sold: Sotheby's, 6.vii.1938, *1076*); J R Abbey (book plate; 'J.A.1810/ 6:6:1938'; sold: Sotheby's, 23.vi.1965, *520*).
REFERENCES: Foot, *Davis*, I, pp. 196, 202, note 21.
LITERATURE: Michon, *Reliures mosaïquées*, no. 6, pl. ii, nos. 12–14, pls xiii–xv; Devauchelle, II, pp. 31–5; Sir Robert Birley, 'The library of Louis-Henri de Loménie, comte de de Brienne, and the bindings of the abbé Du Seuil', *The Library*, 5th series, vol. xvii (1962), pp. 105–31; Foot, *Davis*, I, pp. 192–6; Barber, 'La reliure', pp. 165, 171; for Padeloup: see also Davis 531 (no. 157 below; and literature cited there).

THE HENRY DAVIS GIFT

Same tools on: Dacier, nos. 37–8, pl. 32 (Paris, 1723, 1733); Bodleian Library Oxford, Douce MS19 (MS *Officium BMV*: illustrated in Barber 1994, fig. 1); Davis 478, 532, 479, 538 (nos. 159–62 below).

Note: Augustin Duseuil (1673–c. 1746), apprenticed to Philippe Padeloup, whose daughter he married in 1699; became master: c. 1715; binder to the duc and duchesse de Berry; binder to the king: 1717.

157 *A Paris binding, possibly made by A-M Padeloup, c. 1710*

Office de la Semaine Sainte … à l'usage de Rome et de Paris, Paris: A Dezallier, 1701; ruled in red. 8vo.

197 × 130 × 37 mm. (P 996) Davis 531

Red goatskin over paste boards, tooled in gold to a fanfare design with lines, gouges and pointillé curls, fleurons, leaf-shapes, tailed volutes and dots. Edges of boards: tooled in gold with a zig-zag roll. Doublures of red goatskin, tooled in gold with a fleuron-and-tulip border roll. Edges: gilt and marbled beneath the gold.

Sewn on five (?)cords, laced in, showing as raised bands on the spine, tooled in gold with a zig-zag roll (or pallet); six compartments, tooled in gold with zig-zag rolls (or pallets) near head and tail, fanfare design with pointillé fleurons; title lettered in second compartment. Endbands: double with a bead; pale blue, dark blue and pink silk over (?)rolled paper cores, tied down. Green silk bookmarker.

Endleaves: one free comb-marbled paper leaf (backed) and one free white paper leaf, conjugate with the backing paper, at both ends.

PROVENANCE: Red goatskin label with: MEMOR/FVI/DIERVM/ANTIQVORV[M]'/PS./CXLII; Pichon (sold: Paris, 1897, *55*); Oliver Henry Perkins (book plate); Lucius Wilmerding (book plate; sold: Parke-Bernet, 6.iii.1951, *488*).

REFERENCES: Foot, *Davis*, I, pp. 196, 202, note 22.

LITERATURE: Thoinan, pp. 356–70; De Ricci, *Schiff*; G D Hobson, *Fanfare*, pp. 65–6; Michon, pp. 101–3; Michon, *Reliures mosaïquées*, no. 36, pl. xxii; Devauchelle, II, pp. 37–45, 247; Esmerian sale II, Paris, 8.xii.1972, p. 73; Devaux, pp. 191–2; Foot, *Davis*, I, pp. 193–8; Barber, 'La reliure', pp. 168, 171; Schäfer, p. 100; Barber, 'Around the Padeloup and Derome workshops'.

Same tools (and similar designs) on: Hoe, *176 Bindings*, no. 107 (= Davis 533–535, no. 158, below); Rahir sale I, Paris, 1930, *59* (Paris, 1689); Catalogue: *Bibliothèque René G. D.* (Paris, Palais Galliera, 21–23.iii.1966), *87* (Paris, 1726); Pierre Berès, Catalogue 64, no. 321 (Paris, 1716, attributed to Duseuil); Esmerian sale II, Paris, 8.xii.1972, nos. 46–7 (attributed to A-M Padeloup le jeune).

Compare: Catalogue: *Bibliothèque R Descamps-Scrive* (Paris, Galerie Petit, 1925), no. 68 (Paris, 1666); Gougy sale II, Paris, 7-9.xi.1934, *924* (Paris, n.d.: arms of Louis XIV).

Note: A-M Padeloup le jeune (1685–1758), son of Michel Padeloup; married: 1712; several addresses in Paris (see Thoinan); 'Relieur ordinaire du Roy de Portugal': 1733; succeeded L-A Boyet as royal binder: 1733; married (second time): 1751; he was both a binder and a finisher; the inventory made after his death is printed in Devauchelle, II, pp. 42–4.

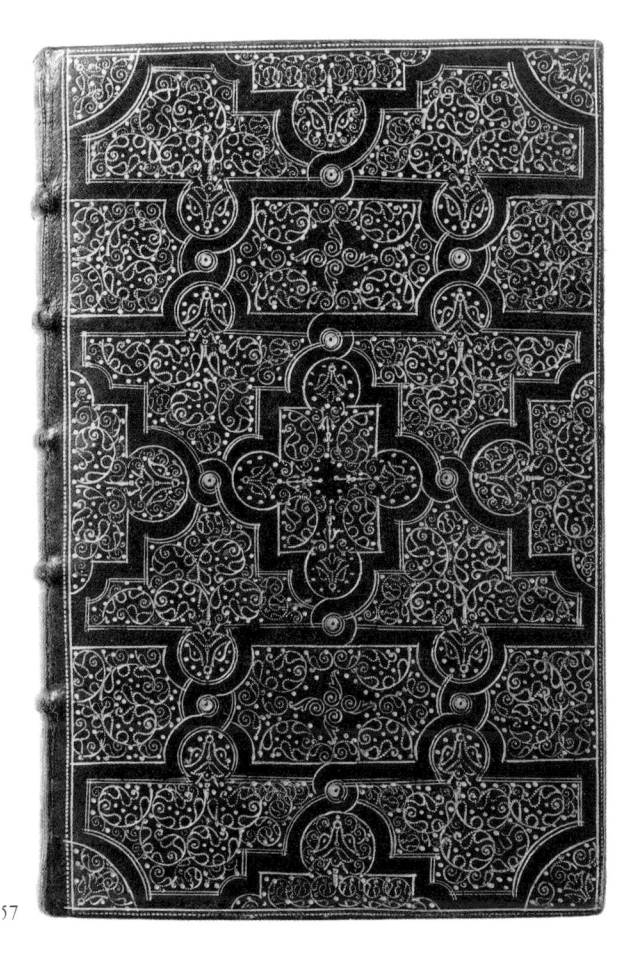

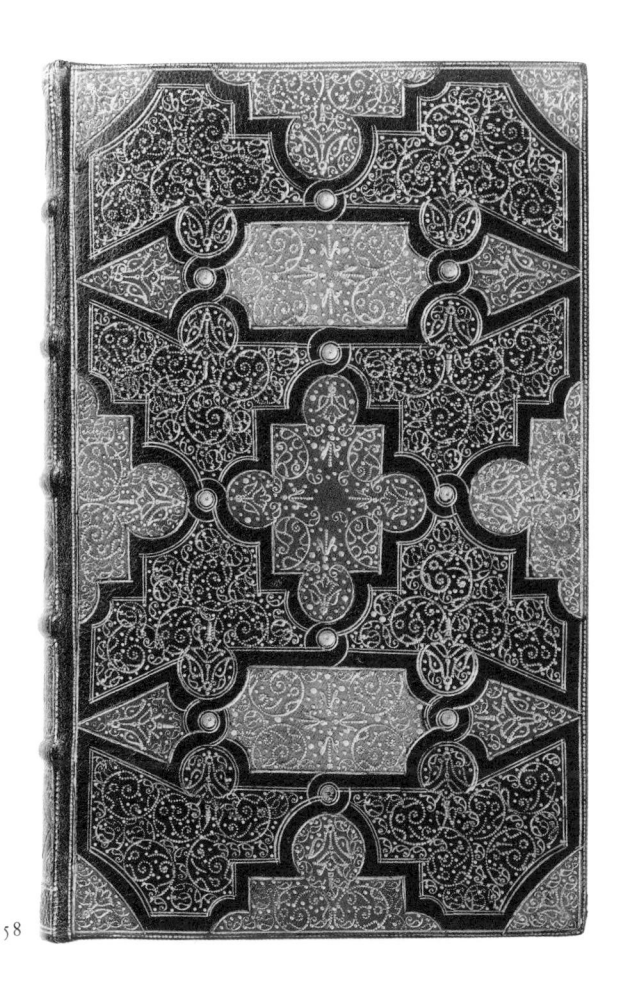

158 *Three Paris bindings possibly made by A-M Padeloup, c. 1710–20*

St John Chrysostom, *Homelies ou sermons de S. Jean Chrysostome ... traduits en françois par Paul A. de Marsilly*, 3 vols, Paris: A Pralard, 1693; ruled in red. 8vo.

195 × 125 × 36/7 mm. (P 1003) Davis 533–535

Black goatskin over paste boards, onlaid in red, citron and light brown goatskin and tooled in gold to a fanfare design with lines, gouges, pointillé curls and fleurons, small solid tools and dots. Edges of boards: tooled in gold with a line; turn-ins: tooled in gold with a roll. Edges: gilt and marbled beneath the gold.

    Sewn on five (?cord) supports, laced in, showing as raised bands on the spine, tooled in gold with dashes; six compartments, onlaid in red and brown and tooled in gold to a fanfare pattern; title lettered in gold on a red label in the second compartment; volume number on an onlay in the third compartment. Endbands: double with a bead; dark blue, pale blue and pink silk over (?)rolled paper cores (cut off), tied down; cord crowning cores. Pink silk bookmarkers.

    Endleaves: white and gold floral paper pastedowns and one free white and gold floral leaf (backed), conjugate with the pastedown, and one free white paper leaf, conjugate with the backing paper, at both ends.

    Repairs: small repairs at head and tail of spine; vol. 1: repair at joint.

THE HENRY DAVIS GIFT

PROVENANCE: On endleaf of vol. I in manuscript: 'par Nic. Fontaine et L maistre de Sacy'; Robert Hoe (book plate; sold: New York, Anderson Galleries, pt. IV, 11.xi.1912, *359*, pl.); Cortlandt F Bishop (book plate; sold: New York, Anderson Galleries, pt. I, 1938, *431*); Lucius Wilmerding (book plate; sold: Parke-Bernet, 5.iii.1951, *170*, pl.).
REFERENCES: Hoe, *176 Bindings*, no. 107; G D Hobson, *Fanfare*, p. 65; Foot, *Davis*, I, pp. 196, 202, note 22.
LITERATURE: Davis 531 (no. 157 above; and literature cited there); see also Culot, *Wittockiana*, p. 47.
Same tools on: Esmerian sale II, Paris, 8.xii.1972, nos. 46, 84 (doublure).

159 *A Paris binding probably made by A-M Padeloup, c. 1714–20*

Office de la Sainte Vierge, Paris: L Josse & C Robustel, 1714; ruled in red. 8vo.

171 × 115 × 32 mm.   (P 1189) Davis 478

Olive goatskin over paste boards, onlaid in red and brown and tooled in gold and blind with lines, gouges, flowers, dots, fleurons, small flame tools and small curls. Edges of boards and turn-ins: tooled in gold with zig-zag rolls. Doublures of red goatskin, tooled in gold with lines and a border filled with curls with fleurons and flames; small triangles roll. Edges: gilt and marbled beneath the gold.

Sewn on five (invisible) supports, probably laced in, showing as raised bands on the spine, tooled in gold with vertical dashes; six compartments, onlaid in different shapes and tooled in gold and blind with small curls, flowers, flame and circle tools, cross-hatching and dots; title lettered in blind on octagonal onlay in second compartment. Endbands: double with a bead; silver thread and blue and pink silk over (?)rolled paper cores, tied down.

Endleaves: a free white paper leaf and a pair of free conjugate paper leaves, at both ends.

PROVENANCE: On endleaf in manuscript: 'Sir Irving Sloter library'; Cortlandt F Bishop (book plate); bought: N Rauch, 30.iii.1955.
REFERENCES: Foot, *Davis*, I, pp. 196, 202, note 21.
LITERATURE: Davis 531 (no. 157 above; and literature cited there).
Same tools on: Davis 474 (no. 156 above), 532, 479, 538 (nos. 160–2 below).

160 *A Paris binding by A Duseuil or possibly by A-M Padeloup, c. 1716*

Office de la Semaine Sainte ... à l'usage de Rome et de Paris, Paris: N Pepie, 1716; ruled in red. 8vo.

201 × 128 × 38 mm.   (P 1324) Davis 532

Olive-brown goatskin over paste boards, onlaid in red and citron goatskin and tooled in gold with lines, dots, dashes, gouges, fleurons, flowers and stars around in the centre: the arms of Louise-Adélaïde d'Orléans, Mademoiselle d'Orléans. Edges of boards: tooled in gold with lines and dashes. Doublures of brown goatskin, tooled in (oxidized) silver with a wide border filled with gouges, flowers, tailed volutes, fleurons, curls, fleurs-de-lis and dots. Edges: gilt and marbled beneath the gold.

Sewn on five cords, laced in, showing as raised bands on the spine, tooled in gold with dashes; six compartments, onlaid in citron or red and tooled in gold to different patterns, with lines, flowers,

159

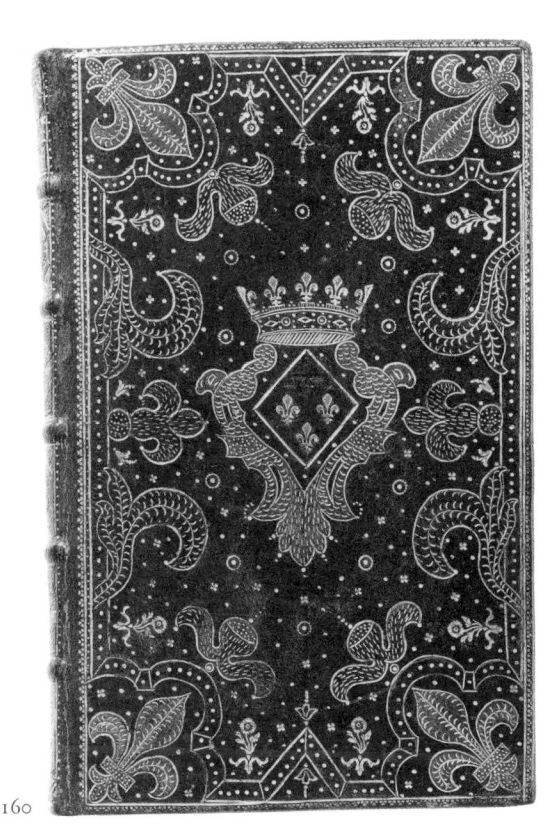

160

fleurons, curls and dots; title lettered on a red octagonal onlay in the second compartment. Endbands: double with a bead; pale blue, dark blue and beige silk over rolled paper cores, tied down occasionally. Blue, green and pink silk bookmarkers.

Endleaves: one free pink satin leaf (backed) and one free white paper leaf conjugate with the backing paper, plus one free white paper leaf and a pair of free conjugate white paper leaves, at both ends.

In a gold-tooled red goatskin case.

PROVENANCE: Louise-Adélaïde d'Orléans; Ripault (sold: January 1924, *11*); R Descamps-Scrive (book plate; sold: Paris, March 1925, I, *198*); Templeton Crocker (book plate); bought from: Lucien Goldschmidt, 8.xii.1959.

REFERENCES: Michon, p. 98; Michon, *Reliures mosaïquées*, no. 149; Romme, *Book Collector*, 1969, p. 24, notes 3–4; Foot, *Davis*, I, pp. 192, 194–6, 202, notes 12–13; *Wormsley*, p. 140.

LITERATURE: Guigard, pp. 109–10; Olivier, 2568 (1); Devaux, pp. 184–5; *Wormsley*, no. 55; Davis 531 (no. 157 above; and literature cited there); see also Davis 474 (no. 156 above; and literature cited there). For editions of the *Office de la Semaine Sainte* see: G. Barber, '"Il fallut meme réveiller les Suisses": Aspects of private religious practice in a public setting in eighteenth-century Versailles', in: N Aston (ed.), *Religious Change in Europe 1650–1914*, Oxford, 1997, pp. 75–101. For a general overview of mosaic bindings see also: Barber, 'La reliure', pp. 166–8 and Barber, 'Parisian fine binding trade'.

Same tools on: Gumuchian, 1930, no. 212; Lardanchet, Catalogue 63 (1970), *189*; Fitzwilliam Museum, Cambridge, Marlay bequest (De Mezeray, Paris, 1668); Waddesdon Manor (Longus, 1718); Davis 474, 478 (nos. 156, 159 above), 479, 538 (nos. 161–2 below).

207

Note: Three copies of this 1716 *Office* were bound in similar bindings, one for: Philippe II, duc d'Orléans (Catalogue: *The Magnificent French Library Formed by the Late Cortlandt F Bishop*, New York, Kende Galleries, 7–8.xii.1948, *220* = Esmerian sale II, Paris, 8.xii.1972, no. 82, attributed to A Duseuil); one for his wife, Françoise-Marie (Michon, pl. xxxvii; Michon, *Reliures mosaïquées,* no. 6, pl. ii), and the third is Davis 532.

Louise-Adélaïde, Mademoiselle d'Orléans (1698–1743), daughter of Philippe II, duc d'Orléans, regent of France, and Françoise-Marie de Bourbon, became a nun in 1717 and abbess of the abbey of Chelles in 1719.

161 *A Paris binding, probably made by A-M Padeloup, c. 1720*

Office de la Semaine Sainte ... à l'usage de Rome et de Paris, Paris: G Dupuis, 1718; ruled in red. 12mo.

173 × 100 × 36 mm. (P 1187) Davis 479

Citron goatskin over paste boards, onlaid in olive-brown and red goatskin and tooled in gold with lines, small flower heads, dots in circles, flowers, pointillé fleurons, solid fleurons, stars, with in the centre a larger flower spray. Edges of boards: tooled in gold with lines; turn-ins: tooled in gold with a zig-zag roll. Edges: gilt and marbled beneath the gold.

Sewn on five cords, laced in, showing as raised bands on the spine, tooled in gold with vertical dashes; six compartments, onlaid in red and brown and tooled in gold with pointillé curls, curved trident tools, lines, and flowers; title lettered on red label in second compartment. Endbands: double with a bead; blue, red and white silk over (?)cord (or possibly rolled paper) cores (cut off), tied down. Blue silk bookmarker.

Endleaves: turquoise, gold embossed, floral paper pastedowns and one free turquoise embossed leaf, conjugate with the pastedown, and two pairs of free conjugate white paper leaves, quired, at both ends.

PROVENANCE: Henri Beraldi (book plate; sold: Paris, Charpentier, June 1934, II, *191* pl.); bought: N Rauch, 30.iii.1955.
REFERENCES: Michon, *Reliures mosaïquées*, p. 72, no. 164; Foot, *Davis* I, pp. 196, 202, note 21.
LITERATURE: Michon, *Reliures mosaïquées,* pls. iii (?trident tool), iv (spine), xii (design), xiii–xvi (tools); Davis 531 (no. 157 above; and literature cited there).
Same tools on: Sale catalogue, Paris, Hôtel Drouot, 6–7.xi.1968, *144* (1746, arms of Marie Leczinska); Esmerian sale II, Paris, 8.xii.1972, nos. 84, 87; Davis 474, 478, 532 (nos. 156, 159, 160 above), 538 (no. 162 below).

162 *A Paris binding, probably made by A-M Padeloup, c. 1720–30*

L Senault, *Heures nouvelles tirées de la Sainte Ecriture*, Paris: Senault & C de Hansy, n.d. [c. 1680]; engraved title-page; engraved throughout; two leaves missing (pp. 231–4). 8vo.

185 × 120 × 21 mm. (P 958) Davis 538

Olive-brown goatskin over paste boards, onlaid in citron and red goatskin and tooled in gold with lines, gouges, pointillé curls and fleurons, solid small tools, flowers, curls and dots. Edges of boards: tooled

161 162

in gold with lines and dashes; turn-ins: tooled in gold with a zig-zag roll (re-tooled at the corners). Edges: gilt and marbled beneath the gold.

Sewn on five cords, laced in, showing as raised bands on the spine, tooled in gold with vertical dashes; six compartments, onlaid in different shapes and tooled in gold with pointillé curls, flower tools, lines, circles; title lettered on red label in second compartment. Endbands: double with a bead; blue, pink and white silk over (?)rolled paper cores, tied down. Pink silk bookmarker.

Endleaves: embossed stencilled (multi-coloured, floral on gold) pastedowns and one free embossed leaf conjugate with the pastedown, at both ends; at the front: one free white paper leaf.

PROVENANCE: On endleaf in manuscript: 'Luton'; H B Wheatley (book plate; sold: Sotheby's, 8.iv.1918, *36*); G D Hobson (manuscript note by Hobson, dated 8 March 1925, about the rayed circle ornament on the spine, a Daphnis and Chloe, 1718, with the arms of the regent, at Waddesdon Manor, and a binding in the *Bulletin Morgand*, I, *3615*; sold: Sotheby's, 22.v.1950, *70*).

REFERENCES: Romme, *Book Collector*, 1969, pl. I (centre); Foot, *Davis*, I, pp. 196, 202, note 21.

LITERATURE: Davis 531 (no. 157 above; and literature cited there).

Same tools on: Esmerian sale II, Paris, 8.xii.1972, nos. 84, 87; Culot, *Wittockiana*, p. 57; Davis 474, 478, 532, 479 (nos. 156, 159–61 above); see also Sotheby's, 19.x.1964, *154* (pl.).

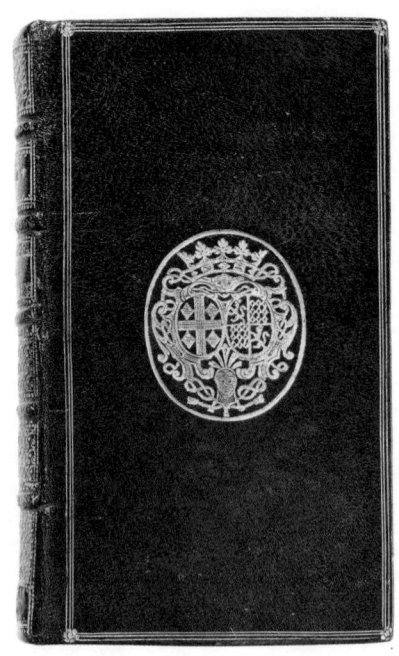

163

163 *Two Paris bindings for the comtesse de Verrue, c. 1712*

Jean Palaprat, *Oeuvres. Nouvelle édition, augmentée de plusieurs comédies*, 2 vols, Paris: P Ribou, 1712. 12mo.

163/4 × 97/8 × 28/36 mm. (P 1074) Davis 475–476

Red goatskin over paste boards, tooled in gold with lines along the border, small rosettes at the corners and in the centre: the arms of Jeanne-Baptiste d'Albert de Luynes, comtesse de Verrue. Edges of boards and turn-ins: tooled in gold with a small roll. Edges: gilt and marbled beneath the gold.

Sewn on three cords, laced in; two false bands, showing as five raised bands on the spine, tooled in gold with a zig-zag roll or pallet; six compartments, tooled in gold with lines, dots and a semis of solid curls; author's name lettered in second compartment; volume number tooled in third compartment; on tail compartment: a brown goatskin label, tooled in gold: '197'; '198'. Endbands: single with a bead; pink and white silk over (invisible) cores (cut off), tied down occasionally. Blue silk bookmarkers.

Endleaves: comb-marbled paper pastedowns and one free comb-marbled paper leaf (backed), conjugate with the pastedown and one free white paper leaf, conjugate with the backing paper, at both ends.

PROVENANCE: Jeanne-Baptiste d'Albert de Luynes, comtesse de Verrue (on endleaf in manuscript: 'Verrue sale cat p. 203'); John Ker, duke of Roxburghe (sold: London, 18.v–vi.1812); C J B Giraud (sold: Paris, 26.iii.1855, *1782*); Solier [Soler?] (1860); Lebeuf de Montgermont (1876); R Hoe (book plate; sold: New York, Anderson Galleries, pt. IV, 11.xi.1912, *380*); Lucius Wilmerding (book plate; sold: Parke-Bernet, 31.x.1951, *701*).
REFERENCES: Foot, *Revue française*, p. 384.
LITERATURE: Guigard, I, p. 206.
Same arms on: BL, C.65.d.18 (Orleans, 1572), C.108.a.21 (Paris, 1626), C.66.a.3 (Cologne, 1688), C.67.a.3 (Paris, 1674), C.66.b.6 (Paris, 1696); Devaux, p. 190; Librairie Laurent Coulet, Paris, Catalogue 35 (2007), p. 10.

164

164 *Two bindings probably made in Paris, c. 1717–20*

Histoire de l'Académie Royale ... avec les mémoires de littérature, 2 vols, Paris: Imprimerie royale, 1717. 4to.

264 × 193 × 53 mm. (P 1047) Davis 536–537

Red goatskin (or possibly sheepskin) over paste boards, varnished and painted with gold and silver paint to a design of a large frame with elaborate curls, corners with Aesculapius, lyre, globe and floral sprays; in the centre within a wreath of palm branches and ribbons: a human face surrounded by (sun)rays. Edges of boards and turn-ins: tooled in gold with a zig-zag roll. Edges: gilt and marbled beneath the gold.

Sewn on five (?)cords (four cords, the centre support may be of tanned leather), laced in, showing as raised bands on the spine; six compartments, painted in gold and silver with a laurel wreath, ornamental curls, fleurons and flowers; title and volume number tooled in second and third compartments. Endbands: double with a bead; white and blue silk over (?)rolled paper cores, tied down; cord crowning core (cut off). Green silk bookmarkers.

Endleaves; gilt-embossed floral paper pastedowns and one free embossed leaf (backed) conjugate with the pastedowns in both volumes, at both ends; vol. I at the front: a pair of free conjugate white paper leaves; at the end: one free white paper leaf conjugate with the backing paper; vol. II: one free white paper leaf, conjugate with the backing paper, at both ends.

In (later) red goatskin cases, lettered on the spine: 'Bignon's copy'.

PROVENANCE: (?)Jean-Paul Bignon; George Hilgrove; Lucius Wilmerding (book plate; sold: Parke-Bernet, 29.x.1951, *155*).

REFERENCES: Foot, *Revue française*, pp. 384–5, note 33.

LITERATURE: Gruel, I, p. 155; L Gruel, *Reliures en vernis sans odeur*, Paris, 1900 (offprint from: *Bulletin du bibliophile*); Oldham, *Shrewsbury School*, p. 129, pl. xxxi; A Ehrman, 'Les reliures vernis sans odeur autrement dit "Vernis Martin"', *Book Collector*, xiv (1965), pp. 523–7; G Barber, 'Note 273. Les reliures vernis sans odeur', *Book Collector*, xv (1966), pp. 351–2; G Colin, 'Foreign bookbindings iii: a "Vernis sans odeur" binding', *Book Collector*, xviii (1969), p. 361; A Rau, 'Note 325. A "Vernis sans odeur" binding', *Book Collector*, xviii (1969), p. 520; M Breslauer, Catalogue 104 (1979), no. 107; Schäfer, p. 160; *Wormsley*, no. 72.

Note: There are two kinds of varnished bindings, those made in the 18th century, mistakenly called 'vernis Martin', and those dating from the early 19th century. The latter are more usually called 'vernis sans odeur'. See Davis 573 (no. 195 below).

Apart from the statement on the cases, there is no indication in the books that they belonged to Bignon. Jean-Paul Bignon (1662–1743) was librarian to the king of France (from 1718); his own library was sold in 1718.

165 *A binding for the duc de Biron, c. 1720–30*

M T Cicero, *De philosophia volumen primum*, Venice: Aldus & A A Socerus, May 1523. 8vo.

164 × 102 × 28 mm.   (P 982) Davis 477

Red goatskin over paste boards, tooled in gold with lines, a wide border filled with small solid curls and fleurons, large marguerite tools in the corners and in the centre the arms of Luc-Antoine de Gontaut, duc de Biron. Edges of boards and turn-ins: tooled in gold with a zig-zag roll. Doublures of black goatskin, tooled in gold with a wide border filled with solid curls, small floral tools and large marguerite tools; on the doublure of the upper cover the monogram HRR has been added. Edges: gilt with a trace of marbling beneath the gold.

Sewn on five cords, laced in, showing as raised bands on the spine, tooled in gold with a zig-zag roll; six compartments, tooled in gold with curls in the corners and a bunch of flowers emanating from a heart in the centre; title lettered in second compartment. Endbands: double with a bead; pink blue and white silk over (?)cord cores (cut off), tied down. Green silk bookmarker.

Endleaves: one free multi-coloured spot-marbled paper leaf (backed) and one free white paper leaf conjugate with the backing paper, at both ends.

PROVENANCE: L-A de Gontaut, duc de Biron; on flyleaf in manuscript: 'aux armes d'Armand Louis de Gontaut Biron, duc de Laugin et de Biron (1747–1793)'; on the title-page a stamp showing two crowned Cs addorsed; Robert Hoe (book plate; sold: New York, Anderson Galleries, 24.iv.1911, *741*); Lucius Wilmerding (book plate; sold: Parke-Bernet, 5.iii.1951, *171*).

LITERATURE: Olivier, 1439.

Note: The binding is more likely to have been made for Luc-Antoine de Gontaut, duc de Biron (1701–1788), who had a military career; became governor of Landrecies: 1740; 'maréchal de France': 1757; governor general of Languedoc: 1775.

165 166

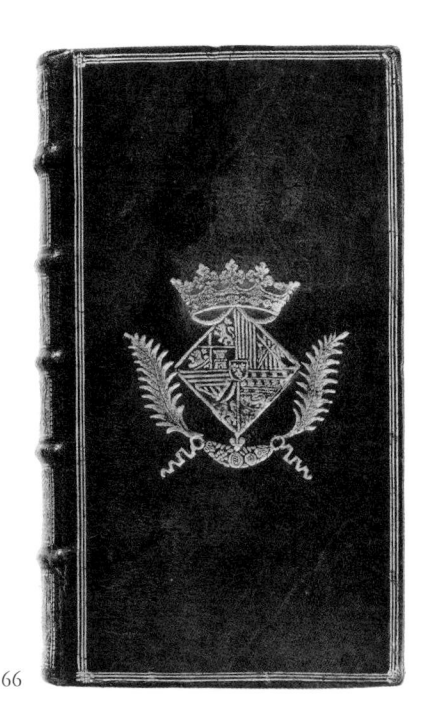

166 *A Paris binding for Marie Anne Victoire, infanta of Spain, c. 1722*

Mémoires sur divers genres de littérature et d'histoire, Paris: La veuve le Febvre, 1722.

Dedicated to Marie Anne Victoire, infanta of Spain, 'Future Reine de France'; engraved frontispiece. 12mo.

159 × 91 × 26 mm. (P 1072) Davis 480

Red sheepskin over paste boards, tooled in gold with three lines along the border, a rosette on the intersections and in the centre the arms of Marie Anne Victoire, infanta of Spain, between two palm branches connected by a garland. Edges of boards and turn-ins: tooled in gold with a small roll. Edges: gilt and marbled beneath the gold.

Sewn on five cords (laced in), showing as raised bands on the spine, tooled in gold; six compartments, tooled in gold with lines, dotted lines and solid and pointillé fleurons; title lettered in second compartment. Endbands: single with a bead; pink and white silk over (?)cord cores (cut off), tied down. Blue silk bookmarker.

Endleaves: comb- and spot-marbled pastedowns and one free marbled leaf (backed) conjugate with the pastedown and one free white paper leaf (probably conjugate with the backing paper), at both ends.

PROVENANCE: Marie Anne Victoire, infanta of Spain; Librairie Morgand & Fatout; Lucius Wilmerding (sold: Parke-Bernet, 31.x.1951, *612*).
REFERENCES: Foot, *Revue française*, p. 385.
Same arms on: BL, C.46.b.4 (Paris, 1723).
Note: Marie Anne Victoire, infanta of Spain (1718–1781), daughter of Philip V of Spain, betrothed to Louis XV of France: 1722; sent to Paris to receive a French education and await the proper age for the marriage to take place; in 1725 she was returned to Spain and diplomatic relations between the two countries were broken off.

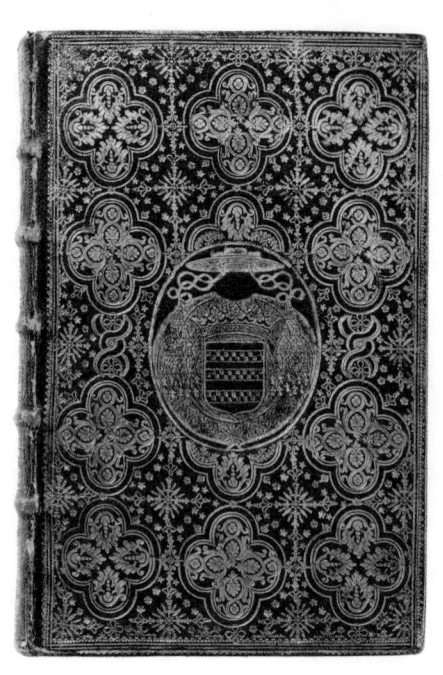

167 *A Paris binding, c. 1727*

L'Office de la Semaine Sainte à l'usage de la maison du roy, Paris: J Collombat, 1727. 8vo.

217 × 143 × 48 mm. (P 1196) Davis 539

Red goatskin (or possibly hair sheep) over paste boards, tooled in gold to a late fanfare design with lines and dotted lines along the border, fanfare ribbons forming compartments filled with large decorative foliage and floral tooling; small solid and pointillé fleurons, flowers, dots and stars. In the centre the arms of a Du Cambout de Coislin prelate. Edges of boards and turn-ins: tooled in gold with small zig-zag rolls. Edges: gilt and marbled beneath the gold.

Sewn on five (?)cords, laced in, showing as raised bands on the spine, tooled in gold with vertical lines; six compartments, tooled in gold with corner curls and fleurons; title lettered in second compartment. Endbands: double with a bead; pink, white and blue silk over (?)rolled paper cores, tied down. Blue silk bookmarker.

Endleaves: purple and gold floral paper pastedowns and one free purple and gold leaf (backed) conjugate with the pastedown, and one free white paper leaf conjugate with the backing paper, at both ends.

PROVENANCE:	Du Cambout de Coislin; bought: Karl & Faber, 12.v.1955, *476*.
REFERENCES:	Foot, *Revue française*, p. 385.
LITERATURE:	Olivier, 618.
Same tools on:	Madame Th. Belin sale, Giraud-Badin, Paris, 1936, *200* (Paris, 1743, with arms of the cardinal of York); N Rauch Catalogue I, *Très beaux livres*, Paris 1948, *246* (Paris 1745, with arms of Madame Marie-Adélaïde of France).
Note:	The arms are not those of Pierre du Cambout de Coislin (1636–1706), bishop of Orléans (Olivier, 618), whose arms can be found on BL, C.46.e.19 (see Davis 469, no. 144 above), but of a later member of the same family.

168

168   *A Paris binding, c. 1731–40*

C Barlaeus, *Poemata*, Leiden: Elzevier, 1631. 12mo.

122 × 74 × 30 mm.   (P 277) Davis 485

Red goatskin over paste boards, onlaid in citron and tooled in gold, with lines, quatrefoils in the corners, ovals with circles along the border, small flowers, dots and circles, a pomegranate tool in each corner and in the centre a cruciform onlay of citron goatskin, tooled in gold with stars, dots and small fleurons. Edges of boards: tooled in gold with lines and dashes; turn-ins: tooled in gold with a small roll. Edges: gilt and marbled beneath the gold.

    Sewn on four (recessed) cords, laced in; smooth spine, tooled in gold to divide into six compartments, each with a differently shaped citron onlay and tooled in gold with corner curls, flowers, a heart with a flower, a fleuron; title lettered in gold on an oval onlay in second compartment; near the tail: a green label lettered: ELZEVIER/1631 (maybe later). Endbands: double with a bead; pink and white silk over (invisible) cores (cut off), tied down sporadically. Blue-green silk bookmarker.

    Endleaves: multi-coloured embossed gilt paper pastedowns and one free embossed leaf (backed) conjugate with the pastedown, and one free white paper leaf conjugate with the backing paper, at both ends.

PROVENANCE:	Paul Hirsch (ex-libris); bought: Heffer, 29.ix.1941.
REFERENCES:	Foot, *Revue française*, p. 385.
LITERATURE:	Michon, *Reliures mosaïquées*, pp. 49–50, pl. xlii.
Same tools on:	John Rylands University Library, Manchester, 15595 (Amsterdam, 1662); Waddesdon Manor (Brussels, 1663); Michon, *Reliures mosaïquées*, nos. 41, 76, ?93, ?206; Whitney Hoff, 164 (pl. lxxxviii); Sotheby's, 22.iv.1958, *112*; Sotheby's, 19–21.xii.1960, *452*; Sotheby's, 19.x.1964, *34*.
Compare:	John Rylands University Library, Manchester, 15607 (Elzevier, 1656); Sotheby's, 19.x.1964, *345*; Sotheby's, 29.xi.1982, *173*.
Note:	Michon attributes several bindings with similar designs and (some) with the same tools to an 'Atelier des petits classiques'.

THE HENRY DAVIS GIFT

169   *Four bindings probably made in Paris, c. 1736–50*

Breviarium monasticum ordinis Sancti Benedicti ad usum congregationis Sancti Mauri in Gallia, 4 parts in 4 vols, Paris: P de Bats, 1736. 12mo.

133 × 80 × 30/25/28/30 mm. (P 204) Davis 481–484

Red goatskin over paste boards, tooled in gold to a dentelle design with lines, a small roll, scallop shells, fleurons and curls, pointillé flowers, dots and circles. Edges of boards: tooled in gold with a line; turn-ins: tooled in gold with a roll. Edges: gilt and marbled (red/blue) beneath the gold.

Sewn on five (?)cords, laced in, showing as raised bands on the spine, tooled in gold; six compartments, tooled in gold with lines, small flower tools, fleurs-de-lis and dots; small rolls near head and tail; title and part number lettered in second and third compartments. Endbands: double with a bead; red and white silk over cord cores (cut off), tied down sporadically. Green silk bookmarkers.

Endleaves: comb-marbled paper pastedowns and one free comb-marbled leaf (backed), conjugate with the pastedown, and one free white paper leaf conjugate with the backing paper, at both ends.

PROVENANCE: H Gordon Selfridge (sold: Sotheby's, 11.viii.1941, *23*, pl.).
LITERATURE: Barber, 'La reliure', pp. 168–9; Barber, 'Parisian fine binding trade'.

170   *Six bindings made in Paris for N-A de Ségur, c. 1738*

[M de Lussan and C J Chéron de Boismorand], *Anecdotes de la cour de Philippe-Auguste*, 6 vols, vols I–III Paris: Veuve Pissot, 1733; vols IV–VI Paris: Veuve Pissot, 1738. 12mo.

vols I–III: 173/2 × 97 × 29/30/26 mm.
vols IV–VI: 172/3/1 × 98 × 22/26/25 mm. (P 1023) Davis 491–496

Red goatskin over paste boards, onlaid in brown, citron and pale olive-brown to different mosaic designs, with gold-tooled lines along the border, onlaid corners and side compartments, and onlaid geometrical, leaf and flower shapes; tooled in gold with small solid tools, lines, dashes, flowers, leaves, circles, curls, dots and stars; vols IV–VI are similar in design; in the centre of all volumes the arms of N-A de Ségur. Edges of boards: tooled in gold with lines; turn-ins: tooled in gold with rolls (same roll on vols I–III, different roll on vols IV–VI). Edges: gilt.

Sewn on five cords, laced in, showing as raised bands on the spine, tooled, vols I–III: in gold with a line, vols IV–VI: in blind with a line, traces of gold; six compartments with hexagonal, round and floral onlays and tooled in gold; title lettered on labels in second compartments; volume numbers on labels in third compartments. Endbands: single with a bead; vols I–III: blue and white silk over (?)rolled paper cores, tied down (pink silk thread among tie-downs); vols IV–VI: pink, white and blue silk over (?)rolled paper or cord cores (cut off), tied down. Vols I–III: blue silk bookmarkers; vols IV–VI: green silk bookmarkers.

Endleaves: gilt-paper pastedowns and one free gilt-paper leaf (backed) conjugate with the pastedown and one free white paper leaf conjugate with the backing paper, at both ends.

PROVENANCE: N-A de Ségur; Lardanchet, Catalogue 45 (1951), no. 1027 bis. (sold: 29.v.1951).
REFERENCES: Michon, *Reliures mosaïquées*, no. 198; Foot, *Revue française*, p. 385, note 34, fig. 6.
LITERATURE: Olivier, 94; Michon, *Reliures mosaïquées*, p. 49, pl. xli, nos. 176, 190.

169   170

Note: Vols I–III were probably bound at the same time and vols IV–VI were also bound at the same time, but a little later; all volumes were probably bound in the same atelier, although the tools are slightly different.
Nicolas-Alexandre de Ségur, president of the Parlement of Bordeaux, died: 1755.

---

171   *A Paris binding attributed to Derome, c. 1745*

L'Office de la nuit, et de laudes. Automne. II. partie, Paris: Libraires associés, 1745; ruled in red. 12mo.

169 × 100 × 38 mm.   (P 1188) Davis 486

Red goatskin over paste boards, onlaid in citron, olive, white, red, brown and black, and tooled in gold; a black onlaid strip along the border, gold tooled lines and small rolls; scallop-shaped onlays in the corners, tooled in gold with dots and circles; a large orchid with leaves and other flowers onlaid in the centre, outlined in gold, gold-tooled circles; a semis of dots. Edges of boards and turn-ins: tooled in gold with a zig-zag roll. Edges: gilt.

Sewn on five (?)cords, laced in, showing as raised bands on the spine, tooled in gold with a line; six compartments, tooled in gold with lines, small trident tools and dots; differently shaped onlays in citron, brown and black, tooled in gold with small tools, dots and circles; title lettered on citron label in second compartment. Endbands: double with a bead; red and grey silk over (?)rolled paper cores, tied down very sporadically.

Endleaves: embossed white on gold floral paper pastedowns and one free white-gold embossed leaf (backed) conjugate with the pastedown, and one free white paper leaf (tipped on at the front; possibly conjugate with the backing paper at the end), at both ends.

217

171

PROVENANCE:	On the title-page a cut-out strip of paper printed: 'Relié par Padeloup le jeune/ place Sorbonne à Paris' [this ticket was used before 1733; it was added later]; Grace Whitney Hoff (book plate); bought: N Rauch, 30.iii.1955.
REFERENCES:	Whitney Hoff, II, no. 331 (pl.); Michon, *Reliures mosaïqées*, no. 227, p. 40, note 3; Romme, *Book Collector*, 1969, pl. 1 (left); Foot, *Davis*, I, p. 200; *Wormsley*, p. 146.
LITERATURE:	Thoinan, pp. 246–56; Hoe, *176 Bindings*, no. 100; G D Hobson, *Thirty Bindings*, pl. xxviii; Devauchelle, II, pp. 53–8, 229; Foot, *Davis* I, pp. 199–200 (and literature mentioned there); Barber, 'La reliure', p. 171; see also Davis 541 (no. 172 below).
Same design:	H Martin *et al.*, *Le Livre français*, exh. cat., Paris, 1924, pl. xcvi; Cortlandt F Bishop sale, New York, Kende Galleries, 1.xii.1948, *152*; Lucius Wilmerding sale, Parke-Bernet, 30.iii.1951, *79*.
Same design and same tools on:	BL, C.48.b.8 (Paris, 1749).
Note:	The Derome family was a large family of binders, working in Paris from the mid-17th century till the first quarter of the 19th century. Jacques-Antoine Derome (c. 1696–1760), master: 1718; three sons: Charles (master: 1740), Nicolas (master: 1748), Nicolas-Denis le jeune (1731–1790), succeeded his father: 1760; master: 1761; 'garde' of the guild: 1773; married a Miss Bradel; was both binder and finisher; inherited his father's tools; was succeeded by Alexis-Pierre Bradel-Derome, his nephew.

---

172 *A Paris binding by J-A or N-D Derome, c. 1748 or after 1760*

L'Office de la Semaine-Sainte, à l'usage de la maison du roy, Paris: J-F Collombat, 1748. 8vo.

216 × 133 × 54 mm.   (P 1319) Davis 541

Red goatskin over paste boards, tooled in gold with lines and a small roll along the border, feathery curls, fleurons, circles with stars, stylized flowers and dots around a centre piece built up of large flowers

172

and curls, a tool showing a sitting bird, facing right and four scallop tools around a rosette. Edges of boards and turn-ins: tooled in gold with a zig-zag roll. Edges: gilt.

Sewn on five cords, laced in, showing as raised bands on the spine, tooled in gold with dashes; six compartments, tooled in gold with floral curls in the corners and a flower tool in the centre; a fleur-de-lis and flower roll near the tail; title lettered in second compartment. Endbands: single with a bead; blue and beige silk over (invisible) cores (cut off); no tie-downs visible.

Endleaves: coloured large-comb-marbled paper pastedowns and one free large-comb-marbled leaf (backed), conjugate with the pastedown, and one free white paper leaf conjugate with the backing paper, at both ends.

PROVENANCE: On endleaf in manuscript: 'Cornellot' (in an 18th–19th-century hand); J R Abbey (book plate; 'J.A.2665/15:10:1945'; sold: Sotheby's, 23.vi.1965, *518*).
REFERENCES: Foot, *Davis*, I, p. 200.
LITERATURE: Foot, *Davis*, I, pp. 199–200 (and literature mentioned there); Devaux, pp. 195–6; Barber, 'Parisian fine binding trade'; Barber, 'Around the Padeloup and Derome workshops', pp. 197–8; see also Davis 486 (no. 171 above).
Same tools on: John Rylands University Library, Manchester, R52200 (blank book); Bodleian Library Oxford, Broxbourne R 945 (1768); BL, C.11.d.6 (with ticket of Derome le jeune), C.19.c.24; Davis 487–90 (no. 173 below) and Davis 545 (no. 184 below); Beraldi sale II, Paris, 1934, no. 98 (Naples, 1723); De Ricci, *Schiff*, nos. 32 (with ticket of J-A Derome), 40 (with ticket of Derome le jeune).
Note: The bird tool facing right was used on bindings with tickets both of J-A Derome and of Derome le jeune.

219

THE HENRY DAVIS GIFT

173 *Paris bindings by J-A or N-D Derome for Dominique de la Rochefoucauld, c. 1750 or after 1760*

Eucologe ou livre d'Eglise imprimé par l'ordre de Monseigneur l'Archevêque de Rouen à l'usage de son diocèse, 4 vols, Rouen: F Oursel, 1739. 12mo.

142 × 85 × 43/34/37/38 mm. (P 988) Davis 487–490

Brown goatskin over paste boards, tooled in gold with a small roll and lines along the border; a dentelle design with curls, fleurons, trident tools, a tool showing a sitting bird, facing right, flower tools and dots; with in the centre the arms of Dominique de la Rochefoucauld. Edges of boards: tooled in gold with a line. Edges: gilt and marbled beneath the gold.

Sewn on five cords, laced in, showing as raised bands on the spine, tooled in gold; six compartments, tooled in gold with curls in the corners and a cross of Lorraine in the centre; small fleurons; title and volume titles (PARTIE DE PRINTEMP/D'ESTE/D'AUTOMNE/D'HYVER) lettered in second and third compartments. Endbands: single with a bead; red, blue and white silk over (?)cord cores (cut off), tied down. Pink silk bookmarkers.

Endleaves: pink silk pastedowns and one free pink silk leaf (backed) conjugate with the pastedown, and one free white paper leaf (?)conjugate with the backing paper, at both ends.

PROVENANCE: Dominique de la Rochefoucauld; part 2: on endleaf in manuscript (modern hand): 'no 2183/4vols/cat 1544' (inserted is a cutting from an (unidentified) catalogue, where no. 1544 = Davis 487–90, pl.); Lucius Wilmerding (book plate; sold: Parke-Bernet, 5.iii.1951, *236*).
REFERENCES: Foot, *Davis*, I, pp. 200, 203, note 55.
LITERATURE: Olivier, 711; Davis 486, 541 (nos. 171, 172 above; and literature mentioned there).
Same tools on: Davis 541 (no. 172 above), 540 (no. 174 below), 545 (no. 184 below).
Note: Dominique de la Rochefoucauld (1713–1800), archbishop of Albi:1747; abbot general of Cluny: 1757; archbishop of Rouen: 1759; cardinal: 1778; after August 1792 he emigrated to Belgium and Germany. The arms are those of an archbishop or a cardinal. Considering the text it is possible that he acquired this copy in or after 1759, in which case a later binding date is more likely.

174 *A Paris binding, probably by J-A Derome for the comte de Langle, c. 1752*

L'Office de la Semaine Sainte … à l'usage de Rome et de Paris, Paris: T de Hansy, E-F Savoye, J-C Chardon fils, 1752. 8vo.

211 × 136 × 35 mm. (P 1132) Davis 540

Dark blue goatskin over paste boards, onlaid in citron, red and olive, and tooled in gold, with lines and a small roll along the border, gouges, curls, small flowers, stars, circles and dots; the centre compartment has been cut out and has the painted arms of the comte de Langle under mica. The upper and lower cover are not absolutely identical. Edges of boards and turn-ins: tooled in gold with a zig-zag roll. Edges: gilt and marbled beneath the gold.

Sewn on five (invisible) supports, uncertain whether all laced in; showing as raised bands on the

173   174

spine, tooled in gold with a zig-zag pallet or roll; six compartments, onlaid alternately in olive, citron and red, and tooled in gold with small and larger flower and acorn tools; fleur-de-lis and leaf pallets (or rolls) near top and tail; title lettered on a red goatskin label in second compartment. Endbands: single with a bead; white and blue silk over (?)rolled cores (cut off), tied down. Blue silk bookmarker.

Endleaves: pink watered-silk pastedowns and one free pink watered-silk leaf (backed) conjugate with the pastedown, and one free white paper leaf (possibly) conjugate with the backing paper, at both ends.

PROVENANCE:	Comte de Langle; on half-title in manuscript: 'Md Briancourt'; in a different hand: 'donné a Me la Baronne de Meugin foudragon'; Aimé Laurent (book plate); bought: Lardanchet (?), 24.xii.1953.
REFERENCES:	*Treasures*, 1965, no. 86; Romme, *Book Collector*, 1969, p. 24, note 2; Foot, *Davis*, I, p. 200.
LITERATURE:	Olivier, 953; see Davis 486, 541 (nos. 171, 172 above; and literature mentioned there).
Same tools on:	G D Hobson, *Thirty Bindings*, no. 28; see also Davis 487–90 (no. 173 above; and bindings with same tools mentioned there).

---

175   *A binding probably made in Paris, c. 1750*

Recueil d'édits, déclarations, ordonnances, arrests et règlements concernant l'Hôtel Royal des Invalides, Paris: Charles Osmont, 1744 [and four other works: Paris 1746–9]. 4to.

262 × 186 × 42 mm.   (P 1136) Davis 542

White calf over paste boards, tooled in gold and decorated with green, yellow and red paint, to a dentelle design with lines and a small roll along the border, large 'carnation' tools in the corners, curls and feathery curls, flowers, acorns and fleurons around, in the centre: the painted German imperial arms; the individual quarterings (Hungary, Bohemia, Old Burgundy, Empire) are painted in the corners, while the escutcheon (Austria) is painted at the sides. Edges of boards: tooled in gold with two lines; turn-ins: tooled in gold with two fleurs-de-lis rolls. Edges: gilt and marbled beneath the gold.

Sewn on five cords, laced in, showing as raised bands on the spine, tooled in gold with dashes; six compartments, tooled in gold with flowers and the painted quarterings of the German imperial arms; title lettered on red goatskin label in second compartment (possibly a later label). Endbands: double with a bead; pink, white and blue silk over white cores (material invisible; cut off), tied down. Pink silk bookmarker.

Endleaves: pink moiré silk pastedowns and one free pink moiré silk leaf (backed), conjugate with the pastedown, and one free white paper leaf, possibly conjugate with the backing paper, at both ends.

Wrapper and box.

PROVENANCE: (?)Maria Theresia, archduchess of Austria; on endleaf in manuscript: 'V.C.33'; ticket (partly printed, partly in manuscript) with: 'A 45/P 4/ No 25' (?); Pierre Berès (ticket; Catalogue 54, *232*, pl.; sold: 29.i.1954).

Note: Both Guigard and Olivier give different arms for Maria Theresia of Austria. Maria Theresia, archduchess of Austria (1717–1780) was empress of Germany (from 1745) and queen of Hungary and Bohemia (from 1737), so she could have used arms with these quarterings.

176

176 *A Paris binding by Lemonnier, c. 1750*

M T Cicero, *De amicitia dialogus ad Atticum; ex recensione J. G. Graevii*, Paris: A V Coustelier, 1749. 32mo.

83 × 54 × 12 mm. (P 1006) Davis 559

White calf over paste boards, inlaid in white, red, olive and brown and tooled in gold to a design showing one large and several smaller flowers; gouges, small sprays, a line along the border, and a semis of dots. In the centre a later green onlay tooled in gold with a sheaf of corn [unidentified crest]. Signed at the foot of both covers: MONNIER FECIT. Edges of boards: tooled in gold with a line; turn-ins: tooled in gold with a small zig-zag roll. Edges: gilt.

Sewn on four (recessed) cords, laced in; smooth spine, onlaid with strips of olive, brown and red, forming 'bands' and a simple floral design, and tooled in gold with small curls and dots. Endbands: single with a bead; blue silk over (?)cord cores (cut off), tied down sporadically. Blue silk bookmarker.

Endleaves: pink watered-silk pastedowns and one free pink watered-silk leaf (backed) conjugate with the pastedown, and one free white paper leaf conjugate with the backing paper and a second free white paper leaf, at both ends.

PROVENANCE: T Seligman, Newton Hall, Cambridge (loose book plate); bought: Sotheby's, 30.iv.1951, *193*.

REFERENCES: Michon, *Reliures mosaïquées*, p. 36, note 1, no. 235; *Treasures*, 1965, no. 85; Romme, *Book Collector*, 1969, p. 24, note 1; Foot, *Davis*, I, pp. 199, 203, note 45.

LITERATURE: Michon, *Reliures mosaïquées*, pp. 33–6; Devauchelle, II, pp. 50–2, 242; Foot, *Davis*, I, p. 199 (and literature mentioned there); Devaux, pp. 192, 194; Barber, 'La reliure', p. 171; Barber, 'Around the Padeloup and Derome workshops', p. 187, colour plate 3; Culot, 'Quelques reliures de l'atelier Lemonnier'; see also Davis 401 (no. 177 below).

Note: The Monnier or Lemonnier family was a family of binders in Paris, the best-known members of which were Louis-François (master: 1737; 'garde': 1756; still alive in 1776)

223

and his son, Jean-Charles-Henri. He became master: 1757; binder to the duc d'Orléans: 1759–after 1780; and 'garde' of the guild: 1769. He lived with his father, possibly sharing his tools. Tessier, who succeeded Lemonnier, apparently used (some of) Lemonnier's tools. His *Catalogue des fers qui sont dans la boête à dorer de Tessier à l'époque de 1789* is in Paris (Bibliothèque des Arts Décoratifs), see: R B Savigny de Moncorps, 'Un catalogue de fers à dorer au XVIIIe siècle', *Le Livre et l'image*, 2 (1893/4), pp. 14–23.

For the sheaf of corn crest see: Devaux, p. 205 (Rouen, 1792).

177 *A Paris binding attributed to Lemonnier, c. 1750*

A Bacci, *De naturali vinorum historia*, Rome: N Mutius, 1597. fol.

316 × 205 × 29 mm. (P 978) Davis 401

Citron goatskin over paste boards, onlaid in red, olive-green and dark green goatskin and tooled in gold with a wide (onlaid and cut-out) border with flower and leaf motifs, gouges, small sprays, small fleurons and a semis of dots; lines and small rolls; onlaid and gold-tooled corners. Edges of boards: tooled in gold with lines and dashes; turn-ins: tooled in gold with crescents. Doublures of red goatskin, tooled in gold with lines and crescents, a wide roll showing feathery leaves winding round plants with berries; a trident tool, feathery curls and fleurons in the corners and along the sides; basket-work tooling. Edges: gilt and marbled (faint) beneath the gold.

Sewn on six (invisible) supports, laced in, showing as raised bands on the spine, tooled in gold with a double line; seven compartments, onlaid in red and brown and tooled in gold with cross-hatching; trident tools, dots; title and date ('1596': as on the engraved title-page) lettered on labels in second and third compartments. Endbands: double with a bead; red, blue and white silk over (?)white (invisible) cores (probably laced in), tied down. Blue silk bookmarker.

Endleaves: one free blue watered-silk leaf (backed) and one free white paper leaf conjugate with the backing paper, at both ends.

PROVENANCE: On title-page in manuscript: 'Philippi Antonij Leonis'; duke of Marlborough (White Knights Library; sold: Evans, 8.vi.1819, *384*); S R Christie-Miller (sold: Sotheby's, 3.v.1920, *468*, pl.); Quaritch; Cortlandt F Bishop (sold: New York, Anderson Galleries, 1938, *165*, pl.); Lucius Wilmerding (book plate; sold: Parke-Bernet, 5.iii.1951, *49*, pl.).
REFERENCES: Michon, *Reliures mosaïquées*, p. 36, no. 72; Foot, *Davis*, I, pp. 192, 197 (pl.), 199, 203, note 47.
LITERATURE: Davis 559 (no. 176 above; and literature cited there).
Compare: Gottlieb, plate 63.

177

178 *A Paris binding by P-P Dubuisson, c. 1750*

Heures nouvelles dédiées à la reine à l'usage de Rome, Paris: C Herissant fils, 1749; ruled in red. 12mo.

171 × 112 × 38 mm. (P 1026) Davis 560

White calf over paste boards, onlaid in red, dark blue and green and tooled and blocked in gold with a line and crescents along the border, and a plaque with a design of intersecting lines, feathery curls, flowers and fleurons; in the centre, a large spray of flowers onlaid and tooled in gold; stylized flowers in circles. Edges of boards and turn-ins: tooled in gold with a zig-zag roll. Edges: gilt and marbled beneath the gold.

Sewn on five (?)cords, laced in, showing as raised bands on the spine; six compartments, tooled in gold with lines and curls, green centre onlays tooled in gold with a fleur-de-lis; small rolls or pallets near top and tail; title lettered on a red goatskin label in second compartment. Endbands: single with a bead; blue and white silk over white cores (material invisible) (cut off), tied down. Blue silk bookmarker.

Endleaves: blue watered-silk pastedowns and one free blue watered-silk leaf (backed) conjugate with the pastedown, at both ends; at the front: one free white paper leaf; at the end: a pair of free conjugate white paper leaves.

In a contemporary green-stained (?)calf (?possibly parchment) pull-off case, tooled in gold; red goatskin label with the title lettered in gold.

PROVENANCE:	On verso of title-page 'Avis': a note in French about editions in different formats to be found in the same bookshop, 'Toutes reliées en veau & maroquin'; on endleaf in manuscript: 'auur avec le Sacq'; Lardanchet (Catalogue 44, 1950, *125*, pl.; sold: 29.v.1951).
REFERENCES:	Romme, *Book Collector*, 1969, p. 24, pl. 1 (third); Foot, *Davis*, I, p. 202, note 34.
LITERATURE:	Gruel, I, pp. 87–9; II, pp. 69–70, pl. B; Michon, pp. 105–6; Devauchelle, II, pp. 46–50, 232; Foot, *Davis*, I, pp. 198, 202 (and literature cited there); Barber, 'La reliure', pp. 169–70; Schäfer, p. 116; Barber, 'Parisian fine binding trade'.
Same plaque on:	Christie's, 23.vi.1982, *72* (with French royal arms in the centre and with Dubuisson's large ticket); Culot, *Wittockiana*, p. 59.
Note:	Pierre-Paul Dubuisson, son of René Dubuisson (master: 1710), became master in 1746; succeeded Padeloup as 'relieur du roi': 1758; he was both a binder and a finisher; died: 1762.

179 *A Paris binding by the 'Atelier à la Tulipe', c. 1752*

Heures nouvelles dédiées aux Dames de S. Cyr, Paris: C Herissant fils, 1752. 12mo.

173 × 103 × 43 mm. (P 1325) Davis 561

Red goatskin over paste boards, onlaid in olive and tooled in gold with lines and a small roll, a dentelle border built up of curls, flowers and fleurons; a large tulip onlaid and tooled in gold in each corner and a pomegranate onlaid and tooled in gold in the centre. Edges of boards: tooled in gold with lines and dashes; turn-ins: tooled in gold with a small roll. Edges: gilt.

Sewn on five (possibly cord) supports, laced in, showing as raised bands on the spine, tooled in gold with dashes; six compartments, tooled in gold with curls, a thistle or a flower; compartments 4 and 6:

178   179

onlaid in citron and tooled in gold with a bunch of grapes or a thistle; title lettered on a citron label in second compartment. Endbands: single with a bead; pink and white silk over rolled paper cores, tied down. Blue silk bookmarker.

Endleaves: curl-marbled paper pastedowns and one free curl-marbled paper leaf conjugate with the pastedown, and one free white paper leaf, at both ends.

PROVENANCE: H Destailleur (book plate); bought: after 1956 (no acquisition details available).
REFERENCES: Foot, *Davis*, I, pp. 196–7, 202, note 28.
LITERATURE: Michon, *Reliures mosaïquées*, pp. 51–2 and no. 223 (same tulip as on Davis 561); Foot, *Davis*, I, pp. 196–7 (and literature cited there); see also Davis 562 (no. 180 below).
Note: Of the bindings listed by Michon as having come from the 'Atelier à la Tulipe', not all have the same tools.

---

180   *A Paris binding by the 'Atelier à la Tulipe' or possibly by A-M Padeloup, c. 1755*

[R de Saint-Sauveur], *Agenda des auteurs ou Calpin littéraire*, [Paris]: 'anonime fertile', 1755 [and] [J F de Bastide], *La Trentaine de Cithère*, London [Paris], 1753. 12mo.

136 × 81 × 30 mm.   (P 1326) Davis 562

Olive goatskin over paste boards, onlaid in red and tooled in gold with lines and a small roll, large onlaid flowers in the corners, an onlaid bouquet of flowers in the centre, small onlaid circles with a gold-tooled pierced heart; background tooled in gold with leaf sprays, flowers, small cocks, small birds, fleurons,

227

180

circles and dots. Edges of boards: tooled in gold with a line and dashes. Doublures of red goatskin, tooled in gold with lines and gouges, flowers, fleurons, birds, floral sprays and in the centre a fan shape surrounded by flowers and trident tools. Edges: gilt.

Sewn on five (invisible) supports (uncertain whether or not laced in), showing as raised bands on the spine, tooled in gold with dashes; six compartments, onlaid in red and tooled in gold with small tools; titles lettered on a red label in second and third compartments. Endbands: stuck on; faded pink in three rows (twisted). Pink silk bookmarker.

Endleaves: two sheets of gold paper pasted together forming a free gilt paper leaf and two free white paper leaves (uncertain whether conjugate: pasted together at the joint), at both ends.

PROVENANCE: V Wassermann (sold: Brussels, 24.x.1921, *1100*); Mortimer Schiff (book plate; sold: Sotheby's, 9.xii.1938, *2180*, pl.); bought: Breslauer, 23.iv.1957.
REFERENCES: Michon, *Reliures mosaïquées*, no. 252; Foot, *Davis*, I, pp. 196, 202, note 25.
LITERATURE: Foot, *Davis*, I, pp. 196–7 (and literature cited there); see also Davis 561 (no. 179 above).
Same tools on: Maggs, Catalogue 489 (1927), *229* (= Michon, *Reliures mosaïquées*, no. 223); Gougy sale I, Paris, 5-8.iii.1934, *507*; Mortimer Schiff sale, Sotheby's, 1938, *458*; Michon, *Reliures mosaïquées*, pl. xliv.

---

181   *Paris bindings by Louis Douceur, c. 1754*

T Lucretius Carus, *Della natura delle cose libri sei* [translation: A Marchetti], 2 vols, Amsterdam: T.° P.°, 1754; engraved title-page. 8vo.

23 1/2 × 14 7/8 × 30/35 mm.   (P 1330) Davis 543–544

Red goatskin over paste boards, tooled in gold to a dentelle design; lines, a small roll and dotted lines

181

along the border, large curls, leaves, acorns, flowers, dots and garlands in the corners and a wide border filled with curls, leaves, acorns, garlands, thistle tools and dots. Edges of boards: tooled in gold with a double line; turn-ins: tooled in gold with a floral roll. Edges: gilt.

Sewn on five cords, laced in, showing as raised bands on the spine, tooled in gold with a line; six compartments, tooled in gold with leaves and thistles; author's name and volume numbers lettered on brown goatskin labels in second and third compartments. Endbands: double with a bead; pink, white and blue silk over (?)rolled paper cores, tied down. Green silk bookmarker.

Endleaves: comb-marbled pastedowns and one free comb-marbled leaf (backed) conjugate with the pastedown and one free white paper leaf, possibly conjugate with the backing paper, at both ends (vol. I: at the end: lacking the free white leaf).

PROVENANCE: T Hugh Cobb (book plate; sold: Sotheby's, 17.vii.1944, *150*); J R Abbey (book plate; 'J.A.6876/25.6.1958'; sold: Sotheby's, 22.vi.1965, *456*, pl.).
REFERENCES: Foot, *Davis*, I, pp. 198, 203, note 38.
LITERATURE: Michon, p. 109; Devauchelle, II, p. 231; Foot, *Davis*, I, pp. 198–9 (and literature cited there); Barber, 'Around the Padeloup and Derome workshops', pp. 191–2.
Note: Louis Douceur, son of François, master: 1721; 'garde de la Communauté': 1737–9; according to Gruel (I, p. 85): succeeded Padeloup (d. 1758) as 'relieur ordinaire du roy' [although Pierre-Paul Dubuisson was 'relieur du roy' from 1758–1762]; died: 1769.

182 *A Paris binding by Nicolas-Denis Derome le jeune, c. 1761*

L'Office de la Semaine Sainte en latin et en françois à l'usage de Rome et de Paris, Paris: G Desprez, 1758. 8vo.

196 × 128 × 36 mm. (P 1328) Davis 564

White calf over paste boards, onlaid in brown, olive and red goatskin and tooled in gold, with lines, gouges, floral, fleuron and leaf tools, decorated with red and blue paint, a semis of dots; large onlaid and gold tooled corner ornaments with cut-out compartments with gold, silver and red paper under mica, and in the centre within a large onlaid and gold-tooled cartouche a cut-out oval with the painted arms of Stanislas Leczinski, (former) king of Poland, under mica. Edges of boards and turn-ins: tooled in gold with zig-zag rolls. Edges: gilt.

Sewn on five cords (uncertain whether or not laced in), showing as raised bands on the spine, tooled in gold; six compartments, onlaid in red and brown goatskin with cut-out centres showing coloured paper under mica, and tooled in gold with small tools; title lettered on brown goatskin label in second compartment. Headband: single with a bead; pink, white and blue silk over white (?)rolled paper cores, tied down sporadically (tailband missing). Green silk bookmarker.

Endleaves: blue silk pastedowns and one free blue silk leaf (backed) conjugate with pastedown, and one free white paper leaf conjugate with the backing paper, at both ends.

PROVENANCE: King Stanislas Leczinski; bought: Breslauer, 2.i.1964.
REFERENCES: Michon, *Reliures mosaïquées*, no. 263; Foot, *Davis*, I, pp. 200, 203, note 58.
LITERATURE: Guigard, I, p. 65; Olivier, 2684; Michon, pp. 109–10; Michon, *Reliures mosaïquées*, pp. 37–43, nos. 150, 248, 256, 257, 259, 265, 268, 297, 334; Foot, *Davis*, I, pp. 199–201 (and literature cited there); Devaux, pp. 195–7; Ract-Madoux, 'Essai de classement'; Barber, 'Around the Padeloup and Derome workshops'; see also Davis 563 (no. 183 below). For Derome family see Davis 486 (no. 171 above).
Same tools on: Beraldi sale II, Paris, 1934, no. 98 (Naples, 1723); Waddesdon Manor, *Heures* (Paris, 1753); compare also Davis 540 (no. 174 above).
Note: Stanislas Leczinski (1677–1766); chosen king of Poland: 1704; consecrated: 1705; defeated by the Russians, fled the country: 1709; his eldest daughter, Marie, married Louis XV and became queen of France. Stanislas was again chosen king of Poland in 1733; abdicated: 1736; duke of Lorraine and Bar: 1737.

183 *A Paris binding by Nicolas-Denis Derome le jeune, between 1761 and c. 1770*

Les Pseaumes en forme de prières, Paris: Savoye & Durand, 1758. 12 mo.

175 × 101 × 30 mm. (P 1327) Davis 563

Black goatskin over paste boards onlaid in citron and red and tooled in gold to a design 'à répétition'. Lines and a small roll along the borders and a repeat-mosaic design onlaid and tooled with lines, gouges, small fleurons, small sprays and dots. Edges of boards: tooled in gold with a line; turn-ins: tooled in gold with a floral roll. Edges: gilt and marbled beneath the gold.

Sewn on five cords, laced in, showing as raised bands on the spine, tooled in gold with a line; six compartments, onlaid in citron and red and tooled in gold; title lettered on a red label in second

182

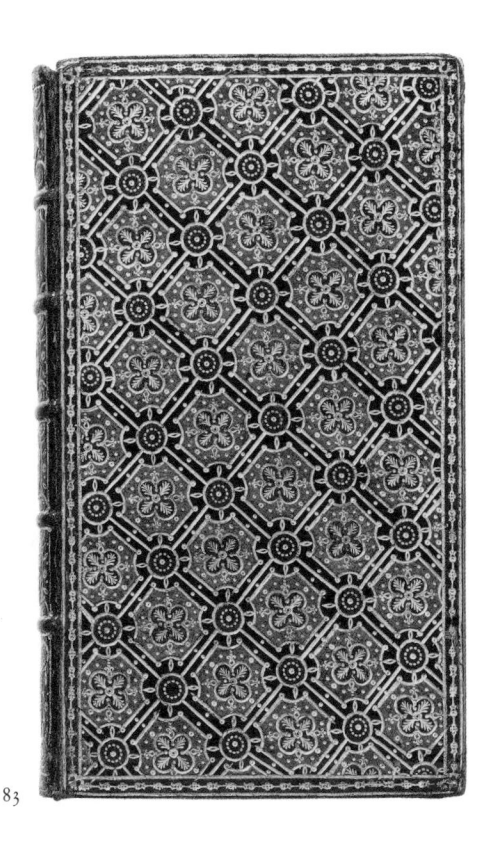

183

compartment. Endbands: double with a bead; red, white and blue silk over cores (material invisible) (cut off), tied down.

Endleaves: gilt paper pastedowns and one free gilt paper leaf (backed) conjugate with the pastedown, at both ends; at the front: two free white paper leaves (possibly conjugate); at the end: one free white paper leaf conjugate with the backing paper and a second free white paper leaf. On endleaf: printed ticket with: 'Relié par DEROME/ le Jeune, rue St. Jacques/ au dessus de St. Benoît,/ seul possédent l'Establissemt./ de Déffunt son Pere'.

PROVENANCE: Bought: Breslauer, 23.iv.1957.
REFERENCES: Foot, *Davis*, I, pp. 200, 203, note 57.
LITERATURE: Foot, *Davis*, I, pp. 199–201 (and literature cited there); Ract-Madoux, 'Essai de classement' (ticket A); see also Davis 564 (no. 182 above; and later literature cited there).

---

184 *A Paris binding by Nicolas-Denis Derome le jeune, after 1761*

P Ovidius Naso, *Le Metamorfosi di Ovidio … con le annotationi di M. G. Horologgi & gli argomenti & postille di M. F. Turchi*, Venice: B Giunti, 1584. 4to.

242 × 175 × 34 mm. (P 987) Davis 545

Dark blue goatskin over paste boards, tooled in gold to a dentelle design with lines and dotted lines, scallop tools in the corners, fan shapes, feathery curls, fleurons, stylized flowers, sitting bird tools

231

184

(looking right), and dots. Edges of boards: tooled in gold with double lines; turn-ins, tooled in gold with floral roll and small drawer-handle roll. Edges: gilt and faintly marbled beneath the gold.

Sewn on five (invisible) supports, laced in, showing as raised bands on the spine, tooled in gold with a line; six compartments, tooled in gold with feathery curls, dots, small stars and a flower tool; small pallets (rolls) near top and tail; title lettered in second compartment. Endbands: double with a bead; pink, blue and white silk over (?)rolled paper cores, tied down. Pink silk bookmarker.

Endleaves: pink watered-silk pastedowns and one free pink watered-silk leaf (backed) conjugate with the pastedown and a pair of free conjugate white paper leaves, at both ends.

PROVENANCE: Holford collection (sold: Sotheby's, 8.xii.1927, *571*, pl.); Lucius Wilmerding (book plate; sold: Parke-Bernet, 5.iii.1951, *208*, pl.).
REFERENCES: Foot, *Davis*, I, p. 200.
LITERATURE: Foot, *Davis*, I, pp. 199–201 (and literature cited there); see also Davis, 564 (no. 182 above; and literature cited there).
Same tools on: Bodleian Library Oxford, Broxbourne R 945; BL, C.2.b.4, C.19.c.24; Davis, 541, 487–90, 563 (nos. 172, 173, 183 above), Davis 546 (no. 185 below); *BFAC*, 1891, pl. cv; Gumuchian, 1930, no. 234.

232

185

185 *A Paris binding by Nicolas-Denis Derome le jeune, after 1761*

Breviarium Parisiense ... pars aestiva, Paris: Bibliopolae usuum Parisiensium, 1745. 8vo.

221 × 146 × 55 mm. (P 851) Davis 546

Olive-brown sheepskin (or possibly hair sheep) over paste boards, tooled in gold to a dentelle design with lines, a drawer-handle (or crescent) roll, scallop tools in the corners, fronds, curls, fleurons, stars, circles, flower tools, dots and bird tools (looking left). Edges of boards: tooled in gold with a line; turn-ins: tooled in gold with a floral roll. Edges: gilt and marbled beneath the gold.

Sewn on five cords, laced in, showing as raised bands on the spine, tooled in gold with a line; six compartments, tooled in gold with flowers; floral rolls near tail; title and part lettered in second and third compartments. Endbands: double with a bead; pale blue silk over (?)rolled paper cores, tied down sporadically. Three pink silk bookmarkers.

Endleaves: comb-marbled paper (large pattern) pastedowns and one free comb-marbled paper leaf (backed) conjugate with the pastedown and one free white paper leaf conjugate with the backing paper, at both ends.

PROVENANCE: Jacob Constant (book plate with 'Ex libris Jacobi Constant Parochi Sti. Trophimi'); bought: Sotheby's 15.ix.1945, *1946*.
REFERENCES: Foot, *Davis*, I, p. 200.
LITERATURE: Foot, *Davis*, I, pp. 199–201 (and literature cited there); Schäfer, pp. 139–41; see also Davis 564 (no. 182 above; and literature cited there).
Same tools on: BL, C.6.a.2, C.9.c.1, C.22.f.3, C.11.d.6 (with N-D Derome tickets); Bodleian Library Oxford, Vet F1c25 (with Derome ticket); Glasgow University Library, Hunt. Bg.2.12, MS Ferguson, 34; Waddesdon Manor (Paris, 1747); Eton College (London, 1773); Davis 545 (no. 184 above); De Ricci, *Schiff*, nos. 38, 39, 40.

186 *A Paris binding, possibly by Nicolas-Denis Derome le jeune, c. 1770–4*

Abbé de Lapérouze, *Poësies sacrées dediées à monseigneur le Dauphin*, Paris: Saillant & Noyon, 1770. 8vo.

200 × 128 × 32 mm. (P 1067) Davis 567

Red goatskin over paste boards, tooled in gold to a dentelle design, with three lines along the border, corners filled with feathery curls, fronds, fleurons and either a fleur-de-lis or a dolphin [dauphin] tool; fleurons, feathery curls and floral tools along the sides; in the centre the arms of (the future) Louis XVI as dauphin. Edges of boards: tooled in gold with a line; turn-ins: tooled in gold with a zig-zag and circle roll. Edges: gilt.

Sewn on five (recessed) supports; smooth spine, tooled in gold with floral pallets near top and tail, the spine divided into compartments, tooled in gold with small curls, flowers and acorn tools; title lettered on a light brown goatskin label. Endbands: double with a bead; pink, blue and white silk over (invisible) cores (cut off), tied down sporadically. Green silk bookmarker.

Endleaves: comb-marbled paper pastedowns and one free comb-marbled paper leaf (backed) conjugate with the pastedown, and one free white paper leaf conjugate with the backing paper, at both ends.

PROVENANCE:	Louis XVI as dauphin [possibly the dedication copy]; Edouard Rey (on title-page in manuscript: 'Paris 18 Juillet 1853 Edouard Rey ce livre qui porte les armes du Dauphin, doit-être l'exemplaire offert à Louis XVI cinq ans avant son avénement'); marginal notes (18th- or early19th-century hand); [Lucius Wilmerding]; bought: Parke-Bernet, 30.x.1951, *$20*.
Same tools on:	Waddesdon Manor (*Grandes Nuits,* with Derome le jeune ticket); BL, C. 30.c.9 (Paris, 1775); Rahir sale I, Paris, 1930, *233* (Paris, 1774 with arms of Merard de St-Just).
Note:	Louis XVI (1754–1793); dauphin: 1765; king of France: 1774; arrested: 1791, imprisoned: 1792; executed: 1793.

187 *Two Paris bindings, c. 1763*

J F Marmontel, *Poétique françoise*, 2 vols, Paris: Lesclapart, 1763. 8vo.

200 × 127 × 34/40 mm. (P 219) Davis 565–566

Red goatskin (or possibly hair sheep) over paste boards, tooled in gold to a dentelle design with lines and a small roll along the borders, a trident tool, feathery curls, fronds, a fleur-de-lis, curls and a flower tool in the corners, feathery curls and fleurons along the sides; in the centre the arms of Louis XV. Edges of boards: tooled in gold with a line; turn-ins: tooled in gold with a zig-zag roll. Edges: gilt.

Sewn on five (?)cords, laced in, showing as raised bands on the spine, tooled in gold with dashes; six compartments tooled in gold with a pallet (or small roll), leaf curls and small flowers; title and volume numbers lettered in second and third compartments. Endbands: double with a bead; blue and white silk over (?)rolled paper cores, tied down. Blue silk bookmarkers.

Endleaves: comb-and-spot marbled paper pastedowns and one free marbled leaf (backed) conjugate with the pastedown and one free white paper leaf conjugate with the backing paper, at both ends.

186 187

PROVENANCE:	Bought: Sotheby's 11.viii.1941, *119* (pl.).
REFERENCES:	Foot, *Reliures françaises*, p. 385, note 35.
Same tools on:	BL, C.47.d.15 (same book with arms of Louis, dauphin, son of Louis XV and Marie-Josèphe of Saxony); Belin, Catalogue: *Riches reliures* (1910), no. 127 (on same book with arms of Louis-Philippe, duc d'Orléans, 1725–1785); Gougy sale I, Paris, 5–8.iii.1934, *511* (same book with arms of the future Louis XVI as dauphin); see also Gumuchian, 1930, no. 211.
Note:	Louis XV (1710–1774), king of France from 1715 (under the regency of Philippe, duc d'Orléans); betrothed: 1722 to Marie Anne Victoire, infanta of Spain (see Davis 480, no. 166 above); married Marie Leczinska: 1725.

188 *A Paris straw binding, c. 1778*

[Almanack] *Étrennes mignones curieuses et utiles … pour l'année 1778*, Paris: C J C Durand, 1778. 24mo.

96 × 60 × 8 mm.   (P 1294) Davis 568

Case binding of strips of straw over thin wood. A border of beige straw, background of strips of dark brown straw; in the centre a large cartouche of curls and floral shapes, decorated with red and gold paint around a panel of strips of beige straw with an embossed bouquet of flowers and leaves, decorated with red and gold paint. Edges of boards: strips of beige straw; inside edges: painted red. Edges: gilt and sprinkled red beneath the gold.

235

188   189

Stitched through the centre fold (the whole work consists of one section of conjugate leaves); smooth spine covered in brown leather (?sheepskin). No endbands.

Endleaves: embossed paper (red floral pattern on gold and green) pastedowns, at both ends.

PROVENANCE: Bought: Heilbrun, 27.xi.1965.
REFERENCES: Barber & Rogers, p. 263, no. 3; Foot, *Reliures françaises*, p. 385, fig. 7.
LITERATURE: Gruel, II, p. 126; Barber & Rogers, pp. 262–5.

---

189   *A Lyon binding by Devers, c. 1780*

T Lucretius Carus, *De rerum natura libri sex*, Birmingham: J Baskerville, 1773; ruled in red. 12mo.

181 × 112 × 17 mm.   (P 1478) Davis 569

Green goatskin over paste boards, onlaid in citron and red and tooled in gold with lines, small zig-zag roll, small fleurons, stars, pointillé gouges, crosses and feathery tools. In the corners: onlaid heart shapes tooled with feathery curls, a small fleuron and a flame tool. Edges of boards: tooled in gold with a line; turn-ins: tooled in gold with a zig-zag roll, dotted line and small border with small tools. Edges: gilt.

Sewn on five recessed cords, laced in; smooth spine, onlaid in red and tooled in gold, dividing the spine into compartments with lines, dotted lines (pallets); author's name lettered on red label; signed near the tail: DEVERS. Endbands: double with a bead; pink and white silk over (invisible) cores (cut off), tied down sporadically. Pink silk bookmarker.

Endleaves: blue watered-silk pastedowns and one free blue watered-silk leaf (backed) conjugate with the pastedown, and one free white paper leaf conjugate with the backing paper, at both ends.

PROVENANCE: J R Abbey (book plate; 'J.A.1837/ 5:7:1938'; sold: Sotheby's, 19–20.vi.1967, *1997*, pl.).

190

REFERENCES: De Ricci, *Schiff*, no. 98; Foot, *Reliures françaises*, p. 385, note 36.
LITERATURE: Devauchelle, II, p. 230; Romme, *Book Collector*, 1972, p. 107 (and literature cited there); Foot, *Davis*, I, pp. 201, 203, note 65.
Note: Devers was a member of a binders' family in Lyon. He worked before 1783.

---

190 *A Paris binding by Bisiaux for Renouard, c. 1785*

Athenagoras Atheniense, *Della risurrettione de' morti, tradotto … da Girolamo Faleti*, Venice: Aldus, 1556. 4to.

210 × 143 × 14 mm. (P 773) Davis 570

Dark blue goatskin over paste boards, tooled in gold with a wide border formed by two leaf rolls, lines and dotted lines, and a floral roll; a narrow inner border made by a small roll. Near the foot of the upper cover: RENOUARD. Edges of boards: tooled in gold with a double zig-zag roll; turn-ins: tooled in gold with a sun roll and a small leaf roll. Edges: gilt (red staining just visible).

Sewn on four (recessed) cords, laced in; smooth spine, tooled in gold; lines dividing the spine into compartments, tooled in gold with a saltire of dotted lines and a leafy tool in the centre; title and imprint lettered on spine. Endbands: double with a bead; red, white and pale blue silk over rolled paper cores, tied down sporadically. Dark pink silk bookmarker.

237

THE HENRY DAVIS GIFT

Endleaves: pink silk pastedowns and one free pink silk leaf (backed) conjugate with the pastedown and one free white paper leaf conjugate with the backing paper, plus one free white parchment leaf, at both ends.

PROVENANCE: On backing paper of first front free silk leaf: a printed ticket: 'Relié par Bisiaux/ Rue du Foin St./ Jacques No. 32.'; Renouard; E P Goldschmidt, Catalogue 73, no. 14 (sold: 1.iii.1944).
REFERENCES: Foot, *Reliures françaises*, p. 385, note 37, fig. 8.
LITERATURE: Gruel, I, pp. 54–6, II, pp. 32–3; Thoinan, p. 207; Whitney Hoff, *463*; De Ricci, *Schiff*, nos. 120–7 (signed Bisiaux bindings), see nos. 120–1, 124, 126–7 (leaf roll as on Davis 570); Ramsden, *French*, p. 33; Devauchelle, II, p. 220.
Signed Bisiaux bindings: BL, C.30.a.26, C.37.e.41 (same roll as Davis 570), C.38.b.33.
Note: Pierre-Joseph Bisiaux, binder in Paris: 1777–1801; in the Rue du Foin St Jacques: 1785. A A Renouard, bibliographer (1765–1853).

191 *A Paris binding, c. 1788*

Les Statuts de l'Ordre du St Esprit establiy par Henri III, Paris: Imprimerie royale, 1788; engraved title-page. 4to.

290 × 218 × 46 mm. (P1103) Davis 547

Red goatskin over paste boards, tooled in gold with a small crescent border roll, lines, in the corners: ornaments containing a dove [St Esprit]; in the centre the arms of Louis XVI. Edges of boards: tooled in gold with a double line; turn-ins: tooled in gold with dashes and dotted lines. Edges: gilt.

Sewn on five cords, laced in, showing as raised bands on the spine, tooled in gold with a line; six compartments tooled in gold with a semis of fleurs-de-lis and flame tools; title lettered on green goatskin label in second compartment. Endbands: single with a bead; white and pink silk over rolled paper cores, tied down. Pale blue silk bookmarker.

Endleaves: blue paper pastedowns and one free blue paper leaf (backed) conjugate with the pastedown, and one free white paper leaf conjugate with the backing paper (at the end; at the front: the backing paper has come off the blue paper and has been pasted to the free white leaf).

PROVENANCE: Duc de Vendôme (book plate); bought: (?)Breslauer, May 1952.
REFERENCES: Foot, *Reliures françaises*, p. 385.
LITERATURE: Olivier, 2495 (3 & 4), 2496 (2 & 3); Guigard, I, p. 26.
Same tools on: BL, C.46.h.1 (Louis XV); N Rauch, Catalogue: *Livres anciens et modernes … de la librairie W S Kundig*, 12–14.v.1952, 346 (on *Statuts*, 1724).
Note: Louis XVI (1754–1793); king of France: 1774 (the same armorial stamp was used for Louis XV and Louis XVI).

192 *A Paris binding, c. 1791–2*

Étrennes intéressantes des quatre parties du monde, et des troupes de France. Année Bissextille 1792, Paris: Langlois père et fils & Deschamps, [1791]. 24mo.

98 × 59 × 10 mm. (P1495) Davis 571

238

191 192

Case binding of red goatskin over paste boards, tooled in gold with three lines along the border, corner fleurons and in the centre a tool depicting two figures on horseback, one seated on a cannon and one standing, two of whom are drinking a toast, below which: Á LA SANTÉ DU ROI/ ET DE LA NATION. Edges of boards and turn-ins: tooled in gold with dashes. Edges: gilt.

Stitched through the centre fold (the whole work consists of one section of conjugate leaves); smooth spine, tooled in gold with dashes dividing the spine into compartments, tooled in gold with dots forming a diamond. No endbands.

Endleaves: embossed paper (green with gilt floral pattern) pastedowns at both ends.

PROVENANCE: Jacques Millot (book plate; sold: Paris, Giraud-Badin/Hôtel Drouot, 18.iii.1958, *126*, pl.).

REFERENCES: Exhibited at the Musée Carnavalet, Paris, 'Cent cinquantenaire de la Revolution', 1939; Foot, *Reliures françaises*, p. 385, note 38.

LITERATURE: Gruel, I, pp. 153–4 (fig. 7); P Gruel, *Les Reliures révolutionnaires de la collection L Gruel au Musée Carnavalet*, Paris, 1917, p. 23, see fig. 12; A Boinet, 'Les reliures révolutionnaires', *Gutenberg Jahrbuch*, 1957, pp. 339–45 (illustration: p. 345); Devauchelle, II, p. 89; Devaux, p. 204; see also Catalogue Jacques Millot, Paris, Giraud-Badin/Hôtel Drouot, 18.iii.1958, *68* (*Almanach*, 1791, with a stamp of the Bastille), *127* (*Étrennes*, 1792, stamp depicting figures and VIVE LA LIBERTÉ).

Note: According to Gruel and Boinet the stamp on Davis 571 commemorates the days of 5 and 6 October 1789 when the women were taken from Versailles to Paris on the canons of the 'Garde', drinking the health of the king and the nation.

193

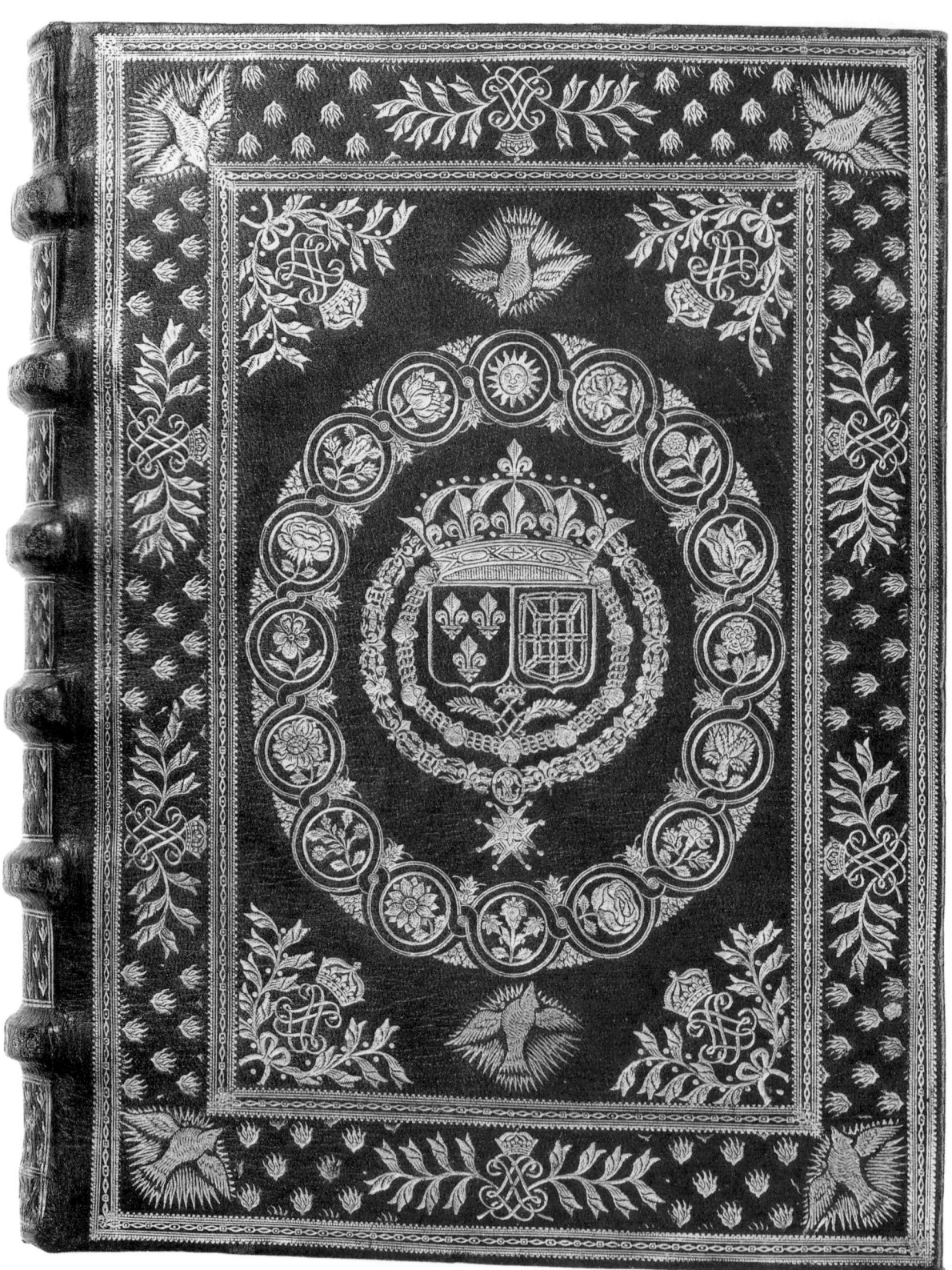

French Bindings

193   *A (?)Paris binding with the arms and cipher of Louis XIV, probably a nineteenth-century imitation*

Creations de Louis XIV dans l'Ordre du Saint Esprit ... de 1654–1663, MS on parchment, interleaved with paper; illuminated; Reims, Fontainebleau, Paris, [Paris, 1665–71].

381 × 288 × 75 mm.   (M 66) Davis 411

Olive goatskin over thick paste boards, tooled in gold with lines, dotted lines and small rolls forming a wide border, filled with flame tools, the cipher of Louis XIV between laurel branches; St Esprit tools at the corners of the panel; the crowned cipher of Louis XIV between laurel branches in the corners, and in the centre the arms of Louis XIV surrounded by a large wreath composed of a fanfare ribbon, large flowers, a sun tool and small solid tools, above and below which a St Esprit tool. Traces of two pairs of ties. Edges of boards: tooled in gold with St Esprit tools and fleurs-de-lis; turn-ins: tooled in gold with a small roll. Edges: gilt.

Sewn on six cords, laced in, showing as raised bands on the spine, tooled in gold with a roll; seven compartments tooled in gold with lines, St Esprit tool or the cipher of Louis XIV on a semis of flame tools. Endbands: double with a bead; pale blue and pink silk over rolled leather (or paper?) cores, (cut off), tied down.

Endleaves: pink satin pastedowns at both ends.

PROVENANCE: (?)A member of the Order of St Esprit (the manuscript); Pierre Berès; bought: Sotheby's. 11.vii.1966, *258*.
REFERENCES: Foot, *Revue française*, p. 384, fig. 5.
LITERATURE: Olivier, 2494 (2).
Note: For a binding with large ciphers between laurel branches and arms within a circle of large flowers see: Meunier, *BN*, pl. 22 (with arms and cipher of Louis de France, son of Louis XIV); see also Whitney Hoff, no. 198, pl. LXII (within a circle of large flowers: the arms, and between palm branches: the cipher, of Charlotte-Elisabeth of Bavaria, wife of the brother of Louis XIV). However, the leather and the tooling of Davis 411 have a 19th-century, rather than a 17th-century look, the thick satin pastedowns are also suspect.

194   *Two Paris bindings made c. 1810*

E F de Lantier, *Contes en prose et en vers, suivis de pièces fugitives et du poème d'Ermine et de métastase à Naples*, 2 vols, Paris: Arthus-Bertrand, 1809. 8vo.

203 × 129 × 21/23 mm.   (P 340) Davis 548–549

Artificially grained red leather over paste boards, tooled in gold with lines, a small border, a fleuron at the corners, and in the centre of the upper cover the crowned cipher of the Empress Marie-Louise. Edges of boards: tooled in gold with a small roll. Edges: gilt.

Sewn on three (recessed) cords, laced in; hollow back; smooth spine, tooled in gold, divided into compartments, filled with small stars; title lettered onto the spine; tooled shield with volume number.

241

194

Endbands: not worked on the book: blue and white silk, the ends stuck down in the inner joint beneath the pastedown. Green silk bookmarker.

Endleaves: green paper pastedowns and one free green paper leaf (backed) conjugate with the pastedown, and one free white paper leaf (uncertain whether conjugate with the backing paper).

PROVENANCE: Bought: Breslauer, i.xii.1941.
REFERENCES: Foot, *Reliures françaises*, p. 387.
LITERATURE: Olivier, 2654, no. 6; Michon, p. 120; for another binding with this monogram see Breslauer, Catalogue 108, no. 40. For another binding with Marie-Louise's monogram (different from that on Davis 548–9) see H P Kraus, Catalogue 126 (1971), no. 98.
Note: Marie-Louise (1791–1847), daughter of Franz Joseph I of Austria; second wife of Napoleon I (married: 1810); later duchess of Parma.

195 *A Paris binding, c. 1810–12*

J B Rousseau, *Oeuvres choisies à l'usage des lycées et des écoles secondaires*, Paris: Mame frères, 1810. 12mo.

147 × 89 × 25 mm. (P 1296) Davis 573

Gold-varnished wooden boards decorated with a painted design showing a border with torches and arrows in black and leaves and wreaths in pale gold; in the centre of the upper cover: an archaic scene of a woman pouring from a jug into a cup a drink for a shepherd, all in black, and branches with leaves in green; on the lower cover: a scene showing a woman holding a flower above a sitting shepherd,

195

painted in black, and two sheaves of corn in dark green. Edges of boards: painted in black with dashes. Edges: gilt.

Sewn on three (recessed) cords, laced in; hollow back; spine strip of dark green leather varnished in gold and painted in black and dark green, spine divided into compartments, painted with dashes, flowers and a pierced heart; title in gold on a red varnished (?)label. Endbands: triple; green, pink, blue and white silk over (invisible) cores, (cut off), tied down sporadically. Green silk bookmarker. Brown calf joints.

Endleaves: red paper pastedowns and one free red paper leaf (backed) conjugate with the pastedown, and one free white paper leaf conjugate with the backing paper, at both ends.

In a slip case of blue, pink, yellow and brown ripple-marbled paper over board; green leather edges; lined with green silk.

PROVENANCE: On endleaf in manuscript: 'de la dernière Dûchesse du jourledan (?) 1812'; bought: Breslauer, 10.vi.1966.

LITERATURE: Michon, p. 118; A Ehrman, 'Les reliures vernis sans odeur autrement dit "Vernis Martin"', *Book Collector,* xiv (1965), pp. 523–7; Devaux, pp. 215, 221; Schäfer, p. 160; for varnish on leather see Davis, 536–7 (no. 164 above).

Compare: (a similar binding of varnished wood on the same book) Beraldi sale III, Paris, 1934, no. 414 (pl.).

196

196 *A Paris publishers' binding by or for Louis Janet, c. 1820*

Hommage aux dames, Paris: Imprimerie de A Firmin-Didot [for] Louis Janet, n.d. [c. 1820]. 12mo.

124 × 79 × 16 mm. (P 954) Davis 574

Case binding of mauve paper over thin boards, embossed in gold with a wide border with a floral design; in the centre: a coloured engraving pasted on, showing, on the upper cover, a gentleman and a beggar and on the lower cover young men (out hunting) with a dog. Edges: gilt.

    Sewn on two (recessed) cords; smooth spine, embossed in gold. No endbands. Remnant of a silk ribbon (attached to the top edge of the upper cover).

    Endleaves: pink ribbed paper pastedowns and one free pink ribbed paper leaf (backed) conjugate with the pastedown and one free white paper leaf conjugate with the backing paper.

    In a case of mauve paper over very thin board; paper embossed in gold with a floral border and a centre ornament showing flowers and leaves in curls.

PROVENANCE: Bought: Sotheby's, 23.v.1950, *121* (through Quaritch).
LITERATURE: Devauchelle, II, p. 239; Fléty, p. 95; Malavieille, *Reliures et cartonnages*, pp. 19–23; see also Davis 572 (no. 197 below).

197

197 *A Paris publishers' binding by Louis Janet, c. 1830*

Jacques Gondar, *Chroniques françoises publiées par F Michel* [and] Charles Nodier, *Recherches sur le style*, Paris: Louis Janet, n.d. [1830]; illuminated title-page. 12mo.

170 × 105 × 21 mm. (P 1031) Davis 572

Red velvet over boards, blocked in blind with a plaque showing an angel surrounded by foliage, holding a shield with the title of the book, below which a small devil. Edges: gilt.

Sewn on three (recessed) cords, (?)laced in; hollow back; smooth spine, blocked in blind with leafy curls surrounding the title, running horizontally up the spine. No endbands.

Endleaves: pale blue ribbed paper pastedowns and one free pale blue leaf (backed) conjugate with the pastedown, and one free white paper leaf conjugate with the backing paper, and one pair of free conjugate white paper leaves, at both ends.

In a contemporary slip case of red straight-grain goatskin, tooled in gold with a line near the edge and tooled in blind with a border with leaves; lined with pink silk.

PROVENANCE: T Seligman (book plate, Newton Hall, Cambridge; sold: Sotheby's, 1.v.1951, *391*); bought: Haywood Hill, 12.vi.1951.
REFERENCES: Beraldi, *XIXe siècle*, I, no. 39 (pl. opp. p. 104).
LITERATURE: Ramsden, *French*, p. 109; G Barber, *Textile and Embroidered Bindings*, Oxford: Bodleain Library, 1971, pl. 30; Malavieille, *Reliures et cartonnages*, pp. 22–3, 242–3; Culot, *Relieurs et reliures romantiques*, pp. 363, 517; see also Davis 574 (no. 196 above; and literature cited there).
Note: Pierre-Claude-Louis Janet (known as Louis), bookseller, publisher and binder (1788–1840), son of Pierre-Étienne Janet (master binder and gilder from 1776), already established in 1810; succeeded his father in 1818.

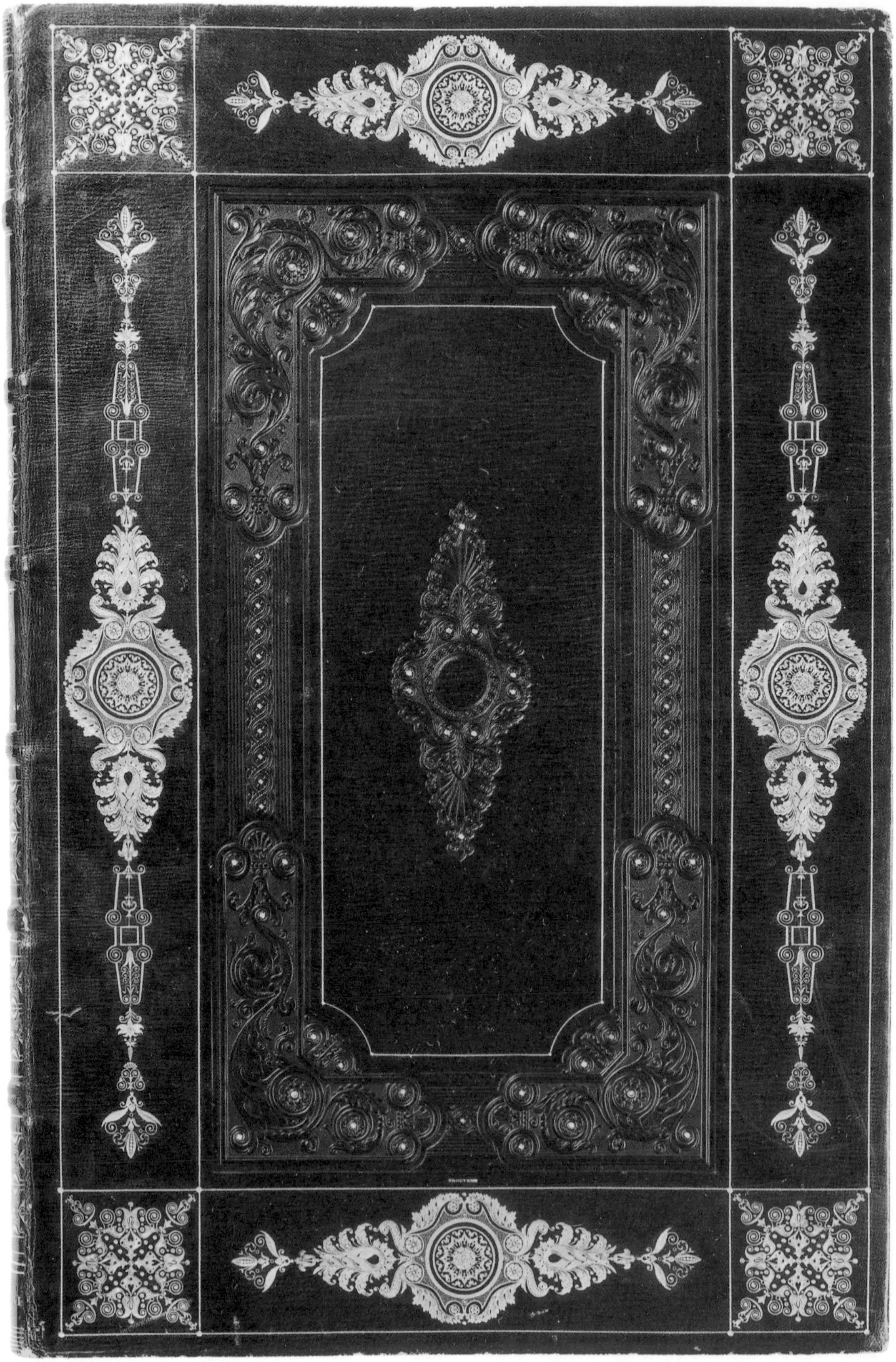

198 Paris bindings by Joseph Thouvenin (l'aîné), c. 1826

P C Tacitus, *Opera*, 4 vols, Paris: C L F Panckoucke, 1826. fol.

549/8 × 367/8 × 36/31/32 mm. (P 1488) Davis 712–715

Purple straight-grain goatskin over paste boards, blocked in blind and gold to a panel design with complex corner ornaments, a wide outer border filled with large blocks, lines and ornamental and floral tools, a wide inner border with large L-shaped corner blocks, blind tooled lines and strapwork and gold-tooled dots; in the centre an ornamental block tooled in blind with gold dots. On the upper cover of vols I and IV, near the tail edge, signed: THOUVENIN. Edges of boards: tooled in gold with a roll; turn-ins: tooled in gold with a zig-zag roll. Edges: gilt.

Sewn on six frayed-out cords, laced in, showing as flat bands on the spine, tooled in blind with lines and dashes; seven compartments, tooled in gold with ribbon and floral ornamental blocks; title, imprint and volume numbers lettered onto the spines; signed near the tail: THOUVENIN (except vol. IV). Endbands: double with a bead; pink and white silk over cord cores (cut off), tied down.

Endleaves: white moiré paper pastedowns and one free white moiré paper leaf (backed) conjugate with the pastedown, and one free white paper leaf (in vols II–IV) conjugate with the backing paper, plus a second free white paper leaf tipped on.

In tan calf envelopes, bound with green ribbon and with leather ties.

PROVENANCE: Bought: Breslauer, 14.x.1961.
REFERENCES: Foot, *Reliures françaises*, p. 387.
LITERATURE: Beraldi, *XIXe siècle*, I, pp. 42–6, 48–9; L Gruel, *Les Thouvenins relieurs français au commencement du XIXe siècle*, Paris, 1898 (offprint from: *Bulletin du bibliophile*); Ramsden, *French*, pp. 5–8, 204–6; Michon, p. 120; Devauchelle, II, pp. 155–69, 251; *La Reliure romantique*, pp. 53–4, pls 2, 8; Devaux, pp. 231, 247 (ornament), 383; R Devauchelle, *Joseph Thouvenin et la reliure romantique*, Paris, 1987; Fléty, p. 168; Schäfer, pp. 170, 175–6; Culot, *Relieurs et reliures romantiques*, pp. 560–2; Médard, p. 198.
Note: Joseph Thouvenin (l'aîné) (1790–1834), apprenticed to Bozerian jeune: 1802; set up on his own: 1813; became successful: 1830; took part in several exhibitions. Joseph Thouvenin (le jeune), brother of Joseph l'aîné, worked probably from 1822; worked mainly: 1806–20; died: 1844; a third brother, François, died in 1832.

199 A Paris jewelled binding by Alphonse Simier, c. 1826

Office de la quinzaine de Pâques suivant le nouveau bréviaire de Paris et Rome, Paris: Crapelet for Louis Janet, 1825. 8vo.

177 × 107 × 33 mm. (P 1525) Davis 550

Blue straight-grain goatskin over paste boards, decorated with gold mounts: gold bars with leaves forming the borders; in the corners gold mounts shaped like Gothic windows, and set with blue, green and red semi-precious stones; in the centre of the upper cover: the initials PL [possibly the cipher of Louis-Philippe] between two leafy branches, all in diamonds; in the centre of the lower cover: a golden mount set with semi-precious stones and diamonds, depicting a chalice with the host surrounded by rays, a cross, a book and the tablets of the law resting on clouds. Doublures of blue

199 200

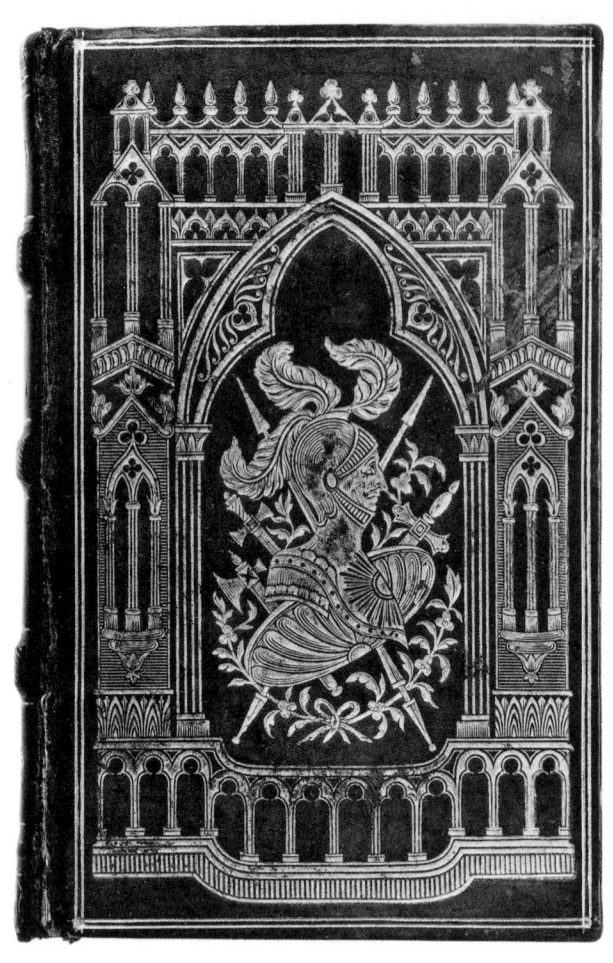

goatskin, blocked in gold with an ornamental border and an ornamental centre plaque. The doublure of the lower cover is signed along the tail edge: SIMIER.R.DU ROI. A large gold clasp in the shape of a church door, set with semi-precious stones, hinges on the lower cover. Edges of boards: tooled in gold with a line. Edges: gilt.

Sewn on four (recessed) cords, probably laced in; smooth spine, tooled in gold with curls and ornamental tools; title lettered in the centre; signed along the tail: SIMIER.R.DU ROI. Endbands: triple; silver thread over (invisible) cores (cut off), tied down. Pink and white silk bookmarkers. Endleaves: one free silver woven-cloth leaf (backed) and one free white paper leaf conjugate with the backing paper, at both ends.

In a blue goatskin box, tooled in gold and with a recess lined in red velvet; signed: NOULHAC REL. 1920.

PROVENANCE: On endleaf in manuscript: 'Rapellez vous dans vos bonnes/ prieres à une amie de votre Mere/ M.A.R[with flourish]' [said to be the autograph of Marie-Amélie, the wife of King Louis-Philippe]; R Descamps-Scrive (book plate; sold: Paris, Galerie Petit, 1925, II, *292*, pl.); bought: Breslauer, November/December 1959.

REFERENCES: *Treasures*, 1965, no. 87; Romme, *Book Collector*, 1969, p. 27, note 26.

248

LITERATURE: Beraldi, *XIXe siècle*, II, pp. 27, 51–2; Ramsden, *French*, pp. 5–8, 190; Devauchelle, II, pp. 150–4, 183, 250, III, p. 274 (Noulhac); *La Reliure romantique*, p. 47; Devaux, pp. 232, 297, 380; Fléty, p. 162 (information differs from that in Devauchelle), see also pp. 136–7 (Noulhac); Schäfer, p. 169; Culot, *Relieurs et reliures romantiques*, pp. 548–53; *Médard*, p. 197; see also Davis 575 (no. 200 below).
Compare: (another jewelled binding by [Alphonse] Simier) Sotheby's, 25.iii.1969, *268*.
Note: René Simier (père), came from Le Mans, set up in Paris: 1798; binder to Empress Marie-Louise: 1809–12; at least from 1818: binder to the king (Louis XVIII); after 1820: Simier, Père et Fils, called: 'Relieurs du Roi, de Madame et du Duc de Bordeaux'; disappeared: 1826; died: 1837. Alphonse Simier (1795/6–1859), son of René, worked with his father, whom he succeeded in 1826; binder to the king, the duchesse de Berry and the duc de Bordeaux; carried on after his father's death till 1847, when he was succeeded by Petit.

Henri Noulhac (1866–1931), born in Châteauroux; went to Paris: 1890; worked in different ateliers; set up on his own: 1894; worked mainly as a forwarder, but later, set up a finishing atelier, where he employed a finisher.

Louis-Philippe, duc d'Orléans (1773–1850), son of Louis-Philippe-Joseph, duc d'Orléans; became duc d'Orléans from 1793; became king in 1830 (as Louis-Philippe I); abdicated in 1848.

200 *A Paris binding by Alphonse Simier, c. 1827*

Miguel de Cervantes Saavedra, *El ingenioso hidalgo Don Quijote de la Mancha*, Paris: J Didot mayor, 1827. 16mo.

126 × 82 × 33 mm.   (P 671) Davis 575

Brown calf over paste boards, blocked in gold to a 'cathedral' design, with lines, a 'cathedral' plaque and in the centre the bust of a knight in armour. Edges of boards and turn-ins: tooled in gold with a small roll. Edges: gilt.

Sewn on three thin cords, laced in; hollow back; three flat false bands, tooled in gold with a zig-zag pallet; four compartments, tooled in gold with a floral pattern; title and EDICION/EN/MINIATURA lettered in second and third compartments. Signed near the tail: SIMIER R. DU ROI. Endbands: single with a bead; pink and white silk over (?)rolled paper cores, tied down sporadically. Blue silk bookmarker.

Endleaves: grey-green marbled paper pastedowns and one free marbled leaf (backed) conjugate with the pastedown, and one free white paper leaf conjugate with the backing paper, at both ends. On endleaf printed ticket with: 'Simier Relieur du Roi … Rue St. Honoré 152 à Paris'.

In a slipcase.

PROVENANCE: Bought: Francis Edwards, 12.viii.1943.
LITERATURE: Davis 550 (no. 199 above; and literature cited there).
Compare: (similar Simier bindings) BL, C.150.k.13 (on same ed. as Davis 575); Sawyer, Catalogue 242 (1957), *47*; Culot, *Relieurs et reliures romantiques*, no. 56.

201   *Two Paris bindings by Ginain, c. 1828*

F de Salignac de la Mothe Fénelon, *Aventures de Télémaque*, 2 vols, Paris: de Trouvé & Cie for Froment & Lequien, 1828. 8vo.

217 × 132 × 28/30 mm.   (P 1300) Davis 551–552

Purple calf over paste boards, tooled and blocked in blind and gold, with two border rolls and a large ornamental centre block. Edges of boards: tooled in gold with a small roll; turn-ins: tooled in gold with a leaf-roll. Edges: gilt.

   Sewn on four (invisible) supports, laced in; four flat false bands, tooled in gold with a line; five compartments, tooled in gold with ornamental and fleuron tools; title lettered in second compartment; volume numbers in fourth compartment; signed near the tail of vol. I: R.[elié] P.[ar] GINAIN. Endbands: double with a bead; pink and white silk over (invisible) cores (cut off), tied down.

   Endleaves: stone-marbled paper pastedowns and one free marbled leaf (backed) conjugate with the pastedown and one free white paper leaf, probably conjugate with the backing paper, at both ends.

PROVENANCE: Bought: Sotheby's, 24.vi.1958, *351A*.
LITERATURE: Ramsden, *French*, pp. 93–4; Devauchelle, II, p. 236; *La reliure romantique*, p. 22; Devaux, p. 360; Fléty, p. 80; Culot, *Relieurs et reliures romantiques*, p. 510; Médard, p. 193.
Note: Ginain, a binder in Paris, who worked for Bozerian jeune, then on his own: c. 1820–49, mentioned as binder to King Louis-Philippe and the prince de Joinville. (Fléty gives his initials as R.P.)

202

202 *A Paris binding by Ducastin, c. 1830(?)*

[F Bertaut, Sieur de Fréauville], *Voyage d'Espagne…Reveu, corrigé & augmenté sur le MS* [and] [R A de Bonnecasse de Saint-Maurice], *Une relation… particuliere de Madrid*, Cologne: P Marteau, 1666. 12mo.

139 × 81 × 30 mm.   (P 1302) Davis 576

Red goatskin over paste boards, tooled in gold and blind with lines, a border roll with trefoils and flowers, and in the centre an ornamental block. Edges of boards: tooled in gold with a small zig-zag roll; turn-ins: tooled in gold with a small roll. Edges: gilt.

Sewn on three (recessed) cords, laced in; hollow back with four false bands, tooled in gold; five compartments, tooled in gold with solid and open tools and small pallets; title lettered in second compartment; in fourth compartment: ELZÉV. 1666; signed in tail compartment: DUCASTIN. Endbands: single with a bead; pink and white silk over (?)cord cores (cut off), tied down. Pink silk bookmarker.

Endleaves: pale blue paper pastedowns and one free pale blue paper leaf (backed) conjugate with the pastedown, and one free white paper leaf conjugate with the backing paper, at both ends.

PROVENANCE: On endleaf in manuscript: 'ce voyage est d'un Sr Fr. Aarsen de Sommerdick'; Sobolewsky library (book plate); Crawford; Margaret, Lady Amherst of Hackney (book plate; sold: Sotheby's, 3.xii.1908, *859*); Tregaskis; Mary Rothes Margaret Baroness Amherst of Hackney (on endleaf in manuscript: 'Bought at the "Crawford sale" by Margaret Lady Amherst of Hackney (and Amhersts wife) sold at the "Amherst of Hackney Sale" 1908— bought by Tregaskis (bookseller in London) bought back from Tregaskis: July 13.1914 by me Mary Rothes Margaret Baroness Amherst of Hackney –wife of Lord William Cecil—'); bought: Raphael King [no date, after 1956].

LITERATURE: Gruel, I, pp. 89–90, II, pp. 70–1; Ramsden, *French*, p. 76; Devauchelle, II, pp. 232–3; Fléty, p. 62; Culot, *Relieurs et reliures romantiques,* p. 497; *Médard*, p. 191.
Note: Ducastin: a family of printers and binders in Paris during the 18th and 19th centuries; Alexis-Jacques: master: 1760; still at work: 1800. Pierre-Alexis (1785–1860) set up on his own: 1812; between c. 1820 and 1831 two binders of that name (père and fils) were at work. Ducastin fils remained active in Paris at least until 1847.

203 *A Limoges publishers' binding, c. 1846*

J B Berger, *Flavien et les fils de Marcomir, épisode de l'histoire des Francs*, Limoges: Barbou frères, 1846. 12mo.

183 × 110 × 20 mm. (P 1455) Davis 582

Case binding of embossed grey flock paper over boards, embossed in gold to a design of knotted branches and leaves along the borders and in the corners, and a large central rectangle with branches and leaves in the centre. Edges of boards: gilt dots; turn-ins: gilt borders. Edges: plain.

Sewn on two (recessed) supports; hollow back(?); spine embossed in gold with a pattern of branches and leaves; title and BARBOU FRERES embossed in gold on gold ground. No endbands.

Endleaves: white paper pastedowns and one free white paper leaf conjugate with the pastedown, at both ends.

PROVENANCE: On pastedown a label with in manuscript: 'Histoire de Belgique 1er Prix decerné a Mlle [name erased] 1ère Classe 2eme [erased] Bruxelles 10 Sbre 18[erased]; ticket with: 'libraire classique de [obscured by label]; Elkin Mathews (Catalogue 144, no. 43, sold: 6.v.1957).
LITERATURE: Malavieille, *Reliures et cartonnages*, pp. 62, 64, 239, compare also pl. XIII, XIV.1; Glénisson, pp. 423–4.
Note: Barbou frères, Henri and Charles, were printers-booksellers and binders in Limoges; binders' atelier: 1840–78. For another binding with a similar prize label, see Davis 580 (no. 207 below).

204 *A publishers' binding by A Mame, Tours, c. 1847*

J de Marlès, *Histoire de Marie Stuart Reine d'Ecosse*, Tours: A Mame et Cie, 1847. 12mo.

185 × 108 × 22 mm. (P 1452) Davis 577

Case binding of embossed dark blue glazed paper over boards, embossed in gold to a panel design with a rococo frame and leaves and flowers around an oval containing a bouquet of flowers. Edges of boards: embossed with a gold line; turn-ins: embossed in gold with half circles and dots. Edges: lightly stained.

Sewn on two (recessed) cords, their ends stuck down beneath the pastedown; hollow back; spine embossed in gold with an arabesque pattern; the title in gold on top of embossed spine decoration. No endbands.

Endleaves: white paper pastedowns and one free white paper leaf conjugate with the pastedown, at both ends.

203   204

PROVENANCE: Elkin Mathews (Catalogue 144, no. 43(n); sold: 6.v.1957).
LITERATURE: Ramsden, *French*, p. 134; R McLean, *Victorian publishers' book-bindings in paper*, London, 1983, pp. 12, 46–8; Malaveille, *Reliures et cartonnages*, pp. 57–62, 87, 209, 244; Glénisson, pp. 417, 420–4; see also Davis 578, 579, 580 and 581 (nos. 205–8 below).
Note: Alfred Mame of Tours (1811–1893), publisher and binder, joined his father Amand: 1833; in association with his cousin Ernest: 1830–45; head of the publishing firm: 1845; in association with his son Paul: from 1859. A Mame et Cie became a very large publishing and binding firm. Davis 577 and 579 (no. 206 below) are part of the series: 'Bibliothèque de la jeunesse Chrétienne'. The British Library's collections contain about 25 Mame et Cie publishers' bindings (Case 109 and in the Olga Hirsch collection of decorated paper).

205   *A binding by A Mame et Cie, Tours, c. 1850*

C Robinet, *Résumé de l'histoire d'Angleterre. Tome 2 – Série historique IV*, Brussels: Delevigne & Callewaert for V Devroede, 1847. 12 mo.

190 × 121 × 16 mm.   (P 1456) Davis 578

Case binding of embossed white paper over boards, embossed in gold to a panel design; within a frame decorated with curls and trefoils, a wide border filled with flowers and leaves; a central rectangular panel containing an oval with arabesque ornament surrounded by curls and flowers; decorated with green paint. Edges of boards and turn-ins: embossed in gold with half circles and trefoils. Edges: plain.

Sewn on three (recessed) cords (stuck down or cut off?); hollow back; spine embossed in gold and decorated with green paint, with leaves and flowers; title embossed in gold and signed near the tail: 'A.Mame/& Cie./Tours'. No endbands.

205　　　　　　　　　　　　　　　　　　　　　　　　　　206

Endleaves: white paper pastedowns and one free white paper leaf conjugate with the pastedown, at both ends.

PROVENANCE: Elkin Mathews (Catalogue 144, no. 43(h); sold: 6.v.1957).
LITERATURE: Davis 577 (no. 204 above; and literature cited there); see also Davis 579, 580 and 581 (nos. 206–8 below).

---

206 *A publishers' binding by A Mame, Tours, c. 1850*

L F, *Les Braconniers ou les dangereux effets de la colère et de la taquinerie*, Tours: A Mame et Cie, 1850. 12mo.

152 × 92 × 15 mm.　　　　　　　　　　　　　　　　　　　　　　　(P 1454) Davis 579

Case binding of embossed white paper over boards, embossed in gold to a design showing a frame, curves, leaves and flowers around a central oval with, on the upper cover, a bee hive amidst flowers on a gold paper ground, and on the lower cover an arabesque ornament. Edges of boards: gilt; turn-ins: embossed in gold with linked half ovals and dots. Edges: plain.

Sewn on four (recessed) cords (ends invisible); hollow back; spine embossed to a flower and ribbon pattern; title printed in gold. No endbands.

Endleaves: white paper pastedowns and one free white paper leaf conjugate with the pastedown, at both ends.

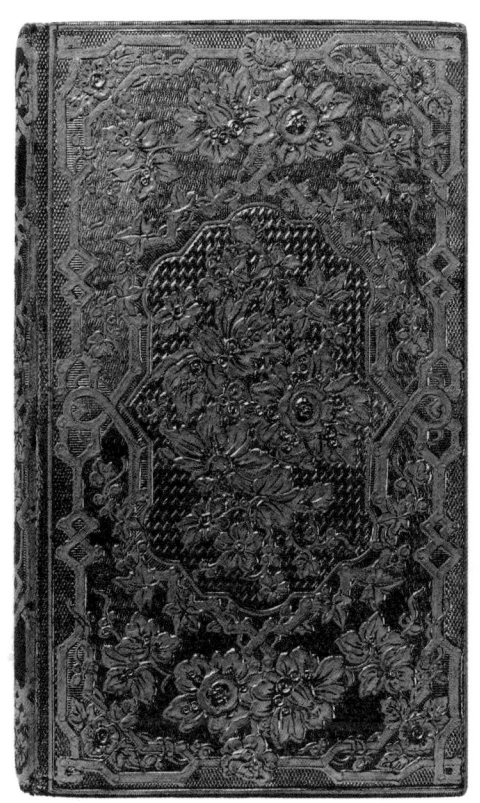

207

PROVENANCE: Elkin Mathews (Catalogue 144, no. 43(g); sold: 6.v.1957).
LITERATURE: Davis 577 (no. 204 above; and literature cited there); see also Davis 578 (no. 205 above), 580 and 581 (nos. 207–8 below).

---

207 *A publishers' binding by A Mame, Tours, c. 1852*

D S, *Vie de Sainte Geneviève patronne de Paris*, Tours: A Mame et Cie, 1852. 12mo.

187 × 111 × 17 mm. (P 1451) Davis 580

Case binding of embossed mauve paper over boards, embossed in gold to an intricate design of interlacing ribbons, flowers, leaves, ivy leaves and a central compartment containing a large bouquet of flowers on a zig-zag background (plate used upside-down on lower cover). Edges of boards: gilt; turn-ins: embossed in gold with a border containing fleurons. Edges: plain (some staining).

Sewn on three (recessed) cords (ends invisible); hollow back; spine embossed to a pattern of flowers and leaves; title and publisher's name embossed in gold on gold ground. No endbands.

Endleaves: white paper pastedowns and one free white paper leaf conjugate with the pastedown, at both ends.

PROVENANCE: Brussels school prize (on pastedown a label with in manuscript: 'Histoire Sacrée 1er Prix décerné à Mlle [name erased] p[remi]ère Clas[erased] 2ème Division [erased]

255

208   209

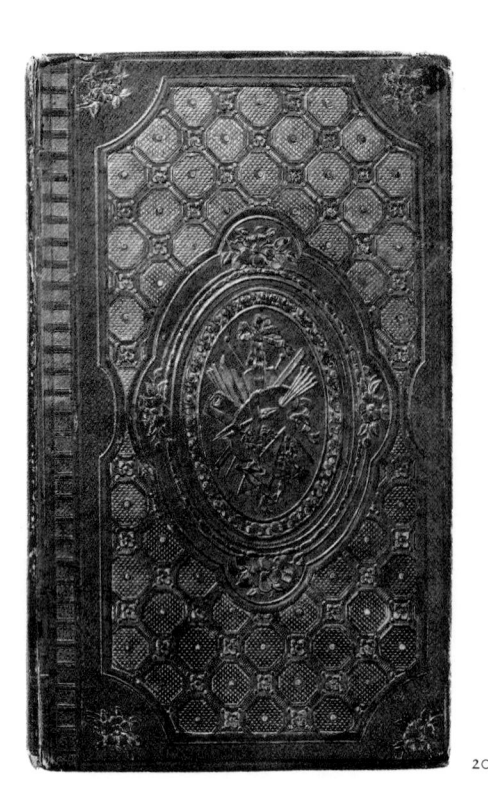

	Bruxelles [erased]'; beneath the label a ticket is just discernible); Elkin Mathews (Catalogue 144, no. 43(e); sold: 6.v.1957).
LITERATURE:	Davis 577 (no. 204 above; and literature cited there); see also Davis 578, 579 (nos. 205–6 above) and 581 (no. 208 below).
Note:	For another binding with a similar prize label see: Davis 582 (no. 203 above).

208   *A publishers' binding by Mame et fils, Tours, c. 1864*

T Ménard [Maynard], *Léon et Alice, correspondance d'un jeune voyageur avec sa soeur*, Tours: A Mame & fils, 1864. 12mo.

187 × 115 × 15 mm.   (P 1457) Davis 581

Case binding of embossed blue paper over boards, embossed in gold to a design with roses in the corners and a large panel with a mosaic pattern round an oval, surrounded by a frame with roses and trefoils and filled with painters' tools. Turn-ins: gilt line. Edges: plain.

  Sewn on two (recessed) supports (invisible ends); hollow back; spine embossed in gold with a pattern of roses, mosaic and the title; place of publication and publisher's name printed in gold. No endbands.

  Endleaves; white paper pastedowns and one free white paper leaf conjugate with the pastedown, at both ends.

PROVENANCE: Prize binding of the Pension Bornigal, Nantes (on pastedown a part printed, part manuscript label: 'Pension Bornigal/ Exercices de l'An 1868/ 1e Classe/ 2e Cours, 2e Division Calcul/ 1e Prix obtenu par/ Mlle Suzanne de Chergé/ Nantes, le 11 Août

256

	1868/ E Bornigal'); given to Henry Davis by Madame Hocq, Paris, March 1971.
LITERATURE:	Davis 577 (no. 204 above; and literature cited there); see also: Davis 578, 579, 580 (nos. 205–7 above).
Note:	From 1859 Alfred Mame took his son Paul (1833–1903) in partnership.

209   *A publishers' binding probably made for Périsse frères, c. 1849*

Abbé Crépon, *Sylvie ou Vie d'une jeune personne*, Lyon: Antoine Périsse for librairie Périsse frères Lyons et Paris, 1849. 12mo.

181 × 106 × 17 mm.   (P 1453) Davis 583

Case binding of embossed white paper over boards, embossed in gold and decorated with pink and green paint, to a design of curls and flowers around a central compartment showing a house in a garden with a dog. Edges of boards: gilt; turn-ins: embossed in gold with a scalloped border. Edges: plain (traces of sprinkling).

Sewn on two (recessed) supports (cut off?); hollow back; spine embossed in gold with a pattern of curls and flowers, decorated with green and pink paint; title and 'Perisse Frères a Paris' printed in green. No endbands.

Endleaves: white paper pastedowns and one free white paper leaf conjugate with the pastedown, at both ends.

PROVENANCE:	Elkin Mathews (Catalogue 144, no. 43(c); sold: 6.v.1957).
LITERATURE:	Fléty, p. 141; for French publishers' bindings in general: see Malavieille, *Reliures et cartonnages* (Périsse fr. only mentioned in lists on p. 46 as publisher in Paris in 1856 and in Lyon in 1846).
Note:	Périsse: bookseller and binder in Paris, worked c. 1830–c. 1860.

210   *A Paris binding by Bacharach, probably for Henri, duc de Bordeaux, c. 1850*

N-P Doubeveijer, *L'appel à la nation ses motifs et ses conséquences*, Paris: Bonaventure et Ducessois for Dentu, 1850. 8vo.

222 × 140 × 11 mm.   (P 1321) Davis 553

Green silk over paste boards, blocked in gold with lines, an over-all pattern of fleurs-de-lis in diamonds and in the centre a cartouche with, on the upper cover: the arms of Henri, duc de Bordeaux, comte de Chambord, and on the lower cover: a crown with the motto TOUS POUR LA FRANCE ET PAR LA FRANCE, and beneath this the initials H B. Edges of boards and turn-ins: tooled in gold with a small roll; green leather joints, tooled in gold. Edges: gilt.

Sewn on four (recessed) supports, laced in; smooth spine, tooled in gold with fleurs-de-lis, fleurons and the title running up the spine. Endbands: single; green silk over (indeterminable) cores (?cut off), tied down sporadically. Green silk bookmarker.

Endleaves: doublures of white watered silk and one free white silk leaf (backed) and three free white paper leaves (uncertain whether any conjugacy), at both ends. Signed on endleaf (with a stamp): BACHARACH RELIEUR.

210

In a green goatskin wrapper, tooled in blind with lines, and with gold-tooled turn-ins; lined with white velvet and watered silk.

Green goatskin box, tooled in blind with lines and in gold with the crowned initials H. B.

PROVENANCE: (?)Henri, duc de Bordeaux; Maggs Bros (label with: 'De la Bibliothèque du Comte de Chambord (Henri V de France, duc de Bordeaux) Né en 1820. Acquise par Maggs Bros. Ltd. de Londres'); Elkin Mathews (Catalogue 144, no. 32; sold: 6.v.1957).
REFERENCES: Foot, *Reliures françaises*, p. 387, fig. 9.
LITERATURE: Maggs Bros, Catalogue 609 (1935), Catalogue 622 (1936); Hobson, *French and Italian*, no. 51; Fléty, p. 15; see also Davis 584 (no. 211 below).
Note: Henri d'Artois, duc de Bordeaux, comte de Chambord (1820–1883), son of Marie-Caroline de Bourbon-Sicile, grandson of Charles X, nephew of the dauphin; after the abdication of Charles X and of the dauphin, proclaimed as Henri V of France: 1830, with Louis-Philippe d'Orléans acting as regent, who soon imposed himself as king of the French; Henri went into exile with Charles X and the dauphin, first to England then to Prague; took up the position of pretender to the French throne: 1843, but the revolution of 1848 and the coup d'état by Louis Napoleon intervened; reaffirmed his claim: 1870–1; died in Frohsdorf (Austria) in 1883.
Bacharach: binder in Paris, mid-19th century.

211

211 *A Paris binding by Petit, probably for Henri, duc de Bordeaux, c. 1854*

A Voysin de Gartempe, *Abrégé de l'histoire de France pendant les dernières années de la restauration,* Paris: J Claye & Cie for Garniers frères, 1854. 12mo.

182 × 120 × 16 mm. (P 1424) Davis 584

Blue artificially grained goatskin (pebble grain) over paste boards, tooled in gold with lines, pointillé curls and fleurons at the corners, fleurs-de-lis in the corners and in the centre the royal arms of France. Edges of boards: tooled in gold with lines; turn-ins: tooled in gold with a zig-zag roll with small leaves and fleurons. Blue goatskin joints. Edges: gilt.

    Sewn on three (recessed) cords, laced in; the spine has five false bands, tooled in gold with lines; six compartments, tooled in gold with corner curls and fleurons; title lettered in second compartment; date near tail; gold tooled dashes on head and tail caps. Endbands: double with a bead; green, red and yellow silk over (?)rolled paper cores, tied down. Green silk bookmarker.

    Endleaves: blue watered-silk doublures, one free blue watered-silk leaf (backed) and one free white paper leaf conjugate with the backing paper, at both ends. Signed on endleaf (with a stamp): 'PETIT SUCCr. DE SIMIER'.

PROVENANCE: Henri duc de Bordeaux, comte de Chambord; Don Jaime de Bourbon, duke of Madrid, Froh(?)sdorf (ownership stamp on title-page); Maggs Bros. (label with: 'De la Bibliothèque du Comte de Chambord ... Acquise par Maggs Bros. Ltd. de Londres'); bought: Sotheby's, 28. ii.1966, *28*.
REFERENCES: Foot, *Reliures françaises*, p. 387.
LITERATURE: Thoinan, p. 372; Ramsden, *French*, p. 154; Devauchelle, II, pp. 154, 248; Fléty, p. 143; see also Davis 550, 553 (nos. 199, 210 above; and literature cited there).

Note: Charles Petit, established: c. 1840; succeeded Alphonse Simier: 1849; his son Petit fils took over the atelier of Jean Simier and then that of his father; still at work in 1884. Don Jaime de Bourbon: Carlist claimant to the Spanish throne; inherited Frohsdorf from the comte de Chambord.

212 *A Paris binding by Marius Michel, c. 1880–5*

Marius Michel, *La Reliure française*, Paris: E Plon for Damascène Morgand & Charles Fatout, 1880 [with extra prints and drawings inserted]. fol.

315 × 225 × 44 mm. (P 1529) Davis 412

Black goatskin over paste boards, onlaid in tan goatskin, outlined by blind tooling, to an overall floral design; within a frame, curls, leaves, flowers and fleurons filling the corners; in a centre cartouche: a large flower with curving tendrils. Turn-ins: tooled in gold with lines; along the tail edge of the upper cover turn-in: signed: MARIUS MICHEL; black leather joints. Edges: gilt.

Sewn on five supports (?cords), laced in, showing as raised bands on the spine; six compartments, onlaid in tan goatskin showing fleurons, curls, lines and floral shapes; title lettered in second compartment. Endbands: single with a bead; green, red and yellow silk over (invisible) cores (cut off); no tie-downs visible.

Endleaves: doublures of green ribbed silk, one free green ribbed silk leaf (backed with comb-marbled paper) and one free comb-marbled paper leaf (backed) conjugate with the backing paper (of the silk leaf), and one free white paper leaf conjugate with the backing paper (of the marbled leaf) and a pair of free conjugate white paper leaves, at both ends.

In a wrapper of marbled paper over leather, gold-tooled leather spine. In a slipcase of marbled paper over board with leather edges.

PROVENANCE: Henri Beraldi (book plate; sold: Paris 1935, pt. IV, *126*, pl.); bought: Breslauer, Catalogue 100, no. 93A (pl.).

REFERENCES: H Beraldi, *Estampes et livres*, 2 vols, Paris: 1892, p. 224, n. 340 (pl.); Romme, *Book Collector*, 1969, p. 43, note 146; Foot, *Reliures françaises*, p. 387, note 39.

LITERATURE: Beraldi, *XIXe siècle*, II, pp. 94–5, 182–9, III, *passim*, IV, *passim*; O Uzanne, 'French bookbindings', *The Studio*, Winter 1899–1900, p. 63; Michon, pp. 127–9; Hobson, *French and Italian*, no. 53; Devauchelle, II, 203–5, III, *passim*; Devaux, pp. 286–93; Fléty, pp. 120–1; Schäfer, p. 193; *Wormsley*, no. 93.

Note: Jean Marius Michel (1821–1890) was apprenticed to a binder-finisher in Lyon, then with Reiss in Paris; worked for Pierre-Paul Gruel: 1839–48; then for Duru and Capé; took his son, Henri, into partnership: 1866; mainly worked as a finisher.
Henri Marius Michel (1846–1925), apprenticed to his father; in partnership with his father: 1866; added a forwarding shop to the finishing shop: 1876; wrote several works on bookbinding; most influential designer of bindings at the end of the 19th century.

212

213 A Paris binding by F Cuzin, 1887

Le Chevalier aus dames, Metz: Gaspart Hochfeder, 1516. 12mo.

186 × 116 × 17 mm.   (P 981) Davis 554

Brown goatskin over paste boards, onlaid in dark brown, green, blue and fawn, and tooled in gold to an imitation 16th-century design of interlacing ribbons, with gouges, open leaf- and fleuron tools. Doublures of white parchment, tooled in gold with lines, small flowers and cherub's heads; signed at the foot: CUZIN. Edges of boards: tooled in gold with lines and dashes; turn-ins: tooled in gold with a small roll; brown goatskin joints. Edges: gilt and gauffered with a pattern of vases, flowers and leaves; trace of colour.

Sewn on five (invisible) supports, laced in, showing as raised bands on the spine, tooled in gold with a line; six compartments, onlaid in dark green, brown, green and fawn, and tooled in gold with gouges; title lettered in second compartment; date near tail. Endbands: double; pink, white and black silk over cord cores (cut off, or possibly: main cores taken down beneath the leather joints), tied down. Red silk bookmarker.

Endleaves: one free white paper leaf and two free (?)conjugate white paper leaves, at both ends.
In a brown goatskin case.

PROVENANCE: T Belin (inserted a partly handwritten bill from 'Francisque Cuzin, 5 Rue Séguier, Paris', dated '26 Novembre 1887', for 'Monsieur Belin libraire' for the binding of this book, with Cuzin's card); William Loring Andrews (book plate); Cortlandt F Bishop (book plate; sold: New York, Anderson Galleries, 7.iv.1938, *424*); Lucius Wilmerding (book plate; sold: Parke-Bernet, 5.iii.1951, *166*).

REFERENCES: Foot, *Reliures françaises*, p. 387.

LITERATURE: Beraldi, *XIXe siècle*, III, pp. 121–31, IV, pp. 44–52, 65–6; Michon, p. 125; Devauchelle, III, pp. 62–7; Devaux, pp. 256–8; Fléty, pp. 50–1.

Note: Francisque Cuzin (1836–1890), apprenticed to Tiersot, binder in Bourg; went to Paris: 1855; worked in several binders' shops; set up on his own: 1861. Cuzin was not a finisher, but used, first Marius Michel père, then Wampflug as finishers; set up his own finishing shop: 1876, where he employed among others: Maillard (1876–1881) and later Mercier. On his father's death, the son, Adolphe, took over; he died: 1892 and was succeeded by E Mercier.

214 A Paris binding by S David, after 1890

V de Voiture, *Oeuvres*, 2 vols bound together, Paris: Veuve de F Mauger, 1681. 12mo.

163 × 95 × 40 mm.   (P 1000) Davis 585

Brown-red goatskin over paste boards, tooled in gold to a pastiche fanfare design with gouges, pointillé curls and fleurons. Doublures of blue goatskin, tooled in gold to a pastiche fanfare design with gouges, pointillé and small solid tools, signed at the foot: S.DAVID. Edges of boards: tooled in gold with lines; turn-ins: tooled in gold with dots; red-brown leather joints. Edges: gilt.

Sewn on five (invisible) supports, laced in, showing as raised bands on the spine, tooled in gold with dots; six compartments, tooled in gold with pointillé tools; head and tail caps: gold-tooled short double lines; title lettered in second compartment; in third compartment: EXEMPL. TAILLEMANT DES/ RÉAUX ANNOTÉ; date near tail. Endbands: double with a bead; green, red and yellow silk over cord cores (?taken down beneath the joints), tied down. Green, red and yellow silk bookmarker.

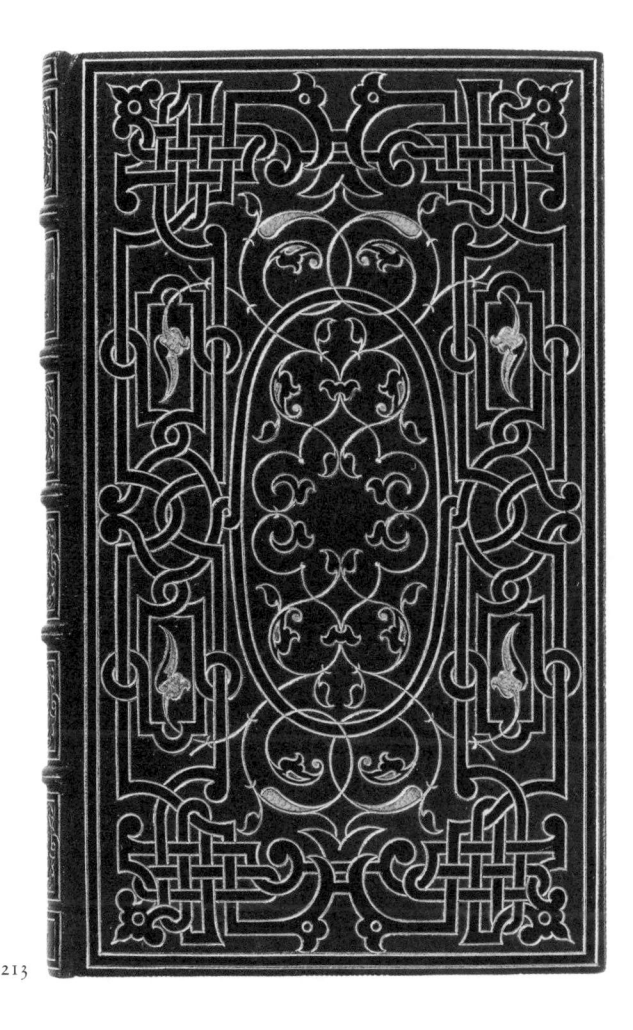

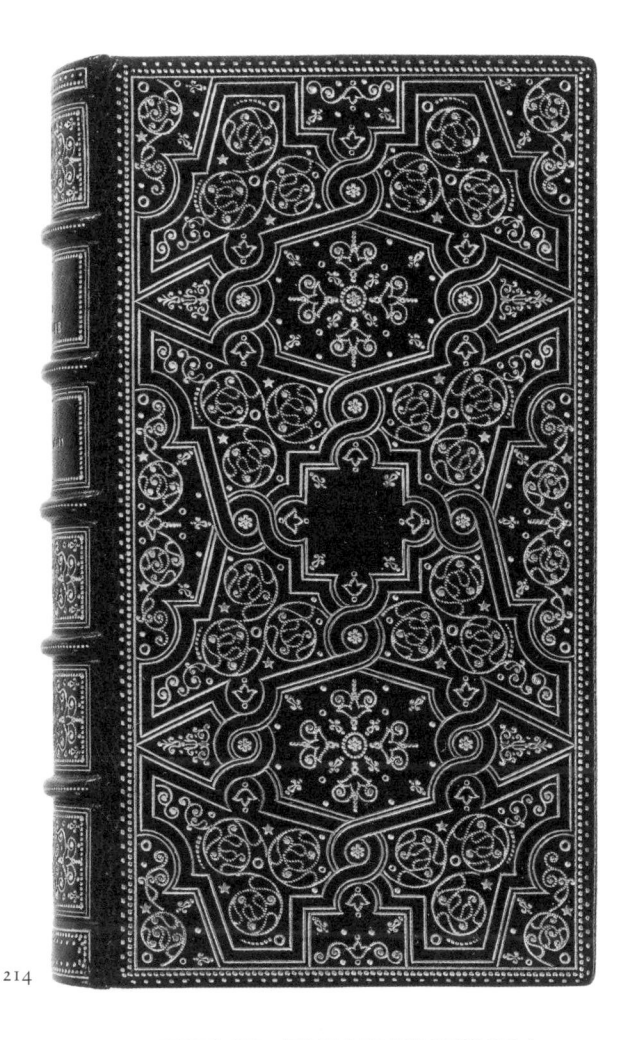

Endleaves: one free red moiré silk leaf (backed with comb-marbled paper) and one free comb marbled paper leaf (backed) conjugate with the backing paper (of the silk), two free conjugate white paper leaves, and one free white paper leaf conjugate with the backing paper (of the marbled leaf), at both ends.

In a brown goatskin case.

PROVENANCE: Tallemant des Réaux; Eusèbe Castaigne (many marginal notes said to be in the hand of Tallemant des Réaux, authenticated by Monmerque, who examined the volume in Angoulême, 30 October 1849; extra blanks bound in with a long manuscript note by Eusèbe Castaigne, dated 15 December 1847); GM (ownership stamp on title-page); Lucius Wilmerding (book plate; sold: Parke-Bernet, 6.iii.1951, *652*).

LITERATURE: Devauchelle, III, p. 253; Fléty, p. 53.

Note: Bernard David (1824–1895), worked in Metz and from 1851 in Paris. His son, Salvador, succeeded him in 1890; died: 1929.

215 *A Paris binding by Léon Gruel, 1890s (before 1896)*

Le Grand Coustumier de France, Paris: Estienne Caveiller for Jehan Ruelle, 1539. 8vo.

173 × 108 × 40 mm. (P 986) Davis 588

Brown goatskin over paste boards, onlaid in green and red and tooled in gold to an imitation 16th-century (François I) design, with lines, a fleurs-de-lis border roll; a panel with the badge of François I surmounted by an arabesque ornament with on the upper cover the title, and on the lower cover the date in a shield; around the panel: LEGE.CVM.PRVDENTIA/ STVDE.CVM.SAPIENTIA/ LABORA.CVM.PATIENTIA/ LÉON.GRVEL. Doublures of pink goatskin. Edges of boards: tooled in gold with a line; turn-ins: tooled in gold with four lines; brown leather joints. Edges: gilt, stained red beneath the gold.

    Sewn on five cords, laced in, showing as raised bands on the spine, tooled in gold with a line; six compartments, tooled in gold with leaves and fleurons, head and tail caps: gold-tooled double dashes; near the tail, signed: GRUEL. Endbands: double with a bead; blue, yellow and red silk over cord cores (cut off), tied down. Blue silk bookmarker.

    Endleaves: one free pale pink watered and ribbed silk leaf (backed) and one free white paper leaf, conjugate with the backing paper, at both ends.

    In a marbled-paper-covered slipcase with brown leather edges.

PROVENANCE: On the title-page in manuscript: owner's name 'H.J.V. La (?)'; Walter Thomas Wallace (book plate); Lucius Wilmerding (book plate; sold: Parke-Bernet, 5.iii.1951, *195*).

216

REFERENCES: Foot, 1977, p. 3.
LITERATURE: Beraldi, *XIXe siècle*, III, pp. 146–7, 155–6; Devauchelle, II, pp. 199–204, III, p. 119; Devaux, p. 361; Fléty, pp. 85–6.
Note: Léon Gruel (1840–1923), son of Pierre-Paul Gruel (d. 1849), taken on by his mother (who continued the firm after her husband's death): 1875–91; Léon became owner of the atelier until 1896, when he retired to Cannes, leaving the business to his son Paul (1864–1954); Léon Gruel had a collection of bindings (given to the Musée Carnavalet in Paris); he wrote his *Manuel* and other works.

---

216 *Paris bindings by Chambolle-Duru, c. 1897*

G H Derby, *Phoenixiana*, 2 vols, Chicago: Lakeside Press for the Caxton Club, 1897; [limited edition, 165 copies, on hand-made paper]. 12mo.

183 × 110 × 20 mm.   (P 209) Davis 586–587

Brown goatskin over paste boards, onlaid in dark brown and tooled in gold to a design of roses and leaves climbing up and around a frame. Doublures of blue goatskin, onlaid in brown, pink and green and tooled in gold, to a design of flowers and leaves in a wide border; signed at the foot of the doublure of the upper cover: CHAMBOLLE-DURU. Edges of boards: tooled in gold with lines; brown leather joints. Edges: gilt.

Sewn on five (invisible) supports, probably laced in, showing as raised bands on the spine, tooled in gold with dots; six compartments, onlaid in dark brown and tooled in gold with leaves and roses; head and tail caps tooled in gold with double dashes; title and volume numbers lettered in second and third compartments; place and date near tail. Endbands: double with a bead; yellow, red and green silk over (?)cord cores (cut off or possibly taken down beneath the joints), tied down. Yellow, red and green bookmarker.

Endleaves: one free flowered pink silk leaf (backed with comb-marbled paper) and one free comb-marbled paper leaf (backed), conjugate with the backing paper (of the silk), and two free white paper leaves (conjugacy not visible), at both ends; these are followed by the original covers of green cloth (laminated with tissue), blocked in gold with the emblem of the Caxton Club, New York.

In a slipcase of brown marbled paper over board.

PROVENANCE: H Gordon Selfridge (sold: Sotheby's, 11.viii.1941, *46*).
LITERATURE: Devauchelle, III, pp. 44–5, 127; Fléty, pp. 40–1; Schäfer, p. 192; see also Davis 585 (no. 214 above) for small similarities (bookmarker, endleaves, tooling of head and tail caps).
Note: René-Victor Chambolle (père) (1834–1898), apprenticed to Delaunay: 1846–52; went to Metz; returned to Paris: 1857; worked in the atelier of Gruel-Engelmann till 1861; in partnership with Duru as Chambolle-Duru: 1861; Chambolle became only owner: 1863, but kept the name Chambolle-Duru. His son, René (1873–1915), apprenticed to Foch; worked with Rousselle; joined his father and succeeded him, keeping the name of Chambolle-Duru.

217 *A Paris binding by E Mercier for Henry Walters, c. 1905*

J de la Fontaine, *Les Amours de Psiche et de Cupidon*, Paris: C Barbin, 1669. 8vo.

187 × 119 × 32 mm. (P 993) Davis 555

Pale brown goatskin over paste boards, onlaid in blue and red and tooled in gold to a 'fanfare-mosaic' design, with lines, gouges and small pointillé curls and fleurons; in the centre the monogram of Henry Walters. Doublures of blue goatskin tooled in gold with an ornamental border; small tools in the corners; signed at the foot of the doublure of the upper cover: MERCIER SR DE CUZIN. Edges of boards: tooled in gold with lines; turn-ins: tooled in gold with a small roll; tan goatskin joints. Edges: gilt.

Sewn on five (?)cords, laced in, showing as raised bands on the spine, tooled in gold with dots (pallet); six compartments, onlaid in blue and tooled in gold to a fanfare pattern with pointillé tools; decorated with red paint; head and tail caps: gold-tooled dashes; title lettered on blue label in second compartment. Endbands: double with a bead; red, green and yellow silk over cord cores (probably taken down beneath the joints), tied down. Pink, purple and yellow silk bookmarker.

Endleaves: one free leaf consisting of two comb-marbled leaves pasted together and one free marbled leaf (backed) conjugate with second marbled leaf, and one free white paper leaf conjugate with the backing paper, plus one free white paper leaf, at both ends.

Brown goatskin box.

217

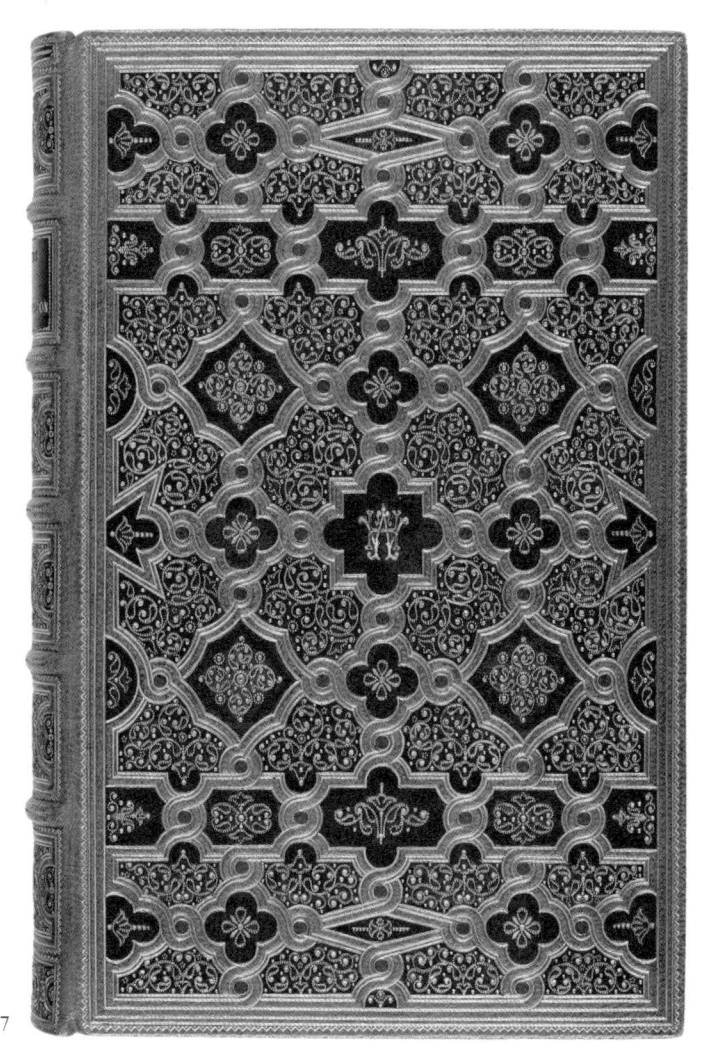

PROVENANCE: Henry Walters; Mrs Walters (sold: Parke-Bernet, 24.iv.1941, *711*, pl.); Lucius Wilmerding (sold: Parke-Bernet, 6.iii.1951, *360*, pl.).
REFERENCES: Romme, *Book Collector*, 1969, p. 43, note 147; Foot, 1977, p. 3.
LITERATURE: Beraldi, *XIXe siècle*, IV, pp. 187–96, 210–12; Devauchelle, II, p. 245, III, pp. 65–7, 117–20, 124–7, 132–3; Devaux, p. 371; Fléty, pp. 126–7; see also: *Ancienne collection des relieurs Émile et Georges Mercier, livres reliés et objets personnels*, sale catalogue, Paris, Hôtel Drouot, 2.iv.1993.
Note: Emile Mercier (1855–1910), apprenticed to C Magnier, also learnt finishing and worked as finisher in several ateliers in Paris; worked with F Cuzin: 1882–90; when Cuzin's son died (1892) Mercier took over the business; president of the Chambre Syndicale de la Reliure: 1901–5; succeeded by his son, Georges: 1910 (d. 1939).
Henry Walters (1848–1931): Baltimore art collector and capitalist; studied in Paris: 1873–5; made annual trips to Continental Europe; lived mainly in New York and Baltimore.

218

218   A Paris binding by Thérèse Moncey, c. 1948

Jean Lurçat, *Géographie animale* [18 lithographs with text], Geneva: A Kundig for A Gonin (Lausanne); lithographs: Zurich: E-J Wolfensberger, 1948 [limited edition of 280 copies, copy n. 13, signed by the artist and publisher, with an extra set of plates on China paper]. fol.

346 × 266 × 30 mm.   (P 1338) Davis 413

Brown goatskin over boards, onlaid in pink and pale grey-blue to a design of a large flying bird (colours in reverse and design upside down and in reverse on lower cover), and tooled in gold with flowing, curving lines. Doublures of pink suede. Edges of boards and turn-ins: plain; signed on turn-in of upper cover: THÉRÈSE MONCEY and on turn-in of lower cover: FACHE, DOREUR; brown leather joints. Edges: gilt.

Sewn on five supports, laced in; smooth spine, lettered in gold with title and author's name. Endbands: double with a bead; pink silk over cord cores (cut off), tied down sporadically.

Endleaves: one free pink suede leaf (backed) and two free conjugate white paper leaves and one free white paper leaf, possibly conjugate with the backing paper, at both ends; at the end: one free leaf conjugate with a stub.

In goatskin wrapper with gilt-paper sides; goatskin slipcase, covered with gilt paper.

PROVENANCE: Breslauer (List, 38, no. 129; sold: 6.v.1966).
REFERENCES: Foot, 1977, p. 3, pl. 1; Foot, *Studies*, p. 82, fig. 6.5.
LITERATURE: Devauchelle, III, p. 274; Arts Council of Great Britain, *Modern British and French Bookbindings from the Collection of J R Abbey*, London, 1965, no. 122; Fléty, p. 131; E van der Vekene, *Reliures d'art du XXe siècle*, Luxembourg, 1994, p. 160; J-C Vrain, *Reliures de femmes de 1900 à nos jours*, Paris, 1995, no. 62.
Note: Thérèse Moncey worked in Paris from 1946 till 1965; in 1950 she won the Grand Prix de la Reliure Française.

219   A Paris binding by J Anthoine-Legrain, c. 1950

M Proust, *A la recherche du temps perdu, tom. 1: Du côté de chez Swann*, Paris: C Colin (Mayenne) for B Grasset, 1914 [title-page: 1914, wrappers and colophon: 1913]. 8vo.

192 × 121 × 36 mm.   (P 1104) Davis 556

Black goatskin over slightly cushioned boards onlaid in green and tooled in blind and gold, decorated with pink paint; a central onlaid circle, curving lines, continuing on the spine; on the upper cover: the name of the author and the title. Doublures of parchment, tooled in gold with a vertical line down the centre. Turn-ins: tooled in gold with a short line along the long sides, signed at the foot of the turn-in of the upper cover: J.ANTHOINE LEGRAIN; black goatskin joints. Edges: gilt.

Sewn on four (recessed) supports, laced in; smooth spine, tooled in gold and blind with the title, some pink paint. Endbands: double with a bead; white and black silk over cord cores (stained black) (cut off), tied down.

Endleaves: one free pink suede leaf (backed) and one free white paper leaf (probably) conjugate with the backing paper, and two free (?)conjugate white paper leaves, at both ends.

The original yellow paper wrappers have been bound in.

219

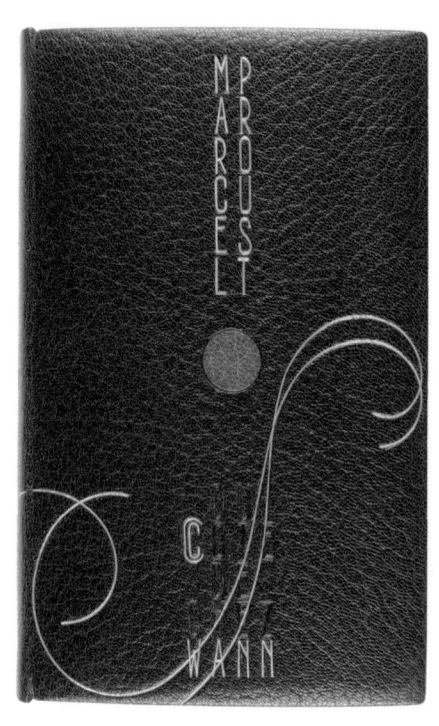

In a black goatskin wrapper, covered in gold-grey marbled paper and lined with tan sheepskin. A box of gold-grey marbled paper over board, with black leather edges.

PROVENANCE: Bound in: one leaf, containing a letter from Marcel Proust (letter continues on the half-title); W S Kundig (sold: N Rauch, Geneva,12–14.v.1952, *581*, pl.).
REFERENCES: Romme, *Book Collector*, 1969, p. 43, note 148; Foot, 1977, p. 3; Foot, *Studies*, p. 82.
LITERATURE: Michon, p. 135; *La Reliure originale*, 1959, pp. 84–7 (nos. 216–29); Devauchelle, III, p. 243; Fléty, p. 12.
Note: Jacques Anthoine (Anthoine-Legrain) (b.1907); worked in Paris from 1929–1950; at the death of his father-in-law, Pierre Legrain (1929) Anthoine-Legrain took over the atelier.

---

220 *A Paris binding by Rose Adler (tooled by André Jeanne), 1957*

Roger Frène, *Les Nymphes. Poème orné de cinq dessins de Modigliani*, Paris: R Davis & Cie, 1921 [limited edition of 130 copies, copy no. 57]. 8vo.

205 × 140 × 10 mm.   (P 1334) Davis 557

Light green and turquoise box calf over boards, onlaid in silver-blue, grey-green and dark green (?)snake skin, tooled in silver (?palladium) with the title. Doublures and joints of olive green suede, onlaid in light green and turquoise, and tooled in silver (?palladium) and white; on the doublure of the upper cover a label with: 'INV.1957 Rose Adler'; on the doublure of the lower cover a label with: 'DOR. A.Jeanne'. Edges: partly silver, partly untrimmed.

Sewn on four (recessed) supports, laced in; smooth spine, tooled in gold with the name of the author; the title lettered in silver and the name of the illustrator lettered in white; head and tail caps: tooled with

220

silver and white dashes. Endbands: triple; pink and green silk over (invisible) cores (cut off, or possibly taken beneath the joints), tied down.

Endleaves: one free green suede leaf (backed) and one free white paper leaf, conjugate with the backing paper, plus two free (?)conjugate white paper leaves, at both ends.

Original wrapper bound in.

In a wrapper of green box calf and decorated paper; decorated paper-covered slip case with green calf edges.

PROVENANCE: Acquired: January 1967 [no further details available].
REFERENCES: Foot, 1977, p. 3; Foot, *Studies*, p. 82.
LITERATURE: Michon, pp. 131, 134; Devauchelle, III, pp. 241–2, 263–4; *La Reliure originale*, 1959, pp. 65–83 (nos. 148–215); *La Reliure originale*, 1961, pp. 7–8; Arts Council of Great Britain, *Modern British and French Bookbindings from the Collection of J R Abbey*, London, 1965, no. 80; C Blaizot, *Reliures françaises contemporaines*, Brussels, 1975, pp. 1–4; Devaux, pp. 347, 363; M Cournault, 'Rose Adler: lettres à Etienne Cournault (1928–1948), reflets d'une vie et d'une oeuvre', *Revue française d'histoire du livre*, no. 37 (1982), pp. 759–72; Fléty, pp. 9–10; J-C Vrain, *Reliures de femmes de 1900 à nos jours*, Paris, 1995, nos. 1–14.
Note: Rose Adler (1890–1959); educated at the École des Arts Décoratifs: 1917; studied under H Noulhac from 1923; worked in Paris: 1923–59 (1924–9 for the collector J Doucet); was influenced by Pierre Legrain; more original and abstract designs: 1929–39; work became more refined, with the use of a variety of materials: 1945–59; founder member of the Société de la Reliure Originale: 1947; was awarded the Légion d'Honneur: 1951.

André Jeanne: educated in Paris at the Collège Technique Estienne; left in 1923; worked for Marius Michel, Pierre Legrain and J Langrand; set up on his own: 1929; worked as a finisher for Rose Adler, Pierre Legrain, Paul Bonet and others; work interrupted: 1942–9; became 'professeur de dorure' at the Collège Estienne.

221   *A Paris binding by P-L Martin, 1961*

P Virgilius Maro, *The Eclogues and Georgics in Latin and English. Vol. I: The Eclogues*, London: Cranach Press (Weimar) for Emery Walker, 1927; woodcuts by A Maillol; printed on Imperial Japanese paper [limited edition, copy no. 1 of 33, with one extra set of plates on Imperial Japanese paper and one extra set of plates on yellow Chinese paper]. fol.

333 × 253 × 30 mm. (P 1528) Davis 414

Olive-brown calf over boards, onlaid in white and fawn; on the upper cover: the name of the author and the title (in Latin) in Roman capitals onlaid in white, and the name of the author, the title (in English) and the date in italics onlaid in fawn; on the lower cover: the author's name and the title (in English) in Roman capitals onlaid in white, and the author's name, the title (in Latin), plus the date (in Roman numerals) in italics onlaid in fawn; all letters are intertwined. Doublures of fawn calf, tooled in gold: at the foot of the upper doublure: P.L.MARTIN and of the lower doublure: '1961'. Edges: gilt.

Sewn on five (recessed) supports, laced in; smooth spine, the name of the illustrator in capitals onlaid in white. Endbands: double with a bead; fawn silk over cord cores (cut off), tied down.

Endleaves: one free fawn calf leaf (backed) and three free white paper leaves (possibly: two conjugate paper leaves and one leaf conjugate with the backing paper), at both ends. Original wrappers bound in.

In calf wrappers with paper sides and slip case.

PROVENANCE: Inserted: a letter from P-L Martin (41 Rue St-André-des-Arts, Paris VI), to Breslauer, dated '2 Fevrier 1961', about this binding to be finished by around 10 February in time for the Arts Council exhibition in London, which was to open on 14 March; Breslauer (Catalogue 94, 1961, *159*, pl.; sold: October 1961).

REFERENCES: *La Reliure originale*, 1961, no. 128; *Times Literary Supplement*, 24 March 1961, 'Modern French Bookbinding'; Romme, *Book Collector*, 1969, p. 43, note 149; Foot, 1977, p. 3; Foot, *Book Collector*, 1987, pp. 244–5; Foot, *Studies*, p. 82.

LITERATURE: *La Reliure originale*, 1959, pp. 121–30 (nos. 360–96); Devauchelle, III, pp. 270–2; *La Reliure originale*, 1961, nos. 105–27; Arts Council of Great Britain, *Modern British and French Bookbindings from the Collection of J R Abbey*, London, 1965, nos. 110–15; Devaux, p. 318; C Blaizot, *Pierre-Lucien Martin*, exh. cat., Brussels: Bibliotheca Wittockiana, 1987; *Reliure française contemporaine*, exh. cat., New York: Grolier Club, 1988, nos. 1–22; Fléty, pp. 122–3.

Note: Pierre-Lucien Martin (1913–1985); educated at the Ecole Technique Estienne (Paris): 1927–31; worked for J Duval, then for A-J Gonon: 1936–40; worked for a while for trade binders; back to Gonon: c. 1936; set up on his own: 1940; produced his first fine bindings: 1945; in later years only designed bindings which were carried out by others; became a member of the Société de la Reliure Originale: 1951.

P. VERGILI MARONIS ECLOGÆ

The Eclogues of Vergil 1927

222 *A Paris binding by Paul Bonet, 1962*

Paul Valéry, Paul Eluard, R Moutard-Uldry, G Blaizot, L-M Michon, *Paul Bonet*, Paris: Frazier-Soye, G Duval & Mourlot frs for A Blaizot, 1945 [copy no. 45 of 50 copies on 'vélin d'Arches', out of a total of 300 copies, with extra plates, including drawings and paper patterns for bindings]. fol.

331 × 254 × 43 mm. (P 1527) Davis 415

Green goatskin over boards, onlaid in orange, red and pale blue-green calf and tooled in gold to a sunburst design. Doublures of red calf with a large panel of green suede; at the foot of the doublure of the upper cover, tooled in gold: PAUL BONET, at the foot of the doublure of the lower cover: 1962; the red calf of the doublures and the green goatskin covering leather meet on the edges of the boards. Red calf joints. Edges: gilt.

Sewn on five (recessed) cords, at least three of which have been laced in; smooth spine, tooled in gold with lines in a zig-zag pattern and with rays; title lettered on spine; head and tail caps: covered in red leather. Endbands: double with a bead; red silk over (invisible) cores (taken down beneath the joints), tied down.

Endleaves: one free green suede leaf, edged with red calf (backed), and two free conjugate white paper leaves and one free white paper leaf conjugate with the backing paper, at both ends. Original paper covers bound in.

In a wrapper of green goatskin and decorated paper, lined with tan calf; slipcase of decorated paper over board with green leather edges, lined with tan calf.

PROVENANCE: Breslauer (sold: 1962).
REFERENCES: Romme, *Book Collector*, 1969, p. 43, note 150; Foot, 1977, p. 3; Foot, *Studies*, p. 82.
LITERATURE: Michon, pp. 135–6; Devauchelle, III, pp. 177–96; *La Reliure originale*, 1959, pp. 88–102 (nos. 230–76); *La Reliure originale*, 1961, nos. 7–26; Breslauer, Catalogue 97 (1963), no. 138; Arts Council of Great Britain, *Modern British and French Bookbindings from the Collection of J R Abbey*, London, 1965, nos. 83–95; C Blaizot, *Reliures françaises contemporaines*, Brussels, 1975, pp. 5–9; Devaux, pp. 310–7; Fléty, p. 27; E van der Vekene, *Reliures d'art du XXe siècle*, Luxembourg, 1994, p. 154.
Note: Paul Bonet (1889–1971); born in Paris to Belgian parents; became electrician: c. 1904, then a maker of models; while still a model maker, devoted his spare time to bibliophily: c. 1920; started to design half-bindings; came under the influence of Pierre Legrain; designed bindings that were executed by others; designs first noticed: c. 1926; career really took off: 1929; worked with several forwarders and finishers; produced first radiating design: 1935; first sun-burst design: 1942. Founder of the Société de la Reliure Originale in 1947.

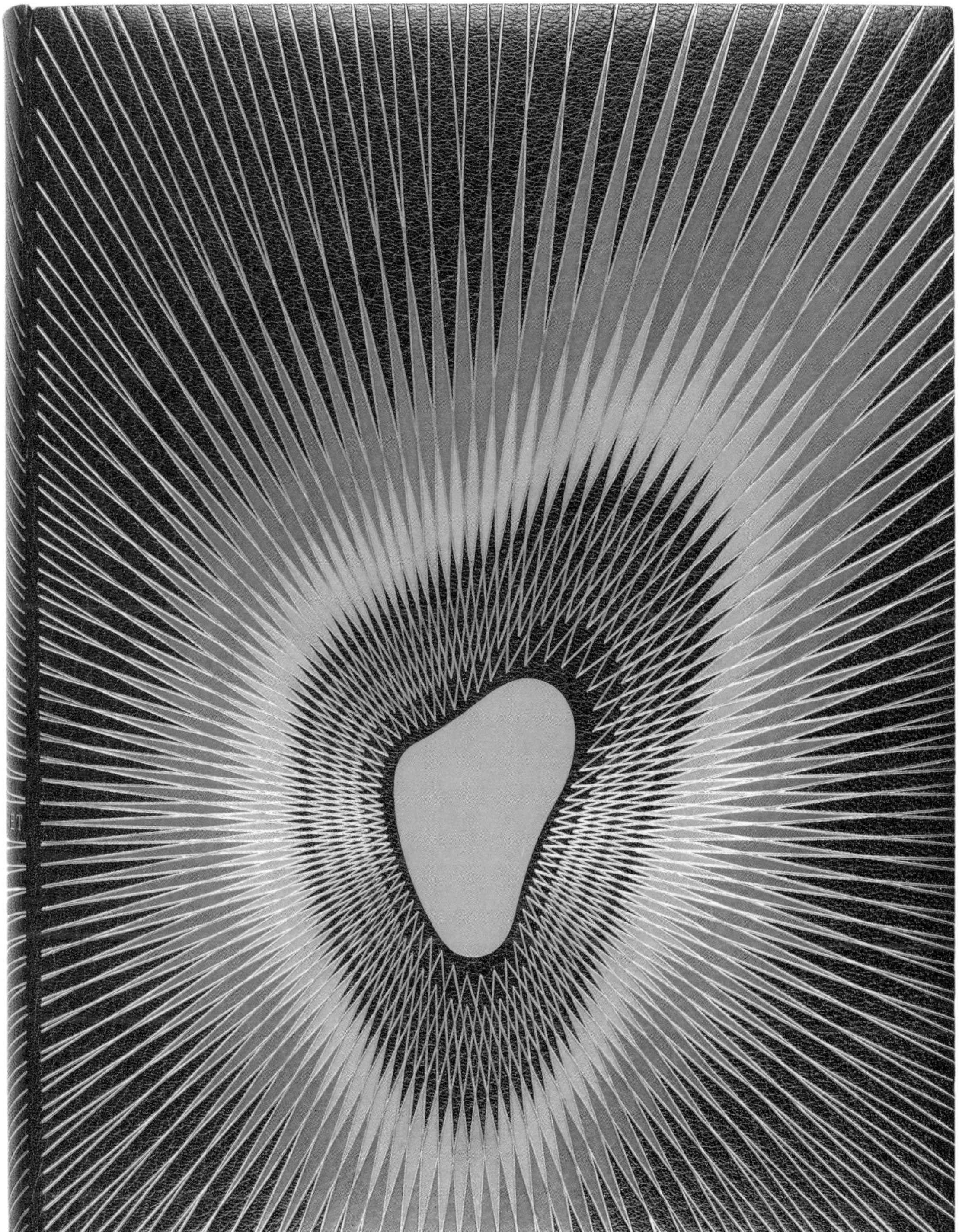

222

223

SWISS BINDINGS

223 *A binding made in Lower Austria or Switzerland, c. 1548*

J Honterus, *Rudimenta cosmographica*, Zurich: Froschover, 1548. 8vo.

163 × 114 × 13 mm. (P 605) Davis 589

Brown goatskin (or possibly hair sheep) over paste boards, tooled in blind to a panel design; blind lines. An outer border with a heads-in-medallions roll. On the upper cover: an inner border, the long sides of which are filled with flower and thistle tools, the top short side tooled in oxidized silver with: COSMOGR., the lower short side: left empty; a central panel, filled with lozenge-shaped tools containing a running animal and small thistle tools. On the lower cover: an inner border with an ornamental roll with human figures; a central panel with two vertical strips of a floral roll. Edges: plain.

Sewn on two supports (invisible, uncertain whether laced in), showing as raised bands on the spine; three compartments, tooled in blind with lines. No endbands.

Endleaves: white paper pastedowns at both ends; at the front: one free paper leaf, possibly conjugate with the pastedown (re-enforced with a paper joint: later).

Repairs at spine and corners.

PROVENANCE: Abraham Iorger [?Torger], 1548 (on upper cover pastedown: manuscript note about planets, etc., signed 'Abraham I[?T]orger 1548'; manuscript note on title-page: 'Abraham I[?T]orger / Lintzij'); in a different hand: 'Σωευδε ξραδεωσ'; Sigismund Ferdinand Engl, Baron Waghain (in a different hand: 'Sum ex lib: Sigis: Ferd: Engl â Waghain Baronis'); in a different hand [partly erased]: 'Bibliotheca Windhaagianie Catalogo inscriptus'; Ioachim, Baron Windhag (book plate) 'A1661'; P Dor (book plate); E P Goldschmidt (sold: 29.iv.1943).
REFERENCES: E P Goldschmidt, Catalogue 67 [1942], no. 94.
LITERATURE: F Warnecke, *Die deutschen Bücherzeichen (ex-libris)*, Berlin, 1890, p. 233, nos. 2490–1.
Heads-in-medallion roll: (possibly) Haebler, II, 24.9 (together with a roll dated: 1547; Basel, 1554).
Note: Several members of the Iörger family are known, among whom Jörger von Tollet, who died in Linz, Austria, in 1631; no Abraham Iörger or Jörger is mentioned (*Deutsche Biographisches Enzyclopädie*, Munich, 1999); Linz: in Austria.

224 *A binding probably made in Geneva, c. 1555–60*

M T Cicero, *Oeuvres*, Lyon: G Roville, 1552 [and] M T Cicero, *Les Epistres familiaires ... traduites en françoys par Estienne Dolet*, Lyon: I Ausoult for G Roville, 1554. 16mo.

122 × 72 × 51 mm. (P 1062) Davis 422

Olive-brown goatskin (or possibly hair sheep) over paste boards, tooled in gold with double lines along

224   225

the border and in the centre a medallion portrait of Julius Caesar, facing right, on a hatched ground. Edges: gilt, gauffered and painted to an arabesque pattern with fleurons.

Sewn on four split alum-tawed supports, laced in, showing as raised bands on the spine, tooled in gold with a line; two kettle stitch bands; seven compartments, tooled in gold with lines; five compartments tooled in gold with a flower. Endbands: single with a bead; traces of primary sewing over leather cores (cut off); secondary sewing of pink silk, tied down occasionally.

Endleaves: white paper pastedowns, two free conjugate white paper leaves, and one free leaf conjugate with the pastedown, at both ends.

PROVENANCE: Marcus Fugger (on pastedown in manuscript: 'Arc.156/Nro.435' [Fugger's library shelf mark]); Princes von Oettingen-Wallerstein (library stamp on title-page; sold: Munich, Karl & Faber, *Auktion VIII (II Teil)*, 6–7.xi.1933, *163*); Lucius Wilmerding (sold: Parke-Bernet, 30.x.1951, *390*).
REFERENCES: Hobson, *Humanists*, p. 142, note 62.
LITERATURE: Hobson, 'Plaquette and medallion bindings', p. 73, pl. 7, pp. 77–8, no. 134 ax); see also Davis 590 (no. 225 below); for Fugger, see also Davis 349, 339, 419, 379 (French, nos. 44, 50, 57, 66).
Same spine tool on: Davis 590 (no. 225 below; see also edge decoration); *same (?)plaquette on*: Lardanchet, Catalogue 45 (1951), no. 1022 (Lyon, 1560, see also edge decoration).
Note: Marcus Fugger (1529–1597), son of Anton Fugger; educated at Louvain; councillor of Augsburg; banker; book collector (see also Davis 349, French no. 44).

225   *A binding, probably made in Geneva, possibly by Schunke's 'Goldast Meister', c. 1560*

J Actuarius, *Opera*, Lyon: I Tornasius & G Gazeius, 1556; 3 vols bound as 1. 16mo.

121 × 73 × 56 mm.   (P 1245) Davis 590

Brown goatskin over paste boards, tooled in gold to a panel design with lines, hatched fleurons at the corners and in the centre a medallion portrait of Nero, in profile facing left. Edges: gilt, gauffered and painted red to an arabesque leaf and fleuron pattern.

   Sewn on four split alum-tawed supports, laced in, showing as raised bands on the spine, tooled in gold with a line; two kettle stitch bands; seven compartments, five of which tooled in gold with a stylized flower. Endbands: single with a bead; blue and yellow silk over cord cores (cut off), tied down.

   Endleaves: white paper pastedowns at both ends; at the front: two pairs of free conjugate paper leaves (quired) and one free leaf conjugate with the pastedown; at the end: one pair of free conjugate paper leaves and one free leaf conjugate with the pastedown, followed by two free paper leaves (uncertain whether conjugate); a section of eight blanks at the end.

PROVENANCE: Marcus Fugger (on endleaf, manuscript note: 'Arc.134./Nro.2.54' [Fugger's library shelf mark]); Princes von Oettingen-Wallerstein (library stamp on title-page; sold: Munich, Karl & Faber, *Auktion IX (III Teil)*, 11.v.1934, *223*); bought: Breslauer, January 1956.

REFERENCES: Foot, *Davis*, I, p. 212; Hobson, *Humanists*, pp. 142 (note 62), 248, no. 133a.

LITERATURE: I Schunke, 'Der Genfer Bucheinband des sechzehnten Jahrhunderts', *Jahrbuch der Einbandkunst*, IV, 1937, pp. 37–64, pl. 4, fig. 3 (attributed to the 'Goldast Meister'); Nixon, *Twelve Books*, pp. 22–4; Schunke, *Palatina*, I, pp. 218–36; Foot, *Davis*, I, pp. 212, 215, note 53 (see also note 56); see also Davis 422 (no. 224 above).

Same tool on: BL, C.108.n.3 (Paris, 1557, with centre block as on St John's College, Oxford, B.3.18 = Bodley, *Exhibition*, no. 110: Geneva Kings' binder); see also Foot, *Davis*, I, p. 215, note 53. One tool is not enough to attribute a binding to a workshop.

226   *A binding, probably made in Geneva, c. 1560*

J Philippson Sleidanus, *Histoire de l'estat de la religion*, [Geneva]: J Crespin, 1557; ruled in red. 8vo.

183 × 110 × 62 mm.   (P 1306) Davis 591

Brown calf over paste boards, tooled in gold with lines and gouges to a pattern of scrolls, interwoven ribbons, two masks, fleuron shapes and a centre cartouche, all on a background with a semis of dots; a central oval filled with a semis of three-dots tools; decorated with black and silver paint. Edges of boards: tooled in gold with lines and dashes; turn-ins: tooled in blind with a line. Edges: gilt and gauffered to an arabesque pattern of curving lines, leaves and fleurons, with traces of red paint.

   Sewn on four (recessed) supports, laced in; smooth spine, tooled in gold with gouges to a pattern of interwoven ribbons on a dotted ground; decorated with black and silver paint. Endbands: double with a bead; blue and yellow silk over (?)alum-tawed leather cores (cut off), tied down.

   Endleaves: white paper pastedowns and one free leaf conjugate with the pastedown, and two free white paper leaves (conjugacy not visible), at both ends.

279

226

PROVENANCE: On title-page in manuscript: erased ownership inscription; Jesuits at Lyon (stamp with: DOMUS LUGDUNENSIS SOC. JESU); Grace Whitney Hoff (book plate; Whitney Hoff, no. 666, pl. cxxix); J R Abbey (book plate; 'J.A.4952/ 12:10:1950'; sold: Sotheby's, 23.vi.1965, *622*, pl.).
REFERENCES: Romme, *Book Collector*, 1969, p. 27, note 27; Foot, 'Geneva Kings' binder', pp. 27–8, pl. 5.
LITERATURE: Chain, Dufour & Moeckli; Nixon, *Pierpont Morgan Library*, no. 40; Toulet, 'L'école lyonnaise', pp. 154–7 (compare fig. 145); Foot, *Davis*, I, pp. 212–13; Needham, *Twelve Centuries*, no. 88; see also Davis 416 (no. 228 below), 507 (French no. 88).

227 *A Geneva binding by the Kings' binder, c. 1560*

S Portius, *De coloribus libellus* [and other works], Florence: L Torrentini, 1548–51 [and] C Mylaeus, *Consilium historiae universitatis scribendae*, Florence: L Torrentini, 1548 [and] S Portius, *De puella Germanica*, Florence: L Torrentini, 1551. 4to.

211 × 140 × 40 mm. (P 1275) Davis 593

Brown sheep over paste boards, tooled in gold, with blind lines, to a panel design, with a centre inlay of dark brown goatskin, tooled in gold with gouges, hatched fleurons, hatched and solid leaf tools and dots; an open fleuron tooled in gold at the top and bottom of the inlay. Turn-ins: tooled in blind with a line. Edges: gilt.

280

227

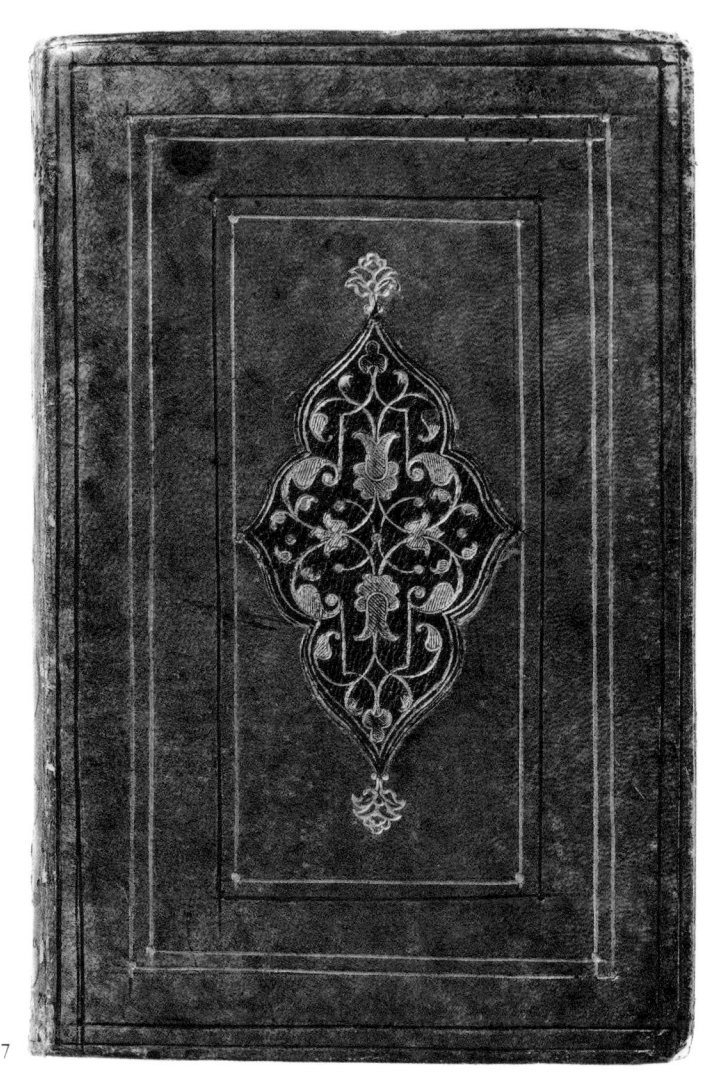

Sewn on four (recessed) (?)cords, laced in; smooth spine, tooled in silver with gouges forming arabesques and hatched tools; title lettered in gold on a red label. Endbands: single with a bead; blue and pink silk over (?)cord cores (cut off), tied down.

Endleaves: white paper pastedowns and one free white paper leaf (tipped on), at both ends.

PROVENANCE: On first title-page: (?)16th-century manuscript notes (referring to other works); on pastedown in manuscript: 'VV48 —zAi (?) Bd.4' and 'καπνοι λιγνυς κνισσα. 47'; on endleaf in manuscript: 'Hugh Hamersley'; in a later hand: 'D. Lincoln'; B H Blackwell, Ltd, Oxford (bookseller's ticket); Kundig (sold: 29.v.1951, no. 115, pl.); bought: Breslauer, 30.x.1959.

REFERENCES: Foot, *Davis*, I, p. 208; Foot, 'Geneva Kings' binder', p. 21, fig. 2.

LITERATURE: Toulet, 'L'école lyonnaise', pp. 154–7; Foot, *Davis*, I, pp. 207–16 (and literature cited there); Needham, *Twelve Centuries*, nos. 88–9; Foot, 'Geneva Kings' binder'; see also Davis 416, 417, 433 (nos. 228–30 below).

228 A Geneva binding by the Kings' binder, c. 1560

Diodorus Siculus, *Bibliothecae historicae libri*, [Geneva]: Henricus Stephanus (H Estienne), 1559. fol.

372 × 244 × 60 mm. (P 1001) Davis 416

Brown calf over paste boards, tooled in gold with lines and gouges, forming an arabesque pattern with fleurons, leaves, cornucopiae and two masks, decorated with silver paint, all on a semis of dots; in the centre, within a large cartouche: an oval filled with gouges and hatched fleuron and leaf tools; traces of black paint. Edges of boards: tooled in gold with lines, dashes and small s-shaped tools. Edges: gilt and gauffered to an arabesque pattern with leaves and fleurons; traces of white paint.

   Rebacked with the original spine strip retained. Sewn on five (recessed) supports (?)laced in; smooth spine, tooled in gold with lines, strips of oblong hatched flower-and-ribbon tools, two pairs of corner tools; a centre ornament of curving lines (gouges) and hatched tools; a semis of fleurs-de-lis. Endbands (probably later): single with a bead; brown and yellow silk over cores (material invisible; cut off); tied down.

   Endleaves: white paper pastedowns and one free white paper leaf, at both ends; at the front: the free leaf is tipped on; at the end: the free leaf is conjugate with the pastedown.

   Repairs: rebacked; repairs at corners of cover.

PROVENANCE: Petrus Uffenbach (on title-page in manuscript: 'Ex dono et liberalitate dni Joannis Caroli renckelij me possidet Petrus Uffenbach d.'); Lucius Wilmerding (book plate; sold: Parke-Bernet, 5.iii.1951, *213*, pl.).

REFERENCES: Sonntag, no. 38, pl. xvii; G D Hobson, *Cambridge*, p. 86, no. ix (of list); Romme, *Book Collector*, 1969, p. 27, note 27; Foot, *Davis*, I, p. 210; Foot, 'Geneva Kings' binder', p. 21, fig. 3.

LITERATURE: Chain, Dufour & Moeckli; E P Goldschmidt, Catalogue 135 (1966), no. 33; Davis 593 (no. 227 above; and literature cited there); *Deutsche biographische Enzyclopädie*, Munich, 1999; see also Davis 417, 433 (nos. 229–30 below).

Note: Petrus Uffenbach (1566–1635), Frankfurt am Main; medical doctor; studied from 1588 in Strasbourg, qualified (MA): 1592; studied in Padua from 1595; DPhil and doctor of medicine in Basel: 1597; became a 'Bürger' and town doctor of Frankfurt; wrote *Thesaurus chirurgicus* (1610, 2nd edn 1635); died in a plague epidemic.

229 A Geneva binding by the Kings' binder, c. 1565

Novum Testamentum, [Geneva]: Henricus Stephanus (H Estienne), 1565; printed dedication to Queen Elizabeth of England, Geneva, December 1564; ruled in red. fol.

395 × 250 × 84 mm. (P 1531) Davis 417

Double boards: brown calf over paste boards, the border tooled in gold with gouges forming interlacing ribbons, painted black, gouges, hatched fleuron and leaf tools; some silver paint; in the corners: sunk medallions with lion's masks (moulded in plaster and painted gold); a sunk centre panel of white calf; tooled in gold with gouges forming an arabesque pattern with in the centre a half-human figure; at the top: a mask with ram's horns; traces of red paint. Edges of boards: tooled in gold with

228

284

230

vertical, slanting and horizontal lines; turn-ins: tooled in gold with a line. Edges: gilt and gauffered with gouges, ribbons, fleurons and masks on a dotted background; traces of red paint.

Rebacked with the original spine strip retained. Sewn on five alum-tawed supports, laced in; smooth spine, tooled in gold with interlacing ribbons, painted black; gouges, hatched leaf and fleuron tools. Endbands: missing.

Endleaves: white paper pastedowns and two free conjugate white paper leaves, at both ends.

Repairs: rebacked; repairs at corners of covers.

PROVENANCE: Beneath the printed dedication in manuscript: 'R T M addictissimus Theodorus Beza Vezelius'; Sir William Curtis Bart. (book plate); J R Abbey (book plate; 'J.A.2723/3:1:1946'; sold: Sotheby's, 22.vi.1965, *502*, pl.).
REFERENCES: Romme, *Book Collector*, 1969, pp. 27–8, note 28; Toulet, 'L'école lyonnaise', p. 154; Foot, *Davis*, I, pp. 207–9; Foot, 'Geneva Kings' binder', p. 21, fig. 1.
LITERATURE: Davis 593 (no. 227 above; and literature cited there); see also Davis 416 (no. 228 above) and 433 (no. 230 below).

---

230 *A Geneva binding by the Kings' binder, c. 1579*

J Servin, *Psalmi Davidis a G. Buchanano versibus expressi. Pars superius*, Lyon [Geneva]: C Pesnot, 1579; dedicated to King James VI of Scotland; ruled in red. (half-sheet) fol.

171 × 225 × 23 mm. (P 1329) Davis 433

Brown calf over paste boards, tooled in gold with lines, large winged sphinx tools in the corner; in the centre: the arms of Scotland; decorated with black paint; a semis of starry flowers. Edges of boards: tooled in gold with s-shaped tools. Edges: gilt. Remnants of four pairs of yellow silk ties.

Sewn on three (recessed) cords, laced in; smooth spine, tooled in gold with floral rectangular tools. Endbands: headband missing, tailband (loose): double with a bead; yellow and blue silk over tanned leather core (broken), tied down.

Endleaves: white paper pastedowns at both ends; at the back: one free white paper leaf conjugate with the pastedown. A fragment of parchment manuscript board lining visible.

PROVENANCE: On last page of text in manuscript: 'Beugeman/de/bou(?)'; in the same hand on the lower endleaf: 'BougomandeboD w[?r]i[?c]B/ Hesboot B(?)'; on title-page in manuscript: 'Johannes Chinnall huius libri possessor est'; H C M Porter (book plate; sold: Christie's, 28.xi.1960, *93*).
REFERENCES: Foot, *Davis*, I, p. 208; Needham, *Twelve Centuries*, no. 89; Foot, 'Geneva Kings' binder', p. 24, fig. 4.
LITERATURE: Davis 593 (no. 227 above; and literature cited there); see also Davis 416, 417 (nos. 228–9 above).
Note: G D Hobson, *Trésors*, pl. lxxxii a, was lot *179* in the Hauck sale: Christie's New York, 27–28.vi.2006 (pl.).

231 *A binding probably made in Geneva, c. 1563*

J I Tremellius, *In Hoseam prophetam interpretatio et enarratio*, [Geneva]: N Barbirius and T Courteau, 1563; dedicated to Frederick III, Elector Palatine; ruled in red. 8vo.

167 × 112 × 28 mm. (P 1540) Davis 592

Brown goatskin over paste boards, tooled in gold with lines decorated with black paint, corner fleurons, a border filled with rectangular hatched fleuron-and-leaf tools, small corner blocks in the corners and in the centre on a semis of three-dots tools: a cartouche surrounding, on the upper cover, the (partly painted) arms of Frederick III, Elector Palatine, and on the lower cover the elector's motto: HERR./ NACH.DE/ INEM. WI/LLEN:. Traces of two pairs of ties. Edges of boards: tooled in gold with small curls, lines and dashes. Edges: gilt.

Sewn on three (recessed) supports, laced in; smooth spine, tooled in gold with lines, decorated with black paint, dividing the spine into wide strips, filled with rectangular fleuron-and-leaf tools, and larger compartments filled with a semis of three-dots tools. Endbands: double with a bead; yellow and blue silk over cord or rolled paper cores, tied down occasionally; cord crowning cores.

Endleaves: white paper pastedowns and two free conjugate white paper leaves and one free leaf conjugate with the pastedown, at both ends.

Repairs: at joints and corners.

PROVENANCE: G Libri (*Monuments inédits*, pl. xxx; sold: Sotheby's, 25.vii.1862, *539*); Samuel Putnam Avery (book plate); L'Art Ancien S.A., Zurich, Haus der Bücher A.G. Basel (sold: *Auktion XXIV*, 27.v.1955, *156*, pl.); J R Abbey (book plate; 'J.A.6776/ 8.1.1957'; sold: Sotheby's, 23.vi.1965, *662*, pl.).
REFERENCES: Romme, *Book Collector*, 1969, p. 28, note 29; Toulet, 'L'école lyonnaise', p. 154.
Note: Frederick III, Elector Palatine (1515–1576), called 'the pious'; brought up in Nancy, Paris, Liège and Brussels; became a Lutheran; married (1): Maria, daughter of Kasimir von Brandenburg-Kulmbach (d. 1567) and (2) Amalia, daughter of Gumbrecht von Neuenahr (d. 1602); six sons and five daughters; became Elector Palatine: 1559.

231

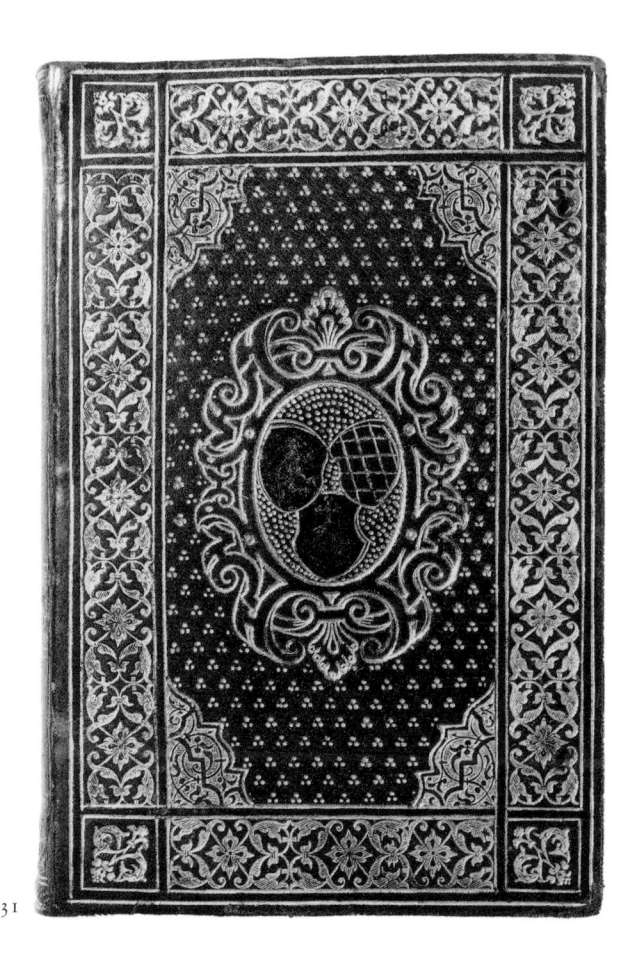

232 *A binding, possibly made in Geneva, 1571*

C Marot & T de Bèze, *Les Pseaumes mis en rime françoise*, Lyon: I de Tournes for A Vincent, 1563 [and] *La Forme des prières ecclesiastiques*, [Lyon: I de Tournes], n.d.; engraved borders; ruled in red. 8vo.

177 × 116 × 44 mm.   (P 1186) Davis 594

Brown calf over paste boards, tooled in gold with lines, a border filled with rectangular hatched interlacing ribbons-fleurons-and-leaves tools; in the centre a block with an arabesque design, above and below which: small mask tools. Edges of boards: tooled in gold with small curls; turn-ins: tooled in blind with a line. Edges: gilt, gauffered and painted (red) to a design of interlacing ribbons with leaves and masks; the fore-edge dated: 1571. Traces of two pairs of ties.

Sewn on three alum-tawed supports, laced in; (?)hollow back [may have come adrift later: spine lined]; smooth spine, tooled in gold with hatched lines near head and tail, lines forming three broad strips with large tools showing interlacing lines, hatched leaves and fleurons; two large compartments with corner pieces and mask tools on a semis of fleurs-de-lis. Endbands: single with a bead; red and white silk over cord cores (cut off), tied down.

Endleaves: white paper pastedowns and one free leaf conjugate with the pastedown, at both ends; at the front: one free white paper leaf; at the back: two free (?)conjugate paper leaves.

Repairs: small repairs at corners.

232

PROVENANCE: Manuscript note by P Lacroix: 'bib. Jacob.' (about the fore-edge date); label with: 'cum/consommaverit/homo/tunc incipiet M E'; Cortlandt F Bishop (book plate; sold: New York, American Art Association, Anderson Galleries, 1948, *254*, pl.); Silvain Brunschwig (book plate; sold: N Rauch, 30.iii.1955, *481*).
REFERENCES: *Treasures*, 1965, no. 75.
Note: The border tools are closely similar to, but not identical with, those used by the Geneva Kings' binder.

---

233 *A binding, possibly made in Geneva, c. 1580*

C Marot & T de Bèze, *Les Pseaumes mis en rime françoise* [and] *La Forme des prières ecclesiastiques*, Geneva: I Stoer, 1576. 16mo.

127 × 82 × 33 mm.   (P 1446) Davis 595

Brown calf over paste boards, tooled in blind with lines, and in gold with a large panel showing a standing female figure, labelled: DIALECTICA, surrounded by vases of flowers, cherubs, tritons, ornaments and curls. Turn-ins: tooled in blind with a line. Edges: gilt and gauffered with a pattern of a curling ribbon and fleurons, traces of two pairs of ties.

288

233

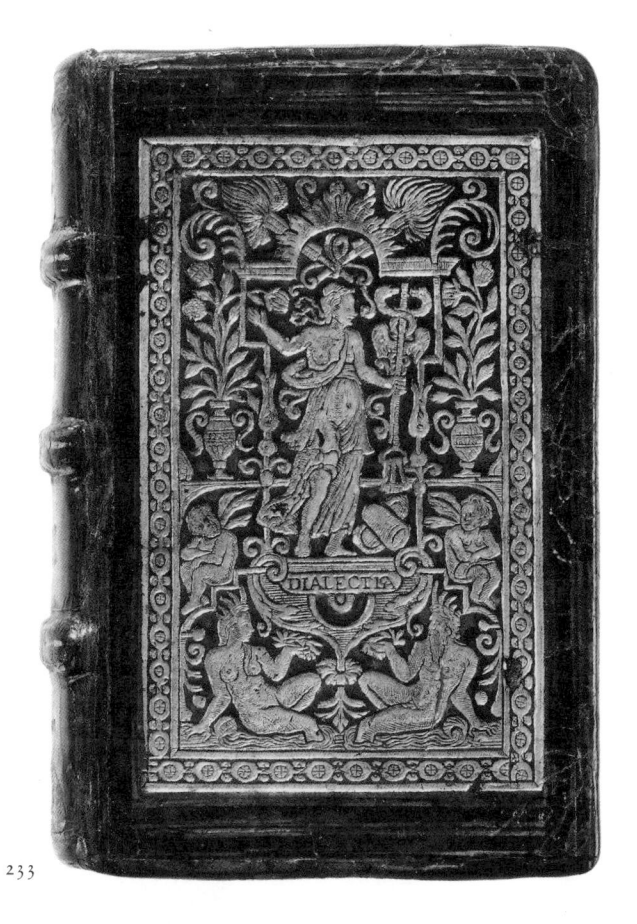

Rebacked with the original spine strip retained. Sewn on three (invisible) supports, laced in, showing as three raised bands on the spine, tooled in gold with a line; four compartments, tooled in gold with an ornamental tool or a stylized flower. Endbands: single with a bead; pink silk over (?)cord cores (cut off), tied down sporadically.

Endleaves: white paper pastedowns and one free leaf conjugate with the pastedown, at both ends.

Repairs: rebacked; repairs at corners and edges of boards.

PROVENANCE: On title-page in manuscript: 'M C'; in a different hand: 'Eliz: Brown/ her Book'; bought: Sotheby's, 24.vi.1958, *498*.

234 *A binding made in Switzerland, or possibly northern Italy, in the last quarter of the sixteenth century*

M T Cicero, [*De partitione oratoria*], M Antonii Maioragii, *In dialogum de partitione oratoria M Tulii Ciceronis, commentarius, ad Petrum Galesinium*, Milan: Pacificius Pontius, 1569. 4to.

222 × 159 × 20 mm. (P 1427) Davis 678

Olive goatskin over paste boards, tooled in blind and gold with parallel lines along the border; a border filled with curling hatched tools; hatched fleurons at the corners; solid floral arabesque tools in the

234

corners; in the centre a shield with: P C and unidentified coat of arms (a chicken holding a cross), surrounded by small hatched leaf tools. Traces of four pairs of blue silk ties. Edges of boards and turn-ins: tooled in blind with lines. Edges: gilt.

Sewn on four (?)leather supports, laced in, showing as raised bands on the spine, tooled in gold; five compartments, tooled in blind and gold with solid and dotted lines and curving and arabesque tools. Endbands: double with a bead; primary sewing over cord cores (once laced in), tied down; secondary sewing of pale blue and dark blue silk.

Endleaves: white paper pastedowns and two free conjugate paper leaves and one free leaf conjugate with the pastedown, at both ends. Printed waste visible beneath pastedown.

PROVENANCE: On pastedown of upper cover: manuscript note (unreadable); on pastedown of lower cover, in manuscript: 'D Balbus'; on endleaf in manuscript: '1f 1578'; on title-page in manuscript: 'Jo. Pauli monti Advocati seno/ gallica'; bought: Sotheby's, 28.ii.1966, *181*.

235

235 *A binding possibly made in Bern, c. 1731*

La Sainte Bible du Vieux et du Nouveau Testament ... avec des préfaces particulières ... tirées de la Bible de Mr Martin, Bern: Jean Bondeli, 1731 [volume I only]. 4to.

260 × 198 × 63 mm. (P 1247) Davis 558

White parchment over wooden boards, tooled in gold with lines and gouges to a design of interlacing ribbons, dividing the covers into compartments, painted pink and green, and filled with gold-tooled curls, leaf sprays, flowers, stars and in the centre a large vase with flowers; decorated with coloured paint. Edges of boards chamfered; turn-ins: painted pink. Edges: gilt and gauffered.

Sewn on four (?alum-tawed) supports, laced in; hollow back; smooth spine, tooled in gold with gouges forming ribbons, curls, fleurons, leaf sprays, stars and small cherub's heads; decorated with pink

291

and brown paint. Endbands: single with a bead; pink and white silk over cord cores (cut off), tied down sporadically. Green silk book marker.

Endleaves: yellow gilt floral embossed paper pastedowns and one free yellow embossed leaf (backed) conjugate with the pastedown, and one free white paper leaf (watermark: the arms of Bern; countermark: NM) conjugate with the backing paper, at both ends.

PROVENANCE: Maggs Bros (Catalogue 830, no. 118, pl.); bought: Quaritch, 12.iii.1956.
REFERENCES: Romme, *Book Collector*, 1969, p. 36, note 98.
Note: For vol. II of this Bible see Hely-Hutchinson sale, Sotheby's, 12.iii.1956, *90* (pl.). Bindings of this type were made in Germany, Austria, Scandinavia, Switzerland and eastern Europe. For a description of how they were produced in Germany, see M M Foot, *Bookbinders at Work*, London, 2006, pp. 97, 100, figs 41–7.

236 *A silver-gilt binding probably made in Zürich, c. 1731*

Das Neüwe Testament [title-page missing] [and] *Die CL Psalmen Davids durch D. Ambros. Lobwasser in teutsche Reimen gebracht*, Zürich: David Gessner, 1731. 8vo.

167 × 92 × 28 mm. (P 1298) Davis 596

Worn black velvet over wooden boards, over which: finely chased silver-gilt covers and spine. The silver-gilt covers show an all-over pattern of arabesques with birds, leaves, flowers, human heads, and in the centre: two pairs of birds eating from a basket of fruit. Edges: gilt. Two pairs of chased silver-gilt clasps, hinging on the upper cover [sic.].

Sewn on four (probably recessed) cords (frayed hemp), laced in; smooth spine. The silver-gilt spine covering also shows a chased pattern like that of the covers and has head and tail extensions covering part of the top and tail edges, showing two birds. Endbands: single (?with a bead); pink silk over (invisible) cores (laced in, no visible tie-downs); possibly: false endbands, consisting of a piece of (?)parchment over-sewn at the top with pink silk; the ends, sewn in pink silk, are laced into the boards.

Endleaves: yellow gold-embossed paper pastedowns (ornamental pattern) and one free white paper leaf (tipped on), at both ends.

PROVENANCE: Viscount Lymington (book plate); bought: Breslauer, 1.vii.1959.
LITERATURE: Whitney Hoff, no. 445; J F Hayward, 'Silver bindings from the J R Abbey collection', *The Connoisseur*, October 1952, no. 14; Sotheby's, 10.v.1985, *30*; Schäfer, p. 121.

236

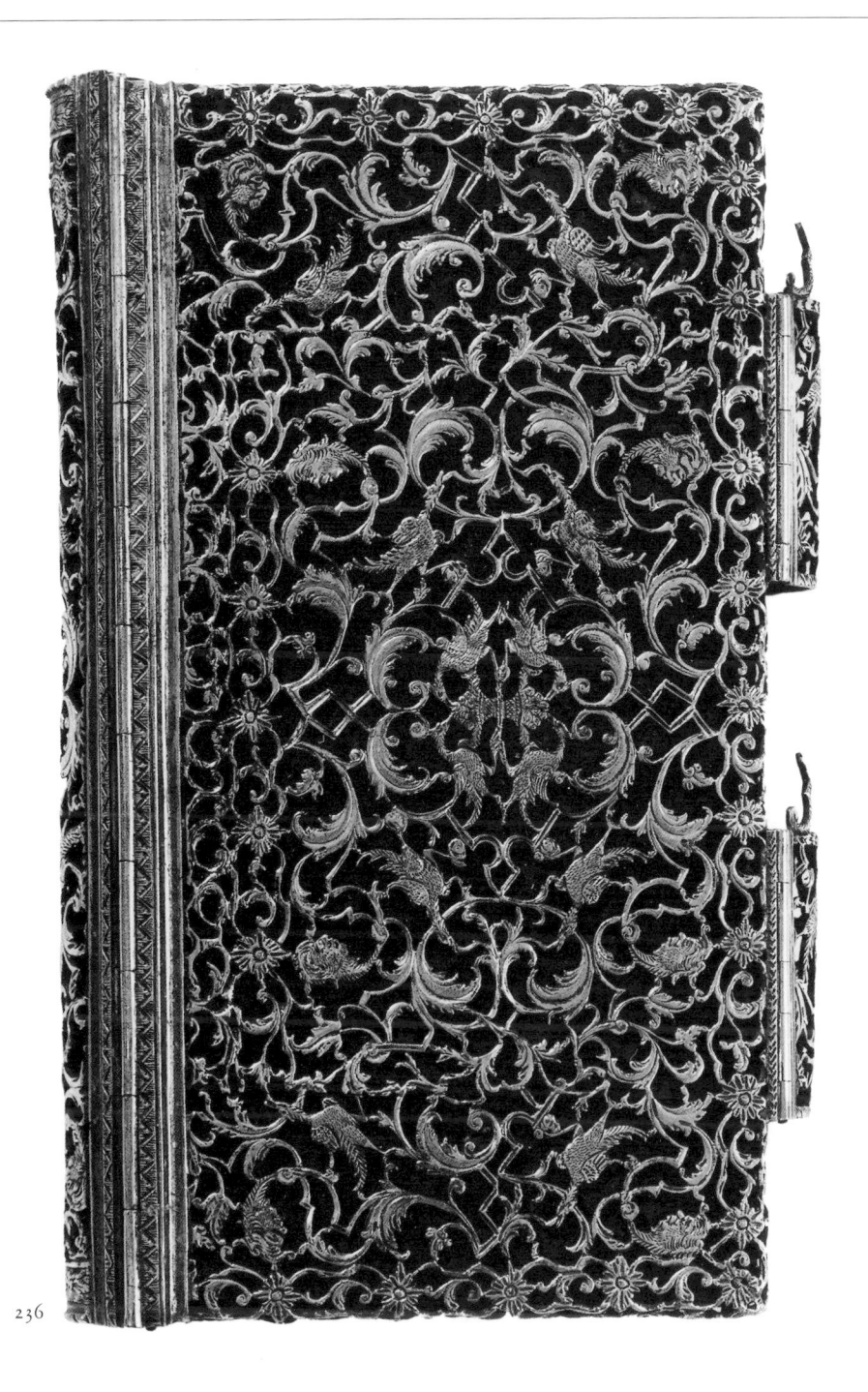

294

ITALIAN BINDINGS

237 *A binding probably made in Naples for Cardinal Oliverius Carafa, c. 1480*

Petrus Balbi, bishop of Tropaea, Dedication of the *Epistola ad Theodosium* to the cardinal of Naples, Latin MS on parchment; illuminated initial. [Italy, before September 1479] [and] Extract of *Dichiaratione sopra il nome di Iesu*, 'stampata in ferrara a presso francisco Rossi nel 1557', MS on paper [copy of part of printed book], four conjugate leaves sewn as one section through the centre fold, sewn in parchment music manuscript wrapper, and [later] tacked onto the kettle stitches and sewing supports of Balbi's manuscript.

185 × 100 × 5 mm. (M 48) Davis 721

Red-brown goatskin over paste boards, tooled in gold, with blind lines, to a panel design with a border and a centre panel filled with strap-work tooling and small starry flowers in blind and gold, to a slightly different design on each cover. Traces of two pairs of ties. Edges: plain.

Sewn, through the centre fold as one section (of eight leaves), on three supports, laced in; smooth spine. Endbands (later, after paper manuscript had been sewn in): single with a bead; pink and blue silk over alum-tawed cores (cut off), tied down.

Endleaves: parchment pastedowns; the Balbi manuscript has a pair of free conjugate parchment leaves (around the eight-leaf section).

Repairs: at spine.

PROVENANCE: Probably Cardinal Oliverius Carafa; manuscript notes on endleaf: 'Andrea da Verracano (?) Cavaliere'; bought: Pierre Berès, 7.v.1955.
REFERENCES: De Marinis, vol. I, p. 9, 209; *Treasures*, 1965, no. 68; Romme, *Book Collector*, 1969, p. 40, note 123, pl. xiia.
LITERATURE: Hobson, *French and Italian*, no. 55.
Compare: Mazal, pl. 77–80; Quilici, no. 51, fig. 28; Pinto, 'Legatura di epoca aragonese', pl. 16.
Note: Oliverius Carafa (c. 1430–1511), cardinal of Naples; created cardinal: 1467.
Petrus Balbi, bishop of Tropaea (d. 1479).

238 *A binding possibly made in Rome or Bologna, c. 1480–90*

P Virgilius Maro, *Opera*, MS on parchment; illuminated initials; painted and decorated border, [Italy, late 15th century].

295 × 195 × 48 mm. (M 73) Davis 767

Brown goatskin over wooden boards, tooled in blind with lines, a border filled with strap-work tools and roundels; a centre panel divided into three compartments, the upper and lower compartments filled with strap-work tooling and roundels; the centre compartment has knot-work tools in the corners, a

238

border filled with small circles and in the centre: an eight-pointed star in a circle, outlined with small circles and filled with strap-work tooling and roundels. Four pair of clasps on blue silk straps, hinging on the upper cover, with catch-plates on the lower cover. The clasps were renewed by Hutchins in 1907. Edges: gilt and gauffered to a pattern of diapers filled with small roses.

Rebacked; the original sewing may have been retained: sewn on four split alum-tawed supports, laced in straight and lying in grooves. Endbands: double with a bead; primary sewing over alum-tawed or leather cores (cut off), tied down; secondary sewing of pink and blue silk.

Endleaves: extensively repaired; parchment pastedowns and one free parchment leaf, may have been conjugate with pastedown, at both ends.

Repairs: extensively repaired by Hutchins in 1907 (as specified on a slip inserted in the book).

PROVENANCE: On fol. 1 in manuscript (17th-century hand): 'Ex lib. Cong. S. Mauri Romae'; on pastedown in manuscript: 'Armario Ord. IV. no. 9.' [library pressmark]; Fairfax Murray (book plate; sold: 1906); C W Dyson Perrins (book plate; sold: Sotheby's, 9.xii.1958, *35*).

239

REFERENCES: G Warner, *Descriptive Catalogue of Illuminated Manuscripts in the Library of C W Dyson Perrins*, Oxford, 1920, no. 82; *Virgil: The Two-Thousandth Anniversary*, exh., British Library, London, 17.ix.1982 – 27.ii.1983, no. 20.

LITERATURE: Warner, no. 81 ([?Rome, c. 1480] with the same provenance as Davis 767: the Congregation of St Maurus in Rome, 'Armario Ord. IV. no. 8', sold: Sotheby's 1.xii.1959, *76*); Pinto, 'Legatura di epoca aragonese', pp. 251, 253, figs 5d, 5e, 6.

Compare: BL, Add. MS 16617; De Marinis, 71, 83, 85, 87; *Legature papali*, nos. 7, 10, 16–18; Hobson, *Humanists*, p. 28, fig. 21; Hobson, 'Bookbinding in Bologna', fig. 1 (tools not identical).

Note: Italian bindings in Mudéjar style were made in Rome, Bologna and Naples in the last quarter of the 15th century.

---

239 *A binding with cut-leather work, possibly made in Venice, c. 1485*

Gregorius IX, *Decretales*, Venice: Andreas Torresanus, Andreus de Asula, et Socii, June 1482 (with MS index). 4to.

255 × 180 × 70 mm. (P 902) Davis 769

Brown goatskin over wooden boards decorated with cut-leather work and tooled in blind with lines and knot-work tooling and circle tools in the corners and upper and lower borders; in the centre a large octagon decorated in cut-leather work with interlacing and floral ornament on a punched ground; small gesso (or white-painted) roundels. Traces of four pairs of clasps, probably having hinged on the upper cover; traces of four corner bosses and a centre boss (or centre piece). Edges of boards: bevelled; tooled in blind with lines. Edges: plain and gauffered (mainly on the top edge) with diagonal lines, forming diapers, and roundels.

Sewn on three split alum-tawed supports (with traces of pink staining), laced into slots and lying in grooves on the outside of the boards (beneath the covering leather); showing as raised bands on the spine, tooled in blind with a line; four compartments, tooled in blind; remnants of a paper label [with library number?] on tail compartment.

Endbands: single with a bead (remnants only); primary sewing over tanned leather cores (broken off; but once laced in and lying in grooves on the inside of the boards), tied down; secondary sewing of pale blue and pink silk.

Endleaves: white paper pastedowns and one free leaf conjugate with the pastedown, at both ends.

PROVENANCE: On first page in manuscript: 'Loci Maciani'; on last page in manuscript: 'Loci Se Me Maciani'; on endleaf in manuscript: 'De Bielignaris' (?); Mensing (sold: Sotheby's, 16.xii.1936, *246*); bought: Sotheby's, 31.v.1948, *958*.

REFERENCES: De Marinis, *Rilegature veneziane*, pl. iv, no. 11. Nixon, *Broxbourne*, p. 21; Hobson, 'Italian fifteenth-century bookbindings', pp. 135–6; Romme, *Book Collector*, 1969, p. 40, note 124.

240 *A Sienese panel, 1488*

[Wooden panel for the accounts of the *Biccherna* of Sienna, painted by Guidocci Cozzarelli, 1488].

500 × 335 mm.   Davis 768

Oil painting on wood, depicting the return of the Noveschi to Siena, showing the armed exiles with their leader, Pandolfo Petrucci on a white horse, before the Porta di Fontebranda. Above the town walls are: (on the left) the Virgin and Child; (on the right) St Mary Magdalen, holding a container for ointment.

Below this scene are the painted coats of arms of the following families: Rocchi, Benucci, Orlandini (twice), Cesari, Beccafumi, Trecerchi and Menghini; (two coats are too damaged to be identified, as are the two small coats of arms at the bottom of the inscription). Inscription: QVESTA E LENTRATA E LVSCITA DELLA BICERNA AL TENPO DELLI SPETABILI/ HVO[MINI] DOMENICO DI GIOVANNI DI M[ISSERE] LORENZO ROCCHI K[AMARLINGO] ANTONIO DI GIO/VANNI BENVCCI NICOLO DI MARIANO ORLANDINI GIOVANNI DI CESARIO CESA[RI]/ FRANCIESSCHO DI GORO CHATASTI DE QVATRO P[ER] LI PRIMI SEI MESI P[ER]LI SICO/NDI LORENZO DANDREA BECCAFVMN [Beccafumi] MINO DI NICOLO TRECERCHI/ DOMENICO DI GVCCIO MENGHINI NICCOLO ORLANDINI GIOVANNI DI/ CHECHO COLONBINI SCRITORE M° CCCCLXXXVIII.

PROVENANCE: Fontange (Montpellier); Figdor (Vienna).
REFERENCES: E Carli, *Le tavolette di Biccherna*, Florence, 1950 (who misidentifies the saint on the right above the wall); Erica S Trippi, 'Matteo di Giovanni: documents and a critical

VESTA E L ENTRATA E L VSCITA DELLA BICERNA AL TENPO DELLI SPETABILI
HVŌ DOMENICO DI GIOVANNI DI M LORENZO ROCCHI E ANTONIO DI GI
VANNI BENVCCI NICOLO DI MARIANO ORLANDINI GIOVANNI DI CESARIO CESA
FRANCIESSCHO DI GORO CHATASTI DE QVATRO P LI PRIMI SEI MESI P LI SIC
NDI LORENZO D ANDREA BECAFVMI MINO DI NICOLO TRECERCHI
DOMENICO DI GVCIO MENGHINI NICOLO ORLANDINI GIOVANNI DI
CHECHO COLONBINI SCRITTORE M°CCCCLXXXVIII

catalogue of his panel paintings', dissertation, University of Michigan, 1987 (where this panel is attributed to Matteo di Giovanni); Foot, *Studies*, pp. 293–5; *Le Biccherne*, no. 76.

LITERATURE: *A Picture Book of Bookbindings, Part I: Before 1550*, London: Victoria and Albert Museum, 1933, nos. 4–5; R W Lightbown, 'The *Tavolette di Biccherna* of Siena', *Journal of the Society of Archivists*, II, 7 (1963), pp. 292 ff. (with further literature); *Le Biccherne*.

Note: Painted wooden covers were used to protect, weigh down and decorate the accounts of the Sienese exchequer; 139 have been described, dating from 1258 to the eighteenth century. The coats of arms and the names are those of the treasury officials.

Pandolfo Petrucci and the Noveschi penetrated the gates of Siena on the night of 21–22 July 1487; Petrucci was particularly devoted to Mary Magdalen, whose feast day falls on 22 July, the day on which he managed to return to Siena.

241 *A (?)north Italian or possibly Venetian binding, c. 1490*

Pius II, *Epistolae in Cardinalatu editae*, Rome: E Silber, [1489–93] [and] Phalaris, *Epistolae* [translated by F Aretinus], Florence: Antonius Francisci, [1487]. 4to.

213 × 144 × 31 mm. (P 252) Davis 770

Brown goatskin over paste boards, tooled in blind to a panel design, with lines, an octagon with a broad border filled with strap-work tooling around a panel with corners filled with small rope tools; in the centre a large knot ornament composed of small strap-work tools; the title of the second work written in ink on the lower cover. Remnants of four pairs of ties. Edges: plain with the title of the first work written on the tail edge ('piccolominei epistole').

Sewn on three split alum-tawed supports, stained pink, laced in straight, showing as raised bands on the spine, tooled in blind with a line; four compartments, tooled in blind with lines; compartments lined with individual pieces of leather, stuck down beneath the pastedowns. Endbands: single; primary sewing over leather cores (now broken off, but traces of lacing-in holes), tied down.

Endleaves: white paper pastedowns at both ends; at the front: one free paper leaf tipped onto a section of eight blank leaves (of a different paper than was used for the text); at the end: a section of eight blank paper leaves and one leaf conjugate with the pastedown.

PROVENANCE: On last page of text in manuscript (15th-century hand): 'Benedicti Capilupi Codex'; Henry Yates Thompson (sold: Sotheby's, 19.viii.1941, *395*).

Compare: *BFAC*, 1891, pl. xxii; Mazal, pl. 72; *Legature papali*, no. 3; Breslauer, Catalogue 110 [1990], no. 3; Quilici, no. 116, fig. 45; Brera, no. 3.

242 *A binding possibly made in Rome in the early sixteenth century*

Diogenes Laertius, *Vitae et sententiae philosophorum*, Venice: [Bonetus Locatellus] for Octavianus Scotus, 15 January [ISTC: 18 December] 1490; woodcut initials. 4to.

214 × 164 × 27 mm. (P 1272) Davis 771

Brown goatskin over paste boards, tooled in blind to a panel design with lines; an outer border filled

241

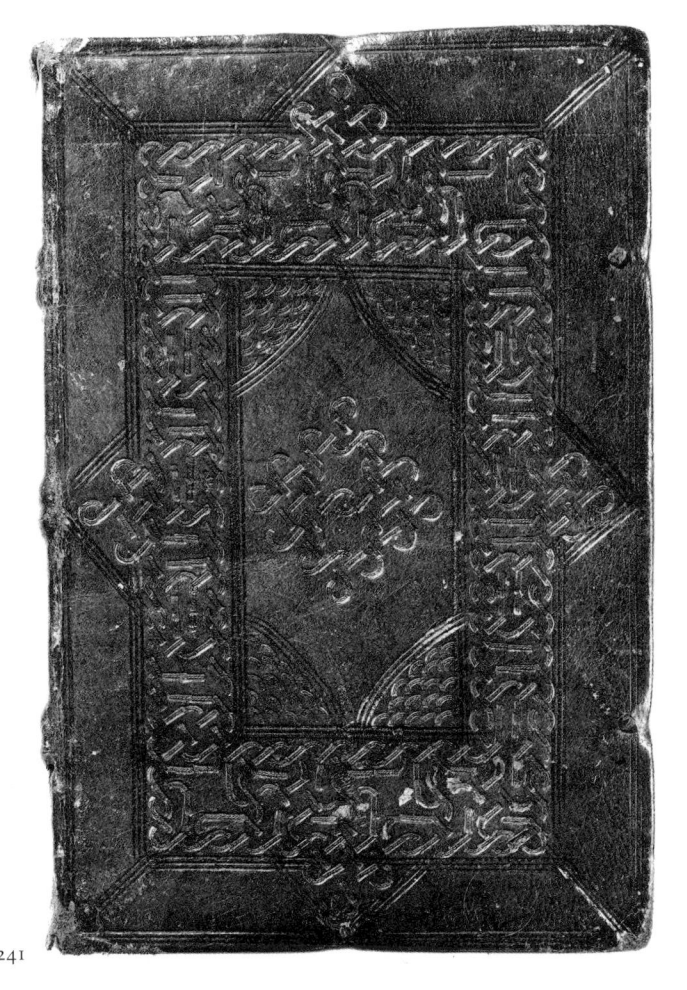

242

with interlinked-circles tools, an inner border with strap-work tools and a centre panel with rows of knot tools. Edges: plain.

Sewn on three supports (material invisible), laced in, showing as raised bands on the spine, tooled in blind with a line; four compartments, tooled in blind with lines. Endbands: single with a bead; primary sewing over leather core (cut off), tied down; secondary sewing of pink silk (fragment of blue silk remaining), tied down (only tail band remains).

Endleaves: white paper pastedowns and one free white paper leaf tipped onto first and last sections, at both ends.

PROVENANCE: Manuscript notes in the margins of the text; on pastedown of lower cover: a manuscript list of books; on pastedown of upper cover in ink: '41' [crossed through], '84'; C S Ascherson (book plate); J R Abbey (book plate, '1933'; sold: Sotheby's, 22.vi.1965, *259*).
LITERATURE: Folger Catalogue, no. 12:1.
Compare: Hobson, *Humanists*, figs 75, 82.

THE HENRY DAVIS GIFT

243   *A Venetian binding of the early sixteenth century*

Flavius Josephus, *De bello Judaico* [and] *De antiquitate Judeorum*, Verona: Petrus Maufer, January [ISTC: December] 1480; with a title-page in manuscript. fol.

138 × 212 × 40 mm.   (P 1290) Davis 786

Brown goatskin (or possibly hair sheep) over paste boards, tooled in gold, with blind lines; a border filled with knot-work tooling; small leaf tools in the corners and around a centre ornamental tool. Traces of four pairs of ties. Edges: plain; on top edge in manuscript: 'Gio: Dadeo'.

Sewn on three split alum-tawed supports, laced in, showing as raised bands on the spine, tooled in blind with lines; four compartments, tooled in blind with lines; on the top compartment: a paper label with the title in manuscript. Endbands: single with a bead; primary sewing over alum-tawed cores (now broken off, but clear traces of lacing in), tied down; remnants of secondary sewing in pink and blue silk, tied down.

Endleaves: white paper pastedowns and one free paper leaf, conjugate with stubs after a8 at the front and before D1 at the end, at both ends; printed waste visible beneath pastedown.

PROVENANCE:	Contemporary manuscript notes on endleaf and in margins of text; Lathrop Harper, Catalogue 19, no. 41 (sold: 7.xi.1964).
Same tools on:	BL, C.108.a.11 (Venice, 1506); De Marinis, 1620 ([Venice], 1490), 2181 (Venice, 1501), 3101bis (Florence, 1523).
Compare:	BL, Add. MS 24897; Pembroke College, Cambridge, 3.29.76 (Dante, n.p., n.d.); Cambridge University Library, Rel.d.51.6 (Venice, 1502); John Rylands University Library, Manchester, 5421 (Venice, 1503); King's College, Cambridge, M.28.REF 46 (Florence, 1514); De Marinis, 1794 (manuscript, 1508), 1921 (Venice, 1506); Hobson, *Humanists*, figs 66, 68.

244   *A binding possibly made in Milan, c. 1501*

A Ianus Parrhasius, *Commentarius in raptum Proserpinae Cl. Claudiani*, Milan: Guillermus le Signerre for Lutius Cotta, 1501. fol.

355 × 248 × 20 mm.   (P 903) Davis 787

Brown goatskin (or possibly hair sheep) over paste boards, tooled in blind to a panel design with lines; an outer border filled with large rectangular floral tools, an inner border filled with rope-work tools; a large lozenge surrounded by a border with flower tools, on the inside: head-tools ('Kopf-Stempel') and in the centre: ornaments made up of knot tools. Traces of four pairs of ties. Edges: plain; title written on tail edge.

Sewn with a long stitch (showing on the outside of the spine), on four alum-tawed supports, laced in; smooth spine; three compartments, top and tail compartments: new. Endbands: none.

Endleaves: white paper pastedowns and one free leaf conjugate with the pastedowns, at both ends. Repairs: at spine and covers.

PROVENANCE: On a1 in manuscript: 'B (?N). Josephi Salaroli de Bon.a' (a: superscript); George Dunn

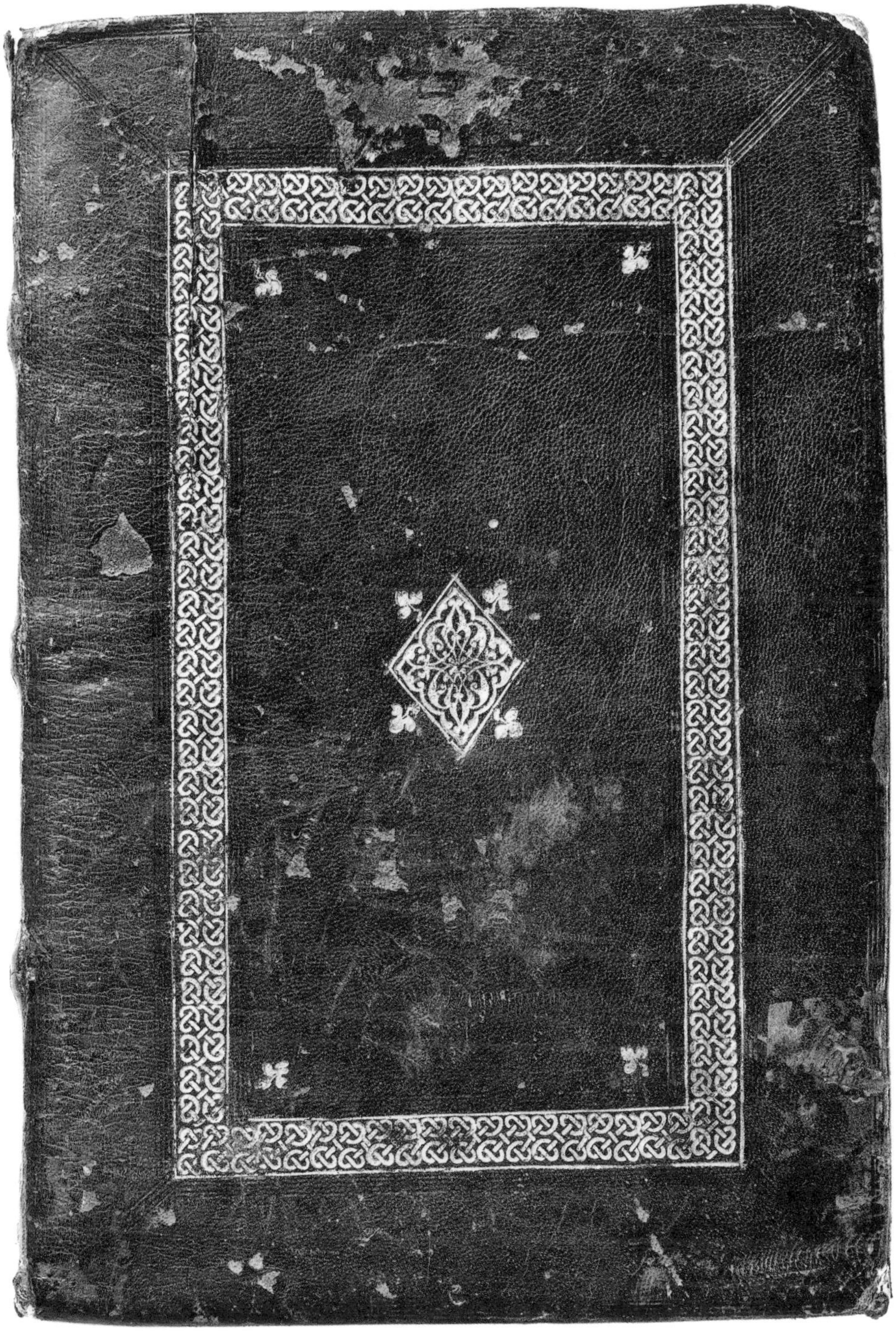

243

244

	(book plate; in Dunn's hand: 'GD/May 1909'); E P Goldschmidt (book plate); bought: Sotheby's, 31.v.1948, *982*.
Same tool on:	Bodleian Library Oxford, Auct I.Q.4.25 (Florence, 1499); De Marinis, 2592 (Milan, 1489).
Compare:	Malaguzzi, *Monferrato*, pls 4, 12, 14; Malaguzzi, *La Valsesia*, pl. 39; Brera, no. 15.

245 *A Milanese binding for Jean Grolier, c. 1509–12*

Procopius, *De bello Gottorum*, Rome: Johann Besickem, 20 June 1506. fol.

290 × 215 × 30 mm.   (P 1131) Davis 788

Brown goatskin (or possibly hair sheep) over paste boards, tooled in blind and gold to a panel design, with blind lines; a border filled with strap-work tooling; fleurons at the corners; small solid fleurs-de-lis tools in the outer border and round a centre plaquette (in blind), showing, on the upper cover: the Judgement of Paris, and on the lower cover: Orpheus playing to the animals. Traces of two pairs of ties. Edges: painted with curving lines and fleurons or fleurs-de-lis; Grolier's arms painted in the centre of the fore edge.

Sewn on three split alum-tawed supports (traces of pink), laced in straight, showing as raised bands on the spine, with traces of blind-tooled lines; four compartments, tooled in blind with lines; title added in blind later. Top and tail of spine: damaged. Endbands: single with a bead; primary sewing over leather cores (laced in; one end is still laced in; rest broken off), tied down.

Endleaves: white paper pastedowns at both ends; at the front: two free conjugate paper leaves and one free leaf conjugate with the pastedown; at the end: two pairs of free conjugate white paper leaves (quired) and one free leaf conjugate with the pastedown.

PROVENANCE:	Jean Grolier (after the colophon, x iiii verso, in manuscript: 'Jo. Grolierij Lugdunensis/ et amicorum', in the same hand: a note in the margin of n ii recto); Edward Synge, bishop of Limerick (on first page in manuscript: 'Dublin febr: 23: 1660 Edw: Lymericensis'); in a different hand: 'Ex dono Richd. Carney'; 'A.A.'; Colonel Cooper (book plate; library label of Makree library, Co. Sligo; sold: Sotheby's, 15.xii.1953, *351*, pl.).
REFERENCES:	De Marinis, 2657; Guignard, 'A propos d'un Grolier inédit', p. 197, no. 21; Nixon, *Grolier*, no. 2 (pl. ii); Romme, *Book Collector*, 1969, p. 40, notes 128, 129; Austin, no. 446.1; Hobson, *Humanists*, p. 230, nos. 52e, 54c; Hobson, *Renaissance*, p. 223, no. 446.1.
LITERATURE:	Molinier, nos. 134, 498; De Marinis, III, pl. E2, nos. 2651, 2652, 2660, 2662; Hobson, *French and Italian*, pp. 5–20; Miner, *Baltimore*, no. 216; Nixon, *Pierpont Morgan Library*, no. 2; Hobson, *Humanists*, pp. 114–20; Hobson, *Renaissance*, pp. 3–69, esp. pp. 11–21; Brera, no. 17.
Same tools on:	Fitzwilliam Museum, Cambridge (*Astronomici veteris*, Venice, 1499); Trinity College, Cambridge, vi.18.25 (Milan, 1499); see also Davis 722 (no. 246 below).

306

246

246 *A Milanese binding for Jean Grolier, c. 1509–12*

J J Pontanus, *Opera*, Venice: Aldus, August 1505; illuminated initials in gold on blue and red ground. 8vo.

171 × 105 × 40 mm. (P 1295) Davis 722

Brown goatskin over paste boards, tooled in gold, with blind lines, to a panel design; stylized flowers in the outer border; corner fleurons; an inner border filled with interlinked-circles tools; ornamental fleurons and triangular tools in the centre. Traces of four pairs of ties. Edges: gilt, and gauffered to a pattern of branches and leaves.

Sewn on three tanned leather supports, laced in straight, showing as raised bands on the spine, tooled in blind with a line; four compartments, tooled in blind to a diaper pattern. Endbands: single with a bead; primary sewing over leather cores (now cut or broken off), tied down; secondary sewing of pink and blue silk.

Endleaves: white paper pastedowns and a pair of free conjugate paper leaves and one free white paper leaf tipped on, at both ends.

Repairs: slight.

PROVENANCE: Jean Grolier (on A ii recto: Grolier's device with the motto: AEQVE DIFFICVLTER and Grolier's arms); Breslauer (Catalogue 67, 1949, no. 81, pls I, IX); De Nobele, Paris (Catalogue IV, 1956, no. 2254).

REFERENCES: De Marinis, 2130 (pl. ccclxxii); Hobson, *French and Italian*, p. 10, no. 6; Nixon, *Grolier*, no. 6; Romme, *Book Collector*, 1969, pp. 40–1, note 130; Austin, no. 429.1; Hobson,

	Renaissance, pp. 11–12 (pl.), p. 223, no. 429.1; D Pearson, *English Bookbinding Styles*, London, 2005, fig. 3.22.
LITERATURE:	See Davis 788 (no. 245 above; and literature cited there); De Marinis, 2652 (pl. ccccrlviii), 2656 (pl. cccclix); J Guignard, 'Notes et hypothèses à propos de Jean Grolier et des débuts de sa collection', in: *Festschrift Ernst Kyriss*, Stuttgart, 1961, pp. 191–225, p. 203, fig. 4; Hobson, *Humanists*, p. 115, note 107, p. 118, fig. 93.
Compare:	John Rylands University Library, Manchester, 18871 (Catullus etc., n.p., n.d.); Fitzwilliam Museum, Cambridge (Petrarch, Venice, 1528).
Note:	Grolier's device has been interpreted as a hand drawing a nail from the top of a hill (Nixon), as God's hand planting a staff ending in a cross on a hilltop (Hobson, *Humanists*), or as a hand holding a stake or a similar object protruding from the top of a mountain (Hobson, *Renaissance*).

---

247 *A binding possibly made in Rome, c. 1510 or later*

[Arnaldus de Nova Villa Avicenna] (attrib.), *Tractatus de virtutibus herbarum*, Venice: Ioannes Rubeus & Bernardinus fratres Vercellensis, 15 March 1509; woodcuts. 4to.

213 × 149 × 25 mm.   (P 257) Davis 772

Brown goatskin over paste boards, tooled in gold to a panel design, with blind lines and corner fleurons; an outer border filled with interlinked-circles tools; an inner border filled with smaller interlinked-circles tools, fleurons in the corners of the centre panel; a centre ornament built up of four corner fleurons; small flower tools. Remnants of four pairs of ties. Edges: gilt and gauffered with a knot-work pattern.

Sewn on three split alum-tawed supports, laced in straight, showing as raised bands on the spine, tooled in blind with lines; four compartments, tooled in blind with lines and, in blind and gold, with small flowers and leaves. Endbands: single with a bead; (?)pink silk over leather cores (now cut off, traces of lacing in holes), tied down.

Endleaves: white paper pastedowns at both ends; at the front: one free leaf conjugate with the pastedown; at the end: one free paper leaf tipped onto last section.

Repairs: small repairs at spine and corners of covers.

PROVENANCE:	On pastedowns manuscript notes in a 16th- or 17th-century hand: (?)'Laymer Houbler'; 'Lau[?w]recius'; J Choul; Fairfax Murray (library label; sold: Sotheby's, 20.vii.1922, *1075*); Henry Yates Thompson (book plate with manuscript note: 'H.Y.T. bought this book on 23/7/1922 at F.M.'s sale: S: July 1922'; sold: Sotheby's, 19.viii.1941, *439*).
REFERENCES:	De Marinis, 610.
Same tool on:	John Rylands University Library, Manchester, 18824 (Venice, 1515).
Compare:	Bodleian Library Oxford, Douce bindings A25; compare also Davis, 774 (no. 251 below); similar tools to the corner tools were used in Rome, see e.g. Hobson, *Humanists*, p. 85, figs 69, 70; De Marinis, 449, 450, 552.

247   248

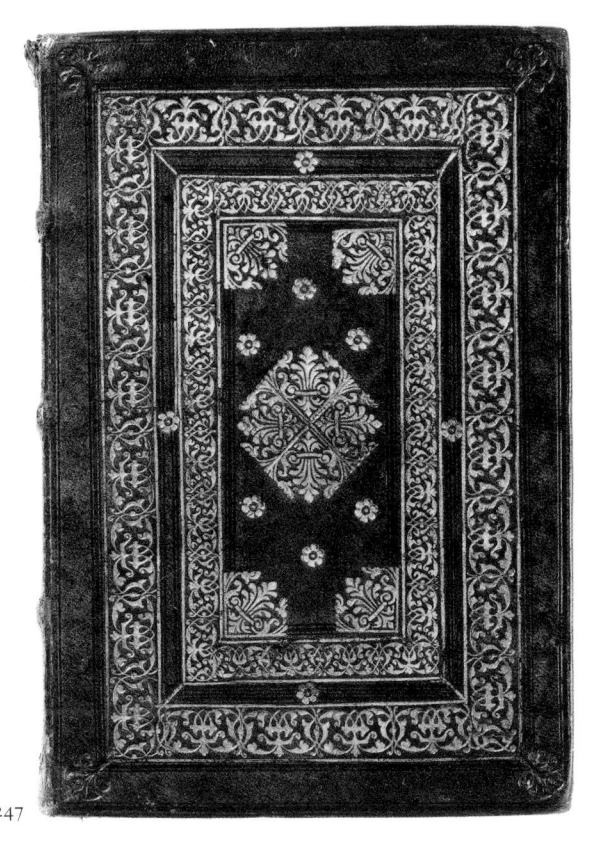

248 *A north Italian binding, c. 1510*

M A Coccius Sabellicus, *Exemplorum libri decem*, Venice: [Georgius de Rusconibus], 19 September 1507; woodcut initials. 4to.

215 × 148 × 30 mm.   (P 836) Davis 773

Brown goatskin over paste boards, tooled in blind and gold to a panel design, with lines, an outer border filled with interlinking ornamental tools in blind; an inner border filled with fleuron tools and dots in gold; in the centre: three circular ornaments built up of fleurons, flowers and other small tools round a knot tool. Remnants of two pairs of clasps, hinging on the upper cover with catch-plates on the lower cover. Edges: gilt and gauffered to a knot-work pattern.

Sewn on three split alum-tawed supports, stained pink, laced in straight, showing as raised bands on the spine; four compartments, tooled in blind with lines; canvas spine lining. Endbands: single with a bead; primary sewing over (?)cord cores (laced in), tied down; secondary sewing of red and blue silk, tied down.

Endleaves: remnants (a stub and cut-off portion) of two free conjugate parchment leaves, at the end. Repairs.

PROVENANCE: Manuscript notes in 16th-, 17th- and 19th-century hands; Loredano Luciani Ranier (library stamp on title-page, with in manuscript '1420'); bought: Sotheby's, 19.xii.1944, 422.
REFERENCES: Romme, *Book Collector*, 1969, p. 41, note 131, pl. xiib.

Same tool on: BL, C.20.b.29 (Venice, 1501); Edinburgh University Library, MS 229; De Marinis, 564, 2966.
Compare: Trinity College, Cambridge, Grylls b.190 (Venice, 1507); De Marinis, 2181, 2689; Hobson, *Humanists*, fig. 124.

249 *A binding possibly made in Venice, c. 1510*

Valerius Maximus, *Dictorum et factorum memorabilium libri novem*, Venice: Aldus, October 1502. 8vo.

159 × 100 × 28 mm. (P 1205) Davis 725

Brown goatskin over paste boards, tooled in gold, with blind lines, with a border filled with strap-work tools, dividing the covers into two panels, each with small stars in the corners, a border filled with small tools, curving and marking off the corners, and a centre ornament formed by four flame tools round a star. Traces of four pairs of ties. Edges: gilt and gauffered to a strap-work pattern.

Sewn on three split alum-tawed supports, laced in straight, showing as raised bands on the spine, tooled in blind with a line; four compartments, tooled in blind with lines. Endbands: single with a bead; primary sewing over leather cores (cut off), sporadically tied down; secondary sewing of pink and blue silk.

Endleaves: white paper pastedowns at both ends; at the end: one free white paper leaf tipped onto the last section.

Repairs: at top and tail of spine and at corners.

PROVENANCE: On pastedown in manuscript: 'J. Weinsheimer' and '8'; bought: Sotheby's, 13.vi.1955, *6*.
Compare: Brera, no. 30.

250 *A binding made in Venice or possibly in Bologna, c. 1510*

C Plinius Caecilius Secundus, *Epistolae*, Venice: Aldus and A A Socerus, November 1508. 8vo.

165 × 100 × 40 mm. (P 1382) Davis 724

Brown goatskin over paste boards, tooled in gold, with blind lines, to a panel design with fleurons at the corners, ivy-leaf tools, and on the upper cover: a blind-fold cupid above a dolphin and the title: .C.PLINII/ SECVNDI/ EPISTOL/ARVM; on the lower cover: Fortuna with her sail above a dolphin. Traces of four pairs of ties. Edges: gilt.

Sewn on three split alum-tawed supports, laced in straight, showing as raised bands on the spine, tooled in gold with a line; four compartments, tooled in blind with lines and in gold with stylized flowers. Spine compartments lined. Endbands: single with a bead; blue and beige silk over alum-tawed cores (now cut off; lacing-in holes visible), tied down.

Endleaves: white paper pastedowns (with conjugate stubs after first and before last sections) and two free conjugate paper leaves, at both ends.

Repairs: small repairs at top and tail of spine and at corners.

PROVENANCE: On endleaf in manuscript: 'Iulij Guiduccij' with a drawing of a leafy branch;

249　　　　　　　　　　　　　　　250

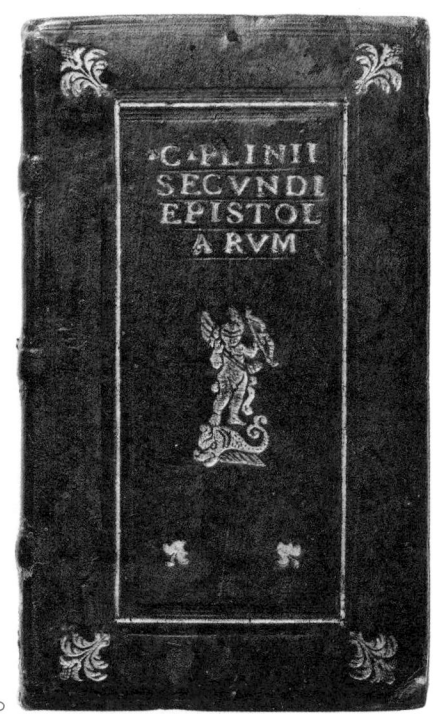

                    underneath in a different hand: 'Narcisco Mazzetti'; on contents page *i in manuscript: 'Hoc mora nec sequies'; on endleaf in pencil [?in G Dunn's hand]: 'Ex dono Paget Toynbee'; George Dunn of Wooley Hall, Maidenhead (library label); bought: Heilbrun, 2.vi.1956.

LITERATURE:　　Hobson, *Humanists*, pp. 260–2 (Fortune and Cupid in Padua: but different tools).
Compare:　　Cambridge University Library, Rel. d.50.1 (Venice, n.d.), SSS.33.16 (Venice, 1513); Edinburgh University Library, W.20.74 (Venice, 1521); Bodleian Library Oxford, Broxbourne R1046, Bodl. 24.17 (Venice, 1541); De Marinis, 609, 819, 1249, 1287, 1352, 1781, 2621; Bodley, *Exhibition*, no. 5; Hobson, *Humanists*, figs 133, 138.

251 *A binding possibly made in Rome, c. 1510–20*

F Vegetius, *De re militari*, Rome: E Silber, 24 October 1494 [and] S I Frontinus, *Strategematicon*, Rome: E Silber, 3 November 1494 [and] Modestus, *De vocabulis rei militari*, n.p., n.d. [and] Onosander, *Ad Q. Veranium de optimo imperatore … officio* [translated from Greek into Latin by Nicolaus Sagundinus], n.p., n.d. 4to.

215 × 158 × 19 mm.　　　　　　　　　　　　　　　　　　　　　　　　　　　　(P 1273) Davis 774

Brown goatskin (or possibly hair sheep) over paste boards, tooled in gold (only traces of gold tooling remain), with blind lines, to a panel design with a border filled with interlinking-circles tools; in the centre panel: the Colonna arms with axe and sword tools, fleurons and a large circle with on the upper cover: MELI/VS EST HO/STEM FAME/ DOMARE:/ QVAM/ PRAE/LIO; on the lower cover: AM/PLIVS/ VALET VIR/TVS: QVAM/ MVLTITV/DO. Traces of four pairs of ties. Edges: gilt and gauffered to a knot-work pattern; title of the first work in manuscript on tail edge.

311

251

Sewn on two split alum-tawed and one tanned leather supports, laced in straight, showing as raised bands on the spine; four compartments, tooled in blind with lines. Endbands: single; primary sewing over alum-tawed core (laced in), tied down; secondary sewing of blue and pink silk, tied down (headband and remnant of tailband only).

Endleaves: white paper pastedowns and one free leaf conjugate with the pastedown, at both ends. Parchment stub (strengthener) visible after free endleaf at both ends.

Repairs: at spine and covers.

PROVENANCE: (?)Member of the Colonna family; Landau (book plate, no. 47906/47910; sold: Geneva, 25.vi.1948, *210*); on upper cover pastedown in manuscript: 'Sc: 7 ux: SSS'; J R Abbey (book plate; 'J.A.4076/ 20:7:1948'; sold: Sotheby's, 23.vi.1965, *671*).
REFERENCES: Hobson, *French and Italian*, no. 57.
Same tools on: Bodleian Library Oxford, Douce bindings A 25; BL, C.19.f.12 (Florence, 1514: De Marinis, 2188); De Marinis, 1794.
Compare: BL, IB 25743 [Ferrara, 1491]; Hobson, *Renaissance*, figs 21, 22.
Note: Hobson suggests as possible members of the Colonna family: Marcantonio (d. 1522), Prospero (d. 1523), Giulio or Pompeo (d. 1532).

252

252 *A binding made in Rome, c. 1510–25*

Philostratus, *De vita Apollonii Tyanei*, n.p., n.d., [?Lyon, ?1504]. 8vo.

163 × 98 × 26 mm. (P 1235) Davis 723

Brown goatskin over paste boards, tooled in blind with lines and blocked in blind with a block showing an arabesque design; in the centre of both covers: a plaquette, showing a cameo portrait of Julius Caesar, laureate, draped bust to the right, behind him a lituus, lettered: (star) DIVI IVLI, traces of gold on plaquette. Traces of two pairs of green ties. Edges: gilt and gauffered to a knot-work pattern.

Sewn on three split alum-tawed supports, laced in straight, showing as raised bands on the spine; four compartments, tooled in blind with lines and roundels. Endbands: single with a bead; primary sewing over alum-tawed cores (laced in at a slight angle), tied down; secondary sewing of pink and blue silk.

Endleaves: white paper pastedowns and one free leaf conjugate with the pastedown, at both ends. Parchment manuscript lining to spine compartments, pasted down beneath pastedowns.

PROVENANCE: On title-page in manuscript: 'Munificentia Celsi Jubilei …' [missing]; Count A Oberndorff (sold: Sotheby's, 6.vii.1955, *135*).
REFERENCES: Romme, *Book Collector*, 1969, p. 40, note 127, Hobson, *Humanists*, p. 221, no. 15k.
LITERATURE: Goldschmidt, no. 92, pl. xl; E Kyriss, 'Plaketten- und Kameen-Bände', *Jahrbuch der Einbandkunst*, III/IV (1929/30), pp. 41–53 (III, pp. 46–7, pl. 18); De Marinis, III, pl. E1, nos. 1658, 1675, 2694; Hobson, *Humanists*, p. 218, no. 8c, p. 221, no. 15 l; Hobson, 'Plaquette and medallion bindings', p. 75, no. 15 lx.

Compare: De Marinis, III, pl. H9, no. 3046bis.
Note: Two examples of this intaglio stamp are in the British Museum: Department of Coins and Medals, MO284 (with two casts: MO283, MO285) and Dept. of Medieval and Later Antiquities, 1915, 12–16, 165. It was apparently modelled on a cornelian gem of Julius Caesar, which belonged to Cardinal Franceso Gonzaga, and was bequeathed by him to Alfonso, duke of Calabria (d. 1483); it is mentioned in Gonzaga's will and in his inventory; see: D S Chambers, *A Renaissance Cardinal and his Worldly Goods: The Will and Inventory of Francesco Gonzaga, 1444–1483*, London: Warburg Institute, 1992, pp. 134, 160–1 (I am very grateful to Dora Thornton for this information).

253 *A binding possibly made in Bologna, c. 1513*

Catullus, Tibullus, Propertius, *Opera*, Venice: Aldus, January 1502. 8vo.

163 × 101 × 21 mm. (P 974) Davis 727

Brown goatskin over paste boards, tooled in blind and gold to a panel design with lines, an outer border filled with interlinked-ovals tools, an inner border filled with interlinked-circles tools; small stars in the corners, in the centre: two knot tools and a rosette composed of a stylized flower surrounded by small triangular tools. Traces of four pairs of ties. Edges: plain.

Sewn on three split alum-tawed supports, laced in straight, showing as raised bands on the spine, tooled in blind with a line; four compartments, tooled in blind with lines. Endbands: single with a bead; primary sewing over alum-tawed cores (laced in), tied down; secondary sewing in blue and pink silk.

Endleaves: white paper pastedowns at both ends; at the front: one free white paper leaf tipped onto first section; at the end: one free white paper leaf conjugate with the pastedown.

PROVENANCE: On lower cover pastedown in manuscript: 'Iohan[n]es gender Alemanus de Norinberga:- An[n]o Christiane salutis MD14/ me[n]se decembris'; on upper cover pastedown in manuscript: '170 francs Giraud'; bought: Sotheby's, 26.ii.1951, *63*.
LITERATURE: Hobson, *Legature bolognesi*, nos. 13, 15, pp. 13–15.
Same tools on: Davis 726 (no. 254 below); John Rylands University Library, Manchester, R52187 (Venice, 1516).
Compare: Hobson, *Legature bolognesi*, pp. 65, 67, nos. 13, 15; Nuvoloni, 'Commissioni Dogali', p. 98, no. 64.

254 *A binding possibly made in Bologna, c. 1513*

C I Caesar, *Commentariorum de bello Gallico libri* [and] *Index eorum*, Venice: Aldus & A Socerus, April 1513; map; woodcuts. 8vo.

170 × 114 × 38 mm. (P 794) Davis 726

Dark brown goatskin over paste boards, tooled in blind with lines, an outer border filled with interlinked-ovals tools, a panel with a lozenge outlined by a border filled with curving leaf tools; stylized flower tools, ivy-leaf tools and in the centre of the upper cover, tooled in gold: COM/CAES; on the

253 254

lower cover in gold: N H. Traces and remnants of four pairs of clasps, hinging on the upper cover. Edges: plain.

Sewn on three split alum-tawed supports, showing as bands on the spine, tooled in blind with a line; four compartments, tooled in blind with lines; compartments lined. Endbands: single with a bead; primary sewing over leather cores (cut off), tied down; remnants of secondary sewing in pink silk.

Endleaves: white paper pastedowns and one free white paper leaf tipped onto first and last sections, at both ends.

Repairs: small repair at corner of spine.

PROVENANCE: Palatine Library, Vienna (on title-page: library stamp: 'Biblioth. Palat. Vindobon. Dupl.'); on pastedown: unidentified book plate with: 'sigillum horatii domitis de orford' [possibly: Horatio Walpole, 4th earl of Orford, 1717–97, visited Italy: 1739–41]; bought: Sotheby's, 17.vii.1944, 2.
LITERATURE: See Davis 727 (no. 253 above; and literature cited there).
Same tools on: Davis 727 (no. 253 above); John Rylands University Library, Manchester, R52187 (Venice, 1516); De Marinis, 1406D.
Compare: BL, C.64.a.13 (Florence, 1510); De Marinis, 563; Esmerian sale I, Paris, 6.vi.1972, *80* (Lyon, 1521); Hobson, *Legature bolognesi*, pp. 65, 67, nos. 13, 15.

255 *A binding probably made in Venice, c. 1514*

M P Cato [and others], *Libri de re rustica*, Venice: Aldus & A Socerus, May 1514. 4to.

221 × 139 × 58 mm. (P 1377) Davis 775

Brown goatskin over paste boards, tooled in blind and gold with lines to a geometrical design of lozenges and triangles. Edges: gilt and gauffered to a strap-work and knot pattern.

    Sewn on three split alum-tawed supports, laced in straight, showing as raised bands on the spine, tooled in gold with a line; four compartments, tooled in blind and gold with lines. Endbands: single; primary sewing over (?)leather cores (cut off), tied down; secondary sewing in pink silk.

    Endleaves: (later) white paper pastedowns and one free leaf conjugate with the pastedown, at both ends.

    Repairs: small repairs at corners and top and tail of spine.

PROVENANCE: On title-page in manuscript: 'J. Bajet & Perre(?)ne'; Bibliotheca Giuliari (book plate); A Lauria, Paris; bought: Sotheby's, 18.ii.1957, *27*.
REFERENCES: De Marinis, 1771.
LITERATURE: (for other bindings with purely geometrical designs) De Marinis, 1227ter, 1772, 1769.

256

256 *A binding possibly made in Rome, c. 1515*

M A Lucanus, [*Pharsalia.*] *Civilis belli libri*, n.p., n.d., [Lyon, c. 1503]. 8vo.

155 × 98 × 20 mm. (P 606) Davis 731

Brown goatskin (or possibly hair sheep) over paste boards, tooled in blind with lines, a border filled with interlinked-circles tools, small star and knot tools, a lozenge filled with strap-work tools and in the centre a small, slightly sunk, medallion with a portrait of a man, bust to left, hair bound with a fillet (probably from an antique coin). Traces of four pairs of ties. Boards flush with the text block. Edges: gilt and gauffered with dots and crosses.

Sewn on three split alum-tawed supports, laced in straight, showing as raised bands on the spine, tooled in blind with lines; four compartments, tooled in blind with lines. Traces of manuscript lining of compartments. Endbands: missing (traces of tie-downs).

Endleaves: white paper pastedowns at both ends; at the front: one free white paper leaf conjugate with the pastedown; at the end: one free white paper leaf conjugate with a stub before the last section; a second stub before the last section is conjugate with the pastedown.

Repairs: at corners, at tail of spine; at covers.

PROVENANCE: On title-page in manuscript: 'Horatij Mugghionij b[?s]itturg[i]ensis'; on pastedown of lower cover: a label with blue border and in pencil: '1/1307'; E P Goldschmidt (book plate with in pencil: 'No 83'; Catalogue 67, no. 106; sold: 29. iv. 1943).
REFERENCES: Goldschmidt, no. 83.
LITERATURE: Hobson, *Humanists*, pp. 92–4.
Same strap-work tools on: Pierpont Morgan Library, M474 (HM Nixon, *Pierpont Morgan Library*, no. 4 = De Marinis, 3040bis).

257 *A binding made in Venice or possibly in Bologna, c. 1515*

M T Cicero, *Orationes a Nicolao Angelio Bucinensi nuper maxima diligentia recognitae et excusae*, Florence: P Iunta, March 1515. 8vo.

163 × 105 × 57 mm.   (P 1012) Davis 728

Brown goatskin over thin wooden boards, tooled in blind to a panel design, with lines, a border filled with curving tools; the panel is divided into two halves, separated by a border filled with curving leaf tools; both halves have corner fleurons and stylized flower tools; in the lower half: a Fortuna tool and a boat; in the upper half: a cupid tool and a burning vase tool. Remnants of two pairs of clasps, hinging on upper cover. Edges: plain; on top edge in manuscript: 'ORATia Cic. ANG.'

Rebacked with the original spine strip retained. Sewn on three (invisible) supports, laced in straight (traces of pegs), showing as raised bands on the spine, tooled in blind with a line; four compartments, tooled in blind with lines. Endbands: missing.

Endleaves: (new) white paper pastedowns and one free paper leaf, at both ends.

Repairs: rebacked, new head and tail caps; repairs at corners.

PROVENANCE: Bought: Leo Olschki, 25.v.1951.
Same tools on: BL, C.68.a.18 (Venice, 1502); Cambridge University Library, SSS 33.16 (Venice, 1513); De Marinis, 608, 2175A, 2262.
Compare: Glasgow University Library, BD2–c.22 (Florence, 1522); John Rylands University Library, Manchester, R4427 (Venice, 1524); BL, G.10968 (Venice, 1532), C.47.e.16 (Venice, 1550); De Marinis, 604, 1249, 1269, 1715, 2252, 2617, 2621; Hobson, *Legature bolognesi*, nos. 19, 23, 50.

258

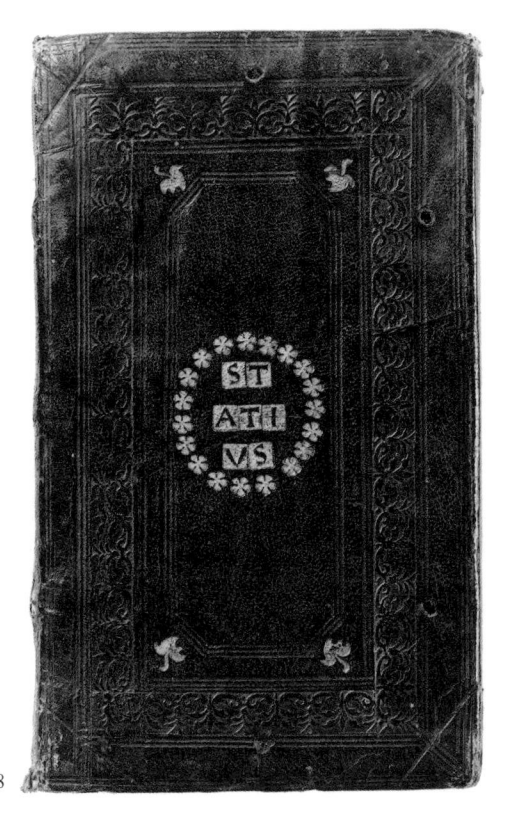

258 *A binding made in Venice, c. 1515*

P P Statius, *Orthographia et flexus dictionum graecarum omnium* [and] Statius, *Sylvarum libri quinque; Thebaidos libri duodecim*, Venice: Aldus, November 1502 [and] Statius, *Achilleidos libri duo*, Venice: Aldus, August 1502. 8vo.

171 × 103 × 40 mm.   (P 1380) Davis 729

Black goatskin over paste boards, tooled in blind and gold to a panel design with lines, a border filled with leafy plant tools, ivy leaves in the corners and in the centre: a circle of small flowers, containing the name of the author (ST/ATI/VS); the lettering tools have been cut in intaglio, with the letters standing out in blind on a gold square. Traces of four pairs of ties. Edges: gilt and gauffered to a ropework and diaper pattern.

Sewn on three split alum-tawed supports, laced in straight, showing as raised bands on the spine, tooled in blind with a line; four compartments, tooled in blind with lines. Endbands: single with a bead; beige and blue silk over alum-tawed cores (three ends cut off, one end still laced in), tied down.

Endleaves: white paper pastedowns at both ends; at the front: one free leaf conjugate with the pastedown; at the end: one free white paper leaf tipped onto and beneath the pastedown and a stub, conjugate with the pastedown, pasted onto verso of endleaf.

Repairs: small repairs at covers.

PROVENANCE: C S Ascherson (inscription on endleaf with: 'L1–1–1917'); J R Abbey (book plate; in manuscript: 'J.A.2708/ 2:1:1946'; sold: Sotheby's, 23.vi.1965, *631*).
Compare: (for intaglio-cut lettering tools used with gold leaf): De Marinis, 1610, 1753.

319

259 *A binding made c. 1516*

Gregory I (Saint, Pope), *Dialogus ... in quattuor libros divisus*, [Paris]: Jean Petit, n.d. [after 1500] [and] Gregory I, *Liber cure pastoralis*, Paris: Jean Petit, 19 March 1516. 8vo.

140 × 100 × 20 mm. (P 1222) Davis 732

Brown goatskin over paste boards, tooled in blind to a panel design with lines, a broad border filled with knot tools and dots, small tulip-shaped tools in the corners and in the centre a shield with: P with (superscript:) Ω, surmounted by a star. Traces of two pairs of ties. Edges: plain.

Sewn on three (?)tanned leather supports, laced in straight, showing as bands on the spine; four compartments, tooled in blind with lines. Spine lined with (?)parchment. Endbands: single with a bead; pink silk over (?)alum-tawed cores (cut off), tied down occasionally.

Endleaves: white paper pastedowns and one free white paper leaf tipped onto section, at both ends.
Repairs: at top and tail of spine, about half the spine leather has been renewed; repairs at corners.

PROVENANCE: On first title-page in manuscript: 'Anno Dni MD' (in a 19th-century hand?); bought: Sotheby's, 6.vii.1955, 74.

260 *A binding made c. 1517*

L A Seneca, *Tragoediae*, Venice: Aldus and A Socerus, October 1517. 8vo.

168 × 100 × 30 mm. (P 1383) Davis 733

Brown goatskin over paste boards, tooled in blind and gold (only traces of gold tooling remain), to a panel design with lines, fleur-de-lis-type fleurons at the corners, a border filled with interlinked-circles tools; a diamond and a saltire dividing the centre panel into lozenges and triangles; trefoils in the lozenges. Remnants of four pairs of leather ties. Edges: plain.

Sewn on three (possibly split alum-tawed) supports, showing as bands on the spine, tooled in blind with a line; four compartments, tooled in blind. Endbands: single with a bead; dark and pink (or beige) silk over leather cores (cut off), tied down sporadically.

Endleaves: (new) white paper pastedowns and one free white paper leaf tipped onto a parchment stub (beneath pastedown), at both ends.

Repairs: at joints and at top and tail of spine; top compartments mostly renewed.

PROVENANCE: Maggs (Catalogue 866, December 1959, no. 5; sold: 3.ii.1960).

261 *A Venetian binding by the 'Mendoza binder', c. 1518*

Aulus Gellius, *Noctium Atticarum libri undeviginti*, Venice: Aldus & A Socerus, September 1515. 8vo.

170 × 95 × 45 mm. (P 1203) Davis 730

Black goatskin over paste boards, tooled in gold, with blind lines, to a panel design with stylized flower tools at the corners, ivy-leaf tools in the corners and on the upper cover: A. GELLIVS./ ALEX.RHA. (with Ωs above the LE and H). Edges: stained black.

259

260

261

321

Sewn on three alum-tawed supports, laced in straight, showing as raised bands on the spine, tooled in gold with dashes; two kettle stitch bands and two false bands alternating with the sewing supports, tooled in gold with dashes; eight compartments, tooled in blind with small rope tools and stylized flowers. Endbands: double with a bead; black-stained thread over alum-tawed cores (still partly laced in), sporadically tied down; crowning cores (laced in).

Endleaves: white paper pastedowns at both ends; at the front: one free white paper leaf conjugate with the pastedown; at the end: one free white paper leaf conjugate with a stub before VI (last section); manuscript strengthener visible beneath pastedown.

PROVENANCE: On pastedown of lower cover in manuscript: 'S 19. 108'; Vernon collection; Holford collection (sold: Sotheby's, 6.xii.1927, *321*); bought: Sotheby's, 13.vi.1955, *2*.
REFERENCES: Hobson, *Renaissance*, p. 246, no. 70.
LITERATURE: Hobson, *Renaissance*, pp. 93–119, Appendix 5; Hobson, 'Was there an Aldine bindery?'; see also Davis 745, 763 (nos. 262, 263 below).
Same tools on: Davis 745 (no. 262 below); Christie's, 9.xii.1981, *173* (Venice, 1515).
Compare: John Rylands University Library, Manchester, 1989 (Venice, 1521).
Note: The 'Mendoza binder' worked in Venice from c. 1518 to c. 1555; the majority of the simple retail bindings from this shop cover Aldine imprints and date from c. 1518/19–1534.

262 *A Venetian binding by the 'Mendoza binder', c. 1523*

M T Cicero, *Secundo volumine haec continentur … De natura deorum libri III. De divinatione libri II. De fato liber I* [and other works], Venice: Aldus & A Socerus, August, 1523. 8vo.

171 × 103 × 26 mm. (P 1213) Davis 745

Brown goatskin over paste boards, tooled in gold, with blind lines, to a panel design with stylized flowers in gold and small leaf tools (in blind) at the corners, ivy-leaf tools in the corners, a knot tool in the centre; on the upper cover: M.T.C. PHI.VOL.II. Traces of four pairs of ties. Edges: gilt and gauffered to a knot-work pattern.

Sewn on three split alum-tawed supports, laced in, showing as raised bands on the spine, tooled in blind with a line; two kettle stitch bands and two false bands alternating with the sewing supports, tooled in gold with dashes; eight compartments, tooled in blind with crescent tools and small stylized flower tools. Endbands: double with a bead; primary sewing over alum-tawed cores (laced in), tied down; secondary sewing in pink and blue silk.

Endleaves: white paper pastedowns and one free leaf conjugate with the pastedown, at both ends (new endleaves at the front; original endleaves at the end).

PROVENANCE: On title-page: ownership inscriptions in manuscript: erased; partly readable: 'B' 'AB' 'S[?f]olde (?) i(?)ta id mio stato soccorno'; bought: Sotheby's, 6.vii.1955, *8*.
REFERENCES: Hobson, *Renaissance*, p. 246, no. 86.
LITERATURE: Davis 730 (no. 261 above; and literature cited there); Davis 763 (no. 263 below).
Same knot-tool on: Davis 778 (no. 272 below); BL, C.108.a.11 (Venice, 1506); De Marinis, 1151, 1213, 1623, 2685, 3101bis; Schunke, 'Venezianische Renaissance-Einbände', pl. 23; Nuvoloni, 'Commissioni Dogali', p. 98, no. 63.

262   263

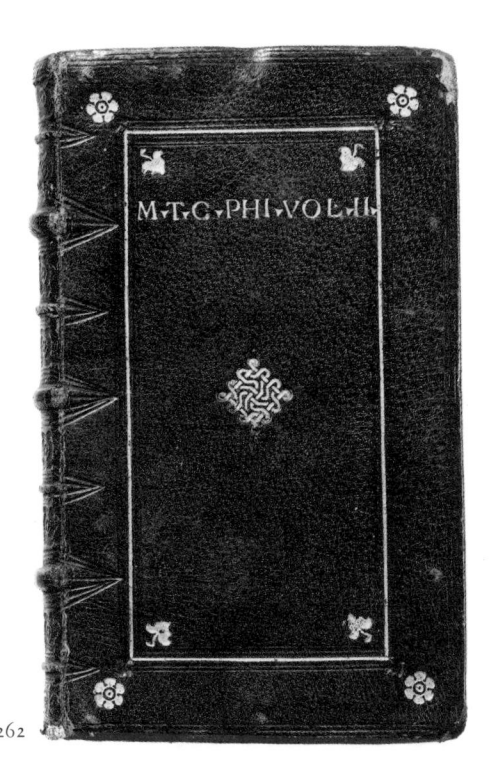

Compare: John Rylands University Library, Manchester, 1989 (Venice, 1521); Christie's, 9.xii.1981, *173*; M Breslauer, Catalogue 107 [1983], no. 260.

---

263 *A Venetian binding by the 'Mendoza binder', c. 1540*

M T Cicero, *Epistolae ad Atticum, ad Brutum, ad quintum fratrem* [and] Paulus Manutius, *In epistolas ad Atticum, ad Brutum, ad quintum fratrem scholia*, Venice: P Manutius, Aldi F., August 1540. 8vo.

215 × 128 × 58 mm.   (P 1378) Davis 763

Red goatskin over paste boards, tooled in gold, with blind lines, to a design of interlacing lines and gouges forming a border with small leaf tools and dots; in the centre: an undulating lozenge containing on the upper cover the painted arms of Cardinal Benedetto Accolti and on the lower cover: the anchor and dolphin device of Aldus's printing house and bookshop. Traces of four pairs of ties. Edges of boards: tooled in gold with a line and dashes. Edges: gilt.

Sewn on three tanned leather supports, laced in, showing as raised bands on the spine, tooled in gold with a line; four false bands alternating with the sewing supports, tooled in gold with dashes; eight compartments, tooled in blind with lines, small interlacing-circles tools and small leaf tools; second compartment: lettered in gold: CICERONIS/ EPIST. AD ATTICUM; third compartment: CH.MAX.; seventh compartment: VENET/ ALDUS 1540 (lettering added later). Endbands: single with a bead; primary sewing over alum-tawed cores (once laced in, now cut off), tied down; secondary sewing of pink silk.

Endleaves: at the front: new pastedowns and one new free leaf conjugate with the pastedown; at the end: white paper pastedowns and one free white paper leaf (?tipped on).

Repairs: at spine and covers.

PROVENANCE: Cardinal Benedetto Accolti; Spencer Compton Cavendish, 8th duke of Devonshire (book plate); bought: Christie's, 30.vi.1958, *26*.
REFERENCES: Brooker, *Book Collector*, 1997, p. 52, fig. 4, p. 65, list: 2.1; Hobson, *Renaissance*, pp. 116, 249, no. 232.
LITERATURE: Davis 730 (no. 261 above; and literature cited there), Davis 745 (no. 262 above); Quilici, no. 270, fig. 113; Brooker, *Book Collector*, 1997; Hobson, *Renaissance*, Appendix 5 (f).
Note: Benedetto Accolti (1497–1549), cardinal of Ravenna: 1527.

264 *A binding probably made in Rome, c. 1520*

C Valerius Flaccus, *C. Valerii Flacci commentarii Pio Bononiensi auctore*, Bologna: Hieronymus Platonicus, May 1519 [and] *Orphei Argonautica Latina*, n.p., n.d. fol.

315 × 210 × 40 mm. (P 1286) Davis 789

Red-brown goatskin over wooden boards, tooled in blind to a panel design with lines, a wide outer border filled with large ornamental tools, an inner border filled with curving leaf tools, two rows of fleurons above and below the centre panel, fleurons and flame or ray tools in the corners, stylized flower tools, and in the centre four impressions of crossed palm and laurel branches. Traces of four pairs of clasps and of four bosses on each cover. Edges: stained a dark green-blue; on the fore-edge: title and date in manuscript; on the top and tail edges: ACAD. LVGD. (a later inscription). Sewn on three split alum-tawed supports, laced in through holes in the edge of the boards and lying in tunnels on the outside of the boards; the supports show as raised bands on the spine, tooled in blind with a line; four compartments, tooled in blind with large ornamental tools and fleurons. Endbands: headband: double with a bead; tailband: single with a bead; pink and blue silk over leather cores (originally laced in, now cut off and repaired), tied down.

Endleaves: white paper pastedowns at both ends; at the front: remnant of a (torn-off) free leaf conjugate with the pastedown.

Repairs: at head and tail of spine, and at covers.

PROVENANCE: On title-page in manuscript: 'Sigre Felippo Bucci'; a stamp with: ACAD. LVGD., overstamped with: 'Ex auct. Curatt. vendidi W.N. du Rieu(?)'; Charles B Lumsden (book plate); Laurence W Hodson of Compton Hall, near Wolverhampton (book plate); bought: Sotheby's, 20.vi.1960, *232* (pl.).
LITERATURE: Hobson, *Humanists*, p. 90, compare fig. 76 (= *Legature papali*, no. 46).
Same tools on: Sotheby's, 21.vi.1967, *2083* (said to be Milanese); De Marinis, 559, 2032.
Compare: BL, C. 47.i.16 (Rome, 1515), C. 36.b.13 (Venice, 1551); Keble College, Oxford, A.62 (Venice, 1502); De Marinis, 449, 1542, 1790, 2621, 2640, 2663, 2721; G D Hobson, 'Dr Theodor Gottlieb', pl. 5A, 6; Hobson, *Renaissance*, pls 19, 21, 22 (but these Milanese versions of the ornamental border tool are quite different from the version on Davis 789); Quilici, no. 149, fig. 59 (Rome; tool: very close to Davis 789).

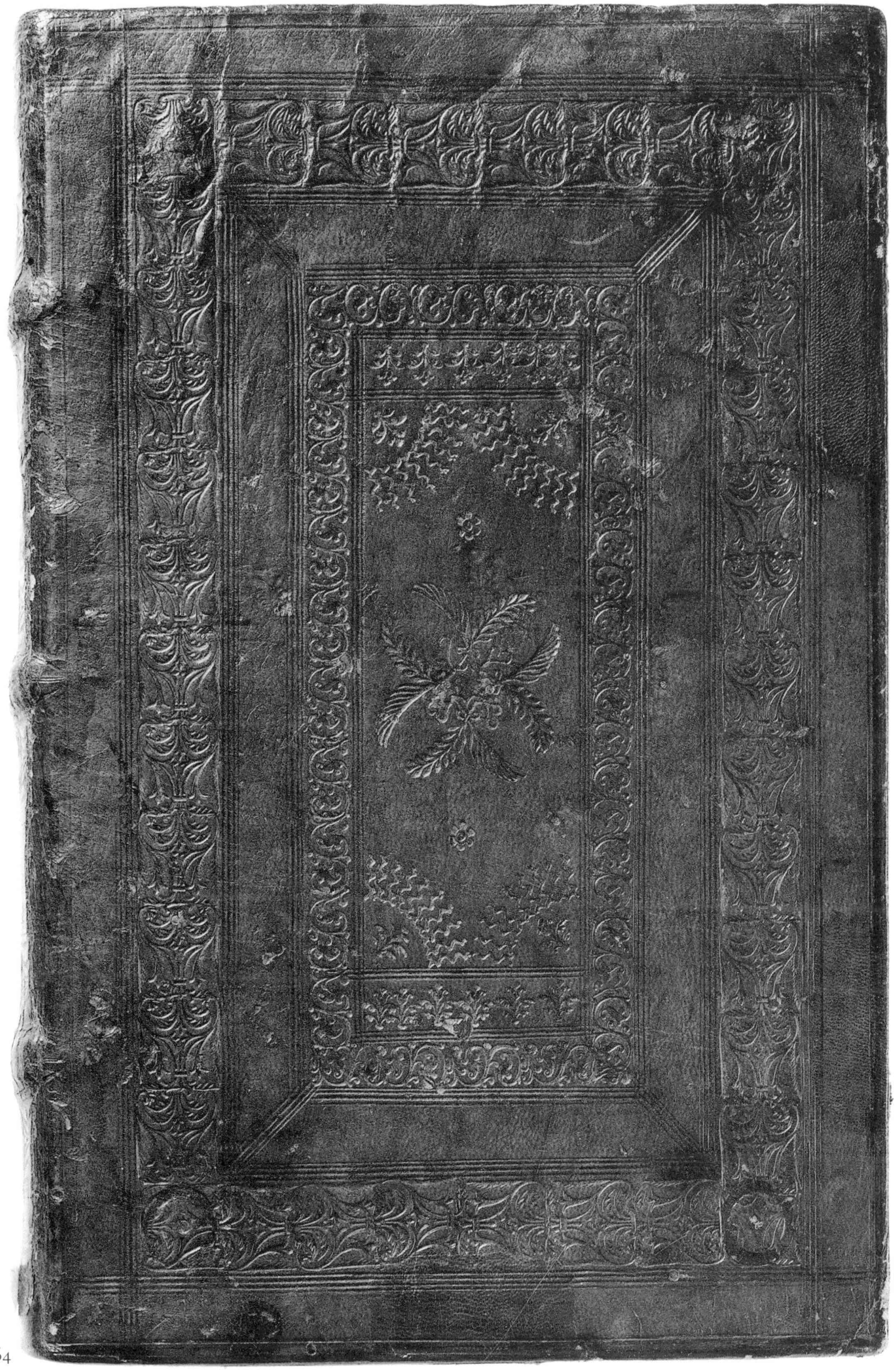

265 *A binding made c. 1520*

M T Cicero, *Officiorum libri iii* [and other works], Venice: Aldus & A Socerus, February 1519. 8vo.

164 × 100 × 27 mm. (P 1381) Davis 734

Black goatskin over paste boards, tooled in blind to a panel design, with lines, stylized leaf tools in the corners and in the centre an ornament built up of four of the stylized leaf tools. Edges: plain; on tail edge in manuscript: 'M.T.C. de officijs'.

Sewn on three alum-tawed supports, laced in, showing as raised bands on the spine; four compartments. Endbands: single; primary sewing over leather cores (now cut off, lacing-in holes visible), tied down.

Endleaves: white paper pastedowns at both ends; at the front: one free leaf conjugate with the pastedown and a pair of free conjugate white paper leaves; at the end: a pair of free conjugate white paper leaves and one free leaf possibly conjugate with the pastedown.

PROVENANCE: On title-page in manuscript [erased]: 'Societatis Jesu Tridenti 1632'; 'Carolus Sarov(?)[...]gc[?e] (?)ia'; bought: Quaritch, 4.vii.1958.

266 *A binding made c. 1520*

C Suetonius Tranquillus, *XII Caesares* [and other works by Sextus Aurelius, Eutropius, Paulus Diaconus], Venice: Aldus & A Socerus, August 1516. 8vo.

157 × 94 × 37 mm. (P 939) Davis 735

Brown hair sheep over paste boards, tooled in blind with lines forming a panel design, corner fleurons and a centre ornament made up of four fleurons. Traces of four pairs of ties. Edges: gilt and gauffered to a knot-work pattern; on the fore-edge gauffered: SVETONIVS.

Sewn on three split alum-tawed supports, laced in straight, showing as raised bands on the spine, tooled in blind with lines; four compartments, tooled in blind with lines. Endbands: single with a bead; brown-stained thread over (?)leather cores (laced in), sporadically tied down.

Endleaves: white paper pastedowns and one free white paper leaf conjugate with a stub after first and before last sections, at both ends.

Repairs: small repairs at corners.

PROVENANCE: On title-page in manuscript: 'Justini Rubei'; in a different hand: 'iv. 380–'; Armand Tonnellier, medical doctor at Auxerre (book plate); bought: Arthur Rau, 1.vi.1949.

267 *A binding made c. 1520*

P P Statius, *Sylvarum libri, Achilleidos libri, Thebaidos libri* [and] *Orthographia et flexus dictionum graecarum*, Venice: Aldus & A Socerus, January 1519. 8vo.

166 × 104 × 35 mm. (P 1384) Davis 736

Black goatskin over paste boards, tooled in blind to a panel design with lines, fleurons at the outer corners and in the corners of the panel, small leaf tools at the corners of the panel; in the centre: a circle

265

266

267

surrounded by rays around four fleurons. On the upper cover: STATII SYL. Vague traces of gold in the rays on the lower cover. Traces of four pairs of ties. Edges: stained black and lightly gauffered with a row of dots.

Sewn on three (?)split alum-tawed supports, laced in, showing as raised bands on the spine, tooled in blind with a line; two kettle stitch bands and two false bands alternating with the sewing supports, tooled in blind with dashes; eight compartments, tooled in blind with lines. Endbands: single with a bead; blue and beige silk over leather cores (cut off), tied down.

Endleaves: white paper pastedowns and one free leaf, conjugate with the pastedown, at both ends.

PROVENANCE: On pastedown of lower cover in manuscript (20th-century hand): '26155'; bought: Quaritch, 14.v.1960.

268 A binding made c. 1520

M V Martialis, *Epigrammata*, Venice: Aldus & A Socerus, December 1517 [and] D J Juvenalis, *Satyrae*, Florence: Haeredes P Iuntae, May 1519. 8vo.

164 × 96 × 33 mm. (P 942) Davis 738

Olive-brown goatskin over paste boards, tooled in gold, with blind lines, to a panel design, the lines outlining the panel forming square knots at the corners, a border filled with curving flower branches; the panel is divided by interlacing lines into two halves; each half has fleurons in the corners and a lozenge with a centre ornament composed of four fleurons. The strip between the two halves is lettered on the upper cover: MARTIALIS; on the lower cover: MAR. ANT. B. Traces of four pairs of ties. Edges: gilt.

Sewn on three alum-tawed supports, laced in, showing as bands on the spine, tooled in blind with a line; four compartments, tooled in blind with lines. Endbands: single with a bead; primary sewing over alum-tawed cores (laced in), tied down; remnants of secondary sewing of pink and blue silk.

Endleaves: white paper pastedowns at both ends; at the front: one free white paper leaf tipped onto the pastedown; a remnant of a stub (conjugate with the pastedown?) after first section; at the end: one free white paper leaf conjugate with a stub before the last section.

Repairs: at head and tail of spine and at corners.

PROVENANCE: (?)Marcus Antonius B; on title-page in manuscript [erased]: 'Ju…Ph.pp…J[?T]el(?)'; Davis and Orioli (Catalogue 132, 1948, no. 85; sold: 17.x.1949, *942*).
Compare: Davis 740 (no. 282 below: for design and corners); De Marinis, 606.

269 A binding possibly made in Bologna, c. 1520

Theocritus, *Opera et commentaria* [Greek], Rome: Zacharias Kallierges, 1516. 8vo.

169 × 112 × 38 mm. (P 1276) Davis 742

Brown goatskin (or possibly hair sheep) over paste boards, tooled in blind with lines forming two rectangles and a lozenge, stylized flowers at the corners and in the centre an ornament built up of cornucopia-and-flower tools. Traces of two pairs of ties. Edges: sprinkled in blue and red.

268　　　　　　　　　　　　　　　　269

Sewn on three split alum-tawed supports, laced in straight, showing as raised bands on the spine; four compartments, tooled in blind with lines. Endbands: single with a bead; primary sewing over alum-tawed cores (laced in), tied down; secondary sewing of pink silk.

Endleaves: white paper pastedowns and three pairs of free conjugate white paper leaves and one leaf conjugate with the pastedown, at both ends.

PROVENANCE: On title-page in manuscript [erased]: 'J. Jo(?)rdani Ga[?r]gani Salutij' (?); on pastedown in manuscript: '3 feb. finis theoc.'; bought: Rauch, 29.iii.1954, *222*.
LITERATURE: Hobson, *Legature bolognesi*, p. 13.
Same tool on: De Marinis, 1244.
Compare: De Marinis, 1287, 1289, 1301; Quilici, no. 287, fig. 122; Hobson, *Legature bolognesi*, pp. 56–7, nos. 4, 5.

270　*A binding possibly made in Venice or Bologna, c. 1520–30*

M T Cicero, *Orationum volumen primum*, Venice: Aldus & A Socerus, January 1519. 8vo.

163 × 102 × 38 mm.　　　　　　　　　　　　　　　　　　　　　　　　(P 1191) Davis 741

Dark brown goatskin over paste boards, tooled in blind to an arabesque design, with lines, corner fleurons and an arabesque centre piece built up of gouges and open tools; in the centre of the upper cover: two leaf tools and .M.T.C./.I.; in the centre of the lower cover: a bust-portrait of a poet crowned with laurel [Cicero?], facing right, tooled in gold. Edges: stained dark; on the tail edge in manuscript: ORATO.CICE; on the top edge in manuscript: 'Lau…'(?) (virtually invisible).

Sewn on three split alum-tawed supports, laced in straight, showing as raised bands on the spine, tooled in blind with a line; four compartments, tooled in blind with lines; spine compartments lined, with the ends pasted down on the inside of the boards. Endbands: single; primary sewing over alum-tawed core (laced in), tied down; remnant of secondary sewing; tailband missing.

Endleaves: none at the front; at the end: two free conjugate white paper leaves.

PROVENANCE: On endleaf in manuscript: 'PM'; Liechtenstein (on title-page: library stamp of 'F. Liechtenstein. Bibliothek'; book plate with 'Ex libris Liechtensteinianis'); on title-page in pencil: '81.6.6', in ink: '66' (?); on inside of upper board in pencil: '(?).L. IIxx2/u [v].13.27' [crossed out]; bought: Sotheby's, 6.iv.1955, *417*.
LITERATURE: Hobson, *Humanists*, pp. 123–5; Hobson, 'Bookbinding in Bologna', pp. 174–5, fig. 16.
Same tools on: De Marinis, 1349
Compare: Cambridge University Library, Rit.e.254.1 (Venice, 1541); De Marinis, 1352; De Marinis, *Fürstenberg*, pp. 106–7; Hobson, 'Bookbinding in Bologna', fig. 16; Hobson, *Legature bolognesi*, no. 47.

271

271 *A binding probably made in Venice, c. 1521*

L Apuleius, *Opera* [and] [Albinus, *Platonicus*], *Ad Platonis dogmata introductio* [Greek], Venice: Aldus & A Socerus, May 1521. 8vo.

170 × 97 × 38 mm. (P 970) Davis 743

Black goatskin over paste boards, tooled in gold with lines, hatched leaf tools, stylized flowers, gouges and dots in the border, fleurons at the corners of the central panel; fleurons in the corners and along the insides of the panel; stylized flowers and four arabesque tools down the centre. Edges: gilt.

Sewn on four cords, laced in; three false raised bands on the spine, tooled in gold with a line; four compartments, tooled in gold with lines, dashes and small flowers. Endbands: single with a bead; pink silk over (?)leather cores (cut off; possibly one end still laced in), tied down.

Endleaves: white paper pastedowns and one free leaf conjugate with the pastedown, at both ends.

PROVENANCE: Bought: Davis and Orioli, 25.x.1950.
Same tools on: De Marinis, 1930, 1931.
Compare: Pembroke College, Cambridge, 3.29.76 (n.p., n.d.); Cambridge University Library, Rel.d.51.6 (Venice, [1502]); John Rylands University Library, Manchester, 5421 (Venice, 1503); G D Hobson, *Maioli*, pl. xv; De Marinis, 1247c, 1953.

331

272

272 *A binding made in Venice, c. 1521*

Dogale [Ducal commission], issued by Leonardo Lauredano, doge of Venice, appointing Antonio Pisauro as captain of Vicenza for one year, or till his successor shall arrive. MS on parchment, [Venice, before 1521]; painted title-page (Lion of St Mark, arms of Lauredano), painted initials in gold on blue or red; ruled in red.

230 × 156 × 8 mm. (M 51) Davis 778

Red-brown goatskin over paste boards, tooled in gold, with blind lines, to a panel design; fleur-de-lis tools at the corners, a border filled with 'dolphin' tools; stylized flowers in the corners of the panel; knot tools in the centre. Traces of four pairs of red ties. Edges: plain.

Sewn (in two sections, each of ten leaves) on two broad parchment supports (probably pasted down beneath the pastedowns); smooth spine. No endbands.

Endleaves: at the front: white paper pastedown and one free leaf conjugate with the pastedown; at the end: parchment pastedown and one free parchment leaf conjugate with the pastedown.

PROVENANCE: Leonardo Lauredano; Antonio Pisauro; bought: Sotheby's, 28.ii.1966, *145*.
LITERATURE: Davis, 745 (no. 262 above; by the 'Mendoza binder'; and literature cited there).

332

273

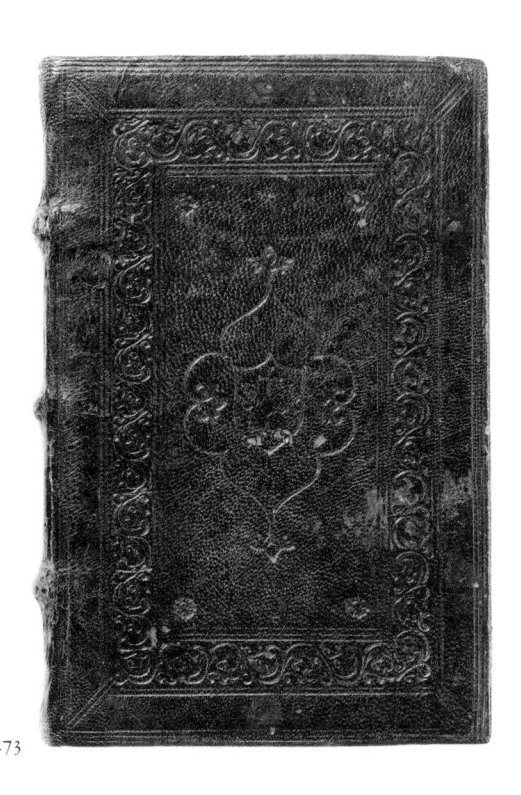

Same tools on:	BL, C.108.a.11 (Venice, 1506); King's College, Cambridge, M28.REF46 (Florence, 1514); De Marinis, 1151, 1213, 1623, 2685, 3101bis; Schunke, 'Venezianische Renaissance-Einbände', pl. 23; *Legature papali*, no. 43; Nuvoloni, 'Commissioni Dogali', p. 98, no. 63.
Note:	Leonardo Lauredano (1438–1521), doge of Venice: 1501.

273 *A binding made c. 1523*

Enchiridion: C Crispus Sallustius, *De coniuratione Catilinae; De bello Iugurtino; Oratio contra M T Ciceronem* [and other works by Sallustius, Cicero and Marcus Porcius Latro], Venice: M Sessa & P de Ravanis, 3 March 1523. 8vo.

153 × 102 × 21 mm. (P 1237) Davis 744

Dark brown goatskin over paste boards, tooled in blind to a panel design with lines, a border filled with curling tools, stylized flowers in the corners; in the centre: gouges and fleurons forming an arabesque centre piece with, on the upper cover: a coat of arms showing three hills surmounted by a cross and two palm branches; on the lower cover: St Michael killing the dragon. Traces of four pairs of ties. Edges: stained blue.

Sewn on three (?)leather supports, (?)laced in, showing as raised bands on the spine, tooled in blind with a line; four compartments, tooled in blind (remnants of original spine strip only retained). Endbands: single; primary sewing over (?)alum-tawed cores (cut off), tied down; (?)woven secondary endbands in blue and white silk.

Endleaves: white paper pastedowns and one free white paper leaf, at both ends.

Repairs: spine heavily repaired; repairs at covers.

PROVENANCE: Count A Oberndorff (sold: Sotheby's, 6.vii.1955, *160*).
Same tools on: John Rylands University Library, Manchester, 4427 (Venice, 1524); Martin Breslauer, Catalogue 38 (1966), no. 9 (Lyon, 1529).
Compare: Cambridge University Library, SSS 33.16 (Venice, 1513); BL, C.55.f.2 (Rome, 1532); De Marinis, 1271, 2252.

274 *A binding possibly made in Verona or in the Veneto, c. 1524–34*

Baldus de Ubaldis, *Lectura super quarto et quinto codicis* [of Justinian], Venice: Philippo Pincio, March 1519. fol.

445 × 285 × 54 mm. (P 1493) Davis 790

Quarter brown goatskin over wooden boards, tooled in blind with a foliage roll and lines forming four compartments, each with a stylized flower in the corners and an arabesque tool in the centre; the upper board is painted in black with: 'Bal. s[uper] 4° / et 5° C' and a large arabesque ornament containing the arms of the Pillone family. Boards bevelled. Four pairs of clasps (metal on leather straps), hinging on upper cover. Edges: plain.

Sewn on four wide alum-tawed supports, laced into holes in the edge of the wooden boards, showing as bands on the spine; five compartments, tooled in blind with lines. Spine compartments lined with strips of parchment, stuck down onto endleaves. Endbands: single; primary sewing over tanned leather cores (were laced in), tied down.

Endleaves: one free leaf consisting of part of a printed page (Latin), at both ends.

PROVENANCE: Pillone library; B Breslauer (Catalogue 101, *233*, pl.; sold: January 1970).
LITERATURE: W Stirling-Maxwell, 'Venetian Library', in: *A Catalogue of the manuscripts and printed books collected by Thomas Brooke, F.S.A. and preserved at Armitage Bridge House, near Huddersfield*, 2 vols, London, 1891, vol. II, pp. 662–81; P Berès, *Bibliothèque Pillone*, Paris, 1957; E Kyriss, 'Bibliothèque Pillone', *Börsenblatt für den deutschen Buchhandel*, 14, no. 32 (22.iv.1958); A R A Hobson, 'The Pillone Library', *The Book Collector*, vol. 7, no. 1 (1958), pp. 28–37; Sotheby's, 21.vi.1967, pp. 182–3, compare *2088*; Pierre Berès, Catalogue 67 (March 1975): 'un groupe de livres Pillone', compare no. 28; Christie's, 3.vi.1998, *54–71*.
Same(?) tool on: BL C.107.bb.12 (1520); Brera, no. 23.
Note: Antonio Pillone, book collector (d. 1533); his son, Odorico Pillone (1503–1594), built the Villa Casteldardo, near Belluno, where the library was kept until it was sold in 1847. The library contained several legal texts bound in quarter goatskin over wood, as well as books with fore-edges painted by Cesare Vecellio or bound in parchment with pen-and-ink drawings on the covers, also by Vecellio, incunabula in contemporary blind-tooled bindings, and a number of German bindings in blind-tooled calf or pigskin.

Sal. s. 4.
et S.

275   *A binding probably made in Florence, c. 1525*

M T Cicero, *Rhetorica ad Herennium*, Venice: Aldus & A Socerus, October 1521. 4to.

222 × 142 × 38 mm. (P 975) Davis 777

Brown goatskin over paste boards, tooled in gold, with blind lines, to a panel design with a wide border filled with tools showing foliage wound around a trunk; a slightly sunk centre medallion inlaid, painted in red, white and black, showing a shield with a Moor's head in profile: the arms of the Pucci family of Florence. Traces of four pairs of ties. Edges: gilt; on the tail edge in manuscript: 'Cicer. Oper. var.'

Rebacked; sewn on three supports, laced in. Endbands: none: new leather headcaps turned over.

Endleaves: (new) white paper pastedowns and a pair of free conjugate white paper leaves, and one free leaf conjugate with the pastedowns, at both ends; one original white paper endleaf at the front (tipped onto new endleaf).

Repairs: rebacked; small repairs at covers.

PROVENANCE: Pucci family of Florence; on original endleaf in manuscript: 'donum ita questa et anima (?)'; second note: 'is o li auagelligr(?)ets[i?]'; Stainton collection (sold: Sotheby's, 26.ii.1951, *66*, pl.).
REFERENCES: De Marinis, 1686.
LITERATURE: Brunet, pl. 82; *BFAC*, 1891, pl. xlvii; Weale, no. 233; Goldschmidt, p. 73; Miner, *Baltimore*, no. 217.
Same arms and border tools on: Cambridge University Library, SSS 39.11 (Venice, 1522).
Compare: Davis 737, 816 (nos. 284, 338 below) for different versions of the border tool.

276

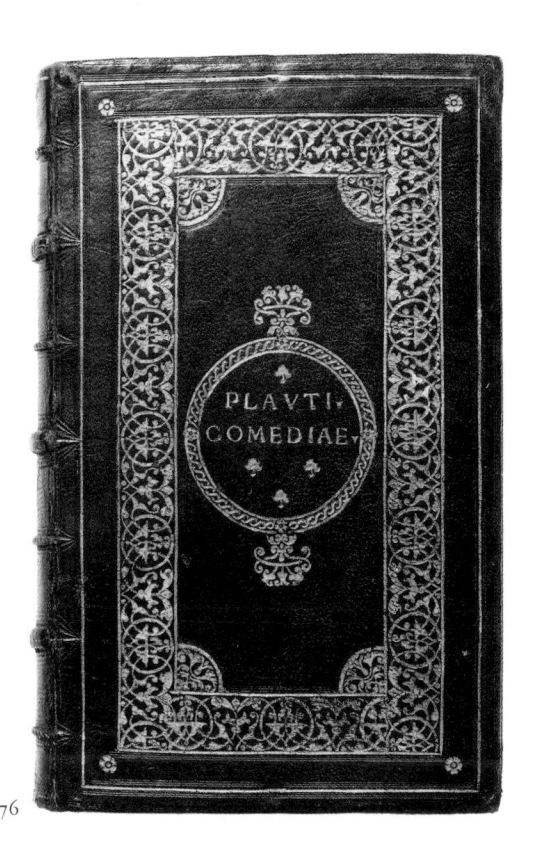

276 *A binding made in Venice, c. 1525*

Plautus, *Ex Plauti comoediis xx quarum carmina magna…restituta sunt*, Venice: Aldus & A Socerus, July 1522. 4to.

223 × 138 × 40 mm.   (P 1145) Davis 779

Brown goatskin over paste boards, tooled in gold, with blind lines, to a panel design; small flowers at the corners, a wide border filled with interlinking-circles tools, fleurons in the corners of the panel and in the centre two fleuron tools above and below a circle with rope-work tooling around, on the upper cover: four ivy-leaf tools and PLAVTI./ COMEDIAE., and on the lower cover: a fleur-de-lis, a flower and an ivy-leaf tool and 'I(superscript:)ΩA. / O(superscript:)ΩB.'. Traces of four pairs of ties (restored away and over-tooled). Edges: gilt and lightly gauffered with a row of dots.

Sewn on three supports, laced in, showing as raised bands on the spine, tooled in gold with a line; two kettle stitch bands and two false bands alternating with the sewing supports, tooled in gold with dashes; eight compartments, tooled in blind with lines; on the second compartment: a red goatskin label, lettered in gold: PLAVTI / COMMEDIAE . XX / Venet. MDXXII. Endbands: stuck-on endbands (not worked, not laced in).

Endleaves: white paper pastedowns and one free leaf conjugate with the pastedown, at both ends.

PROVENANCE: Henry Labouchere (book plate); C S Ascherson (book plate); bought: Nicolas Rauch, 29.iii.1954, *94* (pl.).
Same tools on: BL, C.72.a.14 (Venice, 1521); John Rylands University Library, Manchester, 1989 (Venice, 1521); De Marinis, 1713, 1794, 2020, 2035, 2039, 2095, 2134, 2293.

337

Compare:	Glasgow University Library, Hunt. Bg.3.1 (1493); Cambridge University Library, Rel.c.54.3 (Venice, 1542); Nixon, *Pierpont Morgan Library*, no. 16; De Marinis, 2302, 3102; Christie's, 7.vii.1964, *93*; M Breslauer, Catalogue 107, no. 233A.

277 *A binding made c. 1525*

St Bernardus, *Psalterium Beatae Mariae Virginis ... et Psalterium Beati Hieronymi presbyteri*, Florence: Bartholomeus de Gianettis Brixianus, 1 April 1524; black letter; woodcuts; woodcut initials. 16o.

105 × 72 × 23 mm. (P 477) Davis 746

Brown goatskin over (very thin) wooden boards, tooled in blind to a panel design with lines, stylized flower tools and in the centre a circle with the sacred monogram (upside down on the lower cover). Remnants of two pairs of clasps, hinging on the upper cover.

Sewn on two split alum-tawed supports, taken onto the outside of the boards, showing as bands on the spine; trace of two kettle stitch bands; three compartments, tooled in blind with lines. Endbands: missing (see repairs).

Endleaves: one free white paper leaf tipped onto first and last section, at both ends.

Repairs: at top and tail of spine (new leather in top and tail compartments).

PROVENANCE:	On verso of last leaf (q 8 verso): very faint (unreadable) manuscript note, dated 1700; bought: Sotheby's, 19.viii. 1942, *315*.
Compare:	BL, C.104.dd.16 (Florence, 1524); M Breslauer, Catalogue 107, no. 28.

278 *A binding, possibly made in Venice, c. 1525*

Plautus, *Ex Plauti comoediis xx quarum carmina magna ... restituta sunt*, Venice: Aldus & A Socerus, July 1522. 4to.

208 × 140 × 38 mm. (P 964) Davis 781

Red-brown goatskin over paste boards, tooled in gold to a panel design with lines, a wide border filled with interlinked-circles tools, arabesque corner pieces and an arabesque centre piece, built up of four corner pieces, gouges and small ivy-leaf tools. Traces of two pairs of ties. Edges: sprinkled in black, blue-grey and red.

Sewn on three split alum-tawed supports, laced in, showing as raised bands on the spine, tooled in blind with a line; four compartments, tooled in blind with lines. Endbands: single with a bead; primary sewing over leather cores (once laced in), tied down; remnant of secondary sewing in (?)blue silk.

Endleaves: white paper pastedowns, at both ends; at the front: one free white paper leaf tipped onto first section; at the end: a stub conjugate with the pastedown and one free white paper leaf tipped onto stub. Manuscript strengthener visible beneath pastedowns.

Repairs: at joints and corners.

PROVENANCE:	On title-page: ownership inscription excised; bought: Davis and Orioli, 11.vii.1950.
Compare:	Edinburgh University Library, Wx 28.35 (Venice, 1514); Hobson, 'Bookbinding in Bologna', fig. 7.

277

278

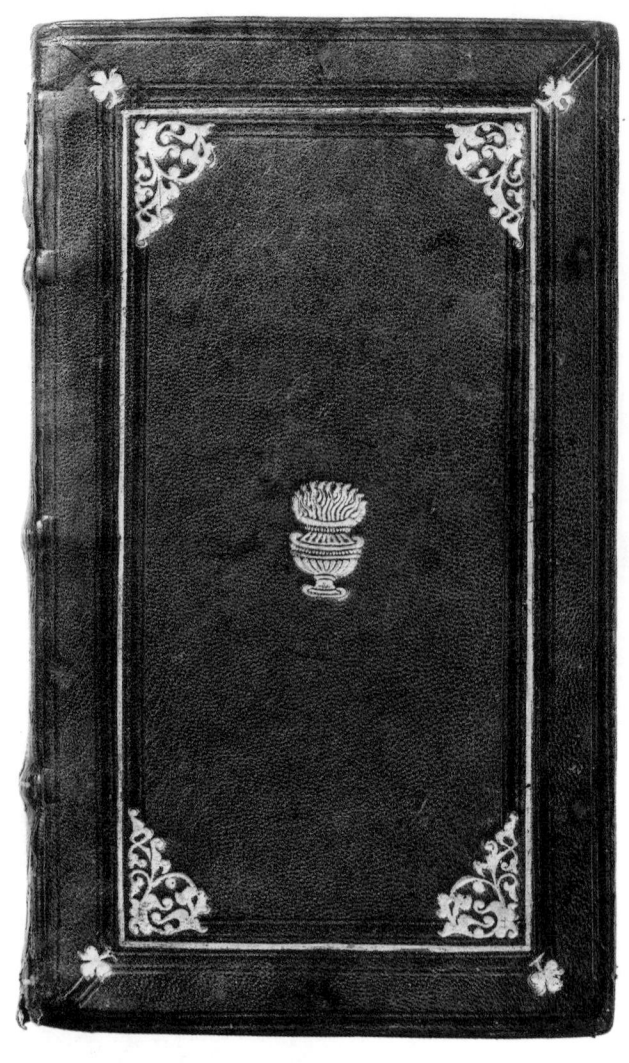

279 *A binding possibly made in Venice, c. 1525*

L A Seneca, *Naturalium quaestionum libri vii*, Venice: Aldus & A Socerus, February 1522. 4to.

222 × 133 × 22 mm.   (P 946) Davis 780

Olive-brown goatskin over paste boards, tooled in gold, with blind lines, to a panel design, with leaf tools at the corners, large curls in the corners, and in the centre a burning vase tool. Traces of four pairs of ties. Edges: sprinkled in black, red and pale blue.

   Sewn on three split alum-tawed supports, laced in straight, showing as raised bands on the spine, tooled in gold with a line; four compartments, tooled in blind. Endbands: single with a bead; primary sewing over alum-tawed cores (cut off), tied down; secondary sewing in pink and blue silk.

   Endleaves: white paper pastedowns and two free conjugate white paper leaves, at both ends; at the front: one free leaf tipped onto preceding leaf; at the end: one free leaf conjugate with the pastedown.

   Repairs: small repairs at the corners, head and tail of spine, and at lower cover.

280

PROVENANCE:	On endleaf in manuscript: 'Vente du comte de Lagondie / mars 1878' [possibly: Joseph-Guilhem, comte de Lagondie (1809–1879)]; bought: Davis and Orioli, 22.xii.1949.
Same tools on:	John Rylands University Library, Manchester, 7595 (Venice, 1514); Cambridge University Library, Rel.c.54.3 (Venice, 1542); Trinity College, Cambridge, Grylls. 6.221.
Compare:	BL, C.47.c.20 (Lyon, 1532); Fitzwilliam Museum, Cambridge (Petrarch, Venice, 1532); De Marinis, 2239, 2258; M Breslauer, Catalogue 110 [1990], no. 23.

---

280   *Bindings, possibly made in Venice, c. 1525*

T Livius, *Ex xiiii T Livii Decadibus. Prima, tertia, quarta*, Venice: Aldus & A Socerus, December 1518. 8vo.
164 × 100 × 45 mm.   (P 641) Davis 748

T Livius, *Decas quarta*, Venice: Aldus & A Socerus, November 1520. 8vo.
165 × 104 × 43 mm.   (P 641) Davis 747

T Livius, *Decadis quintae libri quinque*, Venice: Aldus & A Socerus, March 1521. 8vo.
162 × 100 × 53 mm.   (P 641) Davis 749

Three identical-looking bindings in brown goatskin over paste boards, tooled in gold, with blind lines, to a panel design with fleurons at the corners, a border filled with interlinked-circles tools, fleurons in the corners, small floral, leaf and heart-shaped tools, in the centre of which a circle with: THO / ROVL / ABB. Traces of two pairs of ties. Edges: gilt and gauffered to a strap-work pattern.

341

Sewing structure and endbands differ:

Davis 748: sewn on four alum-tawed supports, laced in (long slips ending in a point, visible beneath pastedowns), showing as raised bands on the spine, tooled in gold with a line; two kettle stitch bands and one false band (above fourth support), tooled in gold with dashes; seven compartments, tooled in blind with lines; gold-tooled lines and dashes below first and fourth support; gold-tooled lines near top and tail. Endbands: missing (top and tail of spine repaired).

Davis 747: sewn on three split alum-tawed supports, laced in straight, showing as raised bands on the spine, tooled in gold with lines and dashes; two kettle stitch bands and two false bands alternating with the sewing supports, tooled in gold with dashes; eight compartments, tooled in blind with lines; gold-tooled lines near top and tail. Endbands: single with a bead; primary sewing over leather cores (cut off), tied down; secondary sewing in pink and blue silk.

Davis 749: sewn on three (?)split alum-tawed supports, laced in straight, showing as raised bands on the spine, tooled in gold with lines and dashes; two kettle stitch bands and two false bands alternating with the sewing supports, tooled in gold with dashes; eight compartments, tooled in blind with lines; gold-tooled lines near top and tail. Endbands: single with (remnant of) a bead; primary sewing over leather cores (cut off), sporadically tied down; secondary sewing in blue silk.

Endleaves: Davis 748: white paper pastedowns and one free leaf conjugate with the pastedowns, at both ends. Davis 747 and 749: white paper pastedowns and one free paper leaf with a conjugate stub after first and before last section, at both ends.

Repairs: at spines, edges of boards and corners.

PROVENANCE: Abbot Thomas Roul.(?); on title-page (of all three volumes) in manuscript: 'Richardi Martialis / Auxilium meum à domino Psal. 120'; Colonel Moss (sold: Sotheby's, 5.iii.1937, *937*, pl.); Lord Keynes (sold: 1.vi.1943).

REFERENCES: Maggs, Catalogue 407 [1921], *403* (pl. cxv).

Note: The identification in the Moss sale catalogue of 'Tho Roul Abb' as Abbot Thomas Pentecost, *alias* Rowlands, last abbot of Abingdon, seems fanciful.

281 *A binding made c. 1525–30*

Asconius Pedianus, *Expositio in iiii Orationes M. Tullii Cic. Contra C Verrem*, Venice: Aldus & A Socerus, December 1522. 8vo.

169 × 102 × 33 mm. (P 1192) Davis 750

Brown goatskin (or possibly hair sheep) over paste boards, tooled in gold, with blind lines, to a panel design with lines, small leaf tools in the corners of the panel and in the centre of the upper cover: a circle with leaf tools, knot tools and dots around ASCONII; in the centre of the lower cover: four arabesque tools. Traces of four pairs of ties. Edges of boards: tooled in blind with a line and dashes. Edges: gilt and lightly gauffered with a row of dots; on the tail edge in manuscript: 'Asconij. ESP. CICERO'.

Sewn on three split alum-tawed supports, laced in, showing as raised bands on the spine, tooled in gold with a line; four false bands, alternating with the sewing supports, tooled in gold with dashes; eight compartments, tooled in blind with lines. Paper labels pasted over top three compartments and over

281 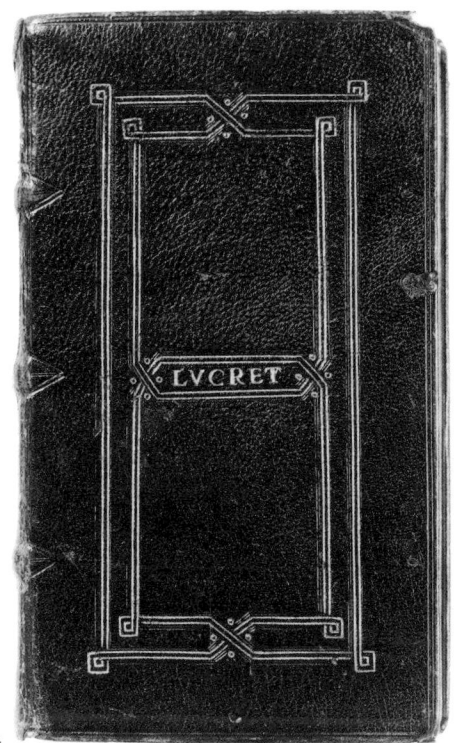 282

tail compartment, with in manuscript: ASCONII / VI. Endbands: double with a bead; primary sewing over (?)leather cores (cut off), tied down; secondary sewing in pink and blue silk.

Endleaves: white paper pastedowns and six free conjugate paper leaves, quired, at both ends; at the end: a seventh free leaf conjugate with the pastedown.

Repairs: at covers.

PROVENANCE: On title-page in manuscript: 'a.38'; 'Be. Car Ravennae'; on pastedowns and endleaves in pencil in manuscript: numbers and 'K. R.22'; Liechtenstein (book plate; on title-page: library stamp with: 'F. Liechtenstein Bibliothek'); bought: Sotheby's, 6.iv.1955, *418*.
Compare: BL, C.130.a.18 (Rome, 1526); De Marinis, 613, 2030, 2843bis.

282   *A binding possibly made in Bologna, c. 1525–30*

T Lucretius Carus, *De rerum natura*, Venice: Aldus & A Socerus, January 1515 [and] C Valerius Flaccus, *Argonautica*, Venice: Aldus & A Socerus, May 1523. 8vo.

171 × 104 × 32 mm. (P 965) Davis 740

Dark brown goatskin over paste boards, tooled in gold, with blind lines, to a panel design of lines, forming square knots at the corners, and roundels, with on the upper cover: LVCRET and on the lower cover: VALER.F. Traces of four pairs of ties. Edges: sprinkled in black-grey and red.

Sewn on three split alum-tawed supports, laced in straight, showing as raised bands on the spine, tooled in blind with a line; four compartments, tooled in blind with lines. Endbands: single with a bead;

primary sewing over alum-tawed cores (were laced in; broken off), tied down; secondary sewing in beige and blue silk.

Endleaves: white paper pastedowns, at both ends; at the front: two free conjugate white paper leaves and one free leaf conjugate with the pastedown; at the end: one free leaf conjugate with the pastedown, one free white paper leaf, tipped onto two free conjugate white paper leaves.

Repairs: at upper cover.

PROVENANCE: On title-page in manuscript: 'Alex. Gulielmj & Amicorum'; on endleaf: manuscript notes in French (modern hand) about the edition; bought: Davis and Orioli, 19.vii.1950.
LITERATURE: Miner, *Baltimore*, no. 221.
Compare: Davis 738 (no. 268 above, for design and corners); De Marinis, 1282, 1282bis; M Breslauer, Catalogue 107 [1983], no. 172.

283 *A binding probably made in Bologna, c. 1527*

J Sannazaro, *De partu Virginis. Lamentatio de morte Christi. Piscatoria* [and other works], Venice: Aldus & A Socerus, August 1527. 8vo.

157 × 100 × 15 mm.   (P 929) Davis 751

Brown goatskin over paste boards, tooled in blind with lines, a border filled with curling leaf tools, large corner curls, rosettes and a centre piece composed of two arabesque tools. Traces of two pairs of ties. Edges: stained blue.

Sewn on three alum-tawed supports, laced in, showing as raised bands on the spine; four compartments, tooled in blind with lines. Endbands: single with a bead; primary sewing over alum-tawed cores (partly laced in), tied down; secondary sewing of red silk (remnants only).

Endleaves: white paper pastedowns, conjugate with a stub, at both ends.

PROVENANCE: On title-page in manuscript: 'Ex libris franc.i Podij'; on pastedown in manuscript: a note referring to an edition of Sannazaro's works, Amsterdam, 1689; on pastedown in manuscript: 'Oct 2 1705 –0–1–0'; bought: Maggs, 27.viii.1948.
Same tools on: BL C.55.c.15 (Rome, 1532).
Compare: Cambridge University Library, Rel. d.50.1; John Rylands University Library, Manchester, R4427 (Venice, 1524); Hoepli, Catalogue, November–December 1925, no. 28 (Florence, 1525); J Baer, Catalogue 690, no. 325 (Rome, 1531); De Marinis, 1269, 1271, 1273, 1279; *Legature papali*, no. 52; Hobson, *Legature bolognesi*, nos. 9, 19.

284 *A binding made in Padua or Venice, c. 1530s*

Aphthonius, *Sophista, In hoc volumine haec continentur, Ausonii praeludia. Hermogenis Rhetorica* [Greek], Florence: P Iunta, July 1515. 8vo.

171 × 102 × 26 mm.   (P 966) Davis 737

Dark brown goatskin over paste boards, tooled in blind with lines, a border filled with tools showing foliage round a trunk; corner curls, and in the centre a slightly sunk medallion with a profile portrait of

283

284

Nero, surrounded by the legend: NERO CLAVD CAESAR AVG GER PM TR P IMP PP; on upper cover: ΕΡΜΟΓΕΝΗΣ; on lower cover: .ΤΙ.ΔΗ. Edges sprinkled in dark blue, grey and red.

Sewn on three alum-tawed supports, laced in straight, showing as raised bands on the spine, tooled in blind with a line; two kettle stitch bands and two false bands alternating with the sewing supports; eight compartments, tooled in blind with lines and interlaced-circles tools. Endbands: single with a bead; primary sewing over (?)alum-tawed cores (cut off), tied down; secondary sewing of pink and dark blue silk.

Endleaves: white paper pastedowns at both ends; at the end: one free leaf conjugate with the pastedown; manuscript waste used as strengthener.

Repairs: small repairs at corner near spine.

PROVENANCE: Small round purple ink stamp with: '[…?] L […?]pis Paris'; bought: Davis and Orioli, 19.vii.1950.
REFERENCES: De Marinis, 1684; Hobson, *Humanists*, p. 222, no. 18b.
LITERATURE: Meunier, *BN*, pl. 69; Mattingley, *Coins*, no. 178; Hobson, *Book Collector*, 1975, pp. 33–6, pl. 8 (a similar Nero plaquette without lettering); Hobson, *Humanists*, p. 233, no. 65 (ditto); Hobson, *Renaissance*, p. 94, pl. 41, no. 5, pl. 43 (ditto).
Same tool on: *Legature papali*, no. 71.
Compare: Davis 777 (no. 275 above), 816 (no. 338 below); Canterbury Cathedral Library, L–4–26 (Venice, 1538); Hobson, 'Italian sixteenth-century bookbindings', no. 3.
Note: The plaquette is taken from a sestertius of Nero.

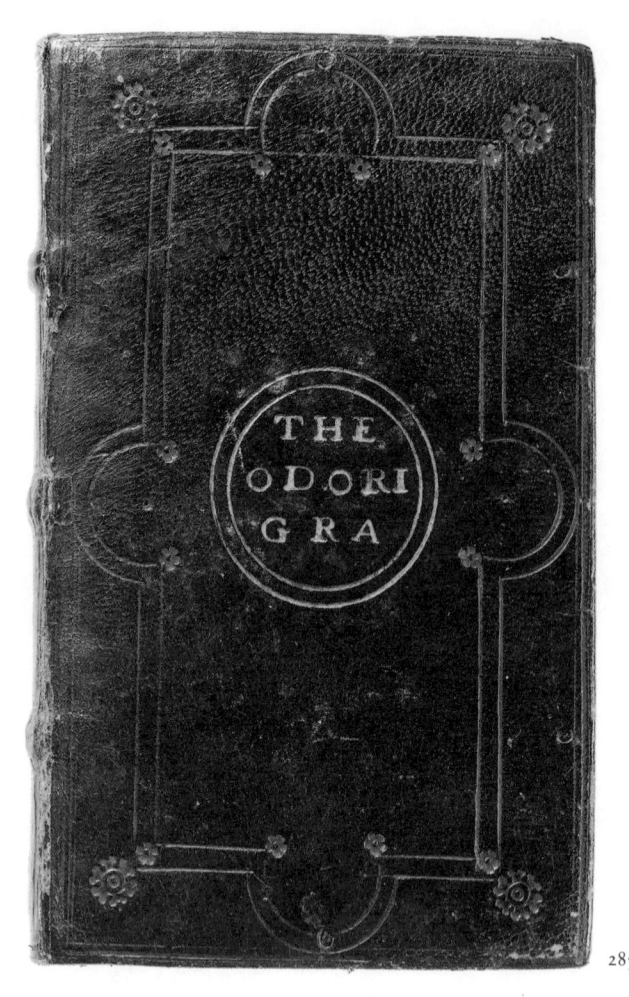

285 *A binding probably made in Venice or possibly in Bologna, c. 1530*

Theodorus Gaza, *Theodori Grammatices libri iiii* [Greek], Florence: Hearedes P Iuntae, 1526. 8vo.

172 × 107 × 29 mm. (P 801) Davis 752

Black goatskin over paste boards, tooled in blind and gold with lines, rosettes, small stylized flowers, and in the centre a circle with, on the upper cover: THE/ODORI/GRA; on the lower cover: an armorial shield with a coat of arms (three fesses or, in chief: crowned double-headed eagle). Traces of four pairs of ties. Edges: gilt and gauffered to a floral pattern.

Sewn on three (?)split (?)alum-tawed supports, laced in, showing as raised bands on the spine, tooled in blind with a line; four compartments tooled in blind with lines. Canvas spine lining. Endbands: single with a bead; green silk over (unidentified) cores (cut off), tied down sporadically.

Endleaves: white paper pastedowns and two free (?)conjugate white paper leaves, at both ends.

PROVENANCE: Erased library stamps on title-page; on endleaf in pencil manuscript: 'Vente Gareia [?Ganeia] iv.82...'; bought: Sotheby's, 17.vii.1944, *59*.
Compare: Davis 751 (no. 283 above); Hobson, *Legature bolognesi*, no. 15.

286

286 *A binding possibly made in Venice or Rome, c. 1530*

Petrus Lombardus, *Textus magistri sententiarum*, Lyon: Joannes David, n.d. [c. 1520]. 8vo.

181 × 121 × 36 mm. (P 1269) Davis 753

Red goatskin over paste boards, tooled in gold, with blind lines, with lines and gouges forming an intersecting border, lettered on the upper cover: MIRA/BILIS. / FACTA. EST. SCIENTIA. TVA./ SVPER. ME. ET./ NON. POTERO. AD. EAM; on the lower cover: IDEO. DA./ MICHI. INTELLECTVM. DO/MINE. ET. SCR/VCTABOR. MANDATA. TVA.; ivy leaves in the corners and in the centre a double circle, lettered: TEXTVS. MAGISTRI. SENTEN., around, on the upper cover: .VBI. and on the lower cover: .IBI. Traces of four pairs of ties. Edges: gilt and gauffered to a knot-work pattern.

Sewn on four split alum-tawed supports, laced in (three supports broken at the joint with the upper cover), showing as raised bands on the spine, tooled in gold with a line; five compartments, tooled in gold with a leaf tool and in blind with lines. Endbands: single with a bead; primary sewing over (?)leather cores (cut off), tied down sporadically; remnants of secondary sewing in blue and pink silk.

Endleaves: white paper pastedowns and one free leaf conjugate with the pastedown, at both ends.

PROVENANCE: J B de Boyveau (book plate); bought: Sotheby's, 18.ii.1957, *35*.
Compare: Sotheby's, 31.x.1949, *467*.

347

287 *A binding possibly made in Venice or Bologna, c. 1530*

Psalterium Graecum [Greek], [Venice]: Aldus Manutius, n.d. [not after 1498]. 4to.

220 × 157 × 29 mm. (P 908) Davis 782

Brown goatskin over paste boards, tooled in blind to a panel design, with lines, a border filled with rectangular tools incorporating an acorn, square tools in the corners and in the centre two arabesque tools surrounding a round tool with the Sacred Monogram in gold. Edges: plain; trace of a red stain; on top edge in ink: 'Greco'.

Sewn on three split alum-tawed supports, laced in, showing as raised bands on the spine, tooled in blind with a line; four compartments, tooled in blind with lines. Endbands: single with a bead; primary sewing over leather cores (cut off), tied down; secondary sewing in pink silk with remnants of blue silk.

Endleaves: white paper pastedowns and one free leaf conjugate with the pastedown, at both ends.

PROVENANCE: On title-page in manuscript: 'federico Giunchi Urbinae'; Dyson Perrins (book plate; library label with in manuscript: '127'; sold: Sotheby's, 18.vi.1946, *229*); bought: Quaritch, 7.vi.1948, *908*.
Compare: Davis 751 (no. 283 above); Breslauer, Catalogue 107, no. 28; Hobson, *Legature bolognesi*, no. 19.

288 *A binding made in Venice by the 'Agnese binder', c. 1530–40*

Dogale [Ducal commission] of the Doge Andreas Gritti to Giovanni Francesco Balbi as Count of Pola, [Venice], 27 September 1529; manuscript on parchment, signed: 'Pet[ru]s Grasolarius Secret[ariu]s; ruled. First page painted in purple, gold and colours, with the Lion of St Mark and the arms of Balbi, medallion portraits of an Evangelist [St John?], Christ and St Francis.

241 × 170 × 18 mm. (M 52) Davis 783

Red-brown goatskin over paste boards, tooled in gold, with blind lines, to a panel design with lines, stylized flowers in the outer corners, a border filled with 'iron-work' (curling leafy branch) tools, ivy-leaf tools in the corners and in the centre a row of knot tools. Traces of four pairs of blue and yellow ties. Edges: plain.

Sewn on three split leather supports, laced in, showing as raised bands on the spine, tooled in blind with a line; four compartments, tooled in blind with lines. Endbands: missing. Remnants of a pink silk cord (to attach a seal).

Endleaves: white paper pastedowns, at both ends; at the front: one free parchment leaf conjugate with a stub, wrapped round first section and pasted down on last leaf of first section.

PROVENANCE: Giovanni Francesco Balbi; Conte Manin (paper library labels with in manuscript: '155' on the spine and 'No 99/ B.Manin' on the upper cover; printed label with: 'Giovanni Lod. Conte Manin'); Amadeus Svajer (paper library label with in manuscript: '126' on the spine; book plate); Lathrop Harper (Catalogue 19, no. 8; sold: 17.i.1964, *470*).

REFERENCES: Hobson, *Renaissance*, p. 262, no. 20.
LITERATURE: Schunke, 'Venezianische Renaissance-Einbände', pp. 123–200 (esp. p. 155); Quilici, no. 266, fig. 111; Hobson, *Renaissance*, pp. 132–6, Appendix 10; Nuvoloni, 'Commissioni Dogali'.
Same tools on: (in addition to the bindings listed in Hobson, *Renaissance*, Appendix 10) BL, C.128.c.1 (Venice, 1521); private collection (Dante, Vicenza, 1529).
Note: Andreas Gritti (1454–1538), doge of Venice from 1523. The 'Agnese binder' was active from c.1510 to c.1545.

289 *A binding possibly made in Rome, c. 1530–40*

Valerius Maximus, *Exempla quatuor et viginti nuper inventa ante caput de omnibus*, Venice: Aldus & A Socerus, October 1514. 8vo.

162 × 101 × 30 mm.   (P 910) Davis 756

Brown goatskin (or possibly hair sheep) over paste boards, tooled in gold, with blind lines, to a panel design with leaf tools at and in the corners, lines and gouges forming a strap-work pattern, with in the centre seven leaf tools forming a centre ornament. Traces of two pairs of ties. Edges: gilt and gauffered to a pattern of knots.

Sewn on three split alum-tawed supports, laced in, showing as raised bands on the spine, tooled in gold with a line; four compartments, tooled in blind with lines and in gold with a leaf tool. Endbands: single with a bead; primary sewing over alum-tawed cores (cut off), tied down occasionally; secondary sewing of pink and green silk.

Endleaves: white paper pastedowns, at both ends; at the front: one free white paper leaf; at the end: two free conjugate paper leaves and a third free leaf conjugate with the pastedown.

Repairs: at upper cover.

PROVENANCE: At end of text (ccviii verso): in manuscript: 'Joh.' (different hand, now erased, over inscription below:) 'Bapt. Prouati' (?); on front endleaf: in manuscript: 'Proua[?t]i' and beneath this [erased]: 'Jo. Jo[sephus?]'; bought: Quaritch, 7.vi.1948, *910*.
Compare: Quilici, no. 151, fig. 60.

290 *A binding made in Venice, c. 1530–40*

Hore Dive Virginis Marie secundum verum usum Romanum, Paris: Thielman Kerver, 24 July 1511; printed on parchment in red and black with coloured initials. 8vo.

180 × 115 × 35 mm.   (P 1190) Davis 755

White parchment over paste boards, painted with an arabesque pattern outlined in black, with flowers and leaf shapes in blue, red, green, yellow and gold; in the centre: a cartouche with the Sacred Monogram surrounded by flowers on a deep blue-green ground (the design shows slight differences

289 290

on upper and lower cover; not a wood block). Traces of two pairs of clasps. Edges: painted in colour with flowers.

Sewn on three leather supports, laced in (taken over the outside of the boards), showing as bands on the spine; four compartments, painted in colour with flowers. Spine lined with textile and leather (possibly later). Endbands: single with a bead; primary sewing over leather cores (now broken off, once laced in), tied down; secondary sewing of pink and white silk.

Endleaves: white paper pastedowns, at both ends.

Damage at upper cover (slight) and at joints and spine.

PROVENANCE: George Hirth; E P Goldschmidt; bought: Sotheby's, 5.iv.1955, *276* (pl.).
REFERENCES: Pitti, exhibition, no. 18; Goldschmidt, no. 192, pl. lxviii; De Marinis, *Rilegature veneziane*, no. 57; De Marinis, 1666; Romme, *Book Collector*, 1969, p. 41, notes 132, 133.

---

291 *A binding probably made in Rome or possibly in Bologna, c. 1530–40*

J J Pontanus, *Centum Ptolemaei sententiae ad Syrum fratrem; De rebus coelestibus; De luna imperfectus*, Venice: Aldus & A Socerus, September 1519. 4to.

222 × 140 × 39 mm. (P 920) Davis 776

Dark brown goatskin over paste boards, tooled in gold, with blind lines, to a panel design with flame tools at the corners, small tools in the borders, in the panel: an arabesque design built up of curving solid tools, with in the centre: two fleurons above and below .G. / .A.C. Traces of four pairs of ties. Edges stained black and lightly gauffered with a row of dots.

Sewn on three split alum-tawed supports, laced in straight, showing as raised bands on the spine, tooled in gold with a line; four compartments, tooled in blind with lines; second and third compartment

291

lettered in gold (later): .PONT.IN / PTO.SEN. Endbands: single with a bead; primary sewing over alum-tawed cores (once laced in; one end still laced in), tied down; secondary sewing of blue and beige silk.
Endleaves: white paper pastedowns and one free leaf conjugate with the pastedown, at both ends.

PROVENANCE: Landau (book plate, with: '47673 / 47675'; sold: Sotheby's, 13.vii.1948, *100*).
LITERATURE: See Davis 739 (no. 292 below; and literature cited there).
Same tools on and compare: Davis 739 (no. 292 below; and references cited there).

292 *A binding probably made in Rome or possibly in Bologna, c. 1540*

Sophocles, *Tragaediae septem cum commentariis*, Venice: Aldus Romanus, August 1502 [and] Aeschylus, *Tragoediae sex*, Venice: Aldus & A Socerus, February 1518 [both Greek]. 8vo.

167 × 105 × 41 mm.   (P 1079) Davis 739

Red goatskin over paste boards, tooled in gold, with blind lines, to an arabesque design, built up of curving solid tools; fleurons at the corners; in the centre: an (unidentified) coat of arms. Traces of four pairs of ties. Edges: gilt and gauffered to a pattern with small stars.
Sewn on three (?)split alum-tawed supports, laced in, showing as raised bands on the spine, tooled in gold with a line; two kettle stitch bands and two false bands, alternating with the sewing supports, tooled in gold with dashes; eight compartments, tooled in blind with lines; in second compartment in

292

manuscript: 'Sophocl./Tragoedi'. Endbands: single with a bead; primary sewing over alum-tawed cores (laced in), tied down; secondary sewing of pink silk.

Endleaves: white paper pastedowns at both ends; at the front: one free leaf conjugate with the pastedown; at the end: two free conjugate white paper leaves and one leaf conjugate with the pastedown.

PROVENANCE: On pastedown in manuscript: 'Armario 9 Scorn. ce muro/ no 3i'; Altemps (on title-page in manuscript: 'Ex biblca Altempsua'); Arthur Kay (book plate; sold: Sotheby's, 29.v.1930, *646b*); bought: Parke-Bernet, 31.x.1951, *861*.
REFERENCES: Hobson, 'Buyers of books', p. 71, no. 3.
LITERATURE: Hobson, 'Buyers of books', pp. 71–2, pl. iii.
Same tools on: Davis 776 (no. 291 above; same design), (possibly same tools on:) Davis 805 (no. 322 below); BL, G. 9030 (Rome [1469] = De Marinis, 2235).
Same coat of arms on: Bodleian Library Oxford, Antiq.f.I.1515/1 (Florence, 1515).
Compare: Schäfer, no. 34; Hobson, *Legature bolognesi*, no. 46.
Note: The Altemps family was a well-known and well-connected Roman family.
Count Annibal d'Altemps, general of the papal army, nephew of Pope Pius IV; Giovanni Angelo Altemps: b. Rome, second half 16th century; d. 1620; 1611 acquired the library of Cardinal Marcello Cervini (Pope Marcello II: 1555), which passed to Cardinal Sirleto and then to Ascanio Colonna, after whose death it was sold. The dukes of Altemps sold their library in Rome and London in 1907 and 1908.
The Altemps arms are not those on Davis 739.
Hobson, 'Buyers of books' describes this binding as being decorated with a panel, however the design appears to have been built up with single tools.

293 *A binding made in Venice by the 'Fugger binder' ('Venetian Apple binder'), c. 1531–2*

Appianus, *Delle guerre civili de Romani*, Florence: Hearedes P Iuntae, 1526 [and] Appianus, *Historia delle guerre esterne de' Romani*, Florence: B Iunta, December 1531. 8vo.

166 × 100 × 59 mm. (P 1280) Davis 754

Brown goatskin over paste boards, tooled in gold, with blind lines, to a panel design with ivy-leaf tools at the corners, stylized flowers, arabesque corner pieces and in the centre within an egg-shaped compartment, on the upper cover: TE/ SOLA SER/VIRO/ FIN CH'/ HAROVI/TA; on the lower cover: CH'/ INTESTA/ IL TOR/MI MORTE/ ET DAR/ MI VI/TA. Traces of four pairs of ties. Edges: gilt and gauffered to a knot-work pattern.

Sewn on two double (or split) supports, laced in, plus a third (false) double band, showing as three raised bands on the spine, tooled in gold with a line; four false single bands, showing as low bands on the spine, tooled in gold with dashes; eight compartments, tooled in blind. Endbands: single (covered in glue and leather dressing); probably: sewn over (?)leather cores (now cut off, lacing in holes visible), tied down sporadically.

Endleaves: white paper pastedowns and one free white paper leaf tipped onto first and last leaves of sections, at both ends.

Repairs: at top and tail of spine and at joints.

PROVENANCE: bought: Sotheby's 17.x.1960, *746*.
REFERENCES: Foot, *Davis*, I, p. 312 (note 57); Hobson, *Renaissance*, p. 256, no. 34.
LITERATURE: Foot, *Davis*, I, pp. 309–22 (and literature cited there); Hobson, *Renaissance*, pp. 119–32 (and literature cited there), Appendix 8; see also Davis 764, 794, 799 (nos. 294, 295, 296 below).
Same motto and corners on: BL, C. 28.a.4 (Florence, 1531); De Marinis, 2161bis (= Hobson, *Renaissance*, Appendix 8, nos. 35, 36).

294   *A binding made in Venice by the 'Fugger binder' ('Venetian Apple binder'), c. 1540*

M T Cicero, *Orationes*, vol. I, Venice: Aldus, Paulus Manutius Aldi F., October 1540. 8vo.

167 × 98 × 32 mm.   (P 1241) Davis 764

Brown goatskin over paste boards, tooled in gold, with blind lines, to a panel design, with lotus tools in the borders, ivy-leaf tools at the corners, corner curls in the corners, an undulating lozenge formed by gouges, fleurons, lotus tools and stars around a centre piece made of curving open tools, decorated with white paint, with in the centre of the upper cover: ORAT./ M.T.C./ I. Traces of four pairs of ties. Edges of boards: tooled in blind with a line and in gold with dashes. Edges: gilt and gauffered to a knot-work pattern.

Sewn on three alum-tawed supports, laced in, showing as raised bands on the spine, tooled in gold with a line; four false bands alternating with the sewing supports, tooled in gold with dashes; eight compartments, tooled in blind. In compartments 3 and 4: later red goatskin labels, tooled in gold: M.T.C./ ORAT./ ALD. 1540. Endbands: single with a bead; blue and white silk over leather cores (cut off), tied down occasionally (white thread only).

Endleaves: White paper pastedowns and one free leaf conjugate with the pastedown and one free paper leaf conjugate with a stub after the first and before the last section, at both ends.

PROVENANCE: Giovanni Paolo Amanio, Latin poet, bishop of Anglona and Tursi (d. 1579/80); papal treasurer of Gregory XIII (on endleaf in manuscript: 'Largitione S.mi D.H. Dni Gregorij Papae/ xiii. ex spolijs ho. Me. Jo. Pauli Amanij/ Gri Anglonen die xix mensis Decembris/ 1579'); on title-page in manuscript: 'Collegij Graecor[um]'; bought: Sotheby's, 12.vii.1955, *574*.
REFERENCES: Foot, *Davis*, I, p. 320, no. 15; Hobson, *Renaissance*, p. 257, no. 57.
LITERATURE: Benvenuti, *Dizionario*, pp. 6–7; Foot, *Davis*, I, pp. 309–22 (and literature cited there); Hobson, *Renaissance*, pp. 119–32 (and literature cited there), Appendix 8; see also Davis 754 (no. 293 above), 794, 799 (nos. 295, 296 below).

295   *A binding made in Venice by the 'Fugger binder' ('Venetian Apple binder'), c. 1541*

B Castiglione, *Il libro del cortegiano*, Venice: Figlivoli di Aldo, 1541. 8vo.

158 × 100 × 23 mm.   (P 909) Davis 794

Brown goatskin over paste boards, tooled in gold, with blind lines, to a panel design with a border formed of interlacing fillets, an ivy-leaf tool at the corners; large curling corner tools; fleurons, and in

295

the centre an empty shield with, at either side: two lotus tools and a small apple tool. Traces of four pairs of ties. Edges: gilt and lightly gauffered with a row of dots.

Sewn on three, probably split (invisible) supports, showing as raised bands on the spine, tooled in gold with a line; four false bands, tooled in gold with dashes; eight compartments, tooled in blind. Endbands: double with a bead; primary sewing over alum-tawed cores (laced in), tied down; secondary sewing of pink and blue silk; cord crowning cores.

Endleaves: white paper pastedowns conjugate with a stub after the first and before the last section, at both ends.

PROVENANCE: On title-page in manuscript: 'J. Ballesdens' surrounded by three S fermés; Lord Viscount Lewisham (book plate); Quaritch (Catalogue 657, 1948, *64*, pl.; sold: 7.vi.1948, *900*).
REFERENCES: Foot, *Davis* I, p. 321, no. 17; Hobson, *Renaissance*, p. 257, no. 61.
LITERATURE: Davis 764 (no. 294 above; and literature cited there); G D Hobson, *Fanfare*, pp. 89, 118; see also Davis 754 (no. 293 above), 799 (no. 296 below).
Note: Ballesdens: see Davis 381–3 (no. 71 above).

296

296 *A binding made in Venice by the 'Fugger binder' ('Venetian Apple binder'), c. 1545*

Procopius, *De la longa & aspra guerra de Gothi libri tre*, Venice: M Tramezino, 1544 [and] L Bruni, *Libro della guerra de Ghotti*, Venice: G Giolito, 1542 [and] L Bruni, *La prima guerra di Carthaginesi con Romani*, Venice: G Giolito, 1545. 8vo.

160 × 98 × 46 mm. (P 769) Davis 799

Olive goatskin over paste boards, tooled in silver (now oxidized), with blind lines; corner curls; gouges forming an arabesque centre piece; lotus tools, fleurons and apple tools; in the centre: a double circle with on the upper cover Fortuna and on the lower cover: an empty shield. Traces of two pairs of ties. Edges: stained dark, lightly gauffered; title painted on fore-edge.

Sewn on three split alum-tawed supports, laced in, showing as raised bands on the spine, tooled in blind with a line; four false bands alternating with the sewing supports, tooled in blind with dashes; eight compartments, tooled in blind. Endbands: double with a bead; primary sewing over alum-tawed cores (laced in), tied down; secondary sewing of blue and white silk; cord crowning cores.

Endleaves: white paper pastedowns and one free paper leaf conjugate with a stub after the first and before the last section, at both ends.

PROVENANCE:	A Perrenot, Cardinal de Granvelle (arms stamped on verso of title-page); Petrus Prost, a priest in Besançon (on endleaf in manuscript: 'Petri Prost./ Sacerdotis Bisuntini/ Villa dej Parochi/ Anno Domini 1702/ ja Augusti'; drawn coat of arms); George Dunn (book plate; sold: Sotheby's, 5.ii.1914, *1517*); Leighton; E P Goldschmidt (book plate; Catalogue 73 [?1944], *156*; sold: 9.ii.1944).
REFERENCES:	Foot, *Davis* I, p. 308 no. 24, p. 321, Appendix III, no. 21, Appendix IV, no. 4; Hobson, *Renaissance*, Appendix 8, p. 257, no. 76 .
LITERATURE:	Davis 764 (no. 294 above; and literature cited there); see also Davis 754, 794 (nos. 293, 295 above); for Granvelle: see Foot, *Davis* I, pp. 313–15 (and literature cited there); see also Davis 800, 801 (nos. 297, 298 below).
Same tools also on:	Brera, no. 36.
Note:	Antoine Perrenot, Cardinal de Granvelle (1517–1586); born in Ornans; studied in Padua; archdeacon of Besançon; bishop of Arras: 1538; archbishop of Malines and Cardina: 1561; archbishop of Besançon: 1584; chancellor of Charles V and Philip II; viceroy of Naples: 1565.

297 *A binding made in Venice by the 'Fugger binder' ('Venetian Apple binder') for Cardinal de Granvelle, c. 1547*

M T Cicero, *Officiorum libri tres* [and other works], Venice: Paulus Manutius Aldi filius, March 1545. 8vo.

167 × 100 × 17 mm. (P 972) Davis 800

Dark brown goatskin over paste boards, tooled in gold, with blind lines, to a panel design with ivy-leaf tools at the corners and on the upper cover: MAR. TVL. CICE./ OFFICIOR/. Traces of four pairs of ties. Edges: gilt and lightly gauffered with a row of dots; on the fore-edge the title painted horizontally in gold on a purple 'label' (background).

Sewn on three, possibly split, alum-tawed supports, laced in, showing as raised bands on the spine, tooled in gold with a line; four false bands alternating with the sewing supports, tooled in gold with dashes; eight compartments, tooled in blind with lines and leafy curls. Endbands: double with a bead; primary sewing over alum-tawed cores (laced in), tied down; cord crowning cores.

Endleaves: white paper pastedowns and one free paper leaf conjugate with a stub after the first and before the last section, at both ends.

PROVENANCE:	Antoine Perrenot, Cardinal de Granvelle (arms stamped in ink on A 2 verso); on A 1 verso in manuscript: 'Will Hamilton'; James Hamilton of Bangour (book plate); bought: Sotheby's, 30.x.1950, *17*.
REFERENCES:	Foot, *Davis* I, p. 321, Appendix IV, no. 11.
LITERATURE:	Foot, *Davis* I, pp. 313–15 (and literature cited there); Hobson, *Humanists*, p. 72; Brooker, *Book Collector*, 1997; Hobson, *Renaissance*, pp. 79, 119–21, 124; Hobson, 'Italian sixteenth-century bookbindings', no. 9; see also Davis 799 (no. 296 above), 801 (no. 298 below).

297 298

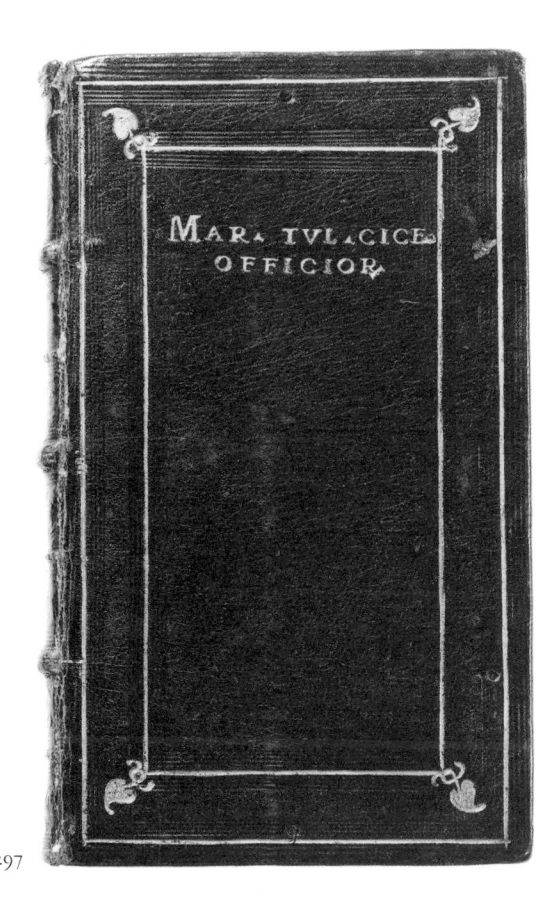

298   *A binding made in Venice by the 'Fugger binder' ('Venetian Apple binder') for Cardinal de Granvelle, c. 1547*

C Claudianus, *Opera*, Venice: Aldus & A Socerus, March 1523. 8vo.

169 × 100 × 23 mm.   (P 1204) Davis 801

Olive goatskin over paste boards, tooled in gold, with blind lines, to a panel design with ivy-leaf tools at the corners and on the upper cover: CLAVDIANVS. Four pairs of (new) green silk ties. Edges: gilt and lightly gauffered with a row of dots; on fore-edge: the title painted horizontally in gold on a purple 'label' (background).

   Sewn on three, possibly split, alum-tawed supports, laced in, showing as raised bands on the spine, tooled in gold with a line; four false bands alternating with the sewing supports, tooled in gold with dashes; eight compartments, tooled in blind with lines and curving branch with a bud. Endbands: double with a bead; primary sewing over alum-tawed cores (laced in), tied down; secondary sewing (new) of green silk; cord crowning cores.

   Endleaves: white paper pastedowns and one free paper leaf conjugate with a stub after the first and before the last section, at both ends.

PROVENANCE: Antoine Perrenot, Cardinal de Granvelle (arms stamped in ink on A3); on endleaf in manuscript: 'Adversana fortuna'; on endleaf in manuscript: 'Brooke's sale 2164');

359

THE HENRY DAVIS GIFT

Heber; Vernon; Holford (sold: Sotheby's, 6.xii.1927, *213*); bought: Sotheby's, 13.vi.1955, *5*.
REFERENCES: Foot, *Davis*, I, p. 321, Appendix IV, no. 9.
LITERATURE: See Davis 800 (no. 297 above; and literature cited there); see also Davis 799 (no. 296 above).

299   *A binding made c. 1535*

Appianus, *Delle guerre civili de Romani*, Venice: Giovantonio & I fratelli da Sabio, 1531. 8vo.

156 × 100 × 33 mm.   (P 1425) Davis 757

Brown calf over paste boards, tooled in gold, with blind lines, to a panel design with small fleur-de-lis tools at the outer corners, a border formed by parallel lines in gold and blind, and a panel filled with an arabesque pattern built up of solid curl, leaf and fleuron tools (the tooling shows slight differences on upper and lower cover; not a block). Traces of two pairs of ties. Edges of boards: tooled in blind with a line. Edges: gilt and gauffered to a knot-work pattern with small stars.

Rebacked and probably resewn; three raised bands, four compartments. Endbands: single; primary sewing over alum-tawed cores (cut off), no visible tie-downs; secondary sewing of beige silk.

New endleaves: white paper pastedowns and one free white paper leaf with a stub after the first and before the last section, at both ends.

Repairs: rebacked; repairs at covers.

PROVENANCE: On title-page in manuscript [erased]: 'Francisco Col[?o]cci'; same [erased] manuscript inscription on k 4 recto; bought: Sotheby's, 28.ii.1966, *82*.

300   *A binding probably made in Rome, c. 1535*

Herodotus, *Delle guerre de' Greci et de' Persi*, Venice: Giovann' Antonio di Nicolini da Sabbio for M Sessa, 1533. 8vo.

157 × 103 × 45 mm.   (P 1475) Davis 758

Brown goatskin over paste boards, tooled in gold, with blind lines, with an interlacing ribbon forming a border and compartments; in the centre compartment: an astrolabe with on a scroll: COL TEMPO. Traces of four pairs of ties. Edges: gilt and lightly gauffered with a row of dots.

Sewn on three split leather supports, laced in, showing as raised bands on the spine, tooled in gold with a line; four compartments, tooled in blind with lines; in the second and third compartment: lettered (vertically): HEROD/OTO. Endbands: single; primary sewing, tied down.

Endleaves: white paper pastedowns and one free white paper leaf conjugate with a stub after the first and before the last section, at both ends.

Repairs: at joints, and top and tail of spine.

PROVENANCE: Prince Diego Pignatelli d'Angio (label); N Rauch (Catalogue 1, 1948, no. 53); J R Abbey (book plate; 'J.A.4798/5:4:1950'; sold: Sotheby's, 20.vi.1967, *1894*, pl.).

REFERENCES:	Pitti, exhibition, no. 487; Hobson, *French and Italian*, no. 64; Hobson, 'Buyers of books', p. 68.
LITERATURE:	E P Goldschmidt, no. 157, pl. lvii (= De Marinis, 2175, now in the Bodleian Library Oxford, Broxbourne collection); G Pollard, 'Changes in the style of bookbinding', *The Library*, 5th series, xi (1956), p. 83; Critien, p. 34; Hobson, 'Buyers of books', pp. 68–9.
Compare:	De Marinis, 1400 (design).
Note:	The E P Goldschmidt and Malta examples also have vertical spine lettering.

301 *A binding made in Venice, dated 1537*

J Apell, *Methodica dialectices ratio, ad iurisprudentiam adcommodata*, Nuremberg: F Peypus, 1535 [and] C Cantiuncula, *Topica*, Venice: G de Fontaneto Montisferrati, 24 December 1534 [and] P A Gammarus, *Dialecta legalis*, Venice: G de Fontaneto, 1533 [and] J Fichardus, *Virorum qui superiori nostroque seculo ... illustres atque memorabiles fuerunt vitae*, Frankfurt: C Egenolph, September 1536 [and] D Erasmus, *Catalogi duo operum*, Basel: H Froben, 1537. 4to.

212 × 154 × 52 mm.   (P 1428) Davis 784

301

Red goatskin over paste boards, tooled in gold, with blind lines, to a panel design with stylized flower tools in the outer corners, ivy-leaf tools in the corners of the panel; on the upper cover: DIALECTA/ LEGALIS./ PHILIPPVS.A.MAVGIS./ M.D.XXXVII. Traces of two pairs of ties. Edges: stained blue; green tabs indicating each new work [may have been added later].

Sewn on three split alum-tawed supports, laced in, showing as raised bands on the spine, tooled in blind with a line; four false bands, tooled in gold with dashes; eight compartments, tooled in blind with lines; title painted in white on first compartment; in ink: '1535'. Spine compartments lined. Endbands: single with a bead; primary sewing over (?)leather cores (partly laced in), tied down; secondary sewing of pale blue and pink silk.

Endleaves: white paper pastedowns and one free leaf conjugate with the pastedown, at both ends.

PROVENANCE: Philippus a Maugis, 1537; manuscript notes in margins of text; on pastedown in manuscript: ownership inscription [erased]: 'Ph…'; Lathrop Harper (Catalogue 25, no. 116, sold: 16.ii.1966).
REFERENCES: Hobson, *Renaissance*, p. 247, no. 100c.
LITERATURE: Hobson, *Renaissance*, Appendix 5 (b).
Note: According to Hobson, *Renaissance*: in the style of the 'Mendoza binder', but by a different binder. Hobson Appendix 5 (b), no. 100b has the same name and date tooled on the cover.

302

302 Four bindings made c. 1540

C Plinius Secundus, *Naturalis historiae. Prima pars*, Venice: Haeredes Aldi & A Socerus, 1536. 8vo.
170 × 105 × 46 mm. (P 1385) Davis 759
C Plinius Secundus, *Naturalis historia. Secunda pars*, Venice: Haeredes Aldi & A Socerus, 1535. 8vo.
171 × 105 × 42 mm. (P 1385) Davis 760
C Plinius Secundus, *Naturalis historia. Tertia pars*, Venice: Haeredes Aldi & A Socerus, 1536. 8vo.
175 × 107 × 40 mm. (P 1385) Davis 761
Index in C Plinii Naturalis historiae libros, Venice: Aldus, 1538. 8vo.
165 × 113 × 35 mm. (P 1385) Davis 762

Four volumes in identical bindings of brown goatskin over paste boards, tooled in (oxidized) silver, with blind lines, to a panel design with a border filled with curving leaf tools and in the centre a row of three stylized flowers. Vol. IV, upper cover: in manuscript in ink: 'Alsauio Philosopho/ Socr Atheniese'. Traces of two pairs of ties. Edges: sprinkled in dark blue and gauffered with dots. Vol. IV: top edge gauffered with curves.

  Sewn on three split leather supports (vol. III: possibly on split alum-tawed supports), laced in, showing as raised bands on the spine; four compartments, tooled in blind with lines. Endbands: single with a bead; primary sewing in dark blue thread over (?)cord cores (laced in), tied down; secondary sewing of pink silk.

  Endleaves: vols I–III: white paper pastedowns and one free leaf conjugate with the pastedown and one free paper leaf conjugate with a stub after the first and before the last section, at both ends; vol.

IV: white paper pastedowns and two free paper leaves, each conjugate with a stub after the first and before the last section, at both ends.

Repairs: vol. III–IV: small repair at corner.

PROVENANCE: On endleaf of vol. I in manuscript: 'Fe Cappni: di.S.Ginnig°'; Oliver Howard (ex-libris in vol. I); vol. III: on endleaf in manuscript: '225'; bought: Quaritch, 27.xii.1962.

303 *A binding made in Rome by Niccolò Franzese for Eurialo Silvestri, c. 1540–5*

Dion Cassius, *Dione historico delle guerre & fatti de' Romani*, Venice: Nicolo d'Aristotile di Ferrara ditto Zoppino, March 1533; woodcut border and title-page; woodcut illustrations. 4to.

214 × 150 × 45 mm. (P 1285) Davis 835

Black goatskin over paste boards, tooled in gold, with blind lines, to a panel design with small fleurons at the corners, an outer border filled with small flower tools, fleurons and gouges; along the top on the upper cover: DIONE HISTORICO; an inner border filled with a chain pattern; solid tools in the corners; gouges and solid leaf and fleuron tools, with in the centre of the upper cover: EVRI/ALVS and on the lower cover: DE/ SILVE/STRIS; outside the outer border on both covers the letters: A R. Traces of two pairs of ties (?). Edges: gilt and gauffered to a knot-work pattern.

Sewn on five supports (probably laced in: invisible), showing as raised bands on the spine, tooled in gold with a line; six false bands, tooled in gold with dashes; twelve compartments, tooled in blind with lines; the two top and two tail compartments: tooled in gold. Endbands: single with a bead; green and pink silk over (?)alum-tawed cores (now cut off); no visible tie-downs.

Endleaves: new pastedowns and one free leaf conjugate with the pastedown, at both ends.

Repairs: at joint and top and tail of spine.

PROVENANCE: Eurialo Silvestri; A R; Libri (sold: Sotheby's, 25.vii.1862, *197*); Clumber (sold: Sotheby's, 23.xi.1937, *248*); J R Abbey (book plate; 'JA1592/ 23:11:1937'; sold: Sotheby's, 22.vi.1965, *260*).
REFERENCES: Libri, *Monuments inédits*, pl. 45; De Marinis, 2982; G D Hobson, *Maioli*, p. 127, list no. 22; Hobson, *Apollo and Pegasus*, pp. 80, 82, list c, no. 37.
LITERATURE: Bignami Odier, pp. 288–9; Hobson, *Apollo and Pegasus*, pp. 69, 76–86, 90–7 (and literature cited there). See also Davis 836, 866 (nos. 304, 305 below).
Note: Eurialo Silvestri arrived in Rome shortly after 1527, became chamberlain to Pope Paul III.
Niccolò Franzese (Fery): bookseller and binder in Rome, employed by the Vatican library; occurs in a list of personnel working for the Vatican library between 1537 and 1550; died: 1570–1.

304 *A binding made in Rome by Niccolò Franzese, c. 1545*

F Petrarca, *Sonetti e canzoni con l'espositione d'Alessandro Vellutello*, Venice: Gabriel Giolito, 1545; woodcut title-page. 4to.

214 × 153 × 32 mm. (P 980) Davis 836

303

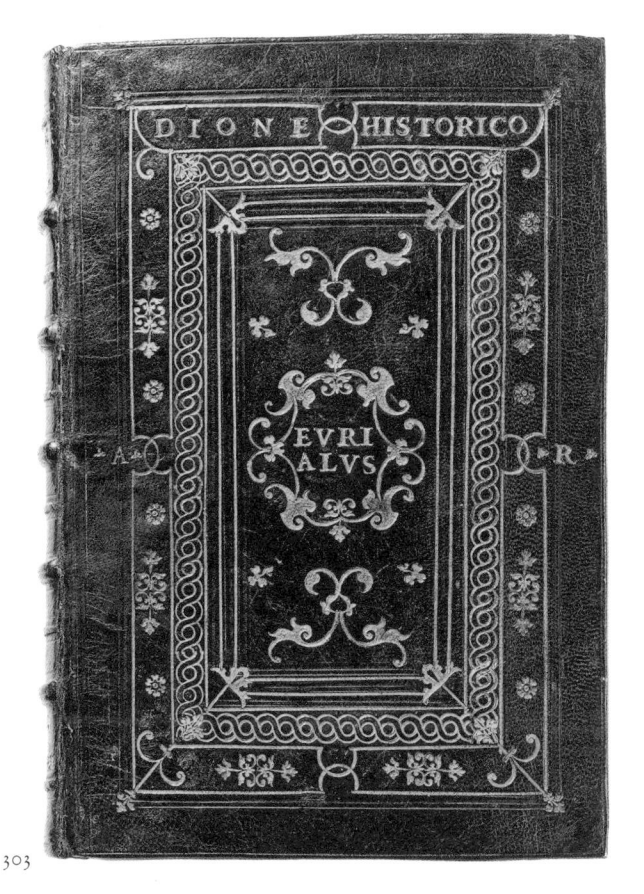

304

Red goatskin over paste boards, tooled in gold, with blind lines, to a design of interlacing ribbons. Small fleurons at the corners; corner ornaments built up of solid tools; roundels and small leafy branches in the border; stylized flower tools, solid curving tools, gouges and dots. The interlace has been painted black. In the centre of the lower cover: IL/ PETR/ARC/HA. Traces of four pairs of ties. Edges: gilt and gauffered to a knot-work pattern.

Sewn on three (?)alum-tawed supports, laced in, showing as raised bands on the spine, tooled in gold with a line; four false bands, laced in, tooled in gold with dashes; eight compartments, tooled in blind with lines and in gold with small solid tools; top and tail compartments: tooled in blind; third compartment: title lettered on spine. Endbands: double with a bead; possibly primary sewing over alum-tawed cores (now cut off), tied down sporadically; secondary sewing of white and pink silk.

Endleaves: later white paper pastedowns and one free leaf conjugate with the pastedowns, at both ends; at the front: four free paper leaves; at the end: two free (?)conjugate paper leaves.

Repairs: at top and tail of spine and corners.

PROVENANCE: On endleaf in manuscript: 'Normandeau[?x]'; 'Mas del presente el dolor Venidero JB'; in a 19th-century hand: 'This Book was purchased at Avignon in the year 1802 by J. Stray Jr. & by him presented to J. Broadly'; Lucius Wilmerding (book plate; sold: Parke-Bernet, 5.iii.1951, *153*).
REFERENCES: Romme, *Book Collector*, 1969, p. 41, note 135; Hobson, *Apollo and Pegasus*, p. 83, no. 54.
LITERATURE: Davis 835 (no. 303 above; and literature cited there); see also Davis 866 (no. 305 below).

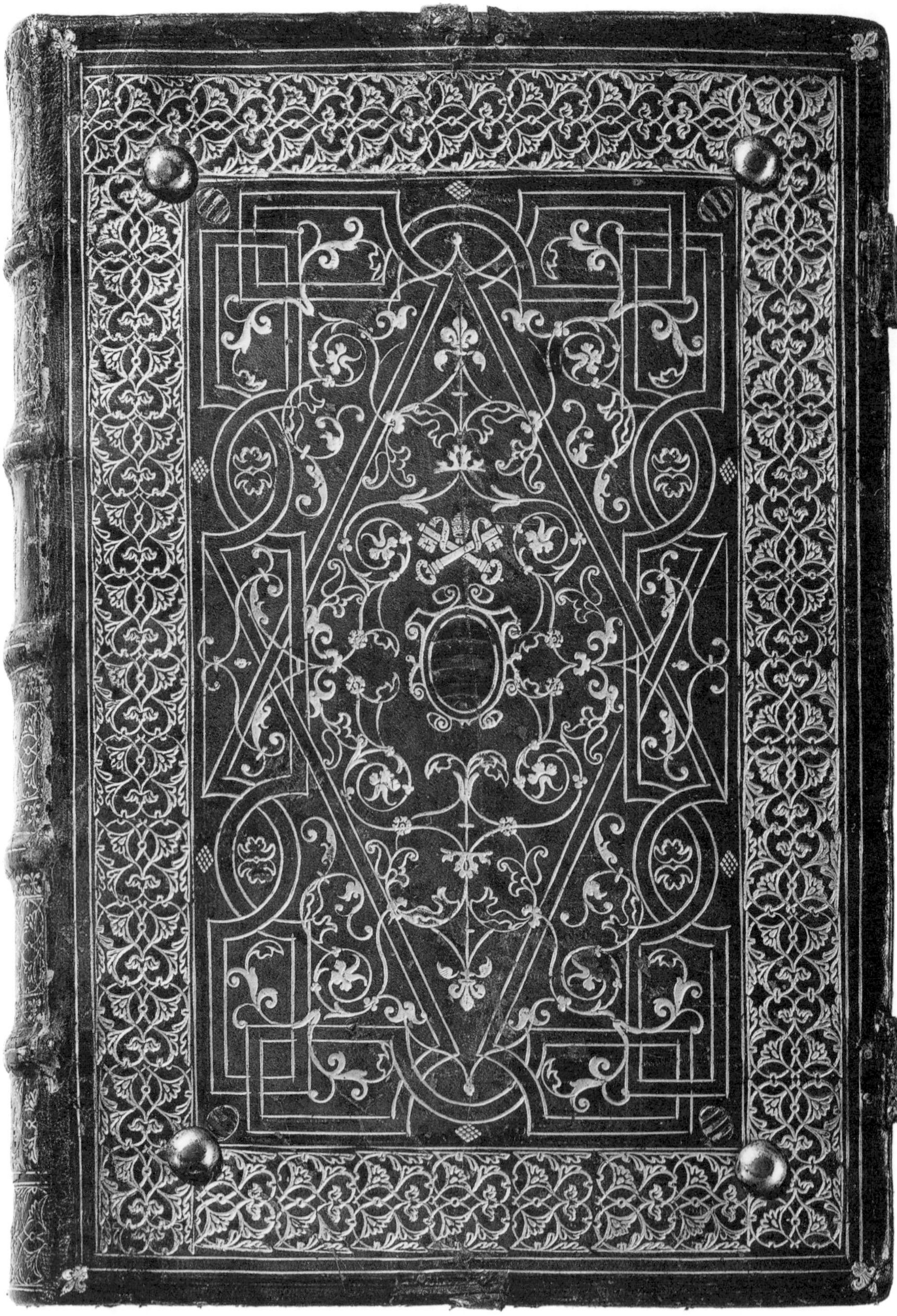

305 *A binding made in Rome by Niccolò Franzese, c. 1555–6*

Biblia Latina [vol. IV: Isaiah-Maccabees], [Venice: Paganino de Paganinis, 1495]. fol.

361 × 250 × 55 mm. (P 886) Davis 866

Red goatskin over paste boards, tooled in gold; a wide border filled with large open curving fleuron tools; interlacing ribbon; gouges, solid and open curving floral and fleuron tools, lotus tools; in the corners and in the centre: the arms of Pope Paul IV. In the upper border of the lower cover: BIBLIA.CV(superscript:)Ω. GLO./ T. IIII. IN. PRO. ET.M. Remnants of four pairs of clasps, hinging on upper cover; four brass bosses on each cover [lectern Bible placed with the lower cover uppermost]. Edges: gilt and gauffered to a knot-work pattern.

Sewn on five split alum-tawed supports, laced in, showing as raised bands on the spine, tooled in gold with a line; seven compartments (tail compartment: new), tooled in gold; third compartment: LIBRI./ PROPHE./TARVM./ MACHA./BEORVM. Endbands: single with a bead; primary sewing over alum-tawed cores (now cut off), tied down; secondary sewing of black and red silk.

Endleaves: white paper pastedowns, at both ends; at the front: two free conjugate paper leaves and one free leaf conjugate with the pastedown; at the end: one free leaf conjugate with the pastedown.

Repairs: at spine and corners.

PROVENANCE: Pope Paul IV; Mortimer Schiff (book plate; sold: Sotheby's, 6.xii.1938, *1370*); bought: Sotheby's, 29.vii.1946, *160* (pl.).
REFERENCES: G D Hobson, *Maioli*, p. 125, list no. 2; Hobson, *Apollo and Pegasus*, p. 95, note 78.
LITERATURE: Davis 835 (no. 303 above; and literature cited there); see also Davis 836 (no. 304 above).
Same tools on: *Legature papali*, no. 102; Quilici, pl. 79, no. 187.
Compare: *Legature papali*, nos. 111, 114; Nardelli, no. 6.
Note: Paul IV elected pope: 1555.

306 *A binding possibly made in Venice, c. 1540–50*: **A Remboîtage**

C Crinesius, *De confusione linguarum, tum orientalium: … tum occidentalium … statuens … concinnatus*, Nuremberg: Simon Halbmayer, 1629. 4to.

195 × 147 × 23 mm. (P 916) Davis 765

Brown goatskin over paste boards, blocked in gold to an oriental design tooled in blind with lines and in gold with small stylized flowers at the corners. Edges: plain.

Sewn on two alum-tawed supports, laced in, taken over the outside of the covers; long slips beneath pastedowns; smooth spine, tooled in gold with flowers and foliage staff tools. Parchment manuscript spine lining between sewing supports. No endbands.

Endleaves: white paper pastedowns, at both ends; at the front: one free leaf conjugate with the pastedown.

PROVENANCE: On endleaf in manuscript (17th-century hand): 'Vivere in Virtute/ mori in fide Janus Kreolas/ Thijapolitanus mpp.'; on title-page in manuscript (same hand): 'Diacoli

306

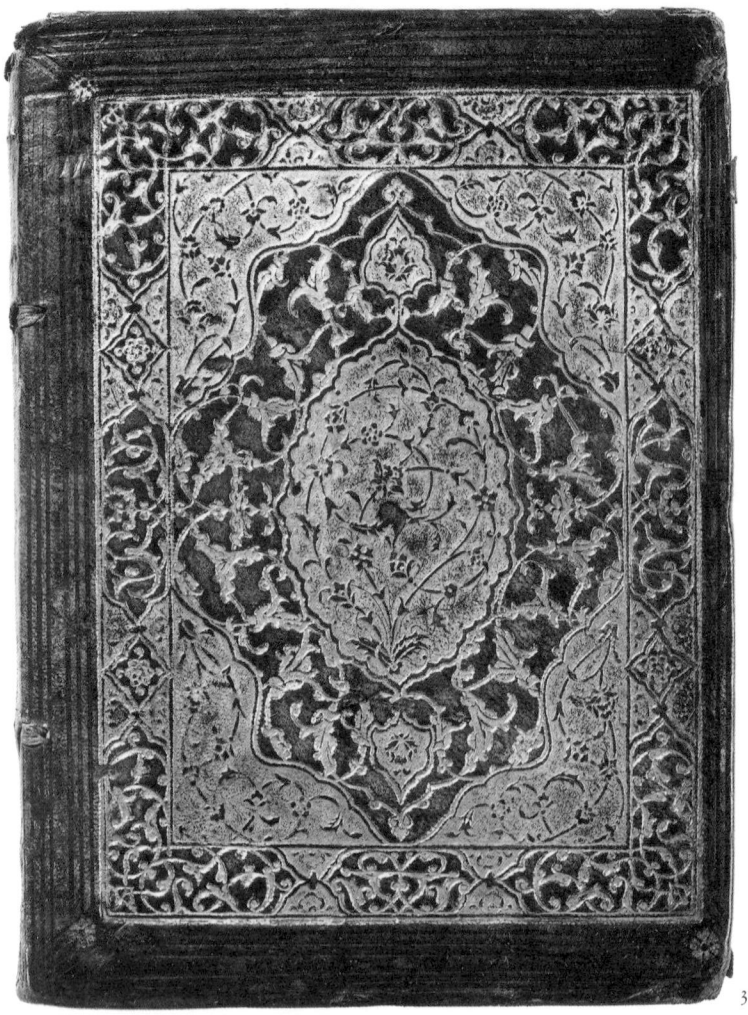

      none/ Aiis veta salis'; Heber (stamp of Heber library); Pickering, bookseller, 196 Piccadilly (book plate); Dyson Perrins (sold: Sotheby's, 10.iii.1947, *606*); Robinson (Catalogue 77, 1948, *146,* pl.; sold: 29.vi.1948).
REFERENCES: *BFAC,* 1981, no. 33.
LITERATURE: Hobson, *Humanists,* pp. 148–54 (but Davis 765 is not decorated with filigree work).
Compare: Fletcher, *Foreign,* xxix; Goldschmidt, no. 217; De Marinis, 1836 (Venice, 1539, for Davis 765 spine tooling).

---

307 *A binding made in Bologna, c. 1540–50*

A Gellius, *Noctium Atticarum libri undeviginti*, Venice: Aldus & A Socerus, 1515. 8vo.

166 × 93 × 46 mm.   (P 940) Davis 791

Red-brown goatskin over paste boards, tooled in gold, with blind lines, to a panel design with small fleurons at the corners; a border filled with curving leafy branch tools; a horizontal strip at top and bottom of the panel filled with small fleurons; a panel divided into lozenges by interlacing rectangles, the sides filled with curving leaf tools; small fleurons in the lozenges. Edges: gilt and gauffered to a knot-work pattern with small flowers.

Sewn on three (invisible, probably split) supports, laced in, showing as raised bands on the spine, tooled in gold with a line; four compartments, tooled in blind with lines and in gold with small fleurons. Endbands: single with a bead; primary sewing over alum-tawed cores (laced in), tied down; secondary sewing of blue and white (beige) silk.

Endleaves: white paper pastedowns and one free white paper leaf with a stub after the first and before the last section, at both ends.

PROVENANCE: On endleaf in manuscript: 'Michaelis'; on last page of text traces of manuscript note: 'Michaelis Bandinij [?et amicorum] 1657/ 20 Maij'; on AA2 ink stamp: 'MB'; on title-page in manuscript: 'Michaelis Bandinij'(?) [erased]; over-written: 'Balthassarius Bandinij'; bought: Quaritch, 28.vi.1949.

Compare: John Rylands University Library, Manchester, R52187 (Venice, 1516); De Marinis, 674bis, 1320, 1406D; De Marinis, *Fürstenberg*, pp. 90–1; Hobson, *Legature bolognesi*, no. 24; Brera, no. 58.

308　Two bindings possibly made in Bologna, c. 1541

M T Cicero, *De philosophia* [and] Paulus Manutius, *Scholia quibus Ciceronis philosophia … corrigitur … explanatur*, 2 vols, Venice: Paulus Manutius, Aldi F., 1541. 8vo.

168 × 100 × 27/25 mm.　　　　　　　　　　　　　　　　　　　　　(P 963) Davis 792–793

Dark brown goatskin over paste boards, tooled in gold, with blind lines; interlacing fillets forming a border with, on the upper cover: .M.T.C. .PHI./ PARS .I. (PARS.II.); in the centre a bust of a poet [?representing Cicero], laureate, to the left. Traces of four pairs of ties. Edges: plain.

　Sewn on three, probably split, alum-tawed supports, laced in, showing as raised bands on the spine, tooled in gold with a line; two false bands (in vol. 2: taken through the joint), tooled in gold with dashes; six compartments, tooled in blind with lines and in gold with leaf tools. Endbands: single with a bead; primary sewing over alum-tawed cores (laced in), tied down; secondary sewing of pale blue and yellow silk.

　Endleaves: white paper pastedowns and one free leaf conjugate with the pastedown, at both ends.

　Repairs: small repairs at corners.

PROVENANCE:　Lardanchet (Catalogue 44, 1950, *49*, pl.; sold: 22.vi.1950).
REFERENCES:　Hobson, *Humanists*, p. 125, note 165.
LITERATURE:　Hobson, *Humanists*, pp. 123–5, compare fig. 97.

309　A binding made in Bologna by the 'Pflug and Ebeleben binder' for Damian Pflug, 1543.

[M T Cicero, *Orationes. Volumen secundum*], Venice: Aldi filii, February 1541 [title-page missing]. 8vo.

166 × 102 × 27 mm.　　　　　　　　　　　　　　　　　　　　　　(P984) Davis 795

Red-brown goatskin over paste boards, tooled in gold, with blind lines, to a design of interlacing ribbons, formed by lines and gouges, with small fleuron, leaf and knot tools; in the centre of the upper cover: DA/MIANVS/ PFLVGK/ CIC. ORAT./ VOLVM./ .:II:. ; on the lower cover: .XX./ FEBRVARII/ .M.D.XLIII./ BONO/NIAE. Traces of two pairs of ties. Edges of boards: tooled in gold with lines, dashes and roundels. Edges: gilt.

　Sewn on three split alum-tawed supports, laced in, showing as raised bands on the spine, tooled in gold with a line; four false bands alternating with the sewing supports, tooled in gold with dashes; eight compartments, tooled in blind with lines and in gold with small tools; spine repaired, original spine strip only partly preserved (covering five bands and six compartments); two tail compartments: renewed. Endbands: single with a bead; primary sewing over alum-tawed cores (cut off), tied down; secondary sewing of blue and pink silk.

　Endleaves: parchment pastedowns, at both ends; at the front: one free white paper leaf pasted onto parchment stub (conjugate with pastedown); at the end: one free paper leaf conjugate with a stub, parchment stub conjugate with pastedown.

　Repairs: spine; top of spine at covers; possibly tailband renewed.

PROVENANCE: Damian Pflug (bought in Bologna, 20 February 1543); on endleaf in manuscript: 'Summo jure possidet/ hunc librum/ Johannes Albertus Samesius/ Hoingensis./ Anno 1661'; in a different hand: 'Summoque etiam jure possidet hunc librum orationum Johannes Georgius ... Hoingensis'; on verso of endleaf in manuscript: 'J.P. B(?)bs 1817 Donum Steubingii'; manuscript notes; Bethmann; E P Goldschmidt; Lucius Wilmerding (sold: Parke-Bernet, 5.iii.1951, *173*).

REFERENCES: Goldschmidt, no. 198, pls lxxii–lxxiii, p. 272, no. 2; Grolier Club, *Exhibition*, 1937, no. 104a; De Marinis, 1396; Romme, *Book Collector*, 1969, pp. 41–2, notes 137–8.

LITERATURE: Foot, *Davis*, I, pp. 299–307 (and literature cited there); Needham, *Twelve Centuries*, no. 52; Hobson, 'Bookbinding in Bologna', pp. 166–70; Hobson, *Legature bolognesi*, pp. 23–6; see also Davis 796, 839, 798 (nos. 310–12 below).

Note: Damian Pflug, a native of Meissen; studied at Leipzig University: 1535; travelled to Paris and Bologna, where he was registered at the university in 1542; went to Siena: 1544; returned to Bologna: 1544–5, thence to Rome: 1546; back in Germany, became councillor to King Ferdinand; created baron.

371

310 *A binding made in Bologna by the 'Pflug and Ebeleben binder' for Nikolaus von Ebeleben, 1543*

M T Cicero, *De philosophia volumen secundum*, Venice: Paulus Manutius Aldi F., May 1541. 8vo.

166 × 100 × 36 mm.   (P 983) Davis 796

Dark brown goatskin over paste boards, tooled in gold, with blind lines, to a design of interlacing ribbons formed by lines and gouges, fleurons in the corners; stylized flowers, fleuron and knot tools; in the centre of the upper cover: .N./ DE/ EBELE/BEN/ CIC./ DE PHIL./ VOL./ .:III:.; on the lower cover: .XX./ IVLII/ M.D.XL/III. BONO/NI/AE. Traces of two pairs of ties. Edges of boards: tooled in gold with lines, dashes and roundels. Edges: gilt.

Rebacked with the original spine strip preserved. Sewn on three split alum-tawed supports, laced in, showing as raised bands on the spine, tooled in gold with a line; four false bands alternating with the sewing supports, tooled in gold with dashes; eight compartments, tooled in gold, with blind lines. Endbands: single with a bead; primary sewing over alum-tawed cores (cut off), tied down; secondary sewing of pink and blue silk. Top and tail of spine renewed.

Endleaves: white paper pastedowns, at both ends; at the front: one free leaf conjugate with the pastedown.

Repairs: rebacked (but probably not resewn); small repairs at covers.

PROVENANCE: Nikolaus von Ebeleben; Bethmann; E P Goldschmidt; Lucius Wilmerding (sold: Parke-Bernet, 5.iii.1951, *172*).
REFERENCES: Goldschmidt, no. 198, pls lxii–lxiii, p. 273, no. 4; Grolier Club, *Exhibition*, 1937, no. 104b; Romme, *Book Collector*, 1969, pp. 41–2, notes 137, 139.
LITERATURE: See Davis 795 (no. 309 above; and literature cited there); see also Davis 839, 798 (nos. 311, 312 below).
Note: Nikolaus von Ebeleben was a cousin of Damian Pflug (see Davis 795); he studied at Erfurt; travelled to Paris: 1540–1, to Bologna (registered at the university: 1542), to Ferrara: 1546, back to Bologna (till 1548); returned to Germany: 1549, became a canon of Meissen, an ambassador to the Elector August, went bankrupt and died in 1579.

311 *A binding made in Bologna by the 'Pflug and Ebeleben binder', probably for Nikolaus von Ebeleben, 1544*

M Cato [and others], *Libri de re rustica*, Venice: Hearedes Aldi et Andreae Soceri, December 1533. 4to.

215 × 134 × 42 mm.   (P 1009) Davis 839

Brown goatskin (or possibly hair sheep) over paste boards, tooled in gold to a design of interlacing ribbons formed by lines and gouges, fleurons in the corners, open curling leaf tools, small leaf tools, solid fleurons, floral tools and knot tools; in the centre of the upper cover: RVS/TICAE/ REI SCRI/PTORES; on the lower cover: BO/NONI/AE/ ANNO/ M.D.XLIIII./ XXVII./ IVN.; the centre of the upper cover has been re-tooled. Traces of two pairs of ties. Edges of boards: tooled in gold with lines, dashes and roundels. Edges: gilt (over red staining) and gauffered to a knot-work pattern.

310   311

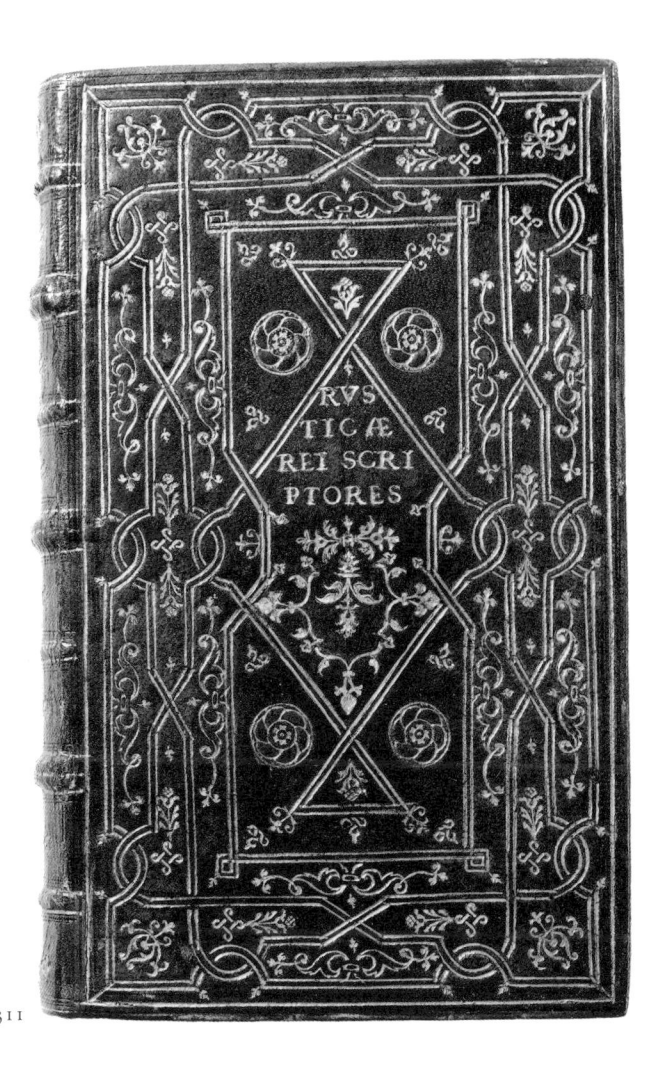

Sewn on three (invisible) supports, laced in, showing as raised bands on the spine, tooled in gold with a line; four false bands alternating with the sewing supports, tooled in gold with dashes; eight compartments, tooled in gold, with blind lines. Endbands: single with a bead; traces of primary sewing over leather cores (cut off), tied down; secondary sewing of blue-green and white silk, tied down.

Endleaves: renewed; white paper pastedowns and two free conjugate paper leaves and a stub conjugate with the pastedown, at both ends.

PROVENANCE: (?)Nikolaus von Ebeleben; on title-page in manuscript: 'Froemmiehen. Nro: 8'; in a different hand: 'August/ Si times Mortem Christus vita est'; manuscript note about this edition; J-L Techener (sold: Paris, 1887, II, *111*); T Seligman, Newton Hall, Cambridge (book plate; sold: Sotheby's, 3.v.1951, *685*, pl.).

REFERENCES: Goldschmidt, p. 273, no. 7; Hobson, *French and Italian*, Appendix C; De Marinis, 1390; Romme, *Book Collector*, 1969, p. 42, note 140; Foot, *Davis*, I, no. 23.

LITERATURE: See Davis 795 (no. 309 above; and literature cited there); see also Davis 796 (no. 310 above), 798 (no. 312 below).

373

312 *A binding made in Bologna by the 'Pflug and Ebeleben binder' for Ranuccio Farnese, 1544*

P Terentius Afer, *Comoediae*, Lyon: S Gryphius, 1544. 16mo.

118 × 73 × 17 mm.   (P 1277) Davis 798

Brown goatskin over paste boards, tooled in gold with intersecting lines, small knot tools, fleurons and floral tools; in the centre: gouges forming a quadrilobe with on the upper cover: TE/RENTI/VS and on the lower cover: RA./ FARN./ ARC. NEAP./ DES/SIG. Traces of two pairs of ties. Edges of boards: tooled in gold with a line, dashes and roundels. Edges: gilt.

Sewn on three split alum-tawed supports, laced in, showing as raised bands on the spine, tooled in gold with a line; four false bands alternating with the sewing supports, tooled in gold with dashes; eight compartments, tooled in gold. Endbands: single with a bead (restored); primary sewing over (?)cord cores (cut off), tied down; remnants of secondary sewing of blue and white silk.

Endleaves: white paper pastedowns at both ends; at the front: one free leaf conjugate with the pastedown; at the end: one free paper leaf.

Repairs: at endbands.

PROVENANCE: Ranuccio Farnese, archbishop designate of Naples; Fairfax Murray (on pastedown of upper cover: '530'); J R Abbey (book plate; 'J.A. 4681./ 17.1.1950'; sold: Sotheby's 23.vi.1965, *648*).

REFERENCES: Davies, *Fairfax Murray*, II, no. 530 (see also no. 529); De Marinis, 1359; Foot, *Davis* I, p. 303, note 33.
LITERATURE: Davis 795 (no. 309 above; and literature cited there); see also Davis 796, 839 (nos. 310, 311 above).
Note: Ranuccio Farnese (b. 1530), son of Pier Luigi Farnese, grandson of Pope Paul III; prior of Venice: 1543; archbishop of Naples: 1544; cardinal: 1545.

---

313 *A binding possibly made in northern Italy, possibly Bologna or Piacenza, for Apollonio Filareto, c. 1545*

P Vettori, *Explicationes suarum in Catonem, Varronem, Columellam Castigationum*, Lyon: S Gryphius, 1542 [and] G Merula, *Georgii Alexandrini enarrationes vocum priscarum in libris de re rustica*, Lyon: S Gryphius, 1541. 8vo.

173 × 110 × 22 mm.   (P 938) Davis 797

Olive-brown goatskin over paste boards, tooled in gold, with blind lines, to a panel design; fleurons at the outer corners, an outer border with small ivy-leaf tools and on the upper cover: P. VICT; an inner border formed by intersecting lines, with small leaf tools; fleurs-de-lis at the corners of the panel; arabesque corner pieces and in the centre of the upper cover: the device of Apollonio Filareto with the motto: ESTE PROCVL; in the centre of the lower cover: curving arabesque tools around APOL/LONII/ PHILA/RETI. Traces of four pairs of ties. Edges of boards: tooled in blind with dashes. Edges: gilt and gauffered to a knot-work pattern.

Sewn on three split alum-tawed supports, laced in, showing as raised bands on the spine, tooled in gold with a line; four false bands, alternating with the sewing supports, tooled in gold with dashes; eight compartments, tooled in blind with lines and in gold with a star tool. Endbands: single with a bead; primary sewing over cord cores (laced in), tied down; secondary sewing of beige-white and blue silk.

Endleaves: white paper pastedowns and one free leaf conjugate with the pastedown, at both ends.

PROVENANCE: Apollonio Filareto; ownership inscription on title-page: erased; Fairfax Murray (on pastedown: printed labels with the numbers: '567' and '598'); bought: A Rau, 1.vi.1949, no. 938A–B.
REFERENCES: Davies, *Fairfax Murray*, II, nos. 567, 598; [Paris, Bibliothèque nationale], *Catalogue de l'exposition du livre italien* (introduction: S de Ricci), Bois-Colombes, 1926, no. 938; G D Hobson, *Maioli*, p. 118, list no. ix; *The Italian Book*, no. 268; De Marinis, 826; Romme, *Book Collector*, 1969, p. 41, note 134; Hobson, *Apollo and Pegasus*, p. 93, no. 11.
LITERATURE: Nixon, *Pierpont Morgan Library*, no. 8; Hobson, *Apollo and Pegasus*, pp. 91–5; Needham, *Twelve Centuries*, no. 48; Hobson, 'Italian sixteenth-century bookbindings', no. 4.
Same tools on: De Marinis, 819, 820.
Compare: Brera, no. 40.
Note: Apollonio Filareto, secretary to Pope Paul III: 1530s; private secretary to Pier Luigi Farnese: 1537–47; spent time in Rome and from 1545 to 47 in the duchy of Parma and Piacenza.

314 *A binding made in Rome by Marcantonio Guillery, c. 1545*

Dante Alighieri, *La Comedia ... con ... espositione di Alessandro Vellutello*, Venice: F Marcolini for A Vellutello, June 1544. 4to.

239 × 160 × 54 mm. (P918) Davis 837

Brown goatskin (or possibly hair sheep) over paste boards, tooled in gold, with blind lines, to a panel design; small leaf tools at the corners, open entwined s-shaped tools in the outer border; three borders, filled with solid 'iron-work' tools and solid fleurons; solid lotus tools at the corners of the panel; in the centre panel: an arabesque block (upside down on the lower cover), with in the centre, tooled in gold: IL/ DANTE and two small curved tools. Traces of four pairs of ties. Edges: gilt.

Sewn on four split alum-tawed supports, laced in straight, showing as raised bands on the spine, tooled in gold with a line; five compartments, tooled in blind with lines and tooled in gold. Endbands: double with a bead; primary sewing over alum-tawed main cores (laced in), tied down; secondary sewing of pink and blue silk, tied down at both ends; cord crowning cores.

Endleaves: white paper pastedowns and one free leaf conjugate with the pastedown, at both ends.

PROVENANCE: Francisci Riccardi de Vernaccia (book plate); Gustavus C Galetti of Florence (library

315

	stamp on title-page); on endleaf in manuscript: 'Gamba Nº 318'; Landau (book plate with: no. 47681; sold: Sotheby's, 12.vii.1948, *41*, pl.).
REFERENCES:	Hobson, *Apollo and Pegasus*, pp. 86, 89, no. 3, 94, note 76.
LITERATURE:	Hobson, *Apollo and Pegasus*, pp. 86–91, 94–5 (and literature cited there); see also Davis 838 (no. 315 below).
Identical binding:	Fitzwilliam Museum, Cambridge (Petrarch, *Opere*, Venice, 1552) [not in Hobson].
Note:	Marcantonio Guillery: bookseller and binder in Rome, active from the mid-1540s to the mid-1560s.

---

315 *A binding made in Rome by Marcantonio Guillery, c. 1548*

P Bembo, *Rime*, Rome: V & L Dorici, October 1548. 4to.

231 × 148 × 18 mm. (P 864) Davis 838

Brown goatskin over paste boards, tooled in gold, with blind lines, to a panel design; different fleurons and curving tools at the corners of the concentric panels; stylized flowers and pomegranate tools in the borders; corner curls, solid curving tools, leaf tools and small dolphin tools, with in the centre a coat of arms (a ram between three six-pointed stars) with the initials F M; on the upper cover: lettered on top of the original tooling: LE DVC DE/NIVERNOIS. Traces of four pairs of ties. Edges: gilt.

Sewn on four, possibly split (invisible) supports, laced in, showing as raised bands on the spine, tooled in gold with a line; five compartments, tooled in gold with a small flower and in blind with lines. Endbands: single; (?)primary sewing over (possibly) cord cores (cut off), tied down; secondary sewing of blue silk, tied down (much covered in dirt and leather dressing).

Endleaves: later: white paper pastedowns and one free leaf conjugate with the pastedowns and one free paper leaf tipped onto the text block, at both ends.

Small repairs.

PROVENANCE: F M; duc de Nivernois; on pastedown of lower cover in manuscript: 'Sidney Sale –June 28 – 1898/ 6.10 Ellis'; R C Fisher (sold: Sotheby's, 21.v.1906. *73*, pl.); Dyson Perrins (sold: Sotheby's, 17.vi.1946, *40*, pl.).
REFERENCES: G D Hobson, *Maioli*, p. 127, no. 27; Hobson, *Apollo and Pegasus*, p. 86, p. 89, no 8.
LITERATURE: Hobson, *Apollo and Pegasus*, pp. 86–9, 94, 104–5 (and literature cited there); Hobson, 'Italian sixteenth-century bookbindings', no. 13; see also Davis 837 (no. 314 above).

316 *A binding made in Rome by Maestro Luigi for Giovanni Battista Grimaldi, c. 1545–7*

G Capella, *Commentarii di M Galeazzo Capella delle cose fatte per la restituzione di Francesco Sforza secondo duca di Milano*, Venice: G Giolito de' Ferrari, October 1539. 4to.

212 × 152 × 17 mm.   (P 240) Davis 766

Red goatskin over paste boards, tooled in gold and blind to a panel design with fleur-de-lis tools at the corners, a wide border filled with interlaced half-circles and small crosses, with larger fleur-de-lis tools in the corners; in the centre solid curl tools above and beneath a centre medallion showing Apollo driving his chariot up Mount Helicon, on which stands Pegasus; on the upper cover: COMENT. DI/ GALEAZZO CAPELLA. Edges of boards: tooled in blind with a line and in gold with dashes. Edges: gilt and lightly gauffered with a row of dots.

Sewn on three split alum-tawed supports, laced in, showing as raised bands on the spine, tooled in gold with a line; four false bands alternating with the sewing supports, tooled in gold with dashes; eight compartments, tooled in gold with a fleur-de-lis. Endbands: single with a bead; primary sewing over cord cores (cut off), tied down; secondary sewing of white and blue silk.

Endleaves: white paper pastedowns at both ends; at the front: one free leaf conjugate with the pastedown; at the end: one free paper leaf (probably conjugate with a stub pasted beneath the pastedown).

Repairs: at top and tail compartment of spine; at corners.

PROVENANCE: G B Grimaldi; J-C Brunet (sold: Paris, 20.iv.1868, *680*); B Quaritch (Catalogue 1889, no. 45, pl. 6); H Yates Thompson (book plate; sold: Sotheby's, 18.viii.1941, *176*, pl.).
REFERENCES: Quaritch, *Facsimiles*, no. 6 (pl. 14); Fumagalli, iv, p. 392, no. 12; G D Hobson, *Maioli*, p. 144, no. xx ; Romme, *Book Collector*, 1969, p. 41, note 136; De Marinis, 754; Hobson, *Apollo and Pegasus*, p. 140, no. 28.

316

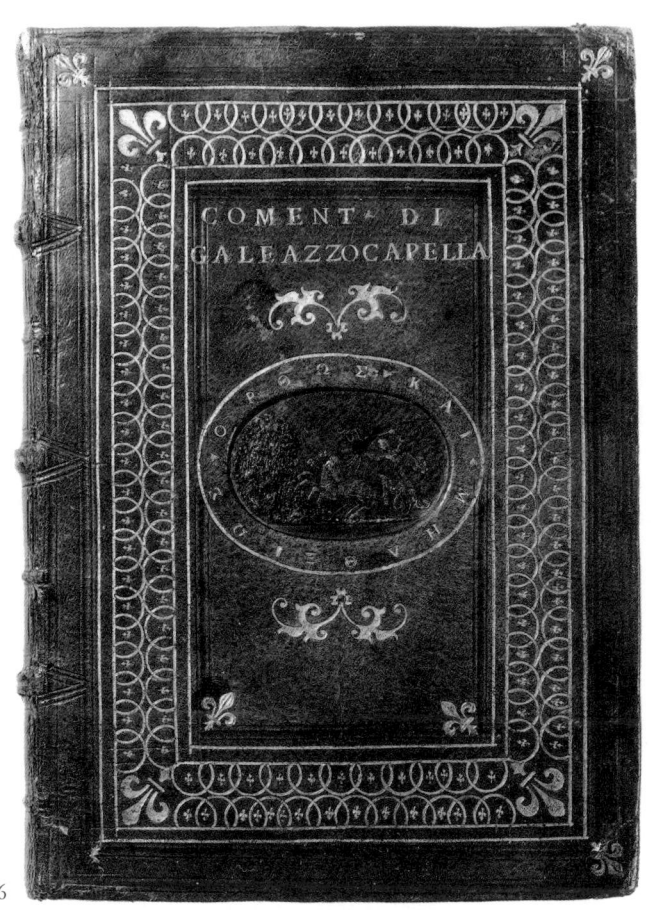

LITERATURE:	Bignami Odier, pp. 289-9; Hobson, *Apollo and Pegasus,* especially pp. 49–76; Hobson, 'Italian sixteenth-century bookbindings', no. 7.
Note:	Giovanni Battista Grimaldi, Genoese nobleman (c. 1524–c. 1612) owner of the Apollo and Pegasus *impresa*.
	Maestro Luigi, binder in Rome, also worked for the Vatican; occurs in a list of personnel working for the Vatican library between 1537 and 1550: he may well have started binding for the Vatican: c. 1542 and continued until 1565.

317 *A binding made in Venice, c. 1545–50*

M T Cicero, *Orationes. Volumen iii*, Lyon: S Gryphius, 1545. 8vo.

173 × 111 × 26 mm. (P 1164) Davis 803

Black goatskin over paste boards, tooled in gold, with blind lines, to a panel design with leaf tools at the corners, a border filled with arabesque tools; fleurons in the corners; in the centre: a large shield containing Fortuna standing on a dolphin; on the upper cover: .OR./ .M.T.C./ .VOL./ .T.; on the lower cover: .P./ MAR./ THO. RAG. Traces of four pairs of ties. Edges: gilt and gauffered to a knot-work pattern.

317

318

Sewn on three (?)tanned leather supports, laced in, showing as bands on the spine; four compartments, tooled in gold with lines and in blind with lines and a roll. Endbands: single with a bead; primary sewing over cord cores (laced in), tied down; secondary sewing of cream and grey silk.

Endleaves: white paper pastedowns and one free leaf conjugate with the pastedown, at both ends. Manuscript waste visible beneath pastedowns.

Small repairs.

PROVENANCE: Thomas Rag(?); on pastedown of lower cover in manuscript: 'perorare secondo l'autico nostro costume'; bought: Sotheby's, 8.xi.1954, *86* (pl.).
LITERATURE: De Marinis, 2257 (identical binding on vol. II of Cicero's *Orationes* = Sotheby's, 27.iii.1956, *431*, where it has been suggested that the inscription on the lower cover stands for: Per Maestro Thomaso Ragusano).
Same tools on: Malaguzzi, *Il Vercellese*, pl. 48 (p. xxxii).
Compare: Fitzwilliam Museum, Cambridge, 5H17A (Paris, 1496).

318 *A binding made in Venice, c. 1547*

[Andrea Baiardo, *Libro d'arme e d'amore nomato Philogine*], [Venice: F Bindoni & M Pasini, 1547] [Lacks prelims, gatherings A, M1, M7–8 (stub of M7 remains)]. 8vo.

154 × 105 × 15 mm. (P 1279) Davis 802

Grey-brown paper over paste boards, with on the upper cover a large printed woodcut depicting two angels holding a vase of lilies and a sheet. Edges: plain.

319

Unsupported sewing (no visible sewing supports), through four sewing holes; smooth spine; some later repairs. No endbands. Endleaves: none.

PROVENANCE: Bought: Sotheby's, 10.xii.1957, *460* (pl.).
REFERENCES: Romme, *Book Collector*, 1969, p. 42, note 141.
LITERATURE: Goldschmidt, p. 74; Needham, *Twelve Centuries*, no. 45; Foot, *Studies*, pp. 280–5 (and literature cited there).
Note: Although most Italian early woodcut paper wrappers or bindings were made in Ferrara in the late 15th and early 16th centuries, they were also produced in Venice during the first half of the 16th century. The same woodcut occurs on the title-page of Bernardus de Gordonio, *Lilio de medicina*, Seville: Meinardus Ungut and Stanislaus Polonus, 18 April 1495.

---

319 *A binding of the (?)mid-sixteenth century*

Jacobus de Clusa, *Tractatus per optimus de animabus exutis a corporibus*, Passau: [B Mayr & C Stahel], September 1482. 4to.

189 × 149 × 8 mm.   (P 1498) Davis 804

Red goatskin over paste boards, tooled in blind and gold, and decorated with yellow and silver paint (now oxidized). A wide border filled with foliage-round-staff tools and flower tools (in blind and decorated with silver paint); in the corners medallion portraits of Alexander the Great, wearing a helmet, bust to right, lettered: ALEXANDER MAG. Open fleuron and curving leaf tools in the corners of the centre panel; open curving leaf tools, decorated with silver paint, a semis of three-dot tools (all in blind) and in the centre surrounded by maple leaves: an oval medallion, impressed in gold, showing the fall of Phaeton with Eridanus, the river god, seated. Corners of panel: painted yellow. Edges: plain.

Rebacked and probably resewn on three flat tapes, laced in; smooth spine, tooled in blind. Endbands: none.

Endleaves: probably later: white paper pastedowns and one free white paper leaf, at both ends.

Repairs: rebacked; repairs at corners of covers.

PROVENANCE: W H Corfield (book plate; sold: Sotheby's, 21.xi.1904, *420*, pl.); Dyson Perrins (sold: Sotheby's, 11.iii.1947, *639*); J R Abbey (book plate; 'J.A.3563/ 11.3.1947'); bought: International Antiquariat Amsterdam, 1.vi.1967, *120*.
REFERENCES: Hobson, *Humanists*, p. 214.
Compare: Molinier, II, no. 747; Hobson, 'Italian sixteenth-century bookbindings', no. 16.
Note: Hobson doubts the authenticity of the plaquettes.

320 *A binding made in Venice in the mid-sixteenth century*

Torellus Sarayna, *De origine et amplitudine civitatis Veronae*, Verona: A Putelleto, 1540; woodcuts. fol.

316 × 215 × 22 mm. (P 1322) Davis 865

Dark brown goatskin over paste boards, tooled in gold, with blind lines, to a panel design, with fleurons at the corners, double-outlined curls in the corners; in the centre: two fillets forming two intersecting squares, resulting in a star, containing a shield with the painted arms of the Grimani family; on the upper cover: ANTIQVITA. DI. VERONA., within a frame formed like a 'tabula ansata'. Traces of four pairs of ties. Edges: gilt and lightly gauffered with a row of dots.

Sewn on three (?)split alum-tawed supports, laced in, showing as raised bands on the spine, tooled in gold with a line; four false bands alternating with the sewing supports, tooled in gold with dashes; eight compartments, tooled in blind with lines and curving acorn tools. Endbands: double with a bead; primary sewing over (?)leather cores (now cut off), tied down; secondary sewing of pale blue and white silk.

Endleaves: white paper pastedowns, at both ends, at the front: a stub; at the end: one free paper leaf conjugate with a stub before the last section.

Repairs: at top and tail of spine and at the joint; small repairs at corners.

PROVENANCE: Grimani; beneath the colophon in manuscript: 'Jacobi Antonij Z[?T]orica et amicorum'; J R Abbey (book plate; 'J.A.6842/ 20:11:1957'; sold: Sotheby's, 21.vi.1967, *2151* pl.); M Breslauer (sold: 1967).
REFERENCES: De Marinis, 2124.
Same tools on: De Marinis, 1812.
Compare: De Marinis, 2162.

ANTIQVITA·DI·VERONA

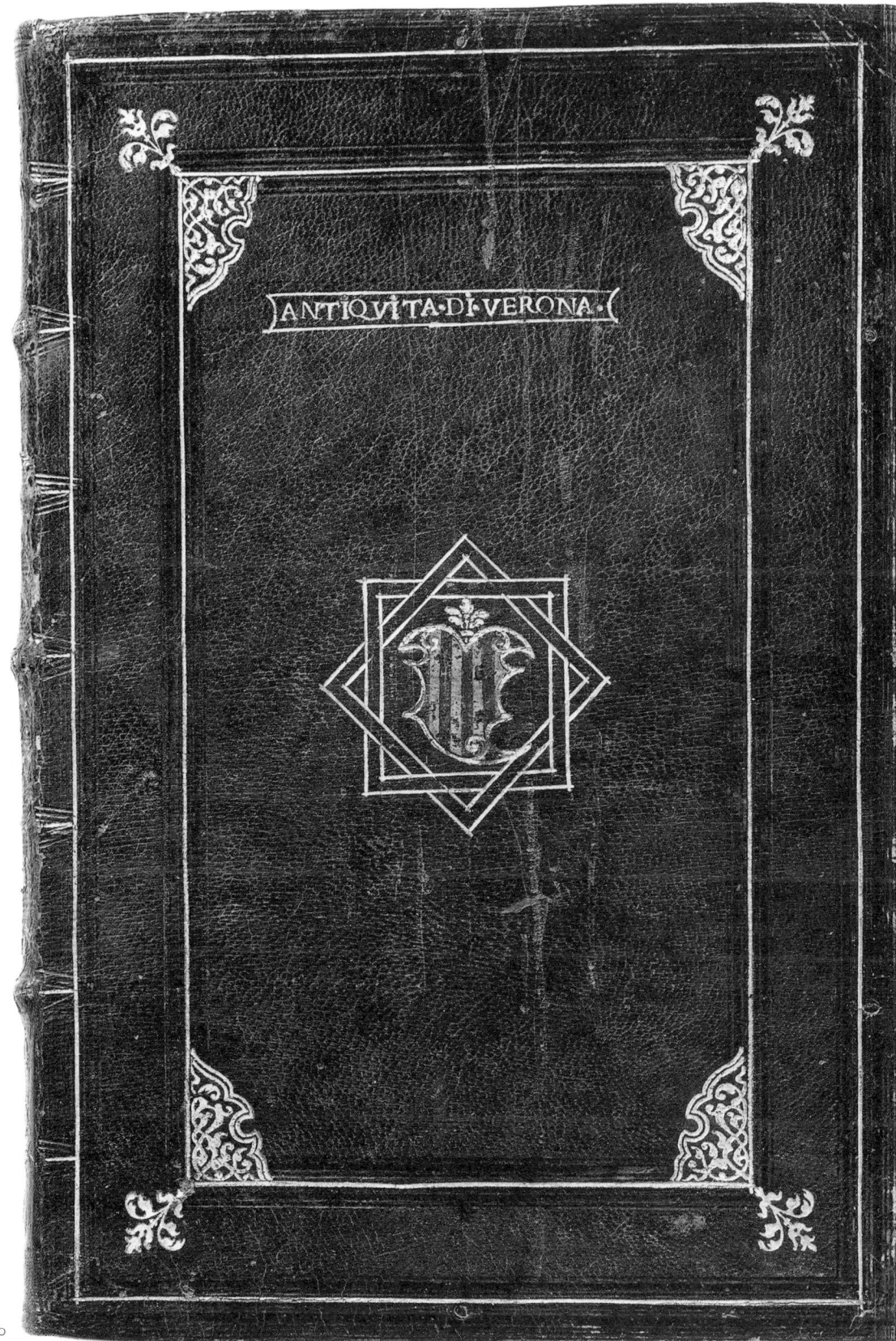

321 *A binding made c. 1550*

P Virgilius Maro, *La Georgica di Virgilio… trad. per B Daniello*, Venice: G Griffio, 1549 [and] Bernardino Daniello, *La Poetica*, Venice: G A di Nicolini da Sabio, 1536; woodcuts and woodcut initials; ruled in red. 4to.

206 × 160 × 28 mm.   (P 1124) Davis 785

Limp parchment, tooled in gold with two lines along the border; a stylized flower at the corners; in the centre: an oval surrounded by a wreath containing an *impresa* showing a hammer striking an anvil, with the motto: ICTA NITESCIT. On upper cover in manuscript (ink): 'Georgica di Virgilio in lengua Italiana'. Traces of two pairs of ties. Yapp edges. Edges: plain gilt.

    Sewn on five split alum-tawed supports, cut off at the joint; smooth spine, tooled in gold with five 'bands' filled with a curving leaf roll or pallet; stylized flower tools in the four 'compartments'; in the top 'compartment' in manuscript in ink: '30[?2]39'. Endbands: remnants only: brown and white silk over parchment slips, (laced through the covers at an angle), traces of tie-downs.

322

Endleaves: white paper pastedowns and one free paper leaf with a stub pasted beneath the pastedown, at both ends.

PROVENANCE: L S Olschki (ex-libris; no. '18951'; in manuscript: 'L. S. Olschki, Firenze, 23 Giugno 1919'); in manuscript: 'Giovanni Manzi, Via Serragli 68, Firenze'; bought: Sotheby's, 23.vi.1953, *296* (pl.).

322 *A binding possibly made in Rome or Bologna, c. 1550*

I da Lezze, *Le ceremonie dei monaci Celestini*, Bologna: A Giaccarelli, 1549; woodcut title-page and initials [and] *Confiteor notato* [with music]. 8vo.

160 × 105 × 21 mm.   (P 774) Davis 805

Brown goatskin or sheep (badly rubbed) over paste boards, tooled in blind with traces of gold leaf. In each corner a roundel surrounded by small curling tools, containing (top, left to right:) the arms of the Benedictine order and a crescent above two stars [possibly the arms of the abbot general of the order at the time of the issue of this book]; (bottom, left to right:) F.P.C. [?Fundator Papa Coelestinus] and on the upper cover: C.O.C. [?Ceremonie Ordo Celestini]; on the lower cover: O.S.B. [Ordo Sancti Benedicti]; solid curling tools, ornamental and flower tools; in the centre of both covers a medallion portrait of a man, facing right, draped bust with tunic. Lettered along the long sides: on the upper cover:

CERI/MONIE; on the lower cover: CELE/STINE. Traces of two pairs of ties. Edges: gilt and gauffered.

Sewn on three split tanned leather supports, laced in, showing as raised bands on the spine, tooled with a line; four compartments, tooled in blind with lines and a fleuron. Endbands: single with a bead; primary sewing over cord cores (laced in at an angle), tied down; secondary sewing of pink and blue silk.

Endleaves: white paper pastedowns and two free conjugate paper leaves and one free leaf conjugate with the pastedown, at both ends.

PROVENANCE: (?)Benedictine monastery; on pastedown in manuscript: 'In pacie mio (?)'; C E Rappaport, Librairie Ancienne, Rome (ticket); E P Goldschmidt (book plate; Catalogue 73, no. 98; sold: 1.iii.1944).
REFERENCES: Goldschmidt, no. 212; De Marinis, 829; Hobson, *Humanists*, p. 218, no. 9d.
Possibly same tools on: Davis 776, 739 (nos. 291, 292 above).

323 *A binding made in Padua or possibly in Bologna for Matheus Herbrot, 1550*

Justinian I, Emperor, *Institutiones iuris civilis*, Venice: Hearedes L A Iuntae, December 1543; woodcuts. 8vo.

174 × 119 × 46 mm. (P 821) Davis 806

Brown goatskin over paste boards, tooled in gold, with blind lines, to a panel design with fleurons in the corners and in the centre of the upper cover the arms of Matheus Herbrot [or Hörbrott]; on the lower cover a cartouche with: MA/THEV/HERB/ROT/.A. On the upper cover: IN STITVTIONES. Traces of two pairs of ties. Edges: stained blue.

Sewn on three split alum-tawed supports, laced in, showing as raised bands on the spine, tooled in gold with a line; four false bands alternating with the sewing supports, tooled in gold with dashes; eight compartments, tooled in blind with lines; parchment manuscript spine lining. Endbands: single with a bead; primary sewing over (?)cord cores (laced in), tied down; remnants of secondary sewing in pink and blue silk.

Endleaves: white paper pastedowns and one free leaf conjugate with the pastedown, at both ends.

PROVENANCE: Matheus Herbrot or Hörbrott (on title-page in manuscript: '1550 Matheus Herbrot Augustanus'; a manuscript note giving Matheus Herbrot's date of birth as 3 April 1532); numerous annotations on endleaves and in margins; on endleaf in manuscript: 'Hans Jacob [...?] 1667'; on title-page in manuscript: 'Jos: Hurth 1777'; E P Goldschmidt (Catalogue 75, no. 84; sold: 20.ix.1944).
REFERENCES: Goldschmidt, no. 209; De Marinis, 2499bis.
Same tool on: Hobson, *Legature bolognesi*, no. 39.
Compare: BL, C.48.b.19 (similar binding for Matheus Herbrot).
Similar cartouche on: Folger Catalogue, p. 196; Hobson, *Legature bolognesi*, no. 57.
Note: A Matheus Herbrot matriculated at the University of Padua in August 1547; the arms (a lion counterchanged) are those of the family of Hörbrott.

324 *A binding made in (?)Rome or Bologna, c. 1550*

C Plinius Secundus, *Historiae mundi libri xxxvii*, Basel: Froben, 1545. fol.

374 × 240 × 95 mm.   (P 1323) Davis 867

Red goatskin over paste boards, tooled in gold, with a few blind lines, to a design formed by intersecting lines and gouges; fleurons; in the centre, surrounded by a circle made of small rope-work and leaf tools: a six-pointed star. Edges: gilt and gauffered to a pattern of large vases, decorated with paint; on the tail edge: PLI/NIVS.

Sewn on four split alum-tawed supports, laced into slots in the edges of the boards, showing as raised bands on the spine, tooled in gold with a line; five compartments, tooled in gold with gouges and lines. Endbands: single with a bead; primary sewing over leather cores (now cut off), tied down; remnants of secondary sewing of pink silk.

Endleaves: white paper pastedowns conjugate with a stub after the first and before the last section, and one free paper leaf conjugate with a stub after the first and before the last section, at both ends; at the front: a separate free paper leaf tipped onto the free endleaf.

Repairs: at top and tail of spine and at corners.

PROVENANCE: On A 2: a manuscript note by Simon de las Cuevas, dated 29 March 1619; on endleaf: manuscript note dated 'Sep. 16 1754'; Sotheby's, 20.vi.1960, *227*; J R Abbey (book plate; 'J.A. 7040/ 20:6:1960'; sold: Sotheby's, 21.vi.1967, *2096*).
REFERENCES: De Marinis, 3055.
Compare: Walters Art Gallery, Baltimore, 8912 (Petrarch, 1547); Mazal, pl. 105.

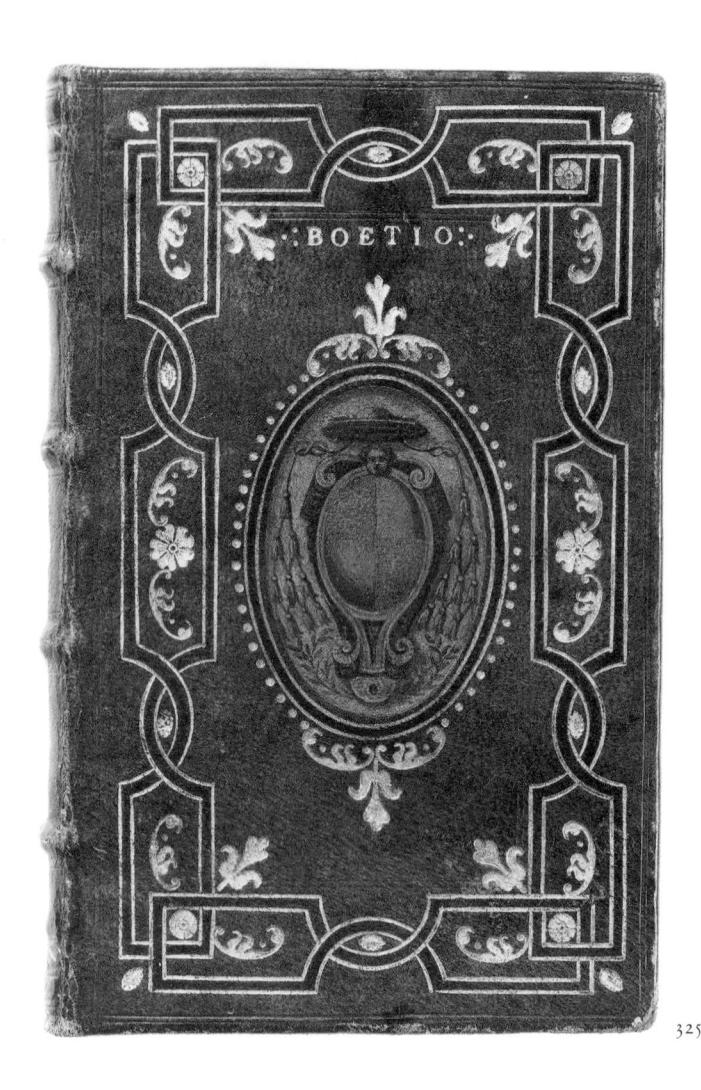

325   *A binding possibly made in Rome, for Cardinal Fulvio Corneo, c. 1551–3*

A M T S Boethius, *Di consolatione philosophica volgare*, Venice: M Sessa, December 1531. 8vo.

155 × 100 × 18 mm.   (P 1142) Davis 807

Red goatskin over paste boards, tooled in gold with blind lines, to a panel design with intersecting lines and gouges forming a border, decorated with black paint, border filled with leaf and flower tools; fleurons in the corners and in the centre a cartouche with on the upper cover the painted arms (quarterly azure and gules) of a cardinal; on the lower cover: two cherub's heads and FVL.COR./ CARD. ET/ EP.PER.; on upper cover: BOETIO. Edges of boards: tooled in gold with dashes. Edges: gilt and lightly gauffered to a rope-work pattern.

   Sewn on four (?)cords, laced in, showing as raised bands on the spine, tooled in gold with a line; two kettle stitch bands, tooled in gold with dashes; seven compartments, tooled in gold with leaves and fleurons, and in blind with lines. Endbands: single with a bead; pink and blue silk over leather cores (cut off), no visible tie-downs.

Endleaves: white paper pastedowns and one free leaf conjugate with the pastedown and one free paper leaf conjugate with a stub after the first and before the last section, at both ends.

Repairs: small repairs to upper cover.

PROVENANCE: Fulvio Corneo; on blank leaf preceding title-page in manuscript: 'Sum Gherar: de Atanasiis et amicor[um] Lugdunensis'; in a different hand: 'Odi profanum vulgus'; Jesuit College at Perpin (on title-page in a different hand: 'Colleg. Perpin (?). Societ. Jesu Catal. adj.'); N Rauch (sold: 29.iii.1954, *110*, pl.).

Note: Fulvio Corneo (1517–1583), nephew of Pope Julius III; bishop of Perugia: 1550–3; cardinal: 1551; according to Chacon (vol. III, col. 769) the arms on Davis 807 are not his arms.

326   *A binding made in Venice, c. 1552*

F Petrarca, *Il Petrarcha, con l'espositione d'Alessandro Vellutello*, Venice: D Giglio, 1552. 8vo.

155 × 103 × 40 mm.   (P 1520) Davis·808

Brown goatskin over paste boards with sunk centre and corner compartments, blocked and painted in gold and red, to an Oriental design, showing curving tendrils and flowers. Doublures: upper cover: brown goatskin painted in gold, with cut-out compartments inlaid in blue paper decorated with a tracery of gold-painted leather; lower cover: red goatskin tooled and painted in gold with curving lines and various flowers; leather inner joints. Traces of four pairs of ties. Edges of boards: painted with a gold line and dashes. Edges: stained blue with traces of gold.

Sewn on three (?)alum-tawed supports, laced in, showing as raised bands on the spine, tooled in gold with a line; four compartments, tooled in gold to a mosaic pattern. Endbands: single with a bead; primary sewing over (?)leather cores (broken off), tied down; secondary sewing of beige silk. Blue silk book marker.

Endleaves: at the front: one free purple paper leaf tipped onto a pair of free conjugate white paper leaves; at the end: a Persian or Turkish marbled paper leaf tipped onto a pair of free conjugate white paper leaves.

PROVENANCE: On title-page in manuscript: 'Costo Doppie e(?)e/ Stephani Marie Pigii'; a (faded) stamp; E P Goldschmidt; J R Abbey (book plate; 'J.A.3003/25:vi:1946'; sold: 23.vi.1965, *542*, pl.).
REFERENCES: [Paris, Bibliothèque nationale], *Catalogue de l'exposition du livre italien* (introduction: S de Ricci), Bois-Colombes, 1926, no. 885; Goldschmidt, no. 217; De Marinis, 1670ter (pl. C31); Romme, *Book Collector*, 1969, p. 39, note 120; Nixon, *Pierpont Morgan Library*, p. 196; Hobson, *Humanists*, p. 150, no. 9.
LITERATURE: Nixon, *Broxbourne*, pp. 91–2; Nixon, *Pierpont Morgan Library*, no. 50; Needham, *Twelve Centuries*, no. 75; Hobson, *Humanists*, pp. 150–4.
Compare: Cambridge University Library, SSS 18.8 (Paris, 1527).

327 *Two bindings made in Genoa by the 'Grimaldi binder', c. 1552*

M T Cicero, *De philosophia*, 2 vols, Venice: Paulus Manutius, Aldi filius, 1552. 8vo.

166 × 103 × 31/27 mm. (P 1292) Davis 809–810

Black goatskin over paste boards, tooled in gold, with blind lines, to a panel design, with fleurons at the corners of the concentric panels; a border formed by parallel and intersecting lines and gouges; in the centre: an oval with a phoenix rising out of a burning vase towards the sun. Traces of two pairs of ties. Edges: gilt and lightly gauffered with a row of dots.

Sewn on three alum-tawed supports, showing as raised bands on the spine, tooled in gold with a line and dashes; four false bands alternating with the sewing supports, tooled in gold with dashes; eight compartments, tooled in blind with lines; gold lines near head and tail (possibly added later); on second compartment: M.T.C./ PHILOSOPH.; vol. 2: top compartment: M.T.C.; second compartment: PHILOS./ TO. II. Endbands: double with a bead; primary sewing over alum-tawed cores (laced in), tied down; secondary sewing of blue and white silk; cord crowning cores (laced in).

Endleaves: Vol. 1: white paper pastedowns and one free leaf conjugate with the pastedown and one free paper leaf tipped on, at both ends. Vol. 2: at front: as vol. 1; at end: white paper pastedown and two free conjugate paper leaves and one free leaf conjugate with the pastedown and one free paper leaf conjugate with a stub in the centre of the two conjugate free leaves.

Repairs: small repairs at top and tail of spines.

PROVENANCE: On endleaf in manuscript: 'P.J.O.'; Lord Vernon (book plate); J R Abbey (book plate; 'J.A.4895/ 23.viii.1950'; sold: Sotheby's, 21.vi.1965, *198*).
REFERENCES: Hobson, *Apollo and Pegasus*, p. 97, no. 4; M Breslauer, Catalogue 102 [1971], no. 55.

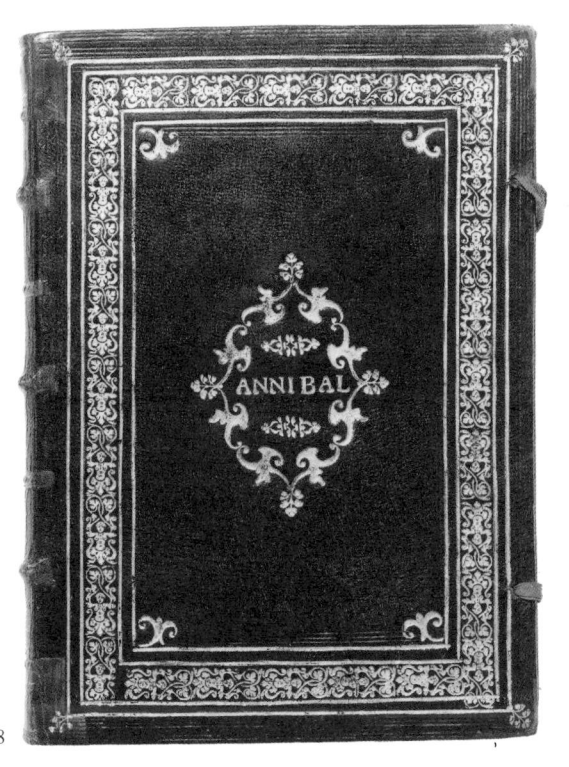

328

LITERATURE: Fumagalli, pl. ix (= De Marinis, 1327, = Hobson, 'Bookbinding in Bologna', p. 171, no. 10); Hoepli, Catalogue, June 1926, xxxix; M Breslauer, Catalogue 67 (1949), no. 28; 74, no. 44; Munby, *Book Collector*, 1952, p. 129; Hobson, *French and Italian*, p. xxxvii; Nixon, *Broxbourne*, no. 32 (= De Marinis, 912bis); De Marinis, 910–13, 1836, 2155, 2270, 2293; De Marinis, *Fürstenberg*, pp. 162–3; Bodley, *Exhibition*, no. 18; Hobson, *Apollo and Pegasus*, pp. 97–9; Hobson, *Renaissance*, p. 127 (especially notes 89, 92); see also Davis 846, 847 (nos. 328, 329 below).

Note: The device of a phoenix rising out of a burning vase towards the sun (which occurs in various versions) is that of Gabriele Giolito de' Ferrari, bookseller in Venice, with branches in Naples, Bologna and Ferrara; it has been suggested that the bindings on which this device occurs were made in Venice, either for sale in Giolito's shop or for his personal library. However, Anthony Hobson thought the device to be an *impresa*, possibly used by the Accademia dei Fenici, founded in Milan in the 1550s, a suggestion later withdrawn.

328 *A binding made in Genoa by the 'Grimaldi binder', c. 1562–5*

St Ambrose, St Jerome, St Augustine, *De virginitate opuscula*, Rome: Paulus Manutius, Aldi filius, 1562. 4to.

215 × 155 × 22 mm. (P 1004(1)) Davis 846

Brown goatskin over paste boards, tooled in gold, with blind lines, to a panel design, with a border filled with tools depicting the trunk of a woman in foliage; curl tools in the corners; in the centre an ornament

391

composed of solid tools and fleurons with on the upper cover: ANNIBAL and on the lower cover: MINALIS. Two pairs of (new) brown woven silk ties. Edges: gilt and gauffered to a knot-work pattern.

Sewn on three alum-tawed supports, laced in, showing as raised bands on the spine, tooled in gold with a line; four false bands alternating with the sewing supports, tooled in gold with dashes; eight compartments, lettered: [TRA]/CTAT/VS. DE/ VIRGI/NITATE/ AMB./ HIE./ [AVG.]. Endbands: single; primary sewing over alum-tawed cores (cut off), tied down; secondary sewing of pink silk.

Endleaves: (new) white paper pastedowns and one free leaf conjugate with the pastedown and one free paper leaf (tipped on), at both ends.

Repairs: top and tail compartments and bands of spine: repaired and covered with strips of new leather; repairs at corners.

PROVENANCE: Hannibal Minale; library stamp on title-page (not identified); Vernon-Holford collections; bought: Quaritch, 17.iii.1951.
REFERENCES: Hobson, *Apollo and Pegasus*, p. 222, no. 8.
LITERATURE: Davis, 809–10 (no. 327 above; and literature cited there); Crollalanza, *Dizionario*; De Marinis, 833, 910; Nixon, *Broxbourne*, no. 32; Hobson, *Apollo and Pegasus*, pp. 97–9; see also Davis 847 (no. 329 below).
Note: For endleaves compare: Briquet, 3251 (Genova, c. 1570). The Minale family was a Genoese family. Matteo Minale was treasurer general of the Church under Pope Pius V; Antonio Minale fl. 1576; Annibale Minale was 'commendatore' of San Giovanni di Pre: 1613 (possibly a later member of the family with the same name?).

329 *A binding made in Genoa by the 'Grimaldi binder', c. 1562–5*

St John Chrysostom, *De virginitate liber*, Rome: Paulus Manutius, Aldi filius, 1562. 4to.

210 × 151 × 17 mm.   (P 1004(2)) Davis 847

Brown goatskin over paste boards, tooled in gold, with blind lines, to a panel design, with a border filled with flower branches; fleurons at the corners; curl tools in the corners; in the centre an ornament composed of solid tools and fleurons with on the upper cover: ANNIBAL and on the lower cover: MINALIS. Two pairs of (new) brown woven silk ties. Edges: gilt and gauffered with interlacing lines.

Sewn on three (?)alum-tawed supports, laced in, showing as raised bands on the spine, tooled in gold with a line; three false bands alternating with the sewing supports, tooled in gold with dashes; seven compartments, lettered: [TRACT]/ATVS. D/ VIRGIN/ITATE/ DIVI. CH/RISOS/[TOMI]. Endbands: double with a bead; primary sewing over cord cores (cut off), tied down; secondary sewing of blue and grey silk.

Endleaves: (new) white paper pastedowns and one free paper leaf conjugate with a stub after the first and before the last section, at both ends.

Repairs: top and tail compartments and bands of spine: repaired and covered with strips of new leather; repairs at corners.

329

PROVENANCE: Hannibal Minale; library stamp on title-page (not identified); Vernon-Holford collections; bought: Quaritch, 17.iii.1951.
REFERENCES: Hobson, *Apollo and Pegasus*, p. 222, no. 8.
LITERATURE: Davis 846 (no. 328 above; and literature cited there); De Marinis, 2198; see also Davis 809–10 (no. 327 above).

330 *A binding possibly made in Rome, c. 1552*

P Bembo, *Lettere ... primo volume*, Venice: Gualtero Scotto, 1552 [and] P Bembo, *Lettere ... secondo volume*, Venice: Aldi filii, 1551 [colophon: October 1550]. 8vo.

165 × 100 × 37 mm. (P 911) Davis 811

Brown goatskin over paste boards, tooled in gold, with blind lines, to a panel design with stylized flowers at the corners; a border filled with fleurs-de-lis and stylized flower tools; curls in the corners of the panel, a fleur-de-lis and a stylized flower tool above and below a centre circle with, on the upper cover: two small stylized flower tools and LETT./ DEL/ BENB.; on the lower cover: VOL.I.II./ P.G/ O. Traces of four pairs of ties. Edges: gilt and gauffered to a knot-work and flower pattern.

Sewn on three split leather supports, laced in, showing as raised bands on the spine, tooled in gold with a line; four false bands, alternating with the sewing supports, tooled in gold with dashes; eight compartments, tooled in blind with interlaced-circles tools and lines. Endbands: single with a bead; primary sewing over leather cores (cut off), tied down; secondary sewing of pink and beige silk.

Endleaves: white paper pastedowns and one free leaf conjugate with the pastedown and one free paper leaf tipped on, at both ends.

Repairs: at top and tail of spine.

PROVENANCE: P G O [possibly the initials of Paolo Giordano Orsini?]; on title-page in manuscript: 'Di P.º F.º Alex(superscript:)ni: et Am.'; bought: Quaritch, 23.vi.1948, *911*.
Same tool on: De Marinis, 839.
Note: All known bindings for Paolo Giordano Orsini (1535–1585) are French (see Hobson, *French and Italian*, no. 18).

331 *A (?)north Italian or possibly Swiss binding, c. 1552–60*

P Giovio, *Le iscrittioni poste sotto le vere imagini de gli huomini famosi* [translated by Hippolito Oris], Florence: L Torrentino, 1552 [title-page imprint date: 1552; colophon: 1551]; ruled in red. 4to.

221 × 149 × 26 mm.   (P 1333) Davis 506

Brown goatskin over paste boards, tooled in gold, with blind lines, with fillets along the border, a hatched fleuron and two hatched leaf tools in the corners; a mandorla-shaped centre piece, formed by gouges, with dots, fleurs-de-lis and hatched, open and solid tools around an oval with small tools, containing three trefoils. Remnants of two pairs of ties. Turn-ins: tooled in blind with a line. Edges: gilt.

   Sewn on four split alum-tawed supports, laced in, showing as raised bands on the spine, tooled in gold with a line; two kettle stitch bands, also with a line in gold; seven compartments, tooled in blind with lines and with a trefoil tooled in gold in each. Endbands: single with a bead; pale blue silk over alum-tawed cores (cut off), tied down occasionally.

   Endleaves: paper pastedowns and a pair of free conjugate paper leaves, plus one free leaf conjugate with the pastedown, at both ends.

   Repairs: small repairs at head and tail of spine.

PROVENANCE: On the title page in manuscript: 'D.P. Degrantrye χρ[Christ]ianissimi Regis oratoris apud Rhetos 1556 [?1566]'; Rudolph August Witthaus A.M.M.D. (book plate); Ioseph

	Martini of Lucerne (book plate; sold: Zurich, 21.v.1935, *105*); bought: Quaritch, 25.iii.1959.
Same tools on:	BL, G 4484 (Giovio, *Istorie*, n.d.: an identical binding with the same provenance inscription, dated 1566); Glasgow University Library, Hunt. G5.24 (Venice, 1560).
Note:	Olivier, 2406, 2407: three trefoils: arms of De Revol (17th- and 18th-century examples); Olivier, 2408: De Brosses, Olivier, 2409: De Rosset (both 18th-century examples); Rietstap has these arms for the Grantis or Grantris family from the Nivernais (Fr).
	'Rhaetia': an area comprising southern Bavaria, most of Tyrol and eastern Switzerland; De Grantrye was probably envoy to Switzerland.

332 *A binding made in Venice, c. 1555*

J Sannazaro, *Arcadia* [and] *Le rime*, Venice: Domenico Giglio, 1553. 12mo.

138 × 76 × 21 mm.   (P 1182) Davis 812

Brown calf over paste boards, tooled in gold with lines, a border filled with arch tools; fleurons at the corners; a second border filled with curving flower-and-leaf tools; the same tools divide the central panel into three compartments; in the corners of each compartment: a cherub's head tool; in the centre of the top and bottom compartments: four fleurons; in the centre of the middle compartment: two clasped hands. Traces of two pairs of ties. Edges: gilt and gauffered to a knot-work pattern.

Sewn on three (?)leather supports, laced in, showing as bands on the spine; four compartments, tooled in gold and blind with lines. Endbands: single with a bead; primary sewing over (?)cord cores (once laced in), tied down; secondary sewing of red and white silk.

Endleaves: white paper pastedowns and one free leaf conjugate with the pastedown and one free paper leaf, at both ends; at the front: the second free leaf is conjugate with a stub after the first section and has been pasted to the verso of the free leaf conjugate with pastedown.

Small repairs at covers.

PROVENANCE:	Ioseph Martini (book plate; sold by Hoepli); Silvain Brunschwig (book plate; sold: Rauch, 29.iii.1955, *261*).
REFERENCES:	G D Hobson, *Maioli*, p. 113, no. c.
LITERATURE:	G D Hobson, *Maioli*, pp. 113–14.
Same tools on:	Libri, *Monuments inédits*, pl. 23; De Marinis, 1713, 2633; Davies, *Fairfax Murray*, no. 10; Malaguzzi, *Aosta*, p. 45, no. 25.

333 *A binding made in Rome or possibly in Genoa, c. 1560*

St Thomas More, *De optimo rei publicae statu, de que nova insula Utopia ...*, [Paris]: Gilles de Gourmont, [1517]. 8vo.

147 × 100 × 20 mm.   (P 995) Davis 813

Red-brown goatskin over paste boards, tooled in gold, with blind lines, to a panel design with a border filled with small leafy branches; fleurons at the corners; in the centre a device showing a key with a serpent coiled round it with the legend: SCILICET. IS. SVPERIS. LABOR. EST. Edges: plain.

332   333

Rebacked with the original spine strip preserved; sewn on three (invisible) supports, laced in, showing as raised bands on the spine, tooled in gold with a line; four compartments, tooled in blind with lines and in gold with flower tools; title lettered on spine. Endbands: single with a bead; primary sewing over (?)leather cores (cut off), tied down; secondary sewing of blue and white silk.

Endleaves: new white pastedowns and one new free leaf conjugate with the pastedown, at both ends; at the front: one (original) free white paper leaf conjugate with a stub after the first section.

PROVENANCE: On (original) endleaf in manuscript: 'Ex copietis (?) Martini Protis'; in a different hand: 'Anfranus Matthias fransonus'; in a different hand: 'Ex Legato[…'?cut out]; on title-page in manuscript: a monogram: 'AMF'; Earl of Rosebery (book plate and stamp; sold: Sotheby's, 26–30.vi.1933, *922*); Lucius Wilmerding (book plate; sold: Parke-Bernet, 6.iii.1951, *469*).

REFERENCES: Hobson, *French and Italian*, p. 182, Appendix D, no. 1; *The Italian Book*, no. 269.

LITERATURE: Hobson, *French and Italian*, no. 66, p. 182: Appendix D; Brera, no. 29; see Davis 814, 840 (nos. 334, 335 below).

For two more bindings with this device (not in Hobson, nor Brera): John Rylands University Library, Manchester, 5980 (Venice, 1558); Sotheby's, 28.ii.1966, *86* (pl.).

Note: Brera, no. 29 has the same early provenance as Davis 813; Davis 814 also belonged to Martinus Protus; the legend is a quotation from the *Aeneid*, book IV, verse 379. The device with legend is illustrated in: C Paradin, *Devises héroïques*, Lyon, 1557, pp. 77–8, but no owner has been postulated.

334

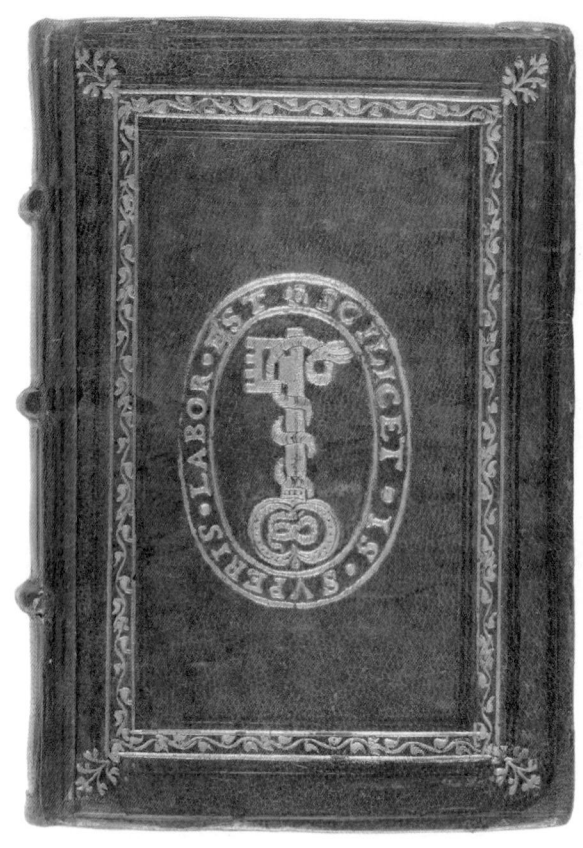

334 *A binding made in Rome or possibly in Genoa, c. 1560*

A T Macrobius, *In somnium Scipionis libri ii. Saturnaliorum libri vii*, Lyon: S Gryphius, 1556. 8vo.

162 × 108 × 30 mm. (P 822) Davis 814

Brown goatskin over paste boards, tooled in gold, with blind lines, to a panel design with a border filled with small leafy branches; fleurons at the corners; and in the centre the same device with legend as occurs on David 813 (no. 333 above). Edges: stained red.

Rebacked. Endbands: later; single with a bead; dark red silk over rolled (?)paper cores (cut off), no visible tie-downs.

Endleaves: White paper pastedowns and one free leaf conjugate with the pastedown (original at the front; new at the end).

PROVENANCE: On (original) endleaf in manuscript: 'Ex copietis (?) Martini Protis'; in a different hand: 'Ex libris Rg(?) Nicolai Hitis' [?Hibis; ?Nitis]; in a different hand: 'Harry Trelawny 1715'; Elton (book plate); duke of Sussex (book plate; in manuscript: 'VII.B.f.10'); on pastedown of lower cover: paper label with in manuscript: '1545'; E P Goldschmidt (Catalogue 75, no. 96; sold: 20.ix.1944).

REFERENCES: Goldschmidt, no. 247, pl. xcvii; Hobson, *French and Italian*, p. 182, Appendix D, no. 7.

LITERATURE: Davis 813 (no. 333 above; and literature cited there); see also Davis 840 (no. 335 below).

335   *A binding made in Rome or possibly in Genoa, c. 1564–5*

J Casa, *Latina monimenta*, Florence: Hearedes B Iuntae, 1564 [and] J Sadoletus, *De laudibus philosophiae*, Lyon: S Gryphius, 1538 [and] S Doletus, *Aurelii carminum libri*, Lyon: [S Gryphius], 1538. 4to.

222 × 152 × 49 mm. (P 1274) Davis 840

Olive-brown goatskin over paste boards, tooled in gold, with blind lines, to a design of intersecting borders, forming two concentric panels with fleurons at the corners; in the centre the same device with legend as occurs on Davis 813 and 814 (nos. 333, 334 above). Edges of boards and turn-ins: tooled in blind with lines. Edges: stained red.

Sewn on three split leather supports, laced in, showing as raised bands on the spine, traces of gold tooling; four compartments, tooled in blind with lines and in gold with lines and leaves; authors' names lettered in first compartment: 'Casa. Sado. Doletvs'. Endbands: single with a bead; white and blue silk over alum-tawed cores (once laced in), tied down sporadically.

Endleaves: white paper pastedowns conjugate with a stub after the first and before the last section, at both ends; at the end: one frcc paper leaf.

Repairs: small repairs.

PROVENANCE: On pastedown in manuscript: 'Mr Annesley'; Maggs Bros (Catalogue 489, 1927, *243*); bought: Breslauer, 4.v.1956.
REFERENCES: Hobson, *French and Italian*, p. 182, Appendix D, no. 10.
LITERATURE: Davis 813 (no. 333 above; and literature cited there); see also Davis 814 (no. 334 above).

336 *A binding made in Venice, c. 1560*

Aeneas Vicus, *Augustarum imagines*, Venice: [P Manutius Aldus], 1558. 4to.

240 × 174 × 23 mm. (P 602) Davis 841

Limp parchment stained purple, painted in gold and silver (oxidized) to a panel design with an arabesque pattern; corner fleurons and a flower in the centre. Edges: painted with curving lines in black and gold.

Sewn on four split alum-tawed supports, cut off; smooth spine; spine panels lined with parchment. Endbands: double with a bead; primary sewing over alum-tawed (main) cores (laced through the turn-ins), tied down; secondary sewing of red and white silk; cord crowning cores.

Endleaves: white paper pastedowns, two free conjugate white paper leaves and one free leaf conjugate with the pastedown, at both ends.

PROVENANCE: On title-page in manuscript: 'Jacobi Joye'; on pastedown: oval paper label with in manuscript: '1605'; on endleaf in manuscript: '87'; R S Cotton (book plate); bought: Sotheby's, 21.iv.1943, *296*.
Note: Italian 16th-century purple-stained parchment bindings are not common. Other examples are: Trinity College, Cambridge, N.1.99 (Venice, 1565); Sotheby's, 28.ii.1966, *102*; Lathrop Harper, Catalogue 10, no. 33; Hobson, *Legature bolognesi*, p. 63, no. 11; Federico Macchi tells me that there is one in the University Library at Pavia, ROT 7 I 1 (which I have not seen).

337 *A binding made in Rome, c. 1560–70*

St Thomas Aquinas, *Tertia pars summae[theologiae] angelici doctoris Sanctae Thome de Aquino*, Rouen: F Regnault, February 1520. 8vo.

155 × 104 × 43 mm. (P 1278) Davis 815

Red goatskin over paste boards, blocked in gold with a plaque showing interlacing ribbons, azured curls and leaf shapes, birds and angels' heads around, in the centre: an empty shield surmounted by a cardinal's hat (possibly: traces of a painted coat of arms on the lower cover). Traces of two pairs of ties. Edges: gilt and gauffered with strips of rope-work and leaf and fleuron rolls.

Sewn on three, possibly split, (?)alum-tawed supports, laced in, showing as raised bands on the spine, tooled in gold with a line; four compartments, tooled in gold with lines and arabesque fleuron tools. Endbands: double with a bead; primary sewing over leather (main) cores (cut off), tied down; secondary sewing of pink and white silk.

Endleaves: white paper pastedowns and one free leaf conjugate with the pastedown, at both ends.

336

337

THE HENRY DAVIS GIFT

PROVENANCE: On title-page in manuscript: 'Oct Sig./ Camillo/ Com./ de Pall(?); sold: Sotheby's, 8.xi.1954, *84* (pl.); J R Abbey (book plate; 'J.A.6316/ 8.11.1954'; sold: Sotheby's, 21.vi.1965, *40*).
LITERATURE: Sonntag, no. 41, pl. xviii; De Marinis, *Fürstenberg*, pp. 78–9; Hobson, 'Italian sixteenth-century bookbindings', p. 55, list no.2; Breslauer, Catalogue 104, pt. II, no. 183 (and literature cited there).
Compare: (spine tool) *Legature papali*, no. 114.

338 *A binding possibly made in Venice*, c. 1561

M T Cicero, *Epistolae ad Atticum, ad Brutum, ad quintum fratrem. Cum correctionibus Pauli Manutii*, Venice: Aldus, 1561. 8vo.

153 × 101 × 42 mm.   (P 672) Davis 816

Brown goatskin over paste boards, tooled in gold, with blind lines, to a panel design with a border filled with tools depicting foliage around a trunk; flowers at the corners; curl tools in the corners; in the centre: fleuron and leaf tools around a stylized flower. On the upper cover: M.T.C. EP. AD ATT. Edges: gilt and gauffered with a strap-work border.

Sewn on three alum-tawed supports, laced in, showing as raised bands on the spine; four false bands alternating with the sewing supports, tooled in gold with dashes; eight compartments, tooled in blind with lines. Endbands: double with a bead; primary sewing over alum-tawed (main) cores (cut off), tied down; secondary sewing of pink and green silk.

Endleaves: white paper pastedowns and one free leaf conjugate with the pastedown, at both ends.

Repairs: at head and tail of spine (top compartment: renewed) and at corners.

PROVENANCE: Frederick Keppel (book plate); bought: Francis Edwards, 12.viii.1943.
Same tools on: Gennadius Library, GC2992 (Venice, 1513); John Rylands University Library, Manchester, 18753 (Cicero, *De officiis*, Venice, 1561: probably part of same set as Davis 816).
Compare: De Marinis, *Fürstenberg*, pp 76–7, 98–9; Quilici, no. 271, fig. 114, no. 291, fig. 124.

339 *A binding made in Venice*, c. 1561–70

Luis de Granada, *Trattato dell' oratione et della meditatione ... tradotto per M. V. Buondi*, Venice: G Giolito, 1561. 8vo.

158 × 100 × 16 mm.   (P 945) Davis 817

Brown goatskin over paste boards, tooled in gold (possibly an alloy) with arabesque, open and solid tools; curl tools in the corners, open leaf tools, apple tools, solid arabesque tools; a circle of gouges, small stars and leaves around a double circle containing an empty shield in the centre. Remnants of two pairs of ties. Edges: gilt and lightly gauffered with rows of dots.

Sewn on three split (invisible) supports, laced in, showing as raised bands on the spine, tooled in gold with a line; four false bands alternating with the sewing supports, tooled in gold with dashes; eight

338 339

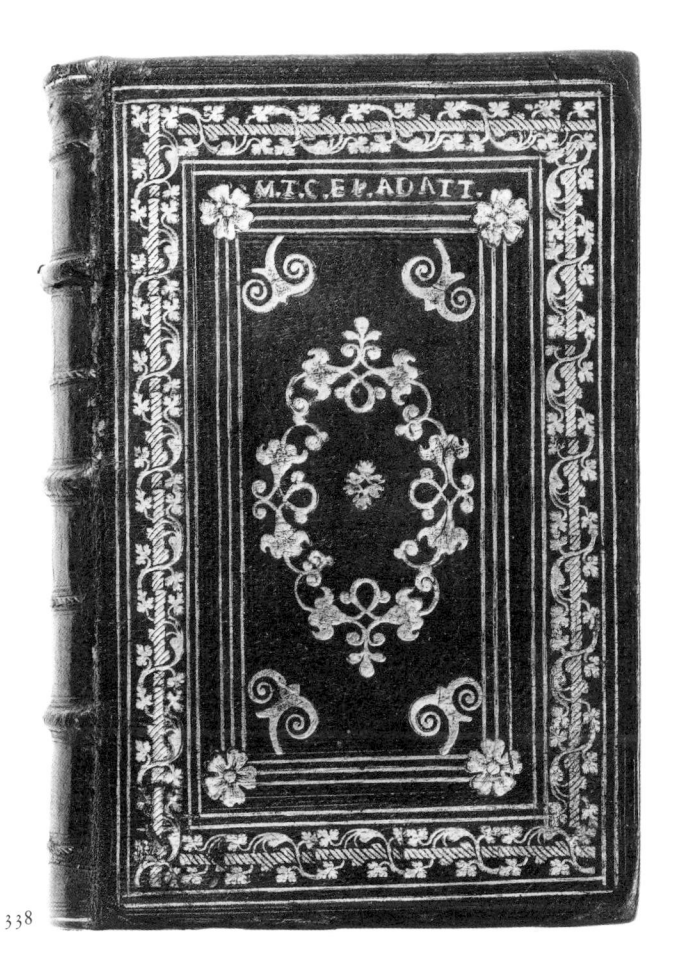

compartments, tooled in blind. Endbands: single; primary sewing over leather cores (cut off), tied down; secondary sewing of pink and white silk (remnant only).

Endleaves: white paper pastedowns and one free leaf conjugate with the pastedown, at both ends.

Repairs: at head and tail of spine (tail compartment: renewed).

PROVENANCE: Bought: Davis and Orioli, 17.x.1949.
REFERENCES: Foot, *Davis*, I, pp. 315, 318–19 (notes 97, 101).
LITERATURE: Foot, *Davis*, I, pp. 318–19, note 101 (for bindings with the same tools).

---

340 *A binding made in Venice, c. 1563*

Dogale [Instructions from the Republic of Venice to an unknown officer], signed: Aloysius Zambius Secretarius, [Venice], 21 April, 1563; MS on parchment, written in red and black; ruled.

239 × 174 × c. 42 mm. (M 47) Davis 842

Red goatskin over paste boards, tooled in gold with lines and small tools; sunk compartments, inlaid in brown calf, blocked in gold with floral compartments in the border; corner compartments blocked with floral branches and three arabesque centre compartments blocked to a design of fleurons and floral

403

branches. Traces of four pairs of ties. Edges of boards and turn-ins: tooled in blind with lines. Edges: gilt and gauffered to a knot-work pattern.

Sewn on three leather supports, laced in, showing as raised bands on the spine, tooled in gold with a line; four compartments, tooled in gold with slanting lines. Endbands: double with a bead; primary sewing over leather (main) cores (cut off), tied down; secondary sewing of pink and blue-green silk.

Endleaves: parchment pastedowns at both ends; at the front: one free parchment leaf conjugate with the pastedown.

Repairs: at joints.

PROVENANCE: Prince Diego Pignatelli d'Angio (N Rauch, Catalogue I, 1948, *69*, pl.); bought: N Rauch, 30.iii.1955, *190*.
REFERENCES: Pitti, exhibition, no. 561; Romme, *Book Collector*, 1969, p. 39, note 121.
LITERATURE: Fletcher, *Foreign*, pl. xxx; Nixon, *Broxbourne*, no. 44; Nixon, *Pierpont Morgan Library*, no. 50; Needham, *Twelve Centuries*, no. 75.
Compare: De Marinis, 1669.

341

341   *A binding made in Bologna, c. 1565*

Le vite de Santi Padri, Venice: Andrea Muscio, 1565; woodcuts. 4to.

203 × 148 × 28 mm.   (P 1198) Davis 843

White calf over paste boards, tooled in gold, with lines, a border roll showing curving floral-leafy branches; interlacing ribbons, fleurons, flowers, arabesque tools, and in the centre of the upper cover: St John the Baptist; in the centre of the lower cover: SVOR/ SVLPITIA/ CAMPEG/GI. Traces of four pairs of ties. Edges: gilt and gauffered to a knot-work pattern.

   Sewn on three split alum-tawed supports, laced in, showing as raised bands on the spine, tooled in gold with a line; four false bands, alternating with the sewing supports, tooled in gold with dashes; eight compartments, tooled in blind with lines. Endbands: single; primary sewing over (?)cord cores (laced in), tied down; remnants of secondary sewing in (?)black and white silk .

405

Endleaves: white paper pastedowns at both ends; at the front: one free paper leaf conjugate with a stub after the first section; at the end: one free leaf conjugate with the pastedown.

PROVENANCE: Sister Sulpitia Campeggi; bought: Karl & Faber, 12.v.1955, *489* (pl.).
LITERATURE: Libri, *Monuments inédits*, pl. xlvii; De Marinis, 1348; Schunke, *Palatina*, I, pp. 170–2, pl. cxxxv (= De Marinis, 1337); Nixon, *Pierpont Morgan Library*, no. 24; Hobson, *Legature bolognesi*, pp. 26–9 (the tools on the bindings listed are not all identical with those on Davis 843).
Compare: De Marinis, *Alcune legature*, no. 16, pl. 18; De Marinis, 1327; De Marinis, *Fürstenberg*, pp. 108–9; Hobson, *Legature bolognesi*, no. 42 .
Note: The Campeggi were a noble family in Bologna, famous during the fifteenth and sixteenth centuries. The family included scholars and influential church officials.

342 *A binding made in Venice by the 'Arabesque outline tool binder', c. 1565–70*

[Andrea Schiavone, *Les Panneaux d'ornaments – suite de 21 estampes*] [a collection of engravings], sixteenth century.

253 × 185 × 10 mm. (P 1011) Davis 844

Red goatskin over paste boards, tooled in gold to a panel design with lines, fleurons at the corners, a border filled with interlinked-circles tools; the centre panel filled with gouges and open tools to an arabesque design; gold-tooled dots. Traces of four pairs of green ties. Edges: sprinkled in red.

Sewn on five (invisible) supports, the centre three of which have been laced in; smooth spine, tooled in blind with lines. No endbands.

Endleaves: at the front: white paper pastedown conjugate with a stub, one free paper leaf pasted onto this stub, and one free paper leaf conjugate with a stub beneath the pastedown; at the end: white paper pastedown and one free paper leaf conjugate with a stub beneath the pastedown.

Repairs: at top and tail of spine and at corners.

PROVENANCE: Bought: Leo Olschki, 25.v.1951.
LITERATURE: Schunke, 'Venezianische Renaissance-Einbände', pp. 182–3, pl. xxv (IV/ 41); Hobson, 'Italian sixteenth-century bookbindings', no. 16; Malaguzzi, *Preziosi*, p. 17, no. 18; Nuvoloni, 'Commissioni Dogali', pp. 92, 94, 99.
Same tools on: BL, Egerton MS 757 (*Dogale*, Venice, 1571); Fumagalli, *L'arte della legatura*, no. 250, pl. xviii; N Rauch, Catalogue I (1948), *48*; De Marinis, 2485; Mazal, pl. 99.
Note: This binder was called by I Schunke the 'Leermauresken Meister' and by A Hobson the 'Arabesque Outline Tool Binder'.

Italian Bindings

342

SECONDO LIBRO
DELLA RECETTORIA
DELLA REVERENDA CAMERA
APPOSTOLICHA DEL
ANO M·D·L·X·V·II

Italian Bindings

343   *A binding made in Rome, c. 1568*

Secondo libro della Recettoria della Reverenda Camera Appostolicha del anno 1567 [second part: 1568], MS on paper [Blank book with manuscript accounts; inscription on first page: signed by Hie[ronymus] de Tarano; second page signed by: Hie[ronymus] de Tarano; seen and endorsed by Hie[ronymus] Maceraten[us] [Hieronymus, bishop of Macerate]; second part: inscription signed by: Cae[sarus] Cappellus; seen and approved by: P Harn[us] (?)], [Rome, 1567–8].

352 × 235 × 45 mm.   (M 56) Davis 868

Brown goatskin over very thin paste boards (semi-limp), tooled in blind and gold. The upper cover: tooled in blind with a border and divided into two panels, each with corner ornaments, leaf and flower tools, fleurs-de-lis, fleurons; in the centre of the upper panel: a large circle outlined by small solid fleuron tools and interlaced-circles tools; in the centre of the lower panel: a large oval, outlined with interlaced-circles tools and containing fleurons, cherub's heads and the title of the manuscript. The lower cover: tooled in blind; divided by a roll into two panels, each with a rectangle and lozenge design, lines, interlinked-circles tools, stylized flowers, fleurons, and fleurs-de-lis. Remnants of two pairs of yellow ties. Edges: plain.

Sewn on two wide alum-tawed supports (cut off; holes for straps or tackets? visible in the spine leather); smooth spine, tooled in blind with small tools. Endbands: single with a bead; primary sewing over leather cores (cut off), tied down; secondary sewing of yellow and pink silk.

Endleaves: conjugate parchment pastedowns (front and back pastedowns: one sheet of parchment) and one free parchment leaf, at both ends, also conjugate (front and back free leaf consists of one parchment sheet wrapped around the textblock).

PROVENANCE: bought: Sotheby's, 19.x.1964, *158*.
LITERATURE: Hobson, 'Two early 16th-century binder's shops', pp. 79–98; Tolomei, 'Reliures romaines', pp. 295–7, pls I, II.
Compare: Davis 869 (no. 344 below: structure); BL, C.64.g.1 (Venice, 1506); De Marinis, 638, 656, 923, 2155; Sotheby's, 10.v.1985, *449*; Tolomei, *Legatura romana barocca*, nos. 6,7.
Note: Tools found on Davis 868 may be identical with those used by Paolo di Bernardino (Rome, until c. 1540).

344   *A binding made in Rome, possibly by Francesco Soresino, c. 1572*

Settimo libro della depositeria generale della Reverenda Camera Appostolica lanno 1572, MS on paper [Blank book with manuscript accounts, every page signed: 'Hic. Mathaeius vera est summa' or 'vera et summa est Mathaeius'], [Rome, 1572].

342 × 230 × 40 mm.   (M 55) Davis 869

Brown sheep over very thin paste boards (semi-limp), tooled in gold and blind. The upper cover: tooled in gold with a border filled with interlinked circles tools; divided into two panels, each with corner ornaments, lion and flame tools, flowers and rosettes; in the upper panel: a circle surrounded by flame tools; in the lower panel: an oval surrounded by flame tools and containing horizontal lines and the title of the manuscript. The lower cover: tooled in blind with a border filled with interlinked circles tools, a wide border filled with separate tools; a centre panel with corner ornaments and a centre lozenge filled

SETTIMO LIBRO
DELLA DEPOSITERIA
GENERALE DELLA
REVERENDA CAMERA
APOSTOLICA
L'ANNO M D LXXII

with stylized flowers and ornamental tools. Remnants of two pairs of pink silk ties. Edges: plain.

Sewn on three pairs of leather supports, cut off at the joint; not every section sewn to every individual support. Spine, lined with layers of paper; holes in spine leather and paper lining, through which parchment tackets (four per pair of supports) fasten the supports to the spine leather. Smooth spine, tooled in blind with individual hand tools. Endbands: single with a bead; primary sewing over leather cores (cut off), tied down; secondary sewing of yellow and pink silk. Three parchment tackets (in tail of spine), holding tailband to the spine leather (knotted on the outside).

Endleaves: two free parchment leaves, at both ends, conjugate (front and back: first free leaves consist of one sheet of parchment, and were probably once pasted down; second pair of free leaves consist of one sheet of parchment wrapped round the textblock with holes for the sewing supports).

PROVENANCE:	Bought: Sotheby's, 19.x.1964, *159* (pl.).
LITERATURE:	De Marinis, 611; Tolomei, 'Reliures romaines', p. 297, pl. VI; see also Davis 822 (no. 356 below; and literature cited there).
Compare:	Davis 868 (no. 343 above: structure); Bodleian Library Oxford, Douce binding A25; De Marinis, 481; Tolomei, *Legatura romana barocca*, no. 6.
Note:	Francesco Soresino was binder to the Vatican after the death of Niccolò Franzese; he bound for the Vatican from 11 August 1575.

345 *A binding probably made in Venice, c. 1573*

B Ferrero, Notarial documents, MS on paper [Blank book in which these documents were transcribed, checked and signed by Joes Dominicus d Licciardo], Palermo 1571–3.

311 × 210 × 20 mm. (M 69) Davis 870

Brown goatskin over paste boards, tooled in gold, with blind lines, with a border filled with palmette-leaf tools, fleurons at and in the corners; in the centre a circle outlined with small knot, fleuron, flame and fleurs-de-lis tools, containing a centre ornament composed of four fleurons and stars. Four pairs of yellow silk ties. Edges: gilt and lightly gauffered with rows of dots.

Sewn on four tanned leather supports, laced in, showing as raised bands on the spine; five false bands (cords, not used as sewing supports, but laced in), alternating with the sewing supports, tooled in gold with dashes; ten compartments, tooled in gold with a small flower and in blind with lines. Endbands: single with a bead; primary sewing over cord cores (laced in), tied down; secondary sewing of pale blue and black silk.

Endleaves: white paper pastedowns and one pair of free conjugate paper leaves and one free leaf conjugate with the pastedown, at both ends.

PROVENANCE:	Ferreri family of Palermo (?); Il Polifilo, Milan (bookseller's ticket); bought: Sotheby's, 14.iii.1961, *441* (pl.).
REFERENCES:	Nixon, *Pierpont Morgan Library*, no. 48; Foot, *Davis*, I. p. 319 (note 101); Breslauer, Catalogue 104, pt. II, no. 172.
Same tools on:	Sotheby's, 27.vi.1956, *630* (pl.); De Marinis, *Fürstenberg*, pl. opposite p. 174 (= Breslauer, Catalogue 90, 1958, no. 36 = Breslauer, Catalogue 92, 1960, no. 103 = Breslauer, Catalogue 104, pt. II, no. 172).
Compare:	De Marinis, *Fürstenberg*, pp. 174–5.

345

346   *A binding possibly made in Padua or in Venice, c. 1576*

[Grant of the degree of Doctor of Philosophy and Medicine at the University of Padua to Sanctiflorius Mundella of Brescia by Nicolaus Galerius, signed by Nicolaus Galerius and Ludovicus Gratianus], Padua, 15 March 1576. MS on parchment, written in black and gold; decorated initial; ruled in gold.

255 × 182 × 8 mm.   (M 57) Davis 871

Red goatskin over paste boards, tooled in gold with lines and gouges; a border filled with leaf, flower and knot tools, decorated with silver paint; fleurons, dots and leaf tools, decorated with silver paint in the corners; the centre panel tooled with gouges to an arabesque pattern with acorns, leaves, flowers and larger hatched curving leaf- and fleuron tools; small ivy-leaf tools and open circles. Four pairs of red silk ties. Edges: gilt.

Sewn on three cords, laced in, showing as bands on the spine, tooled in gold with a line; four false bands alternating with the sewing supports, tooled in gold with dashes; eight compartments, tooled in gold with leaf tools. The silver seal of Ludovicus Manin, doge of Venice, is attached to a red and silver plaited cord, laced through holes in the parchment and in the cover leather, near the tail; silk tassels. Endbands: double with a bead; primary sewing over cord cores (laced in), tied down; secondary sewing of red silk.

Endleaves: two free conjugate parchment leaves, at both ends; at the front: plus two free conjugate parchment leaves.

PROVENANCE: On verso of last page of text in manuscript: 'Criessnei'(?); J R Abbey (book plate; 'J.A.1994/ 10:10:1939'; sold: Sotheby's, 23.vi.1965, *528*).
Note: Nicolaus Galerius: vicar-general of the bishop of Padua.

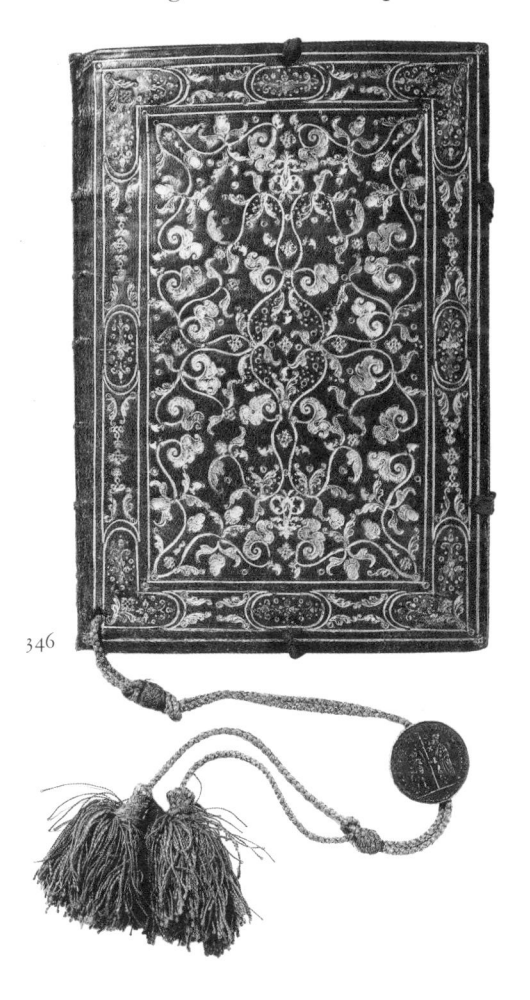

346

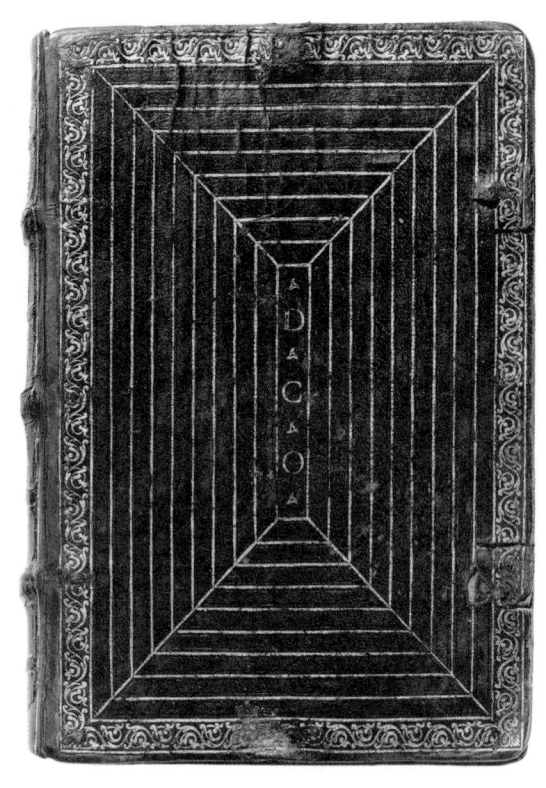

347 *A binding possibly made in Venice, c. 1580*

Missale Romanum, Venice: I B Sessa, 1580. 4to.

237 × 166 × 51 mm. (P 1227) Davis 848

Brown goatskin over wood, tooled in gold, with blind lines, with a border filled with curving leaf tools, in the centre panel a pattern of concentric rectangles and diagonal lines running from the corners, with in the centre rectangle the letters: D C O alternating with small triangular tools. Traces of four pairs of clasps, hinging on the upper cover. Edges: gilt and gauffered to a floral and leaf pattern.

Rebacked with the original spine strip retained; remnants of original sewing on three split alum-tawed supports, laced in; three raised bands on spine, tooled in gold with lines; four false bands alternating with raised bands, tooled in gold with dashes; eight compartments, tooled in gold with vertical lines and flower tools. Endbands: double with a bead; possibly remnants of primary sewing over cord cores (invisible whether once laced in); no visible tie-downs; secondary sewing of blue and yellow silk.

Endleaves: engravings used as pastedowns, at both ends.

Repairs: rebacked; new head and tail of spine; repairs at corners, edges of boards and at upper cover. Repaired by the British Museum in 1969.

PROVENANCE: On title-page in manuscript: 'Luigi R R Rouardis Siamo, inquel tempo an(?)ndo'; in a different hand: 'RRR Romar Sacra e Nor (?)/ (?)Tina Ant.º Ant.º Gas'; 'Jo Ant.º Gasparini (?)'; on pastedown of upper cover in manuscript: 'Collect. Mausane'; bought: Sotheby's, 6.vii.1955, *104*.

348

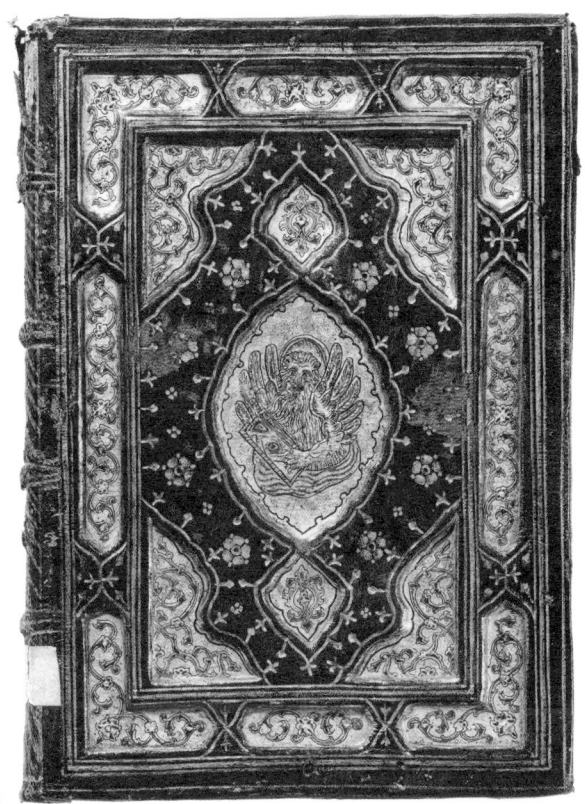

348 *A binding made in Venice, c. 1590*

Dogale [Instructions to Benetto Amoro on becoming a member of the Council], MS on parchment; painted frontispiece with the arms of Benetto Amoro and those of Doge Pasquale Cicogna, [Venice, c. 1590]; ruled.

237 × 170 × 27 mm.   (M 50) Davis 849

Red goatskin over paste boards, floral decoration painted in gold; tooled in gold with small tools. Double boards, sunk compartments, blocked in gold with floral patterns decorated with red, black, mauve and silver paint; in the centre of the upper cover: sunk compartment with the Lion of St Mark; on the lower cover: painted arms of Benetto Amoro. Traces of four pairs of ties. Edges of boards: painted in gold with a line. Edges: gilt.

Sewn on four leather supports, laced in, showing as raised bands on the spine; five compartments painted in gold with lines. Endbands: double with traces of a bead; primary sewing over cord cores (still partially laced in), tied down; secondary sewing (tail band only) of purple and white silk.

Endleaves: block-printed paper pastedowns (gilt, white and pink floral pattern) and one free block-printed leaf (backed), conjugate with the pastedown, at both ends; stub of backing paper after first section and before last section.

PROVENANCE: Benetto Amoro; Stanislaus Count Zamoyski (book plate with date: 1804); Sotheby's, 18.vi.1962, *127* (pl.); Breslauer (sold: 7.vii.1962).
REFERENCES: Romme, *Book Collector*, 1969, p. 39, note 122.

LITERATURE:	Nixon, *Broxbourne*, no. 44; De Marinis, 1917g; Schunke, 'Venezianische Renaissance-Einbände', pl. xxvi; Nixon, *Pierpont Morgan Library*, no. 50; Nuvoloni, 'Commissioni Dogali'.
Compare:	Whitney Hoff, no. 96; Harthan, *V&A Bookbindings*, no. 25; Sotheby's, 20.vi.1967, *1824* (pl.); Esmerian sale I, Paris, 6.vi.1972, *77*.
Note:	Pasquale Cicogna: doge of Venice: 1585–95 (d.).

349   *A binding made in Rome, c. 1590*

Officium B. Mariae Virginis, Venice: Aldus, 1581. 12mo.

150 × 78 × 31 mm.   (P 358) Davis 820

Black goatskin over paste boards, tooled in gold with lines and gouges; small curling tools in the border, gouges, hatched and open leaf and fleuron tools, small flowers and two pineapple tools; in the centre an oval with on the upper cover: the Virgin and Child; on the lower cover: St John the Baptist. Traces of two pairs of ties. Edges: gilt, gauffered and painted, to a curly pattern.

   Sewn on four alum-tawed supports, laced in; smooth spine, tooled in gold with interlinking-circles tools, dashes and small flowers. Endbands: double with a bead; primary sewing over leather cores (cut off), tied down; secondary sewing of blue and white silk.

   Endleaves: white paper pastedowns and two free conjugate paper leaves, at both ends; at the end: one free leaf (probably) conjugate with the pastedown.

PROVENANCE:	Powis (on endleaf in manuscript: 'Powis 1840'; sold: Sotheby's, 22.iii.1923, *588*); bought: Quaritch, 15.xii.1941.
LITERATURE:	Hobson, 'Italian sixteenth-century bookbindings', no. 18 (2).
Same tools on:	BL, C. 29.f.6 (Rome, n.d.), C.42.d.3 (Rome, 1568); Trinity College, Cambridge, Grylls 3.218 (Lyon, 1580); Hoepli, Catalogue 1925, no. 280 (John the Baptist tool).
Compare:	St Catharine's College, Cambridge, c.11.3 (manuscript, n.p., n.d., Aldobrandini arms); BL, C.66.e.16 (Antwerp, 1545), C.46.c.16 (Lyon, 1551); *Legature papali*, nos. 144, 151; Breslauer, Catalogue 104, pt. II, no. 187; Tolomei, 'Reliures romaines', pl. V.

350   *A binding made in Venice or possibly in Rome, 1590*

C S Bergonzo, *Ad Xistum quintum pontificem maximum. Opus in tertium, senten.*, Verona: S dalla Donne, 1590. fol.

325 × 220 × 23 mm.   (P 1049) Davis 872

Brown goatskin over paste boards, tooled in gold, with blind lines, with interlacing fillets, gouges, hatched and open tools; flower tools at and in the corners; border filled with hatched leaf and fleuron tools, solid arabesque tools, open tools and gouges; panel divided into compartments by intersecting fillets and gouges; open and hatched tools, curls and flower tools around, in the centre, a shield with a feather; on the upper cover: XISTO QVINTO; on the lower cover: PONTIFICI MAX° <A> I [over earlier L] VSTIS°. Traces of four pairs of ties. Edges: gilt and gauffered with hatched leaf shapes.

349

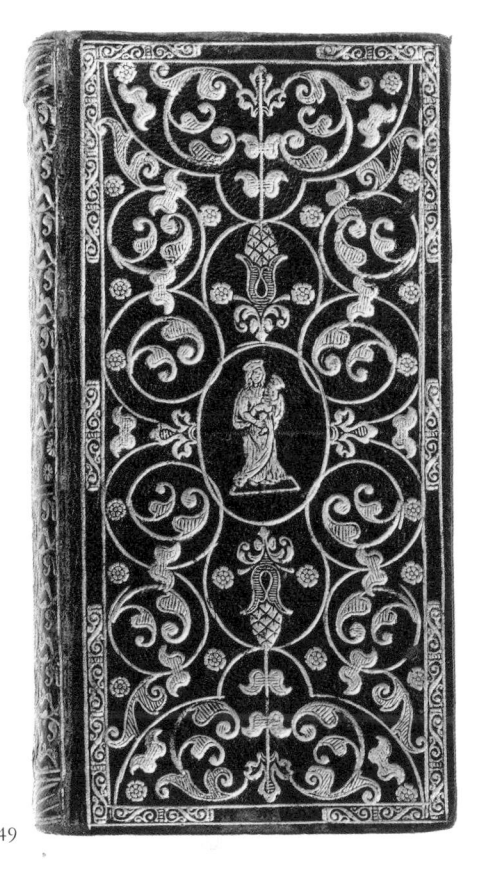

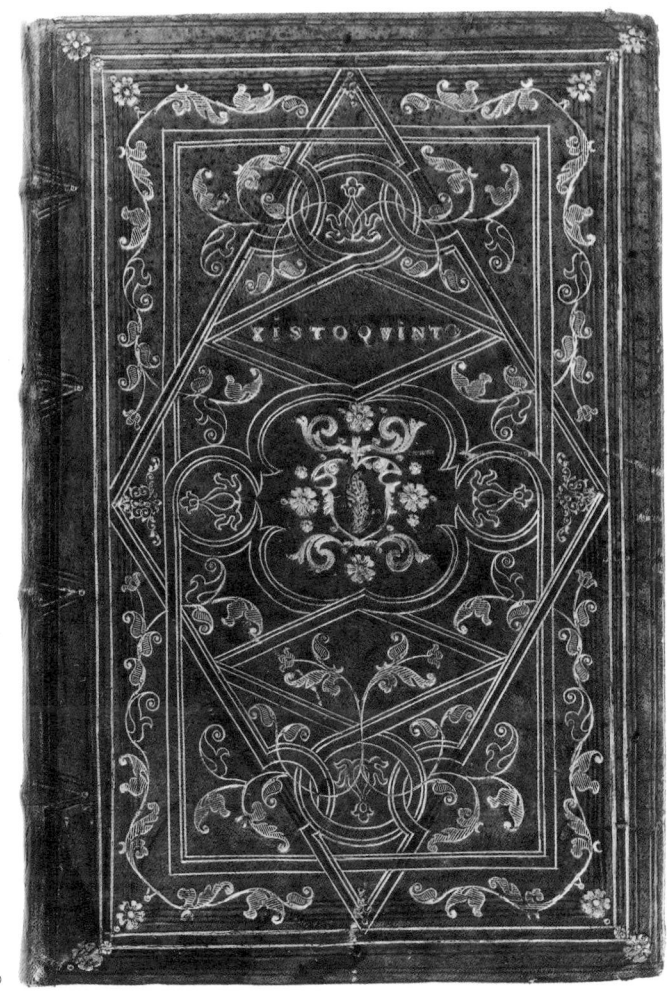

350

Rebacked with part of the original spine strip preserved; resewn on four (invisible) supports, laced in, showing as bands on the spine; five compartments, tooled in gold and blind; in the second compartment: SENT. Endbands: single with a bead; (new) unbleached thread over (?)cord cores (cut off), tied down.

Endleaves: (new) white paper pastedowns and one free white paper leaf conjugate with a stub after the prelims and before the last section, at both ends.

Repairs: spine rebacked and resewn; slight repairs at covers.

PROVENANCE: (?)Pope Sixtus V (or for his Office); on title-page in manuscript: 'Minimitanae monsis princiisma Trinit. bibliotheca'; Lucius Wilmerding (book plate; sold: Parke-Bernet, 29.X.1951, *159*).
Same tool on: Davis 874 (no. 352 below); Fitzwilliam Museum, Cambridge (T Tasso, *Rime et Prose*, Ferrara, 1585).
Compare: Bodleian Library Oxford, Broxbourne R733 (Venice, 1579); *Legature papali*, no. 154; Tolomei, 'Reliures romaines', pl. VI.
Note: Felice Peretti (1521–1590), cardinal: 1570; Pope Sixtus V: 1585.

417

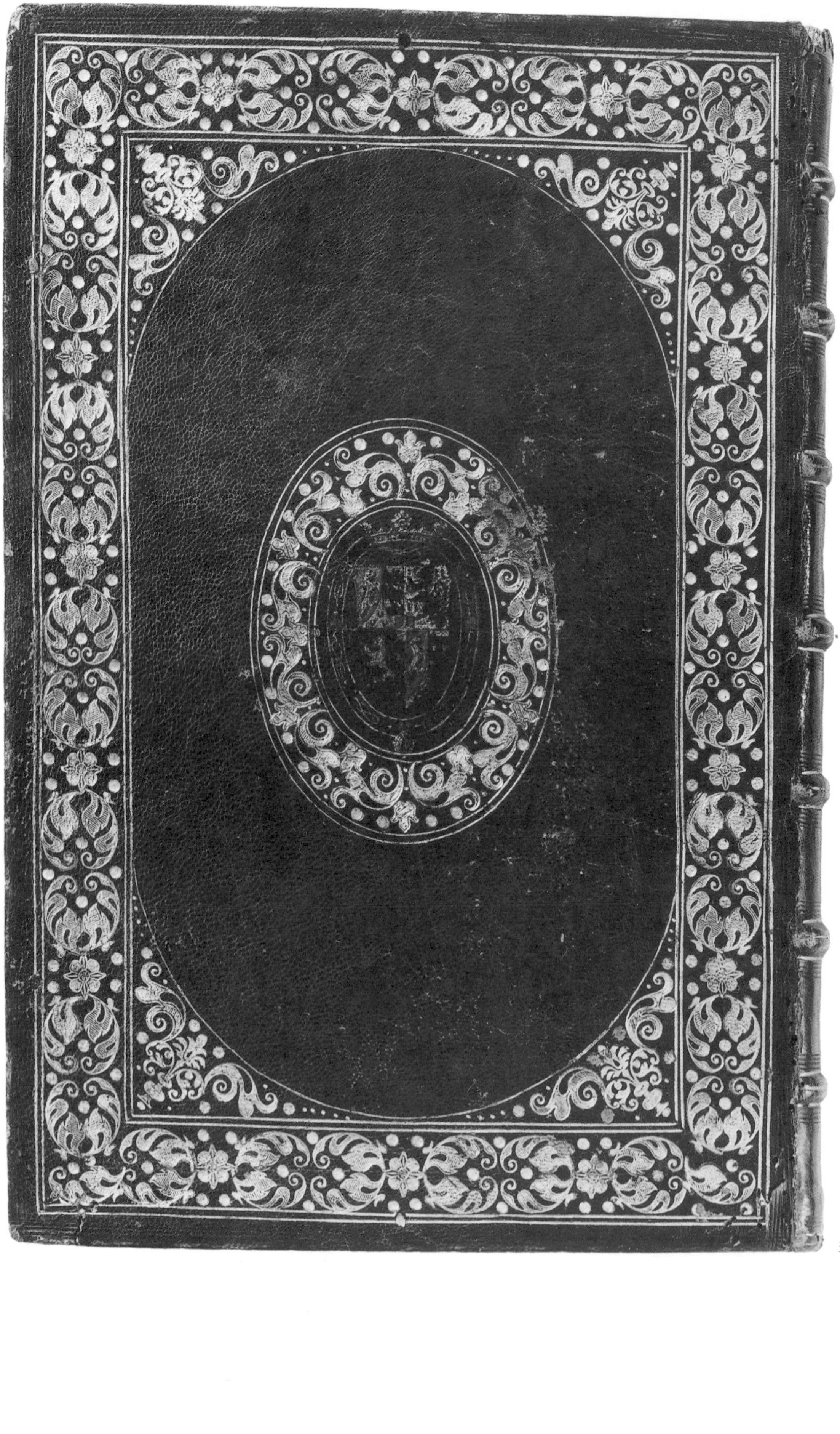

351 A binding probably made in Venice, c. 1593

G Panciroli, *Notitia untraque, dignitatum, cum Orientis, tum Occidentis, ultra arcadij, honorijque tempora* [and] G Panciroli, *De magistratibus municipalibus et corporibus artificum libellus*, Venice: F Senensis, 1593; dedicated to Carl Emanuel, duke of Savoy. fol.

325 × 220 × 33 mm. (P 1233) Davis 873

Red-brown goatskin over paste boards, tooled in gold with lines and gouges; a border filled with curving hatched leaf-shaped tools, solid flower tools and dots; a floral ornament and hatched curling leaf tools in the corners; a centre oval surrounded by hatched curling leaf tools and fleurons, and solid dots around the painted arms of Charles Emanuel I, duke of Savoy. Traces of four pairs of ties. Edges of boards: tooled in gold with part of a roll; turn-ins: tooled in blind with a line. Edges: gilt.

Sewn on seven leather supports, laced in, showing as raised bands on the spine, tooled in gold with lines; eight compartments, tooled in gold with lines and fleurons and in blind with lines. Endbands: double with a bead; primary sewing over alum-tawed (main) cores (laced in), tied down; secondary sewing of yellow and blue silk; cord crowning cores.

Endleaves: white paper pastedowns and two free white paper leaves, (all three) conjugate with stubs after the first and before the last section, at both ends.

PROVENANCE: Charles Emanuel I, duke of Savoy; on upper cover pastedown in manuscript: 'K vi.17'; 'I.x.8' [both crossed out]; 'B.viii.4'; on lower cover pastedown in manuscript: '169'; Count A Oberndorff (sold: Sotheby's, 6.vii.1955, *130*, pl.).
Same tools on: BL, C.46.b.8 (Venice, 1514); Clumber sale: Sotheby's, 6.xii.1937, *933A* (*Dogale*, Venice, c. 1600); Mazal, pl. 101; Brera, no. 56.
Compare: Cambridge University Library, Rel.bb.58.1 (Venice, 1582); sale catalogue, Hôtel Drouot, Paris, 15.xi.1971, *87* (manuscript, Venice, before 1590); Schunke, 'Venezianische Renaissance-Einbände', pls xxiv, xxxi; *Legature papali*, no. 163; *Compare*: (design) Davis 874 (no. 352 below; and literature cited there).
Note: Charles Emanuel I, duke of Savoy (1562–1630); on the throne: 1580.

352 A binding made in Venice, c. 1595

Ordinarium missae pontificalis, Venice, 1595. MS on parchment, part music; written in red and black; gold paint in initials; scribe: Fr. Cyprianus Mantegarrius.

373 × 254 × 30 mm. (M 54) Davis 874

Brown goatskin (or possibly hair sheep) over paste boards, tooled in gold with lines and gouges; two narrow borders filled with small curl tools; a wide border filled with curling leaf tools, vases, clasped hands, fleurs-de-lis, flowers and dots; in the corners a bee and curving floral ornamental tools; fleurs-de-lis; in the centre an oval filled with curving floral ornamental tools, curving leafy tools, small flowers and bees. Traces of two pairs of purple ties. Edges of boards: tooled in gold. Edges: gilt.

Sewn on five (?)leather supports, laced in, showing as bands on the spine, tooled in gold with a line; six false bands, tooled in gold with lines; twelve compartments, tooled in gold. Endbands: single with a bead; primary sewing over (?)alum-tawed cores (cut off), tied down; secondary sewing of pink and white silk.

352

Endleaves: white paper pastedowns and one free leaf conjugate with the pastedown, at both ends. Repairs; at head and tail of spine; at covers.

PROVENANCE: On title-page: painted arms of a cardinal [over-painted]; trace of ex-libris [removed]; printed label with: '154'; Breslauer (Catalogue 90, 1958, no. 38; sold: 29.v.1958).
Same tools on: Davis 872 (no. 350 above); Trinity College, Cambridge, T.16.63 (Venice, 1592); Bodleian Library Oxford, Broxbourne R1370 (Venice, 1593); BL, C.66.h.6 (Venice, 1596); G Michelmore, Catalogue 87, pt. II, no. 122 (Venice, 1593); *possibly*: Corfield sale, Sotheby's, 23.xi.1904, *419*; De Toldo, xiii.
Compare: BL, G 9735 (Venice, 1584), C.64.c.10 (Venice, 1575).

353

353 *A binding of the late sixteenth century*

Uberto Foglietta, *Delle cose della Republica di Genova*, Milan: G Antonio degli Antonij, 1575. 8vo.

157 × 94 × 17 mm. (P 1043) Davis 819

Black goatskin over paste boards, tooled in gold, with blind lines, to a panel design; a wide border filled with large curling tools; fleurons in the corners of the centre panel; in the centre: a tool depicting Diana with a stag. Edges: gilt.

Sewn on four (invisible) supports, possibly laced in, showing as raised bands on the spine; five compartments, tooled in gold with lines and large curling tools. Endbands: single with a bead; primary sewing over leather cores (cut off), tied down; secondary sewing of white and blue silk.

Endleaves: white paper pastedowns and one free white paper leaf tipped onto first and last page, at both ends.

PROVENANCE: Ownership inscription on endleaf erased; on title-page in manuscript: GAR monogram; unidentified cardinal (book plate); Henry B Wheatley (book plate; sold: Sotheby's, 8.iv.1918, *490*); bought: Sotheby's, 7.xi.1951, *468* (pl.).
REFERENCES: Breslauer, Catalogue 107, no. 237 (ref. on p. 176).
Compare: BL, C.183.aa.3 (Venice, 1566).

354

354 *A binding made in Rome, c. 1600*

G Folco, *Effetti mirabili de la Limosina et sentenze degne di memoria appertenenti ad essa*, Rome: F Zanetti, 1586. 8vo.

164 × 103 × 18 mm. (P 1019) Davis 821

Red goatskin over paste boards, tooled in gold with lines, gouges, hatched curving leaf and fleuron tools, cherub's heads and winged caryatides; a centre oval with the painted arms of Orsini. Edges of boards: tooled in gold with dashes; turn-ins: tooled in blind with a line. Edges: gilt.

Sewn on four tanned leather supports, laced in, showing as raised bands on the spine, tooled in gold with a line; five compartments, tooled in gold with circular tools and hatched curving tools. Endbands: single with a bead; primary sewing over alum-tawed cores (cut off), tied down; secondary sewing of blue and yellow silk.

Endleaves: white paper pastedowns, two free conjugate paper leaves and one free leaf conjugate with the pastedown, at both ends.

Repairs: at corners and at head and tail of spine.

PROVENANCE: Orsini; manuscript inscription on title-page: erased; Gumuchian (Catalogue XII [1930], no. 73, pl. xxxi); Grace Whitney Hoff (Whitney Hoff catalogue, no. 104, pl. xxxviii); bought: A Rau, 28.v.1951.

355

355 *A binding made in Rome, c. 1600*

[Sibyls], *Sibyllina oracula ex vett. codd. aucta, renovata, et notis illustrata a D. Iohanne Opsopoeo Brettano*, Paris, 1599. 8vo.

201 × 126 × 60 mm. (P 1268) Davis 850

Red goatskin over paste boards, tooled in gold to a panel design with lines and gouges; flower vases in the corners; wide border filled with solid and hatched leaf and fleuron tools and stars; half-circular extensions to the panel containing leaf tools and cherub's heads; fleurons and hatched leaf tools in the corners of the panel; stars, fleurons and hatched leaf tools around a centre cartouche. Traces of two pairs of (?)yellow ties. Edges of boards: tooled in gold. Edges: gilt and gauffered to a pattern of large diamonds and roundels; traces of red and white paint.

Sewn on four double cords, laced in, showing as raised bands on the spine, tooled in gold with lines; five compartments, tooled in gold with solid and hatched tools. Endbands: double with a bead; primary sewing over cord cores (laced in), tied down; secondary sewing of green and yellow silk.

Endleaves: green block-printed paper pastedowns (floral and dotted pattern) and one free leaf conjugate with the pastedown (backed), at both ends.

PROVENANCE: On title-page: inscription in Aramaic; J R Abbey (book plate; 'J.A.2593/ 4:5:1945'; sold: Sotheby's, 23.vi.1965, *620*).
Compare: *Legature papali*, no. 167.

423

356 *A binding made in Rome by Soresino ('Borghese bindery'), c. 1600–10*

M A Muretus, *Orationes xxiii* [and] *Hymnorum sacrorum liber* [gathering D misbound], Venice: I Alberti, 1586 [and] *Aristoteles Ethicorum … M A Mureto interprete*, n.p., n.d. 8vo.

150 × 93 × 27 mm. (P 1229) Davis 822

Red goatskin over paste boards, tooled in gold with lines; s-shaped tools in the border; floral volutes in the corners; pine-cones and winged caryatides; on the upper cover: the arms of Giovanni Battista Crescenzi and IO. BAP./ CRESCEN; on the lower cover: the arms of Torquato de Cupis with TORQVAT/ CVPIVS. Traces of two pairs of ties. Edges of boards: tooled in gold with dashes near the corners. Edges: gilt.

Sewn on three leather supports, laced in, showing as raised bands on the spine, tooled in gold with lines; four compartments, tooled in blind with lines and in gold with lines and stylized flowers. Endbands: single with a bead; blue and faded pink silk over alum-tawed cores (broken off), tied down.

Endleaves: white paper pastedowns, at both ends; at the end: one free paper leaf conjugate with a stub before the last section.

PROVENANCE: Giovanni Battista Crescenzi; Torquato de Cupis; bought: Sotheby's, 6.vii.1955, *112*.
REFERENCES: Foot, *Davis*, I, p. 326.
LITERATURE: G Baglione, *Le vite de' pittori, scultori ed architetti*, Rome, 1642, pp. 364–7; Bignami Odier, pp. 110, 289, 290, 293; Foot, *Davis*, I, pp. 323–36 (and literature cited there); Tolomei, 'I ferri', pp. 31–2; Quilici, 'Legatoria romana', pp. 21–4; Nardelli, 'Legatori Vaticani', p. 254; Macchi, *Dizionario*, p. 412.
Same cartouche on: Gumuchian, 1930, pl. XLII; Breslauer, Catalogue 107, nos. 95, 262 (but combined with different tools).
Same tool on: Tolomei, 'I ferri', p. 32, a, pl. I; Tolomei, *Legatura romana barocca*, nos. 9, 11, 14.
Compare: *Legature papali*, no. 164; Malaguzzi, *Aosta*, pp. 46–7, nos. 26–7; Quilici, no. 193, pl. 82.
Note: Francesco Soresino bound for the Vatican from 11 August 1575; his son, Prospero, worked for the Vatican from 1588-1593; Baldassarre Soresino, probably Francesco's grandson, also bound for the Vatican, from 19 May 1607-c.1634; he died: 1659. Giovanni Battista Crescenzi (1577–1660): painter and architect; superintendent of works and pictures under Pope Paul V. He designed the mausoleum at the Escorial and the Buen Retiro Palace; left Rome for Spain: c. 1620; died in Madrid. Torquato de Cupis was one of Rospigliosi's teachers at the Collegium Romanum.

357 *A binding made in Venice, 1605*

A Stella, *La vita del venerabile servo d'iddio, il Padre Girolamo Miani nobile venetiano*, Vicenza: G Greco, 1605; woodcut initials. 4to.

205 × 148 × 18 mm. (P 1093) Davis 823

Red goatskin over paste boards, tooled in gold to a panel design, with lines; a wide border filled with leaf tools and in the middle of each side: an oval containing four fleurons, forming a cross; large volutes, fleurons, gouges, solid and hatched flower tools; in the centre: an oval with the painted arms of Marino

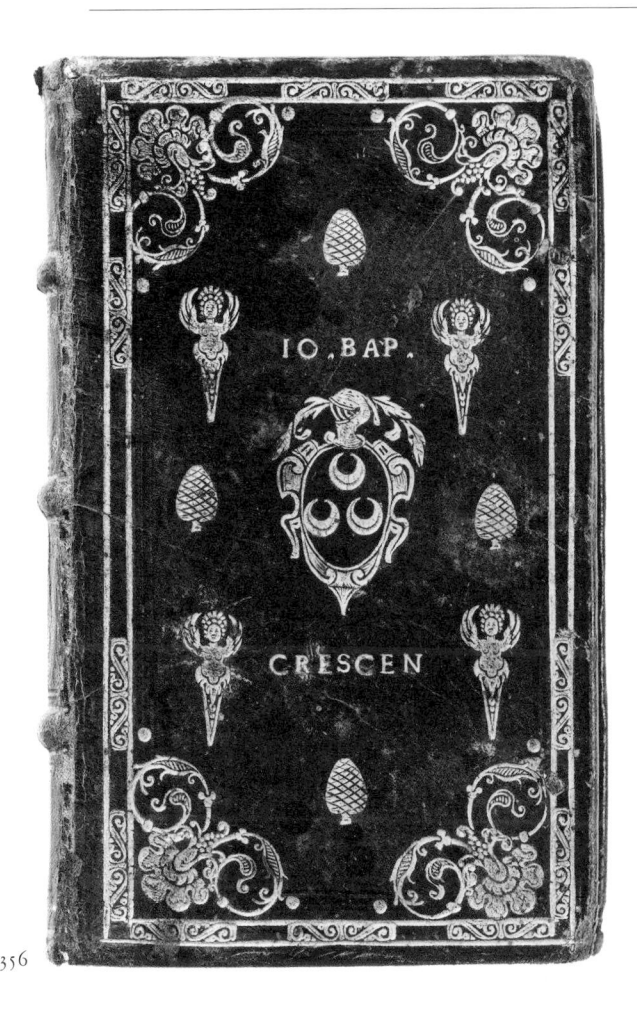

Grimani, doge of Venice (to whom the book is dedicated). Traces of four pairs of ties. Edges of boards: tooled in gold. Edges: gilt and lightly gauffered with a row of dots.

Sewn on four cords, laced in, showing as raised bands on the spine, tooled in gold with lines; three false bands alternating with the sewing supports, tooled in gold with lines; eight compartments, tooled in gold with lines and egg-and-dart tools. Endbands: double with a bead; primary sewing over cord cores (laced in), tied down; secondary sewing of green and red silk.

Endleaves: white paper pastedowns, two free conjugate white paper leaves, and one free leaf conjugate with the pastedown, at both ends.

PROVENANCE: Marino Grimani; Henry S Richardson (book plate); Eduardo J Bullrich (book plate); ink stamp with $\frac{830}{R}$ (in an oval); bought: Sotheby's, 19.iii.1952, *365*.

Note: Marino Grimani, doge of Venice: 1595–1605.

358

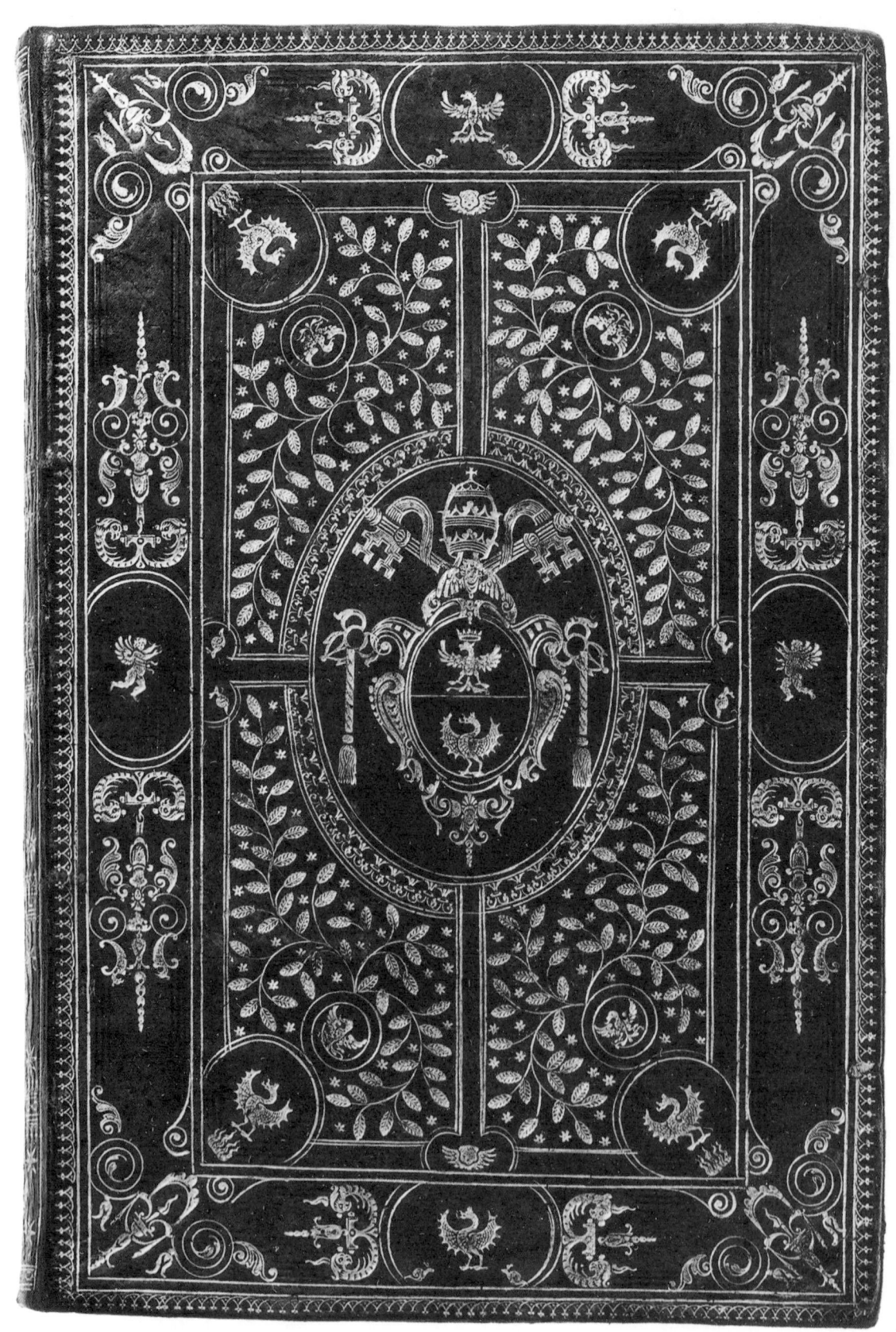

358 *A binding made in Rome for Pope Paul V, c. 1610–20*

Carlo Sigonio, *Historiarum de regno Italiae libri*, Venice: I Ziletto, 1574. fol.

365 × 250 × 48 mm. (P 1288) Davis 876

Red goatskin over paste boards, tooled in gold with lines; a small ornamental outer border; a wide border with baroque ornaments, vase tools in the corners, various curls, hatched tools, pairs of monster [?ram's]-head tools, cherubs and the Borghese eagle; the panel is divided into compartments with Borghese dragons in the corners, small cherub's heads at top and bottom; curving tendrils with leaf tools, and in the centre: the arms of Camilio Borghese, Pope Paul V. Traces of two pairs of ties. Edges of boards: tooled in gold with dashes. Edges: gilt and gauffered with dots.

Sewn on five (recessed) cords, laced in; smooth spine, tooled in gold with lines and small rolls dividing the spine into six compartments, each tooled in gold with a charge from the Borghese arms and four stars. Endbands: single with a bead; red silk, tied down.

Endleaves: white paper pastedowns and one free paper leaf conjugate with a stub after the first and before the last section, at both ends.

PROVENANCE: Pope Paul V; Alphonso Landi (on title-page in manuscript: 'Ex libris Alphonsi Landi'); bought: Breslauer, 14.i.1958.
REFERENCES: Foot, *Davis*, I, pp. 323, 326; Tolomei, 'I ferri', p. 32.
LITERATURE: Foot, *Davis*, I, pp. 323–36 (and literature cited there); Tolomei, 'I ferri', pp. 32–3; see also Davis 824 (no. 359 below).
Compare: *Legature papali*, nos. 179, 182; Tolomei, 'I ferri', p. 33, tools p, u, pls I, III; Tolomei, *Legatura romana barocca*, no. 13.
Note: The tools used on this binding and on Davis 824 (no. 359 below) may be identical with those used by the Soresino shop. Camilio Borghese (1552–1621); Pope Paul V: 1605–21.

359 *A binding made in Rome for Giulio Rospigliosi, c. 1610–20*

[G B Fatio], *Della contemplatione dell' huomo estatico* [and] *Della conversione dell'huomo adio* [and] *Del Madrigale*, Perugia: P Petrucci, 1588 [and] R Cancellieri, *Carmen de iustitia & de hominis conditione in inggressu studij*, Venice: B Iunta, I B Ciottus & Socios, 1611 [and] P Landi, *Dichiaratione dell' impresa dell'Accademia Partenia di Roma*, Rome: L Zanetti, 1594. 4to.

207 × 144 × 17 mm. (P 1429) Davis 824

White limp parchment, tooled in gold with lines; three narrow borders, the outer one filled with small ornamental tools, the second one with chain-tooling; flowers at the corners; floral and spiral tools in the corners; gouges, curving tools, volutes, mask and vase tools; cherubs, flower and leaf tools around a central oval, containing on the upper cover: a grid [?chessboard] and ET/ PRAELIA/ LVDO; on the lower cover: IVLIVS/ ROSPIGLIOSI/VS. Traces of two pairs of ties. Edges: stained red.

Sewn on two tanned leather supports (cut off); smooth spine, tooled in gold with lines and caryatides; title in manuscript (ink). Endbands: single with a bead; primary sewing over alum-tawed cores (cut off), tied down; secondary sewing of pink and blue silk.

359

Endleaves: white paper pastedowns, at both ends; at the front: one free white paper leaf tipped on to the title-page; at the end: one free leaf conjugate with the pastedown.

PROVENANCE: Giulio Rospigliosi; bought: Sotheby's, 28.ii.1966, *105*.
REFERENCES: Foot, *Davis*, I, p. 326.
LITERATURE: See Davis 876 (no. 358 above; and literature cited there).
Compare: Tolomei, 'I ferri', p. 32, l, p. 33, u, pl. III; Tolomei, *Legatura romana barocca*, nos. 20, 24, 26, 27.
Note: Giulio Rospigliosi (1600–1669); cardinal: 1657; Pope Clement IX: 1667–9.

360 *A binding made in Rome by the 'Rospigliosi bindery', 1611*

[Testimony of doctorate, granted to Ioannes Franciscus Rossi], Naples 1611, MS on parchment, parts written in gold, every leaf signed: Joannes Antonius Infrisius; at end of text: 'Ego Joannes Antonius Infrisius Almi Collegij Neap[olita]ni Ads et Sec[retariu]s subsi et signavi infidem et test[imoniu]m premissorum'; decorated with painted borders; painted arms: gu and or, rampant lion counter-changed and three fleurs-de-lis sa.

226 × 152 × 11 mm. (M 43) Davis 852

360

Dark red goatskin over paste boards, tooled in gold with lines; a wide border with caryatides and hatched volutes in the corners; gouges; caryatides, volutes and fleurons; a panel with large volutes ending in mermaids or griffins, curls, fleurons, hatched lotus tools, flower vases, small birds, rampant lions and eagle tools; in the centre an oval with the rampant lion of the Rossi family. Traces of four pairs of ties. Edges: plain.

Sewn on three (recessed?) supports, laced in; smooth spine, tooled in gold with lines dividing the spine into four compartments, tooled in gold with small flowers. Endbands: missing; at head: remnant of cord core, laced in.

Endleaves: white paper pastedowns, at both ends; illuminated manuscript lining beneath part of pastedowns conjugate with a stub after the first and before the last section. Coloured engravings pasted onto pastedowns: inside upper cover: portrait of Pope Paul V with: PAVLVS.V.PONT.OPT.MAX. CREATVS PAPA DIE 16 MA[IVS]; inside lower cover: portrait of Philip III with: PHILIPPVS. III.AVSTRs DEI GRATIA HISPANIAR/ INDIAR/ NEAPOLIS SICILIAE HIEROSOLai etcet REX CATOLs. MEDIOLANI BRABA[N]TIAE BVRGVal etcet DVX.

PROVENANCE: Ioannes Franciscus Rossi (on verso of last leaf in manuscript: 'Rossi'); De Marinis (sold: Milan, Hoepli, xi–xii.1925, *186*, pl.); Gilhofer & Ranschburg (Catalogue 265, Vienna, n.d., *153*; sold: 3.vii.1951).
REFERENCES: Foot, *Davis*, I, pp. 323, 327, 329.
LITERATURE: Bignami Odier, p. 293; Foot, *Davis*, I, pp. 323–36 (and literature cited there); Tolomei, 'I ferri', pp. 32–3 (tool: z), pl. VI; Quilici, 'Legatoria romana', pp. 24–6; Nardelli, 'Legatori Vaticani', pp. 253–4.
Note: Although the 'Rospigliosi binder' has been identified by Monseigneur Ruysschaert with the Andreoli brothers, Davis 852 is too early to have been made in their atelier. Camilio Borghese, Pope Paul V: 1605–21.

361

361 *A binding made in Florence for Cosimo II de' Medici, grand duke of Tuscany, c. 1618*

A Cioli, *Saggi morali opera nuova*, Florence: P Cecconcelli, 1618 [and] *Trattato della sapienza degli antichi*, Florence: P Cecconcelli, 1618. 12mo.

150 × 82 × 23 mm. (P 1421) Davis 825

White parchment over paste boards, tooled in gold with lines and an over-all pattern of crowns, Medici coats of arms, solid curls, and small tools showing mounted horsemen. Edges: gilt.

Sewn on two (invisible) supports; hollow back; smooth spine, tooled in gold with crowns, Medici coats of arms and small solid curls. Endbands: double with a bead; primary sewing over alum-tawed cores (cut off), tied down; secondary sewing of green and beige silk.

Endleaves: (new) white paper pastedowns and one free paper leaf conjugate with a stub pasted beneath the pastedown, at both ends.

PROVENANCE: Cosimo II de' Medici, grand duke of Tuscany (to whom the book is dedicated); on first title-page in manuscript: 'Pitt' ['Pith'?]; 'F.6'; bought: Sotheby's, 28.ii.1966, *109*.
Note: Cosimo II de' Medici, grand duke of Tuscany: 1609–21.

Italian Bindings

362 *A binding made c. 1620*

Missale Romanum, Venice: Iunta, 1618 [and] *Missa propriae festorum ordines fratrum minorum*, Venice: Iunta, 1618. 8vo.

194 × 135 × 37 mm. (P 1232) Davis 851

Black goatskin over paste boards, tooled in gold with lines; an outer border filled with two-linked-floral-circles tools; an inner border with small s-shaped tools; quarter fans in the corners and in the centre a large circular fan, with small circles and fleurons above and below, surrounded by small flying bird tools and stars. Traces of two pairs of green ties. Edges: gilt.

Sewn on four alum-tawed supports, laced in, showing as bands on the spine; five compartments, tooled in gold with two-interlinked-circles tools (traces of labels: removed). Endbands: single; primary sewing over cord cores (laced in), tied down; remnants of secondary sewing in white and pink silk.

Endleaves: white paper pastedowns, at both ends; at the front: one free leaf conjugate with the pastedown; at the end: two free conjugate paper leaves and one free leaf conjugate with the pastedown.

PROVENANCE: On front endleaf in manuscript (modern hand): 'N° 40/1995/P'; bought: Sotheby's, 6.vii.1955, *116*.
Compare: Folger Catalogue, no. 12:12.

363 *A binding made c. 1630*

A Molina, *Instruttione de' Sacerdoti ... tradotta ... per Tomaso Galletti*, Venice: G Sarzina, 1628. 4to.

211 × 152 × 32 mm. (P 877) Davis 854

Red goatskin over paste boards, tooled in gold to a panel design, with lines; three borders outlined with lines and small rolls; second border filled with flowers and leafy branches; gouges forming interlacing ribbons dividing the panel into compartments, filled with solid fleurons, curls, flower tools and small round fans; in the centre a cartouche with the (faded) painted arms of an abbot or bishop (?ar. a rose gu.). Edges of boards: tooled in gold with dashes. Edges: gilt and lightly gauffered with rows of dots.

Sewn on four (recessed) cords, laced in; smooth spine, tooled in gold to a long rectangular panel with small solid tools. Endbands: single with a bead; primary sewing over (?)cord cores (cut off), tied down; secondary sewing (only fragments left) of red silk; black staining.

Endleaves: white paper pastedowns, two free conjugate paper leaves and one free paper leaf tipped on, at both ends.

PROVENANCE: Monastery of Settimo (on title-page and at end of text in manuscript: 'Monasterij & Cellae Abbatis Sep:mi'; the book is dedicated to Attilio Brunacci, abbot of Settimo, but the painted arms on the cover are not those of the Brunacci family); erased note on title-page; R C Fisher (sold: Sotheby's, 23.v.1906, *441*, pl.); bought: Sotheby's, 18.vi.1946, *184* (pl.).

364

364 *A binding probably made in Rome, c. 1640*

[Monte Santo e Loreto], *Compra de Beni in Monte Santo e Loreto* [a collection of legal documents dealing with the purchase of property, dated 1637, 1638 and 1640] [Italy, c. 1640], MS (in Italian and Latin) on parchment.

230 × 165 × 25 mm. (M 53) Davis 855

Red goatskin over paste boards, tooled in gold to a panel design, with lines; an outer border filled with two-linked-floral-circles tools; second border with dog-tooth roll and small solid curl tools; third border with chain roll; at top of panel: -COMPRA- DE-BENI-; at bottom of panel: -IN-MONTE-SANTO-/ -E- LORETO-; a bird tool in the corners of the panel with curls and fleurons; a semis of fleurs-de-lis (?crosses); in the centre of the upper cover: curls, fleurons and leafy sprays around an oval containing a saint holding an arrow and a book, surrounded by stars; in the centre of the lower cover: an elaborately decorated coat of arms (unidentified: per pale, dexter: ear of corn; mount with ?dove; sinister: crab). Two pairs of silver clasps (one partly missing), hinging on upper cover. Edges: gilt.

Sewn on four tanned leather supports, laced in, showing as raised bands on the spine, tooled in gold with dashes; five compartments, tooled in gold with two-linked-circles tools. Endbands: single with a bead; primary sewing over leather cores (cut off), tied down; secondary sewing of yellow and blue silk.

Endleaves: white paper pastedowns and two free conjugate paper leaves, at both ends; at the front: one free leaf conjugate with the pastedown.

PROVENANCE: On endleaf in manuscript: 'Hiermo(?) / Pro MSS. Cap. Jo: Antonio Passaro/ Con(?)/ Q(?)uose[?c]id(?)ig/ die 26. Aplio 1644/ Troianus'; bought: Sotheby's, 18.ii.1957, *37*.
REFERENCES: *Treasures*, 1965, no. 81.
Compare: BL, C.46.f.2 (Rome, 1647); Tolomei, 'I ferri', pl. X; Tolomei, *Legatura romana barocca*, no. 40; Schäfer, no. 85.

365 *A binding probably made in Milan, c. 1648*

G Ripamonti, *Chronistae urbis Mediolani historiae patriae (decadis iii)*, n.p., n.d. [Milan, 1641]; [title-page missing]. fol.

296 × 205 × 82 mm. (P 1283) Davis 875

Light brown goatskin over paste boards, tooled in gold with lines; three borders, filled with small floral and ornamental tools; in the corners: a flower tool and quarter fans built up of small tools; curls, fleurons and small ornamental tools around in the centre: a large fan and two half fans, all built up of small tools. Edges of boards: tooled in gold. Edges: gilt and gauffered to a pattern of half-circles and roundels.

Sewn on three (recessed) cords, laced in; smooth spine, tooled in gold with a strip, formed by lines and two rows of floral tools, dividing the spine into two compartments, each with quarter fans in the corners and a fan in the centre; curl tools. Endbands: single with (the remnant of) a bead; primary sewing over cord cores (laced in), remnants of tie-downs; secondary sewing of green and possibly pink silk (fragments only).

Endleaves: white paper pastedowns, at both ends; at the front: one free paper leaf conjugate with a stub; at the end: two free conjugate paper leaves.

PROVENANCE: On endleaf and first page of text in manuscript: 'Antonij Bendoni'; bought: Sotheby's, 19.xii.1962, *664*.
REFERENCES: Romme, *Book Collector*, 1969, pp. 42–3, note 145.
LITERATURE: Fletcher, *Foreign*, pl. 51; Nixon, *Broxbourne*, no. 68.
Compare: BL, C.24.b.4–5 (Milan, 1643, 1648), C. 46.i.6 (Milan, 1641–8); Sotheby's, 30.xi.1971, *496*.

366 *A binding made in Rome, c. 1650*

N Franco, *Le pistole vulgari*, Venice: A Gardane, 1542. 8vo.

153 × 101 × 31 mm. (P 1179) Davis 826

Red goatskin over paste boards, tooled in gold with lines; a border filled with two-linked-floral-circles tools; a small dog-tooth roll; mask tools and small rampant lions in the corners; fleurons, flowers and curling leafy tools around in the centre: a beaded oval containing a rampant lion. Traces of two pairs of ties. Edges: gilt.

Sewn on four cords, laced in, showing as raised bands on the spine; five compartments, tooled in gold with a rampant lion; title lettered in second compartment. Endbands: double with a bead; primary sewing over cord cores (still partly laced in), tied down; secondary sewing of pink and yellow silk.

Endleaves: white paper pastedowns and one free white paper leaf conjugate with a stub after the first and before the last section, at both ends.

PROVENANCE: Silvain S Brunschwig (book plate; sold: Rauch, 29.iii.1955, *227*).
Compare: *Legature papali*, no. 233; Tolomei, 'I ferri', pl. IV; Tolomei, *Legatura romana barocca*, nos. 19, 22, 23; Quilici, no. 854, pl. 347.
Note: The rampant lion differs from that of the Rossi family on Davis 852 (no. 360 above). Many Italian families have a rampant lion as their coats of arms.

367 *A binding possibly made in Rome, c. 1650*

Blank book [Common-place book, MS in Italian, in two different hands. The first hand, c. 1650, mostly anecdotes of a miraculous or moral kind; the second hand, second half of the 17th century, spiritual exercises and devotions. Two blanks and four stubs at the front; seven blanks at the end], [c. 1650].

159 × 111 × 17 mm.   (P1281) Davis 827

White parchment over paste boards, tooled in gold with lines; a wide border filled with curling tools and small leaf tools; rosettes in the corners; above and below the centre panel: IO. BAPTISTA./ CARDANVS.; small ornamental border roll; flower vases in the corners of the panel; small flower tools and floral curl tools around the arms of the Giustiniani family in the centre. Traces of two pairs of ties. Edges: gilt and gauffered.

435

367

Sewn on four cords, laced in, showing as bands on the spine; five compartments, tooled in gold with small flower vases. Endbands: single with a bead; yellow and beige silk over alum-tawed cores (laced in), tied down.

Endleaves: white paper pastedowns and one free paper leaf tipped on, at both ends.

PROVENANCE: Giovanni Battista Cardani (on endleaf in manuscript: 'Cardanii'); (?)Giustiniani family; J R Abbey (book plate; 'J.A.4080/ 20:6:1948'; sold: 21.vi.1965, *210*).
Compare: BL, C.129.i.5 (Rome, 1681); *Legature papali*, no. 183; Quilici, no. 725, pl. 297.

368 *A binding made in Rome probably by Gregorio Andreoli, c. 1658*

Series actorum omnium in canonizatione Sancti Thomae a Villanova ... a ... Alexandro VII, Rome: Typographia Rev. Camerae Apostolicae, 1658. 4to.

251 × 180 × 22 mm. (P 1284) Davis 853

Red goatskin over paste boards, tooled in gold to a panel design, with lines, a border filled with curling tools, small mask tools in the corners; small dog-tooth roll; quarter fans in the corners of the panel; fleuron and fleurs-de-lis tools, curl tools, and in the centre, partly onlaid in black, the arms of a cardinal (quarterly ?gu. A/VE ?or. and sa. A sun ?or.). Edges: gilt.

Sewn on three (recessed) cords, laced in; smooth spine, tooled in gold to an all-over pattern of small solid tools. Endbands: single with a bead; yellow and (a fragment of) pink silk over cord cores (cut off), tied down.

Endleaves: white paper pastedowns, at both ends; at the front: two free conjugate paper leaves; at the end: one free paper leaf (probably once one of a pair of conjugate leaves).

368

369

PROVENANCE:	On title-page in manuscript: 'Ad (?)usum Phoeb(?)e Augustianensis(?) [erased]; bought: Breslauer, 20.iv.1956.
REFERENCES:	Foot, *Davis*, I, p. 334, no. [36].
LITERATURE:	Bignami Odier, p. 293; Foot, *Davis*, I, pp. 323–36 (and literature cited there); Quilici, 'Legatoria romana', pp. 24–6; Ruysschaert, 'Le legature romane'; Tolomei, 'I ferri', pp. 32–3, pl. IV, V, VIII; Ruysschaert, *Les frères Andreoli*; Nardelli, 'Legatori Vaticani', pp. 253–4; see also Davis 852 (no. 360 above).
Same tools on:	Tolomei, *Legatura romana barocca*, nos. 50, 57, 67, 68, 72; Quilici, nos. 625, 659, 1137, pls 251, 265, 454; *Aussen-Ansichten*, no. 79.
Note:	Gregorio Andreoli, came to work for the Vatican library:1655; appointed binder to the Vatican for his life: 28 September 1665; his brother, Giovanni, appointed to work with him and to succeed him: 7 September 1675. Gregorio died: after 14 January 1696; Giovanni died: 10 September 1699.

369   *A binding probably made in Rome, c. 1660*

P Chifflet, *Concilii Tridendini … canones et decreta*, Cologne: Cornelius ab Egmond, 1656. 12mo.

132 × 80 × 22 mm.   (P 1419) Davis 828

Red goatskin over paste boards, tooled in gold with lines; a small dog-tooth roll; a border filled with two-linked-floral-circles tools; quarter fans in the corners of the panel; small solid tools, and a fan, built up of small tools in the centre. Two shell-shaped brass clasps on gold-tooled leather straps, hinging on the upper cover. Edges: gilt.

Sewn on five cords, laced in, showing as bands on the spine, tooled in gold; six compartments, tooled in gold; second compartment lettered: CONCIL/TRIDENT. Endbands: single with a bead; yellow and red silk over (?)cord (or alum-tawed) cores (cut off), tied down.

Endleaves: red, yellow and blue comb-marbled pastedowns, at both ends; at the front two free conjugate white paper leaves; at the end: one free white paper leaf.

PROVENANCE:	On first free endleaf in manuscript: 'Bernardi Gioanni/ Torino 4 Febbrajo dell' anno 1882'/ 'BG'; on second free endleaf in manuscript: 'G. Bernardi/ Castell Delfino/ BG'; on title-page and at end of index in manuscript: 'BG'; at end of text in manuscript: 'G. Bernardi'; bought: Sotheby's, 28.ii.1966, *115*.
Same tools on:	Chester Beatty Library, 228 (Turin, 1666, with arms of Cardinal Geronimo Farnese); Quilici, no. 661, pl. 266.
Compare:	BL, Add. MS 58853 (Music manuscript, 17th century); Tolomei, 'I ferri', pl. V. VI; Tolomei, *Legatura romana barocca*, nos. 60, 61, 70, 74; *Aussen-Ansichten*, no. 78.

370   *A binding possibly made in Bologna, c. 1668*

U Aldrovandi, *Dendrologiae naturalis scilicet arborum historiae libri duo*, Bologna: J B Ferronius, 1668 [colophon: 1667]; engraved title-page. fol.

360 × 247 × 62 mm. (P 1289) Davis 877

Red goatskin over paste boards, tooled in gold, with lines; a small border roll with floral half-circles; a border roll composed of flowers; a border roll of larger floral half-circles; a fleuron and quarter fan in each corner; the centre panel divided into compartments by single and double fillets (compare 'Fanfare ribbons') and a small floral-half-circles roll; the compartments are filled with floral curls, long leafy sprays, flowers and dots. Traces of two pairs of red ties. Edges of boards: tooled in gold. Edges: gilt.

Sewn on six cords, laced in, showing as raised bands on the spine, tooled in gold; seven compartments, tooled in gold with floral borders, corner curls, and a pointillé flower tool in the centre; title lettered in second compartment. Endbands: single with a bead; yellow and blue silk over leather cores (cut off), tied down.

Endleaves: white paper pastedowns and one free paper leaf conjugate with a stub beneath the pastedown, at both ends.

PROVENANCE:	Paul Menso (ex-libris); library label with: 'Ad Bibliothecam Archi-Episcopalis Presbyterorum & Alumnorum Collegii'; round stamp with: 'M'; in manuscript on endleaf: 'xxxi.A.b.6'; bought: Breslauer, 1.vii.1959.
Same tools on:	Chester Beatty Library, 221 (Bologna, 1612); BL, C.47.i.3 (Venice, 1644), C.128.d.5 (Bologna, 1674); Quilici, no. 856, pl. 348.
Compare:	Tolomei, *Legatura romana barocca*, no. 70; Malaguzzi, *Preziosi*, no. 26.

370

371 *A binding made in Rome, c. 1695*

[Nicolo Vescouo d'Alet], *Trattato della regalia stampatosi d'ordine di Mo[n]sig. Vescouo di Pamies*, n.p., 1680. 4to.

228 × 170 × 27 mm.   (P 1426) Davis 856

Red goatskin over paste boards, tooled in gold to a panel design with lines; large fleurons at the corners; corner curls in the corners of the panel; fleurons; hatched curling tools; small solid tools; in the centre: the arms of Pope Innocent XII. Edges of boards: tooled in gold with a zig-zag pattern. Edges: gilt.

Sewn on six cords, laced in, showing as raised bands on the spine, tooled in gold; seven compartments, tooled in gold; title lettered in second compartment. Endbands: single with a bead; pale and dark blue silk over cord cores (cut off), tied down.

Endleaves: red, yellow, blue and green comb-marbled pastedowns, one free comb-marbled leaf conjugate with the pastedown, and two free white paper leaves each conjugate with a stub beneath the pastedown, at both ends.

PROVENANCE: Pope Innocent XII; on title-page in manuscript: 'X–iiii.n.is/ I. Catta formello di Napoli 1740/ Cavet–'; bought: Sotheby's, 28.ii.1966, *118*.
Same tools on: BL, C.68.c.18 (Rome, 1689); Quilici, nos. 761, 775, pls 316, 328.
Compare: BL, C.47.f.9 (Rome, 1694); Trinity College, Cambridge, A.10.43 (Venice, 1545); Sotheby's, 13.vii.1948, *101*; Tolomei, 'I ferri', pls I, IX; Tolomei, *Legatura romana barocca*, no. 80.
Note: Antonio Pignatelli, Pope Innocent XII: 1691–1700.

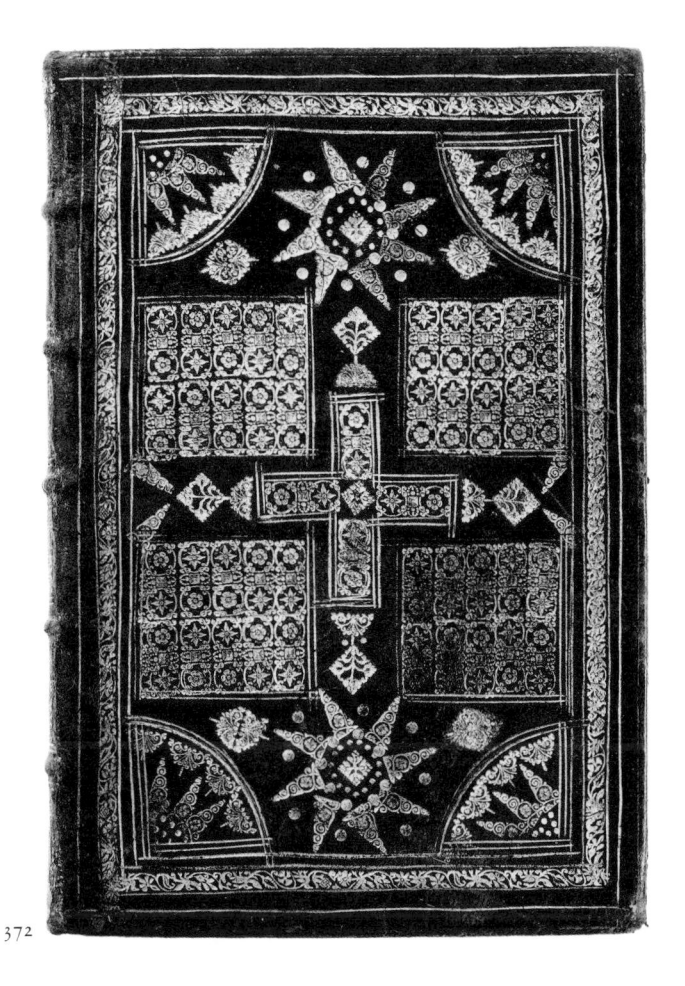

372 *A seventeenth-century binding possibly made in Italy or Spain*

Bible [Italian; incomplete]: vol. II (pp. 361–847) I Chronicles-Malachi, n.p., n.d. 4to.

261 × 182 × 30 mm. (P 1471) Davis 889

Red-brown goatskin over paste boards, tooled in gold with lines; a roll showing birds in floral branches; quarter circular corners filled with spiral curls and small solid fleuron curls; four blocks of linked-floral-circles tools; fleurons; spiral curls; fillets; and in the centre a cross-shape, its arms filled with linked-floral-circles tools. Edges of boards: tooled in gold; turn-ins: tooled in blind with a line. Edges: gilt.

Sewn on five (?)cords, laced in, showing as raised bands on the spine, tooled in gold; six compartments, tooled in gold with corner curls and centre fleurons; in second compartment lettered: BIBBIA./SACRA/P.II. Endbands: single with a bead; primary sewing over (?)rolled-leather cores (cut off), tied down; remnant of secondary sewing of pink and white silk, tied down.

Endleaves: white paper pastedowns and one free leaf conjugate with the pastedown, at both ends.

PROVENANCE: On first page of text: faded blue oval stamp; library label with in manuscript: 'no 2016/815/ AA'; J R Abbey (book plate; 'J.A.2717/ 3:1:1946'; sold: Sotheby's, 21.vi.1965, *150*).

Compare: Tolomei, 'I ferri', pl. V; Quilici, no. 858, pl. 350.

THE HENRY DAVIS GIFT

373 *A binding made in Rome at the end of the seventeenth or the beginning of the eighteenth century*

[A blank book with:] *Libellus in quo diversae Lectiones Antiph[on]ae et id genus alia suis notis acco[mmo]d[a]ta, continentur, prout cantari solent in Ecclesia RR. PP. Servorum B.M.V....edita à Fr. N.N.*, MS on paper [music and text], 1781.

210 × 145 × 14 mm.   (M 33) Davis 861

Brown goatskin over paste boards, tooled in gold with lines and gouges, a small ornamental outer border, a border with a fleuron-zig-zag roll; flower vases and quarter fans in the corners of the centre panel, a small ornamental inner border; curl tools, leafy curls and floral tools around in the centre: a crowned shield with a bend, charged: +.S.P.Q.R. [Senatus Populusque Romanus, the arms of the Populus Romanus]; decorated with black paint. Edges of boards and turn-ins: tooled in gold with small rolls. Edges: sprinkled red.

Sewn on four cords, laced in, smooth spine, tooled in gold with groups of small lozenges. No endbands. Remnants of printed-paper spine lining.

Endleaves: pink, white, green and yellow block-printed paper pastedowns with a striped and floral pattern (printed with paste colours) and one free white paper leaf, at both ends; remnant of printed-paper board lining.

PROVENANCE: W H Corfield (book plate; sold: Sotheby's, 23.xi.1904, *401*); bought: Sotheby's, 16.xi.1943, *150*.
REFERENCES: Foot, *Davis*, I, p. 326, note 42; p. 336, Appendix, no. 90.
LITERATURE: See Davis 853 (no. 368 above; and literature cited there).
Note: The binding of this blank book may predate the contents by over eighty years. It is possible that this binding comes from a successor, or even a later imitator, of the Andreoli brothers.

374 *A Jewish binding, probably made in Italy, c. 1700 (?)*

Cicero, *L'Epistole ad Attico*, Venice: Aldus, 1555. 8vo.

160 × 105 × 57 mm.   (P 570) Davis 888

Red velvet over paste boards with silver mounts. Engraved silver corner pieces and a silver centre piece, left blank on the upper cover and showing on the lower cover [i.e. the upper cover for a Jewish book] beneath a crown: the High Priest's hands lifted in prayer above a dove. Two pairs of engraved silver clasps (one missing), hinging on the lower cover. Edges: gilt.

Sewn on four (invisible) supports, laced in, showing as raised bands on the spine; five compartments. Endbands (possibly later): single with a bead; red silk over flat (?)alum-tawed cores (cut off), sporadically tied down.

Endleaves: white paper pastedowns and one free leaf conjugate with the pastedown and one free white paper leaf, at both ends. Blanks bound in at the end.

PROVENANCE: On title-page: ownership inscription, largely erased; 'nun cest Prospé'; in a later hand: 'Ex libris s.s. ch Sponnieri(?) dms'; bought: Sotheby's, 1.xii.1942, *329*.
LITERATURE: Hobson, *French and Italian*, no. 83.

442

373

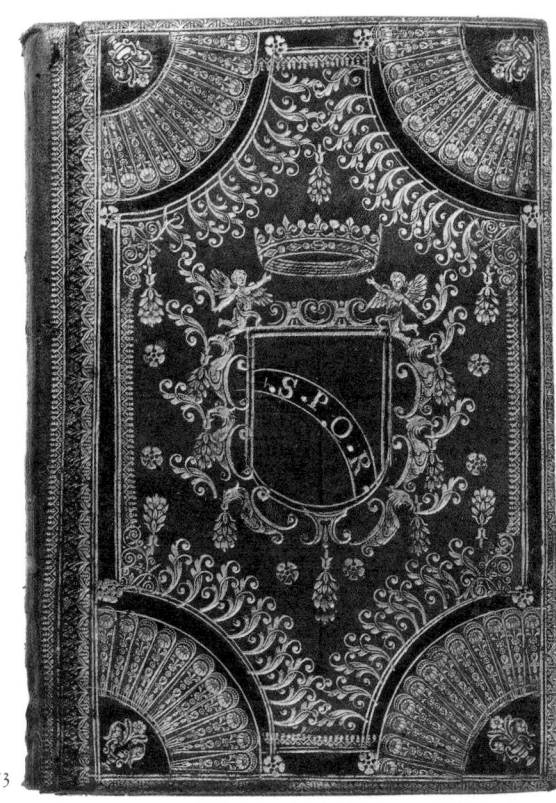

374

443

375   *A binding made in Rome, c. 1700*

[Pair of empty covers]

241 × 176 × 5 mm. (P 1256) Davis 857

Red (?)hair sheep over paste boards, tooled in gold with lines; a small outer border roll, a border roll with curving branches, leaves and flowers; a panel with a small border roll, corners filled with pointillé fleurons, curls and stylized flowers around a fleur-de-lis or an eagle displayed; decorated with silver paint; in the centre: pointillé tools, decorated with silver paint, and small flower tools around, on the upper cover: a crowned shield with a bend charged: +S P Q R [Senatus Populusque Romanus], the crown supported by two cherubs; two small griffins; on the lower cover: crowned arms (unidentified). Two pairs of ties of pink silk with silver thread and traces of two further pairs at head and tail. Edges of boards and turn-ins: tooled in gold.

   Spine strip: tooled in gold to a pattern of leaves.
   Pastedowns: gilt-embossed black paper; floral design.

PROVENANCE: J Hely-Hutchinson (book plate; sold: Sotheby's, 13.iii.1956, *271*).
Same tools on: Chester Beatty Library, 263 (Rome, 1705, with arms of Pope Clement XI).
Compare: BL, C.47.d.30 (Naples, 1703); Critien, p. 38.

376

376 *An embroidered binding, probably made in Rome, c. 1724–30*

[Thomas à Kempis], *De imitatione Christi*, Paris: Typographia Regia, 1640; ruled in red. fol.

373 × 263 × 50 mm. (P 1133) Davis 878

Canvas over paste boards, embroidered with silver thread and coloured silks to a bold design of decorative ribbons, flowers and leaves around in the centre: the arms of Pope Benedict XIII. Edges: gilt; marbled blue and red beneath the gold.

Sewn on six cords, laced in, showing as bands on the spine; seven compartments embroidered with decorative motifs and armorial charges; in the second compartment in silver thread on a blue ground: IMIT/IO. Endbands: lacking; remnants of silver thread and blue silk tie-downs.

Endleaves: purple satin pastedowns and one free satin leaf conjugate with the pastedown (backed), and two conjugate free white paper leaves, at both ends.

PROVENANCE: Pope Benedict XIII; E Quaile (label of the 'Art Treasures Exhibition, Wrexham, 1876', lent by E Quaile); Robert Hoe (book plate; sold: New York, Anderson Galleries, April 1911, *243*); Cortlandt F Bishop (book plate; sold: New York, Anderson Galleries, pt. II, 1938, *1099*, pl.); bought: Lardanchet, 24.xii.1953.
REFERENCES: Libri, *Monuments inédits*, pl. xxxiv; Hobson, *French and Italian*, no. 83, note 6; Romme, *Book Collector*, 1969, p. 42, note 144.
LITERATURE: Hobson, *French and Italian*, no. 83.
Note: Piero Francesco Orsini, Pope Benedict XIII: 1724–30; E Quaile: Edward Quaile of Birkenhead.

377 *An embroidered binding, probably made in Rome, c. 1733*

V Salvi, *Philosophicae theses*, Rome: A de Rubeis, 1733. fol.

408 × 280 × 16 mm. (P 1418) Davis 879

Pink satin over paste boards, embroidered with gold thread to a design of interlacing ribbons, leafy curls and basket-work compartments along the sides and in the corners; in the centre: the arms of Cardinal G A Guadagni. Edges: gilt.

Single quire, sewn through the fold with pink silk, at five sewing stations; sewn twice, the second time at slightly different positions; smooth spine. No endbands.

Endleaves: pink paper pastedowns embossed in gold to a floral design; the two free conjugate white paper leaves at both ends form part of the single quire.

PROVENANCE: Cardinal G A Guadagni (to whom the thesis is dedicated); bought: Sotheby's, 28.ii.1966, *127*, pl.
LITERATURE: Hobson, *French and Italian*, no. 83.
Note: Giovanni Antonio Guadagni (1674–1759), nephew of Clement XII; bishop of Arezzo: 1724; cardinal: 1731.

378 *A binding made in Rome, c. 1740*

Officio della B Vergine Maria dedicato a S Anna, Rome: Eredi del Corbelletti for G M Salvioni, 1707. 8vo.

207 × 135 × 35 mm. (P 1032) Davis 858

Brown stained calf over paste boards, tooled in gold with lines, a small border roll, gouges forming interlacing ribbons, decorated with green and silver paint (silver: now oxidized); palmette tools in the corners; a variety of curling leaf tools, pomegranates and small flower tools. Edges of boards and

377

378

turn-ins: tooled in gold with a small roll. Edges: gilt and lightly gauffered with rows of dots and near endbands.

Sewn on six cords, laced in (probably not every cord laced in), showing as bands on the spine, tooled in gold; seven compartments, tooled in gold with curls and flowers. Endbands: single with a bead; pink and pale blue silk over (?)leather cores (cut off), tied down.

Endleaves: comb-marbled paper pastedowns and one free white paper leaf, at both ends.

PROVENANCE: Marc Antonio Borghese (armorial book plate); Kundig (sold: Catalogue 112, 29.v.1951, *116*, pl.); C Sawyer & Sons (Catalogue 202, no. 55, pl.; sold: 12.vi.1951).
REFERENCES: Hobson, *French and Italian*, no. 79.
Compare: Small roll on turn-ins: Davis 859 (no. 379 below); border roll: Tolomei, *Legatura romana barocca*, no. 76.
Note: Marc Antonio Borghese III (1660–1729) or Marc Antonio Borghese IV (1730–1800)?

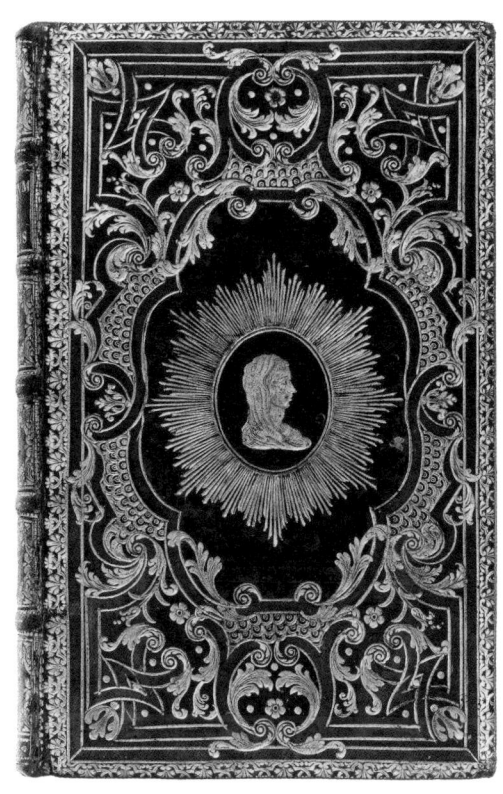

379

379 *A binding made in Rome, c. 1742*

Uffizio della Beata Vergine Maria, Rome: Stamperia Pontificia Vaticana, 1742. 8vo.

209 × 130 × 29 mm. (P 1271) Davis 859

Brown stained calf over paste boards, tooled in gold with lines, a small border roll; gouges forming interlacing ribbons, curling leaf tools, stylized flowers, dots and 'fish-scale' tooling around a centre compartment, stained black and tooled in gold with a profile portrait, depicting the Virgin Mary, surrounded by rays. Edges of boards and turn-ins: tooled in gold with a small roll. Edges: gilt and lightly gauffered with a row of dots and near endbands, and painted in yellow, pink and blue to a floral design.

Sewn on five cords, laced in, showing as bands on the spine, tooled in gold with a line; six compartments, five of which: tooled in gold with corner curls and a large fleuron in the centre; second compartment: gold-tooled red leather title label. Endbands: triple with a bead; pink, pale and dark blue silk over (?)cord cores (cut off), tied down.

Endleaves: pink-sprinkled paper pastedowns and one free sprinkled leaf conjugate with the pastedown, and two free white paper leaves, at both ends.

PROVENANCE: Landau (book plate, with: 'n: 47965'); J Hely-Hutchinson (book plate; sold: Sotheby's, 14.iii.1956, *614*).
LITERATURE: Hobson, *French and Italian*, no. 79 (and literature cited there).
Same tools on: Chester Beatty Library, no. 260 (Rome, 1742); Fletcher, *Foreign*, pl. lix; Maggs, Catalogue 407 (1921), no. 425; Morazzoni, no. 87; Whitney Hoff, no. 366; Sawyer, Catalogue 202 [1951], no. 75.

Compare: Davis 858 (no. 378 above); Fitzwilliam Museum, Cambridge (*Uffizio della B Vergine Maria*, Rome, 1755); BL, C.27.e.18 (Rome, 1758), C.47.i.9 (Viterbo, 1763: Clement XIII); Morazzoni, no. 86; Mazal, pl. 220; Breslauer, Catalogue 104, pt. II, no. 219; Cavalli & Terlizzi, no. 42; Schäfer, n. 115; Malaguzzi, *Preziosi*, no. 192; *Aussen-Ansichten*, no. 56; Bloomsbury Book Auctions, Rome, 6.xii.2006, *131*.

380 *A binding possibly made in Naples, c. 1750–60*

Paolo Giovio, bishop of Nocera, *De piscibus marinis ... liber*, Rome: F Minitius Calvus, 1527. 4to.

200 × 133 × 15 mm. (P 1075) Davis 860

Brown calf over paste boards, tooled in gold to a panel design, with lines, a small outer border roll, two wider borders filled with solid tools, a third border filled with open flower and leaf tools, decorated with silver paint (oxidized); in the corners and centre of the centre panel: open flower and leaf tools, decorated with silver paint; the centre ornament surrounded by a frame of half-circles filled with massed small tooling. Edges of boards: tooled in gold. Edges: stained red.

Sewn on three (recessed) cords; hollow back; smooth spine, tooled in gold; divided into panels in each of which: the front part of a peacock on a branch; two red and brown leather labels lettered in gold with the title and imprint. No endbands.

Endleaves: red, white, blue and orange marbled paper pastedowns and one free marbled leaf conjugate with the pastedown and two free conjugate white paper leaves, at both ends.

PROVENANCE: Lucius Wilmerding (book plate; sold: Parke-Bernet, 31.x.1951, *731*).
Compare: BL, C.68.d.15 (Naples, 1739); Morazzoni, no. 85; *Dalla bottega*, p. 78, pl. 14; Cavalli & Terlizzi, nos. 40, 41; Malaguzzi, *Il Canavese*, pl. 61; Quilici, no. 1133, fig. 449.

381 *A decorated paper binding made in Venice, 1769*

Componimenti poetici per le felicissime nozze dell' ... signor Niccoló Michieli e la signora Elisabetta Gradenigo, Venice: Carlo Palese, 1769. large 4to.

350 × 248 × 10 mm. (P 1287) Davis 880

Block-printed orange paper over thin boards, decorated in grey with a pattern of curving ribbons, flowers and leafy branches; on a fish-scale background, on the upper cover: the arms of the Michieli family; on the lower cover: the arms of Elisabetta Gradenigo. Edges: marbled in red and blue.

Unsupported sewing; two quires sewn through the fold at four sewing stations and linked with a link-stitch; smooth spine, covered in block-printed orange paper with a pattern of flowers and dots. No endbands.

Endleaves: white paper pastedowns at both ends.

PROVENANCE: Niccoló Michieli and Elisabetta Gradenigo on their wedding day [or a wedding guest]; bought: Sotheby's, 18.ii.1957, *41*.
LITERATURE: Hobson, *French and Italian*, no. 84.
Compare: Malaguzzi, *Monferrato*, pls 83–4.

380

381

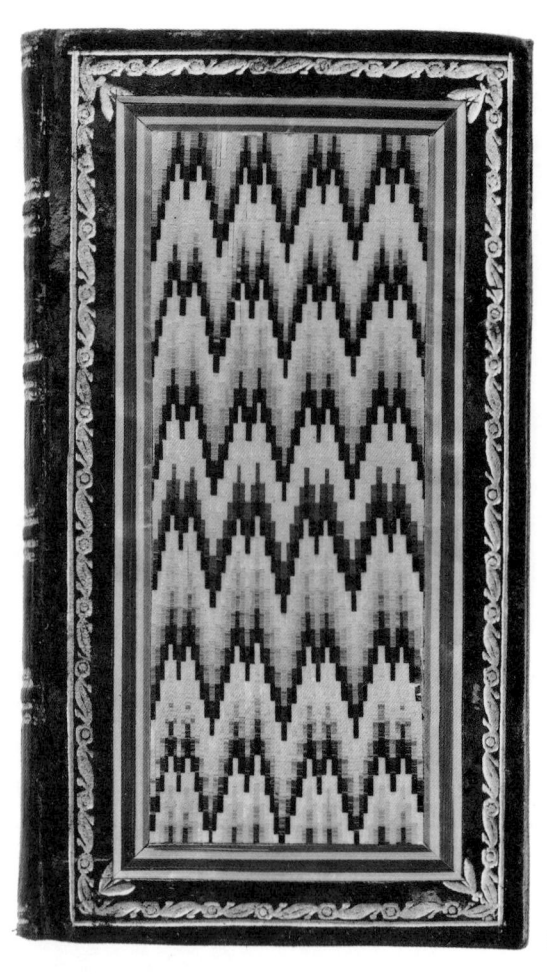

382

382 *A binding possibly made in Faenza, c. 1770*

Apparecchio e ringraziamento per la confessione e comunione, Faenza: Presso Conti, n.d. [c. 1770]. 12mo.

156 × 86 × 20 mm. (P 1293) Davis 829

Brown marbled calf over paste boards, tooled in gold with lines, a small border roll and leaf tools in the corners; inlaid with a large centre panel of strips of coloured straw in a zig-zag pattern. Edges: stained red.

 Sewn on four cords, laced in, showing as bands on the spine; five compartments, tooled in gold with a small roll and tulip tools. Endbands: stuck-on, single: black and beige silk over [invisible] cores. Green silk book marker.

 Endleaves: red, blue and yellow block-printed paper with a pattern of stripes and diapers and one free white paper leaf, at both ends.

 In a contemporary pull-off case of brown marbled calf, tooled in gold with a small border roll (as on spine) and lined with blue and fawn block-printed paper with a floral pattern.

PROVENANCE: J R Abbey (book plate; 'J.A.7052/ 2:10:1960'; sold: Sotheby's, 21.vi.1965, *35*).
REFERENCES: Barber & Rogers, p. 262, no. 1.

452

383

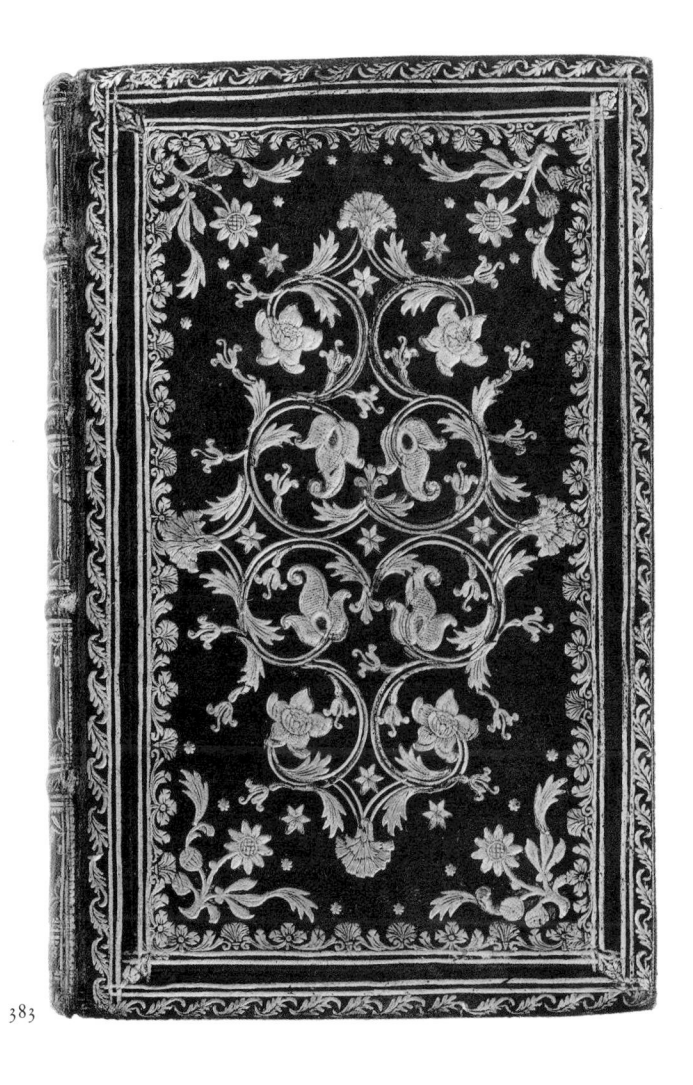

383 *A binding probably made in Rome, c. 1770*

L'Abbandono delle ricchezze di S Filippo Neri componimento sacro per musica, Rome: G Zempel, n.d. [and thirteen other *Componimenti sacri per musica da cantarsi nell'oratorio de' R R Padri della congregazione dell' Oratorio di Roma*, Rome: Stamperia di Pallade, 1767, 1768 (nos. 2,4); Ansillioni, 1752 (no. 3); G Zempel, n.d. (nos. 5–14); with a manuscript table of contents]. 8vo.

184 × 118 × 24 mm. (P 1223) Davis 830

Green sheep (or possibly hair sheep) over paste boards, tooled in gold with lines, an outer border with leaf tools; an inner border with shell-shaped, flower, and leaf tools; large flower tools in the corners and in the centre: a large ornament built up of gouges, stars, leaf tools, fleurons, and solid and hatched flower tools. Edges of boards: tooled in gold with dashes. Edges: gilt and very lightly gauffered with some dots near head and tail of spine.

Sewn on four cords, laced in, showing as bands on the spine, tooled in gold; five compartments, tooled in gold with solid flower tools. Endbands: single with a bead; pink and white silk over cord cores (cut off), tied down. Green silk book markers.

Endleaves: pink sprinkled-paper pastedowns and one free white paper leaf, at both ends; at the end: two free conjugate white paper leaves sewn in with the manuscript table of contents.

PROVENANCE: J de Stuers (book plate, 1901); library label with number in manuscript; bought: Sotheby's, 6.vii.1955, *94*, pl.

Same tools on: Glasgow University Library, BD.14–i.4 (Rome, 1680); Fitzwilliam Museum, Cambridge (F Burlamacchi, *Opere di Santa Caterina da Sienna*, Siena, 1713); Morazzoni, no. 11; Breslauer, Catalogue 104, pt. I, no. 78; Quilici, no. 1114, fig. 441.

Compare: BL, C.52.c.6 (Rome, 1710; Clement XI), C.20.c.4 (Rome, 1711), C.47.e.9 (Landishut, 1719; Clement XI); Chester Beatty Library, N235 (Rome, 1695, with arms of Cardinal Alessandro Albani), N264 (Rome, 1712, with arms of Cardinal A Albani); Sotheby's, 27.x.1975, *465* (Rome, 1725); *Legature papali*, no. 253; Breslauer, Catalogue 104, pt. I, no. 78 (Albani arms); Schäfer, no. 120; Malaguzzi, *Preziosi*, no. 174; Quilici, nos. 1135, figs. 451–2, 1230, fig. 473; Critien, pp. 43, 46; Malaguzzi, *Il Cuneese*, pl. 82.

---

384 *A binding made in Rome, c. 1771*

F A Becchetti, *Della istoria ecclesiastica dell'eminentissimo cardinale G A Orsi … prosequita da Fr F A Becchetti*, vol. II, Rome: P Giunchi, 1771. 4to.

278 × 200 × 36 mm.   (P 1163) Davis 882

Tan goatskin over paste boards, tooled in gold with lines, an outer border with a floral ornamental roll, a second border with leafy curls and palmette tools, an inner border with a floral ornamental roll; in the corners: a palmette tool, leafy curls around 'basket-work' with small stylized flowers; leafy curls and fleurons along the long sides of the centre panel; acorns, pomegranates; in the centre: the arms of Pope Clement XIV, surrounded by leafy curls and with a large fleuron at the bottom of the shield. Edges of boards: tooled in gold. Edges: gilt and lightly gauffered with rows of dots near the spine.

Sewn on five cords, laced in, showing as raised bands on the spine, tooled in gold; six compartments, tooled in gold with 'basket-work' with small flowers; second compartment: title lettered onto spine. Endbands: single with a bead; pink and yellow silk over cord cores (cut off), tied down at front and back only.

Endleaves: pink sprinkled-paper pastedowns, one free sprinkled leaf (backed) conjugate with the pastedown and one free white paper leaf conjugate with the backing paper, at both ends.

PROVENANCE: On title-page in manuscript: 'M.8.23'; on pastedown: manuscript note in Dutch (about the coat of arms); bought: Sotheby's, 8.xi.1954, *72*.

Compare: BL, C.69.aa.13 ([Rome], 1772; Clement XIV), C.64.d.6 (Naples, 1787; Pius VI); Chester Beatty Library, N253 (Rome, 1761), N391 (Rome 1770, with arms of Clement XIV), N249 (Rome, 1771, with arms of Clement XIV); *Legature papali*, no. 260; Schäfer, nos. 119, 136; Malaguzzi, *Preziosi*, no. 182; Malaguzzi, *Il Canavese*, pl. 74.

Note: Giovanni Vincenzo Ganganelli, Pope Clement XIV: 1769–74.

384

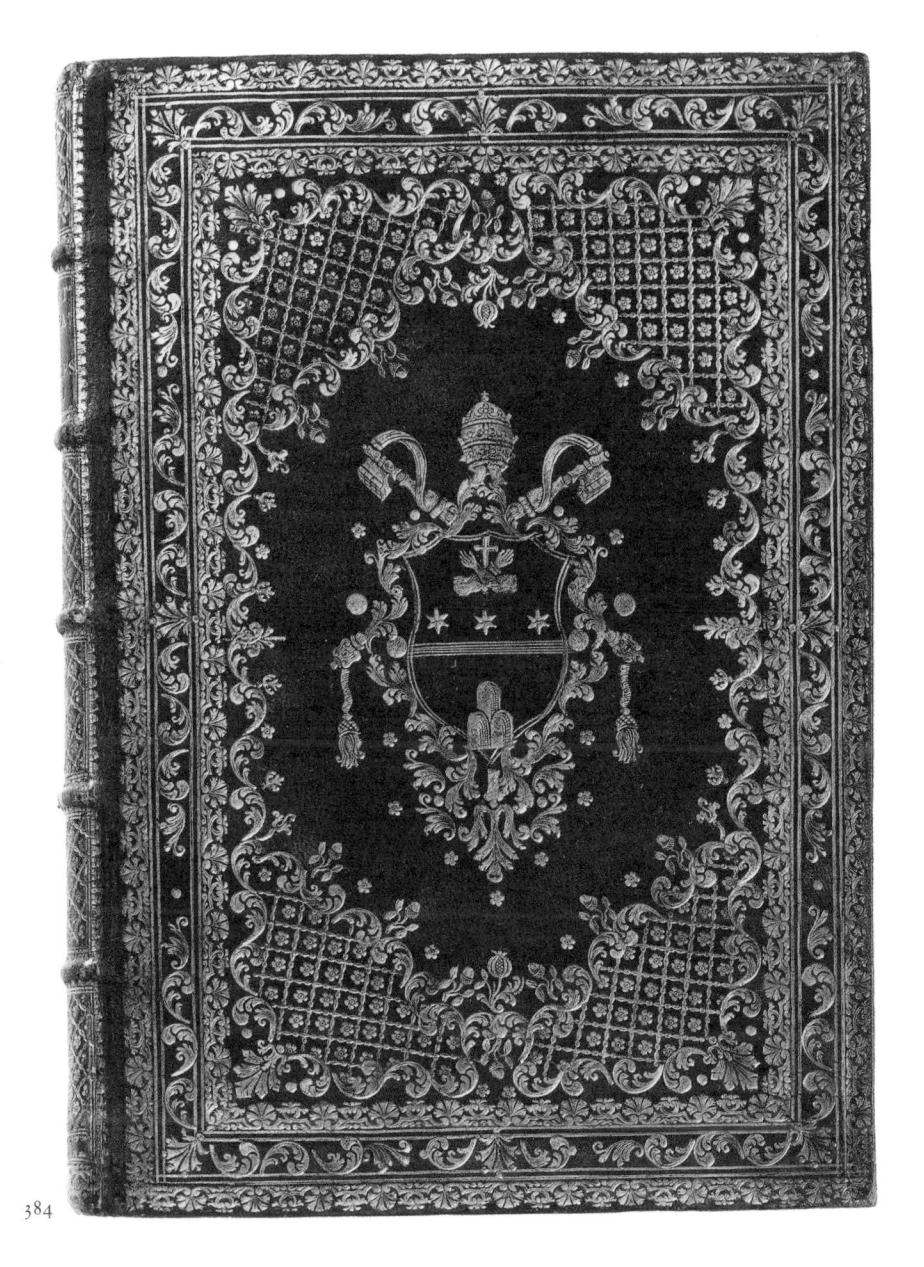

385 *A straw binding possibly made in Italy, 1779*

[Mostly blank book, in manuscript: a few poems in English in 19th- and 20th-century hands].

158 × 98 × 16 mm. (P 953) Davis 831

Strips of green straw over paste boards, surrounded by a small border of brown and fawn straw; an inlaid pattern of branches, leaves and flowers in brown, fawn and red straw; in the centre: a circle of brown straw with, on the upper cover: the monogram MJF in fawn straw; on the lower cover: the Sacred Monogram (IHS) and date: 1779, also in fawn straw. Edges of boards: brown straw; turn-ins: strips of green straw. Edges: gilt, with a touch of red paint at the position of the endbands.

THE HENRY DAVIS GIFT

385

Sewn on three (recessed) cords, laced in; smooth spine covered with strips of green straw with an inlaid pattern of a branch, leaves and a flower in brown and fawn straw. No endbands.

Endleaves: yellow, red and blue curl-marbled paper pastedowns and one free curl-marbled leaf (backed at the end only) conjugate with the pastedown, at both ends; a stub of backing paper at the front.

PROVENANCE: MJF; G D Hobson (sold: Sotheby's, 22.v.1950, *81*).
REFERENCES: Barber & Rogers, p. 263, no. 4.

386 *A binding made in Piedmont, possibly in Turin, c. 1787*

J D Chionius, *Ex jure civili de criminalibus*, Turin: I Soffietti, 1787. 8vo.

194 × 120 × 19 mm. (P 1270) Davis 832

Olive-brown goatskin (or possibly hair sheep) over paste boards, tooled in gold with lines, a small leafy border roll; fan-shapes, leafy curls and bunches of flowers in the corners; flowers, leafy curls and garlands along the long sides; 'basket-work' and flowers along the short sides; in the centre the arms of Charles Emanuel III, duke of Savoy, king of Sardinia. Edges of boards: tooled in gold with dashes. Edges: gilt.

386

Sewn on three (recessed) cords, laced in; smooth spine, tooled in gold with lines, leafy curves and garlands dividing the spine into compartments, tooled in gold with leafy curls and pomegranates. Endbands: stuck-on single: fawn (?silk) over leather cores. Blue silk book marker.

Endleaves: blue marbled (spotted) paper pastedowns, one free marbled leaf (backed) conjugate with the pastedown and one free white paper leaf conjugate with the backing paper, at both ends.

PROVENANCE: Charles Emanuel III [or a member of his court]; bought: Sotheby's, 18.ii.1957, *26*.
LITERATURE: Guigard, I, 82.
Compare: Morazzoni, no. 25; Malaguzzi, *Il Canavese*, pl. 81.
Note: Charles Emanuel III (1701–73); duke of Savoy; king of Sardinia: 1730–73.

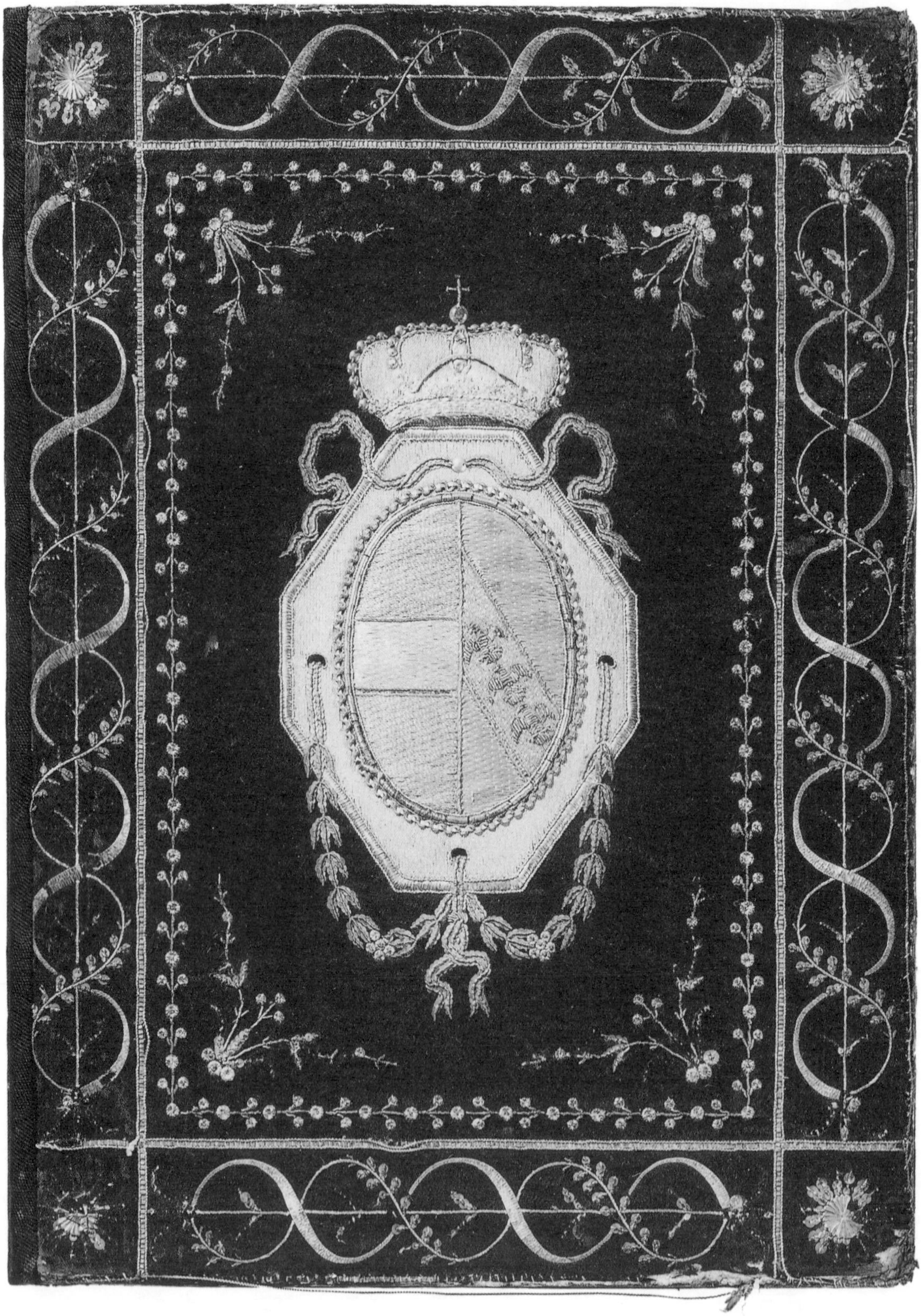

387 *A mourning binding possibly made in Parma, 1789*

B Ridolfi, *In funere Caroli III. Hispaniar. Regis Catholici oratio*, Parma: ex Regio typographeo, 1789. fol.

342 × 255 × 15 mm. (P 1010) Davis 883

Black satin over paste boards, embroidered with gold and silver threads, coloured silks and spangles; a wide border with intertwined leafy branches; circular ornaments at the corners; an inner border of flowers; leaves and flower branches in the corners; in the centre the arms of Austria impaling Loraine. Edges: gilt.

Sewn on four (recessed) cords, laced in; smooth spine covered with a separate strip of black satin. No endbands.

Endleaves: pale blue satin pastedowns, a free satin leaf (backed) conjugate with the pastedowns and one free white paper leaf conjugate with the backing paper, at both ends; at the end: one free white paper leaf (countermark: A.CESINI/ PIORACO: a paper mill near Macerate).

PROVENANCE: For the funeral of Charles III of Spain; bought: L Olschki, 25.v.1951.
LITERATURE: Hobson, *French and Italian*, no. 83.
Compare: O L Shaw, 'Contemporary collectors xxxviii', *The Book Collector*, vol. 13, no. 3 (1964), p. 334, pl. vi; Breslauer, Catalogue 104, pt. II, no. 240; Malaguzzi, *Monferrato*, pl. 117.
Note: Charles III of Spain (1716–1788), son of Philip V of Spain and Elizabeth Farnese; duke of Parma; conquered Naples and Sicily: 1734; king of the two Sicilies; married Maria Amelia, daughter of Frederick Augustus II of Saxony.
Marie Antoinette of Austria (1755–1793) used the arms of Austria impaling Loraine as her escutcheon.

388 *A binding made in Naples, c. 1793*

Manuale sacerdotum pro missa celebranda ... ex missali Romano ... collectis, Naples: V Ursinus, 1793. 12mo.

145 × 92 × 10 mm. (P 1070) Davis 833

Red-brown goatskin over paste boards, tooled in gold with lines, two small border rolls, leafy curls and bunches of flowers; bunches of flowers in the corners; in the centre: the arms of Ferdinand I, king of the two Sicilies. Edges of boards: tooled in blind with dashes. Edges: gilt.

Sewn through the fold at two sewing stations; two kettle stitch positions; smooth spine, tooled in gold with lines dividing the spine into compartments, tooled in gold with small curls and flowers. No endbands.

Endleaves: pink and blue block-printed paper pastedowns, decorated with stripes and a floral pattern, at both ends; at the front: one free white paper leaf; at the end: one free block-printed leaf conjugate with the pastedown and one free white paper leaf.

PROVENANCE: (?)Ferdinand I; C Elton; M A Elton (book plate); Lucius Wilmerding (book plate; sold: Parke-Bernet, 31.x.1951, *584*).
REFERENCES: C I Elton, *A Catalogue of a Portion of the Library of C.I. and M.A. Elton*, London: B Quaritch, 1891, p. 170 (pl.).
LITERATURE: Hobson, *French and Italian*, no. 78.
Note: Ferdinand I (1751–1825), born and died in Naples; king of the two Sicilies.

388

389 *Two bindings made in the later part of the eighteenth century*

Plutarch, *Vite ... de gli huomini illustri Greci et Romani, ... tradotta per M. Lodovico Domenichi et altri*, 2 vols, Venice: G Giolito, 1567–68. 4to.

250 × 177/182 × 58/38 mm. (P 1267) Davis 884–885

White parchment over paste boards, painted in water colour with views of Rome; vol. I: upper cover: landscape with St Peter in the background; lower cover: the Pantheon; vol. II: upper cover: Ponte Sesto; lower cover: Castel Sant' Angelo with St Peter in the background. Edges: stained dark blue.

Sewn on five (recessed) cords, laced in; hollow back; smooth spine with red goatskin labels, tooled in gold with a border of small flowers, the title and volume numbers. Endbands: single with a bead; pink and white silk over rolled parchment cores (laced through the boards and the covers), tied down.

Endleaves: vol. I: white paper pastedowns, at both ends; at the front: one free leaf conjugate with, and folded beneath, the pastedown; at the end: one free white paper leaf conjugate with a stub beneath the pastedown; vol. II: white paper pastedowns and one free leaf conjugate with the pastedown, at both ends.

PROVENANCE: At the end of vol. II in manuscript: 'IVLII. MATTIAE. CARPIAE'; title-page of vol. II: erased manuscript note; bought: Howes, 24.i.1959.

389

389

461

390 *A fake, probably made in Italy in the late eighteenth or possibly early nineteenth century (see Note below)*

G Guidetti, *Cantus ecclesiasticus officii maioris hebdomadae*, Rome: A Phaeus, 1619. fol.

322 × 225 × 19 mm. (P 1109) Davis 886

Red-brown goatskin (or possibly hair sheep) over paste boards, tooled in gold and blind with lines, a border with curly tools (tooled over the blind and gold lines), flowers and fleur-de-lis tools in the corners; the centre tooled with gouges and some solid tools, to a design showing an arch in a brick wall, pillars, a tiled floor, and two bearded and haloed human figures in monastic dress, one holding a staff sprouting leafy branches, their heads and hands: onlaid in painted parchment; traces of darker paint. Traces of two pairs of ties (traces of gold-tooling visible over the cut-off ends of the ties). Edges: gilt.

Sewn on three cords, laced in, showing as bands on the spine; four compartments, tooled in gold with fleurs-de-lis. Endbands: single with a bead; blue and yellow silk over cord cores (cut off), tied down sporadically (tail band: gone, but remains of tie-downs).

Endleaves: white paper pastedowns, at both ends; at the front: two free conjugate white paper leaves; at the end: one free leaf conjugate with the pastedown and one free white paper leaf.

Repairs: to spine.

PROVENANCE: Robert Hoe (ex libris; sold: New York, Anderson Galleries, pt. II January 1912, *231*); bought: Maurice Bridel (Lausanne), 12.vii.1952.
LITERATURE: De Marinis, II, 1249 (pl. 216–17), III, pp. 51–4 (on genuine architectural bindings); Nixon, 'Binding forgeries'; Needham, *Twelve Centuries*, no. 69 (on genuine architectural bindings).
Same curl tools on: Private collection (C Tacitus, *Historia augusta actionum diurnalium: additis quinque libris noviter inventis*, Basel: Froben, n.d.): a genuine 16th-century Italian binding, which has also been made more 'sophisticated' with additional (later) tooling, including the English royal arms, supported by two putti.
Compare: Newbury Library, Chicago: a binding with the figure of Turenne and imitation 'Le Gascon' tools, lower cover: arms of Pope Gregory XIII and Italian-type mask tools in the corners; Hoe sale: New York, Anderson Galleries, pt. I, April 1911, *327* (fake portrait of Henri III, also on a tiled floor, added to a genuine 17th-century French binding).
Note: This is probably a genuine early 17th-century, blind- and gold-tooled, Italian binding to which most of the gold tooling has been added later. The outer border lines (in blind and gold) and the fleur-de-lis tools in the corners may be original; the curl tools have been applied partly on top of the original tooling.

390

391   *Two bindings made in Florence, 1823*

T Tasso, *La Gerusalemme liberata,* 2 vols, Florence: L Ciardetti, 1823. 8vo.

226 × 145 × 35/30 mm.   (P 1040) Davis 862–863

White parchment over paste boards, tooled in gold with a rope-work outer border and a palmette roll forming an inner border; the upper cover of both volumes: painted in brown with views of ancient buildings in Rome; vol. I: the columns of Nerva Forum; vol. II: the Arch of Constantine. Edges: sprinkled in pink and blue.

Sewn on three (recessed) supports, (probably) laced in; hollow back; smooth spine, tooled in gold with small solid tools, curly tools, shells and 'basket work'; two straight-grain goatskin labels: one red, tooled in gold with the title; one green, tooled in gold with a small border and the volume numbers. Endbands: single with a bead; white and blue silk over rolled paper cores (cut off), sporadically tied down. Pink and blue striped silk book markers.

Endleaves: white paper pastedowns and one free leaf conjugate with the pastedown, at both ends.

PROVENANCE: On endleaf of both volumes in manuscript: 'Susan Bayly/ Rome/ 1829'; bought: Quaritch, 30.vii.1951.
Compare: Border roll BL, C.29.m.1 (Rome, 1822).
Note: I am grateful to Chris Michaelides for identifying the scenes on these bindings.

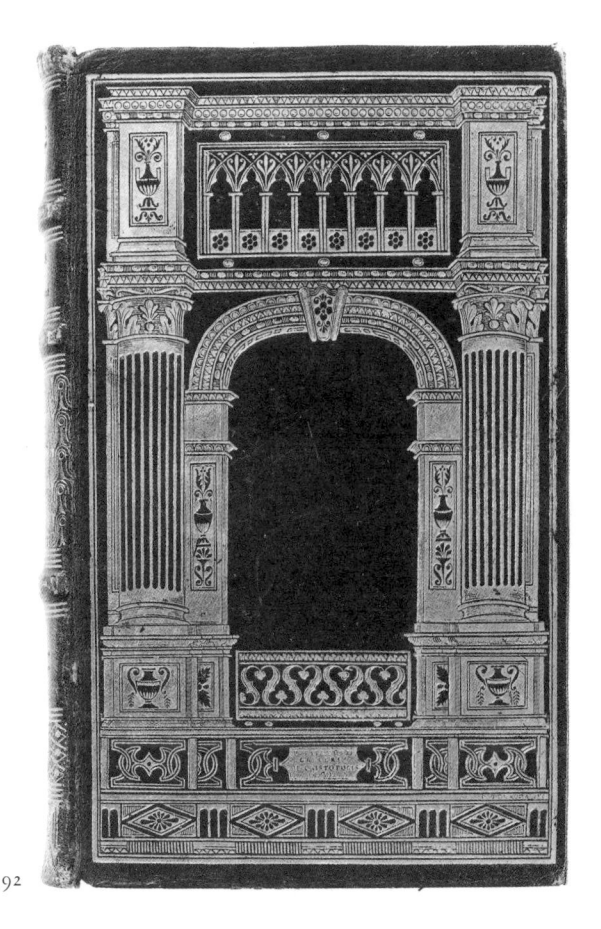

392 *A binding made in Milan by or for P Ripamonti, 1827–8*

Ufficio della settimana santa colla versione italiana di Monsignor M[ar]tini, Milan: P Ripamonti Carpano [1827]. large 16mo.

156 × 98 × 32 mm.   (P 1282) Davis 834

Green goatskin over wood, blocked in gold with a block depicting a façade of high columns, an arch, Gothic windows and an iron-work balcony; signed [small caps]: P. RIPAMONTI/ GALLERIA/ DE CRISTOFORIS/ N20. Edges of boards: tooled in gold with a diaper pattern near the corners. Trace of one clasp. Edges: gilt.

  Sewn on three supports; three false raised bands, tooled in gold; four irregular-sized compartments, tooled in gold; second compartment: title lettered onto spine. Endbands: stuck-on single; green and white ribbon. Pink silk book marker.

  Endleaves: green moiré pastedowns, one free moiré leaf (backed) conjugate with the pastedown and one fee white paper leaf, at both ends.

PROVENANCE: Richard Lane Freer (book plate); label with: 'The Bequest of the Venerable Archdeacon Freer to E.R. Dowdeswell, 1863'; small printed label with: 'E R D / 24 G 19'; Library label of Pull Court Library ('Div. 19, Shelf G, No 7606'); bought: Sotheby's, 19.xii.1960, *475*.

393 *A binding probably made in Florence, c. 1854*

G Antonelli, *Sulla vita e sulle opera di Giovanni Inghirami memorie storiche*, Florence: Tipi Calasanziani, 1854. large 8vo.

225 × 149 × 20 mm.   (P 1464) Davis 864

Blue pebble-grained leather over paste boards, tooled in gold with a line along the border; blocked in gold and blind with blocks showing a mask with leafy curls and flowers above and below a large rectangular central block, showing leafy curls, shell-shapes and palmette ornaments around a circular ornament. Edges of boards: tooled in gold with a line. Edges: gilt.

    Sewn on four supports, laced in, showing as bands on the spine; five compartments, tooled in gold with lines; second compartment: title lettered onto spine. Endbands: stuck-on single; pink silk over paper cores. Blue, red and green striped silk book marker.

    Endleaves: yellow decorated paper pastedowns (floral pattern), one free decorated paper leaf conjugate with the pastedown and one free white paper leaf, at both ends.

PROVENANCE: Bought: Elkin Mathews, 6.v.1957.
LITERATURE: Malaguzzi, *Legature romantiche*.

Italian Bindings

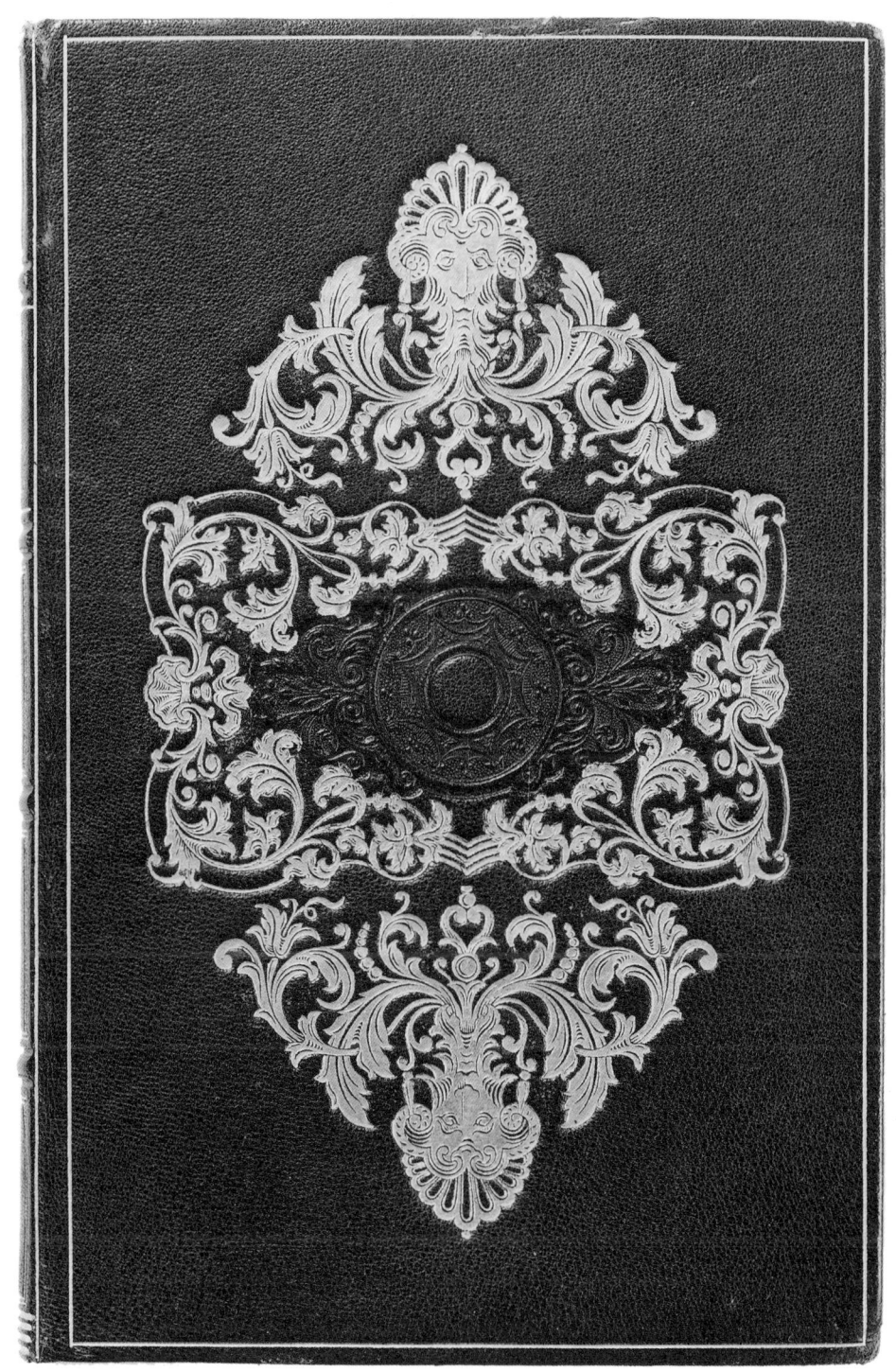

393

468

SPANISH AND PORTUGUESE BINDINGS

394 *A late fifteenth-century Mudéjar binding, probably made in Toledo*

[Breviary for the use of Toledo], MS on parchment; historiated and decorated initials. [Toledo, late 15th century].

225 × 148 × 90 mm. (M 70) Davis 656

Dark brown goatskin over wooden boards, tooled in blind and decorated with gold paint, to a design of interlacing fillets, forming a border, square compartments at the head and tail and in the centre; on the upper cover: a complex interlacing geometrical pattern within a circle; on the lower cover: a knot-work pattern within a circle. All compartments filled with knot-work tooling and dots in blind; fillets and dots are decorated with gold paint. Traces of two pairs of clasps at the fore-edge and traces of a chain fastening (or possibly a third clasp) at the tail edge. Edges: plain.

Rebacked with the original spine strip onlaid. Sewn on five alum-tawed supports, laced in, showing as raised bands on the spine; six compartments, outlined in gold paint and tooled in blind with small strap-work tools and dots; dots decorated with gold paint. Later endbands: single with a bead; brown thread over alum-tawed cores (now cut off), tied down.

Endleaves: parchment pastedowns and one free white paper leaf, at both ends.

Repairs: rebacked; repairs to edges of boards; new endbands.

PROVENANCE: Pearson & Co; Dyson Perrins (book plate with '67'; library label with '115'; sold: Sotheby's, 29.xi.1960, *130*, pl.).

REFERENCES: Sir George Warner, *Descriptive Catalogue of Illuminated Manuscripts in the Library of C W Dyson Perrins*, Oxford, 1920, no. 115, pl. (frontispiece); *Treasures*, 1965, no. 70; Romme, *Book Collector*, 1969, p. 37, note 108, pl. xb; Needham, *Twelve Centuries*, p. 122, note 4; Foot, *Studies*, p. 181, note 4; Foot, *Mirror*, fig. 15.

LITERATURE: Miquel y Planas; Goldschmidt, pp. 138–9; Hueso-Rolland, pp. 31–8, pls ii–xii (esp. pl. vi); Thomas, pls lxi, lxii, lxv, lxix; Nixon, *Broxbourne*, no. 8; Passola; Nixon, *Pierpont Morgan Library*, no. 1; Foot, *Davis*, I, pp. 262, 264; López Serrano, 1972, pls 5–9; Needham, *Twelve Centuries*, no. 34; M Garel, 'Une reliure mudéjar', *Revue française d'histoire du livre*, 37 (1982), pp. 805–10; Wittockiana, *Ocho siglos*, nos. 4–19 (esp. 8, 10); Cockx-Indestege & Storm van Leeuwen, *Quaerendo*, 1987, pp. 246–65; L Avrin, 'The Sephardi box binding', *Scripta Hierosolymitana*, xix (1989), pp. 27–43; *Encuadernaciones españoles*, nos. 15–33, 34b–51, 53–6; Foot, *Studies*, pp. 179–81; Carrión Gútiez, 'Manoscritos', pp. 365–400; V M Pascual, 'El manuscrito de The Metropolitan Museum of Art de Nueva York. Nuevas aportaciones al studio de la lacería en la encuadernación mudejar', *Encuadernación de Arte*, 13 (1999), pp. 26–55; *Els vestits del*

Compare: *saber*, pp. 17–36, 49–69, plates, esp. MSS 446, 447, 735, 736, pp. 107, 109, 131, 133; see also Davis 706, 707 (nos. 395, 397 below).
Thomas, pls lxx, lxxi; Breslauer, Catalogue 109 (1988), *21*.
Note: Bindings in this style, decorated with fillets and the repeated use of one or two small tools to build up intricate strap-work and interlace designs, get their name from the Mudéjares, the Moors who remained in Spain after the Reconquest.

395 *A late fifteenth-century Mudéjar binding*

Pontificale Romanum [edited by Augustinus Patricius and Johannes Burckardus], Rome: Stephanus Plannck, 20 December 1485; printed in red and black [first leaf missing]. fol.

330 × 232 × 65 mm.   (P 1154) Davis 706

Brown goatskin over wood, tooled in blind with fillets and small tools to a different geometrical design on each cover; a border and interlacing ribbons, forming frames and compartments, are filled with rope-work tooling, small stylized flowers and small hatched tools; the upper cover has one central rectangle and the lower cover two central squares with diamonds, filled with small knot-work tooling. Remnants of two pairs of clasps on leather thongs, tooled in blind, hinging on the upper cover; metal catches on lower cover. Edges: gilt and gauffered with: IN OMNIBVS O/PERIBZ TVIS MEMORA/RE NOVISIMA TVA.

 Sewn on five (?)alum-tawed supports, laced in, showing as bands on the spine; six compartments (new leather on five compartments); in the top compartment: remnants of a paper label with the title in manuscript. Manuscript waste used to line boards and possibly also spine. Endbands: primary sewing with unbleached thread over alum-tawed cores (laced in), tied down; (later) secondary sewing of red and green silk over a main alum-tawed core, a second (lower) cord core and a cord crowning core.

 Endleaves: white paper pastedowns at both ends; at the end: one free leaf conjugate with the pastedown.

 Repairs: extensive at spine; repairs at covers; partly new endbands.

PROVENANCE: Davis and Orioli, Catalogue 163 (1960), *130*; Breslauer (sold: 8.ix.1954).
LITERATURE: Miquel y Planas, pl. v; see Davis 656 (no. 394 above; and literature cited there).
Compare: Private collection (Thomas Aquinas, Valencia, 1499); Penney, pl. viii.

396 *A binding, probably made in Spain, c. 1500*

M F Quintilianus, *Institutiones cum commento Laurentii Vallensis: Pomponii ac Sulpitii*, Venice: Peregrinus de Pasqualibus, 18 August 1494 [and] M F Quintilianus, *Eloquentissimi declamationes*, n.p., n.d. fol.

322 × 210 (220 with flap closed) × 50 mm.   (P 1236) Davis 387

Brown goatskin, semi-limp (lined with parchment manuscript), tooled in blind with lines and separate hand tools, forming a border, filled with large thistle tools; the centre panel is divided into two halves by a strip with large thistle tools; triple lines divide the two panels into diamonds and triangles, with crowned fleur-de-lis tools and large rectangular tools showing a crowned hedgehog; the lower cover

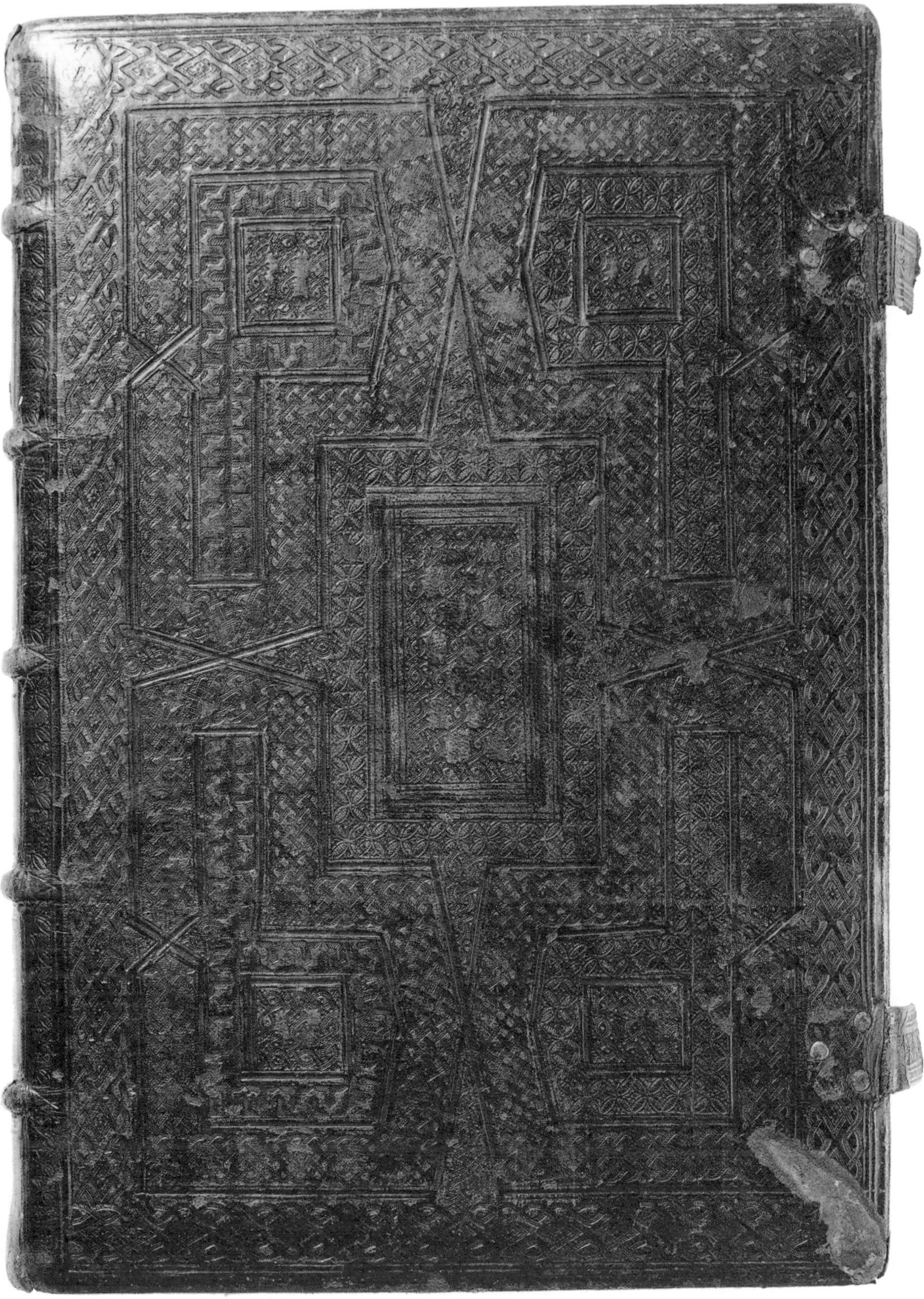

395

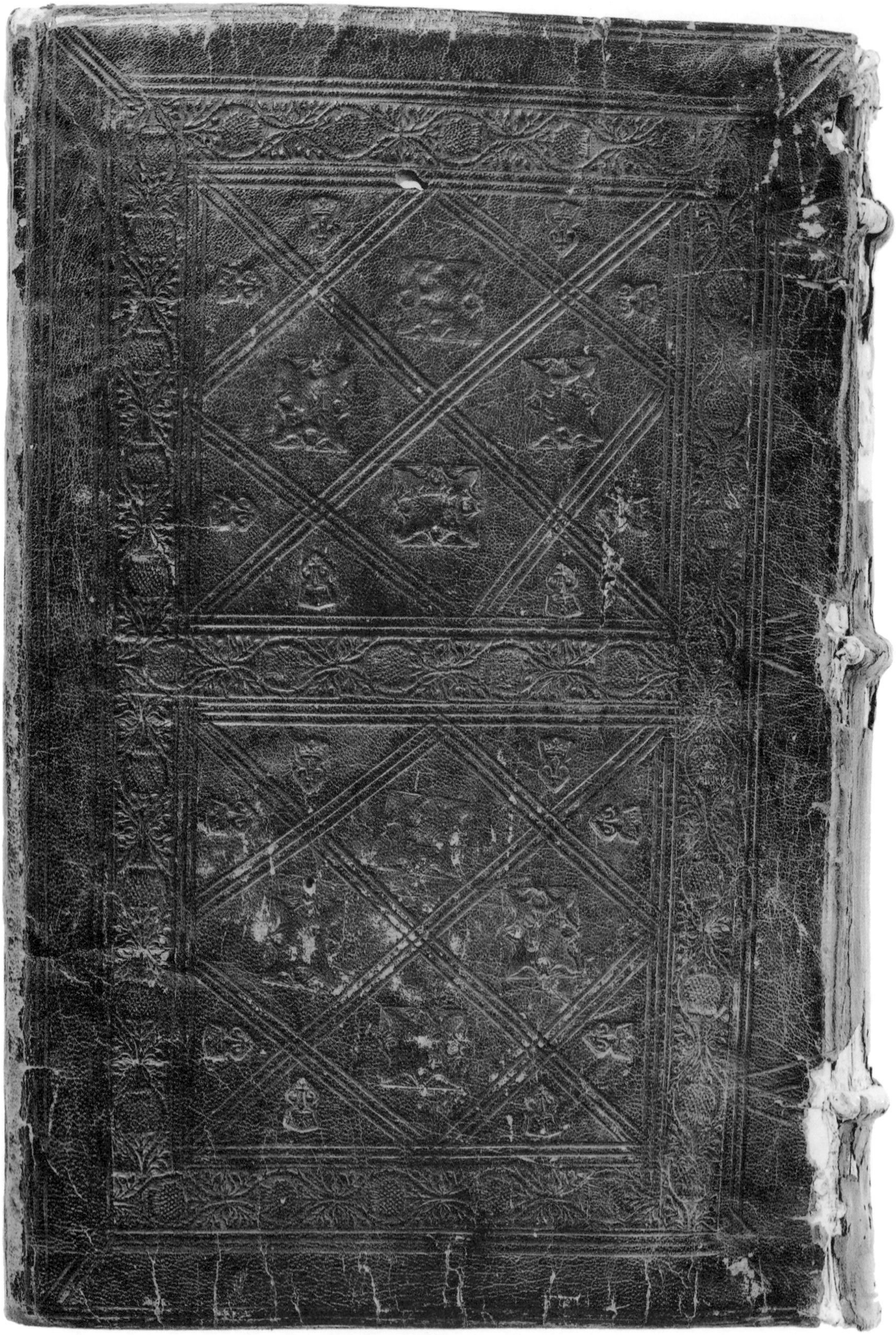

has a flap with shaped corners, covering the fore-edge and c. 55 mm. of the upper cover, tooled in blind with a zig-zag pattern of triple lines and ornamental tools; two times two circular silver eyelets to hold ties (now lost) to fasten the flap through two leather loops on the upper cover. Covers flush with edges of leaves; turn-ins: tooled in blind with lines at top and tail. Edges: plain; titles of both works in manuscript on the tail edge.

Sewn on three tanned-leather supports, once pulled through the leather covers, now broken off, showing as raised bands on the spine; four compartments, tooled in blind with lines; remnant of parchment label with title in manuscript on second compartment. Endbands: single; plain undyed thread over alum-tawed cores (laced through lining of covers), tied down.

Endleaves: one white paper leaf (now free) at both ends.

PROVENANCE: On half-title of *Institutiones* in manuscript: 'Ert [?Evt] 5. Caj.2./n.02' [Shelf mark?]; bought: Sotheby's, 6.vii.1955, *150*.
Same tool on: E J Brill, Catalogue, Leiden, 1984 (Salamanca, 1502).
Compare: BL, C.183.c.17 (Salamanca, 1502).

397 *A Mudéjar binding made in Alcala, c. 1540*

Missale mixtum secundum ordinem alme Primatis ecclesie Toletane, Alcala: J. Brocarius, September 1539; printed in red and black; woodcuts, woodcut borders and initials. 4to.

263 × 190 × 58 mm. (P 1466) Davis 707

Black goatskin over wooden boards, tooled in blind and gold with lines forming concentric borders or frames, filled with strap-work, rope-work, half circles and stylized flowers; rays and fleurons in the corners; fleurons and small circles in inner corners; frames filled with strap-work and rope-work tooling forming the shape of a cross of Lorraine, with in the centre a circle of rays around an ornament formed by lines and leaf tools. Two pairs of metal clasps, hinging on the lower cover; shell-shaped catch plates on the upper cover and shell-shaped hinge plates on the lower cover. Edges of boards and turn-ins: tooled in blind with lines. Edges: gilt and gauffered to a strap-work pattern.

Sewn on five (invisible) supports, laced in, showing as broad raised bands on the spine, tooled in blind with traces of gold; six smaller false bands, alternating with the sewing supports, traces of gold tooling; twelve compartments, tooled in blind with lines and strap-work; first and last compartments: renewed. New endbands: single with a bead; green and white silk over cord cores (cut off); traces of lacing-in tunnels for original endbands.

Later endleaves: white paper pastedowns and one free leaf conjugate with the pastedown, at both ends.

Repairs: new joints; new leather on spine (top and tail compartments); repairs at corners and edges of boards; probably also new endbands and new endleaves.

PROVENANCE: Breslauer (sold: 31.xii.1957).
LITERATURE: Davis 656, 706 (nos. 394, 395 above; and literature cited there).
Same tools on: BL, C.27.g.6 (Saragossa, 1519); Escorial [H Thomas, a collection of photographs in BL] (Alcala, 1541).

397

Compare: BL, Egerton MS 3010 (Miscellaneous offices, Latin, early 16th century), C.36.f.1 (Alcala, 1526), C.64.d.9 (Saragossa, 1528); Miquel y Planas, pls ii, v; Hueso Rolland, pl. xix; Passola, pls 27, 35, 38, 39, 40 (strap-work tools).

398 *A binding possibly made in Spain, c. 1550*

St Joannes Cassianus, *Colla patrum opus, De institutis caenobiorum, origine, causis et remedijs vitiorum, collationibusque patrum*, Lyon: I Giunta, 1542. 8vo.

135 × 94 × 36 mm. (P 598) Davis 657

Brown sheep (possibly hair sheep) over paste boards, tooled in gold and blind to a panel design, with lines forming two concentric borders, filled with the same floral border roll; a centre panel with fleurons

398

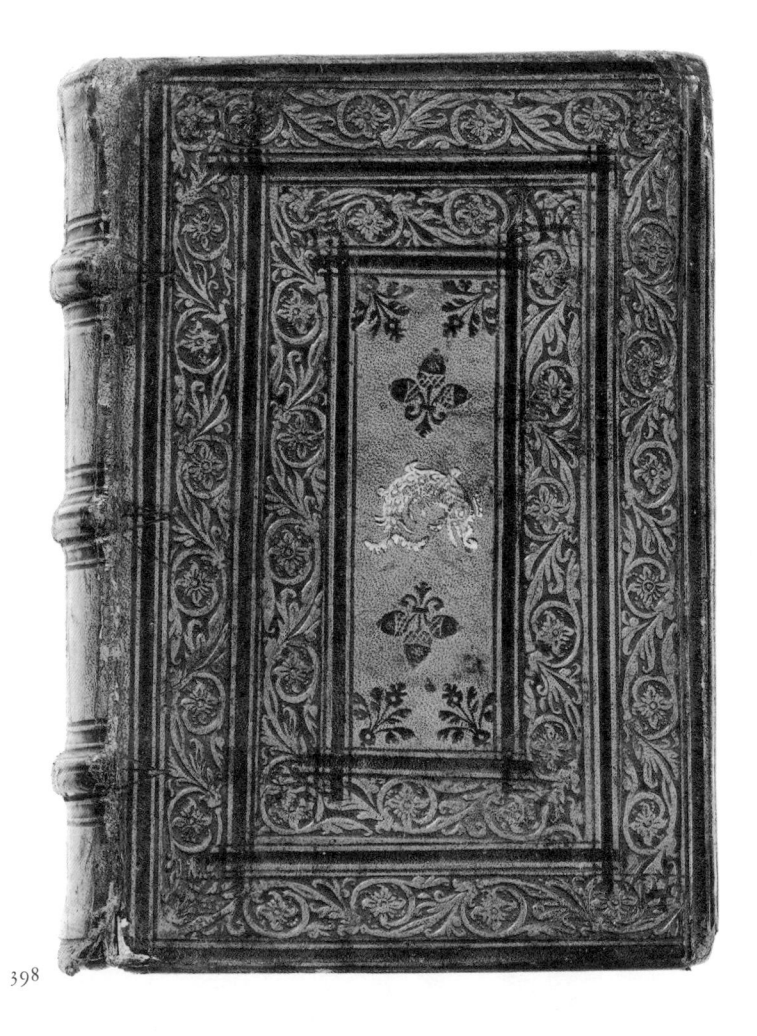

in the corners, two acorn tools and a crowned dolphin in the centre. Edges of boards and turn-ins: tooled in blind with a line. Edges: plain; title in manuscript on the fore-edge.

Sewn on three (?)split leather supports, laced in, showing as raised bands on the spine, tooled in blind with a line; four compartments, tooled in blind with a fleuron. Endbands: single; beige thread over (?)alum-tawed cores (laced in), tied down sporadically.

Endleaves: white paper pastedowns and one free leaf conjugate with the pastedown, at both ends. Printed (?paper) board lining visible beneath pastedowns.

PROVENANCE: On title-page in manuscript [erased]: 'Ex Colegij societatis Jesu'; (in same hand:) 'ovetensin et cyrar(?) Biblotheca' [sic]; (different hand:) 'Dr D. Mar. Serrano de Paz'; Thomas Brooke, FSA, Armitage Bridge (book plate); bought: Sotheby's, 21.iv.1943, *285*.
REFERENCES: Maggs, Catalogue 498 (1927), *36* (pl).
Compare: John Rylands University Library, Manchester, 20318 (Mexico, 1566); BL, C.183.c.15 (Madrid, 1573), C.64.g.4 (Alcala, 1578); Edinburgh University Library, Z.4.14 (Turin, 1582); *Encuadernaciones españolas*, nos. 62, 69; Brera, no. 110.
Note: Ovetum: Oviedo, in Tarracon (Spain).

475

399 *A binding made c. 1565*

Laurentius a Villavicentio, *De recte formando theologiae studio libri quattuor* [and] *De formandis sacris concionibus*, Antwerp: Vidua et Haeredes I. Stelsii, 1565. 8vo.

177 × 107 × 47 mm. (P 1095) Davis 658

Brown calf over paste boards, tooled in blind, with traces of oxidized silver, to a panel design with lines, a pierced heart with leaves at the corners, leafy fleurons at the outer corners of the panel, fir cones in the corners of the panel and in the centre a skeleton holding a lance, above and below which is a bird. Traces of two pairs of ties. Turn-ins: tooled in blind with a line. Edges: plain; author's name in manuscript on fore-edge ('villavincentius. t.j.').

Sewn on four split tanned-leather supports, laced in (now partly broken), showing as raised bands on the spine, tooled in blind with a line; five compartments, the upper three: tooled in blind with a fleuron; two compartments near tail: renewed. Endbands: single with a bead; red and white silk over cord cores (laced in), tied down.

Endleaves: white paper pastedowns and one free leaf, conjugate with the pastedown, at both ends. Parchment manuscript lining of spine panels, stuck down on the inside of the boards beneath the pastedowns.

Repairs: tail part of spine renewed; repairs at top of spine and at corners of covers.

PROVENANCE: On title-page in manuscript: 'Es de la libreria de J. Mrr (?) do Santiago'; 'No es [?g?se] contiere enlos es purgatorios de Rojas J Soto maior en S mrr (?) a 22 de Junio de 1643 Leandro maldonado'; Eduardo Bullrich (book plate; sold: Sotheby's, 19.iii.1952, *395*).
LITERATURE: Hueso-Rolland, pl. xxi (Alcala, 1562).

400 *A binding made in Granada, c. 1570*

Carta ejecutoria apedimjento de Alonso de Mohedas, Granada, December 1570. Single-quire MS on parchment; illuminated frontispiece; decorated initials; ruled in red.

328 × 223 × 22 mm.   (M 45) Davis 708

Black goatskin (or hair sheep) over paste boards, tooled in blind and gold to a panel design, consisting of five concentric frames and a central panel; the frames are formed by lines; the outer frame or border has a roll showing heads in medallions and large flowers, a second frame has individual bird and unicorn tools, a third frame has a roll showing animals and flower branches, a fourth frame has individual stag and monkey tools, and a fifth frame has a roll showing pieces of armour; the same armour-roll links the corners of the frames; the centre panel has corner fleurons and a central row of tools depicting a vase with flowers, a lamb-and-flag, a lion and a bird on a curving branch. On the upper cover is painted in gold paint: OMNIA/ PRO/ VERITATE; 'Aladro./AD. 1570.'; 'Archi^P Foentrabia/ Legi 48.' and an unidentified coat of arms. Traces of four pairs of ties. Turn-ins: tooled in blind with a line. Edges: red with traces of gilding.

Sewn on four alum-tawed supports, laced in, showing as raised bands on the spine; five compartments, tooled in gold with stylized flowers and a lion; blind lines. A red, green, white and yellow cord (to hold a seal) is laced through the centre fold. No endbands.

Endleaves (forming part of the single quire): parchment pastedowns at both ends (now free); the frontispiece is conjugate with the upper pastedown; the last leaf of text is conjugate with the lower pastedown. Printed paper waste used as lining.

Repairs: at top and tail of spine and at spine.

PROVENANCE: Alonso de Mohedas (his coat of arms and that of his wife on fol. 1); Dr Torrez (manuscript note on frontispiece: 'chttr/Eel doctor/torrez'); Breslauer (Catalogue 74, 1951, *43*, pl.; sold: 7.vi.1952).
REFERENCES: Romme, *Book Collector*, 1969, p. 37, note 109; Foot, *Davis*, I, no. 20.
LITERATURE: Foot, *Davis*, I, pp. 261–9 (and literature cited there).
Same tools on: Sourget, Catalogue, May 1987, *48* (*Carta ejecutoria*, 1556); Patrick King, 1980 (*Carta ejecutoria*, Granada, 1569); Breslauer, Catalogue 109 (1988), *13* (*Carta ejecutoria*, Granada, 1578).

Aladro.
AD. 1570.

PRO
OMNIA VERITAT.

Arch⁰ Fuenterabia
Leg⁰ 4 ⁰

Compare: López Serrano, 1942, figs 7, 8; López Serrano, 1972, pl. 16; Brugalla, pl. vi; Carrión Gútiez, 'Incunables', pp. 395–445, pls 15–19; Libreria Jose Porrua Turanzas, *Catálogo de libros y manuscritos antiguos* 46 (Madrid, n.d.), no. 46; see also: Davis 709, 711 (nos. 401, 404 below).

Note: Proceedings on behalf of Philip II of Spain against Don Alonso de Mohedas, citizen of Medellin, for having refused to pay his duties as a nobleman.

401 *A binding of the late sixteenth century*

[Possibly a blank book, now containing:] Appointment of Alonzo Forero to be a 'familiar' of the Inquisition, December 1576, and other documents and privileges issued by the Inquisition in favour of various individuals, written in a variety of hands, dated April 1586–September 1614; last entry signed 'Pedro de camino'. MS on paper; two conjugate parchment leaves with illuminations (St Francis, Crucifixion, Forero's coat of arms).

313 × 217 × 17 mm. (M 34) Davis 709

Dark brown calf over paste boards, tooled in gold to a panel design with three concentric frames; lines, an outer frame or border filled with a roll showing heads in medallions between two birds addorssed; a second frame filled with fleurons and roundels; a third frame with a roll showing heads in medallions and flowers; the centre panel has fleurons in the corners; fleurons, roundels, flowers, three semicircles and an scroll with IHS, inside and surrounding a hexagon, outlined by a frame of lines and a roll of heads in medallions with flowers; the same roll divides the hexagon into two triangles and a central rectangle, with a centre piece of four large fleurons; smaller fleurons in the corners and scrolls with IHS. Traces of four pairs of ties. Edges of boards and turn-ins: tooled in blind with lines. Edges: gilt.

Sewn on four cords, laced in, showing as raised bands on the spine; five compartments, tooled in gold with strips filled with leaves and a large flower. Endbands: single; natural thread over cord cores (laced in), tied down.

Endleaves: white paper pastedowns at both ends; at the front: three pairs of free conjugate white paper leaves (followed by the two parchment leaves with illuminations); at the end: ten blanks [probably part of the blank book].

Repairs: small repairs at corners and top and tail of spine.

PROVENANCE: Alonzo Forero (on second parchment leaf, verso: his coat of arms with 'Forero' and motto: 'Si Dios es. con nos. quien. sera. contra. nos'); on pastedowns: manuscript notes, some dated 1509–99; de Buizo family (on pastedown of upper cover: manuscript notes in various hands in Spanish: announcing the birth of Joseph, son of Joseph de Buizo, 1676; other notes concerning de Buizo family affairs, dated 1676–1760).

REFERENCES: G D Hobson, *Thirty Bindings*, pl. xvi; Romme, *Book Collector*, 1969, pp. 37–8, note 110.
LITERATURE: Davis 708 (no. 400 above, and literature cited there).
Compare: Fletcher, *Foreign*, pl. 43 (= BL, Add. MS 12214); López Serrano, 1942, figs 7, 8; Hueso Rolland, pl. xvii (= *Encuadernaciones españolas*, no. 87); see also Davis 711 (no. 404 below).

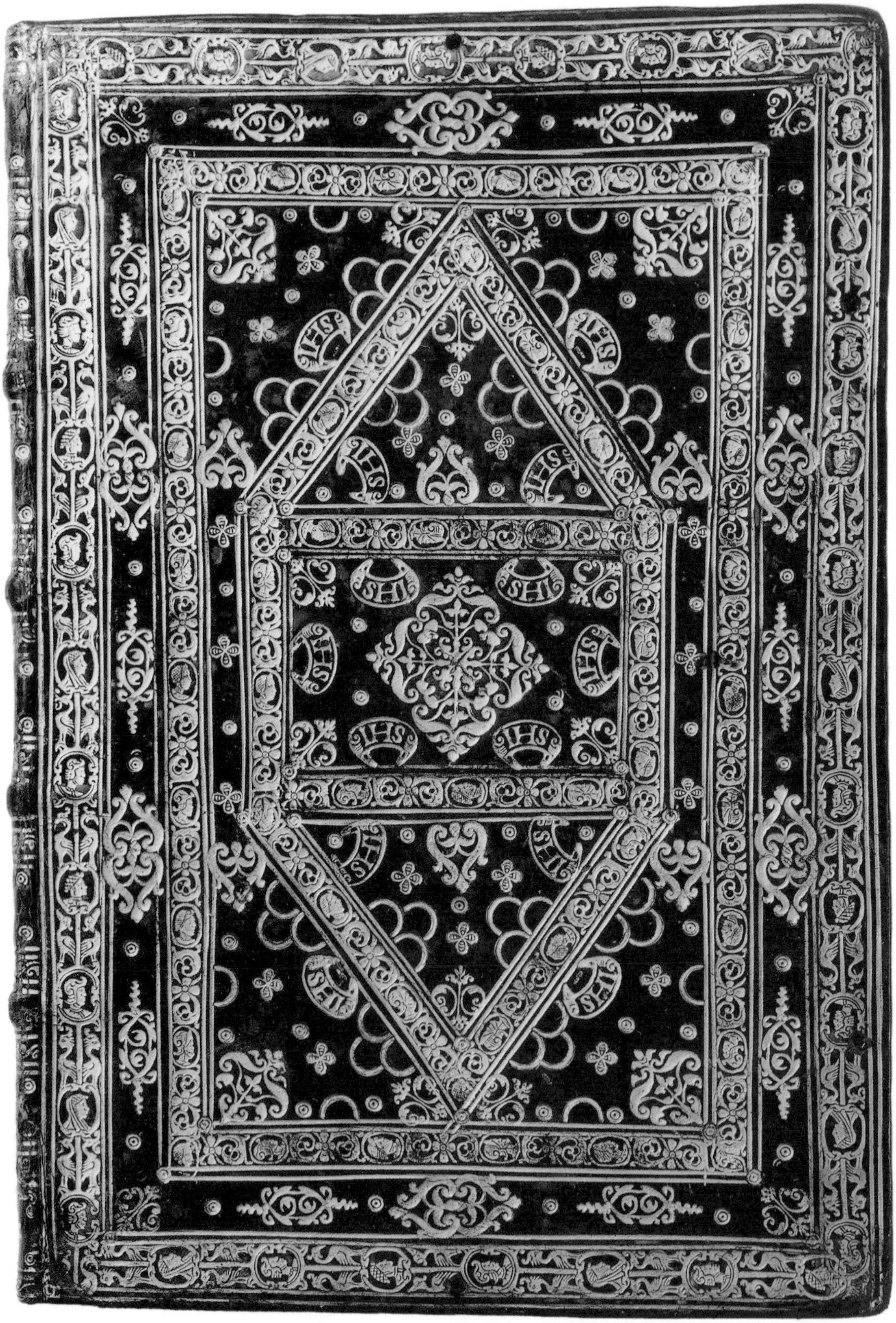

402 *A binding of the late sixteenth century*

Processionarium secundum ritum et morem fratrum predicatorum, Venice: Haeredes L Iuntae, November 1545; printed in red and black. 8vo.

178 × 117 × 36 mm. (P 1243) Davis 659

Brown (?)hair sheep over wooden boards, tooled in gold to a panel design with lines, 'corkscrew' tools in the corners, flower tools at and in the corners of the centre panel; three semicircles and 'corkscrew' tools along the outside frame of the panel; the panel is divided by lines into three rectangles, with smaller flower tools, an armorial shield with the cross of Calatrava in the centre and lettered: S/ YSABEL. ESCHO:/LASTICA. XABAR. Remnants of two pairs of clasps, hinging on the upper cover. Edges of boards: tooled in gold with small curly tools; turn-ins: tooled in blind with a line. Edges: red and gauffered with square ornaments, and small stylized flowers (or dots).

Sewn on four alum-tawed supports, laced in, showing as bands on the spine with traces of gold tooling; five compartments, tooled in gold with stylized flower tools and 'corkscrew' tools. Endbands: single with a bead; white and blue silk over cord cores (now cut or broken off), tied down.

Endleaves: white paper pastedowns at both ends.

Repairs: small repairs at edges of boards and at corners near the spine.

PROVENANCE: Ysabel Xabar [S probably stands for 'Sor': Sister; a Dominican nun?]; manuscript notes in Spanish in various hands on pastedowns; music manuscript on y4 (last page of text); Karl & Faber (Catalogue 51, 12.v.1955, *483*; sold: 27.x.1955).
LITERATURE: Foot, *Davis*, I, p. 265.
Same armorial shield on: Davis 711 (no. 404 below); BL, C.125.g.1 [Dominican rules, n.p., n.d.], C. 69.h.7 (Salamantice, 1524), C.64.g.4 (Alcala, 1578); Hueso Rolland, pls iii, xxx; see also Foot, *Davis*, I, p. 268, note 15.
Compare: Hueso Rolland, pls xxvii, xxix; Penney, pls xi, xviii–xx, xxv.
Note: The order of Calatrava, a military order, was established in 1158 by Raimundo, abbot of the Cistercian monastery of Santa Maria de Fitero (Navarre), who on command of King Sancho III defended the town of Calatrava against the Moors. According to Penney (pl. xi), the Dominicans used the cross of Calatrava as their emblem.

403 *A binding, possibly made in Saragossa, c. 1628–30*

Letras decissorias de Nicolas Mathias de Oña, Señor de Buñales, Saragossa, 11 April 1628; illuminated MS on parchment.

286 × 198 × 18 mm. (M 1) Davis 710

Brown goatskin over paste boards, tooled in gold to an imitation fanfare design, with lines and gouges, a border filled with large curl tools; a ribbon with a double outline divides the covers into compartments, which are filled with fleurons, various flower tools, birds, leafy sprays, large curl tools, dots and pyramids of semicircles. Two pairs of red silk ties. Edges: gilt with traces of red staining beneath the gold.

Sewn on four alum-tawed supports, laced in, showing as bands on the spine; five compartments, tooled in gold with stylized flowers and dots. A red and silver cord (to hold a seal) is laced through the fold and through the bottom half of the spine. Endbands: single with a bead; primary sewing of dark thread over cord cores (laced in), tied down; secondary sewing of pink and yellow silk.

Endleaves: pink silk pastedowns, two free conjugate parchment leaves and a third free parchment leaf, at both ends; at the front: the third free parchment leaf is possibly conjugate with a leaf decorated with a coat of arms that follows the title-page and its conjugate parchment blank leaf, which in turn is followed by a pink silk guard leaf with a stub, pasted down onto the third free parchment endleaf; at the end: the third free parchment endleaf is conjugate with a stub, pasted to the pastedown; two pink silk leaves near the end of the text (before and after p. 27).

PROVENANCE: Bought: Sotheby's, 26.xi.1940, *546* (pl.).

403

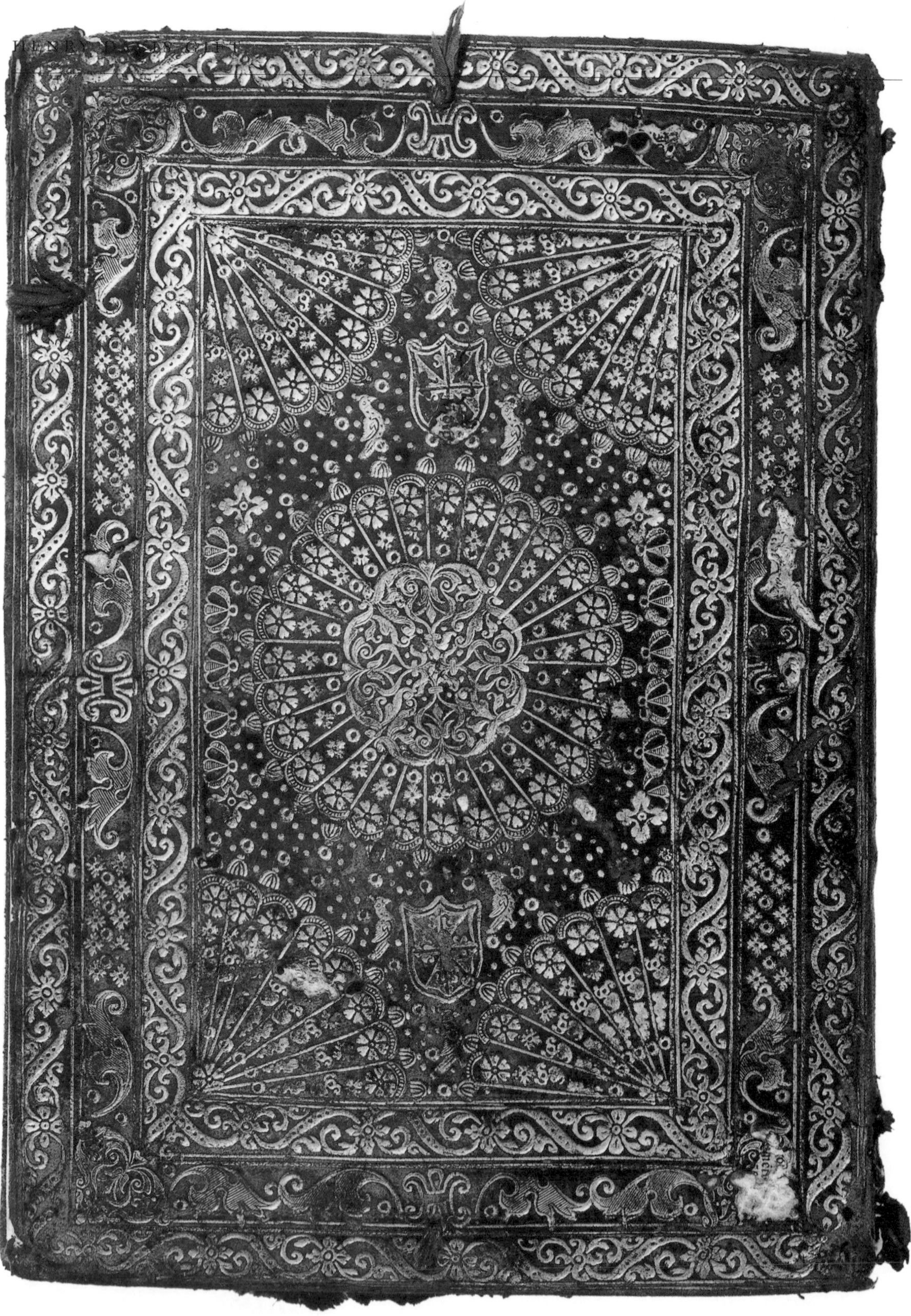

404 *A binding made in Valladolid, c. 1635–40*

Carta ejecutoria de hidalguia de sangre en propriedad apedimjento de Fran[cis]co Calderon, Valladolid, 6 September 1635; decorated MS on parchment.

297 × 208 × 22 mm.　　　　　　　　　　　　　　　　　　　　　　　　　　(M 6) Davis 711

Brown goatskin over paste boards, tooled in gold to a fan design, with lines, an outer border or frame filled with a large floral roll; large hatched corner fleurons; a second frame with large curving hatched tools, open ornamental tools, small stylized flowers and roundels; a third frame with the same large floral roll; a centre panel with quarter fans in the corners, built up of lines and individual flower tools, ivy-leaf tools, 'corkscrew' tools and roundels; a fan-shaped centre ornament composed of four large hatched fleurons, surrounded by fan segments built up of lines and small tools, above and below which are armorial shields with the cross of Calatrava; a background of stylized flowers, parrots, 'parachute'-shaped tools (in two sizes), roundels and dots. Remnants of two pairs of green and two pairs of yellow silk ties. Edges: gilt.

　　Sewn on (?)four cords, laced in; smooth spine, tooled in gold with two strips of the large floral roll. A green, white, yellow and red silk cord is taken over the top of the spine, laced through the joint after the first free endleaf at the front and through the joint after the second free endleaf at the back, and through the spine leather, crossing over on the outside of the spine near top and tail. Endbands: single with a bead; natural thread over cord cores (laced in), tied down.

　　Endleaves: at the front: parchment pastedown (Spanish manuscript) and one free parchment leaf conjugate with the pastedown; at the end: parchment pastedown and a pair of free conjugate parchment leaves. Green silk guard leaf between two illuminated leaves at beginning of text.

PROVENANCE:　Francisco Calderon (his painted coat of arms on fol. 2r); manuscript notes in Spanish on pastedown and on recto of portrait of Philip IV; 'Chancillr Don Joan desolouanos' (?); at end of text: manuscript notes in Spanish in various hands, dated 1605–1754 [Calderon family records?]; bought: Heffer, 21.iv.1941.
REFERENCES:　Foot, *Davis*, I, no. 20.
LITERATURE:　Foot, *Davis*, I, pp. 262–9 (and literature cited there); Cockx-Indestege & Storm van Leeuwen, *Quaerendo*, 1987, pp. 264–9, pl. 12.
Compare:　López Serrano, 1942, fig. 10; *Encuadernaciones españolas*, nos. 94–6; Penney, pls xxvi, xxvii; Wittockiana, *Ochos siglos*, no. 25; see also Davis 708, 709, 659 (nos. 400-2 above).
Note:　Francisco Calderon, of San Esteban de Gormaz and Aranda de Duero, fl. 1635.

405 *A binding made in Madrid by Antonio de Sancha, c. 1783*

Estado militar de España. Año de 1783, [Madrid]: Imprenta Real, 1783. 18mo (in 12s and 6s).

114 × 70 × 10 mm.　　　　　　　　　　　　　　　　　　　　　　　　　　(P 1458) Davis 660

White calf over paste boards, onlaid in black and red and tooled in gold with lines and gouges; cut-out compartments (in the corners and around the centre oval) showing red, yellow, green and silver foil beneath mica; the centre compartments are cut out and painted beneath mica. The black onlaid border is tooled in gold with a small tulip roll; corner onlays and a red onlay surrounding the centre piece are

405

tooled in gold with fleurons, flowers, leafy sprays, curls, dots and circles. The painted oval beneath mica in the centre shows, on the upper cover: a cherub with a bird; on the lower cover: a landscape with a tower, a river and a monument. The white calf has been decorated with red and blue paint and tooled in gold with a semis of dots. The upper cover is signed: SANCHA F[ecit]. Edges of boards and turn-ins: tooled in gold with a zig-zag pattern. Edges: sprinkled (large spots) in red and blue.

Originally stabbed through the inner margin (now broken); two rows of kettle stitches; smooth spine, tooled in gold with strips showing hatching and flower tools. Endbands: none. Blue silk bookmarker.

Endleaves: pink silk pastedowns and one free pink silk leaf (backed) conjugate with the pastedown, and a pair of free conjugate white paper leaves, at both ends. A map guarded in at the front; two fold-out plates guarded in at the end.

In a pull-off case of red goatskin, tooled in gold with lines, dots and a leaf-and-fan roll.

PROVENANCE: J R Abbey (book plate; in manuscript: 'J.A.1692/24:3:1938'; sold: Sotheby's 22.vi.1965, *317*, pl.).

REFERENCES: Romme, *Book Collector*, 1969, p. 38, notes 111, 112; Whitehead, *BLJ*, ix. 2 (1983), p. 140, fig. 1.

LITERATURE: Hueso Rolland, pls li, lii; P Vindel Alvarez, *D Antonio de Sancha, encuadernador*, Madrid, 1935; Nixon, *Broxbourne*, p. 190 (and literature cited there); Penney, pl. lii; López Serrano, 1972, pl. 37; Brugalla, pp. 205, 220; Foot, *Book Collector*, 1979, pp. 256–7 (and literature cited there); Whitehead, *BLJ*; Schäfer, no. 144; Caro & Crespo, p. 6.

Note: Antonio de Sancha, bookbinder, bookseller, printer and publisher in Madrid (1720–1790); binder to the Academy of History: 1757; then binder to the Royal Library and to the Spanish Academy. His son, Gabriel, who worked with his father, used the same finishing tools.

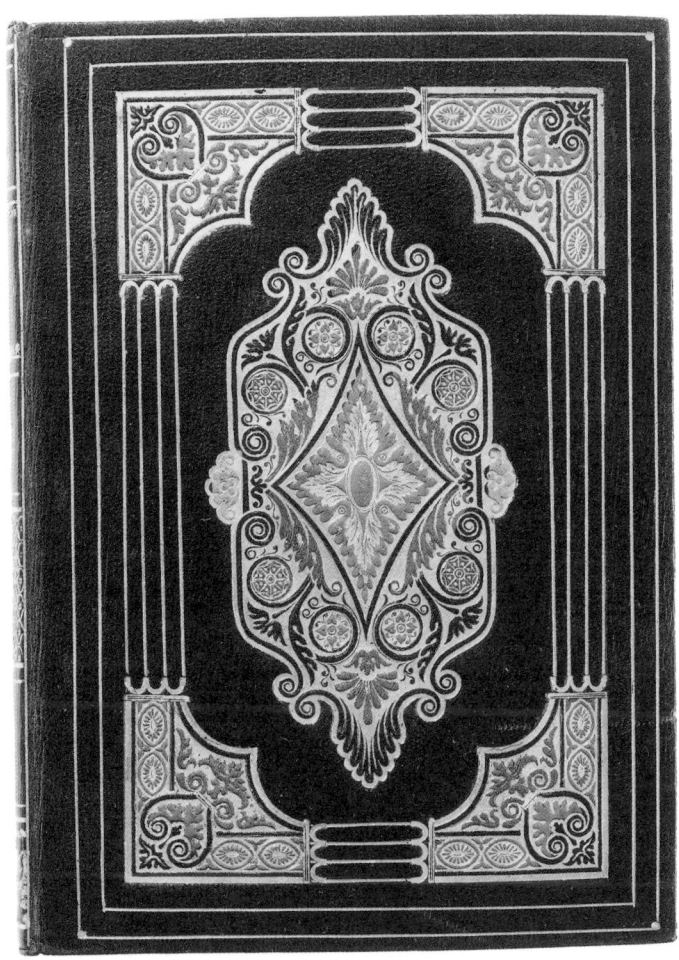

406

406 *A binding made in Madrid by Thomas Cobo, c. 1841*

Don Celestino del Piélago, *Introduccion al estudio de la arquitectura hidráulica*, Madrid: Imprenta Nacional, 1841. 4to.

219 × 159 × 21 mm. (P 1122) Davis 661

Purple straight-grain goatskin over paste boards, tooled and blocked in gold with lines, corner blocks and a large centre block, decorated with red, green, brown and yellow paint; gold-tooled arch-shaped tools and lines connect the corner blocks. Edges of boards: tooled in gold with part of a roll; turn-ins: tooled in gold with a leaf-and-flower roll and a small triangle roll. Thin leather joints. Edges: gilt.

  Sewn on three (recessed) cords, laced in; hollow back; smooth spine, tooled in gold to form compartments with a leaf, a rose and an all-over wavy and dotted pattern, a decorative roll and the title lettered onto the spine in the second 'compartment'. Endbands: single with a bead; green and white silk over (?)rolled (?)paper cores (cut off), tied down.

  Endleaves: coloured and patterned paper doublures (green, gold and red on a pale-blue ground) and one free paper leaf with a ribbed pattern, stamped in gold with a border, followed by a pair of free conjugate white paper leaves and a third free white paper leaf, at both ends.

THE HENRY DAVIS GIFT

PROVENANCE: On pastedown of upper cover: a printed ticket with: 'Enquadernado/ Por/ Thomas Cobo/ Calle de Preciados/ No. 39/ En Madrid'; bought: Sotheby's, 11.v.1953, *51* (reproduction of ticket).
LITERATURE: Hueso Rolland, p. 92, pl. lvii; Castañeda, *Ensayo*, pp. 65–6; López Serrano, 1972, p. 80.
Compare: *Encuadernaciones españolas*, pl. opposite no. 123.
Note: Thomas Cobo, a Madrid binder ('Calle de Preciados, 39'), pupil of Carsí y Vidal, worked for Isabel II and Fernando VII; won a bronze medal at the exhibition of 1831 (Madrid).

407 *A twentieth-century binding made in Barcelona by Emilio Brugalla*

[Robert Persons], *De persecutione Anglicana libellus*, Rome: Vincentius Accoltus; typographia G Ferrarius, 1582. 8vo.

157 × 108 × 16 mm. (P 1499) Davis 662

Red goatskin over paste boards, tooled in gold and blind, to a panel design, with blind lines along the border, outlining the panel and forming a diamond shape in the centre; gold-tooled fleurons at the corners of the panel, a frame with a leafy roll around the panel, small fleurons in the corners and larger fleurons at the top and bottom of the centre diamond. Edges: gilt.

Sewn on three (invisible, probably recessed) supports, laced in; the spine has five false bands (not coinciding with the sewing supports), tooled in gold with a line; six compartments, tooled in blind with lines and in gold with fleurons; title lettered in second compartment; imprint lettered near the tail. Endbands: (not worked) woven, pink and yellow.

Endleaves: brown, blue, white, and pink marbled paper pastedowns and one free marbled leaf (backed) conjugate with the pastedowns, one free white paper leaf conjugate with the backing paper and a pair of free conjugate white paper leaves, at both ends.

PROVENANCE: Manuscript notes (probably 16th century; partly cut-off) on title-page; backing paper of front free marbled leaf: stamped: BRUGALLA; Marquesa Vda de la Mesa de Asta (ex-libris; given by her to Henry Davis in memory of a visit, October 1964).
LITERATURE: Brugalla, *Tres ensayos*; López Serrano, 1972, pp. 102, 105.
Note: Emilio Brugalla Turmo (1901-87); bookbinder and writer about bookbindings, Barcelona.

408 *A Portuguese binding made in Lisbon, c. 1809–10*

Philip [Neri], Saint, *Diario ecclesiastico para o Reino de Portugal ... para o anno de 1809*, Lisbon: Impressam Regia, [1809]. 16mo.

104 × 56 × 12 mm. (P1422) Davis 663

Green silk over thin boards, embroidered with gold and silver thread and coloured silks, sequins and glass beads with a small border, flowers in the corners, bunches of buds, and in the centre: the crowned royal arms of Portugal on purple foil, surrounded by palm leaves. Edges: gilt and gauffered with a cross-hatched pattern.

407　　　　　　　　　　　　　　408

Sewn on two (recessed) cords, stuck down beneath the pastedowns; smooth spine (covered with green silk) embroidered with gold and silver thread and yellow silk to divide the spine into four compartments, each embroidered with a sequin and a cross. Endbands: none.

Endleaves: coloured marbled paper pastedowns and one free marbled paper leaf conjugate with the pastedown, and one free white paper leaf, at both ends. Fold-out map guarded in at the front.

PROVENANCE: Bought: Sotheby's, 28.ii,1966, *175*.
LITERATURE: M Lima, *Encuadernadores portugueses*, Porto, 1956.
Compare: BL, C.108.u.2 (*Diario ecclesiastico para o Reino de Portugal … para o anno de 1829*, Lisbon, 1829); Gumuchian, 1930, no. 317 (*Diario 1823*).

489

HYPERAS

PISTES

MISCELLANEOUS BINDINGS

EASTERN EUROPE

409 *A Cracow binding for Jan Laski, c. 1527*

Desiderius Erasmus, *Hyperaspistes diatribae adversus servum arbitrium M. Lutheri*, Basel: I Froben, 1526 [and] Erasmus, *Hyperaspistae liber secundus adversus librum M. Lutheri*, Basel: I Froben, 1527. 8vo.

165 × 110 × 49 mm.   (P 948) Davis 651

White leather (possibly sheep) over wooden boards, tooled in blind and gold with lines; on the upper cover (tooled in gold), near the top and tail edge: HYPERAS/PISTES, a border filled with linked-circles tools, corner leaf tools and in the centre the arms of Jan Laski (Joannes a Lasco); on the lower cover (tooled in blind, the heat of the tool resulting in dark impressions): lines and Laski's arms in the centre. Remnants of four pairs of clasps, hinging on the lower cover. Edges: plain; title in ink on top edge.

Sewn on three split alum-tawed supports, laced in, showing as raised bands on the spine, tooled in blind with a line; four compartments, tooled in blind with strap-work in the head and tail compartments and floral tools. Parchment manuscript spine lining. Endbands: single with a bead; pink silk over (?)cord cores (laced in), tied down.

Endleaves: white paper pastedowns and one free leaf conjugate with the pastedown, at both ends.

PROVENANCE: Jan Laski (Joannes a Lasco) (on title-page of second work in manuscript: 'Ab Erasmo missus, redditus circiter cal [–: cut off by binder]/ Anni MDXX [—: cut off by binder]/ Νηφε καί άπιστες/ Joannis à Lasco Poloni et amicorum'); Colonel and Mrs Forbes Leith of Whitehaugh (book plate); John Arthur Brooke (book plate; sold: Sotheby's, 25.v.1921, *506*); Arthur Kay (sold: Sotheby's, 26.v.1930, *299*, pl.); G D Hobson (sold: Sotheby's, 22.v.1950, *65*, pl.; with a letter from G D Hobson to Arthur Kay, dated 9 August [19]28).

REFERENCES: G D Hobson, *Cambridge*, p. 65, note 3; *Treasures*, 1965, no. 72; Romme, *Book Collector*, 1969, p. 38, notes 113, 114; Nixon, 1985, p. 65.

LITERATURE: Goldschmidt, pp. 181–2; G D Hobson, *Cambridge*, xxi; Nixon, 1985; see also: E Zwinogrodzka, P Hordinski and J Storm van Leeuwen, *Poolse Boekbindkunst 1400–1800 uit de Jagiellonski bibliotheek, Krakow*, The Hague, 1990 (with further literature).

Note: Jan Laski (Joannes a Lasco) (1499–1560), studied in Bologna, travelled to Basel: 1525 where he stayed with Erasmus; later became inclined to the Protestantism of Zwingli and in 1540 he finally separated from Rome; married, lived in Emden (Frisia); visited England: 1548 and 1550; went to North Germany; returned to Poland: 1556; died in Pińczów.

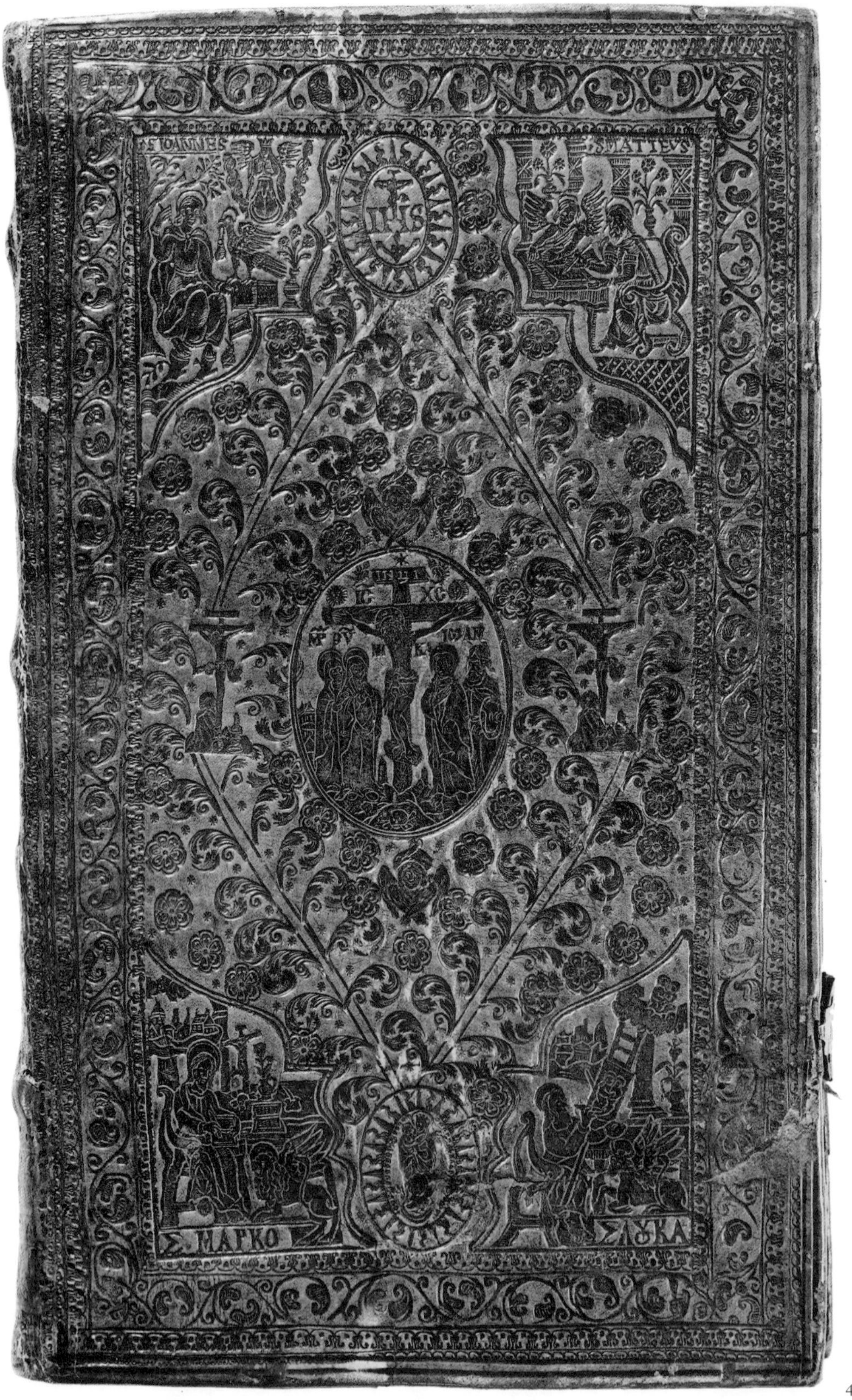
S. IOANNES
S. MATTEVS
IHS
Σ. ΜΑΡΚΟ
ΣΛΥΚΑ

410 *An east-European binding, c. 1725*

[Liturgy of the Ruthenian Uniate Church], Lemberg, 1721; printed in red and black within decorated borders. fol.

307 × 186 × 47 mm. (P 1469) Davis 697

Brown hide or calf over wooden boards, tooled in silver (oxidized) with two very small outer borders, a border filled with curly hatched leaf tools, a small fleuron border roll, large corner pieces showing the four Evangelists: John, Matthew, Mark and Luke, with their names in Latin (John and Matthew) and in Greek (Mark and Luke); near the top an oval with the Sacred Monogram surrounded by rays; near the tail: an oval with the Virgin and child surrounded by rays; in the centre of the upper cover: an oval stamp showing the crucifixion (with inscription in Greek), flanked by two smaller tools of the Crucifixion; in the centre of the lower cover an oval stamp showing King David praying, flanked by two smaller tools showing the Virgin and Child; above and beneath the central stamp: a cherub's head; the background is filled on the upper cover with curving leaf tools and roses, and on the lower cover with curving leaf tools and half-circular tools with flowers. Remnants of two pairs of clasps on leather thongs, hinging on the lower cover; metal catches on the edge of the upper board. Turn-ins: tooled in blind with two lines. Edges: gilt and gauffered with half circles, a fleuron spray and flowers.

Sewn on five cords, three of which (1, 3, 5) have been laced in, showing as raised bands on the spine, tooled with small tools; six compartments, tooled in blind with strips of small rolls and curly hatched leaf tools. Endbands: single with a bead; natural (white) thread over cord cores (laced in), tied down sporadically.

Endleaves: grey paper pastedowns and one free grey paper leaf (not, or no longer, conjugate with the pastedown), at both ends.

Repairs: at top of spine and covers.

PROVENANCE: G J Arvanitidi Byzantini (book plate); Herschel V Jones (book plate); A Ehrman, Broxbourne Library (book plate); bought: Breslauer, 4.v.1962.
REFERENCES: Romme, *Book Collector*, 1969, p. 38, note 115 (I am now less certain that this is a Polish binding).
LITERATURE: Schonath; Klepikov, 1966, pp. 135–42; Laucevičius.
Compare: Schonath, fig. 3; Klepikov, 1966, pls II–III; Laucevičius, nos. 242–3, 248, 267, 269–70, 277, 279, 286, 571–2.
Note: Large corner pieces showing the Evangelists, oval stamps with the Crucifixion or King David are all very common on east-European bindings and can be found in Russia, the Ukraine, Lithuania, Poland, Greece, etc.

411 *Three Russian neo-classical bindings, probably made in St Petersburg in the early nineteenth century*

P Cornelius Tacitus, *Opera*, 3 vols, Parma: Bodoni, 1795. fol.

331 × 253/4 × 40/43/39 mm. (P 1530) Davis 698–700

Red straight-grained sheepskin over paste boards, onlaid in black, yellow and green, and tooled in gold to a neo-classical design with lines, small border rolls, a wide border with floral curls and small tools;

494

roundels in red and gold surrounded by cornucopia tools, ears of corn and small sprigs in the corners. Edges of boards: tooled in gold with lines and dashes; turn-ins: tooled in gold with a floral ribbon. Red leather joints. Edges: gilt.

Sewn on five supports of flat hemp, laced in; smooth spine, tooled in gold with yellow strips onlaid and black-painted strips, forming compartments, with massed gold tooling around a small black-painted roundel in the centre; author's name lettered in second compartment, volume number in fourth compartment. Endbands: double with a bead; blue and white silk over (?)leather cores (cut off), tied down sporadically. Blue silk bookmarker.

Endleaves: brown paper pastedowns, tooled in blind with a small border roll, and one free brown paper leaf (backed) conjugate with the pastedown, and one free white paper leaf conjugate with the backing paper, at both ends.

PROVENANCE: Library of the Russian General Staff (library label); on endleaf of vol. I in manuscript: 'No 3762'; Sotheby's, 9.iv.1963, *460*; Breslauer (Catalogue 97, *114*, pl.; sold: 6.vi.1966).
REFERENCES: Romme, *Book Collector*, 1969, p. 38, note 116.
LITERATURE: Klepikov, 1962, pp. 437–47, pl. iv.
Note: According to a letter from S A Klepikov to G D Hobson (December 1962/January 1963), there are three Bodoni editions of 1799, also in very similar neo-classical bindings in the Lenin Library. Neo-classical bindings of this kind can be found all over Europe; compare for example Staggemeier & Welcher (London), Krauss (Vienna). The Library of the Russian General Staff was founded in 1811.

THE NEAR AND MIDDLE EAST

412 *A (?)fifteenth-century binding, probably made in Dalmatia by Donatus*

Biblia Latina, MS on parchment; historiated initials and decorated initials in red and blue. [French, 13th century].

153 × 102 × 59 mm. (M 40) Davis 654

Brown goatskin over wooden boards, tooled in blind to a panel design with, on the upper cover: small flowers in the corners, lettered in the outer border: ISTA BIBLIA/ EST DO[MI]NI PET/RI CORVI/ PBR DONATVS ME FEC[IT]; on the lower cover: lettered along the top: IESVS CRISTVS; border filled with rope-work tools; central panels filled with strap-work tooling (on both covers) and tiny fleurs-de-lis (on upper cover). Traces of two pairs of clasps (space left in the tooling of the inscription on the upper cover).

Sewn on six alum-tawed supports, laced in, showing as flat bands on the spine, tooled in blind with a line; seven compartments, tooled in blind with lines. Endbands: (later) single; primary sewing of natural (unbleached) thread over leather cores (cut off); secondary sewing with blue and white thread in a < shape, tied down.

Endleaves: parchment pastedowns and one free parchment leaf conjugate with the pastedown, at both ends.

Repairs: at covers, corners of covers, joints, and at head and tail of spine.

412

PROVENANCE: Petrus Corvus; Franciscans of the convent of St Katherine (in manuscript on nine parchment leaves before the text: in two different hands: a list of books of the Bible, a table of Gospels and Epistles, headed: 'Ista Biblia e[st] fr[atru]m c[on]vent[us] s[an]c[t]e Katerine ord[in]is minor[um]'); Henry White JP, DL, FSA (book plate); Michael Tomkinson (book plate; sold: Sotheby's, 3–7.vii.1922, *1085*); P Adam (sold: Sotheby's, 6.vii.1936, *7*); G D Hobson (sold: Sotheby's, 22.v.1950, *61*).

Note: According to the Sotheby's sale catalogue (22.v.1950): a similar binding with knot-work stamps and an inscription of ownership by Bishop Donatus of Ragusa (d. 1482) was in the library of the Franciscans at Kotor (Cattaro).

---

413 *A late fourteenth-century Egyptian binding for the Amir Aytmish al-Bajasī*

Koran (part 25), Arabic MS on paper in Naskhī script; some decorated headings; decorated borders. [Egypt, late 14th century].

373 × 278 × 15 mm. (M 71) Davis 701

Brown goatskin over thin paste boards, tooled in blind and gold, with lines, two borders filled with small tools, rope-work tools and dots, corners filled with rope-work tools and dots, with a large knot tool with dots at the outer point; in the centre a large ornament outlined in blind and gold with gold fleurons at top and bottom, and filled with strap-work tooling, hatching and dots, and with a gold-painted six-pointed star in the centre. The cover near the end of the text [i.e. the upper cover from the west-European point of view] has a pentagonal flap covering part of the cover near the beginning of the text [i.e. the lower cover from the west-European point of view], tooled in blind and gold with borders, strap-work tooling and dots around a central circle with lines forming geometrical shapes, knot-work

497

and dots. Cover of fore-edge: tooled in blind with strap-work and in gold with dots. The covers and flap are lined with blind-stamped leather.

Unsupported sewing with three sewing stations (sewing structure: partly obscured by repairs); flat spine.

Endleaves: two free white paper leaves near beginning of text; one free white paper leaf near end of text.

Repairs: major repairs at joints (inside); repairs at top and tail of spine, at cover of fore-edge; small repairs at covers.

PROVENANCE: [part of a 30-volume Koran, written and bound for the] Amir Aytmish al-Bajasī; Miss P M Bolsworth (sold: Sotheby's, 9.xii.1963, *110*, pl.).

REFERENCES: *Treasures*, 1965, no. 67; Romme, *Book Collector*, 1969, p. 38, note 117, pl. xi; Lings & Safadi, no. 159.

LITERATURE: Ettinghausen, 1954, p. 469, fig. 356; Miner, *Baltimore*, no. 61; Lings & Safadi, no. 160 (= BL, Or 9671); Needham, *Twelve Centuries*, no. 17; James, no. 105; Haldane, no. 13; Raby & Tanindi, pp. 9, 10 (fig. 8).

Compare: Miner, *Baltimore*, no. 68; James, no. 33; Sarre, pl. vi; Bosch, *et al.*, *Islamic Bindings*, nos. 15 and 21 (doublure), 52 (= James, 33), 55–6, 62, 73.

Note: The 30-part Koran, of which this is part 25, was donated to his medrese in Tripoli by the Mamluk Amir Aytmish al-Bajasī, who was executed in 1400 AD; the same binder appears to have worked for Sultan Faraj (reg. 1399–1412), who also owned a Koran in a very similar binding. Other parts of the Koran for Aytmish al-Bajasī in very similar bindings, or fragments/parts of these bindings, are in the Library of Congress, Walters Art Gallery, Baltimore (Miner, 61), British Library (Or 9671), Victoria & Albert Museum (Haldane, 13), Chester Beatty Library, Dublin (James, 105), Freer Gallery, Washington (Ettinghausen, fig. 356); Henry Vever collection, Paris; three were sold at Sotheby's, 12.iv.1976, *176*, 23.v.1986, *283*, 12.x.1990, *209* (now in private hands).

414 *A late sixteenth-century Persian binding*

Nizāmī, *Khusraw u Shīrīn*, Persian MS on paper, written in Nasta'līq script; illuminated, decorated headings. Late 16th century.

253 × 165 × 30 mm.   (M 60) Davis 702

Dark brown sheepskin over paste boards, blocked in gold, with corner blocks and border compartments showing floral garlands; a centre panel decorated with a large block showing trees, birds, animals and a huntsman. The cover near the end of the text has a flap extending over the fore-edge and over part of the cover near the beginning of the text, blocked in gold, to the same design as the cover decoration; a small border decorated with gold paint. Doublures and flap lining of red-brown sheepskin, painted in gold with lines and dashes and decorated with cut-out compartments filled with gold filigree over blue, red and green paper. Leather joints.

Unsupported sewing with two sewing stations; flat spine (rebacked). Endbands: yellow and red silk worked in < shape, tied down.

414

Endleaves: one free white paper leaf at both ends.
Repairs: rebacked; repairs at covers, fore-edge of covers, new hinges.

PROVENANCE: Bought: Sotheby's, 11.xii.1956, *29*.
Compare: Sarre, pls xiii–xiv, xvii; Regemorter, *Chester Beatty*, pls 36, 38 (border decoration); James, no. 63; Haldane, nos. 82, 90, 96, 99, 102–4, 113.

415   *A Persian binding made c. 1630–50*

Koran [with Persian translation], Persian MS, written in Naskhī script on gold ground; illuminated; marginal decoration.

145 × 80 × 25 mm.   (M 14) Davis 652

Brown goatskin over paste boards, border painted in gold with interlacing curving lines; centre panel blocked in gold to a design of interlacing ribbons and small leaves and flowers; decorated with blue paint. Doublures of brown goatskin, tooled in gold with lines in the border.

    Sewing and spine leather missing; traces of four sewing stations for unsupported sewing. Endbands: missing.

    Endleaves: two pair of free conjugate white paper leaves (quired) and two free white paper leaves near beginning of text; one pair of free conjugate white paper leaves near end of text.

PROVENANCE: [believed to have belonged to] Princess Jahānārā; Major D I M Macaulay (sold: Sotheby's, 24.vi.1941, *90*).
Compare: Haldane, nos. 86, 149, 171.
Note: Princess Jahānārā was the daughter of the Emperor Shāh Jahān (reg. 1627–56).

416   *A Persian binding of the second half of the seventeenth century*

Koran [with Persian translation], Arabic MS on paper written in Naskhī and Nasta'līq script; decorated headings; marginal decoration; elaborately decorated opening pages. [17th century].

289 × 170 × 35 mm.   (M 9) Davis 703

Red sheepskin over paste boards, blocked in (oxidized) silver (or low quality gold) and decorated with blue paint; lines, a floral border, a wide border with compartments, blocked with Persian inscriptions, a second floral border; floral corner blocks; a floral centre block above and beneath which are compartments, blocked with Persian inscriptions, and smaller floral tools.

    Unsupported sewing with two sewing stations; flat spine. Endbands: white thread and remnants of pink silk over cord cores (cut off), tied down.

    Endleaves: decorated paper pastedowns (decorated to an over-all pattern of small geometrical shapes in gold, orange and blue) at both ends; near the beginning of text: one free white paper leaf, two pairs of free conjugate white paper leaves (quired) and one pair of free conjugate white paper leaves; near the end of text: five free white paper leaves pasted together and two free conjugate white paper leaves.

PROVENANCE: Major D I M Macaulay (sold: Sotheby's, 24.vi.1941, *79*).
Compare: Sarre, fig. 3; Regemorter, *Chester Beatty*, pl. 36; Lings & Safadi, nos. 163–4; James, no. 63; Bosch, *et al.*, *Islamic Bindings*, p. 70, fig. 11.
Note: The manuscript is believed to have been written by the Emperor Aurangzib-Alamgīr (1659–1707).

415

416

501

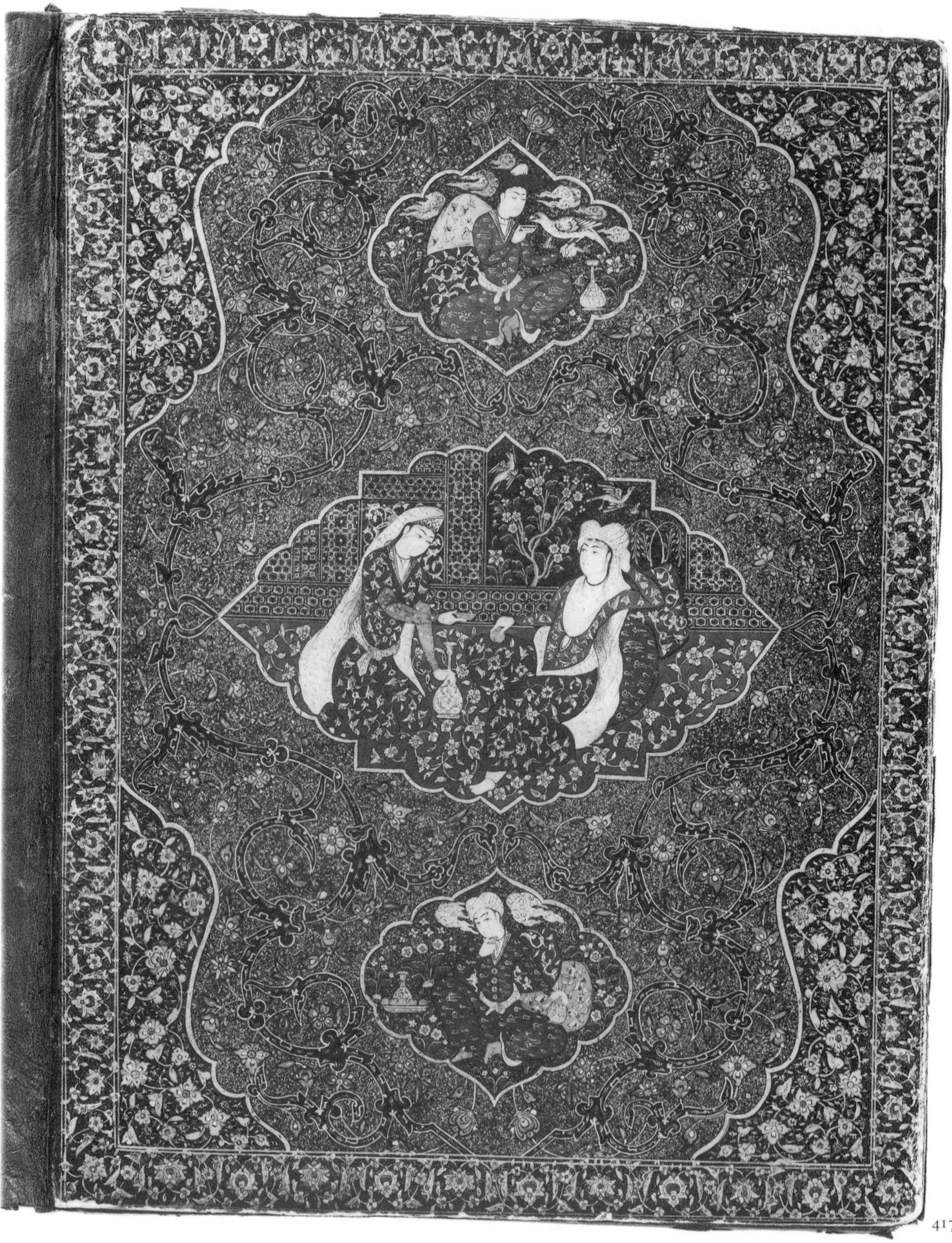

417

417 *A pair of Persian book covers, c. 1650*

[Empty covers].

418 × 323 × 12 (2×6) mm. (P 808) Davis 719

Paste boards, lacquered, painted and covered with clear lacquer. Exterior of finely painted lacquered decoration in red, gold and various colours, showing an outer border with floral decoration, corner compartments with leaves and flowers; three compartments, two of which contain a human figure in different settings, and a larger centre compartment containing two human figures; a gold-powdered background with arabesque branches with coloured leaves and flowers. Doublures of brown goatskin, decorated with gold paint, inlays and cut-out compartments. The outer border is decorated with gold paint, an inner border has cut-out compartments with brown-black, gold and blue paper filigree over fawn or blue; a large centre compartment inlaid in yellow sheepskin, is inlaid in different coloured leathers forming a human figure among flowers; around the centre compartment are fighting animals, large birds, human heads, flowers and foliage, painted in gold.

The covers are connected by a strip of black goatskin.

PROVENANCE: Bought: Sotheby's, 18.vii.1944, *419*.
Compare: Sarre, pls xxv–xxvi, xxvii–xxviii; Haldane, pl. 91.
Note: According to the Sotheby's catalogue, the covers were probably made 'for Shāh Abbas, the Great, and the figures may be attributed to Riza Abbasi (circa 1650 A.D.)'.

418 *A Turkish binding of the last quarter of the eighteenth century*

Tuhid Mungi, Arabic MS on paper written in thuluth script by M Khawaja, 1202 (AD 1787); decorated.

288 × 189 × 8 mm. (M 37) Davis 704

Worn black leather over paste boards, blocked in gold and decorated with red paint; with a deeply impressed centre block with floral branches and two smaller deeply impressed fleuron shapes, painted red and blocked in gold; gold-painted dashes round the edges of the blocks; small gold-tooled twisted rope border roll.

Rebacked; unsupported sewing with three sewing stations (single quire manuscript). No endbands.

Endleaves: marbled pastedowns and one free pale pink paper leaf tipped onto pastedown, at both ends.

PROVENANCE: Bought: Sotheby's 29.vii.1946, *225*.
Compare: St Catharine's College, Cambridge, L.v.86 (Arabic manuscript); Sarre, pl. xviii; Regemorter, *Chester Beatty*, pls 42, 46; James, no. 108; Bosch, *et al.*, nos. 83–5, 90; Haldane, pls 79, 80, 130–2, 134–5, 137–9, 147.

THE HENRY DAVIS GIFT

419

419 *A pair of Persian book covers, painted by Lotfali of Shiraz, 1861*

[Empty covers].

220 × 139 × 4 (2x2) mm. (P 890) Davis 653

Wooden boards, painted and lacquered. Exterior of painted lacquered decoration in gold, green, red and other colours, with a small decorative border, a border with flower garlands in compartments, corner compartments with houses and trees, and a large centre oval with roses and nightingales. Inside of boards: painted and lacquered in gold, red, black and other colours, with a small border with flowers, a second border with leaves and flowers, and a centre panel filled with vines and nightingales, two lotus flowers and a centre compartment showing a hand holding a flowering branch with an inscription in Arabic, reading [in translation]: The humble Lotfali of Shiraz in the year 1278 [AD 1861].

Remnant of red leather (?goat) spine strip.

PROVENANCE: Rt Hon. L S Amery, PC (sold: Sotheby's, 29.vii.1946, *259*).
REFERENCES: Romme, *Book Collector*, 1969, p. 39, note 119.
Compare: Sarre, pls xxvii–xxviii, xxxi; James, no. 103; Bosch, *et al.*, no. 94; Haldane, pl. 123.
Note: Lotfali of Shiraz: a celebrated Persian painter, who worked mainly for the royal court.

THE HENRY DAVIS GIFT

THE NEW WORLD

420 *A Mexican binding made c. 1790*

D Felipe de Zúñiga y Ontiveros, *Calendario manual y guia de forasteros de Mexico, para el año de 1790*, n.p. [Mexico], n.d. [1790]. 12mo.

130 × 76 × 17 mm.   (P 1239) Davis 655

Red sheepskin over paste boards, tooled in gold with lines, a border with stylized leaves, a second border with a roll of intertwined curves, and an inner border of stylized leaves; flower tools in the corners and a centre piece built up of flowers and flower heads. Edges of boards: gold-tooled dashes. Edges: gilt.

Sewn on three (recessed) cords (?laced in, or) stuck down beneath the pastedowns; smooth spine, tooled in gold with lines, flowers, leaves and artichoke tools. No endbands. Green silk bookmarker.

Endleaves: marbled paper pastedowns and one free marbled leaf conjugate with the pastedown and one free white paper leaf, at both ends.

PROVENANCE: Bought: Sotheby's, 6.vii.1955, *209*.
Compare: Manuel Romero de Terreros, *Encuadernaciones artísticas mexicanas*, Mexico, 1932, fig. 5; M López Serrano, *Biblioteca de Palacio*, pl. 34; Thompson, *Libri*, 1960.

421 *A binding made in New York by Wilson & Nichols for Joseph Bonaparte, 1828*

C D Colden, *Memoir, prepared at the request of … the Common Council of the City of New York, and presented to the mayor of the City, at the celebration of the completion of the New York canals*, New York: W A Davis, by order of the Corporation of New York, 1825. 4to.

249 × 202 × 44 mm.   (P 914) Davis 705

Red straight-grain goatskin over paste boards, tooled in gold and blind, with large square corners, built up of small tools; lines, small rolls at both sides of wide border strips filled with a pattern of garlands with plants, leaves and flowers; two inner borders with leafy fleurons and a small leaf roll; corner tools; in the centre the seal with the arms of the City of New York, above and beneath which: PRESENTED BY THE/ CITY OF NEW YORK/ TO/ MONSIEUR LE COMTE/ DE SURVILLIERS/ 1828. Edges of boards: tooled in gold with part of the wide border roll; turn-ins: tooled in gold with a vine roll. Edges: gilt.

Sewn on four (recessed) cords, laced in; six false bands, tooled in gold with lines; seven compartments, tooled in gold; head and tail compartments: with part of the wide border roll; compartments 2, 4 and 6: filled with small tools; title lettered in compartments 3 and 5; signed near the tail: WILSON & NICHOLS BIND. N.Y. Endbands: double; orange, yellow and blue silk over (?)cord cores (cut off), tied down occasionally. Green silk bookmarker.

Endleaves: blue and coloured marbled paper pastedowns and one free marbled leaf (backed) conjugate with the pastedown, one free white paper leaf conjugate with the backing paper, and a second free white paper leaf, at both ends. At the end: facsimiles of manuscript letters (J. Adams, Jefferson, Lafayette, etc.) bound in.

In a contemporary case of red cloth over marbled-paper-covered board, with a red straight-grain goatskin spine, tooled in gold (similar to the tooling on the spine of the book).

Miscellaneous Bindings

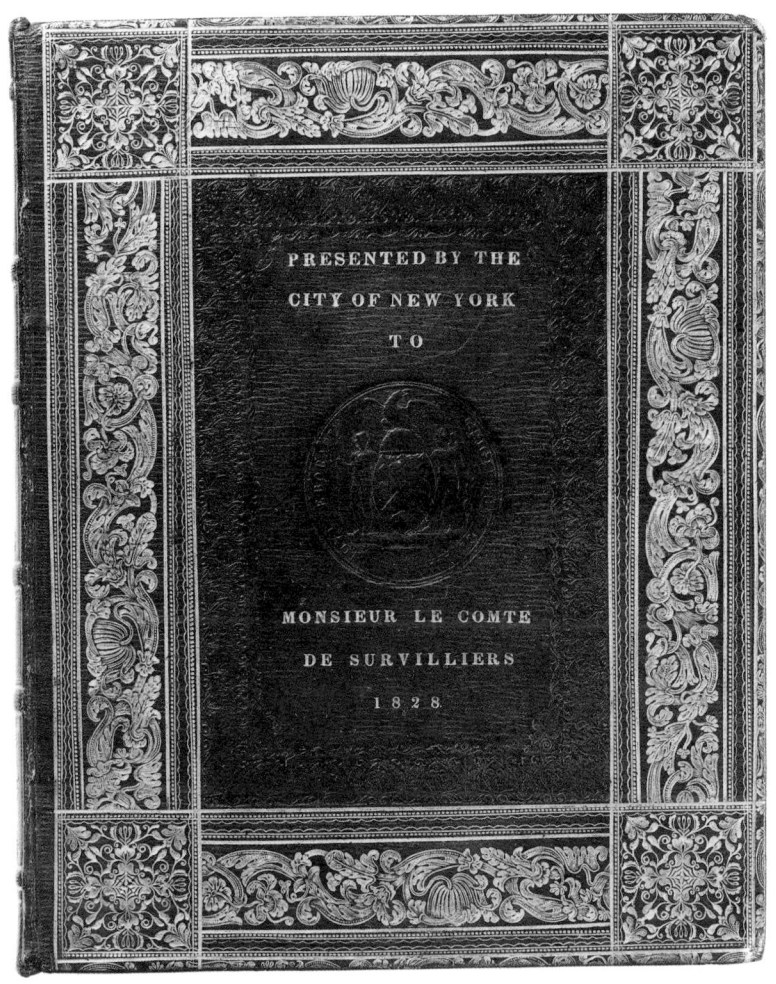

420

421

PROVENANCE: Joseph Bonaparte, comte de Survilliers (on endleaf: manuscript dedication by the Common Council of the City of New York to Bonaparte, 'a distinguished stranger now residing in the United States'); on pastedown of upper cover: library label with $\frac{41}{\text{AIII}}$; bought: Sotheby's, 28.vi.1948. *168* (pl.).

LITERATURE: Andrews, *Bibliopegy*, p. 98 (presentation copy of this book to Lafayette); *Bookbinding in America*, 1967, pp. 81, 93, 110; *Papantonio*, nos. 47 (presentation copy to Thomas Baldock Esq.), 54; Spawn, no. 37. Other presentation copies of this book bound by Wilson & Nichols: Figdor sale, Lucerne, 14.vi.1932, *58* (for Tsar Nicolas I); Sotheby's, 18.xii.1950, *171* = Sotheby's, 21.vi.1965, *204* (for Joseph Harvey Esq., Limerick).

Note: Wilson & Nichols, bookbinders of 2 Pine Street, corner of Broadway, New York, c. 1826. Joseph Bonaparte (1768–1844) went to New York: 1815; he took the title of comte de Survilliers; left for London: 1831; returned to the United States: 1837–9.

THE HENRY DAVIS GIFT

ADDENDA TO VOLUME II

[The following two bindings were inadvertently omitted when *The Henry Davis Gift*, vol. II was compiled.]

ADD I *A German binding of the last quarter of the 1570s*

P A Mattioli, *P A Matthioli ... Compendium de plantis omnibus*, Venice: Valgrisi, 1571. 4to.

220 × 155 × 60 mm. (P 1226) Davis 845

Brown calf over paste boards, tooled and blocked in gold and silver, with lines, a small border, a wide border filled with rectangular blocks, decorated with coloured paint; fleurons in the corners; a semis of stars; fleurons at the corners of a centre block, decorated with gold paint. Traces of two pairs of ties. Edges of boards: tooled in blind with a line; turn-ins: tooled in blind with small tools. Edges: gilt and gauffered to a pattern of knots.

Rebacked, with the original backstrip retained; sewn on four (invisible) supports, (probably) laced in, showing as raised bands on the spine, tooled in blind (trace of gold) with a line; five compartments, tooled in gold with a small border and open fleuron tools. Endbands: single with a bead; pink and green silk (cores and lacing in obscured by new paper inner joints; possible tie-downs: invisible).

Endleaves: new white paper pastedowns and two free white paper leaves, at both ends.

Repairs: rebacked; head and tail of spine: renewed; repairs at corners, at edges of boards and at turn-ins; new joints (repaired by the British Museum in 1969).

PROVENANCE: On title-page in manuscript: 'Joh. Michael Febr. Mdjjj(?)'; bought: Sotheby's, 6.vii.1955, *103*.
Same spine tool on: Trinity College, Cambridge, Grylls 31.263 (Eisleben, 1573).
Compare: Mazal, pl. 160.

Miscellaneous Bindings

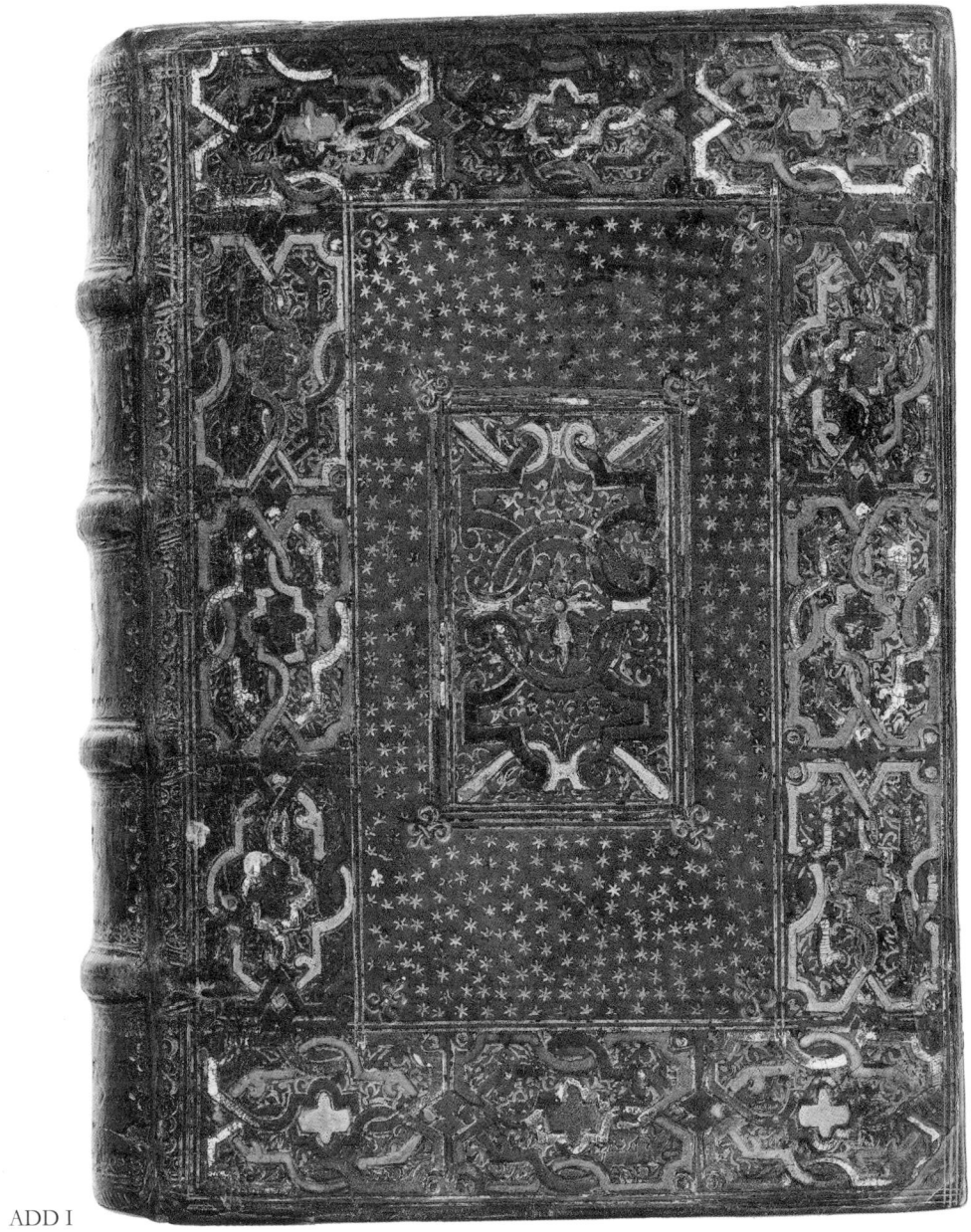

ADD I

THE HENRY DAVIS GIFT

ADD II *A binding made in South Germany or Austria, c. 1770*

V Bellini, *De monetis Italiae medii aevi hactenus non evulgatis, quae in patrio museo servantur, ... dissertatio,* Ferrara: Ioseph Rinaldi, 1767. 4to.

301 × 210 × 25 mm.   (P 1219) Davis 881

Red-brown goatskin over paste boards, tooled in gold with lines, an outer border with shell-shaped and curving tools; two small dog-tooth rolls; two inner borders, one with small stars and one with large drawer-handle tools, clasped hands, and floral and leaf tools; in the corners: bunches of flowers, fleurons and small drawer-handle tools, decorated with black paint. Edges of boards: tooled in blind (or oxidized silver?). Edges: marbled blue.

  Sewn on six cords, laced in, showing as raised bands on the spine, tooled in gold; seven compartments, tooled in gold with small hearts, curls and flowers, decorated with black paint; second compartment: title lettered onto the spine. Endbands: single with a bead; pink and white silk over (?)cord cores (cut off), tied down at front and back only. Green fabric bookmarker.

  Endleaves: pink and green block-printed paste-paper pastedowns, decorated with a pattern of flowers in diamonds, one free block-printed leaf conjugate with the pastedowns, and two free conjugate white paper leaves, at both ends.

PROVENANCE: J de Stuers (book plate, 1901); bought: Sotheby's, 6.vii.1955, *24*.
Same tools on: Jose M Passola, *Artisanía de la piel. Encuadernaciones en Vich, XVI–XX*, Vich, 1969, pl. 139bis, 140.
Note: Although the bindings illustrated in Passola cover Italian imprints, the tools used on these bindings are clearly German or Austrian.

ADD II

INDEXES

Index of Binders

(includes printers, publishers, booksellers, scribes and artists).
Except where otherwise indicated, all references are to entry numbers.

Abbasi, Riza (artist), 417
Adler, Rose, 220
Aesop binder, 91, 92
Agnese binder, 288
Aldus Manutius (printer, publisher, bookseller), *intro. p. 8*; 23, 263
Alexandre, Clement (bookseller, stationer), 8
Alexandre, Jean (publisher, bookseller), 8
Almagest atelier (illuminator), 1
Andreoli, brothers (Giovanni and Gregorio), 360, 373
Andreoli, Giovanni, 368
Andreoli, Gregorio, 368
Anthoine, Jacques *see* Anthoine-Legrain, Jacques
Anthoine-Legrain, Jacques, 219
Arabesque outline tool binder, 342
Arnobius binder *see* Mansfeld binder
Atelier à la Tulipe, 179, 180
Atelier de Fontainebleau, *intro. pp. 8, 9, p. 97*; 23, 63, 64, 69
Atelier des Caumartins, 144
Atelier des petits classiques, 168
Atelier du relieur du roi, *intro. pp. 8, 9, p. 97*; 64, 67, 69
Atelier Louis XII *see* Vostre, Simon
Atelier Louis XII/François I, *intro. p. 7*
Atelier 'Rocolet' *see* Rocolet, Pierre
Aurangzib-Alamgīr, Emperor (scribe), 416

Bacharach, 210
Barbou, Charles (printer, bookseller, binder), 203
Barbou frères, 203
Barbou, Henri (printer, bookseller, binder), 203
Bayfius binder, *intro. p. 7*
Belli, Valerio, of Vicenza (artist), 34
Bernardi, Giovanni, of Venice, 4
Bernardi, Giovanni Desiderio, da Castelbolognese (medallist, engraver), 34
Bernardino, Paolo di, 343
Bisiaux, Pierre-Joseph, 190
Bonet, Paul, 220, 222
Borghese bindery *see* Soresino
Boule, André (bookseller, binder), 5
Boyet, Luc-Antoine, 149, 152, 157
Bozerian, François, *jeune*, 198, 201
Bradel; Bradel-Derome, Alexis-Pierre, 171

British Museum bindery, 347, Add. I
Brugalla, Emilio, 407

Capé, Charles-François, 212
Cassot, Jeanne, *intro. p. 7*
Chambolle, René, 216
Chambolle, René-Victor, 216
Chambolle-Duru, 216
Cobo, Thomas, 406
Cockerell, Douglas & Son, 43
Corberan, Simeon, 129
Cupid's Bow binder, 80, 81, 82
Cuzin, Adolphe, 213, 217
Cuzin, Francisque, 213, 217

David, Bernard, 214
David, Salvador, 214
Delaunay, 216
Derome, Charles, 171
Derome, family, 171
Derome, Jacques-Antoine, 171, 172, 173, 174
Derome, Nicolas, 171
Derome, Nicolas-Denis, *le jeune*, 171, 172, 173, 182, 183, 184, 185, 186
Devers, family, 189
Donatus, Bishop of Ragusa (binder), 412
Douceur, François, 181
Douceur, Louis, 181
Dubuisson, Pierre-Paul, 178, 181
Dubuisson, René, 178
Ducastin, Alexis-Jacques, 202
Ducastin, family, 202
Ducastin, Pierre-Alexis, 202
Dufresnoy, Hélie, binders for, 143
Dupres Lahey, 88
Duru, Hippolyte, 212, 216 *see also* Chambolle-Duru
Duseuil, Augustin, 156, 157, 160
Duval, J, 221

Entrelac binder, *intro. p. 8*
Estienne Bible, binder of, *intro. p. 7, see* Roffet, Etienne
Estienne, Gommar (bookseller, binder), *intro. pp. 7, 8, 9, p. 97*; 55, 63, 64, 65, 66, 67, 68, 69, 71

Ève bindery, 109, 110, 111
Ève, Clovis, 109, 111, 116, 125
Ève, Nicolas (bookseller, binder), *intro. p. 8*; 69, 109

Fache, Jules (finisher), 218
Fery, Nicolas *see* Niccolò Franzese
Fleur-de-lis binder, *intro. p. 7*; 20, 21, 22
Foch, F, 216
Fontainebleau, Atelier de *see* Atelier de Fontainebleau
Fontainebleau binder, *intro. p. 8*; 26
Fugger binder, 293, 294, 295, 296, 297, 298

Geneva Kings' binder, 225, 227, 228, 229, 230, 232
Gilbert, Charles (calligrapher), 155
Ginain, 201
GIR (monogram) *see* Le Rouge, Guillaume
Goldast Meister, 225
Gonon, Alphonse-Jules, 221
Grimaldi binder, 327, 328, 329
Grolier's Arnobius binder *see* Mansfeld binder
Gruel, Léon, 215
Gruel, Paul, 215
Gruel, Pierre-Paul, 212, 215
Gruel-Engelman(n), 216
Guillery, Marcantonio, 314, 315

Henri II, 'grand doreur' of, *intro. p. 8*; 64
Hutchins, 238

Janet, Pierre-Claude-Louis (bookseller, publisher, binder), 196, 197
Janet, Pierre-Étienne (binder, finisher), 197
Jarry, Nicolas (calligrapher), 155
Jeanne, André (finisher), 220

Khawaja, M (scribe), 418
Kings' binder *see* Geneva Kings' binder
Krauss, G F, 411

Landry (engraver), 144
Langrand, Jeanne, 220
Leermauresken Meister *see* Arabesque outline tool binder
Le Gascon (imitation), 390
Legrain, Pierre, 219, 220, 222
Lemonnier, family, 176
Lemonnier, Jean-Charles-Henri, *le jeune*, 176, 177 (?)
Lemonnier, Louis-François, 176, 177
Le Rouge, Guillaume (printer, bookseller), 2
Levasseur, Eloy, 152
Leyden, Lucas van (painter), 118
Lotfali of Shiraz (painter), 419
Louis XII, Atelier Louis XII *see* Vostre, Simon
Luigi, Maestro, 316

Magnier, Charles, 217
Mahieu's Aesop binder *see* Aesop binder
Maillard, Charles (finisher), 213
Malenfant, Jacques de, binder for, 33, 74, 75, 76, 77, 78, 79
  see also Picques, Claude
Mame, A & Cie (publishers, binders), 204, 205
Mame, Alfred (publisher, binder), 204, 206, 207, 208
Mame, Amand (publisher), 204
Mame, Ernest (publisher), 204
Mame et fils (publishers), 208
Mame, Paul (publisher), 204, 208
Mansfeld binder, 87
Mantegarrius, Fr. Cyprianus (scribe), 352
Marius-Michel *see* Michel
Marnef, Jerome de (bookseller, printer, publisher), 93
Martin, Pierre-Lucien, 221
Mendoza binder, 261, 262, 263, 272, 301
Mercier, Emile, 213, 217
Mercier, Georges, 217
Micart, Claude (bookseller, binder), 69
Michel, Henri Marius, 212, 220
Michel, Jean Marius, 212, 213
Moncey, Thérèse, 218
Monnier *see* Lemonnier

Niccolò Franzese (Nicolas Fery), 303, 304, 305, 344
Norvi(n)s, Jehan (possibly bookseller, binder), 9, 10, 11
Noulhac, Henri, 199, 220

Padeloup, A-M, *le jeune*, 156, 157, 158, 159, 160, 161, 162, 171, 178, 180, 181
Padeloup, Michel, 157
Padeloup, Philippe, 156
Pecking Crow binder, 16, 17, 18, 19, 38 *see also* Wotton binder A
Périsse (bookseller, binder), 209
Périsse frères (booksellers), 209
Petit, Charles, 199, 211
Petit, fils (son of Charles), 211
Pflug and Ebeleben binder, 309, 310, 311, 312
Picard, Jean (bookseller, binder), *intro. pp. 8, 9, p. 97*; 23, 24, 25, 64, 69
Picques, Claude (bookseller, binder), *intro. pp. 8, 9, p. 97*; 23, 33, 64, 67, 69, 70, 71, 72, 73, 74, 75, 76, 77, 78, 79, 109

Reiss (finisher), 212
Relieur du roi, Atelier of *see* Atelier du relieur du roi
Ripamonti, P (binder or bookseller, Milan), 392
Rocolet, Atelier, 142
Rocolet, Pierre (printer, bookseller), 142
Roffet, André, *intro. p. 7*
Roffet, Etienne, *intro. p. 7*; 14, 15, 22, 26, 30
Roffet, Pierre (bookseller, binder), *intro. p. 7*; 3, 12, 14

Rospigliosi binder, 360 *see also* Andreoli
Rousselle, E, 216
Ruette, Antoine, 132, 133, 134, 135
Ruette, Macé, 132

Salel binder, *intro. p. 8*; 26, 27, 28, 30
Sancha, Antonio de (bookseller, printer, publisher, binder), 405
Sancha, Gabriel de, 405
Simier, Alphonse, 199, 200, 211
Simier, Jean, 211
Simier, René, 199
Sorbonne Ptolemy, Master of *see* Almagest atelier
Soresino, Baldassarre, 356
Soresino bindery, 358
Soresino, Francesco, 344, 356
Soresino, Prospero, 356
Staggemeier and Welcher, 411
Starry Griffin binder, 1

Tessier, N, 176
Thouvenin, François, 198
Thouvenin, Joseph, *l'aîné*, 198
Thouvenin, Joseph, *le jeune*, 198
Tiersot, of Bourg, 213
Torresani d'Asola, Gian Francesco (bookseller, publisher), 23
Tory, G, 13

Vecellio, Cesare (painter), 274
Venetian Apple binder *see* Fugger binder
Vidal, Carsí y, 406
Vostre, Simon, *intro. p. 7*; 3, 12

Wampflug(h) (finisher), 213
Weiditz, Hans (woodcutter), 29
Wilson and Nichols, 421
Wotton binder A, 37, 38, 39 *see also* Pecking Crow binder
Wotton binder B, 40, 41, 42
Wotton binder C, 43, 44, 45, 46, 47, 48, 49, 50, 51, 52

Index of Owners

and other persons mentioned in the text. Auction houses have not been listed.
Except where otherwise indicated, all references are to entry numbers.

A, A, 245
A, N, 109
Abbey, John Roland, 2, 3, 5, 13, 20, 21, 23, 26, 73, 79, 86, 94, 129, 154, 156, 172, 181, 189, 226, 229, 231, 242, 251, 258, 300, 303, 312, 319, 320, 324, 326, 327, 337, 346, 355, 367, 372, 382, 405
Accademia dei Fenici, 327
Accolti, Benedetto, Cardinal of Ravenna, 263, 281(?)
Acheson, Archibald, Earl of Gosford, 145
Adam, P, 412
Ader, E, 12, 152
Albani, Alessandro (cardinal), 383
Aldenham House, Hertfordshire, library, 86
Aldobrandini (arms of), 349
Aligny, Quarré d', Pierre(?), 61
Altemps, family, 292
Amanio, Giovanni Paolo, Bishop of Anglona and Tursi (poet), 294
Amery, L S, PC, 419
AMF (monogram), 333
Amherst, Margaret, Lady Amherst of Hackney, 202
Amherst, Mary Rothes Margaret, Baroness Amherst of Hackney, 202
Amherst, William Amherst Tyssen, Baron Amherst of Hackney, 45, 55, 202
Amoro, Benetto, 348
Andrew of St-Oyan, Archpriest of Treffort, 1
Andrews, William Loring, 107, 213
Angoulême, Marguérite d', Queen of Navarre, 75
Anne, of Austria, Queen of France, 125
Annécy, Collegium Congregationis S. Pauli, 3
Annesley, Mr, 335
Artois, Henri d', Duke of Bordeaux, Count of Chambord (Henry V of France), 199, 210, 211
Arvanitidi, G J, 410
Ascherson, C S, 26, 242, 258, 276
Ashburnham, Lord, 9
Atanasius, Gherardus de, of Lyon, 325
Athens, Gennadius Library, 18, 338
August, Elector of Saxony, 310
Augustinian Hermits (religious order), 12
Avery, Samuel Putnam, 70, 121, 231
Aytmish al-Bajasī, Amir, 413

B*, Bibliothèque, 54, 152
B, A, 37
B, F, 54
B, Marcus Antonius, 268
Bachelier, 5
Backer, Hector de, 65
Backere, H de, 82
Baer, Jospeh (& Co., bookseller), 25, 87, 283
Bajet, J & Perrene(?), 255
Balbi, Giovanni Francesco, Count of Pola, 288
Balbi, Petrus, Bishop of Tropaea, 237
Balbus, D, 234
Baldock, Thomas, 421
Ballesdens, Jean, 71, 92, 295
Baltimore, Walters Art Gallery, 324, 413
Bandinius, Balthasar, 307
Bandinius, Michael, 307
Barbançon, Marie de, 115
Barbet, A, 55, 111
Baudaire, Mathurin, 142
Bavaria, Charlotte-Elisabeth of, 193
Bayly, Susan, 391
BBYY (monogram), 146
Beatty, Sir Alfred Chester (library of) see Dublin
Beaulieu, 18
Beckford, William, 86
Belin, Madame Théophile, 36, 54, 167
Belin, T (bookseller), 106, 187, 213
Belton House see Brownlow, Earls of
Bendonus, Antonius, 365
Benedict XIII, Pope (Piero Francesco Orsini), 376
Benedictines (religious order), 322
Benedictines, Paris, 147
Beraldi, Henri, 161, 172, 182, 195, 212
Berbis, Claude, 79
Bérenger, Marquis of, 22
Berès, Pierre, 51, 61, 110, 153, 157, 175, 193, 237
Bernardi, G, 369
Berruyer, 64
Berry, Duchess of see Bourbon, Marie-Caroline de
Berry, Duchess of see Orléans, Marie-Louise-Elizabeth d'
Berry, Duke of see Charles de France
Bethmann, Baron L (Paris), 309, 310

518

Beugeman de bou (?), 230
Bielignaris (?), de, 239
Bignon, Jean-Paul, 164
Bigot, F(?), 54
Bigot, Louis-Emeric, 54
Bird, Godfrey J, 39
Biron, Duke of *see* Gontaut
Bishop, Cortlandt F, 101, 107, 121, 124, 158, 159, 160, 171, 177, 213, 232, 376
Blackwell, B H (bookseller), 227
Bochetel, Jeanne, 91
Bodleian Library *see* Oxford
Boisset, 143
Bolsworth, Miss P M, 413
Bonaparte, Joseph, Count of Survilliers, 421
Bordeaux, Duke of *see* Artois
Borden, M C D, 22
Borghese, Camilio *see* Paul V, Pope
Borghese, Marc Antonio, 378
Bornigal, Pension, Nantes, 208
Bourbon, Antoine de, 113
Bourbon, Françoise-Marie de, Duchess of Orléans, 144, 160
Bourbon, Jaime de, Duke of Madrid, 211
Bourbon, Marie-Caroline de Bourbon-Sicile, Duchess of Berry, 199, 210
Bourges, Jean de, 51
Boyveau, J B de, 286
Brabant, Dominicus, 12
Braeker, W D, 22
Brédeault, G, 93
Brereton, J, 119
Breslauer, Bernard *see* Breslauer, Martin
Breslauer, Martin (bookseller), 14, 19, 43, 55, 64, 82, 113, 122, 124, 139, 151, 180, 182, 183, 191, 194, 195, 198, 199, 212, 218, 221, 222, 225, 227, 236, 241, 246, 262, 273, 274, 276, 277, 279, 282, 287, 320, 327, 335, 345, 348, 349, 352, 353, 356, 358, 368, 370, 379, 383, 387, 394, 395, 397, 400, 410, 411
Bressiens, Monsieur & Madame de, 18
Bretby Hall, Derbyshire, library, 40, 47 *see also* Herbert, George Edward
Brézé, Louis de, 61
Briancourt, Md, 174
Bridel, M, 15, 124, 390
Bridges, John, 82
Brill, E J (bookseller), 396
Brinon, Jean, de Villaines, 23
British Library *see* London
British Museum *see* London
Britwell Court, library *see* Miller, S R Christie
Broadly, J, 304
Brooke, 298
Brooke, John Arthur, 409
Brooke, Thomas, FSA, 10, 116, 119, 398

Brown, Elizabeth, 233
Brownlow, Earls of, 149
Broxbourne Library *see* Oxford, Bodleian Library
Brunacci, Attilio, Abbot of Settimo, 363
Brunet, J-C, 316
Brunschwig, Silvain S, 232, 332, 366
Bry, Michel de, 12, 152
Bucci, Felippo, 264
Buizo, de, family, 401
Buizo, Joseph de, 401
Bullrich, Eduardo J, 10, 16, 36, 357, 399
Bure, J J de, 55
Burns, John, 33
Butler, Charles, 64

C, D, 31
C, G A (?), 291
C, M, 233
C, P, 234
C, R, 100
Cabazac, C, 97
Calabria, Alfonso, Duke of, 252
Calatrava, Order of, 402, 404
Calderon, family, 404
Calderon, Francisco, 404
Cambridge, Fitzwilliam Museum, 107, 141, 160, 245, 246, 279, 314, 317, 350, 379, 383
Cambridge, King's College, 34, 243, 272
Cambridge, Pembroke College, 34, 243, 271
Cambridge, St Catharine's College, 349, 418
Cambridge, Trinity College, 245, 248, 279, 336, 349, 352, 371, Add. I
Cambridge, University Library, 54, 107, 144, 243, 250, 257, 270, 271, 273, 275, 276, 279, 283, 326, 351
Campeggi, Sister Sulpitia, 341
Canterbury, Cathedral, 5, 284
Capilupus (Capilupi), Benedictus, 241
Carafa, Oliverius (cardinal), 237
Cardani, Giovanni Battista, 367
Carew, Sir George, 119
Carnarvon, Earl of *see* Herbert, George Edward
Carney, Richard, 245
Carpia, Julius Mattias, 389
Carthusians (religious order), Louvain, 11
Carysfort, Earl of *see* Proby
Castaigne, Eusèbe, 214
Castellau, Charles de, Abbot of St Epure (Toul), 146
Catta, I, 371
Cavendish, Spencer Compton, 8th Duke of Devonshire, 263
CC (monogram), 165
CC/RD, 150
Cecil, Lord William, 202
Cecil, Robert, Earl of Salisbury, 119

Chadwyck-Healey, Sir Charles Edward H, 27
Chalon, René de, 87
Chalon-sur-Saône, College, 141
Chambord, Count of *see* Artois
Chandon de Briailles, Count Henry, 55
Charles III, King of Spain, 387
Charles V, Emperor, 87
Charles VIII, King of France, 51
Charles IX, King of France, *intro. p. 8*; 69, 78
Charles X, King of France, 210
Charles de France, Duke of Berry, 156
Charles Emanuel I, Duke of Savoy, 351
Charles Emanuel III, Duke of Savoy, King of Sardinia, 386
Chelles, abbey of, 160
Chergé, Mademoiselle Suzanne de, 208
Chesterfield, Earls of *see* Stanhope
Chicago, Newbury Library, 390
Chinnall, John, 230
Choul, J, 247
Christie-Miller, S R *see* Miller
Churchill, George Spencer, Duke of Marlborough, 177
Cicogna, Pasquale, Doge of Venice, 348
Clement IX, Pope (Giulio Rospigliosi), 359
Clement XI, Pope (Giovanni Francesco Albani), 375, 383
Clement XII, Pope (Lorenzo Corsini), 377
Clement XIII, Pope (Carlo della Torre Rezzonico), 379
Clement XIV, Pope (Giovanni Vincenzo Ganganelli), 384
Clermont, Bishop of, 110
Clermont, Church of, 110
Clermont, College of, 136
Clinton, Henry A D P, 7th Duke of Newcastle, 303, 351
Clinton, Lord, 13
Clumber library *see* Clinton, Henry
Cobb, Thomas Hugh, 181
Coislin, Du Cambout de, family, 167
Coislin, Pierre du Cambout de, Bishop of Orléans, 144, 167
Colbert, Jean-Baptiste, 71
Colocci, Francisco, 299
Colonna, family, 251
Colurieu (?), Claude de, 128
Conflans *see* Villeroy, library
Congrégation des Pénitents [de l'Annonciation Notre-Dame], 110, 111
Constant, Jacob, 185
Cooper, Colonel, 245
Corfield, W H, 118, 319, 352, 373
Cornellot, 172
Corneo, Fulvio (cardinal), 325
Corvus, Petrus, 412
Cossé-Brissac, Marie Marguerite de, Duchess of Villeroy, 152
Cotton, R S, 336
Coulet, Laurent (bookseller), 163
Cracherode, C M, 78

Crawford, W H, 202
Crescenzi, Giovanni Battista, 356
Crevenna, Pietro Antonio Bolongaro, 55
Crocker, Templeton, 160
Cupis, Torquato de, 356
Curtis, Sir William, Bart., 68, 229

D, René G, 157
Dartmouth, Earl of *see* Legge
Datigni, 79
Daucombe, P H Pauncefort, 8
Davis and Orioli (booksellers), 62, 77, 126, 268, 271, 278, 279, 282, 284, 339, 395
DCO, 347
Degrantrye, D P, 331
De Marinis, Tammaro, 360
Dent, John, 81
Descamps-Scrive, René, 157, 160, 199
Deschamps, Petrus Augustinus Alexander (Pierre-Augustin-Alexandre), 14
Des Maisour, Claude, 89
Des Maisour, Guillaume, 89
Desportes, Philippe, 78
Destailleur, H, 179
Devonshire, Duke of *see* Cavendish, Spencer Compton
Dominicans (religious order), 402
Dor, P, 223
Double, J P F, 111
Double, Leon, 65
Double, Léopold, Baron, 111
Double, P M M, Monseigneur, Bishop of Tarbes, 111
Doucet, J, 220
Dowdeswell, E R, 392
Dowdeswell, family, 392
Dresden, Sächsische Landesbibliothek, 63
Druot, Antoine, 141
Dublin, Chester Beatty Library, 369, 370, 375, 379, 383, 384, 413, 414, 416, 418, 419
Du Choul, Guillaume, 55
Duff, E Gordon, 6
Dufresnoy, Hélie, 143
Dunn, George, 9, 33, 244, 250, 296
Duodo, Pietro, 116
Dupuis, L, 142
Du Rieu, W N, 264

E, M, 103, 232
Ebeleben, Nikolaus von, 310, 311
ED (monogram), 112
Edinburgh, National Library of Scotland, 54
Edinburgh, University Library, 248, 250, 278, 398
Edward VI, King of England, 83
Edwards, Francis (bookseller), 200, 338
Ehrman, Albert, 410

Index of Owners

Elizabeth I, Queen of England, 38, 74, 83, 105, 229
Ellis, F S (bookseller), 315
Elton, 334
Elton, C, 388
Elton, M A, 388
Engl, Sigismund Ferdinand, Baron Waghain, 223
Erasmus, Desiderius, 409
Esmerian, Raphael, 54, 95, 120, 144, 152, 157, 158, 160, 161, 162, 254, 348
Este, Alessandro d' (cardinal), 121
Eton College, 185
Evans, John, 38
Exeter, Cathedral Library, 7

F, M J, 385
Faraj, Sultan, 413
Farnese, Elizabeth, 387
Farnese, Geronimo (cardinal), 369
Farnese, Pier Luigi, 312, 313
Farnese, Ranuccio, Archbishop of Naples, 312
Faucigny de Lucinge, Count, 51
Ferdinand, King of Naples, 87
Ferdinand I, King of Germany (later Emperor), 309
Ferdinand I, King of the two Sicilies, 388
Ferdinand VII, King of Spain, 406
Ferreri, family, of Palermo, 345
Fière, Louis, of Romans, Drôme, 1
Figdor Collection (Vienna), 240
Filareto, Apollonio, 313
Filleau, Jean, of Poitiers, 6
Finali, Signora H, 60
Firmin-Didot, Ambroise, 87, 96, 97
Fisher, R C, 315, 363
Florence, Public library, 36
Folger Library *see* Washington DC
Fontaine, Nicolas, 158
Fontainebleau, Royal library at, 64
Fontange Collection (Montpellier), 240
Forbes, Lord, 87
Forbes Leith, Colonel and Mrs, 409
Forero, Alonzo, 401
Fouquet, Nicolas, Viscount of Melun & Vaux, Marquis of Belle Isle, 136, 142
Franciscans (religious order; convent of St Katherine), 412
Franciscans, Kotor (Cattaro), 412
François I, King of France, *intro. p. 8*; 3, 12, 15, 29, 215
François II, King of France, *intro. p. 8*; 69, 89
Fransonus, Anfranus Matthias, 333
Franz Joseph I, Emperor of Austria, 194
Frederick III, Elector Palatine, 231
Frederick Augustus II, Duke of Saxony, 387
Freer (archdeacon), 392
Freer, Richard Lane, 392
Fresnoy, Elie du *see* Dufresnoy

Fugger, Anton, 44, 224
Fugger, Marcus, 44, 50, 57, 64, 66, 224, 225

Galerius, Nicolaus, 346
Galetti, G C, of Florence, 60, 314
Gancia, collection, 118
Ganganelli, Giovanni Vincenzo *see* Clement XIV, Pope
GAR (monogram), 353
Gasparini, J A, 347
Gennadius Library *see* Athens
Gilgen, Luwig zur, 72
Gilhofer & Ranschburg (booksellers), 360
Gioanni, Bernardi, of Turin, 369
Giolito de' Ferrari, Gabriele (bookseller), 327
Giraud, C J B, 163, 253(?)
Giuliari, library, 255
Giunchi, Federico, 287
Giustiniani, family, 367
Glasgow, University Library, 91, 185, 257, 276, 331, 383
Goldschmidt, E P, 4, 6, 8, 9, 11, 27, 31, 32, 74, 190, 223, 244, 256, 290, 296, 300, 306, 309, 310, 322, 323, 326, 334
Goldschmidt, Lucien, 160
Gontaut, Armand-Louis de, Duke of Laugin and Biron, 165
Gontaut, Luc-Antoine de, Duke of Biron, 165
Gonzaga, Francesco (cardinal), 252
Gosford, Earl of *see* Acheson, Archibald
Gostling, George, 78
Gougy, Lucien, 54, 153, 157, 180, 187
Gradenigo, Elisabetta, 381
Graham, Carol, 72
Gramont, 112
Granvelle, Cardinal *see* Perrenot, A
Graux, Lucien, 122
Gregory XIII, Pope (Ugo Boncompagni), 294, 390
Grimaldi, Giovanni Battista, 316
Grimani, family, 320
Grimani, Marino, Doge of Venice, 357
Gritti, Andreas, Doge of Venice, 288
Grolier, Antoine, 102
Grolier, François, 102
Grolier, Jean, *intro. pp. 7, 8*; 22, 23, 24, 38, 55, 64, 71, 81, 84, 86, 87, 91, 102, 245, 246
Gros, Anne de, 87
Gruel, L, 94, 99, 117, 128
Guadagni, Giovanni Antonio (cardinal), 377
Guarre, Madame François, 79
Guiduccius (Guiducci), Julius, 250
Guise, Duke of *see* Lorraine, François de
Gumucian & Cie (booksellers), 106, 160, 184, 187, 354, 356, 408

H, N, 254
Halincourt, Charles de Neufville Halincourt, Duke of Villeroy, Marquis of Alaincourt, 120

Hamersley, Hugh, 227
Ham House, Surrey *see* Tollemache
Hamilton, James, 297
Hamilton, William, 297
Hamilton-Bruce, R T, 136
HARA, 17
Harper, Lathrop C, 243, 288, 301, 336
Harris, Henry, 3
Harvey, Joseph, 421
Hauck, C J, 230
Haywood Hill (bookseller), 197
Heber, Sir Richard, 298, 306
Heffer, W (bookseller), 116, 168, 404
Heilbrun, Georges (bookseller), 188, 250
Hely-Hutchinson, John W, 235, 375, 379
Henri II, King of France, *intro. p. 8*; 55, 61, 63, 69, 96, 113
Henri III, King of France, *intro. p. 8*; 69, 103, 109, 110, 111, 390
Henri IV, King of France, 109, 113, 116, 121, 125, 151
Henri V, King of France, 210 *see also* Artois, Henri d'
Henry, Prince of Wales, 119
Herbert, George Edward, Earl of Carnarvon, 40, 41, 42, 46, 47, 83
Herbrot (Hörbrott), Matheus, 323
Hilgrove, George, 164
Hirsch, Olga *see* London, British Library
Hirsch, Paul, 21, 25, 43, 63, 116, 168
Hirth, George, 290
Hobson, G D, 91, 162, 385, 409, 412
Hocq, Madame, 208
Hodson, Laurence W, 264
Hoe, Robert, 15, 49, 126, 157, 158, 163, 165, 376, 390
Hoepli, U (bookseller), 283, 332, 349, 360
Hoff, Mrs Grace Whitney, 117, 132, 135, 144, 152, 168, 171, 193, 226, 348, 354, 379
Holford Collection *see* Holford, Sir George
Holford, Sir George, 26, 71, 101, 143, 184, 261, 298, 328, 329
Hörbrott *see* Herbrot
Houbler, Laymer (?), 247
Howard, Oliver, 302
Howes (bookseller), 15, 389
HRR (monogram), 165
Huberdeau, Pierre, 128
Hurth, J, 323

Innocent XII, Pope (Antonio Pignatelli), 371
Iorger (Iörger), Abraham, 223
Isabel II, Queen of Spain, 406

Jahān *see* Shāh Jahān
Jahānārā, Princess, 415
James I, King of England, 230
James II, King of England, 144, 154
James VI, King of Scotland *see* James I

Jesuits (religious order), Lyon, 226
Jesuits, Nivelles, 87
Jesuits, Oviedo, 398
Jesuits, Paris, 52, 55, 136
Jesuits, Perpin, 325
Jesuits, Pont-à-Mousson, 126
Jesuits, Trent(?), 265
John V, King of Portugal, 157
Joinville, Prince of, 201
Jones, Herschel V, 410
Jourdin, 142
Jourledan (?), Duchess of, 195
Joye, Jacob, 336
Julius III, Pope (Giovanni Maria del Monte), 325
Jusani, M (?), 146

Kann, Edouard, 132
Kay, Arthur, 10, 292, 409
Kehr, Freye von der, 43
Kehr, Margaretha von der, 43
Kehr, Richard von der *see* Kher
Keppel, Frederick, 338
Ker, John, Duke of Roxburghe, 163
Kergounadech, family, 112
Kerr, Philip Henry, Marquis of Lothian, 105
Keynes, Lord, 280
Kher, Richard von der, 43
King, Patrick (bookseller), 400
King, Raphael, 202
Kraus, H P (bookseller), 95
Kreolas, Janus, 306
Krishaber, 154
Kundig, W S, 191, 219, 227, 378

L, H, 15
L, J, 80
L, P, 199
La Baume le Blanc, Louis César de, Duke of La Vallière, 3
Labouchere, Henry, 276
La Chastre, Gasparde de, 115
Lacroix, P, 232
Lafayette, M J P, 421
Lafond Laferté, 58
Lagondie, Joseph-Guilhem, Count of, 279
Lambonne, G, 108
Landau, Baron Horace de, 53, 60, 251, 291, 314, 379
Landi, Alphonso, 358
Langan, F de, Sieur d'Éstival, 112
Langle, de, Count, 174
Lardanchet (bookseller), 15, 57, 58, 67, 69, 90, 99, 122, 123, 126, 130, 143, 160, 170, 174, 178, 224, 308, 376
Lareche (?), Monsieur de, 18
La Rochefoucauld, Dominique de (archbishop, cardinal), 173

Index of Owners

Lasco, Joannes a *see* Laski, Jan
Las Cuevas, Simon de, 324
Laski, Jan, 409
Laubespine, Claude II de, 91
Laubespine, Claude III de, 78, 91
Laubespine, François de, 91
Laubespine, Madeleine de Laubespine-Villeroy, 78, 103
Lauredano, Leonardo, Doge of Venice, 272
Laurent, Aimé, 174
Lauria, A, 255
Laurin, Marc, 64, 65, 82
La Vallière, Duke of *see* La Baume le Blanc, Louis César de
LDLP, 137
Le Bar, Monsieur, 18
Lebeuf de Montgermont, Louis, 77, 114, 163
Le Court, Benoît, 31, 32
Leczinska, Marie, Queen of France, 161, 182, 187
Leczinski, Stanislas, King of Poland, 182
Legge, Viscount Lewisham, Earl of Dartmouth, 295
Le Gros, frater Joannes Petrus, 19
Leighton, J&J, 29, 64, 92, 296
Lenin Library *see* Moscow
Leo, Philippus Antonius, 177
Leoncourt, Antoine de, 126
Le Riche, Antoine, 153
Le Tellier, François Michel, Marquis of Louvois, 143
Le Tellier, Michel, 143
Lewisham, Viscount *see* Legge
Libri, A R, 303
Libri, Guglielmo, Count, 231, 303, 332, 376
Liechtenstein, Princes of, library, 270, 281
Lignerolles, Count, 15
Liliis, Ludovicus a *see* Gilgen, Ludwig zur
Lincoln, D, 227
Lionne, 131
London, British Library, Department of Manuscripts, 109, 238, 243, 342, 369, 397, 401
London, British Library, Department of Oriental Manuscripts and Printed Books, 413, 416
London, British Library, Department of Printed Books, 5, 33, 83, 92, 103, 107, 109, 115, 116, 120, 131, 141, 142, 144, 148, 149, 150, 163, 166, 167, 171, 172, 184, 185, 186, 187, 190, 191, 200, 204, 225, 243, 248, 251, 254, 257, 262, 264, 272, 273, 274, 276, 277, 279, 281, 283, 288, 292, 293, 323, 331, 343, 349, 351, 352, 353, 364, 365, 367, 370, 371, 375, 379, 380, 383, 384, 391, 396, 397, 398, 402, 408
London, British Library, Department of Printed Books, Olga Hirsch Collection, 204
London, British Museum, Department of Coins and Medals, 252
London, British Museum, Department of Medieval and Later Antiquities, 252
London, National Art Library, Victoria and Albert Museum, 107, 348, 413, 414, 415, 417, 418, 419

Longepierre, Baron *see* Requeleyne, Hilaire-Bernard de
Lorraine, François de, Duke of Guise, 49
Lothian, Marquis of *see* Kerr, Philip Henry
Louis XII, King of France, *intro. p. 7*; 51
Louis XIII, King of France, 109, 118, 121, 124, 125, 132, 144
Louis XIV, King of France, 71, 132, 136, 142, 144, 147, 151, 157, 193
Louis XV, King of France, 156, 166, 182, 187, 191
Louis XVI, King of France, 186, 187, 191
Louis XVIII, King of France, 199
Louis de France, Prince, 193
Louis Joseph, Duke of Vendôme, 151
Louis Napoleon, 210
Louis-Philippe I, King of France, Duke of Orléans, 199, 201, 210
Louvain, Carthusian monastery, 11
Louvois, Marquis of *see* Le Tellier, F M
Lumsden, Charles B, 264
Lurde, Count of, 148
Lussau, 86
Luton, 162
Luttrell, Narcissus, 100
Luynes, Jeanne-Baptiste d'Albert de, Countess of Verrue, 163
Lymington, Viscount, 236
Lyon, Academy, 264
Lyon, Collège de, 120

M, 36, 370
M, F, 315
M, G, 214
M, P, 270
M, R T, 229
Macaulay, D I M (major), 415, 416
Madrid, Academy of History, 405
Madrid, Escorial Library, 397
Madrid, Royal Library, 405
Madrid, Spanish Academy, 405
Maggs Bros. (booksellers), 48, 85, 89, 180, 210, 211, 235, 260, 280, 283, 335, 379, 398
Mahieu, Thomas, 64, 71, 84, 85, 86, 91
Mahuet, Joannes, 126
Makree, library *see* Cooper
Malenfant, Jacques de, 33, 75, 76, 77, 78
Manchester, John Rylands University Library, 53, 107, 168, 172, 243, 246, 247, 253, 254, 257, 261, 262, 271, 273, 276, 279, 283, 307, 333, 338, 398
Manin, Count, 288
Manin, Giovanni L, Count, 288
Manin, Ludovicus, Doge of Venice, 346
Mansfeld, Peter Ernst, Count of, 87
Manzi, Giovanni, of Florence, 321
MAR *see* Marie-Amélie de Bourbon
Marchthal, abbey, 43

Marduel, Jean Baptiste, of Lyon, 3
Marguerite, of France, Queen of Navarre, 113
Maria Theresia, Archduchess of Austria, Empress of Germany, Queen of Hungary & Bohemia, 175
Marie-Adélaïde de France, Madame, 167
Marie-Amélie de Bourbon, 199
Marie Anne Victoire, Infanta of Spain, 166, 187
Marie Antoinette, Archduchess of Austria, Queen of France, 387
Marie-Josèphe of Saxony, Dauphine of France, 187
Marie-Louise, Empress of France, Duchess of Parma, 194, 199
Marinis *see* De Marinis
Marlborough, Duke of *see* Churchill, George Spencer
Marlborough Fine Arts, 104
Marly, library of, 65
Marmius, Antonius Franciscus, 36
Martialis, Richardus, 280
Martini, Ioseph, of Lucerne, 331, 332
Mathews, Elkin (bookseller), 203, 204, 205, 206, 207, 209, 210, 393
Maugis, Philippus a, 301
Mausane, collection, 347
Maynard, Charles, Lord, 73
Mazarin, Cardinal, 71
Mazzetti, N, 250
Medici, Cathérine de', Queen of France, *intro. p. 8*; 61, 69, 84, 91
Medici, Cosimo II de', Grand duke of Tuscany, 361
Medici, Marie de', Queen of France, 113, 121
Mensing, 96, 239
Menso, Paul, 370
Merard de St-Just, 186
Mesa de Asta, Marchioness Vda de la, 407
Meugin Foudragon, Baroness of, 174
Michelmore, G & Co. (booksellers), 352
Michieli, Niccoló, 381
Milan, Accademia dei Fenici, 327
Miller, S R Christie, 81, 133, 177
Milliner, 45
Millot, Jacques, 192
Minale, Antonio, 328
Minale, Hannibal (Annibale), 328, 329
Minale, Matteo, 328
MJF (monogram), 385
Modena, Mary of, Queen of England, 154
Mohedas, Alonso de, 400
Moira (John Rawdon, Earl of Moira?), 119
Montgermont *see* Lebeuf de Montgermont
Montille, L de, 93
Montmorency, Anne de, 64, 91
Morgand, Damascène (bookseller), 24
Morgand & Fatout (bookseller), 166
Moscow, Lenin Library, 411

Moss, Lieutenant-Colonel W E, 48, 280
Mugghionius, Horatius (?), 256
Mundella, Sanctiflorius, of Brescia, 346
Murray, Charles Fairfax, 154, 238, 247, 312, 313, 332

Napoleon I, Emperor, 194
National Art Library *see* London
National Trust: Waddesdon Manor *see* Rothschild, Ferdinand J de, Baron
Neufville *see* Halincourt
Neufville, François de, Duke of Villeroy, 152
Newton Hall (Cambridge) *see* Seligman
New York, Common Council of, 421
New York, Pierpont Morgan Library, 18, 256
Nicolas I, Tsar of Russia, 421
Nivernois, Duke of, 315
Nobele, F de (bookseller), 246
Nouvellet, Joseph, 120
Novini (?), Nicolaio, 60

O, B, 4
O, P G, 330
O, P J, 327
Oberndorff, Count A, 18, 252, 273, 351
Oettingen-Wallerstein, Princes of, 44, 50, 57, 66, 224, 225
Olschki, Leo (bookseller), 257, 342, 387
Olschki, L S (booksellers), 321
Orléans, Françoise-Marie, Duchess of *see* Bourbon, Françoise-Marie de
Orléans, Louise-Adélaïde, Mademoiselle d', 160
Orléans, Louis-Philippe, Duke of *see* Louis-Philippe I, King of France
Orléans, Louis-Philippe, Duke of, 176, 187
Orléans, Louis-Philippe-Joseph, Duke of, 199
Orléans, Marie-Louise-Elizabeth d', Duchess of Berry, 156
Orléans, Philippe II, Duke of, 160, 187
Ormathwaite, 67
Orsini, family, 354
Orsini, Paolo Giordano, 330
Orsini, Piero Francesco *see* Benedict XIII, Pope
Oxford, Bodleian Library, 27, 106, 107, 144, 156, 172, 184, 185, 244, 247, 250, 251, 292, 344, 350, 352
Oxford, Keble College, 264
Oxford, Manchester College, 139
Oxford, St John's College, 225

Paris, Benedictine monastery, 147 *see also* Jesuits
Paris, Bibliothèque des Arts Décoratifs, 176
Paris, Musée Carnavalet, 215
Passaro, J A, 364
Paul III, Pope (Alessandro Farnese), 303, 312, 313
Paul IV, Pope (Giovanni Pietro Carafa), 305
Paul V, Pope (Camilio Borghese), 356, 358, 360
Paulus, J, 234

Index of Owners

Pavia, University Library, 336
Pearson & Co. (bookseller), 394
Peiresc, Nicolas-Claude Fabri de, 129
Perkins, Oliver Henry, 157
Perrenot, Antoine, Cardinal de Granvelle, 296, 297, 298
Perrins, Charles William Dyson, 2, 29, 118, 238, 287, 306, 315, 319, 394
Pesant, frère Gideon, 5
Petrucci, Pandolfo, 240
Pflug, Damian, 309, 310
Phelypeaux, 121
Philip II, King of Spain, 400
Philip III, King of Spain, 360
Philip IV, King of Spain, 404
Philip V, King of Spain, 166, 387
Pichon, Jérome, Baron, 157
Pickering (bookseller), 306
Pickering, Hester, 83
Pickering, Sir William, 83
Pierpont Morgan Library *see* New York
Pigius, Stephanus M, 326
Pignatelli, Antonio *see* Innocent XII, Pope
Pignatelli d'Angio, Prince Diego, 300, 340
Pillone, Antonio, 274
Pillone, Odorico, 274
Pins, Jean de, Bishop of Rieux, 3
Pisauro, Antonio, 272
Pius V, Pope (Michele Ghislieri), 328
Pius VI, Pope (Giovanni Angelico Braschi), 384
Podius, Franciscus (?), 283
Poitiers, Diane de, Duchess of Valentinois, 61, 64
Pol, Antoine, 1
Polifilo, Il (bookseller, Milan), 345
Pont-à-Mousson, Jesuit College *see* Jesuits
Porter, H C M, 230
Portugal, Royal arms of, 408
Powis, Earl of, 56, 349
Pratley, 35
Pratt, Lieutenant-Colonel E R, 85
Prieur, Jean Louis (priest), 30
Primrose, Earl of Rosebery, 333
Proby, William, Earl of Carysfort, 108
Prost, Petrus (priest of Besançon), 296
Protus, Martinus, 333, 334
Prouatus (Provatus?), B, 289
Pucci, family, of Florence, 275
Pull Court Library *see* Dowdeswell

Quaile, Edward, of Birkenhead, 376
Quaritch, Bernard (bookseller), 7, 21, 29, 39, 41, 45, 52, 54, 56, 58, 68, 80, 81, 83, 114, 115, 118, 123, 177, 196, 235, 265, 267, 287, 289, 295, 302, 307, 316, 328, 329, 330, 331, 349, 391

R, A, 303
Rabot, Laurent, 22, 55
Rag (?), Thomas, 317
Rahir, Edouard, 49, 61, 77, 92, 95, 96, 114, 148, 157, 186
Raimundo, Abbot of Santa Maria de Fitero (Navarre), 402
Ranier, Loredano Luciani, 248
Rappaport, C E (bookseller), 322
Rau, A (bookseller), 117, 132, 135, 144, 266, 313, 354
Rauch, Nicolas (bookseller), 93, 95, 99, 102, 129, 150, 159, 161, 167, 171, 191, 219, 232, 269, 276, 300, 325, 332, 340, 342, 366
Ravenna, Cardinal of, (probably Benedetto Accolti), 281
Renard, J, 120, 146
Renckel, Joannes Carolus, 228
Renouard, A A, 52, 71, 101, 190
Requeleyne, Hilaire-Bernard de, Baron of Longepierre, 148, 149, 150
Rey, Edouard, 186
Riccardus, Franciscus, of Vernaccia, 60, 314
Richardson, Henry S, 357
Ricordeau, A, 31
Ripault, Collection, 160
Ris, Count L Clément de Ris, 145
RM (monogram), 138
Robinson, W H (bookseller), 49, 306
Rochefoucauld *see* La Rochefoucauld
Rohan-Soubise, library, 115
Rome, Collegium Graecorum, 294
Rome, Congregation of St Maurus, 238
Rome, Populus Romanus (arms of), 373, 375
Ronsard, Pierre de, 78, 103
Rosebery, Earl of *see* Primrose
Rospigliosi, Giulio (cardinal), 356, 359 *see also* Clement IX, Pope
Rossi, family, 360, 366
Rossi, Ioannes Franciscus, 360
Rothschild, Ferdinand J de, Baron, 131, 160, 162, 168, 182, 185, 186
Rouardis, Luigi R R, 347
Roul (?), Thomas (abbot), 280
Rubeius, Justinus, 266
Russian General Staff, library *see* St Petersburgh

S, A, 53
Sacy, L, maistre de, 158
St-Claude du Jura (abbey), 1
St Esprit, Order of, 193
St Mary Magdalen, 240
St Maurice, Sieur de, 62
St Maurus, Congregation of, Rome, 238
St Michel, Order of, 63
St Petersburgh, library of the Russian General Staff, 411
Salarolus, Josephus (?), 244
Salisbury, Earl of *see* Cecil, Robert

THE HENRY DAVIS GIFT

Salutis, Jordanus Garganus (?), 269
Salvaign de Boissieu, D de, 18, 22
Samesius, Johannes Albertus, of Hoingen/Höingen, 309
Samuell, Mr, 133
Sancho III, King of Spain, 402
Sandys, Lord, 34
Sanesin, Carolus, 126
Santiago, J M (?) do, 399
Sardou, Victorien, 65
Sauvage, Count, 114
Sawyer, Charles [& Sons] (bookseller), 121, 200, 378, 379
Schäfer, Otto, 364, 379, 383, 384
Scheffer, Sebastian, 9
Schiff, Mortimer L, 130, 134, 155, 156, 172, 180, 185, 189, 305
Schneider, P, of Erlangen, 10
Séguier, Pierre, 71
Ségur, Nicolas-Alexandre de, 170
Selfridge, Henry Gordon, 24, 127, 145, 169, 216
Seligman, J, 59, 138
Seligman, Theodore, 59, 138, 176, 197, 311
Serrano de Paz, Dr D M, 398
Settimo, Monastery of, 363
Seuret, J (?), 93
Shāh Abbas, the Great, 417
Shāh Jahān, Emperor, 415
Sidney, 315
Silvestri, Eurialo, 303
Sixtus V, Pope (Felice Peretti), 350
Sloter, Sir Irving, 159
Smith, J M, 78
Smythe, Clement J, 39
Sobolewsky, library, 202
Solier (Soler?), 163
Solouanos, Don Joan de, 404
Sourget, Patrick & Elisabeth (booksellers), 400
Spencer, Charles, 3rd Earl of Sunderland, 21, 77
Sponnieri (?), Ch, 374
Stainton, Mrs Evelyn, 275
Stanhope, Earls of Chesterfield, 19, 40, 41, 46, 47
Stanhope, Henry Lord Stanhope, 40, 83
Stanhope, Philip, 1st Earl of Chesterfield, 40, 83
Steubing, 309
Stray, J, 304
Stuers, J de, 383, Add. II
Sulz see Tours, O de
Sunderland, library see Spencer, Charles, Earl of Sunderland
Surreau, 51
Sussex, Augustus Frederick, Duke of, 334
Svajer, Amadeus, 288
Synge, Edward, Bishop of Limerick, 245

Tallemant, Gédéon, Sieur des Réaux, 214
Tapin, Claude, 141

Techener, Joseph-Léon, 49, 311
Thomas, Mr (bookseller), 89
Thompson, Henry Yates, 72, 80, 85, 92, 99, 241, 247, 316
Thou, Jacques-Auguste de, 81, 103, 107, 115
Thüngen, Bernhardt von, 43
Thüngen, Conrad von, Bishop of Würzburg, 43
Thüngen, Hubert von, 43
Thüngen, Simon von, 43
Thüngen, Theoderic von, 43
Tibuaul, library, 23
Tiersonnier, S, 4
Tisserand, Claude, 141
Tollemache, Sir Lyonel, 75, 76, 118
Tomkinson, Michael, 4, 412
Tonnellier, Armand, MD, 266
Torrez, Dr, 400
Tours, O de (general), 151
Toynbee, Paget, 250
Tregaskis (bookseller), 202
Trelawny, Harry, 334
Trivulzio, Giorgio Teodoro, 14
Turanzas, Jose Porrua (bookseller), 400
Turner, Robert Samuel, 114

Uffenbach, Petrus, 228

Vendôme, Duke of see Louis Joseph
Vendôme, Duke of, 191
Vernon, Collection see Vernon, George John Warren
Vernon, George John Warren, 5th Baron Vernon, 26, 71, 261, 298, 327, 328, 329
Verracano, Andrea da, 237
Verrue, Countess of see Luynes
Vesey, Mrs Elizabeth, 74
Vever, Henry, 413
Victoria & Albert Museum see London
Vienna, Palatine Library, 254
Villeroy, Duchess of see Cossé-Brissac
Villeroy, Duke of see Halincourt; see Neufville, François
Villeroy, library, 78 see also Laubespine
Villeroy, Nicolas de Neufville de, 78, 103
Villers (artillery officer), 126

Waddesdon see Rothschild, Ferdinand J de, Baron
Waghain see Engl
Waillet, Eugene, 72
Wallace, Walter Thomas, 215
Walpole, Horatio, 4th Earl of Orford, 254
Walters, Henry, 217
Walters, Mrs, 217
Washington DC, Library of Congress, 413
Washington D C, Folger Shakespeare Library, 122, 323, 362
Washington DC, Freer Gallery, 413
Wassermann, V, 180

Index of Owners

Pavia, University Library, 336
Pearson & Co. (bookseller), 394
Peiresc, Nicolas-Claude Fabri de, 129
Perkins, Oliver Henry, 157
Perrenot, Antoine, Cardinal de Granvelle, 296, 297, 298
Perrins, Charles William Dyson, 2, 29, 118, 238, 287, 306, 315, 319, 394
Pesant, frère Gideon, 5
Petrucci, Pandolfo, 240
Pflug, Damian, 309, 310
Phelypeaux, 121
Philip II, King of Spain, 400
Philip III, King of Spain, 360
Philip IV, King of Spain, 404
Philip V, King of Spain, 166, 387
Pichon, Jérome, Baron, 157
Pickering (bookseller), 306
Pickering, Hester, 83
Pickering, Sir William, 83
Pierpont Morgan Library *see* New York
Pigius, Stephanus M, 326
Pignatelli, Antonio *see* Innocent XII, Pope
Pignatelli d'Angio, Prince Diego, 300, 340
Pillone, Antonio, 274
Pillone, Odorico, 274
Pins, Jean de, Bishop of Rieux, 3
Pisauro, Antonio, 272
Pius V, Pope (Michele Ghislieri), 328
Pius VI, Pope (Giovanni Angelico Braschi), 384
Podius, Franciscus (?), 283
Poitiers, Diane de, Duchess of Valentinois, 61, 64
Pol, Antoine, 1
Polifilo, Il (bookseller, Milan), 345
Pont-à-Mousson, Jesuit College *see* Jesuits
Porter, H C M, 230
Portugal, Royal arms of, 408
Powis, Earl of, 56, 349
Pratley, 35
Pratt, Lieutenant-Colonel E R, 85
Prieur, Jean Louis (priest), 30
Primrose, Earl of Rosebery, 333
Proby, William, Earl of Carysfort, 108
Prost, Petrus (priest of Besançon), 296
Protus, Martinus, 333, 334
Prouatus (Provatus?), B, 289
Pucci, family, of Florence, 275
Pull Court Library *see* Dowdeswell

Quaile, Edward, of Birkenhead, 376
Quaritch, Bernard (bookseller), 7, 21, 29, 39, 41, 45, 52, 54, 56, 58, 68, 80, 81, 83, 114, 115, 118, 123, 177, 196, 235, 265, 267, 287, 289, 295, 302, 307, 316, 328, 329, 330, 331, 349, 391

R, A, 303
Rabot, Laurent, 22, 55
Rag (?), Thomas, 317
Rahir, Edouard, 49, 61, 77, 92, 95, 96, 114, 148, 157, 186
Raimundo, Abbot of Santa Maria de Fitero (Navarre), 402
Ranier, Loredano Luciani, 248
Rappaport, C E (bookseller), 322
Rau, A (bookseller), 117, 132, 135, 144, 266, 313, 354
Rauch, Nicolas (bookseller), 93, 95, 99, 102, 129, 150, 159, 161, 167, 171, 191, 219, 232, 269, 276, 300, 325, 332, 340, 342, 366
Ravenna, Cardinal of, (probably Benedetto Accolti), 281
Renard, J, 120, 146
Renckel, Joannes Carolus, 228
Renouard, A A, 52, 71, 101, 190
Requeleyne, Hilaire-Bernard de, Baron of Longepierre, 148, 149, 150
Rey, Edouard, 186
Riccardus, Franciscus, of Vernaccia, 60, 314
Richardson, Henry S, 357
Ricordeau, A, 31
Ripault, Collection, 160
Ris, Count L Clément de Ris, 145
RM (monogram), 138
Robinson, W H (bookseller), 49, 306
Rochefoucauld *see* La Rochefoucauld
Rohan-Soubise, library, 115
Rome, Collegium Graecorum, 294
Rome, Congregation of St Maurus, 238
Rome, Populus Romanus (arms of), 373, 375
Ronsard, Pierre de, 78, 103
Rosebery, Earl of *see* Primrose
Rospigliosi, Giulio (cardinal), 356, 359 *see also* Clement IX, Pope
Rossi, family, 360, 366
Rossi, Ioannes Franciscus, 360
Rothschild, Ferdinand J de, Baron, 131, 160, 162, 168, 182, 185, 186
Rouardis, Luigi R R, 347
Roul (?), Thomas (abbot), 280
Rubeius, Justinus, 266
Russian General Staff, library *see* St Petersburgh

S, A, 53
Sacy, L, maistre de, 158
St-Claude du Jura (abbey), 1
St Esprit, Order of, 193
St Mary Magdalen, 240
St Maurice, Sieur de, 62
St Maurus, Congregation of, Rome, 238
St Michel, Order of, 63
St Petersburgh, library of the Russian General Staff, 411
Salarolus, Josephus (?), 244
Salisbury, Earl of *see* Cecil, Robert

Salutis, Jordanus Garganus (?), 269
Salvaign de Boissieu, D de, 18, 22
Samesius, Johannes Albertus, of Hoingen/Höingen, 309
Samuell, Mr, 133
Sancho III, King of Spain, 402
Sandys, Lord, 34
Sanesin, Carolus, 126
Santiago, J M (?) do, 399
Sardou, Victorien, 65
Sauvage, Count, 114
Sawyer, Charles [& Sons] (bookseller), 121, 200, 378, 379
Schäfer, Otto, 364, 379, 383, 384
Scheffer, Sebastian, 9
Schiff, Mortimer L, 130, 134, 155, 156, 172, 180, 185, 189, 305
Schneider, P, of Erlangen, 10
Séguier, Pierre, 71
Ségur, Nicolas-Alexandre de, 170
Selfridge, Henry Gordon, 24, 127, 145, 169, 216
Seligman, J, 59, 138
Seligman, Theodore, 59, 138, 176, 197, 311
Serrano de Paz, Dr D M, 398
Settimo, Monastery of, 363
Seuret, J (?), 93
Shāh Abbas, the Great, 417
Shāh Jahān, Emperor, 415
Sidney, 315
Silvestri, Eurialo, 303
Sixtus V, Pope (Felice Peretti), 350
Sloter, Sir Irving, 159
Smith, J M, 78
Smythe, Clement J, 39
Sobolewsky, library, 202
Solier (Soler?), 163
Solouanos, Don Joan de, 404
Sourget, Patrick & Elisabeth (booksellers), 400
Spencer, Charles, 3rd Earl of Sunderland, 21, 77
Sponnieri (?), Ch, 374
Stainton, Mrs Evelyn, 275
Stanhope, Earls of Chesterfield, 19, 40, 41, 46, 47
Stanhope, Henry Lord Stanhope, 40, 83
Stanhope, Philip, 1st Earl of Chesterfield, 40, 83
Steubing, 309
Stray, J, 304
Stuers, J de, 383, Add. II
Sulz see Tours, O de
Sunderland, library see Spencer, Charles, Earl of Sunderland
Surreau, 51
Sussex, Augustus Frederick, Duke of, 334
Svajer, Amadeus, 288
Synge, Edward, Bishop of Limerick, 245

Tallemant, Gédéon, Sieur des Réaux, 214
Tapin, Claude, 141

Techener, Joseph-Léon, 49, 311
Thomas, Mr (bookseller), 89
Thompson, Henry Yates, 72, 80, 85, 92, 99, 241, 247, 316
Thou, Jacques-Auguste de, 81, 103, 107, 115
Thüngen, Bernhardt von, 43
Thüngen, Conrad von, Bishop of Würzburg, 43
Thüngen, Hubert von, 43
Thüngen, Simon von, 43
Thüngen, Theoderic von, 43
Tibuaul, library, 23
Tiersonnier, S, 4
Tisserand, Claude, 141
Tollemache, Sir Lyonel, 75, 76, 118
Tomkinson, Michael, 4, 412
Tonnellier, Armand, MD, 266
Torrez, Dr, 400
Tours, O de (general), 151
Toynbee, Paget, 250
Tregaskis (bookseller), 202
Trelawny, Harry, 334
Trivulzio, Giorgio Teodoro, 14
Turanzas, Jose Porrua (bookseller), 400
Turner, Robert Samuel, 114

Uffenbach, Petrus, 228

Vendôme, Duke of see Louis Joseph
Vendôme, Duke of, 191
Vernon, Collection see Vernon, George John Warren
Vernon, George John Warren, 5th Baron Vernon, 26, 71, 261, 298, 327, 328, 329
Verracano, Andrea da, 237
Verrue, Countess of see Luynes
Vesey, Mrs Elizabeth, 74
Vever, Henry, 413
Victoria & Albert Museum see London
Vienna, Palatine Library, 254
Villeroy, Duchess of see Cossé-Brissac
Villeroy, Duke of see Halincourt; see Neufville, François
Villeroy, library, 78 see also Laubespine
Villeroy, Nicolas de Neufville de, 78, 103
Villers (artillery officer), 126

Waddesdon see Rothschild, Ferdinand J de, Baron
Waghain see Engl
Waillet, Eugene, 72
Wallace, Walter Thomas, 215
Walpole, Horatio, 4th Earl of Orford, 254
Walters, Henry, 217
Walters, Mrs, 217
Washington DC, Library of Congress, 413
Washington D C, Folger Shakespeare Library, 122, 323, 362
Washington DC, Freer Gallery, 413
Wassermann, V, 180

Webber, F, 35
Weinsheimer, J, 249
Well, Gabriel, 87
Wells, Gabriel, 105
Wharton, Margaret, 48
Wharton, Philip, Baron Wharton, 48
Wheatley, Henry B, 162, 353
White, Henry, JP, DL, FSA, 412
Williams (?), Alexander, 282
Wilmerding, Lucius, 22, 40, 42, 44, 46, 47, 49, 50, 54, 57, 65, 66, 70, 71, 74, 75, 76, 85, 87, 89, 96, 101, 103, 107, 108, 111, 112, 114, 119, 120, 136, 142, 143, 147, 148, 149, 155, 157, 158, 163, 164, 165, 166, 171, 173, 177, 184, 186, 213, 214, 215, 217, 224, 228, 304, 309, 310, 333, 350, 380, 388
Wilmot, Earl of Lisburne, 80
Wilson, William, 140

Windhag, Ioachim, Baron, 223
Witthaus, Rudolph August, MD, 331
Wittock, Michel, 75, 162, 178
Wittockiana, Bibliotheca *see* Wittock
Wotton, Catherine, 40, 83
Wotton, Edward, 1st Baron Wotton, 48, 83
Wotton, Thomas, 38, 39, 40, 41, 42, 45, 46, 47, 48, 83
Wright, J, 62

Xabar, Ysabel, 402

Yemeniz, N, 72, 96

Zamoyski, Stanislaus, Count, 348
Zorica (?), Jacobus Antonius, 320